The Global History of Childhood Reader

"An excellent and very useful addition to the literature on the history of childhood. It is thoughtful, well and broadly conceived, and addresses a need in the area of teaching the history of children and childhood."

Paula S. Fass, *University of California, USA*

"Heidi Morrison makes a forceful case for the advantages of looking beyond the national boundaries usually adopted by historians of childhood, encouraging us to think in comparative and global terms. Her choice of material for this reader moves beyond the usual emphasis on the Western experience to include a wealth of examples from the rest of the world. No less importantly, her commentary draws attention to the insights to be gained from a historical perspective on the campaign launched during the twentieth century for the recognition of children's rights."

Colin Heywood, *University of Nottingham, UK*

The Global History of Childhood Reader provides an essential collection of chapters and articles on the global history of childhood. The Reader is structured thematically so as to provide both a representative sampling of the historiography as well as an overview of the key issues of the field, such as historicizing childhood as a social construct, delineating commonalities and differences globally, and understanding why the twentieth century was not the "century of the child" for most of the world's children. The Reader is divided into four parts:

1. Theories and methodologies of the history of childhood
2. Constructions of childhood in different times and places
3. Children's experiences in different times and places
4. Usage of the past to articulate solutions to problems facing children today.

Topics covered include education, gender, disability, race, class, religion, violence, labor and illiteracy. With introductions that contextualize each of the four parts and the articles, further reading sections and questions, this is the perfect guide for all students of the history of childhood.

Heidi Morrison is an Assistant Professor of History at the University of Wisconsin – La Crosse. Her research focuses on the history of childhood in the Middle East. She is currently working on a book about childhood in early twentieth-century Egypt.

Routledge Readers in History

The

Global History of

Childhood Reader

Edited by

Heidi Morrison

 Routledge
Taylor & Francis Group

LONDON AND NEW YORK

For Carmen and Marie-Sarah

First published 2012
by Routledge
2 Park Square, Milton Park, Abingdon, Oxon OX14 4RN

Simultaneously published in the USA and Canada
by Routledge
711 Third Avenue, New York, NY 10017

Routledge is an imprint of the Taylor & Francis Group, an informa business

British Library Cataloguing in Publication Data
A catalogue record for this book is available from the British Library

Library of Congress Cataloging in Publication Data
The global history of childhood reader / edited by Heidi Morrison.
    p. cm. – (Routledge readers in history)
Includes bibliographical references and index.
1. Children – History   2. Children – Cross-cultural studies.   3. Children – Social conditions.
I. Morrison, Heidi.
HQ767.87.G56 2012
305.23 – dc23

2011039362

ISBN: 978-0-415-78248-7 (hbk)
ISBN: 978-0-415-78249-4 (pbk)

Typeset in Perpetua and Bell Gothic
by RefineCatch Limited, Bungay, Suffolk

MIX
Paper from
responsible sources
FSC
www.fsc.org   FSC® C004839

Printed and bound in Great Britain by the MPG Books Group

Contents

PART 4: Use of the past to articulate solutions to problems facing children today

Acknowledgements

Part 1:

1. Ariès, Philippe. "The Discovery of Childhood" in *Centuries of Childhood: A Social History of Family Life* translated by Robert Baldick (New York: Alfred A. Knopf, 1962), pp 33–49. Copyright © 1962 Jonathan Cape Ltd. Originally published in French as *L'Enfant et la vie familiale sous l'ancien regime*. Copyright © 1960 by Librairie Plon, Paris. Used by permission of Alfred A. Knopf, a division of Random House, Inc.

2. Thorne, Barrie. "Re-visioning Women and Social Change: Where Are the Children?" in *Gender & Society* (Vol. 1, No. 1, March 1987), pp 85–109. Copyright © 1987, Sociologists for Women in Society. Reprinted by permission of Sage Publications.

3. Shorter, Edward. "Bastardy in South Germany: A Comment" in *JIH* (Winter 1978, VIII: 3), pp 459–69. Reprinted from *The Journal of Interdisciplinary History,* with the permission of the editors of *The Journal of Interdisciplinary History* and the MIT Press, Cambridge, Massachusetts. © 1978 by the Massachusetts Institute of Technology and The Journal of Interdisciplinary History, Inc.

4. Milanich, Nara. "Historical Perspectives on Illegitimacy and Illegitimates in Latin America" in *Minor Omissions: Children in Latin American History and Society* edited by Tobias Hecht. Wisconsin: The University of Wisconsin Press, 2002, pp 72–101. ©2002 by the Board of Regents of the University of Wisconsin System. Reprinted by permission of The University of Wisconsin Press.

5. Aronsson, Karin and Bengt Sandin. "The Sun Match Boy and Plant Metaphors: A Swedish Image of a 20th-Century Childhood" in *Images of Childhood* edited by C. Philip Hwang, Michael E. Lamb, Irving E. Sigel. New Jersey: Lawrence Erlbaum Associates, 1996. Copyright © 1996. Reproduced with permission of Taylor & Francis Group LLC – Books in the format Textbook via Copyright Clearance Center.

6. Wu, Pei-yi. "Childhood Remembered: Parents and Children in China, 800 to 1700" in *Chinese Views of Childhood* edited by Anne Behnke Kinney (Honolulu: University of Hawaii Press, 1995), pp 129–56. © 1995 University of Hawaii Press. Reprinted with permission.

7. Gil'adi, Avner. "Infants, Children and Death in Medieval Muslim Society" in *Children of Islam: Concepts of Childhood in Medieval Muslim Society* (London: Macmillan / St Antony's College Series, 1992), pp 69–93, 145–52. Copyright © 1992, Palgrave Macmillan. Reproduced with permission of Palgrave Macmillan.

8. Saxton, Martha. "Introduction" in *Journal of the History of Childhood and Youth* (Winter 2008, 1.1), pp 1–3. © 2008, The John Hopkins University Press. Reprinted with permission of The John Hopkins University Press.

9. Sigel, Irving E. "Integrative Summary" in *Images of Childhood* edited by C. Philip Hwang, Michael E. Lamb, Irving E. Sigel. New Jersey: Lawrence Erlbaum Associates, 1996. Copyright © 1996. Reproduced with permission of Taylor & Francis Group LLC – Books in the format Textbook via Copyright Clearance Center.

Part 2:

10. Najmabadi, Afsaneh. "Crafting an Educated Housewife in Iran," in *Remaking Women: Feminism and Modernity in the Middle East*, ed. Lila Abu-Lughod (Princeton: Princeton University Press and Cairo: American University in Cairo Press), 1998, pp 91–125. © 1998 Princeton University Press. Reprinted by permission of Princeton University Press.

11. Kociumbas, Jan. "Children in Chains: Juvenile Convicts" in *Australian Childhood*. Australia: Allen and Unwin, 1997, pp 21–37. © 1997 Allen and Unwin. Reprinted with permission of Allen and Unwin Pty Ltd. www.allenandunwin.com

12. Illick, Joseph E. *American Childhoods*. Philadelphia, Pennsylvania: University of Pennsylvania Press, 2002, pp 36–54. © 2002, University of Pennsylvania Press. Reprinted with permission of the University of Pennsylvania Press.

13. Browning, Don and Marcia Bunge, eds. *Children and Childhood in World Religions: Primary Sources and Texts*. NJ: Rutgers Press, 2009, pp 1–14. Copyright © 2009 by Rutgers, the State University. Reprinted by permission of Rutgers University Press.

14. Safford, Elizabeth and Philip Safford. *A History of Childhood and Disability*. Teachers College Press, 1996, pp 286–300. Copyright © 1996 by Teachers College Press, Columbia University. All rights reserved. Reprinted by permission of the Publisher.

15. Grier, Beverly Carolease. *Invisible Hands: Child Labor and the State in Colonial Zimbabwe*. Heinemann, 2005, pp 69–110. Reprinted with permission. Copyright © 2006 by Beverly Carolease Grier. Published by Heinemann, Portsmouth, NH. All rights reserved.

16. Fortna, Benjamin. "Emphasizing the Islamic: Modifying the Curriculum of Late Ottoman State Schools" in *Enfance et jeunesse dans le monde musulman* edited by Francois Georgeon and Flaus Kreiser. France: Maisonneuve & Larose, 2007, pp 193–209.

17. Stearns, Peter. *Childhood in World History*. New York: Routledge, 2011, second edition, pp 143–55. Copyright © 2011 Taylor & Francis. Reproduced by permission of Taylor & Francis Books UK.

Part 3:

18. Cooter (Pollard) Juliet, "A Most Remarkable Phenomenon: Growing Up Métis: Fur Traders' Children in the Pacific Northwest" from *An Imperfect Past: Education and Society in Canadian History*, J. Donald Wilson ed, from: Vancouver: Centre for the Study of Curriculum

and Instruction, UBC, 1984, pp 120–40. Reprinted by permission of the Centre for the Study of Curriculum and Instruction, UBC. The author's doctoral dissertation, "The making of the Metis in the Pacific Northwest fur trade children: Race, class, and gender" (The University of British Columbia, 1990) contains a more detailed examination of the children mentioned in the article.

19. Davin, Anna. *Growing Up Poor: Home, Street, and School in London 1870–1914*. Rivers Oram Press, 1997, pp 97–111. © 1997, Rivers Oram Press. Reprinted with permission of Rivers Oram Publishers Ltd.

20. Kelly, Catriona. "Thank You for the Wonderful Book: Soviet Child Readers and the Management of Children's Reading, 1950–75" in *Kritika* Journal (Vol. 6, No. 4, Fall 2005), pp 717–53. Reprinted with permission of *Kritika: Explorations in Russian and Eurasian History*.

21. Humphries, Jane. *Childhood and Child Labour in the British Industrial Revolution*. London: Cambridge University Press, 2010, pp 172–209. © Jane Humphries 2010, published by Cambridge University Press. Reproduced with permission.

Part 4:

22. The United Nations Convention on the Rights of the Child (CRC), UNICEF. 1989.

23. Cunningham, Hugh. *Children and Childhood in Western Society Since 1500*. Great Britain: Pearson, 2005, pp 137–70. © 2005 Pearson Education Limited. Reprinted with permission.

24. Stephens, Sharon. Introduction to *Children and the Politics of Culture*, edited by Sharon Stephens. New Jersey: Princeton University Press, 1995, pp 3–24. © 1995 Princeton University Press. Reprinted by permission of Princeton University Press.

25. Lohmann, Ingrid and Christine Mayer. "Lessons from the History of Education for a 'Century of the Child at Risk'" in *Paedagogica Historica*. Vol. 45, No. 1/2, pp 4–11. February 2009. Copyright © Stichting Paedagogica Historica reprinted by permission of Taylor & Francis Ltd, http://www.tandf.co.uk/journals on behalf of Stichting Paedagogica Historica.

26. Uno, Kathleen S. *Passages to Modernity: Motherhood, Childhood and Social Reform in Early Twentieth Century Japan*. Hawaii: University of Hawaii Press, 1999, pp 19–46. © 1999 University of Hawaii Press. Reprinted with permission.

27. Schrumpf, Ellen. "From Full-Time to Part-Time: Working Children in Norway from the Nineteenth to the Twentieth Century" in *Industrious Children: Work and Childhood in the Nordic Countries* edited by Ning de Coninck-Smith, Bengt Sandin, and Ellen Schrumpf. Denmark: University Press of Southern Denmark, 1997, pp 47–78. Reprinted with permission.

28. Odem, Mary E. "Statutory Rape Prosecutions in California" in *Delinquent Daughters: Protecting and Policing Adolescent Female Sexuality in the United States, 1885–1920*, (North Carolina: The University of North Carolina Press, 1995), pp 63–81. Copyright © 1995 by the University of North Carolina Press. Used by permission of the publisher.

29. Postman, Neil. "The Disappearing Child" in *The Disappearance of Childhood*. New York: Vintage Books, 1994, pp 120–42.

Prologue

A FEW YEARS AGO, I WANTED TO TEACH an undergraduate course on my research specialty, which is childhood in modern Middle East history. I quickly realized that there might not be enough material to adequately cover an entire semester, as the history of childhood is a relatively uncharted subfield of Middle East Studies. I decided to fill in the empty space on my syllabus by including histories of childhood in other parts of the world. Compared to non-western regions of the world, a seeming abundance of literature exists for childhood in western history. I do not see this imbalance in literature as a negative. The fact that a critical mass of historians cares about childhood is important in itself, since adults in all parts of the world customarily marginalize children. *The Global History of Childhood Reader* responds to the need of many instructors who currently lack a comprehensive textbook that builds on, but is not limited to, the body of literature on childhood in western history.

Throughout my academic career and while attending conferences in the USA and Europe on the history of childhood, I continue to find myself one of few non-western specialists in attendance. While I appreciate being included in the conferences, I often yearn for a more diverse setting in which to engage my research. Flying to a conference in Europe recently, I wondered, "When will the day come in which the sounding board for my research is not only the western child's experiences, but also the Central American's, the African's, etc.?" Academic conferences, books, courses, and workshops on the history of childhood tend to be region specific, not making thematic interrogations and comparisons across place. For instance, historians of twentieth-century American childhoods have taken little initiative to discuss with colleagues of twentieth-century Middle Eastern childhoods how their works relate and diverge. The same case could be made in reverse and for any combination of geographical locations.

The Global History of Childhood Reader pushes the intellectual boundaries of the field of the history of childhood by attempting to interweave into one dialogue histories of childhoods in different regions of the world. The word "global" emphasizes the interconnectedness of living beings on our planet. Until recently, many histories of childhood have accepted the western child's experience as normative. However, as this Reader details, there have been several fissures, even within the so-called west. This Reader pulls together scholarship that usually is not linked to global history, but instead to regional histories of childhood. Many of the authors in this Reader might not primarily identify their work as being a part of the field called the global history of childhood. This Reader encourages students and scholars to use this collection of articles to see patterns – commonalities as well as differences – in childhood. Children do not exist in national or regional vacuums, and as such narratives on childhood should be thought of in terms of global processes, such as imperialism, globalization, and war. A global perspective on the past opens the door for new trajectories in the history of childhood by asking questions such as: Is there a different set of ideas – besides the tenets of the modern western model of childhood – which historians can use to compare childhoods? How have western conceptions of childhood been influenced by realities of and perceptions of non-western conceptions of childhood? Can there be one global history of childhood?

Within higher education and academic research, there is an increasing desire to include the global history of childhood. Yet, there is currently little historical scholarship on global childhood, save for a few encyclopedias. *The Global History of Childhood Reader* provides an essential collection of publications on the global history of childhood, focusing primarily on the modern era. The term childhood in this Reader generally refers to ages 6–12. In a few cases, when literature is lacking, articles dealing with infancy or adolescence are included. The Reader is structured thematically so as to provide both a representative sampling of literature as well as an overview of the key issues of the field. The Reader is divided into four parts, each of which contains a general introduction and reading questions.

The first part of the Reader seeks to define the history of global childhood as a field that is still in its infancy. Historian Peter Stearns recently published his second edition of *Childhood in World History*, which articulates historical markers for changes in childhood conceptions and experiences. In 2010, Rutgers University Press published an edited volume entitled *Girlhood: A Global History* that takes a thematic approach to the topic of children in history, focusing particularly on how gender and age impact girls in the domains of politics, identities, education and work. The *Global History of Childhood Reader* builds on both of these initiatives, but goes a step further by mapping out the historiography of the field, as well as its goals and trajectories.

The second part of this Reader addresses the idea that childhood is a social construct shaped by time and place. What distinguishes the history of childhood from other histories is that age is the primary category of analysis. However, age is not the only factor that people use to delineate childhood from adulthood. Societal notions about what does and does not constitute a child vary based on such global and regional forces as class, religion, and labor. This Reader encourages readers to break down commonly held ethnocentric notions that the modern conception of childhood began in Western Europe and North America and that all other regions replicated it. Instead, the Reader emphasizes that the concept of childhood throughout the world developed both within and alongside the European and North American models. This Reader also contextualizes our understanding of the history of childhood in Western Europe and North America. As the modern models of middle-class childhood became dominant within these societies in the eighteenth and nineteenth centuries, a quite different set of changes affected children in many other parts of the world, due in large part to slavery, colonization, and the concomitant exploitation-based globalized economies.

The third part of the Reader deals with children's experiences in different times and places. The global history of childhood is not just about how adults think about children, but also how children create and understand their own lives. Looking at the past through the eyes of the child forces world historians – traditionally concerned with topics such as trade relations and migration – to take a more intimate look at the human experience over time. The history of childhood is not just about childhood, it is also about larger themes in history, such as gender, imperialism, globalization, the environment, religion and spirituality, nationalism, poverty, consumerism, and warfare.

The fourth part of the Reader addresses children's rights. Historians of childhood can contribute to the international movement for children's rights in many ways. They can use the past to articulate solutions to problems facing children today. A global history of childhood reveals that for most of the world's children, the twentieth century was not the "century of the child," as many progressive thinkers hoped it would be. The global history of childhood reminds us of the interconnectedness of children's conditions worldwide. As Paula Fass remarks, "A global perspective makes clear that no children are protected when there are others who are vulnerable."[1]

Finding solutions to the problems facing children in the world today requires more assistance from academics. The global history of childhood can contribute to the improvement of the conditions of many children in contemporary society. Professors can inspire students to care about children's rights, and they can train students in the critical-thinking and problem-solving skills necessary to turn that care into action. Historians of global childhoods can serve as consultants for activists and policy-makers seeking historical parallels to issues facing children today. Historians can also trace the roots of problems, such as exploitive labor and violence. Destitute and needy children should not be blamed for their conditions. The *Convention on the Rights of the Child* (CRC) provides general standards and tools that the world community works with to help children today, but it is sometimes criticized as being modeled around the ideal western child. A global perspective will help children's rights advocates expand their tool kit for the future.

Note

1   Fass, P. (2006) *Children of a New World*, New York: New York University Press, p. 256.

PART 1

What is the global history of childhood?

THE GOAL OF THIS FIRST PART OF THE Reader is to introduce the field of the global history of childhood through key articles on the subject. Part 1 does not attempt to survey the history itself, for which there exists only one such comprehensive attempt.[1] This section asks: what does it mean to write a history of childhood and what does it mean to make that history global? In answering these questions, this section presents important debates that pertain to this growing field's methodologies. The term childhood in this Reader generally refers to ages 6–12. In a few cases, when literature is lacking, articles dealing with infancy or adolescence are included.

There are four paradigm shifts that have shaped the evolution of the field: first, the recognition in the 1960s and 1970s that western children have a history and merit a narrative of their own; second, the realization in the 1990s that childhood is a social construct and hence there are multiple types of childhoods in western history; third, the contemporaneous jump from exploring the diversity of childhoods in western history to exploring the diversity in world history; and lastly, the opening up of the field to other disciplines.

Childhood discovered

The first turning point was the discovery by historians in the 1960s and 1970s that children have a history. Before that, other scholars produced research that related tangentially to the topic. Ethnologists touched upon children through studies on rites of passage, for example. Legal specialists came upon children through their look at disappearance and custody cases. Literary scholars historicized children's changing place in the novel and explored literature written explicitly for children.

Research on the history of childhood was minimal until French historian Philippe Ariès' groundbreaking book *Centuries of Childhood* (published in 1960 in France and translated into English in 1962). Ariès began the discussion on the history of childhood when he theorized that medieval western civilization did not perceive a transition period between infancy and adulthood, and instead launched children into manhood and womanhood the moment they could survive without the care and attention of mothers or nannies, somewhere between the ages of

5 and 7. He said that the pre-modern west lacked a conception of childhood and had no special emotions for children. Ariès used as evidence medieval art that depicted children as adults on a smaller scale or that left out children altogether.

During the 1960s and 1970s, four factors fostered the interest of historians in taking their research in the new trajectory of children. First, demographers became interested in children when they realized that population studies must include birth rates, death rates, infanticide, and abortion. Second, there was a new curiosity among social historians to move from the study of grand economic classes, such as the bourgeoisie and nobility, to study smaller social groups and people who fell outside pre-defined social-economic categories. As historian of childhood in the USA Paula Fass articulates, " . . . by the 1960s, American historians, together with their British and Continental colleagues, were no longer satisfied to concentrate exclusively on the more visible topsoil of historical research."[2] Third, Michel Foucault's work in the 1960s on control sought to explain the forces that act on people to create a disciplined society. Foucault posited that society imposes through the school, home, and family a normalized type of behavior that children internalize. Lastly, aspects of the women's movement problematized the construction of identity in men versus women and this forced scholars to look at how those identities were shaped in childhood. Parts of the women's movement also brought attention to children in their efforts to challenge the hegemonic structures that loom over seemingly powerless actors in society. The article by sociologist Barrie Thorne, published in 1987, reflects the impact that the women's rights movement had on fostering the nascent field of the history of childhood. Thorne says that feminist scholars can better understand the fate of women by understanding the fate of children. She also encourages liberating the child from the subordination of adult-centered knowledge, much like women must be liberated from men.

Although Ariès opened the floodgates of scholars ready to study children in the past, his theory that there was no place for childhood in the medieval world was proven wrong a few decades later. He gave a false start to the field. Most notable among his critics was historian Shulamith Shahar whose book *Childhood in the Middle Ages* argues that Ariès' theory is wrong simply because no society could physically survive without a tradition of child-nurturing, ways of transmitting knowledge, and socialization of the young. Shahar claims that just because children in the Middle Ages were closely involved in adult society does not mean the conception of childhood was non-existent. Universal elements, such as recognizing the needs of children, ensure a society's survival.

Perhaps the most important contribution Ariès made to the history of childhood was not only in periodizing childhood's existence but also in signaling the dangers of present-centered visions of history. Historian of European childhoods Colin Heywood states, "Most people assume that their own ideas and practices concerning childhood are 'natural,' and are shocked to discover that other societies diverge from them."[3] Scholars today generally agree that the conception of childhood did exist in the Middle Ages, but the conception was radically different than that which would come later in the West. For instance, child historian James A. Schultz finds that in the German High Middle Ages adults did not think, as people generally do today, that their treatment of children affected children's outcome as eventual adults. But adults thought that childhood was important because it can reveal to a discerning eye the traits in the child that will remain with him/her as an adult.[4]

Childhood as a social construct

The attempts in the 1970s to write a history of childhood focused on the institutional level, such as school systems, infant welfare services, child labor legislation, and specialized agencies for juvenile delinquents. Adult attitudes towards children were at the center of such narratives, and hence children's experiences and actions were often overlooked. Historians viewed the history of childhood as one of progress in which children's lives had improved over time. Edward Shorter's work on illegitimacy illustrates this style, which is now generally out-dated. His work on bastardy was important for its time because he moved away from studying elites in history to studying average people. Shorter was one of the first scholars to acknowledge the presence of bastard children in history. But, his institutional, adult-centered approach to studying childhood was indicative of the historiography of the era. Shorter's work was a precursor to the work for the historian P. Laslett who dutifully calculated illegitimacy rates without ever asking whether they are a relevant social category in the societies in question in the first place.

During the 1980s, diversity was of critical concern to feminist and post-modernist scholars, as well as to cultural historians. As a result, many historians of childhood shifted from studying institutions for children to studying children as individuals defined by their class, race, and gender. Paying attention to the multiple constructions of childhood in time and place is the second major paradigm transformation in the historiography of the field and remains an important trope in the field today. Historians are concerned with what ideas different cultures attach to childhood and how those ideas vary with the environment in which a child is raised. Such histories often privilege the experiences of children because they look at the impact of adult attitudes on children as well as the relationships between members of different generations.

Nara Milanich's article, published in 2002, exemplifies this type of historiography, which is still prevalent in the field today. Viewing childhood as a social construct is a critical aspect of the global history of childhood. This article illuminates the changes in the historiography of the field since the time of Shorter. Milanich shows that illegitimate children do not share a single experience. She also goes beyond looking at institutions made for children and adults' attitudes towards children to look at children's experiences in their own words.

Historians employ a wide range of written and non-written evidence. Children leave few records of their own because of their historic preponderance for illiteracy. Archives, statistical collections, official reports, and administrative correspondence often do not talk directly about intimate attitudes of private life. However, historians of childhood claim that they are not at a disadvantage when focusing on children because, as Paula Fass clarifies, "[historians of childhood realize that] no historical subjects ever spoke plainly in their own voices or acted entirely freely."[5] The field of the history of childhood often relies on oral history, diaries, material culture, and autobiographies.

Historians of childhood use material culture to access information about their subjects. Karin Calvert's book *Children in the House*, published in 1992, served as a sounding bell for the use of objects with physical substance to articulate a history of childhood. Calvert historically contextualizes walking stools and swaddling clothes. Karin Aronsson and Bengt Sandin's article provides an example of the use of visual images to write a history of childhood in Sweden. In this article, the authors interpret an image on a box of matches to uncover 1930s' Swedish cultural values on childhood. The matches were sold to Swedish households as part of a philanthropic child welfare campaign.

Global childhoods

Accounts of the history of childhood outside of Europe and North America are fewer because the history of childhood has been defined and developed by historians as a "western" narrative of modernization. That is to say, historians of childhood in Europe and North America have been concerned traditionally with the moment when the notion of childhood appeared within their own modernity, i.e. with the nineteenth-century ideas of the Romantics about the natural/innocent child; the replacement of charity/philanthropy with state welfare for children; the separation of children from adults and the legal protection of children from wage-work. Moreover, this notion is deeply related to industrialization and the emergence of the rising middle class that some western countries saw as the core of a universal modernity.

The history of children in non-western regions has often been ignored due to pre-existing stereotypes. Based on their knowledge (or lack thereof) about children in different regions of the contemporary world, people sometimes only associate children in non-western regions with dire children's rights issues. Media representations of children in Africa, for example, portray AIDS orphans, child soldiers, and raped girls. Children in Africa, like any region of the world, have a long and rich heritage that needs to be studied.

The history of childhood outside the western cultural sphere was also generally ignored because, since the 1960s, historians of this region paid less attention to minor actors within their own histories and more concern to studying why the regions were economically "under-developed" according to modernization theory.[6] Historian Ping-chen Hsiung points out in a historiographical essay on the history of childhood in China that historians from China who focus on the history of childhood are still rare and have often only written a one-time essay or conducted a limited study as a tangential aspect of their larger intellectual pursuits.[7]

Children and childhood as a distinct category of analysis is still in its formative stages in non-western regions, but this is changing. As the historical conception of childhood has begun to be investigated over the last two decades as a cultural construct in western history, historians began as well to acknowledge the diversity in childhoods worldwide. The increasing production of narratives on non-western childhoods created the global history of childhood. World historian of childhood, Peter Stearns, divides the field into three branches: accounts, patterns, and globalization (how conditions of childhood are impacted by global forces).[8] Since the number of historical accounts of non-western childhoods is few in comparison to the West, it is difficult to find commonalities, differences, and links in children's experiences and childhood through time and space. Stearns is the only historian who has attempted to pinpoint the global patterns in how childhood has modernized, claiming that all countries – even those hostile to western values and institutions – have moved towards the modern conditions of childhood found in the West, i.e. education, lower birth rates, and the increase in value of the child for his/her emotional (and not economic) worth. Neither inside nor outside the modern paradigm, the non-western model has developed *alongside* it.

This Reader looks at what western and non-western accounts of the history of childhood offer in terms of engaging in debates on cultural constructions of childhood and the experiences of being a child. The articles by Pei-yi Wu and Avner Gil'adi taken together or separately, exemplify what it means to *do* a global history of childhood. Each article provides an account of the way a certain civilization dealt with the death of children in pre-modern times. The former focuses on China and the latter on the Muslim Middle East. These pieces underscore the diversity in attitudes towards childhood throughout time, urging readers to reflect on similarities and differences in global conceptions of childhood. The conception of childhood existed in pre-modern non-western societies, a finding which dispels ethnocentric myths that the West was the first civilization to discover childhood and develop a sophisticated conception of it.

Making the field multidisciplinary and multigenerational

The fourth paradigm shift in the history of childhood is the move to open up the field to other voices, be they in the form of different academic disciplines or the newest generation of children. The inaugural volume of the *Journal of the History of Childhood and Youth* includes a milestone article by Martha Saxton that encouraged historians of childhood to engage with disciplines as seemingly remote from their work as neurobiology, anthropology, and economics.

Historical research on children requires understanding how children learn (cognitive science), how children negotiate the global and local (anthropology), and how children engage through work in family decision-making (economics). The article in this Reader by Irving Sigel explores how different disciplinary outlooks on images of children provides a rich understanding of the conception of childhood in different times and places.

In addition to the new dialogue emerging in the global history of childhood between scholars from many different disciplines, there is a new dialogue emerging between children and scholars. Tobias Hecht, in his edited volume on children in Latin American history, argues that young people themselves need to participate in research. This will ensure that better records are left for future generations of historians. Through drawings and written and audio diaries children can record their experiences with violence, hunger, sexuality, and work. Including children can also inspire methods of information gathering that are different than those ordinarily employed by academics.

Articles

1.   Ariès, Philippe. "The Discovery of Childhood" in *Centuries of Childhood* translated by Robert Baldick (New York: Alfred A. Knopf, 1962), pp 33–49.

The foundation of a field

- What is innovative about Ariès' work?
- What is Ariès' theory about childhood in the past?
- What are the strengths and weaknesses to the evidence Ariès uses to make his argument?
- Make an argument for why Ariès' theory is incorrect based on the following idea: Biological immaturity of children is a fact of life, but the ways this immaturity are understood and made meaningful is an act of culture.

2.   Thorne, Barrie. "Re-visioning Women and Social Change: Where Are the Children?" in *Gender & Society* (Vol. 1, No. 1, March 1987), pp 85–109.

Impact of women's studies on the field

- According to Thorne, what are the problems with how children are studied?
- What can the field of women's studies teach us about re-visioning the field of childhood studies?
- Why study children?
- How is children's studies different than women's studies?

3.   Shorter, Edward. "Bastardy in South Germany: A Comment" in *JIH* (Winter 1978, VIII: 3), pp 459–69.

Viewing childhood through adult eyes

- What makes Shorter's article innovative for its era?
- Find examples from the article that illustrate Shorter's institutional approach to writing about children in history.

- Find examples from the article that illustrate Shorter's adult-centered approach to writing about children in history.
- What are the weaknesses to Shorter's approach?

4.   Milanich, Nara. "Historical Perspectives on Illegitimacy and Illegitimates in Latin America" in *Minor Omissions* edited by Tobias Hecht. Wisconsin: The University of Wisconsin Press, 2002, pp 72–101.

Childhood as a social construct

- In what ways is the child placed at the center of this article on illegitimacy?
- How does the author show illegitimacy to be a social construct?
- What is the value in placing the child at the center of the narrative on illegitimacy?
- Compare Milanich's approach to Shorter's. How might we account for the differences?

5.   Aronsson, Karin and Bengt Sandin. "The Sun Match Boy and Plant Metaphors: A Swedish Image of a 20th-Century Childhood" in *Images of Childhood* edited by C. Philip Hwang, Michael E. Lamb, Irving E. Sigel. New Jersey: Lawrence Erlbaum Associates, 1996.

Material culture as a source

- What sources do the authors use?
- What do these sources reveal about the conception of childhood in the period under review?
- What are some of the benefits to using material culture in understanding the history of childhood?

6.   Wu, Pei-yi. "Childhood Remembered: Parents and Children in China, 800 to 1700" in *Chinese Views of Childhood* edited by Anne Behnke Kinney (Honolulu: University of Hawaii Press, 1995), pp 129–56.

7.   Gil'adi, Avner. "Infants, Children and Death in Medieval Muslim Society" in *Children of Islam* (London: Macmillan, 1992), pp 69–93, 145–52.

Doing a global history of childhood

- How did people react to the death of children in pre-modern China, according to the Wu article? Cite some of the author's sources.
- What were some of the emotional reactions to death of infants and children in pre-modern Muslim society, according to the Gil'adi article? Cite some of the author's sources.
- What similarities are there between the findings of these two articles? Differences?
- How do these two articles dispel the myth that the West was the first civilization to discover childhood?

8.   Saxton, Martha. "Introduction" in *JHCY* (Winter 2008, 1.1), pp 1–3.

The importance of the field

- Why study the history of childhood?

9. Sigel, Irving E. "Integrative Summary" in *Images of Childhood* edited by C. Philip Hwang, Michael E. Lamb, Irving E. Sigel. New Jersey: Lawrence Erlbaum Associates, 1996.

Prospects for the future

● In your opinion, what are the pros and cons to studying children through an interdisciplinary lens?

Suggestions for further reading

Bargach, J. (2002) *Orphans of Islam: Family, Abandonment, and Secret Adoption in Morocco*, Lanham, MD: Rowman and Littlefield

Dore, R. (2011) *Education in Tokugawa Japan*, London: Routledge

Farquhar, M. (1999) *Children's Literature in China: From Lu Xun to Mao Zedong*, Armonk, NY: M.E. Sharpe

Gutman, M. and de Coninck-Smith, N. (eds.) (2008) *Designing Modern Childhoods: History, Space and the Material Culture of Children*, New Brunswick, NJ: Rutgers University Press

James, A. and Prout, A. (1997) *Constructing and Reconstructing Childhood: Contemporary Issues in the Sociological Study of Childhood*, Washington, DC: Falmer Press

Jenks, C. (2005) *Childhood*, New York: Routledge

Lohmann, I. and Mayer, C. (2009) Lessons from the History of Education for a 'Century of the Child at Risk', *Paedagogica Historica: International Journal of the History of Education*, Taylor & Francis Online, 45 (1, 2), pp.1–16

Scheper-Hughes, N. (1992) *Death Without Weeping: The Violence of Everyday Life in Brazil*, Berkeley: University of California Press

Wicks, A. (ed.) (2002) *Children in Chinese Art*, Honolulu: University of Hawaii Press

Wyness, Michael G. (2006) *Childhood and Society: An Introduction to the Sociology of Childhood*, New York: Palgrave Macmillan

Zelizer, V. (1985) *Pricing the Priceless Child: The Changing Social Value of Children*, New York: Basic Books

Notes

1   Stearns, P. (2010) *Childhood in World History*, New York: Routledge.

2   Fass, P. (2006) *Children of a New World*, New York: New York University Press, p.2.

3   Heywood, Colin (2001) *A History of Childhood: Children and Childhood in the West from Medieval to Modern Times*, Cambridge: Polity Press, p.612.

4   See the work of Schultz, James A. (1995) *The Knowledge of Childhood in the German Middle Ages, 1100–1350*, Philadelphia: The University of Pennsylvania Press.

5   Fass, P. (2006) *Children of a New World*, New York: New York University Press, p.5.

6   Similar to in the West, early twentieth-century Latin America, Asia, and Africa scholars typically did not use childhood as their main focus of study, but instead information about childhood came as a byproduct of studies on such topics as marriage rites. One example is the publication, first published 1933, of Gilberto Freyre's classic *The Masters and the Slaves: The Development of Brazilian Civilization*, republished 1953, New York: Knopf. Freyre studied Brazilian civilization through slave plantation households. He located social reproduction in relationships involving children, implicitly showing

that the history of Brazilian racial identity and a history of childhood are conceptually linked.

7   Ping-chen, H. (2008) Treading a Different Path? Thoughts on Childhood Studies in Chinese History, *The Journal of the History of Childhood and Youth*, 1 (1), p.80.

8   Stearns, P. (2010) *Childhood in World History*, New York: Routledge.

Chapter 1

Philippe Ariès

THE DISCOVERY OF CHILDHOOD

Mediaval ART UNTIL ABOUT THE twelfth century did not know childhood or did not attempt to portray it. It is hard to believe that this neglect was due to incompetence or incapacity; it seems more probable that there was no place for childhood in the medieval world. An Ottonian miniature of the twelfth century provides us with a striking example of the deformation which an artist at that time would inflict on children's bodies.[1] The subject is the scene in the Gospels in which Jesus asks that little children be allowed to come to Him. The Latin text is clear: *parvuli*. Yet the miniaturist has grouped around Jesus what are obviously eight men, without any of the characteristics of childhood; they have simply been depicted on a smaller scale. In a French miniature of the late eleventh century the three children brought to life by St Nicholas are also reduced to a smaller scale than the adults, without any other difference in expression or features.[2] A painter would not even hesitate to give the naked body of a child, in the very few cases when it was exposed, the musculature of an adult: thus in a Psalter dating from the late twelfth or early thirteenth century, Ishmael, shortly after birth, has the abdominal and pectoral muscles of a man.[3] The thirteenth century, although it showed more understanding in its presentation of childhood, remained faithful to this method.[4] In St Louis's moralizing Bible, children are depicted more often, but they are still indicated only by their size. In an episode in the life of Jacob, Isaac is shown sitting between his two wives, surrounded by some fifteen little men who come up to the level of the grown-ups' waists; these are their children.[5] When Job is rewarded for his faith and becomes rich once more, the illuminator depicts his good fortune by placing Job between an equal number of cattle on the left and children on the right: the traditional picture of fecundity inseparable from wealth. In another illustration in the Book of Job, some children are lined up in order of size.

In the thirteenth-century Gospel-book of the Sainte-Chapelle, in an illustration of the miracle of the loaves and fishes, Christ and one of the Apostles are shown standing on either side of a little man who comes up to their waists: no doubt the child who carried the fishes.[6] In the world of Romanesque formulas, right up to the end of the thirteenth century, there are no children characterized by a special expression but only men on a reduced scale. This refusal to accept child morphology in art is to be found too in most of the ancient civilizations. A fine Sardinian bronze of the ninth century B.C. shows a sort of Pietà: a mother holding in her arms the somewhat bulky body of her son.[7] The catalogue tells us: 'The little masculine figure could also be a child which, in accordance with the formula adopted in ancient times by other peoples, had been represented as an adult.' Everything in fact would seem to suggest that the realistic representation of children or the idealization of childhood, its grace and rounded charms, was confined to Greek art. Little Eroses proliferated in the Hellenistic period, but childhood disappeared from iconography together with the other Hellenistic themes, and Romanesque art returned to that rejection of the special features of childhood which had already characterized the periods of antiquity before Hellenism. This is no mere coincidence. Our starting-point in this study is a world of pictorial representation in which childhood is unknown; literary historians such as Mgr Calvé have made the same observation about the epic, in which child prodigies behave with the courage and physical strength of doughty warriors. This undoubtedly means that the men of the tenth and eleventh centuries did not dwell on the image of childhood, and that that image had neither interest nor even reality for them. It suggests too that in the realm of real life, and not simply in that of aesthetic transposition, childhood was a period of transition which passed quickly and which was just as quickly forgotten.

Such is our starting-point. How do we get from there to the little imps of Versailles, to the photographs of children of all ages in our family albums?

About the thirteenth century, a few types of children are to be found which appear to be a little closer to the modern concept of childhood.

There is the angel, depicted in the guise of a very young man, a young adolescent: a *clergeon*, as Père du Colombier remarks.[8] But how old is this 'little clerk'? The *clergeons* were children of various ages who were trained to make the responses in church and who were destined for holy orders, seminarists of a sort in a period when there were no seminaries and when schooling in Latin, the only kind of schooling that existed, was reserved for future clerks. 'Here', says one of the *Miracles de Notre-Dame*, 'there were little children who had few letters and would rather have fed at their mother's breast [but children were weaned very late at that time: Shakespeare's Juliet was still being breast-fed at three] than do divine service.'[9] The angel of Reims, to take one example, is a big boy rather than a child, but the artists have stressed the round, pretty, and somewhat effeminate features of youths barely out of childhood. We have already come a long way from the small-scale adults of the Ottonian miniature. This type of adolescent angel was to become extremely common in the fourteenth century and was to last to the very end of the Italian *Quattrocento*: the angels of Fra Angelico, Botticelli and Ghirlandajo all belong to it.

The second type of child was to be the model and ancestor of all the little children in the history of art: the Infant Jesus, or the Infant Notre-Dame, for here childhood is linked to the mystery of motherhood and the Marian cult. To begin with, Jesus, like other children, is an adult on a reduced scale: a little God-priest in His majesty, depicted by Theotokos. The evolution towards a more realistic and more sentimental representation of childhood begins very early on in painting: in a miniature of the second half of the twelfth century, Jesus is shown wearing a thin, almost transparent shift and standing with His arms round His mother's neck, nestling against her, cheek to cheek.[10] With the Virgin's motherhood, childhood enters the world of pictorial representation. In the thirteenth century it inspires other family scenes. In St Louis's moralizing Bible,[11] there are various family scenes in which parents are shown surrounded by their children with the same tender respect as on the rood-screen at Chartres: thus in a picture of Moses and his family, husband and wife are holding hands while the children (little men) surrounding them are stretching out their hands towards their mother. These cases, however, remained rare: the touching idea of childhood remained limited to the Infant Jesus until the fourteenth century, when, as is well known, Italian art was to help to spread and develop it.

A third type of child appeared in the Gothic period: the naked child. The Infant Jesus was scarcely ever depicted naked. More often than not, like other children of His age, He was chastely wrapped in swaddling-clothes or clad in a shift or a dress. He would not be undressed until the end of the Middle Ages. Those few miniatures in the moralizing Bibles which depicted children showed them fully dressed, except in the case of the Innocents or the dead children whose mothers Solomon was judging. It was the allegory of death and the soul which was to introduce into the world of forms the picture of childish nudity. Already in the pre-Byzantine iconography of the fifth century, in which many features of the future Romanesque art made their appearance, the bodies of the dead were reduced in scale. Corpses were smaller than living bodies, In the *Iliad* in the Ambrosian Library the dead in the battle scenes are half the size of the living.[12] In French medieval art the soul was depicted as a little child who was naked and usually sexless. The Last Judgments lead the souls of the righteous to Abraham's bosom in this form.[13] The dying man breathes the child out through his mouth in a symbolic representation of the soul's departure. This is also how the entry of the soul into the world is depicted, whether it is a case of a holy, miraculous conception – the Angel of the Annunciation presenting the Virgin with a naked child, Jesus's soul[14] – or a case of a perfectly natural conception: a couple resting in bed apparently quite innocently, but something must have happened, for a naked child can be seen flying through the air and entering the woman's mouth – 'the creation of the human soul by natural means'.[15]

In the course of the fourteenth and particularly the fifteenth century, these medieval types would develop further, but in the direction already indicated in the thirteenth century. We have already observed that the angel-cum-altar-boy would go on playing its part, without very much change, in the religious painting of the fifteenth century. On the other hand the theme of the Holy Childhood would never cease developing in both scope and variety from the fourteenth century on – its popularity and fecundity bearing witness to the progress, in the collective consciousness, of that idea of childhood which only a keen observer can distinguish in the thirteenth century and which did not exist at all in the eleventh century. In the group of Jesus and His mother, the artist would stress the graceful, affectionate, naive aspects of early childhood: the child seeking its mother's breast or getting ready to kiss or caress her, the child playing the traditional childhood games with fruit or a bird on a leash, the child eating its pap, the child being wrapped in its swaddling-clothes. Every gesture that could be observed – at least by somebody prepared to pay attention to them – would henceforth be reproduced in pictorial form. These features of sentimental realism would take a long time to extend beyond the frontiers of religious iconography, which is scarcely surprising when one remembers that this was also the case with landscape and genre painting. It remains none the less true that the group of Virgin and Child changed in character and became more and more profane: the picture of a scene of everyday life.

Timidly at first, then with increasing frequency, the painters of religious childhood went beyond that of Jesus. First of all they turned to the childhood of the Virgin, which inspired at least two new and popular themes: the theme of the birth of the Virgin – people in St Anne's bedroom fussing over the new-born child, bathing her, wrapping her in swaddling-clothes and showing her to her mother – and the theme of the Virgin's education: a reading lesson, with the Virgin following the words in a book held by St Anne. Then came other holy childhoods: those of St John, the Infant Jesus's playmate, St James, and the children of the holy women, Mary Zebedee and Mary Salome. A completely new iconography thus came into existence, presenting more and more scenes of childhood, and taking care to gather together in similar groups these holy children, with or without their mothers.

This iconography, which generally speaking started with the fourteenth century, coincided with a profusion of priors' tales and legends, such as those in the *Miracles de Notre-Dame*. It continued up to the seventeenth century and its development can be followed in painting, tapestry and sculpture. We shall in any case have occasion to return to it with regard to the religious practices of childhood.

From this religious iconography of childhood, a lay iconography eventually detached itself in the fifteenth and sixteenth centuries. This was not yet the portrayal of the child on its own. Genre painting was developing at this time by means of the transformation of a conventional allegorical iconography inspired by the antiquo-medieval concept of Nature: ages of life, seasons, senses, elements. Subject pictures and anecdotal paintings began to take the place of static representations of symbolic characters. We shall have cause to deal with this evolution at some length later on.[16] Let us merely note here that the child became one of the characters most frequently found in these anecdotal paintings: the child with his family; the child with his playmates, who were often adults; the child in a crowd, but very definitely 'spotlighted' in his mother's arms, or holding her hand or playing or even piddling; the child among the crowds watching miracles or martyrdoms, listening to sermons, or following liturgical rites such as presentations or circumcisions; the child serving as an apprentice to a goldsmith or a painter or some other craftsman; or the child at school, an old and popular theme which went back to the fourteenth century and would go on inspiring subject paintings up to the nineteenth century.

These subject paintings were not as a general rule devoted to the exclusive portrayal of childhood, but in a great many cases there were children among the characters depicted, both principal and secondary. And this suggests the following ideas: first, children mingled with adults in everyday life, and any gathering for the purpose of work, relaxation or sport brought together both children and adults; secondly, painters were particularly fond of depicting childhood for its graceful or picturesque qualities (the taste for the picturesque anecdote developed in the fifteenth and sixteenth centuries and coincided with the appreciation of childhood's charms), and they delighted in stressing the presence of a child in a group or a crowd. Of these two ideas one now strikes us as out of date, for today, as also towards the end of the nineteenth century, we tend to separate the world of children from that of adults; the other foreshadows the modern idea of childhood.

* * *

The origins of the themes of the angel, the holy childhoods, and their subsequent iconographical developments date as far back as the thirteenth century; two new types of child portrayal appeared in the fifteenth century: the portrait and the *putto*. The child, as we have seen, was not missing from the Middle Ages, at least from the thirteenth century on, but there was never a portrait of him, the portrait of a real child, as he was at a certain moment of his life.

In the funeral effigies listed in the Gaignières Collection,[17] the child appeared only at a very late date, in the sixteenth century. Curiously enough, his first appearance was not on his own tomb or that of his parents but on that of his teachers. On the tombs of the masters of Bologna, the teacher was shown surrounded by his pupils.[18] As early as 1378, Cardinal de La Grange, the Bishop of Amiens, had the two princes he had tutored portrayed at the ages of ten and seven on a 'handsome pillar' in his cathedral.[19] No one thought of keeping a picture of a child if that child had either lived to grow to manhood or had died in infancy. In the first case, childhood was simply an unimportant phase of which there was no need to keep any record; in the second case, that of the dead child, it was thought that the little thing which had disappeared so soon in life was not worthy of remembrance: there were far too many children whose survival was problematical. The general feeling was, and for a long time remained, that one had several children in order to keep just a few. As late as the seventeenth century, in *Le Caquet de l'accouchée*, we have a neighbour, standing at the bedside of a woman who has just given birth, the mother of five 'little brats', and calming her fears with these words:

'Before they are old enough to bother you, you will have lost half of them, or perhaps all of them.'[20] A strange consolation! People could not allow themselves to become too attached to something that was regarded as a probable loss. This is the reason for certain remarks which shock our present-day sensibility, such as Montaigne's observation: 'I have lost two or three children in their infancy, not without regret, but without great sorrow',[21] or Molière's comment on Louison in *Le Malade imaginaire*: 'The little girl doesn't count.' Most people probably felt, like Montaigne, that children had 'neither mental activities nor recognizable bodily shape'. Mme de Sévigné records without any sign of surprise[22] a similar remark made by Mme de Coetquen when the latter fainted on receiving the news of her little daughter's death: 'She is greatly distressed and says that she will never again have one so pretty.'

Nobody thought, as we ordinarily think today, that every child already contained a man's personality. Too many of them died. 'All mine die in infancy', wrote Montaigne. This indifference was a direct and inevitable consequence of the demography of the period. It lasted until the nineteenth century in the depths of the country, in so far as it was compatible with Christianity, which respected the immortal soul in every child that had been baptized. It is recorded that the people of the Basque country retained for a very long time the custom of burying children that had died without baptism in the house, on the threshold, or in the garden. Here we may perhaps see a survival of ancient rites, of sacrificial offerings, or rather it may be that the child that had died too soon in life was buried almost anywhere, much as we today bury a domestic pet, a cat or a dog. He was such an unimportant little thing, so inadequately involved in life, that nobody had any fears that he might return after death to pester the living. It is interesting to note that in the frontispiece to the *Tabula Cebetis* Mérian has placed the little children in a sort of marginal zone, between the earth from which they have emerged and the life into which they have not yet entered, and from which they are separated by a portico bearing the inscription *Introitus ad vitam*.[23] This feeling of indifference towards a too fragile childhood is not really very far removed from the callousness of the Roman or Chinese societies which practised the exposure of new-born children. We can now understand the gulf which separates our concept of childhood from that which existed before the demographic revolution or its preceding stages. There is nothing about this callousness which should surprise us: it was only natural in the community conditions of the time. On the other hand, there are grounds for surprise in the earliness of the idea of childhood, seeing that conditions were still so unfavourable to it. Statistically and objectively speaking, this idea should have appeared much later. True, there was the taste for the picturesque, pleasing aspects of the little creatures, the idea of the charms of childhood and the entertainment to be derived from the ingenuous antics of infancy: 'puerile nonsense', as Montaigne said, in which we adults take an interest 'for our amusement, like monkeys'.[24] But this idea could quite easily go hand in hand with indifference towards the essential, definitive personality of the child: the immortal soul. The new taste for the portrait indicated that children were emerging from the anonymity in which their slender chance of survival had maintained them. It is in fact quite remarkable that at that period of demographic wastage anyone should have felt a desire to record and keep the likeness of a child that would go on living or of a child that was dead. The portrait of the dead child in particular proves that that child was no longer generally considered as an inevitable loss. This solicitous attitude did not exclude or elimi-nate the opposite attitude, that of Montaigne, the neighbour at the mother's bedside, and Molière: down to the eighteenth century they coexisted. It was only in the eighteenth century, with the beginning of Malthusianism and the extension of contraceptive practices, that the idea of necessary wastage would disappear.

The appearance of the portrait of the dead child in the sixteenth century accordingly marked a very important moment in the history of feelings. This portrait was a funeral effigy to begin with. The child was not at first portrayed alone, but on his parents' tomb. Gaignières's records show the child by his mother's side and very tiny, or else at his parents' feet.[25] These tombs all date back to the sixteenth century: 1503, 1530, 1560. Among the interesting tombs in Westminster Abbey, let us note that of the Marchioness of Winchester, who died in 1586.[26] The recumbent figure of the Marchioness is life-size; represented on the front of her tomb on a smaller scale are her husband the Marquess, kneeling, and the tiny tomb of a dead child. At Westminster too, on a tomb dating from 1615 to 1620, the Earl and Countess of Shrewsbury are represented in a pair of recumbent figures, with their little daughter kneeling at their feet, her hands folded in prayer. It should be noted here that the children who surround the dead are not always dead themselves: the whole family is gathered round the heads of that family, as if it were at the time when they breathed their last. But beside the children who are still alive the sculptor has portrayed those who are already dead; there is always an indication to distinguish them: they are smaller and they hold a cross in their hands (as on John Coke's tomb at Holkham, 1639) or else a skull (on Cope of Ayley's tomb at Hambledon, 1633, there are four boys and three girls around the dead parents, and one boy and one girl are holding a skull).

At Toulouse in the Musée des Augustins there is an extremely interesting triptych that comes from the Du Mège Collection.[27] The volets are dated 1610. On either side of a 'Descent from the Cross' the donors, a husband and wife, are depicted on their knees, together with their ages. Both are sixty-three. Next to the man there is a child, wearing what was then the fashion for very little children, under five years of age: a girl's dress and pinafore and a big bonnet with feathers. The child is dressed in bright, rich colours, green brocaded in gold, which throw into relief the severity of the donors' black clothes. This woman of sixty-three cannot possibly have a child of five. It is clearly a dead child, no doubt an only son whose memory the old couple treasured and whom they wanted to show beside them in his best clothes.

It was a pious custom in the old days to present churches with a picture or a stained-glass window, and in the sixteenth century the donor had himself portrayed with his whole family. On the walls and pillars of German churches one can still see a great many pictures of this kind which are in fact family portraits. In St Sebastian's in Nürnberg, in a portrait from the second half of the sixteenth century, the father is shown in the foreground with two full-grown sons behind him and then a scarcely distinguishable bunch of six boys crowded together, hiding behind each other so that some of them are barely visible. Surely these must be dead children.

A similar picture, dated 1560, and kept in Bregenz Museum, has the children's ages recorded on the banderoles: three boys, aged one, two and three; five girls, aged one, two, three, four and five. But the eldest girl of five has the same size and dress as the youngest of one. She has been given her place in the family group just as if she had gone on living, but she has been portrayed at the age when she died.

These family groups are naive, clumsy, monotonous works without style; their painters, like their models, remain unknown or obscure. It is a different matter when the donor has obtained the services of a celebrated painter: in such instances art historians have carried out the research required to identify the figures in a famous painting. This is the case with the Meyer family which Holbein portrayed in 1526 at the Virgin's feet. We know that of the six people in the picture three had died in 1526: Jacob Meyer's first wife and her two boys, one of whom were dead at the age of ten and the other, who is shown naked, at an earlier age.

Here in fact we have a custom which became widespread in the sixteenth century and remained so until the mid-nineteenth century. Versailles Museum has a picture by Nocret portraying the families of Louis XIV and his brother; this painting is famous because the King and the princes are half-naked – the men at least – like gods of Olympus. We would draw attention to one detail here: in the foreground, at Louis XIV's feet, Nocret has placed a framed picture showing two little children who had died in infancy.

Gaignières's records note as early as the end of the sixteenth century some tombs bearing effigies of children on their own: one dates from 1584, the other from 1608. The child is shown in the costume peculiar to his age, in a dress and bonnet, like the child in the Toulouse 'Descent from the Cross'. When within the two years of 1606 and 1607 James I lost two daughters, one when she was three days old and the other at two years of age, he had them portrayed fully dressed on their tombs at Westminster, and he gave instructions that the younger should be shown lying in an alabaster cradle in which all the accessories – the lace of her swaddling-clothes and her bonnet – should be faithfully reproduced to create the illusion of reality. The inscription on the tomb gives a good idea of the pious feeling which endowed this three-day-old child with a definite personality: *Rosula Regia prae-propero Fato decerpta, parentibus erepta, ut in Christi Rosario reflorescat.*

Apart from these mortuary effigies, portraits of children shown separately from their parents were a rarity until the end of the sixteenth century: witness the painting of the Dauphin, Charles Orlando, by the Maître de Moulins, another instance of the pious regard felt for children who had died at an early age. On the other hand, they became very common at the beginning of the seventeenth century; it is clear that it had become customary to preserve by means of the painter's art the ephemeral appearance of childhood. In the portraits of this period the child parted company with the family, just as a century earlier, at the beginning of the sixteenth century, the family had parted company with the religious section of the presentation portrait. Henceforth he would be depicted by himself and for himself: this was the great novelty of the seventeenth century. The child would be one of its favourite models. There are countless examples among the leading painters of the period: Rubens, Van Dyck, Franz Hals, Le Nain, Philippe de Champaigne. Some of these painters portray little princes, as in the picture of Charles I's children by Van Dyck or that of James II's children by Largillière; others, the offspring of great lords, such as the three children painted by Van Dyck, the eldest of whom is wearing a sword;[28] and others, well-to-do bourgeois such as those depicted by Le Nain or Philippe de Champaigne. Sometimes there is an inscription giving the child's name and age, as used to be the custom for adults. Now the child is all alone (see Philippe de Champaigne's work at Grenoble), now the painter gathers together several children from the same family. This last is a popular type of portrait, favoured by a great many anonymous painters, and often to be found in provincial art-galleries or in antique-shops. Henceforth every family wanted portraits of its children, and portraits painted while they were still children. The custom originated in the seventeenth century and is still with us. Photography took over from painting in the nineteenth century: the idea remained the same.

Before finishing with the portraits, we must mention the pictures of children on *ex-votos*, the plaques placed in churches to record the making or granting of a prayer. There are some in the museum of Puy Cathedral, and the Eighteenth Century Exhibition of 1958 in Paris revealed an astonishing portrait of a sick child which must also be an *ex-voto*.

Thus, although demographic conditions did not greatly change between the thirteenth and seventeenth centuries, and although child mortality remained at a very high level, a new sensibility granted these fragile, threatened creatures a characteristic which the world had hitherto failed to recognize in them: as if it were only then that the common conscience had discovered that the child's soul too was immortal. There can be no doubt that the importance accorded to the child's personality was linked with the growing influence of Christianity on life and manners.

This interest shown in the child preceded by more than a century the change in demographic conditions which can be roughly dated from Jenner's great discovery. Correspondences such as that of General de Martange[29] show that certain families insisted at that time on having their children vaccinated; this precaution against the smallpox reveals a state of mind which must have favoured other hygienic practices at the same time, producing a reduction in the death-rate which was counterbalanced to some extent by an increasingly widespread control of the birth-rate.

* * *

Another type of child portraiture unknown to the Middle Ages is the *putto*, the naked child. The *putto* made its appearance at the end of the fourteenth century and obviously represented a revival of the Hellenistic Eros. The theme of the naked child was immediately welcomed with extraordinary enthusiasm, even in France, where Italian art was encountering a certain native resistance. The Duc de Berry, according to his inventories, had a 'children's room', in other words a room hung with tapestries decorated with *putti*. Van Marle wonders 'whether sometimes the scribes responsible for the inventories did not use the word "children" to denote these semi-pagan angels, these *putti* who so often adorned the foliage of tapestries in the second half of the fifteenth century.'[30]

In the sixteenth century the *putto* invaded the world of painting and became an ornamental motif which was repeated ad nauseam. Titian in particular used or rather abused it: witness the 'Triumph of Venus' in the Prado.

The seventeenth century showed no sign of tiring of it, whether in Rome, in Naples, or at Versailles, where the *putti* still kept the old name of *marmousets*. Religious art succumbed to them, thanks to the transformation of the medieval angel-cum-altar-boy into a *putto*. Henceforth, with one exception (the guardian angel) the angel would no longer be the adolescent still to be seen in Botticelli's paintings: he too had become a little naked Eros, even if, in order to satisfy post-tridentine modesty, his nudity was concealed behind clouds, mists and veils.

The *putto*'s nudity spread even to Jesus and the other holy children. If the artist was reluctant to adopt this complete nudity, he simply made it a little more discreet, taking care not to give Jesus too many clothes: He was shown with His mother undoing His swaddling-clothes,[31] or His shoulders and His legs were uncovered. Père du Colombier has already pointed out with regard to the paintings by Lucca della Robbia in the Hôpital des Innocents that it was impossible to portray childhood without stressing its nudity.[32] The taste for child nudity was obviously linked with the general taste for classical nudity which had even begun to affect modern portraiture. But it lasted much longer and it affected the whole of ornamental art: witness Versailles or the ceiling of the Villa Borghese in Rome. The taste for the *putto* corresponded to something far deeper than the taste for classical nudity, something which can be ascribed only to a broad surge of interest in childhood.

Like the medieval child – a holy child, or a symbol of the soul, or an angelic being – the *putto* was never a real, historic child in either the fifteenth or the sixteenth century. This is all the more remarkable in that the theme of the *putto* originated and developed at the same time as the child portrait. But the children in fifteenth and sixteenth century portraits are never, or scarcely ever, naked children. Either they are wrapped in swaddling-clothes even when they are portrayed kneeling in prayer,[33] or else they are shown wearing the dress of their age and station. Nobody could visualize the historic child, even when he was very small, in the nudity of the mythological and ornamental child, and this distinction remained in force for a long time.

The final phase of child iconography was to be the application of the *putto*'s ornamental nudity to the child portrait, and this too was to take place in the seventeenth century. True, a few portraits of naked children are to be noted in the sixteenth century, but they are comparatively rare. One of the oldest is probably the child in Holbein's painting of the Meyer family who had died in infancy (1521). Then too, in one of the halls in Innsbruck Palace, there is a fresco in which Maria Theresa wanted to gather together all her children: next to the living, a dead princess is portrayed in a very chastely draped state of nudity.

In a picture by Titian of 1571 or 1575,[34] Philip II in a dedicatory gesture is shown holding out to Victory his son, the child Ferdinand, who is completely naked: he looks like Titian's usual *putto*, and he seems to be finding the situation extremely funny: the *putti* were often depicted at play.

In 1560 Veronese in accordance with custom portrayed the Cucina-Fiacco family in front of the Virgin and Child: three men, including the father, one woman – the mother – and six children. On the far right a woman is almost cut in half by the edge of the picture: she is holding a naked child in her arms just as the Virgin is holding the Holy Child, a resemblance stressed by the fact that the woman is not wearing the dress of her time. Pushed to one side as she is, she cannot be the mother of the family: perhaps she is the wet-nurse of the youngest child.[35] A mid-sixteenth century painting by the Dutchman P. Ærtsen shows a family: the father, a boy about five, a girl of four, and the mother sitting with a naked child in her lap.[36]

There are sure to have been other cases which more extensive research would bring to light, but they were not numerous enough to create a general taste.

In the seventeenth century, portrayals of this sort became more numerous and more typical: witness the portrait at Munich of Helen Fourment carrying her naked son, who is distinguished from the ordinary *putto* not only by the resemblance to his mother but also by a plumed bonnet of the sort that children wore at the time. The youngest of Charles I's children painted by Van Dyck in 1637 is shown next to his brothers and sisters, naked, and half covered by the linen on which he has been laid.

'When, in 1647,' writes L. Hautecoeur, 'Le Brun portrays the banker and collector Jabach in his Rue Saint-Merri house, he shows us this powerful man casually dressed, with his stockings pulled on anyhow, displaying his latest acquisition to his wife and son . . . his other children are present: the last-born, naked as an Infant Jesus, is lying on a cushion, and one of his sisters is playing with him.'[37] The little Jabach, more than the naked children of Holbein, Veronese, Titian, Van Dyck and even Rubens, has exactly the same pose as that of the modern baby in front of the studio photographer's camera. Henceforth the nudity of the little child was to be a convention of the genre, and all the little children who had always been so ceremoniously dressed up in the time of Le Nain and Philippe de Champaigne would be depicted naked. This convention is to be found both in the work of Largillière, the painter of the upper middle-class, and in that of Mignard, the court painter: the Grand Dauphin's youngest child, in the painting by Mignard in the Louvre, is lying naked on a cushion by his mother, just like the little Jabach.

Either the child is completely naked, as in Mignard's portrait of the Comte de Toulouse,[38] where his nudity is scarcely veiled by the loop of a ribbon which has come undone for the occasion, or in Largillière's portrait of a child holding a billhook;[39] or else he is dressed not in a real costume similar to the clothes generally worn at the time but in a *négligé* which fails to cover his nudity and indeed often reveals it: witness the children's portraits by Belle in which the legs and feet are bare, or Mignard's Duc de Bourgogne, dressed in nothing but a flimsy shift. There is no need to follow any further the history of this theme, which by now had become conventional. It can be found again at its conclusion in the family albums and studio photographers' shop windows of yesterday: babies baring their little bottoms just for the pose – for they were normally carefully covered, swaddled or breeched – and little boys and girls who were dressed for the occasion in nothing but a pretty transparent shift. There was not a single child whose likeness was not preserved in a nude study, directly inherited from the *putti* of the Renaissance: a remarkable example of the persistence in the collective taste (bourgeois as much as lower-class) of a theme which was originally ornamental. The Eros of antiquity, rediscovered in the fifteenth century, went on serving as a model for the 'artistic portraits' of the nineteenth and twentieth centuries.

* * *

The reader of the preceding pages will not have failed to notice the importance of the seventeenth century in the evolution of the themes of childhood. It was in the seventeenth century that portraits of children on their own became numerous and commonplace. It was in the seventeenth century too that the family portrait, a much older genre, tended to plan itself around the child. This concentration on the child is particularly striking in the Rubens family group in which the mother is holding the child by the shoulder while the father has him by the hand,[40] and in the works of Franz Hals, Van Dyck and Lebrun, whose children kiss, cuddle and generally enliven the group of serious adults with their games or their affection. The baroque painter depended on them to give his group portrait the dynamism that it lacked. In the seventeenth century too, subject painting gave the child a place of honour, with countless childhood scenes of a conventional character: the reading lesson, in which the theme of the Virgin's lesson survived in lay form from the religious iconography of the fourteenth and fifteenth centuries, the music lesson, and groups of boys and girls reading, drawing and playing. One could go on indefinitely listing these themes which were extremely common in painting, especially in the first half of the century, and in engraving later. Finally, as we have seen, it was in the second half of the seventeenth century that nudity became an essential convention in child portraiture. No doubt the discovery of childhood began in the thirteenth century, and its progress can be traced in the history of art in the fifteenth and sixteenth centuries. But the evidence of its development became more plentiful and significant from the end of the sixteenth century and throughout the seventeenth.

This is confirmed by the interest shown at that time in little children's habits and 'jargon'. We have already noted, in the preceding chapter [see original reading], how they were given new names: *bambins, pitchouns* and *fanfans*. People also amused themselves by picking up their children's expressions and using their vocabulary, that is to say, the vocabulary used by their nannies when speaking to them. It is a rare thing for literature, even of the most popular kind, to preserve traces of children's jargon. Yet some such traces are to be found in the *Divina Commedia*: 'What further glory will you have if you leave an aged flesh than if you had died before you had stopped saying *pappo* and *dindi*.'[41] *Pappo* is bread. The word existed in the French language of Dante's time: *le papin*. It is to be found in one of the *Miracles de Notre-Dame*, that of 'the little child who feeds the picture of Jesus in Our Lady's arms'. But is the word *papin* really confined to childhood, or does it not rather belong to the familiar speech of everyday life? Be that as it may, the *Miracles de Notre-Dame*, like other sixteenth-century texts, bears witness to a certain taste for childhood painted from life. But references to children's jargon are unusual before the seventeenth century. In the seventeenth century they are to be found in abundance. To take one example, a collection of prints by Bouzonnet and Stella, dated 1657:[42] this collection contains a series of engravings showing *putti* at play. There is nothing original about the drawings, but the captions, written in appalling doggerel, speak the jargon of infancy and also schoolboy slang, for the limits of infancy were still anything but clear at the time. A plate showing *putti* playing with hobby-horses is entitled 'Le Dada'.

> Some *putti* are playing at dice.
> One goes away, and number two
> Consoles himself with his *toutou*.

The *papin* of the fourteenth and fifteenth centuries must have been dropped, at least from the speech of French bourgeois children, possibly because it was not confined to infancy. But other childish words had appeared which are still in use today: *toutou* and *dada*.

Apart from this nursery language, the *putti* also use school slang or the slang of military academies. In the caption to a drawing of a sledge game the word *populo*, from school Latin, is used. In the same childish sense, Mme de Sévigné would refer to Mme de Grignan's children as *ce petit peuple*. One child who shows exceptional skill is referred to as *ce cadet*, a term used in the academies where young gentlemen at the beginning of the seventeenth century were taught fencing, riding and the arts of war. Under another picture, we are told that children go and play tennis as soon as they have *campos*: an academy expression, a military term, which means 'to have leave'. It was widely used in everyday speech, and can be found in Mme de Sévigné. Again, we are shown some children bathing and are told that the others are drinking to the health of their *camarades*. This term, which was also new or at least did not date back further than the late sixteenth century, was obviously of military origin (possibly it came from the Germans or German-speaking mercenaries) and went through the academies. Incidentally it would always be more or less confined to the familiar speech of the French middle class. It is still not used in French lower-class speech, which prefers the older word *copain*, from the medieval *compaing*.

But let us return to the jargon of infancy. In Cyrano de Bergerac's *Le Pédant joué*, Granger calls his son his *toutou*: 'Come and kiss me, come my *toutou*.' The word *bonbon*, which I suppose originated in nannies' jargon, was admitted to everyday speech. And attempts were even made to give onomatopoeic renderings of the speech of children who had not yet learnt to talk. Thus Mme de Sévigné laboriously noted the noises made by her little daughter and reported them to Mme de Grignan who was then in Provence: 'She talks most amusingly: titota, tetita, y totata.'[43] Already, at the beginning of the century, Heroard, Louis XIII's doctor, had carefully recorded in his diary his charge's childish pronunciation of certain words: *vela* for *voilà*, *équivez* for *écrivez*, and so on.

When she describes her little daughter, her 'little darling', Mme de Sévigné paints genre pictures similar to those of Le Nain or Bosse, with the pretty affectation of late seventeenth-century engravers and eighteenth century artists besides. 'Our daughter is a dark-haired little beauty. She is very pretty indeed. Here she comes. She gives me sticky kisses, but she never screams.' 'She kisses me, she recognizes me, she laughs at me, she calls me just plain *Maman* [instead of *Bonne Maman*].' 'I simply adore her. I have had her hair cut: it is a happy-go-lucky style now which is just made for her. Her complexion, her chest and her little body are admirable. She does a hundred and one different things: she caresses, she slaps, she makes the sign of the cross, she begs pardon, she drops a curtsy, she blows a kiss, she shrugs her shoulders, she dances, she strokes, she holds her chin: in a word she is pretty in every particular. I watch her for hours on end.'[44] Countless mothers and nannies had already felt the same way. But not a single one had admitted that these feelings were worthy of being expressed in such an ambitious form. These literary scenes of childhood correspond to those of contemporary genre painting and engraving: each reflected the discovery of infancy, of the little child's body, habits and chatter.

Notes

1   Gospel-book of Otto III, Munich.
2   'Vie et miracle de saint Nicolas', Bibliothèque Nationale.
3   Psalter of St Louis of Leyden.
4   Compare the scene, 'Suffer the little children to come to me', in Otto's Gospel-book and in the *Bible moralisée de saint Louis*, f° 505.
5   *Bible moralisée de saint Louis*, f° 5. A. de Laborde, *Bibles moralisées illustrées*, 1911–21, 4 vols of plates.
6   Gospel-book in the Sainte-Chapelle; scene reproduced in H. Martin, *La Miniature française*, plate VII.
7   *Exposition des bronzes sardes*, Bibliothèque Nationale, 1954, no. 25, plate XI.
8   P. du Colombier, *L'Enfant au Moyen Age*, 1951.
9   *Miracles de Notre-Dame*, edited by G. F. Warner, 1885.
10   *Manuscrits à peinture du VIIe au XIIe siècle*, Exhibition at the Bibliothèque Nationale, 1954, no. 330, plate XXX.

11   See note 5.
12   *Iliad*, Ambrosian Library, Milan.
13   Rampilly.
14   See note 5.
15   *Miroir d'humilité*, Valenciennes, f° 18, early fifteenth century.
16   See below, Part III, Chap. II [see original reading].
17   Gaignières, *Les Tombeaux*.
18   G. Zaccagnini, *La vita dei maestri e degli scolari nella studio di Bologna*. Geneva, 1926, plates IX, X.
19   Before this, the representation of children on tombs was rare.
20   *Le Caquet de l'accouchée*, 1622.
21   Montaigne, *Essais*, II, 8.
22   Mme de Sévigné, *Lettres*, August 19th, 1671.
23   Mérian, *Tabula Cebetis*, 1655. Cf. Lebègue, 'Le Peintre Varin et le Tableau de Cebes', *Arts*, 1952, pp. 167–71.
24   Montaigne, *Essais*, II, 8.
25   Gaignières, *Les Tombeaux*.
26   F. Bond, *Westminster Abbey*, London, 1909.
27   Musée des Augustins, no. 465 in the catalogue.
28   Van Dyck, K. d. K., plate CCXIV.
29   *Correspondance inédite du général de Martange*, 1756–82, edited by Bréard, 1898.
30   Van Marle, op. cit., vol. I, p. 71.
31   Baldovinetti, 'Virgin and Child', Louvre.
32   P. du Colombier, op. cit.
33   'Virgin Enthroned', supposedly portrait of Beatrice d'Este, 1496.
34   'Glorification of the Victory of Lepanto', Prado.
35   Dresden, Pinakothek.
36   Reproduced in H. Gerson, *De nederlandse Shilderkunst*, 2 vols, 1952, vol. I, p. 145.
37   L. Hautecoeur, *Les Peintres de la vie familiale*, 1945, p. 40.
38   Versailles Museum.
39   Rouches, 'Largillière, peintre d'enfants', *Revue de l'Art ancien et moderne*, 1923, p. 253.
40   About 1609, Karlsruhe.
41   *Purgatorio*.
42   C. Bouzonnet-Stella, op. cit.
43   Mme de Sévigné, *Lettres*, January 8th, 1672.
44   September 18th, 1671; December 22nd, 1671; May 20th, 1672.

Chapter 2

Barrie Thorne

RE-VISIONING WOMEN AND SOCIAL CHANGE: WHERE ARE THE CHILDREN?

FEMINISTS HAVE RE-VISIONED WOMEN as active subjects in knowledge by granting them agency and diversity and by challenging divisions like public versus private. But both feminist and traditional knowledge remain deeply adult centered. Adult perspectives infuse three contemporary images of chilldren: as threats to adult society, as victims of adults, and as learners of adult culture ("socialization"). We can bring children more fully into knowledge by clarifying ideological constructions, with attention to the diversity of children's actual lives and circumstances; by emphasizing children's agency as well as their subordination; and by challenging their conceptual privatization. The re-visioning of children involves complex issues of gender, generation, autonomy, and relatedness.

Critical scholars have revealed deep sources of bias masked by claims that knowledge is "objective" and without standpoint; the experiences and interests of the privileged have shaped not only the choice of topics but also conceptual frameworks and methods of study (Smith 1979). Feminists entered this process of critique by placing women at the center, as subjects of inquiry and as active agents in the gathering of knowledge. The result has been a rethinking of basic concepts in many disciplines.[1] But while feminists challenged the hegemony of men's experiences, we have often assumed the standpoints of white, class-privileged, heterosexual, and Euro-American women.[2] The process of critique—of attending to diversity among women, and among men, and of theorizing intersecting patterns of domination and their effects on knowledge—has become a complex project.

I want to add to that complexity by pursuing a relatively simple observation: Both feminist and traditional knowledge remain deeply and unreflectively centered around the experiences of adults. Our understanding of children tends to be filtered through adult perspectives and interests. How can we bring children more fully into our understanding of social life, including processes of social change? Because the fates and definitions of women and children have been so closely tied, our re-visioning of women may provide useful leads for recentering our knowledge of children. Broadened understanding of children will, in turn, enhance feminist visions of and strategies for change.

To illustrate our re-visioning of women, I will briefly review challenges to traditional conceptions of work and production that emerged by granting women conceptual autonomy and placing them at the center of study. I will then argue that we need a similar re-visioning of children; their full lives, experiences, and agency have been obscured by adult standpoints. We may discover leads for rethinking children both by examining *parallels* between their situations and those of women, and by gaining clarity about ideological and actual *connections* between women and children. Finally, I will discuss limits of the analogy between our re-visioning of women and potential re-visioning of children. In the concluding discussion, I will try to clarify the discomfort that accompanies the granting of conceptual autonomy to women and to children—a discomfort that perhaps should, but rarely does, accompany the granting of autonomy to men.

Placing women at the center: the re-visioning of work

Within traditional sociology, whatever the theoretical school, the assumption was always made that workers were adult men. (I use the past tense, but we should remember that androcentric knowledge still flourishes in many quarters.) Marxist frameworks—tracing the changing organization of production, the emergence of industrial capitalism, and processes of class conflict—emphasized the industrial proletariat and the owners of capital. Both groups were assumed to be men. Women (and children) were relegated to the margins of history, to privatized domestic units, assumed to be relatively static and reactive. Men were granted a direct position in production and class struggle, and hence in the making of social change. Unless engaged in wage work (and even then, Marxists only peripherally attended to women), women were located in the class structure via their husbands or fathers.

The sociology of occupations and professions—a different way of casting the study of work—also equated work with paid work, and workers with adult men. Empirical studies focused on an array of professional, managerial, white-collar, and blue-collar occupations, but in nearly all of them, men predominated. Women's occupational experiences were either ignored or included as an afterthought. For example, sociologists coined the term "semi-professions" to encompass "women's fields" like social work and nursing. The gender assumption—that women could never be full professionals, but were destined, almost by definition, to remain "semi"—was tacit but never clarified or analyzed.

The contemporary feminist movement developed along with a dramatic increase in women's labor force participation that made it difficult to ignore women's work. Seeking to make women visible and to revalue and articulate their experiences, feminist sociologists, economists, and historians directed attention to women's varied experiences of labor. For example, feminist scholars pursued the fact that as workers in early textile mills, women were the first industrial proletariat. Women were also the first workers to experience the process of deskilling as their traditional work of spinning and weaving was reorganized and routinized for someone else's profit (Kessler-Harris 1982). In the nineteenth century, when wage labor became more prevalent, it was increasingly relegated to men, but large numbers of immigrant, black, and poorer white women continued to work for wages. Women have been active participants, and sometimes leaders, in labor movements and other forms of collective action (Milkman 1985).

Fuller attention to women's lives also encouraged more research on women's experiences in a variety of occupations (e.g., see Lopata, with Miller and Barnewolt 1984). This has included jobs in which women traditionally have predominated, such as clerical work, elementary school teaching, paid domestic labor, routine assembly work, and subsistence farm labor in developing countries, and the experiences of women tokens in male-dominated occupations such as police enforcement, construction work, law, and medicine.

The experiences of women workers don't always fit comfortably into categories, either Marxist or non-Marxist, honed out of the experiences of men. This lack of fit helped clarify male bias and has led to efforts to reformulate basic concepts such as social class (Acker 1978; Eisenstein 1979), occupational mobility (Acker 1978), relationships to employment (Feldberg and Glenn 1979), and models of organization (Kanter 1977) and of economic development (Beneria 1982).

Feminists' efforts to understand the whole of women's lives also challenged the equation of work with paid work. Broadening their conception of "work," feminists illuminated various forms of unpaid "invisible labor" (Glazer 1984; Kahn-Hut et al. 1982). Such labor—housework, subsistence farming, the knitting together of kin, volunteering in community institutions, shopping for consumer goods, care of children and the frail elderly—tends to be overlooked and devalued in part *because* it is usually done by women.

By taking gender as a basic category of analysis, feminists have raised new questions about relationships among class, race, and gender hierarchies; gender segmentation of the labor force; the gender typing of occupations; wage gaps between men and women; sexual harassment and other informal ways in which men control women in work settings; and relationships between paid and unpaid work, and work and families. This scholarship looks not only at the constraints imposed on women as subordinates in the gender hierarchies basic to every social institution but also at ways in which women of varying circumstances actively try to shape the conditions of their lives.

Women, in short, have been re-visioned as active, speaking subjects. Feminist re-visioning of women in varied economic, family, political, cultural, and social contexts has highlighted several basic themes:

(1)   Women's subordination to men is basic to their experiences. But women are not just passive victims; they are also agents, actors, creators of culture, and participants in the making of history. Their consciousness needs to be understood directly, rather than filtered through ideologies or stereotypes created by men.

(2)   Like other subordinates, women have often been defined by their social category and treated as a singularity ("the woman problem"), while men, as dominants, have been granted individual status. Feminists have challenged this ideology; we have argued that men's lives are as deeply structured by gender as are those of women, and we have placed increasing emphasis on diversity among women by social class, race, culture, sexuality, and age.

(3)   Women are actors and participants in all social institutions, and the study of gender should be basic not only to conceptualizations of more "private" institutions such as family and community (with which women have ideologically been associated) but also to the study of more "public" institutions—the wage economy, bureaucracies, the state, and political movements (Stacey and Thorne 1985). The very distinction between public and private or domestic is problematic and needs to be explored.

How do we think about children?

Children lurk at the edges of the knowledge I have briefly reviewed. They worked alongside women in the early textile mills, and in traditional thought, notions like "the family" and "the domestic" have encapsulated children along with women. Feminist challenges of public/domestic divisions have opened new angles of vision that have not been as fully developed for children as for women. Like the traditional theorists such as Marx and Parsons, from whom we borrowed analytic tools while also rebelling, feminist theorists have assumed the standpoints of adults. Adult interests and perspectives infuse three contemporary images of children: as threats to adult society, as victims of adults, and as learners of adult culture.

Children as threats and as victims

Within sociological, feminist, and popular thought, children rarely appear on *public* agendas unless they are defined as a social problem. Adults do the defining, using imagery that vacillates between two sometimes interrelated poles: children as a threat to adult society and children as victims of adults. In both views, the experiences of children are filtered through adult concerns.

In nineteenth-century England and the United States, state agencies first began to intervene in families in response to perceived problems of juvenile crime (Eekelar et al. 1982; Gordon forthcoming). Children, especially from working-class households, were seen as potential threats to social order. Emphasis on protection of adults *from* children later shifted to protection *of* children from specific adults—parents who abused and neglected them. Thus, in Western legal and social history, children, especially from working-class households, were defined as threats before they were defined as victims. A variety of reformers— charity workers, evangelicals, municipal authorities, and feminists—shaped these changing definitions. Nineteenth-century feminists were especially active in movements to protect children from adult abuse (Gordon forthcoming).

In the changing construction of social problems, images of children as threats and as victims have continued to appear and reappear. In the United States in the 1950s, juvenile delinquency became a spectre in popular consciousness. The theme of children as menacing to adult society continued in images of "hippie" youth culture in the 1960s (in this case the imagery was of adolescents, who generally seem less innocent and more threatening than younger children). Within the last decade, there has been striking emphasis on children as victims. The media, buttressed by social science findings, have given visibility to the problem of adult physical abuse of children, and, in recent years (due in part to efforts of the contemporary women's movement), to the prevalence of adult sexual abuse of children (McCormack 1985). Startling statistics about the growing impoverishment of children in the United States add to a sense of alarm about the victimization of children.

The popular media use portrayals of victimized young children as a rhetorical strategy to convey the severity of problems that adults often face as well. Since children are defined as innocent, their presence suggests that at least some of the victims cannot be blamed. For example, when the media began to emphasize the presence of children among the urban homeless, the reports assumed new urgency and a shift from victim blaming. The evils of apartheid in South Africa—and the limits of blaming the victims—are often dramatized by referring to the large number of black children, some as young as seven, who have been arrested or killed by the government. In a primary arena of contemporary victim blaming, stories about children who have contracted AIDS counter moralists who claim that all AIDS victims have chosen their fates.

A recent wave of books with almost interchangeable titles—*The Disappearance of Childhood* (Postman 1982), *Children Without Childhood* (Winn 1983), *The Hurried Child* (Elkind 1981), *Our Endangered Children* (Packard 1983), *The Erosion of Childhood* (Suransky 1982)—portray contemporary children as generalized victims, deprived of adult protection and subjected to unhealthy competitive and bureaucratic pressures, sex, drugs, and too much television. These authors also believe children are victimized by divorce, the large number of mothers in the work force, and the shortage of good alternative sources of nurturance and security.

These are compelling issues, and my intent is not to undermine their importance. I want rather to observe that it is *adults* who construct the imagery of children both as quintessential victims *and* as threats to adult society. In both cases, children tend to be constructed as "the other," to be regarded with emotions of pity or fear. Neither portrayal allows much room for understanding children's consciousness and actions within their sometimes difficult circumstances. Our current images of agency are deeply adult centered.

Children as learners: the "socialization" approach

Apart from the social problems tradition, children have mostly been considered under the rubric of "socialization" in both traditional sociology and in feminist thought. The core insight is reasonable and even compelling: Born without language or knowledge of social organization, children become slowly inducted into the social worlds around them. This process of induction addresses a basic sociological question: How is society possible? The socialization answer posits that new members internalize culture and learn the rules of adult society. An enormous and in many ways useful body of research informs us about the ways children acquire language, conceptions of social organization, the capacity for friendship, religious beliefs, political attitudes, and the outlooks of their social class.

Mainstream sociologists and psychologists often give positive weighting to processes of socialization and "child development." Kagan et al. (1978, p. 5) observe that experts in child development usually assume "orderly, organized change toward a hypothetical ideal." That ideal, or *telos*, is presumed to be friendly; developmental psychologists emphasize "flexibility, control, self-consciousness, strength, coordination, task competence, freedom of choice, and speed of cognitive processing," all of which seem to increase with age. The authors observe that "depression, chronic anxiety, guilt, ambivalence, insomnia, vacillation, and hatred" also become more common with age. But these more negative states are rarely assumed to be the endpoints of development.

Feminists have used the socialization approach not to ask "How is society possible?" but rather to demonstrate that gender divisions (man/woman; masculine/feminine) and male dominance are not "natural" and hence immutable, but are socially constructed. As learners of culture, children become drawn into, and thus help reproduce, the gender organization of their society. Critical of this endpoint, feminists argue that the structure and content of socialization should be changed.

For example, feminist psychoanalytic theorists, such as Nancy Chodorow (1978) and Gayle Rubin (1975), have connected the learning of gender identity—the molding of "feminine" and "masculine" personalities—with family structure. Through childhood experiences, social conventions of sex and gender, including men's greater power, become inscribed within individuals (Rubin 1975). According to these theorists, if gendered divisions of labor were altered and men were more involved in caring for children, then society, culture, and personality would become more equitable and less repressive.

The learning of gender has proven to be a rich topic, and I believe that feminist proposals for changing socialization indeed have emancipatory possibilities. But "socialization" frameworks—within traditional knowledge *and* within feminist thought—embed what Matthew Speier (1976) calls "the adult ideological viewpoint." Children are imaged primarily as learners of adult culture, their experiences in the present continually referred to a presumed future, the endpoint (to use the term from developmental psychology) of adulthood.

Studies of the socialization of gender start with adult arrangements—feminine and masculine personalities, gendered divisions of labor, and gender hierarchies. Children's lives are then referred to that outcome, with the basic question: How do children become shaped by and inducted into the (adult) sex/gender system? The result is a conceptual double standard: Adults are understood by their present actions and experiences in the world; children are understood more by their becoming, as adults-in-the-making.

Socialization frameworks are deeply teleological, referring children's present lives to their presumed adult futures. They also assume an ontology, a division between the supposedly completed nature of the adult and the incomplete child (Jenks 1982). In a classic article, Ruth Benedict (1938) observed that in our culture, adults go to great extremes to define themselves as different from children. Adults consider themselves responsible, dominant, and sexual, and assume children to be irresponsible, submissive, and asexual. Earlier in Western history, adult/child dichotomies were less sharply drawn (Aries 1962). As Arlene Skolnick (1980) argues, our contemporary social practices, such as the restriction of children to age-graded institutions, may help to construct some of the very patterns psychologists have posited as universal "stages of development."

Jerome Kagan (1984) makes a related point: Cultures project onto infants and young children a nature opposite to the qualities prized in adults. Valuing independence, we define children as dependent; the task of socialization is to encourage independence. In the nineteenth century, when parental authority was idealized, adults defined children as willful, and the goal of socialization was to teach obedience. The Japanese, who value interdependence, define infants as too autonomous and needing to be tempted into dependence.

Thus, conceptions of adulthood and childhood vary cross-culturally and change historically, just as definitions of gender do. But whatever the conception of children, adults do the defining. Currently, adults use children to define themselves, in an ideological process of dominance and self-definition analogous to the way in which men have defined women and colonialists have defined those they colonized, as "the other" (DeBeauvoir 1953; Fanon 1967). Adult power over children, including the power of definition, constitutes the usually unspoken context within which modern studies of socialization and child development take shape.

Socialization approaches have other problems. The logic is forward looking, taking a long temporal sweep by referring children's experiences in the present to their presumed distant futures. Although temporal, this approach tends to be abstracted from historical time. It entails what Kagan (1984, p. 11) calls a "faith in continuity," a belief that "life is an unbroken trail" on which one can trace a particular quality or presumed outcome to its beginning. He observes that personal change is sometimes abrupt, due to biological maturation or unexpected social events. War, economic crisis, environmental disasters, and even a shift from the situations of elementary school to those of junior high, may quickly alter the behavior and experiences of people of any age. The functionalist and determinist assumptions of many socialization theories pose obstacles to understanding the dynamics of social structure, human agency, and historical change (Brittan and Maynard 1984).

To highlight limitations of the underlying logic, I have etched a sharp portrayal of the socialization approach. In fact, within the last few decades many socialization theorists have taken a less determinist perspective, assuming that children are not passive recipients of culture, but that they actively construct and interpret the world. Piaget (1952), Vygotsky (1978), and Mead (1934), for example, all emphasize the activities of children who, in the process of socialization, take the role of the other, discover and interpret the world, engage in practical activities, and hence help shape their own experiences of development (for a useful theoretical synthesis, see Corsaro 1985; also see Denzin 1977).

Inspired by these theoretical traditions, a growing number of researchers have used tools of ethnography, sociolinguistics, and open-ended interviewing to uncover the complex nature of children's experiences. They organize their insights around the theme of children's active participation in processes of socialization. For example, in empirical studies of children's interactions in same-gender play groups, Lever (1976) and Fine (1981) focus their analyses upon the question of what adult skills children's interactions teach. Because these studies are richly empirical and allow for the agency of children, their discoveries spill beyond the conceptual container of socialization. But other lines of interpretation are not developed. The socialization framework has the effect of translating doing into learning, locating experience in abstracted developmental rather than in historical time, and conveying a preoccupation with the reproduction of adult social order. Studies of socialization and child development are useful, but limiting; we need to develop more fully other frameworks for understanding children.

Some researchers have dislodged the conventional socialization framework by turning it on its head, asking not how adults shape children, but rather how children influence adults. For example, Beverly Purrington (1980) asked parents to discuss the effects on their lives and consciousness of having preschool-aged children. Daily contact with young children renewed the parents' access to play and memory, provided a close-up "mirror" that altered their self-reflection, enlarged their range of emotions (including intense rage and joy), and pressed them to make decisions they might otherwise put off. Elise Boulding (1980) found that college students could remember specific ways in which, as children, they had actively nurtured their parents. Studies of this kind challenge the assumption that adults are self-sufficient and complete; they also indicate that adult-child relations may involve considerable mutual influence.

Rethinking ideological constructions of children

How can we move beyond the limitations of adult-centered frameworks and bring children more fully into sociological and feminist thought, including our conceptions of human agency and social change? Because the fates and definitions of children have been closely tied with those of women, feminist re-visioning of women may provide leads for similar re-visioning of children. One fruitful source of insight comes from feminist analyses of gender ideologies, which are often intertwined with ideological constructions of children and adults. With more clarity about the distorting effects of such ideologies, we will ask better questions about the complexity of children's lived experiences.

Feminists have traced the changing social and cultural construction of gender dualisms like man/woman and feminine/masculine. Age-based dualisms like adult/child are also socially constructed. When either gender or age is highlighted, the other dimension often recedes from conscious view. For example, in probing varied definitions of "adult" and "child," Kagan (1984) neglects gender; and in starting with gender, feminist scholars often do not reflect upon their assumptions about age.

Beneath surface meanings, however, age and gender categories are complexly intertwined. For example, a frequently cited study of the late 1960s (Broverman et al. 1970) found that therapists viewed the psychologically healthy adult as a healthy man—as competent, independent, and objective; the healthy woman was seen as more dependent, submissive, and less objective, qualities associated with children. The unraveling of contemporary gender stereotypes often reveals an adult/child strand.

Adult/child dualisms—especially the authority of parents (and within that, the authority of fathers) over children—are often invoked to justify other forms of social inequality. Different types of power—of kings over subjects, slave owners over slaves, and men over women—have been justified by defining the subordinates as "like children," inherently dependent and vulnerable, less competent, incapable of exercising full responsibility, and in need of protection. Each of these forms of domination and its supporting ideology has, in turn, been challenged; political subjects, blacks, and women are *not* "like children," and their subordination is not legitimate.

The use of adult/child dualisms to justify inequality should be pushed a step further. Do children—given their great variability in age, culture, and circumstance—have a singular "child-like nature" that legitimates their subordination to adults? As discussed earlier, definitions of children are socially constructed and historically changing; a reified notion like "the child" should be critically examined. Furthermore, the challenging of women's subordination has led to questioning of family hierarchies and patterns of "intimate oppression" (see Thorne, with Yalom 1982), with important, but underdeveloped implications for rethinking the subordination of children.[4]

In some ideological constructions, women are *likened to* children. In other constructions, women are *closely and unreflectively tied* with children; womanhood has been equated with motherhood in a mixing of identities that simply does not occur for men and fatherhood. Nancy Chodorow and Susan Contratto (1982) have observed that a definition of "mother" entails a definition of "child," but feminist writers, who have opened the topic of motherhood to fresh understanding, have been relatively unreflective about the assumptions they make about children. For example, Ruth Bloch (1978) traces the rise of "motherhood" ideologies in the United States in the late eighteenth century and early nineteenth century. In the colonial period, women were depicted as wives and Christians, and motherhood was not idealized. Over the course of the eighteenth century, as men gradually shifted to wage labor, many women and children became economic dependents and public/domestic divisions became more sharply marked. A new maternal ideal gained ascendancy in the middle class, and women were increasingly defined by ideologies of motherhood and domesticity. Bloch raises, but does not develop, the point that this altered view of women entailed a redefinition of children as domesticated, dependent, and needing constant maternal care.

Between 1870 and 1930 the ideology of domesticated mothers and children expanded across social classes, in a process analyzed by Viviana Zelizer (1985), who emphasizes changing definitions of children. Child labor laws and compulsory public schooling further privatized children. Through considerable conflict that often pitted working-class women and men against middle-class reformers, an earlier view of the useful wage-earning child was replaced by a view of the child as "economically worthless, but emotionally priceless" (Zelizer 1985, p. 21). Children became sentimentally defined, their "proper place" narrowed to families and schools. The field of child development also emerged in this period, providing "expert" definitions of the nature and needs of children, and charging mothers with the work of deliberately "developing" the child (Ehrenreich and English 1979; Kessen 1979).

Modern ideologies of motherhood and childhood are far from monolithic, but in various twists of definition and labeling—which in the United States often embed structures of social class and race—women and children have been repeatedly defined in terms of one another. Linda Gordon (1985) shows that the labeling of "single mother" and "neglected child" developed as interrelated conceptions imposed by child welfare agencies between 1880 and 1920. Bias against single mothers, who violated ideals of family life, shaped definitions of child neglect. In a comparative study of the United States and Italy, Chiara Saraceno (1984, p. 352) argues that the "policies of welfare states which concern children always embody a definition of mothers; and the policies which concern women always assign them responsibility for the children." For example, definitions of "the day care child" have been closely linked to constructions of "the working mother."

Ideological constructions both shape and distort the varieties of lived experience. By uncovering gender ideologies and questioning their assumptions (e.g., that women have no lives apart from children, and that mother and child exist in an isolated dyad), feminists have cleared space for examining the actual, enormously varied experiences of women. If we turn fuller attention to the "child" side of these ideologies, we would also clear space for better understanding of *their* enormously varied experiences. For example, feminists have shown that the practice of blaming the mother for every sort of problem distorts women's experiences and neglects other circumstances that help shape the lives of children. We have paid less attention to the other side of the ideological coin: that mother-blaming *also* distorts children's experiences of the world, denying their intentionality and capacity for action within circumstances that extend beyond ties with mothers.

Contemporary sentimental definitions trivialize and domesticate children's activities and objectify them as "cute." Conceptualizing children in terms of development and socialization imposes an adult-centered notion of structured becoming upon children's experiences in the present. Both ideologies tend to collapse children into a singularity—"the child" (perhaps subdivided into "developmental stages")—and deflect attention from children's varied circumstances, experiences, and social relations. These ideologies also mask the harsh realities of children's subordination: Placing children on the pedestal of sentimentality helps obscure the ways in which adults abuse and exploit them, and government policies contribute to their growing impoverishment. Conceptualizing children as victims *does* reveal these harsh realities, but that view—when it fails to acknowledge children's worlds of meaning and their capacities for action and survival—also distorts. In short, we need fuller understanding of the social contexts in which different ideological constructions of children are evoked, the effects of adult definitions on children's own experiences of themselves, and more attention to children's abilities to act within and upon the world.

Re-visioning children

Feminists have emphasized women's active presence and consciousness in the world—agency rendered invisible in male-centered knowledge. They have also challenged divisions like public/private that obscure women's presence and structures of gender in varied institutions. Working by analogy, I have argued that our ways of thinking about children reflect adult interests and limit understanding of children's experiences and actions. Like women, children have been treated as a singularity—"the child." And they have been conceptually privatized.

Within sociology, the study of children has largely been confined to a few subfields: the family, education, and social psychology—arenas in which socialization frameworks flourish. Anne-Marie Ambert (1986) documents the near absence of children in writings of classical sociological theory, recent introductory sociology textbooks, and eight widely read sociology journals. At most, textbooks have one chapter on children, usually under the rubric of socialization. At the top of the journals in the proportion of space devoted to children, *Journal of Marriage and Family* had only 3.6 percent and *Sociology of Education* only 6.6 percent of articles on children.

Before the challenges posed by the women's movement and feminist theory, sociological research on women was also sparse and limited to a few subfields, notably, family and community. Studies of women, and attention to gender relations, can now be found in the literature on work, social organization, political and urban sociology, social movements, and stratification. But children remain relatively invisible in most sociological *and* feminist literature. To bring children more fully into knowledge, we will need to rethink their conceptual privatization. Age relations, like gender relations, are built into varied institutions and social circumstances. The experiences of children may be illuminated by, and in turn may challenge, our frameworks for understanding not only families and schools but also politics, work, poverty, social class, organizations, bureaucracy, urban life, social stratification, and social change. One can argue, as Joan Kelly (1979, p. 21) did for women, that children's place is "not a separate sphere or domain of existence but a position within social existence generally."

Of course, in contemporary Western societies children are largely excluded from public politics and paid work; in many ways they are literally relegated to a separate sphere of family, neighborhood, and schooling. But in situations of intense political conflict, as in South Africa and Nicaragua, even young children may be directly involved in actions conventionally defined as "political." Children may also be canny political observers. Through respectful listening to children, Robert Coles (1971, 1986) has revealed complex political and ethical sensibilities that make psychologists' "stages of moral development" seem highly artificial.

And in relations with adults, as well as within their social groups, children collaborate to further their interests, engaging in conflicts and gestures of partisanship that not only may be understood as socialization for later, more full-fledged political life but also as a form of politics itself (Maynard 1985). Attention to children may expand our overall notions of "the political."

In contemporary Western societies, children do relatively little paid work. But in studies of political economy and development, we should attend more closely to the productive labor of children in Third-World countries, in earlier historical times, and, in our own society, in contexts like those of migrant farming (Coles 1971). Feminist scholars developed concepts like "invisible work" to focus attention on women's everyday lives. Children also do invisible work; they nurture others (Boulding 1980); they construct culture and social organization (Corsaro 1985; Goodwin 1980; Maynard 1985); they participate in negotiations and conflicts about and in some of the actual doing of housework (Wittner 1980). As with adults, children's visible and invisible labor tends to be divided by gender (Medrich et al. 1982). These activities are not simply socialization for adult work life; they have their own consequence and meanings in the present and should become more central to our overall conceptualizations of work.

On the other hand, sociologists and feminists may have stretched the metaphor of "work" too far. Because work is unquestionably an arena of agency, feminists have drawn upon that metaphor ("caring work," "interaction work") to lend weight to activities that absorb women's time and attention but tend to be ignored. But the processes of caring for others and facilitating conversations are both like—and *not* like—work. We need to develop more complicated ways of thinking about human activity.

We often assume that adults work and children "play," a conceptual separation that tends to bracket children's activity from "serious" life. Clinical psychologists and sociologists have called play "the work of little children" (Denzin 1977)—a shift of metaphors intended, like feminist renaming, to rescue activities from invisibility and trivialization. Indeed, children's play *is* often serious and purposive. But we should question the very dichotomy between work and play, a dichotomy, imposed by adults and perhaps distinctively Western, that masks great variety in the experiences of people of all ages. As Suransky (1982) observes, young children do not experience a play/work dichotomy; they work while playing and play while working. Wonderfully detailed studies of children at play (reviewed in Schwartzman 1978) reveal multiple layers of meaning in children's activities. Such complex phenomenological understanding—the result of revaluing children and attending closely to their experiences—may inspire fresh approaches to adult life.

Closer attention to children and their diversity can also deepen our understanding of social stratification. In an ethnographic study of working-class "lads" in a vocational school in England, Paul Willis (1977) connects daily interactions with the organization of institutions and with structural contradictions of age, social class, and gender. Resisting the authority structure of their school, the "lads" develop an oppositional culture of aggression and joking that resembles the masculine, working-class culture of factory work—their ultimate, albeit unintended destination. While they resist social-class domination, they ironically end up reproducing the class structure, and doing so partly through a specific form of masculinity.

Inspired by Willis's approach, later researchers have examined strategies of accommodation and resistance used by girls as well as boys, and they have begun to explore dimensions of race as well as social class (e.g., Anyon 1983; Connell et al. 1982; Fuller 1980). In these studies, children are not defined as undergoing socialization, but rather as human actors negotiating within and sometimes resisting institutional structures—schools, families, wage labor. These studies emphasize both agency and structure; they bridge between public and private institutions; and they trace complex, sometimes contradictory intersections of class, gender, race, and age.

These varied examples suggest leads for recentering our knowledge of children. They move beyond the conceptual container of socialization, showing that age relations and children's experiences may be relevant to a variety of sociological and feminist questions. While acknowledging the effects of structural constraints and the importance of children's subordination, they grant children agency and seek to understand the complexity of their experiences. The most compelling of these studies attend to gender, race, and class, as well as to age; they challenge the ideological singularity of the child.

Epistemological issues

It is not by chance that the most suggestive empirical research on children—revealing them to be complex actors, strategists, performers, users of language, creators of culture—is based on qualitative and interpretive approaches. Open-ended interviewing (e.g., Coles 1971, 1986; Wittner 1980), participant-observation (e.g., Willis 1977), and the tools of sociolinguistics (e.g., Corsaro 1985; Goodwin 1980; Maynard 1985) assume the importance of human action and the daily construction of meaning. They are especially helpful in uncovering experiences and forms of agency that have been suppressed by dominant ideologies.

Reflexive and interpretive approaches also help researchers grapple with a fundamental fact: "virtually all studies of children have been done by adults" (Boocock 1975, p. 426). Adult women, blacks, and Hispanics can bring their missing voices into knowledge by speaking and writing about their own experiences. But while children may help with research (Boocock 1981), they will never be in central positions of knowledge-creation. That fact suggests one limit to the analogy I have been pushing between the re-visioning of women and the re-visioning of children in knowledge.

On the other hand, although feminists often emphasize the truth-telling of personal experience, we have wrestled with the challenge of understanding women of varied economic and cultural circumstances. Scholars have long confronted the challenge of learning across lines of difference, of trying not to impose their own assumptions but to make room for varied experiences. The tools for such learning—critical awareness of distorting ideologies, continual reflection about relationships between researcher and those being researched, openness to hidden dimensions of experience—can also be used by adults who study children. Experience never enters knowledge direct and unmediated; we need to reflect continually about processes of representation.

There is an added and distinctive twist in the study of children: All adults were once children themselves. Whereas those of different genders or races rarely cross social categories, in this case the subject/other division masks a running process: children, the subordinates and the other, are daily moving toward adulthood, the dominant position. And the dominants were once subordinates. This structure may hold special promise for understanding: Adults may know from their own experience what it is like to be a child. On the other hand, the child within—suffused with the distortions as well as insights of memory and threatening when it contradicts idealized adulthood—may also pose obstacles to seeing children clearly. Furthermore, the special ties of affection, power, and authority that mark relationships between adults and children may have profound effects on the construction of knowledge.

Conclusion: the limits of autonomy

My emphasis on conceptual autonomy may have glossed over the depth and intensity of young children's dependence upon, and relationships to, adults. The power of adults—partly

inherent in greater physical capacities, but greatly magnified by economic and social organization and cultural beliefs—has both positive and negative dimensions. Having resources to
provide responsible care to those who are more vulnerable and dependent (the positive side
of greater adult power) is essential to ensuring children's survival and growth. But adults also
use their greater power to dominate, exploit, and abuse children. Debates over "children's
rights" divide on the problem of how to enhance adults' nurture, while diminishing their
abuse of power.

Those who stress the oppression of children see "adult protection" as a euphemism for
control. They advocate empowering children by granting them self-determination and
"liberty rights." Others argue that when taken to an extreme, granting formal equality to
children—in effect, treating them like adults—results in their exploitation. Children, especially young children (the issue of relative competence and vulnerability becomes crucial),
are inherently dependent on adults. Children's needs for adult care and protection are best
expressed through "claim rights" that place duties on adult caretakers and the state.

The most sensible writings I have seen on children's rights steer a course between these
two positions. For example, Michael Wald (1979) identifies different types of claims made
under the rubric of "children's rights" and points to areas of conflict. In some circumstances,
children may need more protection, but in others they benefit from autonomy. The often
contradictory relationships between individuals, families, and the state must be carefully
sorted out. Finally, the entire "rights" approach to deeply structural problems has serious
limitations.

I mention the debate over children's rights mostly to suggest the complexity of power
relations between adults and children, a complexity that needs to be taken into account in
our re-visioning of children. The domination of men over women and of adults over children
are both analogous *and* very different. The debate over children's rights also bears on my
overall argument because children's claim rights are often assumed to place many more
duties upon women than upon men. Once again, gender assumptions lie barely beneath the
surface of a discussion about "adults" and children.

The recent wave of books about "children without childhood" generally fall on the
protect-the-child side of the debate over children's rights. To varying degrees, each of these
books takes traditional gender divisions of labor for granted, holding mothers uniquely
responsible for nurturing, caring for, and protecting children. Working mothers (but not
working fathers) are included among the forces depriving contemporary children of their
"right to childhood." This message echoes a theme dear to the heart of the New Right—that
the autonomy of women is necessarily gained at the expense of children. A related, albeit
modified, line of argument emerges in writings that Judith Stacey (1983) has called "the new
conservative feminism."

In an article titled "The 'War Over the Family' Is Not Over the 'Family,'" Susan Cohen
and Mary Katzenstein (forthcoming) argue that political encounters between feminism and
the right, while sometimes phrased in terms of the needs and interests of children, primarily
concern the gendered division of labor and the issue of women's autonomy within and from
the family. The New Right assumes that "woman's place" should primarily be defined by
motherhood; public/private divisions, male dominance in all institutions, and men's relative
absence from the care of children are taken for granted. Feminists challenge these assumptions. While the welfare of children *should* be a matter of widespread concern, to find solutions in "defense" of a romanticized nuclear family with a stay-at-home mother at its symbolic
core, is to ignore reality (few households fit that model), as well as gender and generational
hierarchies (see Thorne, with Yalom 1982). Feminists seek a more realistic and complex
understanding, struggling simultaneously to empower women, *and* to empower and ensure
the welfare of children. Improved understanding of children, in all their diversity and in

varied institutional contexts, will strengthen feminist visions of and strategies for social change.

Granting women, and children, conceptual autonomy is essential if we are to bring their experiences into knowledge that has been shaped by dominant groups. The autonomy of men is usually taken for granted; they are assumed to be separate—perhaps *too* separate—and self-defining. Drawing on women's and children's experiences of relatedness, a number of feminist theorists (e.g., Chodorow 1978; Flax 1983; Harding 1986; Hartsock 1983) have criticized what they regard as a "masculinist" ideal of self defined through separation. If our theorizing began with selves defined through relationships with others, retaining full awareness of social hierarchies, and if that approach were developed into a full critique of existing institutions, we might thoroughly overturn traditional knowledge.

Notes

1   For discussions of feminist transformation of knowledge, with examples from varied disciplines, see DuBois et al. (1985), Harding (1986), Millman and Kanter (1975), Sherman and Beck (1979), Spender (1981), and Stacey and Thorne (1985).

2   Analyses of racist bias in feminist writings can be found in Hooks (1981) and Zinn et al. (1986). Rich (1980) discusses heterosexual bias; Nash and Fernandez-Kelly (1983) and Duley and Edwards (1986) point to questions raised by more global frameworks.

3   Suransky (1982) argues that increased bureaucratization of children's lives, especially in many day care centers, is eroding a positive "separate space of childhood," and she tends to romanticize "the family." In these respects, her book is like the others. But her criticisms of adult control of children and her imaginative use of ethnographic methods to learn directly about children's experiences and agency set this book apart. In Suransky's theoretical and empirical account, children are much more than victims.

4   In a founding work of feminist theory, Shulamith Firestone (1970) argued that the oppression of children is tied to the oppression of women. There are many problems with her way of thinking about children (e.g., see criticisms in Suransky 1982). But in making the liberation of children a central concern, Firestone is relatively unusual among feminist writers (a point made by Jaggar 1985).

References

Acker, Joan. 1978. "Issues in the Sociological Study of Women's Work." Pp. 134–61 in *Women Working*, edited by A. Stromberg and S. Harkess. Palo Alto, CA: Mayfield.

Ambert, Anne-Marie. 1986. "Sociology of Sociology: The Place of Children in North American Sociology." Pp. 11–31 in *Sociological Studies of Child Development*. Vol. 1, edited by P. Adler and P. A. Adler. Greenwich, CT: JAI Press.

Anyon, Joan. 1983. "Intersections of Gender and Class: Accommodation and Resistance by Working-Class and Affluent Females to Contradictory Sex Role Ideologies." Pp. 1–19 in *Gender, Class and Education*, edited by S. Walker and L. Barton. Sussex: Falmer Press.

Aries, Philippe. 1962. *Centuries of Childhood*. New York: Vintage Books.

Benedict, Ruth. 1938. "Continuities and Discontinuities in Cultural Conditioning." *Psychiatry* 1:161–67.

Beneria, Lourdes. 1982. *Women and Development*. New York: Praeger.

Bloch, Ruth H. 1978. "American Feminine Ideals in Transition: The Rise of the Moral Mother, 1785–1815." *Feminist Studies* 4:100–126.

Boocock, Sarane Spence. 1975. "The Social Context of Childhood." *Proceedings of the American Philosophical Society* 119:419–29.

—— 1981. "The Life Space of Children." Pp. 93–116 in *Building for Women*, edited by S. Keller. Lexington, MA: Lexington Books.

Boulding, Elise. 1980. "The Nurturance of Adults by Children in Family Settings." Pp. 167–89 in *Research in the Interweave of Social Roles*. Vol. 1, edited by H. Lopata. Greenwich, CT: JAI Press.

Brittan, Arthur, and Mary Maynard. 1984. *Sexism, Racism and Oppression*. New York: Basil Blackwell.

Broverman, Inge K., Donald M. Broverman, Frank E. Clarkson, Paul S. Rosenkrantz, and Susan R. Vogel. 1970. "Sex-role Stereotypes and Clinical Judgments of Mental Health." *Journal of Consulting and Clinical Psychology* 34:1–7.

Chodorow, Nancy. 1978. *The Reproduction of Mothering*. Berkeley: University of California Press.

—— and Susan Contratto. 1982. "The Fantasy of the Perfect Mother." Pp. 54–75 in *Rethinking the Family: Some Feminist Questions*, edited by Barrie Thorne with Marilyn Yalom. New York: Longman.

Cohen, Susan, and Mary Katzenstein. Forthcoming. "The 'War Over the Family' Is Not Over the 'Family.'" In *The New Families*, edited by Myra Strober and Sanford Dornbusch. New York: Guilford Press.

Coles, Robert. 1971. *Migrants, Sharecroppers, Mountaineers*. Boston: Little, Brown.

—— 1986. *The Political Life of Children*. Boston: Atlantic Monthly Press.

Connell, Robert W., Dean J. Ashenden, Sandra Kessler, and Gary W. Dowsett. 1982. *Making the Difference: Schools, Families, and Social Division*. Boston: Allen & Unwin.

Corsaro, William. 1985. *Friendship and Peer Culture in the Early Years*. Norwood, NJ: Ablex.

DeBeauvoir, Simone. 1953. *The Second Sex*. New York: Knopf.

Denzin, Norman K. 1977. *Childhood Socialization*. San Francisco: Jossey-Bass.

DuBois, Ellen, Gail Kelly, Elizabeth Kennedy, Carolyn Krosmeyer, and Lillian Robinson. 1985. *Feminist Scholarship: Kindling in the Groves of Academe*. Urbana: University of Illinois Press.

Duley, Margot I., and Mary I. Edwards, eds. 1986. *The Cross-Cultural Study of Women*. New York: Feminist Press.

Eekelaar, John M., Robert Dingwall, and Topsy Murray. 1982. "Victims or Threats? Children in Care Proceedings." *Journal of Social Welfare Law*: 68–82.

Ehrenreich, Barbara, and Deirdre English. 1979. *For Her Own Good*. Garden City, NY: Doubleday Anchor.

Eisenstein, Zillah, ed. 1979. *Capitalist Patriarchy and the Case for Socialist Feminism*. New York: Monthly Review Press.

Elkind, David. 1981. *The Hurried Child*. Reading, MA: Addison-Wesley.

Fanon, Frantz. 1967. *Black Skin, White Masks*. New York: Grove Press.

Feldberg, Roslyn L., and Evelyn Nakano Glenn. 1979. "Male and Female: Job Versus Gender Models in the Sociology of Work." *Social Problems* 26:524–38.

Fine, Gary Alan. 1981. "Friends, Impression Management, and Preadolescent Behavior." Pp. 29–52 in *The Development of Children's Friendships*, edited by Steven R. Asher and John M. Gottman. New York: Cambridge University Press.

Firestone, Shulamith. 1970. *The Dialectic of Sex*. New York: Morrow.

Flax, Jane. 1983. "Political Philosophy and the Patriarchal Unconscious: A Psychoanalytic Perspective on Epistemology and Metaphysics." Pp. 245–81 in *Discovering Reality*, edited by S. Harding and M. B. Hintikka. Dordrecht, Holland: D. Reidel.

Fuller, Mary. 1980. "Black Girls in a London Comprehensive School." Pp. 52–65 in *Schooling for Women's Work*, edited by R. Deem. London: Routledge & Kegan Paul.

Glazer, Nona Y. 1984. "Servants to Capital: Unpaid Domestic Labor and Paid Work." *Review of Radical Political Economics* 16:61–87.

Goodwin, Marjorie H. 1980. "He-Said-She-Said: Formal Cultural Procedures for the Construction of a Gossip Dispute Activity." *American Ethnologist* 7:674–95.

Gordon, Linda. 1985. "Single Mothers and Child Neglect, 1880–1920." *American Quarterly* 37:173–92.

——— Forthcoming. *Family Violence and Social Control: Boston 1880–1960*. New York: Pantheon.

Harding, Sandra. 1986. *The Science Question in Feminism*. Ithaca: Cornell University Press.

Hartsock, Nancy. 1983. *Money, Sex and Power*. New York: Longman.

Hooks, Bell. 1981. *Ain't I a Woman? Black Women and Feminism*. Boston: South End Press.

Jaggar, Alison M. 1985. *Feminist Politics and Human Nature*. Totowa, NJ: Rowman & Allenheld.

Jenks, Chris. 1982. "Introduction: Constituting the Child." Pp. 9–24 in *The Sociology of Childhood*, edited by Chris Jenks. London: Batsford Academic.

Kagan, Jerome. 1984. *The Nature of the Child*. New York: Basic Books.

——— Richard B. Kearsley, and Philip R. Zelazo. 1978. *Infancy: Its Place in Human Development*. Cambridge, MA: Harvard University Press.

Kahn-Hut, Rachel, Arlene Kaplan Daniels, and Richard Colvard, eds. 1982. *Women and Work*. New York: Oxford University Press.

Kanter, Rosabeth Moss. 1977. *Men and Women of the Corporation*. New York: Basic Books.

Kelly, Joan. 1979. "The Doubled Vision of Feminist Theory." *Feminist Studies* 5:216–27.

Kessen, William. 1979. "The American Child and Other Cultural Inventions." *American Psychologist* 34:815–20.

Kessler-Harris, Alice. 1982. *Out to Work: A History of Wage-Earning Women in the United States*. New York: Oxford University Press.

Lever, Janet. 1976. "Sex Differences in the Games Children Play." *Social Problems* 23:478–87.

Lopata, Helena, with Cheryl Miller and Debra Barnewolt. 1984. *City Women: Work, Jobs, Occupations, Careers*. Vol. 1. New York: Praeger.

Maynard, Douglas. 1985. "On the Functions of Social Conflict Among Children." *American Sociological Review* 50:207–23.

McCormack, Mary. 1985. "Silenced No More: The Emergence of Child Sexual Abuse as a Social Problem." Unpublished paper, Sociology Department, Michigan State University.

Mead, George Herbert. 1934. *Mind, Self and Society*. Chicago: University of Chicago Press.

Medrich, Elliott A., Judith Roizen, Victor Rubin, and Stuart Buckley. 1982. *The Serious Business of Growing Up*. Berkeley: University of California Press.

Milkman, Ruth. 1985. *Women, Work and Protest*. Boston: Routledge & Kegan Paul.

Millman, Marcia, and Rosabeth Moss Kanter, eds. 1975. *Another Voice: Feminist Perspectives on Social Life and Social Science*. Garden City, NY: Anchor Books.

Nash, June, and Patricia Fernandez-Kelly, eds. 1983. *Women, Men and the International Division of Labor*. Albany: SUNY Press.

Packard, Vance. 1983. *Our Endangered Children*. Boston: Little, Brown.

Piaget, Jean. 1952. *The Construction of Reality in the Child*. New York: Basic Books.

Postman, Neil. 1982. *The Disappearance of Childhood*. New York: Delacorte Press.

Purrington, Beverly T. 1980. "Effects of Children on Their Parents: Parents' Perceptions." Ph.D. dissertation, Michigan State University.

Rich, Adrienne. 1980. "Compulsory Heterosexuality and Lesbian Existence." *Signs: Journal of Women in Culture and Society* 5:631–60.

Rubin, Gayle. 1975. "The Traffic in Women: Notes on the 'Political Economy' of Sex." Pp. 157–210 in *Toward an Anthropology of Women*, edited by R. Reiter. New York: Monthly Review Press.

Saraceno, Chiara. 1984. "The Social Construction of Childhood: Child Care and Education Policies in Italy and the United States." *Social Problems* 31: 351–63.

Sherman, Julia, and Evelyn T. Beck, eds. 1979. *The Prism of Sex: Essays in the Sociology of Knowledge*. Madison: University of Wisconsin Press.

Schwartzman, Helen B. 1978. *Transformations: The Anthropology of Children's Play*. New York: Plenum Press.

Skolnick, Arlene. 1980. "Children's Rights, Children's Development." Pp. 138–74 in *Children's Rights and Juvenile Justice*, edited by L. T. Empey. Charlottesville: University of Virginia Press.

Smith, Dorothy. 1979. "A Sociology for Women." Pp. 135–87 in *The Prism of Sex*, edited by J. A. Sherman and E. T. Beck. Madison: University of Wisconsin Press.

Speier, Matthew. 1976. "The Adult Ideological Viewpoint in Studies of Childhood." Pp. 168–86 in *Rethinking Childhood*, edited by A. Skolnick. Boston: Little, Brown.

Spender, Dale, ed. 1981. *Men's Studies Modified: The Impact of Feminism on the Academic Disciplines*. New York: Pergamon Press.

Stacey, Judith. 1983. "The New Conservative Feminism." *Feminist Studies* 9:559–83.

—— and Barrie Thorne. 1985. "The Missing Feminist Revolution in Sociology." *Social Problems* 32:301–16.

Suransky, Valerie Polakow. 1982. *The Erosion of Childhood*. Chicago: University of Chicago Press.

Thorne, Barrie, with Marilyn Yalom, eds. 1982. *Rethinking the Family: Some Feminist Questions*. New York: Longman.

Vygotsky, Lev. 1978. *Mind in Society*. Cambridge, MA: Harvard University Press.

Wald, Michael. 1979. "Children's Rights: A Framework for Analysis." *University of California, Davis Law Review* 12:255–82.

Willis, Paul. 1977. *Learning to Labor*. New York: Columbia University Press.

Winn, Marie. 1983. *Children Without Childhood*. New York: Pantheon.

Wittner, Judith G. 1980. "Domestic Labor as Work Discipline: The Struggle over Housework in Foster Homes." Pp. 229–47 in *Women and Household Labor*, edited by S. F. Berk. Newbury Park, CA: Sage.

Zelizer, Viviana A. 1985. *Pricing the Priceless Child: The Changing Social Value of Children*. New York: Basic Books.

Zinn, Maxine Baca, Lynn Weber Cannon, Elizabeth Higginbotham, and Bonnie Thornton Dill. 1986. "The Costs of Exclusionary Practices in Women's Studies." *Signs: Journal of Women in Culture and Society* 11:290–303.

Chapter 3

Edward Shorter

BASTARDY IN SOUTH GERMANY:
A COMMENT

L EE HAS RECENTLY ARGUED IN THESE PAGES that the startling increase in illegitimacy which took place in Bavaria between 1750 and 1850 resulted not from a "sexual revolution" but from an increase in real wages, which made it easier for people to support children born out of wedlock.[1] I am certainly sympathetic to his wage arguments, and to much of the logic of the article. But no sexual revolution at all? Not even a touch of saucy rebelliousness, an angry-young-person-against-the-*Hofbauerntum* syndrome?

His argument partly depends, of course, on what we mean by a "sexual revolution." If we insist on a dramatic breakaway from previous sexual styles, on homosexuality, oral intercourse, and the bondage-and-domination scene, then *d'accord*: no "sexual revolution" in early nineteenth-century Bavaria. But if we take this mildly sensationalist notion of a "revolution"—which I myself am partly responsible for foisting upon the trade—to mean the sudden rejection by a whole generation of young people of their parents' values towards premarital intercourse, I think that such a revolution *did* occur in Bavaria, and all over Europe, between the middle of the eighteenth and the middle of the nineteenth centuries.

Here Lee and I differ. He argues that "this illegitimacy did not imply a dramatic change in behavioral norms. . . . It did not conflict, in the opinion of the peasantry, either in the late eighteenth or early nineteenth centuries, with traditional moral norms" (416). This, I think, is simply wrong.

The mainstay of Lee's case is that the Bavarian peasantry had always accepted illegitimate children as more or less full-fledged family members, and that at the village level no one became very upset about out-of-wedlock conceptions. Illegitimate and legitimate children would inherit alike, work side by side, and enjoy roughly equal moral status in the local community. Because, according to Lee, this continued to be true in 1850 as well as in 1750, the great upsurge in bastardy had in no way conflicted with accepted local mores. Hence, no sexual revolution.

In my view, Lee has confused two types of illegitimacy. He studied Oberbayern, one of Bavaria's seven right-bank-of-the-Rhine provinces. And his Oberbayern peasants, in this large-farm, impartible inheritance region, represent perfectly the first type of illegitimacy: betrothal license, which meant men and women who were firmly engaged to marry and so went ahead and had sex, producing out-of-wedlock children because the ceremony could not take place until the man inherited his father's farm at age 34. In southern Bavaria, Austria, and German Switzerland marriage had always been late, high proportions of the population had always remained single, and illegitimacy had always been substantial compared to other parts of Europe.[2] Because engagements could run as long as a decade, betrothal license within such a context was thoroughly "traditional." Accidents happened, but were not so serious because a secure economic place awaited the infant. Normally the only other unwed mothers were rape victims.[3]

Lee so focused upon this first type that he has missed the second, more "modern" variety of illegitimacy. The point I wish to make is that "modern" illegitimacy was mainly responsible for the great bastardy explosion on which his article concentrates. "Modern" means men and women having sex not within the accepted context of delayed inheritance but within the context of wage labor. In the "modern" form young people have no prospects of a decent settlement, no hope of gaining an established situation as large-peasants or master craftsmen in the local community, but they go ahead and have sex anyway. The revolutionary element here is that before 1760 or so the journeymen craftsmen, agricultural laborers, and live-in hired hands who later produced the illegitimacy boom seem to have stayed continent until marriage, or at least if not, the women did not get pregnant.[4]

After 1760 or so these numerous subpeasant groups started to change their minds about waiting chastely for a marriage that might never take place. They began sexual relations in their early-to-mid-twenties—to go by statistics on the mother's age at the first illegitimate birth.[5] And because they did not practice birth control (married couples did not, at least), a tremendous increase in illegitimacy eventuated.

Contrary to Lee's theory, this boom in bastardy among the propertyless evoked loud complaints from the village elders. In no way was it accepted as "normal" by the established community, and the infants born to these furtive unions underwent fates much worse than those of their legitimate counterparts. I would therefore argue that two forms of bastardy nestled side by side in Bavaria: the "traditional," premarital births of the *Hofmark* (large farms in Oberbayern) which continued over the years at a relatively stable level, and the explosively growing *Concubinate* and *Winkelehen* (backstairs coupling) of the propertyless.

Various evidence indicates that bastardy increased most rapidly among the propertyless. Phayer, for example, who studied the illegitimacy boom in the parish of Dietramszell, which is not far from Lee's Kranzberg, found that "all illegitimate births occurred to members of the better-off working class [*gehobene Unterschicht*] and the lower class [*untere Klasse*]." The illegitimacy ratio (number of illegitimate births as a percent of all births) among the former was 20 percent, among the latter 28 percent. "In every instance the people involved were the young, unmarried sons and daughters of little" shopkeepers, shoeing smiths, weavers, and the like."[6] Phayer concludes that by 1817 "a new orientation predominated among the rural populace," leading to sexual behavior that would have been unthinkable in the old regime.

A second way to confirm this hypothesis is to observe the social profile of illegitimacy in a more systematic way—across Bavaria as a whole. The census of 1840 lets us correlate the number of illegitimate children alive in that year (measured as a percent of all children under 14) with various other variables indicating property ownership and social status. The following table shows some of the correlations [see original reading].

It is clear, then, that by 1840 illegitimacy in Bavaria as a whole was closely associated with the presence of a large lower-class population of rural craftworkers, agricultural servants, and laborers. An *inverse* association exists between illegitimacy and large-holding peasants—people with enough land to avoid having to take on supplementary work and who had been the main group associated with bastardy in the preexplosion period.

Another indication that illegitimacy was interwoven in the lives of the landless lower classes is that a goodly number of contemporary observers *said* that it was. As the Bishop of Regensburg complained in 1839, "Yet scarcely forty to fifty years ago only one or two illegitimate children were to be found in a community. . . . Now there are communes, especially around the patrimonial iron foundries [*Hammer- und Fabrikgüter*] in which one encounters 45–50 and still more illegitimate children."[7] Such laments could be pulled by the dozen from the austere administrative correspondence of the early nineteenth century. The entire corpus of social commentary in the years before 1848 hammers away at the point that illegitimacy was coterminous with misery.[8] It happened among the marginal people who were trapped on the fringes of the social order. The following list of unmarried mothers apparently living alone in 1836 in the village of Neudrossenfeld highlights precisely that group most typical of the world of bastardy:

— Agnes Kummerer, age 36, 3 children, no property, "is not able to support herself."
— A group of five people, all with different family names, two children, living in the same house, "these families live in the most needy condition and the commune must pay the school fees for the children."
— Katharina Ebert, age 53, one child, occupation spinning, no property, lives in rented room.
— Magdalene Kufner, age 44, two children, occupation knitting, no property, "is totally impoverished and the commune must pay 3 gulden, 12 kreuzer school fees for the two children."
— Three women named Hofmann, ages 26, 40, and 48, three children, occupation spinning and knitting, no property, "support themselves scantily, whereby the commune must pay the school fees for the children."
— Margarethe Geierin, age 36, two children, no property, occupation "Vagabunda," must be completely supported by the commune.[9]

These wretched, trapped women were leagues removed from the solid peasantry that Lee describes, tolerant of bastardy as a normal part of the social order.

It is possible that these thousands of unfortunates really were accepted at the village level, regardless of what the Bishop of Regensburg and the government bureaucrats thought. If Lee is correct, it is to the villagers themselves, not the nation's social authorities, that we must go. And here opinion is mixed. I have encountered a considerable amount of testimony to the effect that many villagers considered bastardy no great offense. Joseph Hazzi, for example, a government bureaucrat on tour of Oberbayern around 1800, observed of the population of Marquartstein County: "They are eager to marry early and produce many children, among them so many illegitimate that it is considered not so much a sin as a good deed."[10] The provincial government of Unterfranken argued in 1839 that "among the rural population, especially among the so-called middle class [*Mittelstande*] . . . the view has gained predominance that the natural satisfaction of the sex drive is no longer forbidden by the police and morally not terribly sinful either."[11] Judge Puchta of Erlangen County had grown so accustomed to the idea of out-of-wedlock pregnancy among his clientele that in notarizing marriage contracts he would normally ask whether illegitimate children were present.[12] Yet these were middle-class officials looking from the outside in; to them illegitimacy doubtlessly seemed acceptable because so much of it was occurring.

When we let the village fathers themselves speak, a fearful, condemnatory vision of bastardy emerges which is as different from Lee's picture of indifferent acceptance as night is from day. Many "little people" had an opportunity to express their views on the root causes of poverty in the social order when, in 1848, King Max ordered an essay contest to be held on that subject. The bundles of responses are packed with illiterate, semilegible missives from what appear to be ordinary villagers. Jacob Giel, a schoolteacher in Mörlbach bei Uffenheim, described how illegitimacy happened: "Some fellow from village X buys a little house in village Z. His fiancée has a little money too, and like the man has also been for a long time in service, having now several illegitimate children." But the village administration, for complicated reasons, denied the couple permission to marry. "So their fortune runs out. They sell the dwelling again, with a loss. They produce another batch of illegitimate children. The man tries to forget his woes for a few minutes with drink. A few more years in service flow by and you have—a proletarian. No! Four or five proletarians now!"[13]

Michael Genssperger, a cottager (*Söldner*) from Ottering in Dingolfing County, had a less enlightened analysis: "As for the maintenance of illegitimate children, a very irksome matter for communities, the trouble would be easily alleviated if the father had to pay a 7 gulden penalty into the community chest and the mother were punished with open humiliation or monetary fines, as used to happen, because now the illegitimate children have become far too many, and often some light-headed young thing [*liederliche Dirne*] will have given birth to 6, 8 and 10 and still more children, heeding no warnings, not even of the clergy. . . . "[14]

What so many respondents wanted was a return to the old regime, when the village as a whole could deal ruthlessly with out-of-wedlock conception, humiliating the "whores," as one writer put it, "making them wear a blue sign for ridicule," keeping the premarital fornicators away from the maypole dances, having the local seigneur "give speeches in praise of the virtuous maidens while mocking the scoundrels and whores [*Schelmen* and *Huren*], who crept away for shame." But after 1806, when such fornication penalties were made illegal, things became different, the writer continued, "and now it's the *Schelmen* and *Huren* who are the dancing masters."[15]

In these bundles of scratched-off briefs, any hint of the "full accommodation of high illegitimacy rates on the local level" of which Lee speaks is difficult to discern (425). For these village essayists, burning with fire and brimstone, bastardy was anything but a matter of "social indifference."

What happened in reality was the bifurcation of these little communities over sexual morality. Within them a sizable portion of established opinion clung to the traditional peasant notion that premarital sex was bad unless the couple could count on inheriting a farm or craftshop. Yet a growing "subculture," composed precisely of the propertyless young men and women whose sexual drives had previously been so brutally repressed, were challenging this "charter culture" view of no-sex-unless-you-have-an-establishment and proceeding to seize the options for sexuality and "happiness" that an increasingly romanticized, individualized, popular culture was holding out. That all this premarital sex might end in later wretchedness of the Neudrossenfeld variety was doubtlessly obscure to them.

Joseph Walther, a retired schoolteacher in Saal (Königshofen County), made clear how deeply this cultural rift over sexual matters divided so many villages and small towns. "A community of 94 families elects its reeve every three years," he wrote. "And each time the question comes up: should we choose someone who's strict about morality and order, who puts limits on abuses and fooling around [*Ausschweifungen*], and who conscientiously enforces the laws of the land? Twenty-eight would desire this fervently, but sixty-six are horrified by it, and elect one of their own. Then for entire nights the village bars are full of drinkers and the streets full of night-time roamers [*Streuner*], the houses full of shameless and seduced daughters . . . the villages full of illegitimate children." And what can the government do about it? asked Walther rhetorically. "Whoever wants to be re-elected has to look the other way."[16]

Lee's final argument is that, not only at the level of the village but in the family itself, illegitimate children enjoyed equal status with legitimate children. That they could inherit property and otherwise participate in family life is, according to him, one of the signs of a "matrifocal" family system. Leaving aside for the moment the question of whether Bavaria was in fact a "matrifocal" society, let us see if the assertion is true that Bavarians were "generally indifferent to the principle of legitimacy" because parents treated both legitimate and illegitimate alike. Lee's view is that both were treated equally *badly*, in a culture where "children were seldom regarded as individuals" (423). My view would be that, however poor the quality of marital "mothering," that of non-marital was considerably worse, reflecting a fundamental inequality in the situation of the illegitimate.

For one thing, relatively few bastards were absorbed into the circle of family life, to go by statistics on legitimation. Only about a fifth of the illegitimate babies ever ended up legitimated, 15 percent from 1835 to 1859, 20 percent from 1882 to 1884.[17] Because many of these children died before legitimation could take place, the real percentage of survivors who found themselves legitimated is probably more like a third.[18] An additional fraction of bastards doubtlessly lived in a family situation, although unlegitimated by their unmarried parents, if we may go by the sudden spurt in legitimation which took place in the mid-1860s as Bavaria's marriage legislation became liberalized.[19] But the main fact remains that, far from being a "functional" or "accepted" part of rural society, a majority of bastards remained unlegitimated social outcasts.

And they were treated as outcasts, being, for example, breast-fed less often. "The highest mortality of the illegitimate Bavarian children in 1871–74 falls not in the first month of life but in the second and third, a result of the fact that already in these months the breast-feeding of the children has been terminated, and the injuriousness of worse treatment is making itself apparent."[20]

Although Lee argues that both kinds of children received equally poor treatment, in fact illegitimate infants perished considerably more frequently than legitimate ones. This discrimination started with the birth process: whereas over the years from 1835 to 1859 only 3.0 percent of legitimate infants were stillborn, 3.7 percent of the illegitimate were. And in Unterfranken the figures were 2.6 percent for legitimate, 3.7 percent for illegitimate. Many more bastards died in the first year of life: 31 percent of the legitimate (in itself, a horrifying rate), and 37 percent of the illegitimate in the kingdom as a whole over the period from 1835 to 1859. Childbearing in general meant a slaughter of the innocents among these Bavarians, but with the illegitimate babies mortality had an expressly cruel edge.[21]

The surrounding community made even less tolerable the hostile start which illegitimate infants received in life. Although the Catholic Church officially deplored the practice, individual priests would often refuse to baptize bastards, because the local parish would not want to take responsibility for the infants' subsequent poor relief should their parents fall destitute. So, for example, the priest in Grunthal (Wasserburg County) denied baptism to the newborn child of Barbara Gogg, a laborer's unmarried daughter who had been in service locally. Gogg was obliged to carry the child "three hours' distance" to Mühldorf for baptism. In a similar case a Fraham mother had to carry her child to Rottenkirchen for baptism, seeing it then die on the trek home.[22]

Most illegitimate children, unlike those Lee studied in Kranzberg County, grew up poor, usually unwanted, and were prone to commit petty crimes and violent acts.[23] "If a single woman has several children, it is difficult for her to find work, and the community can only support her with alms or let her subsist on minor theft from the fields and woods [*Flur-und Waldfrevel*], or place her children in foster homes at its cost. The sort of upbringing the children receive in the former case is only too well known: they grow up without any fatherly discipline, and so does it happen that the girls soon follow the footsteps of their mother."[24] Illegitimate dynasties arose in this way, such as that started around 1800 in the village of Neunkirchen when an unwed mother gave birth to a son who, immediately after reaching puberty, himself impregnated two women. He had learned the weaver's trade but never settled down to regular work, earning his way instead as a sometime pack-peddlar. He went on to sire three illegitimate children with a third woman, and after she died he produced yet another by a fourth woman, who already had one bastard child herself. At the time of the report, this woman was pregnant again, she and her husband living from "deception and petty theft."[25]

Here we have the core of the illegitimacy explosion, a mushrooming lower-class population that existed from wage work and hovered on the threshold of vagrancy. Family ties were unstable and uncertain; the offspring were rejected by the established social order, and their origins were judged a blatant affront to all the values of prudence and economic security which traditional peasant society represented. It is these people, not that minority of farmers' sons born out of wedlock under betrothal license, who were behind the stunning increase of illegitimacy in Oberbayern—Lee's chosen ground—from 4 percent in 1760, to 18 percent in 1825, to 28 percent in 1860.[26]

Did this great rise in bastardy involve a "sexual revolution"? If the sexual activation of an entire generation of single, lower-class young people in the space of thirty years, the passage of tens of thousands of servants and laborers from chastity to nonvirginity, can be judged a sexual revolution, I would say that Bavaria had one. Why, exactly, remains unclear.

Notes

1   W. R. Lee, "Bastardy and the Socioeconomic Structure of South Germany," *Journal of Interdisciplinary History*, VII (1977), 403–25.

2   Although no overall study of this homogenous region exists, numerous local monographs have recently become available. On Switzerland sec Silvio Bucher, *Bevölkerung und Wirtschaft des Amtes Entlebuch in 18. Jahrhundert* (Lucerne, 1974); Markus Schürmann, *Bevölkerung, Wirtschaft und Gesellschaft in Appenzell Innerrhoden im 18. und frühen 19. Jahrhundert* (Appenzell, 1974). On the persistence of these features into a more recent period, see John Friedl and Walter S. Ellis, "Celibacy, Late Marriage and Potential Mates in a Swiss Isolate," *Human Biology*, XLVIII (1976), 23–35. On Austria see Klaus Arnold, "Der Umbruch des generativen Verhaltens in cinem Bergbauerngebiet," in Heimold Helczmanovszki (ed.), *Beiträge zur Bevölkerungs—und Sozialgeschichte Österreichs* (Vienna, 1973); Franz Fliri, *Bevölkerungsgeographische Untersuchungen im Unterinntal* (Innsbruck, 1948); Gisela Winkler, *Bevölkerungsgeographische Untersuchungen im Martelltal* (Innsbruck, 1973). See also Inge Rohn, "Bevölkerung und Landwirtschaft in Kitzbühel," in Eduard Widmoser, *Stadtbuch Kitzbühel* (Kitzbühel, 1967), I, 197–222, for a demographic analysis which discusses both the town and the surrounding countryside. The most recent work on Bavaria seems to have been done by non-Bavarians: John Knodel, "Two and a Half Centuries of Demographic History in a Bavarian Village," *Population Studies*, XXIV (1970), 353–76; Jacques Houdaille, "Quelques résultats sur la démographie de trois villages d'Allemagne de 1750 à 1879," *Population*, XXV (1970), 649–54. (One of the three villages, Kreuth, is in Bavaria.)

3   Jacques Rossiaud's important article, "Prostitution, jeunesse et société au XVe siècle," *Annales; ESC*, XXXI (1976), 289–325, makes clear how often out-of-wedlock pregnancy in the premodern era was the result of rape. A good discussion of "traditional" illegitimacy in Upper Bavaria may be found in Hanns Platzer, *Geschichte der ländlichen Arbeitsverhältnisse in Bayern* (Munich, 1904), 186–93.

4   I have elsewhere rehearsed the justification for concluding that this particular rise in illegitimacy was caused by a rise in premarital intercourse, and not—as Lee suggests—by an increase in fecundity or a decrease in abortions. See Shorter, *The Making of the Modern Family* (New York, 1975), ch. 3.

5   The Oberpfalz government, for example, reported in 1863 that "on the basis of statistical . . . surveys, illegitimate births occur on the average at the age of 24." Bavarian Hauptstaatsarchiv in Munich, Ministerium des Innern (MI) 52139, 20 June, 1863, report to Interior Ministry.

6   Fintan Michael Phayer, *Religion und das Gewöhnliche Volk in Bayern in der Zeit von 1750–1850* (Munich, 1970), 98.

7   MI 46556, 25 April, 1839, communication to Interior Ministry.

8   See Shorter "Social Change and Social Policy in Bavaria, 1800–860," unpub. Ph.D. diss. (Harvard University, 1968).

9   MI 53272, excerpt from report of 3 Nov., 1836. The implication of the report is that these women were unmarried.

10   *Statistische Aufschlüsse über das Herzogthum Baiem* (Nürnberg, 1801), III, 657.

11   MI 46556, 30 Feb., 1839, report to Interior Ministry.

12   MI 46556, 22 Feb., 1837, report from Mittelfranken government to Interior Ministry.

13   Hauptstaatsarchiv, Ministerium des Handels (MH) 9616, no. 491, Jan., 1849.

14   MH 9612, no. 22, n.d.

15   Letter from Johann Fink, "Bauer," in Weissenbrunn, Altdorf County, 27 Jan., 1849.

16   MH 9614, no. 231, 16 Jan., 1849.

17   *Beiträge zur Statistik des Königreichs Bayern,* XI (1863), 87; Friedrich Lindner, *Die unehelichen Geburten als Sozialphänomen Ein Beitrag zur Statistik der Bevölkerungsbewegung im Königreich Bayern* (Leipzig, 1900), 188.

18   *Generalien-Sammlung der Erzdiozese München und Freising. Die oberhirtlichen Verordnungen und allgemeinen Erlässe von 1821 bis 1846,* (Munich, 1856), II, 411, an estimate of Munich's episcopal chancellery.

19   The percent legitimated rose from 15 in 1862 to 22 by 1868. Josef Kaizl, *Der Kampf um Gewerbereform un Gewerbefreiheit in Bayern von 1799 bis 1868* (Leipzig, 1879), 159.

20   L. Pfeiffer, "Die Kindersterblichkeit," in A. Jacobi *et al.* (eds.), *Hygiene des Kindesalters* (Tübingen, 1882; 2nd ed.), I, 287, 327.

21   *Beiträge zur Statistik des Königreichs Bayern,* XI (1863), 91, 96, 97.

22   These examples are from Ordinariatsarchiv Munich, Pfarr-Matrikel, 1749–1845, letter from Magistrat Mühldorf of 1 March 1844. I am grateful to Phayer for this reference.

23   For a typical description, see the letter from the local cleric in Haag to the Oberfranken government, 12 Feb., 1834, in Kreisarchiv Bamberg K3 718.

24   MI 52137, 23 June, 1853.

25   MI 46556, 3 April, 1838, Archbishop of Bamberg to Munich.

26   Data on the period 1760 to 1825 from Phayer's compilation of statistics in the manuscript Pfarrmatrikel at the Ordinariatsarchiv in Munich. The 1860 ratio is from Lindner, *Uneheliche Geburten,* 218.

Chapter 4

Nara Milanich

HISTORICAL PERSPECTIVES ON ILLEGITIMACY AND ILLEGITIMATES IN LATIN AMERICA

I N 1783 A YOUNG MAN NAMED RODOLFO brought a case before a court in the provincial town of San Felipe, Chile. His goal was to prove his birth origin and, in so doing, become eligible for an inheritance. Rodolfo claimed that he was the illegitimate son of the recently deceased Doña María Alzamora, a woman from a family of some social standing, who had given him up shortly after birth. The witnesses who testified in the case provide us with a glimpse of the itinerant path of Rodolfo's first years of life. Alejo, a mulatto slave of Doña María's parents, declared that he had seen María give birth to Rodolfo and could affirm that he was her son. Then, Alejo recounted, Doña María gave him the baby, "ordering him to take him out of the house and to find some woman to raise him; that she would pay for the rearing." Alejo gave the baby to an Indian named Isabel Herrera but did not know what had become of him thereafter.

Another witness, a family member, picked up the story from there, recounting that the newborn had remained in this first adoptive home for just a few days. Rodolfo would spend his next years circulating among a welter of households, across social and racial cleavages, to relatives and nonrelatives alike, in a seemingly endless rotation of caretakers: from Isabel's house, Rodolfo's father gave him to his sister-in-law, who placed him in the house of one Pablo Jiménez ("whose wife cared for him for three months"); next he was given to Doña Rosa Orellana, the wife of the witness, where he spent eight months; then he was taken in by some "mulattos named Escobar," where he remained for a few days; and finally he went to live in "the house of María Regalato, in the valley of Putaendo, where they finished nursing him and maintained him until a little before the death of his mother" (Cavieres 1995: 233–34).

It would be an exaggeration to suggest that the extraordinary saga of Rodolfo's early years was typical of childhood in late-eighteenth-century Chile, or in any other Latin American society of the past. Yet one aspect of the youngster's identity that clearly conditioned his experience—his out-of-wedlock birth—was not at all unusual. For reasons that are rarely straightforward, and with consequences that are just beginning to be explored by historians, illegitimacy rates in Latin American societies have historically been very high. One way to appreciate the magnitude of the statistics is to compare them with those of European societies of the time. European illegitimacy rates ranged from a low of 1 to 2 percent in seventeenth-century England to a high of 5 to 9 percent in nineteenth-century France.

Compare these numbers with those of Latin American societies, where out-of-wedlock births accounted for 30, 40, or even 50 percent of all births in some communities at certain times. Rates could be even higher among particular subpopulations, such as slaves.

Not surprisingly, illegitimacy rates fluctuated significantly over time and from place to place. Some historians have postulated a positive relationship between illegitimacy and urbanization (Cavieres 1995: 226; Kuznesof 1986). Others (for example, Pérez Brignoli 1981; and Sánchez Albornoz 1974) suggest the phenomenon is inextricably linked to miscegenation, or racial mixing, a hypothesis that will be explored in this chapter. A third explanation attributes widespread illegitimacy to the ineffectiveness of church- and state-imposed social strictures concerning marriage and morality.

Another significant characteristic of illegitimacy is that different social, racial, and ethnic groups often exhibited strikingly different rates of out-of-wedlock birth. A study of parish records in early-seventeenth-century Guadalajara, Mexico, for example, found an overall illegitimacy rate of about 40 percent. But a closer look at the data reveals considerable variability: whereas about one-fourth of Spaniards were born out of wedlock, two-thirds of *castas*, or peoples of mixed racial descent, were illegitimate, and four-fifths of African slaves were so registered (Calvo 1982; 60). Moreover, Indian communities from Mexico to Chile have historically had lower rates of illegitimacy than their white or *casta* counterparts (Borah and Borah 1966; Morin 1977; Salinas and Salinas 1988). Finally, illegitimacy was also tied to social class. While historians have explored the widespread existence of illegitimacy among elites (Nazzari 1998; O'Phelan Godoy 1998; Twinam 1999), it is likely that illegitimacy rates were higher among the poor. In the late nineteenth century, moreover, the association between poverty and illegitimacy appears to have strengthened (Milanich 2002).

But amid a canvas of social and geographic variation and change over time, at least one general trend is clear. In comparison with Europe—the standard against which Latin American commentators judged their own societies until the twentieth century—and North America, the rates of illegitimate birth in Latin America have been very high. One author has suggested that no single factor—urbanization, miscegenation, or the nature of social control—can explain illegitimacy throughout the region because the phenomenon was not everywhere and at all times the product of a single logic. Rather, it is necessary to examine "the fine and dense social mesh of relations between men and women . . . in each historical moment in order to be able to interpret what meanings [illegitimate birth] had" (Moreno 1997–98: 65). While this chapter will touch on the "macro causes" of illegitimacy, it is less concerned with the statistical frequency of out-of-wedlock birth than with the cultural significance and social position of illegitimate children. In other words, what did it mean to be born illegitimate? How did societies regard such children? Did children like Rodolfo experience a different life course because of their out-of-wedlock birth status? One pattern that will be given special attention is the circulation of illegitimate children. By circulation, I refer to the fact that, like Rodolfo, many children in Latin American societies were raised outside of their natal homes by people other than their biological parents and that they might be shifted frequently from one household to another. The phenomenon of circulation is a crucial aspect of childhood in Latin America.

Just as it is difficult to generalize about the rates or causes of illegitimacy among diverse societies and social groups, so too is it risky to generalize about the meanings of illegitimacy and the status of illegitimates. There was no single experience shared by all such children; rather, illegitimacy was mediated by class status and racial and ethnic identity as well as by more fortuitous factors such as the parents' attitudes and circumstances and the relationship between a child's progenitors.[1] What becomes apparent in examining these diverse experiences, however, is that in the colonial and republican societies of Latin America, one's birth status as legitimate or illegitimate, a status that in Spanish and Portuguese was often referred to as "filiation" (*filiación*, or *filiação*, respectively), functioned in concert with these other factors as a marker of social hierarchy. As a result, it had important consequences for individual experience and for the structure of society in general.

[. . .]

Illegitimate children and their families

The experience of illegitimacy was powerfully shaped by the nature of the family into which a child was born. But what kinds of family formations gave rise to out-of-wedlock birth? What kinds of relationships between men and women produced illegitimate children? One category of social relationships that was associated with illegitimacy had its roots in the doctrines of *limpieza de sangre* and the culture of honor discussed above [see original reading]: these were unions between men and women considered socially or racially unequal. From the dawn of the colonial enterprise, Iberian men formed relationships with Indian and African women whom they never married.[2] The children born of these unions were both illegitimate and of mixed racial identity. Thus, in the colonial imagination, illegitimacy became inseparably identified with miscegenation—so much so that illegitimates and people of mixed race were often considered two virtually interchangeable categories. As a bishop from Huamanga, Peru, declared, "The most common situation is that . . . *mestizos* [people of mixed Indian-European parentage] are illegitimate" (cited in Castañeda 1981:235). Similarly, in the late colonial period the *cabildo* (town council and court of first instance) of Caracas, Venezuela, defined the racial category *pardos* in this way: they "are descended of slaves, their filiation is illegitimate, and they have their origin in the union of white men with negresses" (cited in Martínez-Alier 1989: 167). In other words, racial identity and birth status were understood to be intertwined.

Racially mixed concubinage was perhaps especially common in slave societies. Studies of colonial Brazil and nineteenth-century Cuba, for example, reveal that white men readily established relations with free and slave women of color and had children with them, yet they rarely married such women and indeed were likely to marry and engender legitimate children with a white partner concurrently or afterward (Martínez-Alier 1989; Nazzari 1996). What about the progeny of unequal unions? We can imagine that such children—marked by the stigmas of mixed race and inferior birth status—would have had minimal material or affective claims on their fathers. It follows that the children of such racially or socially unequal unions were among the most vulnerable of illegitimates. The seventeenth-century will of Francisco Arce de la Parra, an unmarried merchant from Madrid who resided in Lima, reveals how race influenced his behavior as a parent. Arce de la Parra recognized four illegitimate children in his will. He clearly maintained close relations with all of them, naming one executor of his will, leaving dowries to his two daughters, and carefully specifying that in addition to a monetary inheritance, his youngest son, who was fourteen and lived with him, should receive "a canopy from the bed in which I sleep and all the linens and four shirts of mine and four white pants"—objects of symbolic value that expressed paternal affection for the youngster. Arce de la Parra identified the three mothers of these four children by name and specified that they were all single. But he then went on to expressly repudiate paternity of two other children. Although a mulata named Felipa de Montoya attributed paternity of her son Josephe to him, the testator declared, "He is not [my son] nor do I recognize him as such." He also denied paternity of a six- or seven-year-old *mestizo* child, Ugenio, who had briefly lived in his house (Mannarelli 1993: 177–78).

Whether or not Arce de la Parra was telling the truth, the fact that he felt compelled to identify the "inferior" racial status of the mothers and children he refused to recognize, in contrast to his silence about the racial status (presumably white) of the children he did recognize, suggests the significance of racial identity in a parent's relationship to illegitimate offspring (Mannarelli 1993: 178). Indeed, the authorities charged with monitoring morality encouraged just such behavior. While the colonial Brazilian church counseled marriage as a resolution to the sinful state of concubinage, when confronted with the reality of interracial unions, it ignored its own teachings and admonished the sinners to separate immediately, a policy that almost certainly had negative consequences for any children the couple might have. In 1779, an ecclesiastical court accused Miguel Raposo, a lieutenant in Guarulhos, a town in the state of São Paulo, Brazil, of living in concubinage with his slave Quitéria. The couple had been together for over fifteen years and had five children, whom Raposo acknowledged as his own. Nevertheless, the court ordered him to sell Quitéria; what became of her or the couple's children is unknown, but for the court, the need to terminate the sinful affair took precedence over the dictates of paternal responsibility or the well-being of the children (Nazzari 1996: 6). White fathers in colonial Brazil rarely recognized illegitimate children of color, and even when they did, the courts were reluctant to reward such offspring their rightful inheritance (Silva 1993: 194–95). In addition to racial prejudice, this fact may also reflect the stigma attached to mothers' unfree status.

Such patterns of selective recognition and acceptance of illegitimate children by fathers based on the (inferior) status of their mothers endured into the twentieth century and involved class prejudices as well. One well known Chilean doctor who directed the Santiago foundling home in the 1920s deplored the wealthy mistresses who forced their maids to abandon children they had engendered with the sons of the household. He described how, spinning a web of lies about the baby's identity, the typical mistress would recur to the orphanage to dispose of "the grandchild of whom she is ashamed and whom she secretly curses" (Calvo Mackenna 1928: 207). Even as sexual and affective relations between men and women routinely crossed the racial, ethnic, status, and class cleavages that undergirded Latin American societies, social and legal norms of endogamy (the principle that like marry like) endured, swelling the ranks of the illegitimate and contributing to the social marginalization of these individuals.[3]

The offspring of consensual unions

Concubinage by no means always involved socially or racially unequal unions. The consensual union of couples who lived together "as if married," as the documents routinely phrase it, was a widespread and enduring social institution, one that was rooted in medieval Iberian tradition.[4] For example, early Iberian legal codes both recognized and permitted consensual unions, defining them as inferior to marriage but conceding certain rights and obligations to concubines and their children that set the practice apart from more casual unions (Elizarrarás Rendon 1951: chapter 2). Latin American legal codes never went so far, but such unions nevertheless existed at all levels of the social hierarchy, though they were almost certainly more common among nonelites. In Latin America, many couples could not or did not, for any number of economic, social, or personal reasons, formalize their union. Periodic crises that in many places constituted structural aspects of the economy made it difficult to secure the material prerequisites of marriage, such as the dowry. Even the marriage ceremony (whether ecclesiastical or, after the late nineteenth century, civil) involved significant and sometimes prohibitive expenses. The inhabitants of late-eighteenth-century Bogotá could expect to pay more than fourteen pesos to be wed, at a time when three-quarters of the city's households earned between four and fifteen pesos a year (Dueñas Vargas 1997: 165–67). In any case, propertyless people would have relatively little incentive to legitimate their unions for purposes of inheritance. Moreover, the fact that natural children possessed significant inheritance rights, and that legitimated children could enjoy equal inheritance with legitimate siblings, meant that in some cases there might have been a weak incentive to marry, even for the propertied.[5]

In addition, the relative weakness of the Catholic Church and of colonial and republican states, especially in remote rural areas, impeded attempts to impose the dominant morality on a wayward populace (Potthast-Jutkeit 1991). Evidence indicates the existence of popular moral codes vis-à-vis consensual unions and out-of-wedlock births that were very different from those espoused by church and state. In the colonial period, the Inquisition prosecuted individuals such as Gaspar Fernandes and Belchior Preto, who were brought before authorities in Pernambuco, Brazil, in the 1590s for making statements deemed blasphemous. The two had asserted that "sleeping with a black woman or a single woman is not a mortal sin" (cited in Schwartz 1997: 65).[6] Likewise, one historian (Moreno 1997–98: 73–74) has found that as illegitimacy became increasingly widespread on the pampas of Buenos Aires Province, Argentina, in the early 1800s, people stopped using condemnatory terms like "illicit relations" or "illicit friendship" to describe extramarital relationships, instead employing phrases like "living together" (*vivir juntos*) or "we got together" (*nos juntamos*). The value-neutral language suggests that people had begun to attribute a moral legitimacy to such unions. Again, popular norms in such instances seem strikingly independent of official and elite beliefs about honor, sexuality, and illegitimacy.

If their parents recognized them and remained together, and if they did not go on to engender legitimate children, the children born of stable, consensual unions, while technically illegitimate, probably remained largely unaffected by their birth status. They would grow up with parents, siblings, and other family members, and they were likely to use both their father's and mother's last names (in Iberian naming practice, people use both their mother's and father's last name, but illegitimates, especially those unrecognized by their father, often used only their mother's name). Finally, if their parents had anything to bequeath to them, they would not be in competition with the superior rights of legitimate siblings or half siblings. While their filiation may have exposed them to some measure of social stigma, the examples from the Brazilian Inquisition and the nineteenth-century pampas suggest that such prejudices did not exist everywhere and among all social groups.

We have a portrait of one such family in Santiago, Chile, in 1902. The family of Tránsito X, Rafael X, and their seven children became the subject of *Monograph of a Working-Class Family*, a sociological study conducted by two university students (Errázuriz Tagle and Eyzaguirre Rouse 1903) interested in the nature of urban poverty. At the time of the study, Tránsito and Rafael had been together for over twenty years and had had twelve children, five of whom had died. When asked why they had never formalized their union, the couple explained that such measures were only "a necessity for people who have wealth, so that they can make out their wills" (16). With no possessions to speak of, Tránsito and Rafael had little incentive to marry, and their children were consequently illegitimate. Yet in this case, it is clearly the grinding poverty in which the couple's children were born and raised and not their filiation that fundamentally shaped their chances for survival, their life course, and their future prospects. It is impossible to determine how common such unions were historically or what proportion of illegitimate children grew up in such families. What is clear is that not all, and perhaps relatively few, consensual unions were as enduring as that of Tránsito and Rafael. For reasons that vary from place to place, relationships between men and women in many Latin American societies, in particular among nonelites, were characterized by pervasive instability. In short, it was difficult to establish and maintain an enduring domestic union. While it is impossible to talk about "typical" cases when we are dealing with such a diverse group of societies over centuries of time, the experience of Narcisa Checa and Juan López, who lived on the pampas of Buenos Aires province, Argentina, in the early nineteenth century, can at least be regarded as illustrative of the patterns of flux that characterized gender relations and family formation in many Latin American societies. While young, Checa had been widowed and left with children to support on her meager earnings as a seamstress. She had had relationships with several different men but eventually met Juan López, who, in his words, "went to live with her and to establish a friendship [relationship]." The couple agreed that as long as López remained with Checa, he would contribute to the rent of the farm and provide for "her subsistence and that of a spurious child and two natural children who lived with her."[7] The couple lived together for an unspecified period, but at some point López moved on, leaving Checa and her children behind. It seems reasonable to suppose that he would not be her last partner (Moreno 1997–98: 76).[8] As the couple's story shows, nonelite families were perpetually shedding and gaining members. Men made fleeting appearances in families, only to disappear, as in this case; in other instances, women might dissolve their households to become live-in domestic servants, only to reestablish them when they could; and in a practice that will be discussed below, children were born, sent to other households to be raised, or abandoned at foundling homes, but subsequently reclaimed if circumstances permitted.

Such instability was in many places the result of pervasive migration. In colonial Brazil, for example, male migration to mining areas, the excursions of *bandeirantes* (quasi-military parties that penetrated the backlands in search of Indians and gold), and military impressment all contributed to the mobility of the populace and to the instability of family structures (Silva 1993). Migration could result in notable sexual imbalances in the population. In many cases, women migrated to cities to find work as domestic servants, resulting in a "demographic surplus" of women in urban centers, as in seventeenth-century Guadalajara, Mexico, late colonial Bogotá, Colombia, and São Paulo, Brazil, or nineteenth-century Santiago, Chile, and Asunción, Paraguay. In turn, agricultural and mining areas attracted male labor, such that labor markets kept men and women in perpetually separate orbits. In addition, at some moments, high mortality rates among men, often due to warfare, would have contributed to these tendencies.

Illegitimates and matrifocal families

The result of these realities is that many children grew up in matrifocal households, in which women were the enduring authorities and breadwinners. One indication of the secondary importance of fathers is the low rate of paternal recognition of illegitimate offspring. As previously stated, recognition was a legal act that gave illegitimate children much expanded legal and civil rights. But it was also a deeply significant cultural act, for in recognizing their offspring, parents acknowledged material, social, and affective obligations to them. María Mannarelli's (1993) study of seventeenth-century baptismal records from Lima, Peru, reveals that about a third of illegitimate children were recognized by both parents at birth but that an additional 40 percent were recognized only by their mothers; in 16 percent of cases, neither parent recognized the child, and 3 percent of the time fathers alone recognized the child. Meanwhile, an examination of thousands of baptismal records from late-nineteenth-century Chile reveals only one father who recognized his illegitimate child at birth (other illegitimate children might be recognized later in life, of course, and even parents who never legally recognized their offspring might still love and care for them).

Such patterns had important consequences for the social and ethnic identity of illegitimate children. In colonial Bogotá, Colombia, few illegitimate children received formal paternal recognition and most were assimilated into and more closely identified with the community, family, and ethnic or racial group of the mother. Here as elsewhere, illegitimates also acquired the mother's class status, regardless of the father's socioeconomic position

(Dueñas Vargas 1997). Female-headed families were similarly widespread in nineteenth-century São Paulo, Brazil. There, although relations between men and women were by definition fleeting, extended matrifocal families of older women and their daughters and grandchildren provided some measure of continuity and stability to domestic organization. It was in this environment that many illegitimate children were raised (Dias 1995: chapter 6).

Elite social commentators tended to associate matrifocal families and the children reared in them with disorder, laziness, and delinquency. "Because of the fact that legitimate children are raised by a father and a mother, they are more educated, deferential, and apply themselves to work," opined Don Manuel Samper Sanzo, a lawyer of the Real Audiencia of Santafé de Bogotá in 1791 (cited in Dueñas Vargas 1997: 155). Such views were strikingly persistent. In a 1929 article on "the deficiencies of the home as a factor in the delinquency of minors," a Chilean jurist and juvenile court justice declared, "The father's authority tends to be indispensable to direct the behavior of the children, and frequently the mother's weakness is impotent to replace it" (Gajardo 1929: 204). Such doubts about mothers were also inscribed in the law. Through the doctrine of *patria potestad*, fathers exercised exclusive control over their legitimate children, controlling their property, education, and legal transactions. They did not, however, enjoy *patria potestad* over illegitimate offspring. But the law did not grant mothers *patria potestad* over illegitimate children either. Thus, according to the law, the mothers who raised illegitimates were essentially guardians, not parents, of their children.[9]

The lack of legal recognition of maternal authority had important consequences for the illegitimate children over whom single mothers exercised de facto custody. In societies that valued the labor of children, such provisions made illegitimates vulnerable to removal from their mothers' control and hence more easily exploited. The report of a nineteenth-century official reflects the claims public authorities could assert over the illegitimate children of single mothers: "I have been ordered . . . to investigate those women vagabonds who live in our district without means of subsistence; principally, those who maintain illicit relations and have many illegitimate children. . . . The local inspector orders that the children of those women . . . be deposited in homes of respectable individuals" (cited in Salazar 1985: 289–90).

Meanwhile, the judicial archives provide evidence that single mothers' custody of illegitimate children was challenged not just by public authorities but also by private individuals. In the provincial town of San Felipe, Chile, in 1898, Secundina Brito placed her fifteen-year-old illegitimate daughter, María del Rosario, as a servant in the home of Paulina Carrasco in order that she learn some domestic skills. Carrasco was to pay her daughter four pesos a month, give her periodic raises, allow the mother to visit when she wanted, and "care for her and watch over her as befits a girl of fifteen who leaves her home for the first time to assume employment." The practice of placing children as servants in other people's homes was common, especially among families whose economic situation made it difficult to support their offspring. But in this case, the arrangement quickly turned sour. Brito declared that Carrasco had not paid the girl the agreed-upon wage, failed to attend to her and keep her out of trouble, and, worst of all, "deprived me of the prestige and authority of a mother" by inciting her to disobedience. Brito sought to regain custody of her daughter, but Carrasco rebuffed her (AJSF).[10] Such disputes were frequent in late-nineteenth- and early-twentieth-century Chile, and it is telling that they consistently involved illegitimate children. Even more explicitly, a defendant opposing a woman's attempt to reclaim her five-year-old son from his care conceded "the boy is son of the complainant," but then challenged her claim by immediately adding "but he is not legitimate" (AJL).[11]

The pattern is echoed elsewhere. In one municipality in nineteenth-century Northeast Brazil, the gradual abolition of slavery made the labor of "orphans," that is, fatherless children, increasingly important. Such children were assigned guardians who were charged with protecting their well-being and in exchange benefited from the children's labor; according to the law, only widows who lived morally upright lives had custody over their fatherless children. Unmarried mothers, whose morality was by definition suspect, could be automatically denied guardianship of their children. In a period of high labor demand, potential guardian-employers had a clear incentive to impugn the morality of single women and thereby gain access to their children (Meznar 1994: 507). Thus, because of the lack of legal or social recognition of maternal authority, illegitimate children made easy targets for those seeking to exploit their labor.

At the same time that single mothers were deemed an immoral influence on their children, there existed a parallel belief that illegitimate children were somehow bad for their mothers. Some charitable societies who worked for the moralization of the poor, for example, even sought to remove the fruits of sinful relations in order to rehabilitate fallen mothers. This could be a rationale for sending illegitimate children to orphanages—sometimes against their mothers' will. "The salvation of the mother depends on the placement of these children," wrote the member of one society to the nuns of the foundling home in Santiago, Chile (Libros Entradas).[12] In even starker terms, another declared, "I am sending you the baby Rejina del Carmen . . . daughter of Rosalia, a very young girl; it has been necessary to take the baby from her mother, since she is the cause of her perdition" (Libros Entradas).[13] In this discourse, illegitimate children were not only the products of sin but by their very existence also fomented it.

"Sending out to be raised": the circulation of illegitimates

The separation of illegitimates and their mothers was not always blatantly coercive. Owing to stigma, poverty, or the demands of wage earning, many single mothers were unable or unwilling to keep their children. In this case, they might engage in a cultural practice with roots far back in Western culture, temporarily or permanently relinquishing the child to be raised by someone else. The mother would place the child with a neighbor, friend, kinswoman, or relative or even with a perfect stranger. Sometimes this arrangement would be for a stipulated period (for example, until weaning), other times it would last indefinitely, and often there was an exchange of money. While any child might be reared under such circumstances, evidence suggests the practice was especially common with illegitimate children, who lived disproportionately in poor, female-headed households unable to maintain them and who in some social circles occasioned stigma. When five-year-old Luis Alberto Acevedo died in 1885 in a rural Chilean community he was being cared for by Paulina Liberona, a tenant farmer's wife who had four grown children and several young grandchildren of her own. She identified the boy as the "illegitimate son of Rozenda Acevedo, who sent [him] to be raised five years ago, leaving one year's anticipated payment, and afterward I never saw her again" (AJR).[14] While Luis Alberto never knew his mother, other parents maintained ties with their children and eventually reclaimed them.

Young children like Luis Alberto were first sent out to be nursed. Slightly older ones were placed in homes to be "educated" or to work as servants (activities that were often synonymous). The status of children reared in such families was ambiguous. In the best of scenarios, the children were adopted into families. Such was the case of Ignacia Naranjo, whom Tránsito Figueroa remembered in her 1851 will: "Given the love and affection I have had and have for the youngster Ignacia Naranjo, a girl I raised since her tender years . . . I order that upon my death my executor give the said Naranjo thirty pesos in silver . . . and an image of the Virgin of Tránsito" (ANS).[15] But they might also be incorporated into these "foster" families as servants—sometimes in a lifelong capacity. Archival documents abound with young people who refer to the people who reared them since infancy not as "mother" and "father" but as "master" and "mistress."[16]

At the other end of the social hierarchy, some elite parents, such as those in seventeenth-century Lima and eighteenth-century Brazil, anonymously "abandoned" their own illegitimate children to relatives or kinspeople in order to conceal out-of-wedlock births and salvage their honor. If they maintained discretion in their comportment, they might even be able to maintain contact with the children, who could grow up unaware of their true origins. The parents of such children might surreptitiously serve as their godparents, and illegitimates might even be "taken in" by their own biological parents who disguised their true identity by calling them foundlings (see chapter 4 [see original reading]).[17] Such subterfuges were plausible precisely because it was so common for households to raise abandoned or unrelated children.

The circulation of illegitimate children, then, was a generalized practice and involved the poorest and wealthiest of households. Children "sent to be raised" often crossed class and ethnic boundaries; such was the case with Rodolfo (whose story is recounted at the beginning of this chapter), who was born of a well-to-do family but passed through households of varying social levels and ethnic identities. Children could also circulate upward, as when poor youngsters were taken in by wealthy households who acted out of charity. The extended patriarchal households of Iberian tradition, "inclusive entities" that assimilated a wide array of individuals into their fold, were uniquely suited for such eventualities (Schwartz and Lockart 1995: 7). Perhaps the quintessential patriarchal household was the sugar plantation of Northeast Brazil described by Gilberto Freyre, which absorbed large numbers of dependents, including illegitimates, abandoned children, and adopted ones (categories that often overlapped), poorer relatives, servants, and slaves. On such plantations, abandoned or illegitimate youngsters might grow up to become *agregados*, permanent residents who were integrated into the landowner's paramilitary force or given work not entrusted to slaves (Freyre 1956 [1933]; Mesgravis 1975: 405).

The circulation of illegitimate children was not simply an informal, private custom among households, however. It was also an institutionalized, public practice actively fomented by church and state through the functioning of foundling homes. Vast numbers of children were interned in orphan asylums (for example, one of every ten children born in turn-of-the-century Santiago was sent to the city's largest orphanage). And while legitimate children could also be abandoned, the majority—sometimes the vast majority—of children left at these institutions were born out of wedlock, for the same reasons illegitimates made up a disproportionate share of those "sent out to be raised" (in the Santiago foundling home, over 80 percent of children were illegitimate) (Delgado Valderrama 1986; Salinas Meza 1991).[18] Perhaps the most striking feature of such institutions was their almost unimaginably high mortality rates. To cite figures from late-nineteenth-century Santiago once again, death rates of young infants left at the institution routinely surpassed 80 percent and in one particularly bad year, 1892, reached an astounding 97 percent (Casa de Huérfanos 1892). Thus, abandonment to an asylum and the premature death it often brought about were common fates for illegitimates in many Latin American cities, as discussed in the next chapter of this volume [see original reading].

Illegitimacy and social hierarchy

Adoption by poor foster mothers, rearing in the homes of relatives or neighbors as "anonymous foundlings," incorporation into large, extended households as *agregados*, or abandonment to a foundling home all provided for the assimilation of illegitimate children into networks of social relations and patron-client hierarchies. But while these mechanisms provided a social niche for the extensive population of illegitimates and may have mitigated the potential dangers of a rootless, alienated group of individuals, they were also frequently associated with social marginalization. Indeed, quite apart from the bureaucratic or occupational discrimination illegitimates suffered in colonial society and the legal discrimination they endured in the republican period, the everyday cultural practices societies availed themselves of in providing for illegitimate children were themselves frequently associated with social subordination.

Even an illegitimate ostensibly incorporated as one more member of his or her biological family did not necessarily enjoy a status equal to the household's legitimate children. Parents who bequeathed possessions to natural children sometimes framed the transaction not in terms of love and affection or even in terms of concern for the child's well-being but in recognition of services or labors rendered. When Doña Gerarda Berríos dictated a will in 1775, she described how for more than twenty years she had raised her illegitimate son, Antonio Muñoz, who "has accompanied me and served myself and my husband personally with total obedience and subjection." She then stated, "I declare that for his personal service he be given half of the plot that I leave as my goods . . . charging him not to leave Cayetano Zamora, my legitimate son, and to accompany and assist him as he has done with me as the good and obedient son who until today he has been, since the aforementioned [Cayetano] is infirm and cannot . . . personally support himself" (Cavieres 1995: 238–39).[19] The will leaves starkly clear the inferior status Antonio enjoyed vis-à-vis Cayetano, his legitimate half brother and Doña Gerarda's principal beneficiary. Whether Antonio is more a son or a servant is difficult to say.

Indeed, illegitimacy might be associated not only with subordination in the context of the family but with downward social mobility, a fact nowhere more strikingly illustrated than in cases of illegitimates born to high-status parents like Don Pedro Antonio Ramíres. Don Pedro was a very wealthy and politically powerful landowner in mid-nineteenth-century central Chile. A local official, he owned a number of haciendas (landed estates), on which numerous peons labored, and he held additional properties in the cities of Santiago and La Serena. Although married, Ramíres also fathered four illegitimate children (only two of whom survived) with his wife's niece. Immediately following her clandestine birth, Don Pedro's first illegitimate child, Lucinda, was anonymously abandoned in the middle of the night near the house of two low-level employees on one of his haciendas. The couple's son discovered the baby, and their adult daughter agreed to care for her. Lucinda lived with her foster mother for some nine years. For several years, Don Pedro paid for Lucinda's upbringing, but he explained it was "out of charity" to an "anonymous" foundling that he did so, never admitting his paternity. Surely the adoptive family was not so easily duped. Don Pedro's second illegitimate child, Wenceslao, was born several years later. Don Pedro claimed the boy had been given to him by a stranger in Santiago, and he offered the young Wenceslao to the overseer of one of his haciendas, suggesting that the child "could serve him."

The fate of Don Pedro's illegitimate children is striking: the two who survived infancy were incorporated into the families of their elite father's humble and illiterate employees. Born of elite parents who had engaged in a relationship considered both illicit and execrable (they were not only illegitimates but, worse still, *adulterinos*—born of a married father—and *incestuosos*—children, in this case, of relations between a man and his wife's niece), the highborn Lucinda and Wenceslao were stripped of their natal social rank and inserted into the lowest rungs of the hacienda's social hierarchy (AP).[20]

The association of illegitimacy and subordinate class status is a recurring one. A witness in a case concerning the inheritance of the illegitimate offspring of a wealthy Bahian captain-major defended their rights by noting, "The captain-major never sent nor consented to send his sons or grandchildren to any mechanical trade once he had legitimized them, treating them always according to the law of nobility" (Pinho 1982:179–80). The comment is a particularly clear articulation of the relationship between illegitimacy and inferior social status: here the act of legitimizing a natural son is tantamount to conferring on him a higher class status. An illegitimate, even one born to a wealthy captain-major, is considered fit for the humble mechanical trades.

But the most vulnerable of all in this regard were children of color in slave societies. While late colonial provisions in Brazil declared all foundlings, regardless of their color, to be automatically free, these mandates were often ignored.[21] Children sent out to wet nurses by foundling homes might disappear forever, becoming integrated into the ranks of the enslaved. In some places a trade in foundlings of color evolved. In 1830, lawmakers in Rio de Janeiro considered the enslavement of abandoned children enough of a problem to pass a decree declaring that "whoever sells or enslaves foundlings will suffer the penalty of 30,000 réis, and eight days in jail, which will also be applicable to those who buy in bad faith, if they are proven to be aware of the fraud" (Marcílio 1998: 275; Venâncio 1999:131–36),[22] Once again, patterns of circulation intersected with existing hierarchical structures to produce the subordination of illegitimate children.

The early twentieth century: scientific compassion and the state

If illegitimacy had always been a legal issue, at the turn of the twentieth century it became a public health one as well. Public officials and a nascent corps of professional physicians began to take an interest in illegitimacy because it was believed that children born out of wedlock suffered unusually high rates of mortality. The conclusions of Ecuadorian doctor Antonio J. Bastidas (1933) in his study "Illegitimacy: A factor in infant mortality" were typical: illegitimate children suffered a mortality rate double that of their legitimate counterparts. An Argentine advocate elaborated: "All the problems of childhood become more acute in the case of the illegitimate child: it is he who swells the statistics of infant mortality . . . it is he who, crowding the asylums. . . . transmits infections that devastate the population" (Nelson 1927: 220). Thus, a traditional moral preoccupation with out-of-wedlock birth was assimilated into a new, positivist world view, and illegitimacy came to be seen as a public health problem and social crisis.

Many commentators questioned the traditional stigma attached to illegitimacy. Whereas once out-of-wedlock birth had been a "stain" or an "infamy," now illegitimates were increasingly regarded as blameless victims of circumstance. Thus, the illegitimate child could be characterized as "the scapegoat of others' vices, of seduction, inexperience, ignorance, superstition, individual and social egoism" and even as a "tender victim . . . a silent social reformer" (Nelson 1927: 221). But illegitimacy continued to be heavily laden with negative associations. In the positivist discourses of the era, it was associated with delinquency, crime, disease, and, above all, infant mortality. Illegitimacy rates were even read as indicators of a country's rank on an imagined scale of civilization: "In the most civilized countries of Europe more than 90 percent of births are legitimate, [which] shows that . . . the legally constituted family is the basis of . . . the progress of peoples," declared a Chilean congressman (Rubio 1928). "On the contrary, where illegitimacy reigns, populations . . . are closer to a primitive state . . . and backwardness prevails."

More helpful in explaining trends in filiation than the congressman's dubious notion of "civilization" is the evolution of state formation in Latin America. Expanding twentieth-century states began providing new benefits to their citizens, including war pensions, civil service jobs, and social welfare programs, but made these benefits contingent on formal marriage and legitimate filiation. As the purview of their action expanded, states were probably more powerful arbiters of family formation than ever before. Still, the history of illegitimacy is by no means one of linear decline. In fact, recorded illegitimacy rates in the late twentieth century were in many places as high as or higher than they had ever been.[23]

Conclusion

It is of course difficult to generalize about social and legal attitudes toward illegitimacy or the experience of illegitimates over the course of five centuries and across the diverse societies of Latin America. But it is possible to draw several general conclusions about the significance of illegitimacy in the region's history. Like the categories of race, ethnicity, and gender, filiation is a socially constructed designation that has been fundamental to the production of social hierarchy since the beginning of the colonial enterprise in Latin America. Illegitimacy has endured as a culturally significant category because, historically, family order has been perceived as essential to social order, and filiation has been perceived as integral to the very existence of the family. As an Argentine commentator put it in the 1920s, "undoubtedly the complete equalization of the illegitimate child with the legitimate one . . . would lead to the beginning of the dissolution of the family as we now know it" (Nelson 1927: 227). His comment sums up a conviction that has endured among many political, religious, and social authorities from the colonial period to the present.

Second, it is clear that while birth status had important consequences that lasted a lifetime, those most immediately affected by the practices and prejudices associated with illegitimacy were children. Illegitimates faced the very real possibilities of subordination, downward mobility, enslavement, and, in the context of the foundling home, premature death. On the other hand, the widespread circulation of children and informal cultural practices at all social levels of taking in unrelated children also meant that illegitimates separated from their families of origin could become sons and daughters, or at least servants and dependents, in other households. Subordinated within the social order, they were not necessarily marginalized from it.

Today, many of the social realities associated with illegitimacy endure. The matrifocal households in which many illegitimates grew up continue to be a prevalent family form in many Latin American societies. Meanwhile, the practices of child circulation that have historically transferred children, especially illegitimate ones, into the homes of kin, neighbors and strangers, are very much alive in poor Brazilian communities (Cardoso 1984; Fonseca 1998) and in some Caribbean societies.[24] One Brazilian author has suggested that international adoption is a contemporary transnational manifestation of the historical pattern (Fonseca 1998).

Commentators continue to debate the causes, meanings, and consequences of illegitimacy. Perhaps the most visible recent debate erupted in Chile in 1998 in the context of the proposed New Filiation Law. The law, one of the most significant reforms of the Chilean Civil Code since its promulgation in 1855, eliminated the legal discrimination against illegitimates and instituted new provisions for paternity investigation. The proposal provoked heated debates, with those against it marshalling traditional arguments about the threat it posed to the integrity of the family and those in favor invoking newer ideas about children's inalienable rights to a mother and a father.

Ultimately, the New Filiation Law was passed, and as of 1999 Chilean newborns no longer have their birth certificates stamped "legitimate" or "illegitimate," categories that have shaped the experience of Latin American children for centuries. While the debate in Chile is not yet over—critics have charged that judges have been slow to apply the law and have unfairly dismissed many rightful paternity claims (Solicitan 2000)—it is nevertheless safe to say that today illegitimates across the continent enjoy more legal rights than ever before. But the debates serve as a reminder that the waning of illegitimacy as a legal category in Latin America does not mean it has ceased to be a deeply significant cultural one.

Notes

1   As Mannarelli (1993: 175) suggests of colonial Lima, "an illegitimate man was different from a woman of the same status; an illegitimate Spaniard was incomparable to a slave born out of wedlock."

2   Such refusal can be attributed to social and racial prejudice, economic self-interest, and even legal prohibition. In any case, by the end of the colonial period in Spanish America the cultural disapproval of unequal marriages was inscribed into law. The Royal Pragmatic on Marriage, which took effect in 1778, gave parents unprecedented authority to control their children's marriages, precisely in order to stymie legitimate unions between unequal partners.

3   Nazarri (1996) suggests that norms prohibiting exogamy contributed to illegitimacy because biracial couples were unable to marry and simply procreated out of wedlock.

4   The notion of "consensual union" sets concubinage among social equals apart from the unequal unions discussed above; the latter were not necessarily "consensual" at all.

5   In other words, as Lewin (1992) notes, illegitimate unions could produce heirs, so in terms of inheritance law, marriage was not technically obligatory.

6   Obviously, the fact that black women, regardless of their marital status, are placed in the same category as single ones starkly illustrates the role of race in delineating the parameters of these practices. In addition, the reference to single women suggests that engendering natural children with an unmarried woman is more acceptable than engendering *adulterinos* with a married one.

7   That López distinguishes between Checa's natural and spurious children suggests that in this particular context, the distinction was important not only in the law but also in popular attitudes. The spurious child to whom he refers could be the offspring of a priest or, more likely, of an adulterous affair (the term "spurious" in this usage probably included all unions in which the parents were not single and marriageable), The natural children were presumably born once Checa was widowed.

8   The couple's story was recorded in the judicial archives when Checa filed a case against López to receive economic support from him.

9   This situation prevailed in many countries into the twentieth century, when women were only gradually granted equal authority over children. Even when women were granted equal authority over legitimate children, neither parent was necessarily given *patria potestad* over illegitimates. A partial but important exception to this trend was in Mexico, where civil codes in the 1870s and 1880s granted women *patria potestad* over natural children (though not over other kinds of illegitimates), contingent on their good behavior (Arrom 1985). It is unclear how these changes affected such families in practice, however. On *patria potestad* in nineteenth-century Argentina, see Guy (1985).

10 The judicial record is incomplete, and we do not know whether Brito was able to get her daughter back (Secundina Brito contra Paulina Carrasco, 1899, caja 115).

11 Melinda Vásquez con Ropajito Astudillo por entrega de un niño, 1925, legajo 301, expediente 41.

12 1896, Card, M.M. Larrain, número 11987–88.

13 1909, Letter, Magdalena Márquez, número 6734.

14 Indagación sobre la muerte de un niño encontrado en el canal Rafaelino [?] en Codegua, 1885, legajo 911, expediente 490.

15 1851, tomo 51, foja 53.

16 According to Szuchman (1988), child labor of this kind was also rampant in early-nineteenth-century Buenos Aires.

17 See the fascinating cases from late colonial Brazil discussed in Nazzari (1998). This pattern is also discussed for Brazil by Silva (1993: 185–87) and for colonial Lima by Mannarelli (1993: 273–77). Twinam (1999) gives many examples of creative subterfuge among colonial elites.

18 The proportion of illegitimates in Brazilian institutions was considerably lower (Marcílio 1998).

19 Silva (1993:197) reproduces a similar statement from a late-eighteenth-century Brazilian will.

20 This course of events may well have been derailed when the children's existence was revealed during a lengthy and ultimately successful divorce suit his wife, Doña Juana Josefa Madariaga, filed against

Don Pedro. "Doña Juana Josefa Madariaga con Don Pedro Antonio Ramíres por divorcio perpetuo." 1867/68, rollo 1855307, legajos 813–14.

21   The Alvará of 1775, confirmed in 1823, declared Brazilian foundlings free.

22   In addition, Meznar (1994: 504–5) discusses parents' fears that children of color would be enslaved in the wake of the abolition of the slave trade in Brazil.

23   According to FLACSO (2001), 27 percent of Uruguayan children were illegitimate in 1987; 30 percent of Paraguayan children in 1985; over 33 percent of Chilean children in 1988; 41 percent of Costa Rican children in 1991; and 58 percent of Argentinian children in 1990.

24   In Haiti, illegitimate children abandoned by their parents may be reared by another household as *"restaveks"* literally "stay-withs," children impressed into a deeply exploitative form of servitude in their adoptive household. See Cadet (1998) for the poignant autobiography of a *restavek* as well as chapter 8 in this volume [see original reading].

References

AJL (Archivo del Juzgado de Letras de Menor Cuantía de Linares [Chile]).

AJR (Archivo Judicial de Rancagua [Chile]).

AJSF (Archivo Judicial de San Felipe [Chile]).

ANS (Archivo Notarial, de Santiago [Chile]).

AP (Archivo del Provisor, Asuntos Matrimoniales, Arzobispado de Santiago [Chile]).

Arrom, Silvia. 1985. Changes in Mexican family law in the nineteenth century: The Civil Codes of 1870 and 1884. *Journal of Family History* 10 (3): 305–17.

Bastidas, Antonio J. 1933. La ilegitimidad, factor de letalidad infantil. *Boletín del Instituto Internacional Americano de Protección a la Infancia* VI (4): 357–85.

Borah, Sherburne Cook, and Woodrow Borah. 1966. Marriage and legitimacy in Mexican culture: Mexico and California. *California Law Review* 54: 946–1008.

Cadet, Jean-Robert. 1998. *Restavec: From Haitian slave child to middle-class American.* Austin: University of Texas Press.

Calvo, Thomas. 1982. Familia y registro parroquial: el caso tapatío en el siglo XVIII. *Relaciones: Estudios de Historia y Sociedad* 3 (10): 53–67.

Calvo Mackenna, Luis. 1928. La profilaxia del abandono del niño y el Servicio Social. *Servicio Social* año II. Vol. 1 (3): 200–214.

Cardoso, Ruth C. L. 1984. Creating kinship: The fostering of children in favela families in Brazil. In *Kinship ideology and practice in Latin America*, edited by R. T. Smith. Chapel Hill: University of North Carolina Press.

Casa de Huérfanos. Various. Memorias de la Casa de Huérfanos. Santiago, Chile.

Castañeda, Paulino. 1981. Facultades de los obispos indianos para dispensar de ilegitimidad. *Missionalia Hispánica* 38 (113): 227–47.

Cavieres, Eduardo. 1995. Consensualidad, familia e hijos naturales: Aconcagua en la segunda mitad del siglo XVIII. *Cuadernos de Historia* 15 (diciembre): 219–39.

Delgado Valderrama, Manuel. 1986. Marginación e integración social en Chile: Los expósitos, 1750–1930. Masters diss., Instituto de Historia, Universidad Católica de Valparaíso, Chile.

Dias, Maria Odila Silva. 1995. *Power and everyday life: The lives of working women in nineteenth-century Brazil.* New Brunswick: Rutgers University Press.

Dueñas Vargas, Guiomar. 1997. *Los hijos del pecado: Ilegitimidad y vida familiar en la Santafé de Bogotá colonial.* Bogotá: Editorial Universidad Nacional.

Elizarrarás Rendon, Delfino. 1951. El problema jurídico del concubinato. Law diss., Universidad Autónoma de México, Mexico City.

Errázuriz Tagle, Jorge and Guillermo Eyzaguirre Rouse. 1903. *Estudio social: Monografía de una familia obrera de Santiago.* Santiago: Imprenta Barcelona.

FLACSO (Facultad Latinoamericana de Ciencias Sociales). 2001, Mujeres latinoamericanas en cifras. www.eurosur.org/FLACSO/mujeres. (Website consulted on 10 December.)

Fonseca, Claudia. 1998. *Caminos de adopción*. Translated by J. C. Radovich. Buenos Aires: Eudeba.

Freyre, Gilberto. 1956 [1933], *The masters and the slaves: A study in the development of Brazilian civilization*. Translated by S. Putnam. New York: Alfred A. Knopf.

Gajardo, Samuel. 1929. Las deficiencias del hogar como factor de delincuencia de menores. *Servicio Social* II (3).

Guy, Donna. 1985. Lower-class families, women and the law in nineteenth-century Argentina. *Journal of Family History* 10 (3): 305–17.

Kuznesof, Elizabeth. 1986. *Household economy and urban development in São Paulo, 1765–1836*. London: Westview Press.

Lewin, Linda. 1992. Natural and spurious children in Brazilian inheritance law from colony to empire: A methodological essay. *The Americas* 48 (3): 351–96.

Libros Entradas. Libros de Documentos de Entradas de la Casa de Huáerfanos. Santiago, Chile.

Mannarelli, María Emma. 1993. *Pecados públicos: La ilegitimidad en Lima, siglo XVII*. Lima: Ediciones Flora Tristán.

Marcílio, Maria Luiza, 1998. *História social da criança abandonada*. São Paulo: Editora HUCITEC.

Martínez-Alier, Verena. 1989. *Marriage, class and colour in nineteenth-century Cuba*, 2d ed. Ann Arbor: University of Michigan Press.

Mesgravis, Laima. 1975. A assistência à infância desamparada e a Santa Casa de São Paulo: A roda dos expostos no século XIX. *Revista de História* 52 (103): 401–23.

Meznar, Joan. 1994. Orphans and the transition to free labor in Northeast Brazil: The case of Campina Grande, 1850–88. *Journal of Social History* 27 (3): 499–515.

Milanich, Nara. 2002. Culture, class, and family in Chile, 1857–1930. Ph.D. diss., Yale University.

Moreno, José Luis. 1997–98. Sexo, matrimonio, y familia: La ilegitimidad en la frontera pampeana del Río de la Plata, 1780–1850. *Boletín del Instituto de Historia Argentina y Americana "Dr. Emilio Ravignani"* tercera serie (16/17): 61–84.

Morin, Claude. 1977. Démographie et différences ethniques en Amérique Latine coloniale. *Annales de Démographie Historique*: 301–12.

Nazzari, Muriel. 1996. Concubinage in colonial Brazil: The inequalities of race, class, and gender. *Journal of Family History* 21 (2): 107–24.

———. 1998. An urgent need to conceal. In *The faces of honor: Sex, shame, and violence in colonial Latin America*, edited by L. Johnson and S. Lipsett-Rivera. Albuquerque: University of New Mexico Press.

Nelson, Ernesto. 1927. El problema de la ilegitimidad. *Boletín del Instituto Internacional Americano de Protección a la Infancia* 1 (2): 221–48.

O'Phelan Godoy, Scarlett. 1998. Hijos naturales "sin impedimento alguno." La ilegitimidad en el mineral de Hualgayoc, Cajamarca (1780–1845). In *El norte en la historia regional: siglos XVIII–XIX*, edited by Y. Saint-Geours and S. O'Phelan Godoy. Lima.

Pérez Brignoli, H. 1981. Deux siècles d'illégitimité au Costa Rica, 1770–1974. In *Mariage et remariage dans les populations du passé*, edited by E. H. J. Dupâquier, P. Laslett, M. Livi-Bacci, S. Sogner. London: Academic Press.

Pinho, Wanderley. 1982. *História de um engenho do Recôncavo*. 2d ed. São Paulo: Companhia Editora Nacional.

Potthast-Jutkeit, Barbara. 1991. The ass of a mare and other scandals: Marriage and extramarital relations in nineteenth-century Paraguay. *Journal of Family History* 16 (3): 215–39.

Rubio, Santiago. 1928. Cámara de Diputados [Chile]. 2a Sesión Ordinaria, 28 May 1928.

Salazar, Gabriel. 1985. *Labradores, peones y proletarios*. Santiago: Ediciones Sur.

Salinas, Rolando Mellafe, and René Salinas. 1988. *Sociedad y población rural en la formación de Chile actual: La Ligua 1700–1850*. Santiago: Ediciones de la Universidad de Chile.

Salinas Meza, René. 1991. Orphans and family disintegration in Chile: The mortality of abandoned children, 1750–1930. *Journal of Family History* 16 (3): 315–29.

Sánchez Albornoz, Nicolas. 1974. *The population of Latin America: A history*. Berkeley: University of California Press.

Schwartz, Stuart B. 1997. Pecar en las colonias. Mentalidades populares, Inquisición, y actitudes hacia la fornicación simple en España, Portugal y las colonias americanas. *Cuadernos de Historia Moderna* 18: 51–67.

Schwartz, Stuart B., and James Lockhart. 1995. *Early Latin America. A history of colonial Spanish America and Brazil*. Cambridge: Cambridge University Press.

Silva, Maria Beatrix Nizza da. 1993. *Vida privada e quotidiano no Brasil: na época de D, Maria I e D. João VI*. Lisboa: Editorial Estampa.

Solicitan cambios a ley de filiación. 2000. *El Mercurio* (Santiago), 23 June.

Szuchman, Mark D. 1988. *Order, family, and community in Buenos Aires, 1810–1860*. Stanford: Stanford University Press.

Twinam, Ann. 1999. *Public lives, private secrets: Gender, honor, sexuality, and illegitimacy in colonial Spanish America*. Stanford: Stanford University Press.

Venâncio, Renato Pinto. 1999. *Famílias abandonadas: Assistência à criança de camadas populares no Rio de Janeiro e em Salvador, séculos XVIII e XIX*. Rio de Janeiro: Papirus.

Chapter 5

Karin Aronsson and Bengt Sandin

THE SUN MATCH BOY AND PLANT METAPHORS: A SWEDISH IMAGE OF A 20TH-CENTURY CHILDHOOD

FOR MANY YEARS, A POSTWAR BABY, a little prince born in 1946, was the favorite photo object of Swedish ladies' magazines. He was portrayed on his own or at play with his four elder sisters, or as a sweet fatherless orphan, held by the hand of his grandfather, King Gustaf Adolf VI. Blue-eyed and blonde, with curly hair, this little prince (*lill-prinsen*) matched Nordic fairy tale notions of little princes. He was often portrayed in different play activities, wearing different garments, such as a chef's hat, an aviation pilot uniform, ski clothes, an American Indian costume, and so on. He and his sisters, the wee princesses at Haga (*sessorna på Haga*), presented images of the ideal childhood in Sweden: eternally playing in rural settings, yet practicing their future roles as adults.

However, this prince never attained the coverage of another little boy, although looking curiously like the growing boy-prince in many ways. In every Swedish household from the 1930s onward, one could find pictures of the sun match boy (*solstickepojken*), a little child who by 1976 appeared on two thirds of all Swedish matchboxes. This sun match boy was the symbol for a philanthropic child welfare campaign.[1]

Unlike the little prince, the sun match boy never changed clothing. He was forever portrayed half-naked, running on his own on a sun-lit scene. For more than 50 years, this child image has dominated the matchbox imagery in Sweden.

In this chapter, we discuss the image of the sun match boy set in contrast to other images of childhood and in relationship to social and political changes in Sweden during the 20th century as well as to underlying notions, metaphors, as it were, of child development. The political changes in the creation of the Swedish welfare state are central for the understanding of development of new images of childhood.

Contrasting images

Public representations of different kinds can be read as markers of cultural values. What is shown and what is not shown? What images are chosen in large-scale commercial and publicly sponsored campaigns? Media representations of children may be instrumental in the creation of images of childhoods. These images naturally relate in a complex manner to social and political changes, both as expressions of certain realities and values as well as being agents around which realities and values are created. We do not claim that the images that we discuss here are representative in the meaning that they are the only or most important notions of a certain time. However, they are examples from a body of similar images with a considerable circulation and as such they can serve as focal points for an understanding of childhood in Sweden. Foremost, they relate to each other and indeed represent different aspects of modern images of social changes in Swedish social life. Thus, this chapter is based on the contrast between different and conflicting understandings of childhood. We set the little match boy toddler in contrast to social realistic images, widespread during the early 19th century.

The match boy image has indeed been very widely spread. The boxes with the little boy toddler began to be sold in 1936 and by the late 1970s more than two thirds of all matchboxes sold in Sweden carried this image. The illustration was made by Einar Nerman, a celebrated illustrator of children's books and a portrait artist. Thus, this little piece of art was so widely distributed that the concept of matchbox became almost synonymous with the boy walking toward the sun with his arms stretched forward. The revenues brought in by the sales of these boxes were used for welfare projects of different kinds. This philanthropic campaign was somewhat ironically launched during the formative years of the Social-Democratic welfare policies. Policies that in due time would terminate the need for many of the philanthropic agencies created during the early 19th century and drawing on funds from campaigns of this nature. The conflict between these different modes of bringing welfare to the people should not be overstated, however. In many cases, philanthropy and state agencies worked close together (Olsson, 1990; Seip, 1984). The matchbox foundation gave support to projects that were classical arenas where both the state and the philanthropic interests participated, such as summer camps and maternity clinics. The idea was inspired by British and other welfare projects involving matchboxes sold for specific welfare purposes. The price was set in such a way that it would not prevent anyone from buying the sun matches instead of other matches. The foundation was set up by incomes from a marginal percentage of the matchbox sales. Voluntary work was part of the foundation's original design. The county governors would generally be the ones in charge of administering sun match money for specific counties. These incomes steadily increased. In 1937, a marginal percentage of all matchboxes sold were sun matchboxes (10%). After a few years, this marginal share had increased to almost one third of the Swedish matchbox sales (30% in 1941). In postwar Sweden, the majorities of all matchboxes sold were sun matchboxes (57% in 1947, and 70% in 1976).

The sun match was sold for the stated purpose to be for "the benefit of children and old people." Now let us turn to the image in itself. What does the picture convey about modern Swedish images of childhood (see Fig. 9.1 [see original reading])?

The toddler boy of the matchbox emblem is portrayed in profile, walking swiftly with outstretched arms, facing the sun. His hair is a little unruly and there is a prominent curl that sways on the top of his head (a blonde curl that reminds the spectator of the curly head of the little prince). He is half naked. The only piece of clothing is a little shirt that is tied in the back with a ribbon that blows as the child moves. What does this movement convey? It is the movement of a free child. He moves bravely out into the open with outstretched arms, as if he is ready to grasp what is there. He is not held by the hands of his big sisters or grandfather (as the little prince in the ladies' journals' iconography of early postwar Sweden). Neither does anyone hold him in the lap as in the traditional madonna–child paraphrases that permeate snapshots and family life albums (Holland, 1992). In many ways, he can be seen to represent the independent, self-contained child, free to ramble on his own. On the matchbox, there is an association between the child and the sun (nature), not between the child and a parent or some other caregiver.

The boy seems happily unaware or unashamed of his nudity. He has not cared to get fully dressed before running out into the open. He is natural and impulsive, not yet hindered by cultural restrictions about getting dressed before going out. His nudity conveys naturalness in that he has not cared to get dressed. Yet, it is an asexual nudity. First, the profile projection does not make it possible to discern whether the child is a boy or a girl. The short wavy hair can be that of a boy or a girl. The ribbon of the little shirt may suggest a girl. Yet, the confident stride is that of a self-assertive little boy. Moreover, the toddler period is not marked by stereotypically gendered traits.

The history of the picture partly explains its gender neutrality or asexuality. The original model was the painter Einar Nerman's son, Tom, at the age of 2, who acted as a model for an illustration of H. C. Andersen's little fairy tale girl, Tummelisa. About 20 years later in 1936 this illustration was then adapted for the sun matchbox project. The sun match boy is thus originally a boy acting girl as it were. In other words, in terms of its own history, the sun match boy is thus a girl–boy. Naked but asexual. This asexuality can also be seen to be linked to the child's young age. The sun match boy is not a baby but a 2-year-old. Somehow, his little baby shirt makes him more nude than if he had been entirely naked. Yet, his pose is far from coquettish or sexually inviting. This type of portrayal can be placed within a romantic tradition that seems to idealize the child's original purity. He moves swiftly and without any coy smile at the onlooker; apparently with no intent to charm or seduce. In many ways, he thus embodies natural purity that, of course, adds to his very charm.

The sun match boy is linked to what is natural in one more way. He faces a radiant red sun with white sun rays. His body is white like the sun rays. The sun rays and the toddler are bright against a darker blue background. The sun and the boy may thus be seen as one of a kind, nature's light representations. The text "the sun match" is set against a yellow background frame with three red stars. Framed by the sun and the star, the match boy is thus enclosed by nature's light (sun and night light). The sun match boy is also close to nature in that he is a summer boy. He does not need any clothing as he moves in a setting of eternal summer (half naked in the sun). He is obviously too young for the summer camps for school-age children. However, he apparently does not need this type of camp for health reasons. His outer appearance is that of a well-fed and energetic healthy child (if anything, the ideal result of a sun match summer camp). He is a "natural" child in that he is healthy.

Moreover, the match boy can be viewed as a natural Swede. The child's complexion has the fair color of a prototypical Swede. Moreover, the blue color of the matchbox is that of the Swedish flag, even if the flag is cast in a different hue. The sun match boy is "natural" in the sense that he is all Swedish. Nothing is as Swedish as the internationally renowned Swedish match company with their "safety matches." No doubt, this is a little Swede. And he is a good boy who does not roam the streets. A welfare child who does not need to beg or work.

This image has to be read in the light of its stark contrast to another image of childhood, that of the poor, sickly, and undernourished child in the philanthropic propaganda of the early 20th century. This image was almost as prevalent in the public's mind during the 1920s and 1930s, as are today's pictures of starving and homeless Third World children. One representative picture of such propaganda of the philanthropy movement of the early 20th century can be found in an issue of the annual magazine *Barnens Dag* (*Children's Day*) in 1907. This picture appears as the vignette to a joint appeal by a series of distinguished child specialists and social reformers, educators, medical doctors, for better housing and better conditions for mothers, and so on, in a feature paper for children's rights under the assuming heading of *J'accuse*. One of the signers was Hjalmar Branting, an important Social-Democratic statesman, who was at the time, leader of the Social-Democrats of the second chamber of the Swedish Parliament, and later a legendary prime minister. The accompanying illustration of *J'accuse* is one of two dirty children with ragged clothes and bare feet (see Fig. 9.2 [see original reading]).

In this illustration, nudity is associated with a lack of clothing, not with impulsivity or summer life. Similarly, wildness is associated with the life of unprotected street children, orphans, and not with children happily roaming around in a summer setting. The two street children are set against an urban landscape, emblematic for culture and the potential pollutions of city life.

These two ways of presenting childhood were not historically unrelated. In fact, they are two sides of the same coin. The poor starving child represented a project for the philanthropist, a reality to be changed. The sun match boy was an ideal to be created. The tie between these images was that the money brought in by this symbolic child was to be spent on summer camps and other welfare measures for poor children. And from these would spring physically strong and morally healthy children.

Historical contexts

The two contrasting images represent different childhoods but one underlying set of ideals. What is shared is an implicit understanding of the value of growing up in nature, a childhood not constrained by lack of food, bad urban dwellings, or hard child labor (or physical ailments).

In Sweden, the 20th century has seen a romantic adoration of sun and free summer life. During the early part of the century, the Swedish bourgeoisie bought big summer houses in the Stockholm archipelago and other countryside areas. The Swedish tourist association wanted to open up the magnificent Swedish mountains and countryside for tourism. Urban social problems should be countered by allowing workers to settle in private housings (*egna hem*) outside the cities, and through the creation of allotments, the Swedish workers would get a stake in the system (allotments are little garden plots where the workers could grow vegetables, which would contribute to their household incomes). This was no doubt a part of the nationalist project to develop people's love for their home country. The celebration of "natural" summer life also corresponded with other movements, such as campaigns for greater hygiene and greater health. Fresh air and outdoor life were important in fighting diseases like tuberculosis. At the core of this project was a struggle to overbridge class conflict and create national identity (Larsson, 1977). In that situation and with that ambition, the living condition of children came in strong conflict with the ideals.

In fact, the nature of childhood was in the center for an intensive public debate in Sweden that formed the ideals of the welfare state. Criminality among the young was increasing at a disconcerting rate it was claimed, and there was a serious shortage of publicly controlled institutions for delinquent and criminal children. Conditions in the schools were criticized, and grave doubts were expressed about the ability of working-class families to look after their own children (Key, 1900). The number of single mothers was much too large for a sound society. An extension of obligatory school education was necessary to keep children off the streets; another measure was the organization of leisure activities. Attention was drawn to the harsh conditions for foster children in the towns and the boarding out of poor children and orphans in rural areas. Children's work in the countryside conflicted with the demands for schooling and should be banned, it was argued. People questioned the wisdom of part-time schooling for farmers' children. The high infant mortality rate highlighted the need for efforts by voluntary organizations and later by local and central authorities. Maternity care required state support, according to some; mothers could not cope with the care and upbringing of their own children. They should listen to the advice of professionals (the male doctors)—the pediatricians ("The Child," 1907; Sandin, 1992a, 1992b; Weiner, 1992).

This struggle for the children and thus also over the nature of childhood was fought around the turn of the century and paved the way for new initatives about how to care for the children. This could take the form of issuing milk to poor children, sending them to summer camps in rural settings, founding children's hospitals, organizing leisure activities, and so forth. The list could be made very long. It was important to send the children away from the cities. The country air would strengthen the morals of the delinquent and the body of the weak. This opinion had its counterparts outside Sweden. In both England and the United States, similar organizations played a major role in molding public opinion and instigating legislation about children (Platt, 1969).

The movement in Sweden also tried to engage local and central authorities. In many cases, the activities came under the responsibility of the municipalities or the state. The state took a major part in legislating centrally for the welfare of the populous and in protecting children from abuse. The rights of the child were thus protected by the state. It should be underlined that this development had its base in the changes that took place in Sweden prior to the beginning of the long period of Social-Democratic power. Professional interest groups, doctors, teachers, and priests declared themselves to be particularly qualified to advise parents about childrearing. In fact, some did claim that parents were not very suitable at all for the task of childrearing. In a manner of speaking, the children stood alone, without the family, protected by the state and the professionals that worked through its agencies. Childhood (i.e., the good childhood) was a creation of the professionals and the state. Institutions were created and new laws were passed to support and control child care in the home (Donzelot, 1980; Hatje, 1974; Hirdman, 1989; Ohrlander, 1992). The welfare state provisions did not only bring help to families, it also made the children visible in their homes as the welfare provisions are based on supervision of individual children's physical and mental growth and status. Helping thus also entailed registration and control. In this process, a new attitude toward childhood was formed, and a new concept of childhood was developed.

The tighter control over school attendance around the turn of the century (1900) and a higher school leaving age meant a new reality for children from the lower classes. It created a whole new childhood. It was no longer possible to stay at home looking after younger siblings, or to leave school when there was chance for a job. New requirements to satisfy the routines of the school were formulated as absolute demands. Breaches of the rules were punished, being seen as a visible expression of a fundamentally moral problem, which emphasized the importance of new efforts to get children to attend school. At the same time, the children became visible in another way. Apart from school truancy and other conflicts between school and home, children's other flaws were revealed. Diseases, deviations of a physical, mental, and not least moral kind were exposed in urban environments and in the schools. Steps were taken to change the curriculum, to delouse children, to tighten control of school attendance. The right to a "good" childhood could be seen as an egalitarian right, but also as a moral obligation. It was now important to weed out the "delinquent" and "morally depraved" children (Dahl, 1978; Sandin, 1992b; Sundkvist, 1993). Childhood was normalized and standardized.

For working-class families, the new demands on the children also involved demands on the families. The mothers were expected to be able to send clean, healthy children to school or social welfare institutions at the right time. It was important to create a proper childhood (a long childhood). The ideal of motherhood that was so strongly emphasized in the national sentiment at the turn of the century corresponds to this development of a new image of childhood, the idea of a nonuseful child, dependent on a breadwinning father and a caring mother. The new emotionality in the family, the caring element, is a consequence of this kind of change. The moral demands also increased now that set criterias for a "normal" childhood of general validity had been established against which deviation could be measured. It was now essential for everyone to benefit from what was considered to be the blessings of childhood (Armstrong, 1983; Sandin, 1992b; Zelitzer, 1985).

Child welfare in its various aspects increasingly became a public concern, which was eventually to encompass all children. Welfare was not to deal exclusively with the needy children, the ragged or the obviously poor, but with all children, that was the novelty and a key aspect of the social engineering of the Swedish model (Hirdman, 1989). The boundary between public and private in the matter of childrearing was thus shifted after the turn of the century, bringing greater public responsibility for things that had previously been part of the private sphere (Halldén, 1990a, 1990b).

In the 20th century, the broader social undertakings of the school, family counseling, and parental education are expressions of this process, as are maternity centers and child-care centers. In many respects, this has also meant a questioning of the family's ability to meet society's new demands regarding children and childrearing. Regardless of how this development is described, it is obvious that the emergence of new professional groups and professional child care, has changed social relations and relations of power between parents, children, and institutions (Donzelot, 1980; Lasch, 1977). But most fundamentally, this development has in Sweden been based on the image of a childhood protected and partly guaranteed by the state.

In the 1930s, when the match boy saw the light of day, much political discussion centered on the declining birthrate and policies to counter that trend with political reforms. The nation needed more children of better quality (Kälvemark, 1980). The sun match boy seemed to represent not only the need to do something for poor children but also the image of the ideal normal child as he appeared in pediatric books on child health or for that matter in family photo albums. Under ideal conditions, he would be well taken care of. This history of child protection has created a legacy that still marks Swedish legislation and social life; bicycle helmets and kitchen stove safety grids are more or less obligatory attributes in the lives of Swedish children. Child safety has been an important part of the official agenda since the 1940s; partly influenced by the public administration of the Children's Environment Council (*Barnmiljörådet*) which is now part of the recently appointed Children's Ombudsman (*Barnombudsman*).

Child safety is partly propagated through child-care clinics (*barnavårdscentraler,* BVC). In Sweden, pregnant women attend free health checkups at the maternity health clinic (*mödravårds-centralen*, MVC) at times escorted by the father-to-be (for lessons or for breathing excercises). When the child is born, mother and child attend free health checkups at the BVC. More than 97% of all families with small children employ this service. These checkups are not obligatory but voluntary, although many parents think that they are obligatory, as they have become part of Swedish institutional life (Olin Lauritzen, 1990, 1993), Mothers are sent welcome notes with dates for their first visits. The first visits are biweekly, or monthly then more seldom. There is a time chart of special visits, for instance, at the age of 6 months, 8 months, 10 months, 18 months, and 4 years. During these checkups, nurses and doctors at the BVC check the child's weight, height, sight, hearing, greeting routines, vocabulary, figure drawings, and general medical status (Sundelin Wahlsten, 1991). If anything abnormal is discovered, the child is referred to more qualified experts for further checkups. Moreover, polio vaccinations are administered at regular intervals. In preschools and schools, the child's psychological well-being is diagnosed and discussed in so-called *kvartssamtal* (literally, 15-minute conversations), that is, scheduled staff–parent talks about the child's progress.

The sun match boy is thus carefully observed and the poor begging children are no longer seen. Children are free to roam around, but different medical professionals carefully watch their adventures at a distance, ready to intervene if they transcend the limits of what is adventurous to the "right" degree (Swedish *lagom*), not too little, not too much.

The plant metaphor, guardian angels, and other images in the description of childhood

Notions of childhood are shaped in historical contexts but also by psychological models of what a child is. Folk theories of childhood and childrearing are at times linked to metaphors (positioning the child as dependent/independent, etc.). In the following, we discuss plant metaphor. Swedish images of childhood are related to Japanese images as they involve related but still somewhat different imagery.

Academic models of child development often tend to foreground growth or formation. The child is primarily seen as a growing plant, developing according to some inherent biological plan, not as someone who is formed by teachers, parents, or other childminders. Harkness (chap. 2, this volume [see original reading]) differentiates between different root metaphors in psychological theories on child development, A pervasive root metaphor in scientific theorizing as well as in ethnotheories is that of the child as a plant. Root metaphors of a plant type surface in terms such as *growing up, budding talent, fertile environment, sweet as a rose bud, run wild* (Swedish: *vildvuxen*; literally, grown wild). Plant metaphors are, of course, related to cultural conceptions of nature (as safe vs. dangerous; as pure vs. polluted; as good vs. bad). Within the rhetoric of organicist theories like that of Piaget (Piaget & Inhelder, 1966), concepts linked to teaching or scaffolding are often more or less taboo, whereas concepts like *developing, growing,* or *unfolding* are the preferred or accepted terms.

Children may be seen to be close to nature in different ways. On the one hand, they can be seen as natural in the sense that they are yet not socialized (wild or pure). In some cultures, purity is linked to ideas about proximity to the gods or related ideas about "good" nature. For instance, in traditional Japanese culture it is said that children under the age of 7 belong to the gods (Chen, 1992). Relatedly, wildness is at times linked to ideas about children as close to dark forces or devils in that they are yet not fullbodied members of society, which accounts for "bad" or uncivilized nature. Both conceptions draw on the underlying idea that children are closer to nature than adults, that is less civilized but the evaluative inferences are completely different. Similarly, children may be seen as close to nature in that they are dynamic rather than static. Young children have yet not attained their ultimate shapes (physically or intellectually), which at times creates unpredictable action or chaos. At the very least, children's growth involves change in contrast to the more static and stable forms of adult maturity (growing plants being nature's counterpart to childhood and fossils to maturity).

Different cultures celebrate different notions of child and nature. In his paper on Japanese childhood, Chen (1992) showed how plant cultivation is an emic metaphor for child development that has been used for several hundred years in Japan, Childhood is not a state to be rushed through, but something to be savoured and cherished. Chen referred to Japanese upbringing as a type of plant cultivation in contrast to cash-crop breeding or animal training. Discipline is not meaningful per se. Rather, the childminder tries to preserve childlike qualities in the child, much as the gardener grows a beautiful chrysanthemum. In the cultivation of plants, timing is important in that the gardener must observe when it is time to erect supportive splints, and to prune deformed branches or when it is timely to put the plant in a more suitable soil. Time and timing are crucial in this process. Growth should be facilitated but not speeded up, as in cash-crop growth.

The Japanese child is thus viewed as a plant that is to be tenderly nourished and protected. The young Japanese child is kept close to adults (Chen, 1992; Hendry, 1986). It is a child that grows in close contact with others, rather than on his or her own. As shown by Chen (1992) cosleeping and cobathing are common practices, and children are carried up to the age of 3 or 4. Japanese children are seen as belonging to the gods (and to nature). Yet they represent a type of nature that must be pruned and protected. Physical proximity, as in bodily contact, provides one type of protection. Careful surveillance another.

Physical closeness is linked to human interdependence. In Western cultures, such as Sweden and the United States, independence is often highly valued in the young child's psychological make up. In contrast, there is a strong focus on interdependence in Japanese child care (Doi, 1973; LeVine & White, 1986). Through positive experiences of loving dependence, the child will develop his or her sense of empathy and responsibility. These analyses are not grounded in discourse studies on Japanese mother–child dialogues. However, there is some recent work that seems relevant to the idea of Japanese thinking on interdependence. It has, for instance, been shown how Japanese mothers gradually introduce empathy training (which stresses human interdependence). In a pioneer study, Clancy (1986) showed how Japanese mothers voice stuffed animals, guests, siblings, or other family members as a way of making the child sensitive to the wishes of others. A related finding is that, in comparison with Americans, Japanese mothers make more than three times as many appeals to the feelings of others (Azuma, Hess, Kashigawa, & Conroy, 1980). The Japanese model of empathy training obviously requires close surveillance in that the mother must be close at hand in order to take the perspective of others in relation to the child. Plant cultivation is Chen's key concept for Japanese childrearing. Japanese children could thus be construed as God's beautiful flowers to be pruned (e.g., empathy trained) and protected (physical contact) in order to better reveal their underlying beauty. Obviously, this type of plant cultivation metaphor implicitly requires a gardener, someone who will carefully observe and monitor the plants.

On an underlying level, all plant metaphors, of course, focus on children's proximity to nature. The sun match boy is close to nature in quite a literal sense in that he is portrayed facing a big sun. In Swedish folk culture, nature is often equated with summer landscape representations (in songs, poems, art, etc.), and the sun match boy is indeed an active summer child.

If Japanese children belong to the gods, children in Protestant societies may belong to the gods or to the devil, as man's nature is construed as Janus-faced (good and evil), In the British evangelist tradition of the 19th century, children's evil nature was seen as a societal problem, whereas the child-saver movement and modern public mentality, tend to construe the young child as innocent (Cunningham, 1991). Similarly, the 18th-century Protestant literature on childrearing in Sweden argued that young children need harsh physical punishment as they are born evil (Norberg, 1978). Is the sun match boy good or bad? He is obviously free and independent. He may be running away from his custodians. Yet, this type of cheekiness need not be seen as bad. In Swedish culture, there are distinguished fictional children, celebrating wild and even anarchistic behavior.

The sun match boy seems to run into the future, outstretched arms and open eyes, bravely facing the unknown. His unorganized clothing may even suggest that he is perhaps running away from his custodians (away from the structured and organized life of the welfare state). What is the character of his freedom and independence? Could he perhaps be a bad boy?

Pippi Longstocking, the wild baby, and other wild boys

Tomboys or wild boys are cherished characters in children's literature, which is a major Swedish export product. Astrid Lindgren's celebrated Pippi Longstocking is an anarchist figure of carnivalesque dimensions, as has been shown by Vivi Edström (1992). Pippi Longstocking has been translated into most major languages, and she is probably the most well-known figure in Swedish children's fiction both outside Sweden and within the country.

Pippi Longstocking is the exception who proves the rule in that most "wild" and unruly heroes in Swedish literature tend to be boy heroes. For instance, Astrid Lindgren has also created a popular mischievous boy hero, Emil. Pippi is a rebel girl with magic powers, such as being able to carry her horse. Emil in Lönneberga is of a different kind. Some of his adventures are quite picaresque. Yet, they do not transcend the limits of what is possible (at least in a chaos-prone setting). Emil thus represents a familiar unruly type, including other wild and untamed boys, like Richard Crompton's wild Bill or Mark Twain's Huckleberry Finn.

Most of the traditional wild boys are schoolboy heroes. In Swedish children's fiction, there is also a well-known and much loved small wild boy, the "wild baby" who first appeared in 1980 and who has gained a wide readership.[2] The wild baby, created by Barbro Lindgren (author) and Eva Eriksson (illustrator) represents something new in that he is quite a young boy, a toddler rather than a schoolboy. He runs away from home, takes a swim in the kitchen sink, etc. His adventures are related to those of other little rascals of children's fiction, such as Max and Moritz or Stumpelpetter, but he is not portrayed as "naughty." As his name, the "wild baby" suggests, he is merely wild, a natural uninhibited child, not yet restrained by school or other regimenting influences. His mother does not stop him. Like Pippi Longstocking, he creates his own egalitarian world.

The sun match boy is about the same age as the wild baby. If we inspect the energetic gait of the sun match boy, it could be that of a child about to do something mischievous, not because he is naughty but because he is an active, natural (free) child, out on his own, free to follow his impulses. An early cousin of the wild baby?

In several ways, the sun match boy reflects Swedish images of an ideal chilhood as a period of freedom and active independence (see Table 9.1 [see original reading]). But there is an inherent contradiction in that the sun match boy is freed from poverty, diseases, and the like, and is also independent of his family ties but consequently, he is then also dependent on support from the welfare agencies and various professional groups. The irony of such a historical process in that certain types of freedom create new ties and dependencies of a different kind.

Wild boys and guardian angels

In folk etymology, sweet rascals are at times referred to as "little devils." This is yet another reminder of children's proximity to nature in folk images of the child as well as in scientific models, such as in the psychoanalytic discussion of aggressive impulses.

In the popular romantic iconography of Protestant and Catholic Europe in the 19th century, children were often protected by guardian angels (Johannesson, 1987). In the prototypical guardian angel painting, a child is seen exploring dangerous grounds, such as the verge of a cliff, a suspension bridge or something equally dangerous, protected by a guardian angel. However, Johannesson demonstrated how the guardian angel iconography of Catholic countries or regions tends to deviate from that of Protestant regions. In the Catholic iconography, the child is, for instance, led by the hand of his or her guardian angel or the angel touches the child's shoulder. In contrast, the Protestant guardian angel does not touch its protégée. This prototypical northern angel carefully watches the child at a distance, ready to intervene if necessary. Guardian angels may assist the child (particularly in Catholic-type thinking) but ultimately, the child is on his or her own.

A Japanese guardian angel, were it to exist, would most likely carry its protégée, not watch at a distance in the manner of the prototypical Protestant guardian angel. The sun match boy has no guardian angel or other adult in sight. He is independent, moving on his own. Yet, being a Swedish preschooler, he is well protected by a system of remote control. As shown in our discussion on the preschool panopticon, child health (psychological and medical) is well controlled. The absence of visible protectors could also be seen as a deliberate choice. The prototypical modern Swedish guardian angel would not hold the child or touch him or her. Children's independence, and independent exploration is highly valued in Swedish preschool philosophy, as demonstrated for instance in the the report of the State Commissions on Child Care (SOU, 1972).

Childminders as gardeners or botanists

To some extent, Japanese society, as described by Chen (1992) seems to hold similar images to those of Swedish society in that the child's impulsivity and naturalness is cherished. Yet, nature is construed somewhat differently in the two countries. We argue that, in Chen's description of Japanese childhood, the child's "nature" is foremost a cultivated type of nature, nature in relation to good gardening. For instance, emic descriptions of childrearing refer to the proper cultivation of chrysanthemums. In contrast, the child's nature in Swedish models is perhaps rather that of wild nature. Wildflowers were, for instance, highly cherished by Carl von Linné, the 18th-century botanist, as well as in Swedish traditional culture, as reflected in songs, poems, folk dances. Quite symbolically, Linné lent his name to a wildflower, the linnaea (twinflower).

One important difference between Swedish and Japanese upbringing has to do with society's view on children's independence. Swedish images of childhood, as expressed in, for instance, the free-roaming match boy, seem to celebrate an independent child. Similarly, official discourse on adult–child interaction generally discusses how adults are to understand children better, not how children are to understand others. The so-called dialogue pedagogy (Swedish: *dialogpedagogik*) discusses how child-care staff are to understand children and their ideas (SOU, 1972; for a critical discussion see Aronsson & Evaldsson, 1993; Kallos, 1978). Adults are seen more as listeners, not as talkers. Adults are to listen to the child and not the reverse. In their analyses of Western Samoa, New Guinea, and U.S. White mainstream ideologies of mother–child talk, Ochs and Schieffelin (1984) showed how U.S. mainstream culture puts less emphasis on the child's empathy training and more emphasis on adults' perspective taking or capacity to listen to the child. The dialogue pedagogy of the Swedish 1970s and 1980s is thus quite typical for U.S. White mainstream and other modern Western pedagogies, that are child-centered, and independency oriented.

The Japanese plant metaphor of childhood links child development to proper pruning. A child is to be held, and protected in close and loving proximity to adults, and he or she is to listen to others at an early age. Empathy and interdependence is thus more focused than independence. In the Swedish panopticon of barnombudsman, children's right legislation, and child-care control, the child is, however, never left to drift away from the normal or desirable growth. Our discussion suggests that the sun match boy is emblematic for a healthy, free, and independent modern welfare child. Somewhat paradoxically, the match boy representation is at the same time intimately linked to an important philanthropic fundraising project launched during the first half of the 20th century, In the thinking of the Swedish child savers, as well as in modern child-care philosophy, proper growth requires protective surveillance, such as the child-care clinical checkups, covering physical as well as psychological growth (checking if children are independent, active, and so forth), In contrast to the Japanese gardener, Swedish caretakers are rather botanists, who carefully watch their children but who do not prune or interact with their precious specimens. The sun match boy is close to nature, precious to behold, but he is not a chrysanthemum, tenderly pruned by a gardener. If anything, he is a wild and healthy flower. Through the years, the benevolent gaze of child experts follow the sun match boy, and other wild children on their active and "independent" exploits.

Acknowledgment

We would like to thank Gunilla Halldén for helpful comments on an earlier version of this chapter.

Notes

1   Figures and facts about the sun match campaign are drawn from: *Solstickan trettio år* (1966); *Solstickan fyrtio år* (1976); *Solstickan femtio år* (1986), and from Helgeland (1990).
2   Lindgren's and Eriksson's *Mamman och den vilda bebin* (The Mummy and the Wild Baby) was first published in 1980. In 1991 it was printed in its 128,000th edition. *Den vilda bebiresan* (The Wild Baby Trip) was first published in 1982. In 1990 it was printed in its 93,000th edition. *Den vilda bebin får en hund* (The Wild Baby Gets a Dog) was first published in 1985. All books are printed in Stockholm by Rabén and Sjögren, a major publisher of books for children.

References

Armstrong, D. (1983). *Political anatomy of the body. Medical knowledge in Britain in the twentieth century*. Cambridge: Cambridge University Press.

Aronsson, K., & Evaldsson, A-C. (1993). Pedagogic discourse and interaction orders. Sharing time and control. In N. Coupland & J. F. Nussbaum (Eds.), *Discourse and lifespan identity* (pp. 103–31). Newbury Park, CA: Sage.

Azuma, H., Hess, R. D., Kashigawa, K., & Conroy, M. (1980). *Maternal control strategies and the child's cognitive development: A crosscultural paradox and its interpretation*, Paper presented at the International Congress of Psychology, Leipzig.

Chen, S-J. (1992, September). *Positive childishness. Images of child development in Japan*. Paper presented at the conference on images of childhood, Sätra Bruk, Sweden.

The child: "I accuse." (1907). *Children's Day*, pp. 2–6.

Clancy, P. (1986). The acquisition of communicative style in Japanese. In B. B. Schieffelin & E. Ochs (Eds.), *Language socialization across cultures* (pp. 213–50). Cambridge: Cambridge University Press.

Cunningham, H. (1991). *The children of the poor. Representation of childhood since the seventeenth century*. Oxford: Basil Blackwell.

Dahl, T. S. (1978). *Barnevern og samfundsvern* [Child protection and social protection] (Doctoral dissertation). Oslo: Pax.

Doi, T. (1973). *The anatomy of dependence*. New York: Harper & Row.

Donzelot, J. (1980). *The policing of families*. London: Hutchinson.

Edström, V. (1992). Astrid Lindgren. *Vildtoring och lägereld* [Astrid Lindgren: The wild thing and the campfire]. Stockholm: Rabén & Sjögren.

Halldén, G. (1990a). Barnen som tillhöriga privat eller offentlig sfär. Historiska perspektiv på föreställningar om barn [Children as private or public belongings: Historical perspectives on images of children]. In T. Englund (Ed.), *Politik och socialisation. Nyare strömningar i pedagogisk historisk forskning* (pp. 93–110). Uppsala: Pedagogiska Institutionen, Uppsala Universitet.

Halldén, G. (1990b). Alva Myrdals första föräldracirkel 1931—en pedagog beskriven via sina anteckningar [Alva Myrdal's first parent's circle, 1931: A pedagogy as described in her notes]. I G. Halldén (Ed.), *Se barnet. Tankegångar från tre århundraden* (pp. 145–77). Stockholm: Rabén & Sjögren.

Hatje, A-K. (1974). *Befolkningsfrågan och välfärden* [The question of population and welfare]. Stockholm: Allmänna Förlaget.

Helgeland, H. (1990). Solstickan tändes för barnhemsbarnen. *Barn i Hem-Skola-Samhäile,* 5, 52–60.

Hendry, J. (1986). *Becoming Japanese.* Manchester: Manchester University Press.

Hirdman, Y. (1989). *Att läga livet tillrätta. Studier i svensk folkhemspolitik* [Putting life back in order: Studies in local Swedish politics]. Stockholm: Carlsson.

Holland, J. (1992). *What is a child? Popular images of childhood.* London: Virago Press.

Johannesson, L. (1987). " . . . I skapelsen en länk, från englarne till djuren . . . ". En 1800-tals ikonografi [" . . . in the creation, a link between the angels and the animals . . . " An 18th century iconography]. In H. Brander Jonsson, H. Broberg, & L. Johannesson (Eds.), *Historiens vingslag* (pp. 232–60), Stockholm: Atlantis.

Kallos, D. (1978). *Den nya pedagogiken. En analys av den s k dialogpedagogiken som svenskt samhälls-fenomen* [The new pedagogy, An analysis of the so-called pedagogy of dialogue as a Swedish social phenomenon]. Stockholm: Wahlström & Widstrand.

Key, E. (1900). *Barnets århundrade* [The century of the child]. Stockholm: Bonniers.

Kälvemark, A-S. (1980). *More children of better quality? Aspects on Swedish population policy in the 1930's.* Uppsala: Studiea Historica Upsaliensia 115. Almqvist & Wiksell International.

Larsson, J. (1977). *"En ny nationell effektivitet". Historieforskning på nya vägar* [A new national efficacy: Historical research on new ways]. Lund: Studentlitteratur.

Lasch, C. (1977). *Haven in a heartless world. The family besieged.* New York: Basic Books.

LeVine, R. A., & White, M. (1986). *Human conditions. The cultural basis of educational developments.* New York: Routledge & Kegan Paul.

Lindgren, B. (1980). *Mamman och den vilda bebin* [The mummy and the wild baby], Stockholm: Raben & Sjögren.

Lindgren, B. (1982). *Den vilda bebiresan* [The wild baby trip]. Stockholm: Raben & Sjögren.

Lindgren, B. (1985). *Den vilda bebin får en hund* [The wild baby gets a dog]. Stockholm: Raben & Sjögren.

Løkke, A. (1990). *Vildfarende børn—om forsomte og kriminelle børn mellem filantropi og stat 1880–1920* [Lost children: About ignored and criminal children between philanthropy and the state, 1880–1920]. Holte: Forlaget Soc. Pol.

Norberg, A. (1978). *Uppfostran till underkastelse. En analys av normer för föröldra-barnrelationer i religiös litteratur om barnuppfostran i Sverige 1750–1809* [Raised for undermining: An analysis of norms in child–parent relationships in religious literature on Swedish childrearing]. Lund: Gleerups.

Ochs, E., & Schieffelin, B. (1984). Language acquisition and socialization practices. Three developmental stories. In R. Schweder & R. LeVine (Eds.), *Culture theory and essays on mind, self and emotion* (pp. 276–320). Cambridge: Cambridge University Press.

Ohrlander, K. (1992). *I barnens och nationens intresse. Social liberal reform politik 1903–1930* [In the interests of the children and the nation: Liberal social reforms 1903–30], Unpublished doctoral dissertation, Studies in Education and Psychology, Stockholm University, Stockholm.

Olin Lauritzen, S. (1990). Hälsovård som rutin eller relation [Preventive health care. Routine or relation]. Unpublished doctoral thesis, Department of Education, Stockholm University, Stockholm.

Olin Lauritzen, S. (1993). Coping with health hazards: Parents' and professionals' perspectives on child health surveillance. In B, Mayall (Ed.), *Family life and social control. Discourses on normality.* London: Social Science Research Unity, Institute of Education, University of London (Conference Proceedings).

Olsson, S. E. (1990). *Social policy and welfare state in Sweden.* Lund: Arkiv.

Piaget, J., & Inhelder, B. (1966). *La psychologie de l'enfant* [The psychology of the child], Paris: Que Sais-je.

Platt, A. (1969). *The child savers. The invention of delinquency*. Chicago: University of Chicago.

Sandin, B. (1992a). *The century of the child. On the changed meaning of childhood in the twentieth century* (A research program).

Sandin, B. (1992b). *Education, social change, and "the discovery of normality" in urban Sweden 1850–1910*, Paper presented at the SSHA Conference, Chicago.

Seip, A-L. (1984). *Sosialhjelpstaten blir til. Norsk Sosialpolitikk 1740–1920* [The welfare state turns into Norwegian social policy, 1740–1920]. Oslo: Gyldendahl.

SOU. (1972). Statens Offentliga Utredningar [State Research Bureau]. Preschool, parts 1 and 2. Consideration before 1988 of research on child care centers. Liber: Allmänna Förlaget. SOU:26, SOU:27.

Sundelin Wahlsten, V. (1991). *Uweckling och överlevnad. En studie av barn i psykosociala riskmiljöer* [Development and survival: A study of children in risky psychosocial environments]. Unpublished doctoral dissertation, Stockholm University, Stockholm.

Sundkvist, M. (1993). *Parental strategies, state rights and a new childhood, Interventions in family life in a Swedish town 1903–1925*. Paper presented at SSHA, Chicago.

Weiner, G. (1992). De 'olydiga' mödrarna. Konflikter om spädbarnsvård på en mjölkdroppe [The mothers who don't listen: Conflicts about infant care on a drop of milk]. *Historisk Tidskrift*, 4, 488–501.

Zelitzer, V. (1985). *Pricing the priceless child. The changing social value of children*. New York: Basic Books.

Chapter 6

Pei-yi Wu

CHILDHOOD REMEMBERED: PARENTS AND CHILDREN IN CHINA, 800 TO 1700

A MAJOR PROBLEM CONFRONTING HISTORIANS of premodern Chinese childhood is that of source material. In spite of the massive written records of the past, there was nothing in China that could even remotely compare to the diary of the court doctor Jean Héroard, who kept a day-to-day account of the infancy of the future King Louis XIII (1601–43), beginning with the accouchement. Everything that a modern social historian likes to know can be found in it, often in minute detail: food, clothes, corporal punishment, toilet training, infantile sexuality, weaning, parental interactions, education. No wonder, then, that the history of childhood, for the last thirty years or so one of the most lively fields in Western history, began in France and still lags in China. Nonetheless, in the vast store of traditional Chinese writings there are several categories of materials that can be made to yield useful information on various aspects of Chinese childhood. Accordingly, this essay explores several genres, primarily mourning literature, for descriptions of childhood and facts on related topics.

Biography

One may begin with biography, the most voluminous of all genres of Chinese prose writings, for the obvious reason that since childhood is an inevitable stage of life, any writing about a life is likely to touch on this matter. Biography, however, turns out to be of little use to us. What we would recognize as biography today went under a variety of names in traditional China. The subgenre that enjoyed the widest vogue and most resembled the modern form is the *zhuan*. In its verbal form the word means "to transmit," and it was used in its nominal form to denote a commentary or an exegesis of a canonical text. Hence even in its earliest days the didactic function of the *zhuan* had already been foreshadowed: it should contain what was worthy of transmission to posterity, and its contents should illustrate or demonstrate general principles. This fact contributed to the highly selective principle governing the type and quantity of incidents that could be included in a biography.[1] It is not surprising, then, that childhood is often completely neglected in traditional biographies, even in subgenres other than the *zhuan*. When childhood is touched at all, it is usually represented by a few standard topoi such as early signs of precocity or commendable acts of filial piety.[2]

Biographers writing about a subject's childhood tend to rely upon standard formulas even when, or especially because, the author knew the subject well. The brothers Cheng Hao (1032–85) and Cheng Yi (1033–1107) were so close to each other philosophically that they were often mentioned in the same breath by their Neo-Confucian disciples and admirers. The only survivors among six boys, the two, born just a year apart, grew up together and remained almost inseparable as adults. After Cheng Hao died his younger brother wrote a biography for him that, running to some five thousand characters, is unusually long. The following is the childhood section in its entirety:

> The master, born with superb endowment, was different from ordinary children. One day he was carried by his great-aunt Lady Ren in her arms. As she was walking, her hairpin dropped without her knowledge. She did not look for it until several days later. The master was too young to talk, but he started to point with his finger. Lady Ren followed his directions and in the end found the hairpin. Everyone was amazed by the incident. When the master was not quite ten years old he could recite the *Book of Poetry* and the *Book of Documents*. His power of memory was unsurpassed. When he was ten years old he could compose poetry and rhymed prose. In his early teens he stayed in the school dormitory where he comported himself like a mature adult. None could see him without respect and admiration.[3]

Autobiography

Autobiography, often taking its cue from biography, is not much more helpful than biography in providing information on Chinese childhood. Occasionally we are given a brief outline of the autobiographer's schooling. The Tang historiographer Liu Zhiji (661–721) seems to have had a less auspicious beginning than the Song master Cheng Hao:

> As a child I received instructions from my father and had an early exposure to the classics. When I was a little older I was taught the *Book of Documents* in the ancient script version. As I was troubled by the text, which I found difficult and vexatious, I was unable to chant or memorize. I could not master it even though I was frequently beaten. In the meantime my father was explaining to my older brothers the *Zuo zhuan* version of the *Spring and Autumn Annals*. When I heard him I dropped the book I was supposed to study and listened. Every time he finished his session I would take over and expound the lesson for my older brothers. I sighed and said to myself: "If all the books were like this, I would not be as slow as I have been." Impressed, my father began to teach me the *Zuo zhuan*, and in a year's time I finished reading and memorization. I was then just twelve years of age. Although my comprehension of my father's explanations was by no means profound, I understood the general idea of the book. My father and older brothers wanted me to read all the commentaries on the book so as to achieve a thorough mastery of this classic. I declined on the ground that this book did not cover the events that have occurred since the death of Confucius. Instead I begged that I might be allowed to read other books of history, thus broadening my knowledge of the field.[4]

Strange as it may seem, it is a rare father who is accorded an important place in the son's auto-biography. Tao Qian (365–427), Deng Huoqu (1498–1570), and Chen Jiru (1558–1639) never mentioned their fathers; Mao Qiling (1623–1716), Hu Zhi (1517–85), Deqing (1546–1623), and Wang Jie (1603–82?) did so only in passing once or twice. In this respect, the contrast between autobiography and biography is conspicuous. Biography seldom begins without a genealogy, and the biographer almost always finds something worthy of notice in the father of the subject. On this point even autobiographies that are otherwise virtually self-written biographies often differ from their models. Some of the fathers of autobiographers were quite prominent, pillars of the state or masters of learning, and presumably exemplars for all, but they rarely earned an acknowledgment from the sons, as if emulation, the fundamental tenet of Confucian education, could be practiced only from afar. The most glaring case is that of Han Chang (799–855), the son of Han Yu (768–824). In his autonecrology, Han Chang describes his literary apprenticeship under two mentors, but his father, the great defender of Confucianism, an innovative poet and the most celebrated essayist of the Tang, merits no more than a mention—and that only in the list of ancestors.[5] Although it is true that Han Yu, exiled by the emperor to the south, was an absent father during three years (803–6) of the autobiographer's early childhood, still the son must have benefited from the father's company from 807 on.[6]

The mother, however, is often remembered with affection and sometimes credited with the early education of the son. Mao Qiling begins his long autobiography with a dream that his mother had on the eve of his birth. She dreamt that a foreign monk came into the chamber and hung on the wall a monk's certificate, on the borders of which was a drawing of five dragons linked in a circle. After his birth she chose his name on the basis of a poetic allusion to the five mythic beasts. It was again the mother who acted as the first teacher:

> When I was five years of age I expressed a wish to begin reading books. As no tutor was available, my mother recited the *Great Learning* and I repeated after her. After I succeeded in committing the text to memory, I asked her what the corresponding characters were. My mother bought a popular edition of the book and told me to read the text by myself, using my memorized version as the guide. After two readings there was no character that I could not recognize.[7]

The father, a prominent man of letters in his own right, is mentioned only very briefly near the end of the long autobiography. It is extraordinary that neither he nor the grandfather had anything to do with the naming of the boy. His place in the life of the son, like that of so many fathers in biographies and autobiographies, is further diminished by the topos of the prophetic dream. On the eve of his birth, the child's future is typically prefigured: there may be a variety of signs and portents, for example, or he is shown to be a gift from a divinity or the reincarnation of another man. Under such circumstances, the father cannot have much to say about either the essential nature of the boy or how the course of the son's life will turn out.

This topos and the teleological principle of Chinese biography—that the adult traits are discernible in the child—tend to reinforce each other. Mao's life story is a case in point. As his narrative states, the significance of the certificate became clear to the mother twenty-two years later, when she learned that a monkish disguise saved her son from certain death. Later, during another crisis in Mao's life, a monk, who came from a border region, appeared in an outlandish habit. He saved Mao from his worst troubles, and the magic was wrought through the instruction of how to read the *Great Learning* in a new way. Although Mao does not specify what the dragon in his mother's dream prefigures, this symbol of elusiveness and swift trans-formations was quite appropriate for a decade of constant motion and frequent changes of disguise. The mythic creature also possesses other attributes that Mao shares: vigor, expansiveness, creative powers. No wonder that his early display of ease in memorizing texts and mastering the written language was repeated many times in adulthood.

The monk Deqing, also known as Hanshan, gives us the most detailed representation of premodern childhood in an autobiography—or for that matter in any kind of Chinese writing. As I have discussed him fully elsewhere, I shall not repeat his story, which combines all the themes—the mother's prophetic dream just before the birth of the child, her prominent role in the formation of the future adult, and the enigmatic absence of the father—mentioned in this section.[8]

Writings about the wet nurse

Here we are exploring not a genre but a group of miscellaneous writings on a very important aspect of childhood. As there are references to the wet nurse in the *Shiji*, the first dynastic history, and in the canonical classics such as the *Liji* and the *Yili*, the practice of wet-nursing must have begun before the Han, probably even before the dawn of history. Although in recent years there has been much literature on her in the history of European childhood, nowhere else has she played so important a role as in China. From the Han dynasty to the Ming, there were numerous cases of emperors lavishing noble titles and other favors on their wet nurses and members of their families. Sometimes the bond between the charge and his nurse was so strong that she never left the palace. One does not have to be a Freudian to appreciate the closeness, both physical and psychological, children feel toward the women who suckle them. When such children grew up and ascended the imperial throne, their wet nurses often enjoyed a share of the absolute power. Some nurses are believed to have abused their positions of power by interceding with the emperor on the behalf of relatives and acquaintances and by interfering (usually through their allies) in the affairs of the state. The most notorious among them was Dame Ke (?–1628), whose faction dominated the court for three years. In a bitter struggle with Confucian ministers who led the opposition, hundreds were killed and more were exiled. The country never recovered from the resulting decimation of experienced and competent officials, and historians tend to hold the Ke faction at least partly responsible for the decline and fall of the Ming.

It is generally believed that among major dynasties the Ming had the worst emperors, and the childhood of the Ming sovereigns can be shown as an element in the formation of the deplorable traits they subsequently displayed as adults. The key may lie in their early separation from their mothers, their isolation from their siblings and from children of their age, their ritualistic and formal relationship with their tutors, the hostility or at best the indifference of their fathers, the claustrophobic palace environment rife with intrigues and suspicions, and, finally, the resultant dependence on their wet nurses and eunuchs. However important this topic may be, a detailed study of the childhood of Ming emperors must await a future occasion. Here we shall concern ourselves only with the Ming system of choosing imperial wet nurses. Little is known about the system in other dynasties, but we can obtain much information about its operation during the Ming from the memoir of a sixteenth-century magistrate of Wanping county, which had jurisdiction over much of Peking and its western suburbs.[9]

To qualify as a candidate for the position of wet nurse in the imperial household, a woman had to satisfy several stringent requirements. She had to be a presentable married woman, between fifteen and twenty years of age, with husband and children all alive. At the time of selection she was supposed to have given birth to a child about three months earlier. A physical examination of her was to be administered by an official midwife to ascertain the absence of hidden diseases and the adequacy of her lactation. Forty candidates were selected for each season, half of them having recently delivered boys and the other half girls. They along with their infants were then housed in the Bureau of Imperial Nurses, located just outside Dongan Gate. Another eighty qualified women were designated alternates. When a birth in the imperial household was imminent, a number of candidates would be called into the Forbidden City. The imperial infant would be suckled by several nurses for a month or so, and then one of them would be chosen. Thereupon the rest would be dismissed. Once a nurse was kept beyond the tryout period, she would stay in the palace to wait on her charge for the rest of her life. If the imperial infant was a boy, only nurses who had recently delivered girls were kept for the tryout period; for an infant princess, the reverse obtained.[10]

In more humble households the wet nurse was just as ubiquitous. Pediatric treatises often suggest standards by which wet nurses are to be chosen. She is also mentioned in other types of writings. Sometimes she played a role equivalent to that of the loyal masculine retainer, whose heroism and selflessness have long been sung in Chinese literature. The biography of Hou Yi in the *Songshi* discloses that when his son's whole family was massacred by rebels, only his infant grandson survived. The child owed his life to his wet nurse, who had replaced him with her own son—literally a case of killing one child to save another. Carrying the infant in her arms, the woman begged her way to the capital and returned her charge to his grandfather.[11]

The nurse's bond with her charge and her employers was so strong that often she would stay in the household to the end of her life. Two prominent men of letters wrote tombstone inscriptions for their wet nurses in which they expressed their gratitude. Han Yu, orphaned during his infancy, wrote:

> Nurse Xu . . . grew old among the Hans. She lived to see Yu, the child she once suckled, obtain the highest degree and rise through the ranks, marry, and have two sons and five daughters of his own. On every feast day Yu would lead his wife and children to offer felicitations to her, honoring her just as they would his mother.[12]

The wet nurse of Su Shi (1037–1101) filled several roles. For thirty-five years she waited on Su's mother as servant and seamstress. Earlier she had suckled Su's elder sister, and later she took care of Su Shi's three sons. The loyal retainer stayed in Su's employment as he moved from official post to post until she died at seventy-two in Huangzhou.[13]

However devoted the wet nurse and her charge may have been to each other, her own children could not but suffer the cruel consequences of her employment. This fact cannot long escape any keen observer, wherever he may be. Montaigne had the following to say:

> For a slight profit, we tear . . . their own infants from their mothers' arms, and make these mothers take charge of ours. We cause them to abandon their children to some wretched nurse, to whom we do not wish to commit our own, or to some goat, forbidding them not only to be breastfed . . . but also to care for them in any way, so that they will be able to devote themselves completely to ours.[14]

In China there was no shortage of criticism of the practice on the same grounds. Hong Mai (1123–1202) and several authors of the popular genre termed "family instructions" advocated the abolition of wet-nursing.[15] Others suggested various reforms. Among the Neo-Confucian master Cheng Yi's many sayings recorded by his disciples, there is the following:

In most cases employing a wet nurse is unavoidable. If the mother is unable to feed her child, someone must be employed. However, it is wrong to kill another mother's child as a result of feeding one's own child. If a wet nurse is absolutely necessary, employ two so that the milk for two babies can be used to feed three. If one of the wet nurses becomes sick or even dies, there will be no harm to one's own child and one will not be killing another person's child as a result of feeding one's own. The only thing is that it is expensive to employ two.[16]

Chen Longzheng (1585–1645) had a different solution:

The rich like to spare themselves the trouble of suckling their young. The poor will substitute for them, in exchange for food, clothing, and cash which they will use to support their family. Such an arrangement is beneficial to both. However, in nursing other people's children the poor have to part with their own, entrusting them to childless families. Such families, usually poor, will soon find the undertaking a great inconvenience. Although they have agreed to it at the beginning, gradually they will come to resent the children. Resented, very few infants will survive. During my lifetime my family have hired more than ten wet nurses. When I was young I never thought about it. As I grew older I became very sorry for their hapless children. Our practice is no different from killing other people's children on behalf of our own children. Every time I thought about it, I broke out in sweat. Yet for a long time I could not find a way to save those children. The following is a tentative solution. Before anyone hires a wet nurse the employer should first find a family among her relatives where there is surplus milk and where her child is welcome. Beyond the contractual three-year wage paid to the woman there should be a subsidy of two and a half taels of silver to be paid to the foster family. The first payment will be in the amount of half a tael. After three months the child will be brought to the employer's house to be inspected by the mother. If she is satisfied with the condition, one tael will be paid to the foster parents. The procedure will be repeated at the end of the first year.

Infancy is the most hazardous time for a child. The mother probably does not hire herself out until her child is several months old. After three months with the foster family the child will be more than six months old. After another year the child will be twenty months old. At the very beginning the foster parents may not feel much affection for the child. But tempted by the silver, they would put up with the trouble. From the age of one on, the child can laugh, stand, and walk. The foster family will cherish such a child even if they are not of the same flesh and blood. There is even more reason for them to take good care of their charge when the final tael is in sight.[17]

One might note that what Chen recommended as a solution for the care of the wet nurse's child was essentially the same practice that wealthy European families had for their own children. Another difference between the two systems is the longer period of nursing on the part of the Chinese.[18] Chen mentions a thirty-six-month contract with a wet nurse, while a sixteenth-century Chinese handbook on child care suggests that a child should be weaned at four or five *sui*.[19] In contrast, a 367 B.C. Greek document shows a twenty-four-month contract with a wet nurse. Lloyd deMause has prepared a table of "age in months at full weaning." Of the twenty-five cases he has collected, beginning with the Greek contract and ending with a German statistical study made in 1878–82, only three indicate full weaning taking place beyond twenty-four months. In five cases the children were weaned at nine months or younger.[20]

Parents writing about children

In recent years scholars have repeatedly asserted that childhood is a modern discovery. In Europe, "except for brief glimpses . . . children rarely appear in classical literature." Furthermore, they "seldom appear in medieval imaginative literature; when they do appear they tend to be precocious."[21] I shall not discuss the situation in early China as it is fully covered elsewhere in this volume. From the Tang to at least the fifteenth century, children were more written about in China than in Europe. We can find useful information about children in two types of writings. More and more poets from the Tang onward poured out their sorrows of parting from their children and mourning their deaths. The other type, closely linked to ritual, I shall call necrology for the lack of an established term. It includes the requiem (*jiwen*), grave notice (*kuangzhi*), tombstone inscription (*muzhih ming*), and other lesser-known genres. A necrology usually consists of two parts—a prose preface followed by a eulogy in verse—but sometimes one part by itself suffices. Its length varies from several lines to several thousand characters. Given the Chinese emphasis on death rites and the manner in which the past was remembered, necrology had a special place and constituted a sizable portion of traditional Chinese literature.[22]

There was an initial reluctance, both in classical Europe and ancient China, to accord children more than a minimum recognition in death rituals. But in China, as time went on, parents became increasingly ready to extend the same honor and care to dead children as to dead adults. There was not only a growing presence of children in necrology but also an increasingly sentimental representation of them. The trend was too consistent and too durable to be dismissed as simply a reflection of a shifting literary vogue. We shall proceed to explore these two types of Chinese writings in the hope of gaining a few insights into a most important topic: the parental attitude. As Lawrence Stone puts it, "the history of childhood is in fact the history of how parents treated children."[23]

The growing tendency to write about children with deep affection probably began with the ninth century. The case of Han Yu (768–824), mentioned earlier, was typical. Early in 819, Han Yu, then vice-minister of justice, remonstrated with the emperor against the plan of welcoming into the palace a relic bone of the Buddha. Offended by Han's bold language, the emperor demoted him to a minor post in the south. After his departure, his family was expelled from the capital as well. His fourth daughter Na, aged twelve, died en route and was hastily buried. The following year the emperor relented and appointed Han chancellor of the national university. On his way back to the capital, Han made a stop at his daughter's grave and wrote a moving poem of mourning. When he became mayor of the capital in 823, he had his daughter's remains removed to Heyang for reburial in the ancestral cemetery. For the removal he wrote a requiem (*jiwen*) and for the reburial he wrote a grave notice (*kuangzhi*). Han was not the first poet mourning the death of children, nor was his daughter the first child accorded a burial with two literary accessories. Before the Tang, however, it was a rare child whose death would occasion *both* kinds of commemoration. Another distinction is that in all three works Han displayed a more intense grief than had ever been expressed in previous literature. The requiem is especially moving:

> On such a day, such a month, and such a year, your dad and mom send your wet nurse to your grave with pure wine, seasonal fruit, and a variety of delicious food to be offered to the spirit of Nazi, their fourth daughter.

Alas, you were gravely ill just when I was about to be exiled to the south. The parting came so suddenly that you were both startled and grieved. When I caught my last glimpse of you, I knew death would make our separation permanent. When you looked at me, you were too sad to cry. After I left for the south, the family was also driven out. You were helped into a sedan chair and traveled from early morning to night. Snow and ice injured your weakened flesh. Shaken and rocked, you did not have any rest. There was no time to eat and drink, so you suffered from frequent thirst and hunger. To die in the wild mountains was not the fate you deserved. It is usually the parents' guilt that brings calamities to their children. Was I not the cause of your coming to such a pass?

You were buried hastily by the roadside in a coffin which could hardly be called a coffin. After you were interred the group had to leave. There was no one to care for your grave or watch over it. Your soul was solitary and your bones were cold. Although everyone must die, you died unjustly. When I traveled back from the south I made a stop at your grave. As I wept over you I could see your eyes and face. How could I ever forget your words and expressions?

Now on an auspicious day I am having you moved to our ancestral cemetery. Do not be frightened or fearful: you will be safe along the way. There will be fragrant drink and sweet food for you, and you will arrive in your permanent resting place in a nice new coffin. Peace will be with you for ten thousand years![24]

Although the requiem (*jiwen*) is a literary genre represented even in the earliest Chinese anthologies, its origins go back to ancient death rites. It began as a performative text accompanying sacrifices and libations to the dead. Han Yu's piece was obviously written before the burial party set out, and it was the usual practice to leave the exact date of the service blank. Also remarkable about this requiem is that even four years after the death of the daughter her wet nurse's association with the family had not been severed. Apparently she acted as the parents' surrogate at the exhumation service. The grave notice (*kuangzhi*), however, indicates that at the reburial ceremony the wet nurse shared her functions with Han Yu's son or sons—the eldest was born in 799—and other family members of the younger generation.

Han Yu's innovations must be seen in the light of the hierarchical order of traditional Confucian society, which stipulated gradations in the elaborateness of the funeral and mourning ritual for each individual, depending on the age, station, gender, and generational ranking of the dead relative to the mourner or mourners. In the section on death rites the Confucian canonical classic, the *Yili*, compiled probably during the first century, divides *shang*, the mourning for those dying before adulthood, into three descending categories: *zhangshang*, for those aged sixteen to nineteen; *zhongshang*, for those aged twelve to fifteen; and *xiashang*, for children eight to eleven years old. Children who die before reaching the age of eight can be mourned by the parents, but not with outward ceremony. The length of the mourning period depends on the age of the child. For each month the child lived there will be a day of mourning: "An infant is given a name by the father when it is three months old. A father may weep at the death of a child with a name. He will not weep if the child is not yet named."[25] Coincidentally, Plutarch, who was more or less a contemporary of the compilers of the Confucian canonical classic just quoted, shared some of the same ideas. In his letter to his wife on the death of their young daughter Timoxena he states:

It is not our way to pour out libations for children who die in infancy nor to perform the other ceremonies which the living do for the dead. This is because these infants are in no way involved with earth or earthly things; and so people do not stand around long at their funerals or keep watch at the tombs or at the laying out or at the side of the bodies.[26]

However much Plutarch may have cherished his young daughter, he did not challenge Roman conventions. On the other hand, the Confucian rules may not have been observed consistently. As Wu Hung's essay in this volume (Chapter 3 [see original reading]) indicates, as early as A.D. 170 there was a fairly elaborate burial for a five-year-old boy. Nevertheless the tension between a parent's love and the force of convention seems to have persisted. Some parents would acknowledge the canonical stipulations; others would simply ignore them. An early example of this tension is seen in the case of the infant daughter of Cao Rui (205–39), Emperor Ming of the Wei. When the princess died before she completed her first year, the grieving father lavished all commemorative honors on the infant. He decided to accompany the cortege to the imperial burial mound, which was some distance outside the capital. A minister objected: since the emperor did not attend the burial of his father and mother, he argued, how could he now go out of the city "for a babe still in swaddling clothes"? The emperor prevailed.[27]

The same dilemma confronted the poet Li Shangyin (812–58?) when he mourned the death of his little niece and prepared a full-dress reburial for her: "I know I am doing more than what proprieties would allow for a child, but how can I do less than my deep feelings demand?" Again feelings triumphed over convention and Li wrote a long requiem for the five-year-old girl. In format the "Requiem for My Little Niece Jiji" does not differ much from Han Yu's piece, but I shall quote it in full because it contains descriptions of several children:

> On the twenty-fifth day of the first month your uncle, with fruit and toys, brings back the body and soul of Jiji for burial in the family cemetery.
>
> After you were born you were not taken to your hometown until four years later. After just a few months, alas, you were suddenly returned to nothingness. You had hardly lived beyond infancy, but the sadness you left behind is limitless. Why did you come, and what was the cause of your departure? Seeing you play as a little girl, who would have predicted the day of your death? At that time I moved the family to the capital, waiting for a transfer of office. Pressed constantly by events, I did not notice the fleeting of time. Five years had passed since your bones were temporarily interred here, amid pallid grass and withered roots next to an unused, weed-choked road. When you were hungry in the morning, who would hold you in his arms? At night who would find water to quench your thirst? It was my fault that your desolation was unrelieved. Now that I am planning to bury the remains of second elder sister in the family cemetery, I have the occasion of moving your coffin as well. With the help of geomancers I have chosen a plot for your grave and a tombstone with an inscription. I know I am doing more than what proprieties would allow for a child, but how can I do less than my deep feelings demand?
>
> Since you died I have been blessed with several nephews and nieces. Clad in colorful swaddling clothes or short jackets, they often play with their hobby-horses and jade hoops in the courtyard. Under the sun and in the breeze, they fondle flowers and crowd around me. Only you are missing and I wonder where your spirit has gone. I am even more fond of my nephews and nieces now that I have had no children with my second wife. My heart burns with longing for the dead and love for the living.
>
> Your great grandfather and grandfather are not far from you. Just look above the Rong River and next to the Tan Hill, you can see the thick grove of

pines surrounding their resting places. Your oldest and second-oldest aunts are just next to you. Wandering about, you will not be frightened of anything. Come and enjoy the pretty dresses, sweets, and fragrant drink that I have brought for you. Your uncle is making the offering to you and your father is weeping for you. Jiji, my sad child, are you there?[28]

Tang poets often wrote about the death of their children. But their classical allusions and ornate language seldom allow a modern reader either a clear view of their feelings or a vivid description of the children. Against this background Li Shangyin's requiem stands out. While Li the poet yields to none in deliberate obscurity and allusiveness, as a grieving uncle he anticipates the expressiveness of a much later age.

With Song poetry a change occurred. Simple words, direct observation, and plain narration give great immediacy to the representation of family life in an everyday setting. In 1084 poverty forced Chen Shidao (1053–1102) to send his wife and their three children to the care of her father, who had prospered as a judge in a distant province. No parting scene—the father's sorrows, the daughter's fears, the older son's fumbling attempt to be brave and dutiful—is depicted with greater poignancy in Chinese poetry:

> My daughter was just old enough to have her hair tied,
> Yet she already knew the sadness of parting.
> Using me as a pillow she refused to get up
> For fear that getting up she would have to let me go.
> The older son was just learning to talk.
> Unused to adult ceremonies, he had to struggle with his clothes
> When he took formal leave of me, saying: "Dad, I am going now."
> How can I ever bear to recall these words?
> The younger son was still in swaddling clothes.
> He was carried by his mother when they left.
> His cry is still ringing in my ears:
> Can anyone else understand how I feel?[29]

The poet Lu You (1125–1209) must have been a loving father, too, for even in his old age he dreamt he had another brood of children:

> In my dream I had a little son and a little daughter,
> For whom I felt boundless love.
> I took them to doctors whenever there was anything wrong;
> I bored every visitor with tales of their cleverness.
> The morning rooster suddenly woke me up:
> How can my love still be there?
> Life is but a web of entanglements—
> With a laugh I free myself of these fetters.[30]

His quick recovery from a sense of loss should not be seen as a sign of callousness. A few years earlier a daughter was born to him, but the girl lived no more than a year. The tombstone inscription he wrote for his daughter shows clearly that on that occasion Lu was not happy at all to have one entanglement dissolved:

> I came to Xinding as county magistrate in the seventh month of the Bingwu year
> of the Chunxi reign [1186]. On the Dingyou day of the eighth month a daughter

was born to me. She was first given the name of Runniang, then Dingniang. I loved her dearly because she was the youngest of my children. I called her "Nünü" rather than by her formal name. She was graceful and regal. Not given to tears or laughter, she was unlike other children. She grew two teeth in the seventh month of the following year. She fell ill and died on the Bingzi day of the eighth month. Her body was coffined in the Chengqi Monastery, northeast of the city. On the Renyin day of the ninth month she was buried on North Ridge. When she died I was much grieved. I shed tears inside the coffin and said: "They are my parting gifts to my daughter." Everyone who heard it wept bitterly. The mother of Nünü Yangshi, is a native of Huayang of Szechwan.

The verse:

> By a deserted hill and over a desolate ravine,
> Amid frost and dew and surrounded by thorns and brush,
> Lies my hapless daughter in a solitary grave.
> No neighbor is seen in any direction.
> When she was alive she never left the house.
> In her death she is abandoned in a place like this.
> How unkind I am![31]

That a girl from a commoner family and so young—Nünü was not quite a year old—was given a formal burial with all the trappings is a clear indication that by the twelfth century it was possible, at least among the educated, to depart from two conventions: minimum mourning for the very young and the favoring of sons over daughters. Whatever the practice of the populace, the mourning literature shows that daughters, at least in death, were just as cherished as the sons, if not more. There are even several cases of bias in favor of the daughter. Four sons and two daughters of the Song writer and statesman Ouyang Xiu (1007–72) died in childhood, but only one, a daughter who perished at eight, was mourned in poetry. She was obviously his favorite child, for the relation between father and daughter seems to have been easy and close: "In the evening when I came home she would welcome me with a big smile. / In the morning when I was leaving she would pull me by my jacket. / The instant after she jumped into my arms she would dash away."[32] Ouyang was a prolific writer of necrologies, but he wrote none for his children. Perhaps the inhibition came from his knowledge of epigraphy—he was a passionate student and collector of stone and bronze inscriptions from previous dynasties. There were so few early precedents—none in his collection—for composing necrologies for the young.

In general, young daughters were depicted with more individuality than young sons. The reason for this bias may lie in differences in parental expectations. It was easier for little girls to be "children," while little boys were expected to behave in an exemplary manner, in a way that would prefigure the future men. The Song loyalist Wen Tianxiang (1236–83) wrote during his last imprisonment by the Mongols a suite of six laments over the destruction of his family. His two sons are represented entirely by metaphors and allusions, but the daughters are given more specifics:

> Daughters I have two, both bright and sweet.
> The older one loved to practice calligraphy
> While the younger recited lessons sonorously.
> When a sudden blast of the north wind darkened the noonday sun
> The pair of white jades were abandoned by the roadside.

> *The nest lost, the young swallows flitted in the autumn chill.*
> *Who will protect the girls, taken north with their mother?*[33]

One could go on and on. I shall just cite one more case of an apparent partiality for a daughter. Ye Xianggao (1562–1627) had a distinguished official career, serving for several years as both minister of rites and grand secretary. Of his six sons, only one lived into adulthood. When his third daughter Jiang, born in 1590, died in 1602 he wrote a long grave notice in which he states: "As I am deficient in virtue, many of my children have died young. But I have never wept as bitterly as I do for this daughter."[34]

Another stereotype—the distant father who leaves child care to the women in the household—is contradicted in at least two cases. Huang Xingzeng (1490–1540) wrote a grave notice (*kuangzhi*) for his son who had lived less than a month.[35] This short necrology reveals an impoverished but loving father trying desperately to save a newborn child. The mother, herself weakened by undernourishment, struggled to care for the sick child. The father moved the infant to his bed, hoping to offer better care. Too poor to seek professional medical help, he delved into a Tang pediatric classic but to no avail. Huang, a Neo-Confucian scholar, followed the terminology laid down in the Confucian classic *Yili* and referred to the son as "dying under the age of *shang*," but he certainly ignored the canonical advice against a ceremonial burial for so young a child.

The other case had to do with Zhou Rudeng (1547–1629), another prominent Neo-Confucian. He lost his five-year-old youngest son on the day he was scheduled to set out for a new post in a distant city. In the grave notice for his son he describes his profound grief over the boy's death. After five days of indecision he was set to bury the son and begin the journey, but at the last minute could not bear the abrupt separation between father and son: "I had the coffin carried with me and after traveling for ten days we arrived at Jinghai. I dried my tears and said, 'This is where my son's bones will have a resting place.'" Zhou blames his career as an official for his son's illness:

> Ever since he was born I had personally attended to his feeding and clothing. Without reason I would never leave his side. He had not been sick for one day. After I became an official I was fully occupied with work. There were long periods when I saw very little of him.[36]

The cult of the child

Both Huang Xingzeng and Zhou Rudeng were members of the Wang Yangming school of Neo-Confucianism. In fact Huang received instructions from the master himself. It was perhaps no accident that they were so solicitous of the welfare of their young children, for the child had a special place in the discourse of his school. Although no Confucian would have believed in the sinful state of the newborn, strict discipline and a didactic approach to elementary education had until this time been the staple of the Confucian attitude toward children.[37] With the Wang school the entire approach shifted. The innocence of children was strongly reaffirmed, and the preservation of this quality became more important than the mere acquisition of knowledge.

We shall begin with the founder of the school, Wang Shouren (1472–1529), better known as Wang Yangming. A corollary of Wang's theory of innate knowledge, the cornerstone of his teaching, is the elevation of the child in the Confucian hierarchy. "Everybody, from the infant in swaddling clothes to the old, is in full possession of this innate knowledge," Wang announced to his disciples.[38] When one disciple quoted an opinion that a child was incapable of the investigation of things, the starting point of the Confucian regimen as taught in the canonical classic the *Great Learning*, the master refuted him, saying: "When I speak of the investigation of things, it is the same endeavor from the child to the sages."[39] It is this affirmation of the child that led Wang to entertain a rather modern view of elementary education:

> It is in the nature of children to indulge in play and dislike restraint. It is like the budding of a plant. If it has plenty of freedom to expand, it will proliferate. If it meets with hindrance and obstruction, it will wither. When we teach children we must kindle their enthusiasm and make everything a joy. Then they will advance of their own accord without ceasing. It is just like plants nourished by timely rain and spring breezes. They will grow exuberantly. If they are visited upon with ice and frost, they will lose their vital force and weaken daily.[40]

Some followers of the Wang school, especially those in the Taizhou sect, to which Zhou Rudeng belonged, went even further, approaching what may be called a cult of the child—a similar trend appeared in Europe about two centuries later.[41] Lou Rufang (1515–88) contrasted infants and adults by using a traditional opposition, the yin and the yang: "During infancy the yang forces are strong and the yin forces are weak. Although infants are not without thoughts, they depend on physical functions. Therefore they smile like the warm sun; they are open and cheerful like the dawn, vivacious like a fresh breeze."[42] Adults, however, having too much yin, tend to be stiff, anxious, and confused.

Li Zhi (1527–1602) wrote an article entitled "On the Heart of the Child" (*Tongxin shuo*) in which he exalted the child to an unprecedented level: "The heart of the child is absolutely not false but pure and true (*jue jia chun zhen*). . . . If one loses the heart of the child then he loses his true heart."[43] Li advocated that everyone should try to preserve the heart of the child. To him the highly educated were at the greatest risk of losing their "heart of the child" because he believed that learning and experience tend to corrupt. Yuan Hongdao (1568–1610), too, equated the innocence of the child with perfection. In his literary criticism he selected the nebulous word *qu*, which means something like "taste" or "understanding," and assigned to it new and lofty aesthetic and metaphysical connotations. Here again the child is accorded a privileged status:

> *Qu* is more a matter of nature than of learning. When one is a child, one does not know that one has *qu*, but whatever a child does always has to do with *qu*. A child has no fixed expression in the face, no fixed gaze in the eyes. He babbles in trying to speak while his feet jump up and down without stopping. This is the time when the joy of life is unsurpassed. This is what is meant by Mencius when he speaks of "not losing [the heart of] the newborn infant" or by Laozi when he speaks of "the power of the babe." Theirs is the highest level of *qu*, the superior understanding, and the supreme enlightenment.[44]

Concurrent with the vogue of the Wang school was the proliferation of mourning literature commemorating the death of children. Not only did more and more parents write about their bereavements, but their unabashed avowal of affection and their unrestrained outpourings of grief contrast with the measured and succinct expressions in earlier centuries. If the romantic view of the purity of child in the West—beginning with Rousseau and going through Wordsworth and Dickens—led to the sentimental view of children in the nineteenth century, the Wang school, the most powerful intellectual and spiritual movement during the Ming, must have had a similar impact on the Chinese attitude as reflected in the mourning literature. This literature, scarce in early China but growing steadily after 800, took a sharp upturn around 1520 and reached its apex just before 1680. Infant mortality was probably high in all premodern societies, but now it was no longer accepted stoically and silently as a matter of course.[45] Lu Shen (1477–1544) lost eleven of his thirteen children. He poured out his sorrows for them all in his writings, and his collected works include necrologies for four daughters and two sons. Qu Dajun (1630–96) repeatedly mourned the death of his young children and wrote more than twenty poems for his four-year-old daughter. The desperate cries of the distraught parents and the detailed accounts of the death scene sometimes border on maudlin sentimentalism. But if grief sometimes compels a total or near total recall, then we are the gainers because for the first time there was the possibility of a full portrayal of the child. We shall conclude our study with a discussion of a long necrology that makes the most of this possibility.

The necrology of Shen Azhen (1616–19)

Exactly eight hundred years after Han Yu's daughter Hana died, another young girl perished. The child's seventeenth-century father, Shen Cheng (1588?–1624), an obscure man of letters, also expressed his grief and tried to calm the departed soul with a requiem. The two compositions could not be more unlike. The circumstances surrounding the two untimely deaths, the stations of the fathers, the ages of the two daughters—all differ. But the great contrast between the two requiems also reflects a number of cultural changes that occurred during the intervening eight centuries.

The increasingly affective attitude toward children—for which the Wang school of Neo-Confucianism may have been responsible—constitutes, I believe, one major difference between the articulateness of the two fathers. The other change is that of narrative style. Although Shen's is in four-character verse, his language is much closer to the vernacular than Han's. It is well known that the growth of vernacular literature from the twelfth century on changed both the perception and the representation of reality. Preferring a narrative style leaning toward mimesis (showing) rather than diegesis (telling), the readers of popular fiction and the audience of theater all demanded that everyday life be depicted with greater specificity. Moreover, as the society was becoming more and more egalitarian, so too were the topics and characters of literature. A ninth-century father of Shen's station would not even have thought of composing a requiem for so young a daughter, much less filling the composition with numerous quotidian details. It is those humble particularities that situate the young girl in the reality of an urban household, with all the accoutrements and activities attendant to her care and then to her death.

If Han Yu's necrology represents the beginning of a trend, Shen Cheng's composition is its culmination. Han Yu may have felt just as strongly about his daughter as Shen Cheng, but the ninth-century girl was a shadowy figure passively enduring her fate. While her father could still "see her eyes and face" when he stood over her temporary grave, the reader cannot share the vision. There is nothing in the text to suggest a real person. Even the standard topoi are absent. But the seventeenth-century girl, perishing after only three short years in this world, is nevertheless the most fully realized child in all traditional Chinese literature. Self-assured and perhaps a bit spoiled, she was playful, agile, and totally engaged with all the people, young or old, who came her way. Her individuality and complexity are lovingly recalled by her father: her innocent wiles and revelries, her little games and amusing mimicries, her quick though simple comprehension of the adult world, even her importunities. Why this became possible has been the heart of our story. The following is the complete text of the requiem:

On the twenty-third day of the eleventh month of the *jiwei* year in the Wanli reign [1619], the eldest daughter Azhen of Shen Cheng died of complications from smallpox. She was temporarily interred in North Cemetery. Her mother, Madame Bo, chanted Buddhist scriptures daily in the hope of gaining merit for her. In addition, she urged me to write a plea for her, but I could not for some time bear to touch the pen. On the third seventh day of my daughter's death, having prepared food for offering to her, I wrote the following as a way of mourning for her. The text was to be burned on the playground where she used to romp.

Alas, what a sad occasion! You were named Azhen because you were born in the year *binchen* [1616]. The character *zhen* was a combination of *bin* and *chen*. When you were born I was not pleased. A man over thirty wanted a son, not a daughter. But you won me over before you had completed your first year. Even then you would respond with giggles each time I made a face at you. You were then cared for by nurse Zhou. Whenever you became hungry, you were brought to your mother to be suckled. After you were fed, your nurse would carry you back to her room. As she had to get up many times during the night, she stayed in her day clothes all night. Because of you, she went through a great deal of hardship. Your mother would be angered if you were brought to her too often, but you would cry if your wish was not immediately gratified.

Last year, *wuwu* [1618], was a bad year for me. As I had to leave for the examinations, I parted from you reluctantly several times. Nurse Zhou died, and I failed my examinations. When I came home you greeted me by holding onto my sleeves and demanding gifts of toys. With you by my side my unhappiness was relieved. As you grew more teeth, you became more intelligent. Addressing your parents, you pronounced the words "dad" and "mom" perfectly. You often knocked on the door and then quickly went inside and asked: "Who is there?" When my nephew came you called him "brother." He teased you by pretending to snatch your toys; you darted and dashed away. When your mother's brother came, you seized him by his jacket while gleefully shouting, "Mom! Mom!" When your uncle came you acted the part of host. Holding up a wine cup, you invited your honored guest to drink. Everybody burst out laughing. After you were born your grandfather went to the country and then you went to Soochow. As a result you had not seen each other for more than a year. When you two met again you were asked if you knew who he was. Without hesitation you responded: "By his white hat and white beard I know he is my grand-dad." Your maternal grandfather you had never seen before. As soon as you saw him for the first time you pronounced that he came from Peking. Your maternal grandmother loved you as if you had been her own child. Several times she took you back with her to Soochow. There in the middle of the night you would ask her for toys, and at dawn you would demand fruit. When your parents wanted to keep you home you refused, saying to me: "Granny will miss me."

In the sixth month of this year you developed a skin rash. I went to Soochow to bring you home. You kept rubbing the troubled spots and looked sad. But you dared not cry, thinking that crying would displease us.

Every time you reached for fruit or candy you always watched the reaction of your parents. You would not put the food into your mouth unless there was a sign of approval. During your play you would sometimes injure one of your hands. Your little eyes would glower at the wound, but you would hide your hand when you saw adults approaching.

Your mother was too strict. From time to time she would discipline you for fear that your habits would be carried into adulthood. Although I agreed with her, I said to her when you were not around: "A little child cannot be expected to know right and wrong. Let her be until she is a little older."

When you were still in Soochow your parents were about to return home in Loudong. You were asked whether you would go back with them. You couldn't make up your mind. When you did come back I was overwhelmed with joy. We played together—I taunted you and surprised you, and you would play along by feinting dumb. You carried jujubes in a small basket and sipped porridge in a low chair. Sometimes you recited the *Great Learning* while bowing to Amit'ofo. Sometimes you would play a guessing game with me and the winner would chase the loser around the house. When you finally caught me you laughed jubilantly and clapped your hands. Who would have believed that not quite half a month later you would breathe your last? Was it decreed by heaven, or was it simply fate? Who could fathom the mystery?

When you were stricken I sent for the doctors. Some said you had measles while other believed it was the flu. It did not seem to be the flu, and it may have been measles. Looking back, I still cannot understand what happened. You had always been an articulate child but then you could not talk. Your voice was gone and you could hardly breathe. You could do nothing but open or shut your eyes. The family surrounded you and wept, and tears also flowed from your eyes. Alas, it is too painful to say any more!

It is the way of the world that one does not weep over the death of a daughter. But a man like me, who is still poor and friendless in his prime, should be content to have only daughters. He should have been happy to have a daughter as intelligent as you. Who would have expected the gods to treat me so cruelly! Ten days before you were stricken your sister A-hsün, younger than you by two years, came down with the same illness. Three days after she died, you too were gone.

Now that you no longer have playmates, you should at least have the company of your sister, whom you knew well. You can walk now but she is still unsteady on her feet. Hold her by the hand wherever you go. Be nice to her and compete not! If you meet your nurse again, ask her to guide you to your father's first wife, Madame Gu, and his mother, Madame Min. They will take you girls in. That was why I had you temporarily interred next to Gu. She will look after you, while you must take good care of your baby sister. In the future I shall choose a plot and make a permanent resting place for all of you.

I have been thinking of you all the time. If you know how much I miss you you will come back, again and again, in my dreams. If fate permits, be reborn as my next child. For such hopes I am sending you a copy of the Diamond Sutra as well as other books of spells and incantations. There are also offerings of meat and paper money for your use. When you see the King of the Underworld, kneel down with raised hands and plead for mercy. Say the following to him:

"Although I die young, I am truly guiltless. I was born into a poor family, and I never complained about the hardships. Fearing the God of Thunder, I never wasted even a grain of rice. I have always worn my simple clothes with care. I am too young to bring suitable gifts for Your Majesty. Please have pity on me and shield me from the exactions of ghosts."

Just say the words to him and don't cry or be noisy. You must not forget that the underworld is different from home.

> I am writing this but you cannot read. I shall call your name and let you know that your father is here. Azhen, Azhen, your sad father is mourning you.[46]

Notes

1   On Chinese biography see Pei-yi Wu, *The Confucian's Progress: Autobiographical Writings in Traditional China* (Princeton: Princeton University Press, 1990), pp. 4–5 and 20.

2   An interesting theme is the role of the mother in the education of the son. *GJTSJC*, 324:28a–37b, records twenty-six cases of prominent figures who were taught by their mothers, and even more cases of the mother as role model or disciplinarian.

3   "Mingdao xiansheng xingzhuang," in *Er-Cheng wenji* (*Congshu jicheng* ed.), p. 147. Throughout this chapter I follow the Chinese way of reckoning age; e.g., here I translate *shisui* as "ten years old."

4   *Shitong tongshi* (*Universals in History* with collected annotations), ed. Pu Qilong (Taipei: Shijie shuju, 1962), p. 138.

5   *LDW*, 2:339–41.

6   It is beyond the scope of this study to attempt a psychological portrait of the Han family. As we shall see, Han Yu, orphaned at an early age, was raised by his wet nurse. When it came to daughters, he seems to have been a loving father.

7   Mao Qiling, *Mao Xihe xiansheng quanji* (1761), 11:1a.

8   Wu, *Confucian's Progress*, pp. 142–59.

9   Shen Bang, *Wanshu zaji* (Beijing: Xinhua shuju, 1961), pp. 74–76. The Ming editions of the book are no longer extant in China. The modern book is based on a copy of the 1593 edition preserved in a Japanese library.

10 Whatever the scientific justifications for this sort of symmetrical arrangement, it probably had behind it the long-held Chinese belief in the yin/yang complementarity. Yet a contemporary French physician, Laurent Joubert, arrived at exactly the same idea a continent away, which he recommended to the public in his *Traité des erreurs populaires* (Lyon: 1608), p. 515. His student, Jean Héroard, attended the future Louis XIII and kept a detailed journal about the daily life of the dauphin from birth to adolescence. See Lloyd deMause, ed., *The History of Childhood* (New York: Harper & Row, 1974), pp. 264 and 284. An anonymous reader for the University of Hawai'i Press suggests that in both instances the symmetrical arrangement was designed to prevent the wet nurse from switching her own child for her employer's.

11 *GJTSJC*, 324:40b.

12 *Changli xiansheng ji* (*SBBY* ed.), 35:4b.

13 *GJTSJC*, 324:39b.

14 Quoted in David Hunt, *Parents and Children in History: The Psychology of Family life in Early Modern France* (New York: Basic Books, 1970), p. 104.

15 *GJTSJC*, 324:39a.

16 *Reflections on Things at Hand: The Neo-Confucian Anthology Compiled by Chu Hsi and Lü Tsu-ch'ien,* trans. Wing-tsit Chan (New York: Columbia University Press, 1967), p. 178.

17 *GJTSJC*, 324:39a. Chen Longzheng's compassion and earnestness represent the best of Song-Ming humanitarianism. It would take us too far afield to delve into the devices invented and efforts expended by the elite in improving the lot of abandoned or neglected children. Here I shall cite only one incident. When Ye Mengde (1077–1148) served as prefect in western Honan, a bad flood sent many refugees into his region. To feed the needy and starving he opened up all the "ever-level granaries" under his jurisdiction, and more than 100,000 lives were thus saved. "But I was unable to reach all the abandoned children. One day I asked my staff, 'Why is it that all those who are childless do not adopt the children?' They replied, 'People fear that sooner or later—no later than the first bumper crop—the parents will find their way to them and reclaim the children.' Examining the laws and precedents I discovered a stipulation to the effect that parents who abandoned their children during natural calamities could make no future claims to them. The man who made this law must have been a man of kindness. . . . I thereupon had the text of this stipulation printed on thousands of forms and distributed in all the districts and neighborhoods within and without the city. Whoever adopted a child would write down the circumstances on one of those forms, which in turn would be notarized in my office. Those who adopted a large number of children would receive awards as well as surplus food from the ever-level granaries. The poor adoptive parents would receive appropriate subsidies.

Altogether there were 3,800 forms notarized. This was the number of children who were rescued from a death in the ditches and placed in caring homes. Although this was only a trifle not worth talking about, I keep telling prefects and magistrates about it for fear that at the time of an emergency they may not be aware of this particular law or the way of making the most effective use of it." *Bishu luhua* (*Congshu jicheng* ed.), pp. 13–14.

18 Both circumstances tended to reinforce the Chinese dependency on the wet nurse. After the European child returned to the household of the parents, whatever bond there may have once been would gradually dissolve.

19 Liu Xi, *Huoyou bianlan* (Handbook for the preservation of children) (Xin'an, 1510), 1:6a.

20 DeMause, *The History of Childhood*, p. 36.

21 Leah S. Marcus, *Childhood and Cultural Despair: A Theme and Variations in Seventeenth-Century Literature* (Pittsburgh: University of Pittsburgh Press, 1978), pp. 9–10, 12.

22 The Europeans tended to be lithic; the Chinese, literary. See Pei-yi Wu, "Memories of K'ai-feng," *New Literary History* (Spring 1994): 47–60.

23 "The Massacre of the Innocents," *New York Review of Books*, November 14, 1974, p. 30.

24 *Changli xiansheng ji* (*SBBY* ed.), 35:3b–4a.

25 *Yili* (*SBBY* ed.), 11:14a.

26 Quoted in Robert Pattison, *The Child Figure in English Literature* (Athens: University of Georgia Press, 1978), p. 6.

27 *GJTSJC*, 712:41b. There were of course emperors who did not depart from conventions. For instance, the Chenghua Emperor (1447–87) of the Ming lost his oldest son in 1466 and the next oldest in 1472. The funerals for the boys, who perished at a very early age, were very simple, conforming to the rules laid down in the *Yili*, the father's affection for the second son notwithstanding—the boy was made crown prince before he was even three years of age. The emperor heeded the advice of the minister of rites, who made an explicit reference to the stipulations in the canonical classic. See *Ming shilu leizuan*, eds., Li Guoxiang and Yang Chang (Wuhan: Wuhan chubanshe, 1992), pp. 195 and 197.

28 *Li Shangyin xuanji*, ed. Zhou Zhenfu (Shanghai: Guji chubanshe, 1986), pp. 350–51.

29 *Houshan jushi wenji* (Shanghai: SHGJCBS, 1984), 1:2b–3a.

30 *Jiannan shigao* (*SBBY* ed.), 60.3b.

31 *Weinan wenji* (*SBBY* ed.), 4b–5a.

32 *Ouyang Xiu quanji* (Beijing: Zhongguo shudian, 1986), p. 408.

33 *Wenshan xiansheng quanji* (*SBCK* ed.), 14:23b. Wen's "Six Laments" are modeled on Du Fu's "Seven Laments." The two compositions are similar in format and style down to the last detail, but Du (712–70) said nothing in his laments about his suffering children—one of them, a young son, had died of hunger four years earlier. Wen devotes the third lament to his daughters and the fourth to his sons. Although Du in his voluminous writings often shows great affection for his children, there is no indication of any necrological attention to the dead boy.

34 *Cang xia cao* (National Library of Peiping microfilm), 10:5b–6a.

35 *Wuyue shanren ji* (NCL microfilm, EcF 6067), 38:138a–14b.

36 *Dong Yue zhengxue lu* (Taipei: Wenhai chubanshe, 1970), 2:1061–62.

37 See Pei-yi Wu, "Education of Children During the Sung," in W. Theodore de Bary and John Chaffee, eds., *Neo-Confucian Education: The Formative Stage* (Berkeley: University of California Press, 1989), pp. 307–24.

38 *Wang Yangming quanshu* (Taipei: Zhengzhong shuju, 1955), 1:79. The term "innate knowledge" (*liangzhi*) comes originally from *Mencius* VIIA:15: "The ability possessed by men without having been acquired by learning is innate ability and the knowledge possessed by them without deliberation is innate knowledge." Translated by James Legge, *The Chinese Classics*, vol. 2, p. 456.

39 Ibid, p. 71.

40 Ibid.

41 For a sampling of sixteenth-century French attitudes toward children see Hunt, *Parents and Children in History*, p. 185: "Montaigne wrote bluntly that they had 'neither movement in the soul, nor recognizable form in the body, by which they could render themselves lovable.' Charron went so far as to claim that 'the faculties of the soul are opened' only after the child had reached the age of four or five. Bérulle summed up the opinions of a century when he characterized childhood as 'the meanest and most abject state of the human condition.'"

42 Huang Zongxi, *Mingru xuean* (Taipei: Shijie shuju, 1965), p. 350.

43 *Feng shu* (Beijing: Zhonghua shuju, 1961), p. 97.

44 *Yuan Hongdao ji qianjiao*, Qian Bocheng ed. (Shanghai: Shanghai guji chubanshe, 1981), pp. 463–64.

45 The increasingly affective parental attitude implied by the proliferation of mourning literature may suggest, paradoxically, a downward trend in infant mortality in late Ming China. Grieving parents

were more inconsolable if they had been led to hope for more or if fewer neighbors and acquaintances suffered the same deprivations. See Lawrence Stone, *The Family, Sex and Marriage in England 1500–1800* (abridged ed.) (New York: Harper & Row, 1979), p. 57: "Even if mortality rates in England were lower than those of France, this will not alter the fact that to preserve their mental stability parents were obliged to limit the degree of their psychological involvement with their infant children. . . . It was very rash for parents to get too emotionally concerned about creatures whose expectation of life was so very low." Chinese parents in late Ming times do not seem to have been deterred from emotional involvement with their young children.

46   "Ji Zhennü wen," in *Jindai sanwen chao*, ed. Shen Qiwu (Hong Kong: Tianhong chubanshe, 1957), pp. 262–64.

Chapter 7

Avner Gil'adi

INFANTS, CHILDREN AND DEATH IN MEDIEVAL MUSLIM SOCIETY

DEATH AMONG INFANTS AND CHILDREN and the adults' reactions to this phenomenon are essential aspects of the history of childhood in any given society. Indeed these issues have been repeatedly raised and dealt with by historians of family and childhood, particularly with regard to the classical world and Europe from the Middle Ages to modern times.

The rates of infant and child mortality and their causes shed light on environmental, social and cultural conditions under which children in the past lived. Moreover, adults' reactions to their death reflect various types of concepts of childhood and attitudes towards children.

It is well-known that in pre-modern societies, particularly among new-born infants, infants of less than two years, and children of the lower strata, the death rates were very high. This was also the case with medieval Middle Eastern societies as well as with the European ones with which our findings are occasionally compared.[1] It was not until the end of the nineteenth century, with the attainment of the knowledge necessary for effective treatment of children's diseases, that essential changes began to take place.[2]

[. . .]

Reactions to infant and child death

Two levels of reactions to the death of infants and children in medieval Muslim society are referred to here: religious–theoretical and emotional. While juridical and theological discussions of the death of children reflect the *'ulamās''* awareness of the uniqueness of children as well as the religious problems connected with their death, there are genres which mirror the emotional confrontation with the phenomenon. They are mainly consolation treatises for bereaved parents and poems of lamentation. Studying these sources while keeping in mind the above-mentioned [see original reading] descriptions of violence, abandonment and infanticide (which, on the face of it, support Ariès's 'thesis of indifference') one comes to the conclusion that the adults' attitudes towards infants and children in medieval Muslim society were much more varied and complex than those attributed by Ariès and his followers to adults in medieval Europe.

Juridical and theological discussions of infant and child mortality

Infant and child mortality as a frequent occurrence in medieval Muslim society is clearly reflected in juridical as well as theological writings dealing with the ways in which deceased infants and children should be treated, and their fate in the Hereafter. The focus of legalistic considerations is whether or not the child is to be regarded as a human being in the full sense of the word. The answer given by some well-known jurisconsults is in the affirmative. Thus, al-Sarakhsī, the Ḥanafī jurisconsult of the eleventh century, maintains that the coffin of a dead child should be borne by people, not on the back of an animal 'since by lifting (the coffin) on to a beast's back we liken it to the carrying of a burden. However, carrying (the coffin) by hand is the way to honour the dead. Children should be regarded as human beings and should be honoured like adults'.[3] Also, in al-Sarakhsī's view, the washing of an infant's corpse and the prayer for him should be exactly the same as the washing and the prayer for a deceased adult.[4] According to Ibn Qayyim al-Jawziyya, this opinion is supported by a vast majority of *ḥadīth* reports describing the Prophet's prayer for Ibrāhīm, his son who died in infancy.[5]

Al-Manbijī devotes a special chapter to this topic,[6] and his own view is already expressed in its title: '(Muslims) should pray for every Muslim infant (who has died) and for his parents'. This right is, as he puts it, 'great tidings for bereaved parents', who, naturally, wish to secure the future of their children in the Hereafter by means of prayer. According to al-Manbijī, the majority of the religious scholars uphold this right although others reject it, claiming that only a child who has become mature is entitled to a prayer after his death. This opposing opinion is backed up by another *ḥadīth* report which describes Muḥammad as not praying for his son Ibrāhīm.[7]

Among the references cited by al-Manbijī to support what he regards as the general opinion, there are some interesting reports. One of them (taken from an authoritative *ḥadīth* collection, namely, al-Bukhārī's *Ṣaḥīḥ*) urges one to pray for the soul of every infant who was born Muslim, including the child of a prostitute.[8] Another (included in several *ḥadīth* collections) permits a prayer for an aborted foetus.[9]

It should be mentioned, however, that those scholars who, in principle, allow prayer for a dead infant or aborted foetus are not unanimous as to certain preconditions. For instance, disputes arise concerning a prayer for the soul of an infant who was born dead.[10] Those who do not regard a foetus as a human being would also reject the prayer for such an infant, including him in the same category as the foetus. Most of the supporters of the prayer for an aborted foetus insist on one condition, namely, that the foetus had been in his mother's womb for at least four months. This reflects the view adopted by all jurists that the foetus is 'ensouled' after 120 days of pregnancy[11] and, as such, is expected to be resurrected on the Day of Judgement.[12] Interestingly enough, some scholars, who seem however to be in a minority, argue that every aborted foetus is entitled to be prayed for regardless of the point at which the abortion took place.[13]

In any case, it seems that prayers for children's souls were actually offered up. We have at least two clear testimonies to support this. The first is included in Ibn Taghrī Birdī's account of burial during the plague epidemic of 833/1429–30 in Cairo: 'The child of an individual in our service named Shams al-Dīn al-Dhahabī died, and we went out with him to the oratory. The boy was less than seven years old, and when we set him down to pray over him among the dead, a large number of others were brought, until their numbers went beyond counting. Then prayer was over them all.'[14]

Al-Yūnīnī (d. in Damascus, 1326) describes a similar case of a deceased child being treated like an adult and lamented. He mentions, moreover, that the memory of the child was kept in the hearts of the members of his family who missed him.[15]

On the other hand, it seems that deceased children, as opposed to adults, did not have the privilege of having gravestones on their tombs,[16] and there are a few hints to the effect that dead infants and aborted foetus were sometimes buried in domestic yards.[17] But, as claimed by Wilson, in the context of European history, this does not necessarily imply parental indifference towards the death of their offspring.[18]

It could be argued that very little can be inferred from purely juridical discussions about attitudes towards living children. Nevertheless, it seems likely that some of the opinions expressed by religious scholars concerning infant mortality are connected with attitudes towards children in general. Thus, it is reasonable to assume that the recurring exhortations to honour the deceased child and to regard him as an adult resulted from a situation in which living as well as dead children were not always looked upon as human beings in the full sense of the term. On the other hand, these exhortations reflect the awareness of religious scholars to the necessity of change.

Children's fate in the afterlife is mostly discussed in the context of rather abstract theological considerations of divine justice, mercy and knowledge.[19] Qur'ān commentators, theologians, and heresiographers deal with issues such as whether or not children are questioned in the grave, whether children of unbelievers are sent by God to Hell, whether God punishes children in the Hereafter, and the exact status of Muslim children in Paradise. However, discussions of this sort were not always irrelevant to actual life and in some cases they mirror, albeit implicitly, certain concepts of childhood and attitudes towards children.

In the first place, the abstract theological discussions look more relevant when they appear in treatises written to console parents distressed by the loss of a child or children, finding it hard to accept. Here the theological discussions play an important psychological role in supporting the bereaved parents by assuring them that their children's place in Paradise is secured.[20] Thus, the chapter entitled 'On placating parents concerning (the fate of) the children' in al-Manbijī's *Tasliya* opens by quoting a Qur'ānic verse (52:21) in which Allāh promises the believers 'to join their seed with them (in Paradise)'. Al-Manbijī ignores the complexity of the theological problems raised by the verse and the various suggestions made by Qur'ān commentators on this issue.[21] His main concern is rather the practical psychological value of the verse in consoling parents. From this point of view the most important message of the verse is that 'the progeny will reach the ranks of their fathers in the Garden, even though they have not by their own works achieved those ranks . . . '.[22]

The idea that the child is an innocent creature – since he had not committed sins before his death – and a potential believer is supported by commentaries to other Qur'ānic verses,[23] and by various interpretations of the term *fiṭra* (lit. 'natural disposition') which are dealt with in a special section within the above-mentioned chapter[24] Al-Manbijī accepts the notion that *fiṭra* means 'monotheism and Islam'. Since all children – including those of unbelievers – are born in a state of *fiṭra*, they are entitled to enter the Garden when they die in childhood, although they cannot yet be credited with good works.[25] In another chapter al-Manbijī consoles parents who lost an infant by assuring them that the baby's suckling period will be completed in Paradise. He cites an unidentified narration to the effect that on a certain tree in Paradise a breast is hung from which the infants are suckled.[26]

As mentioned above, some concepts of childhood are reflected even in writings in which questions connected with infant mortality are discussed in a purely theological context. Thus, the basic assumption of the Muslim religious scholars in considering the issue of the questioning of children in the grave[27] is that children are lacking *tamyīz* (lit. 'the ability to discriminate between good and bad, right and false', etc). That means, in this context, that they do not have the intellectual ability to comprehend the basic principles of faith.[28]

Those believing in the questioning of children, while accepting the above-mentioned assumption, try to explain away the contradiction by arguing that Allāh 'completes' the children's intellect in the grave and reveals to them the right answers by means of inspiration.[29] The opponents of the idea of children being questioned in the grave emphasise the child's innocence and non-accountability: 'And Allāh does not punish anyone who has not committed a sin. The meaning of the punishment of the grave is apparently the pain caused to the dead by the (behaviour of) others, not (necessarily) a punishment for any of his own acts.'[30]

This theological debate had practical implications as well. One's position in it could determine whether the basic articles of faith should be passed on to a dying child (talqīn)[31] and whether special supplications should be offered to save him from suffering in the grave.[32] It is likely that the recommendation to teach every Muslim child the articles of faith even before he could understand their real meaning[33] was the result of the awareness of the rather poor survival prospects of children.

Ibn Qayyim al-Jawziyya sees an essential difference between the situation of the deceased child in the grave, on the one hand, and in the Hereafter, on the other. Regarded as non-accountable, due to his intellectual inability, the child is exempted from being questioned in the grave. In the next world, however, his intellectual development being accomplished, he is expected to accept the angel's instructions and to obey God; otherwise, he will not escape the divine punishment.[34] The idea that children's intellect becomes complete in the next world was concomitant with the concept of children, when entering Paradise, changing physically and becoming adults.[35]

Not many theologians of earlier periods, however, endorsed distinctions such as this and, to them, the fate of children in the other world remained a controversial issue. Some Muslim groups, especially Mu'tazilites and Shī'ites, crediting children with innocence and a state of religious 'neutrality' and emphasising God's justice, held that children are admitted to Paradise regardless of their parents' fate. That meant that even the infant children of unbelievers were entitled to enter the Garden. Yaḥyā b. Al-Ḥusayn al-Hādī ilā al-Ḥaqq (859–910), the founder of the Zaydī dynasty in Yemen,[36] is an outstanding representative of this attitude. The discussion of the question of children's fate in the Hereafter in his *Majmū'* concludes as follows:

> From these and from similar verses it is known that God will not torture infant children on the day of Resurrection, He will not punish them for their parents' sins nor for the sins He knows they themselves could have committed (if they had lived). This is the case with the infant children of believers as well as of unbelievers, and also with adulterers' infants and madmen who became mad in their childhood and remained so till their death.[37]

The concept of children's innocence and 'neutrality' was so deeply rooted that even some of the extreme opponents of the Mu'tazila,[38] among them certain subgroups of the Khawārij,[39] were not unanimous concerning the fate of children in the world to come. While one group (al-Azāriqa) believed that the legal status of the infant children of polytheists was the same as that of their parents, and they would be punished in the Fire,[40] many members of another group (the Ibāḍiyya) were described as

> hesitating concerning the suffering of the children of polytheists in the world to come. They considered it permissible to assume that God would make them suffer in the other world, but not in the way of retribution (for having been unbelievers). Others considered it permissible to assume that, as an act of kindness, God admitted children into Paradise. Still others held that God made them suffer by necessity and not by choice.[41]

Similarly, the Sunnis are not categorical as to the fate of infant children of the polytheists. The Prophet is credited with the statement that only God knows how these children would have acted had they lived. Therefore Muḥammad himself refused to rule whether they are admitted to Paradise or sent to Hell. In the eleventh century, al-Ghazālī was still perplexed by these questions. He suggests that unbelievers' children, just like madmen, enjoy an intermediate status in the Hereafter: on the one hand, they are not punished; on the other, they are precluded from eternal happiness. Nevertheless, he avoids any clearcut decision and refers to the contradictory reports concerning their fate.[42] Ibn Taymiyya, citing the above-mentioned Prophetic statement in one of his *fatāwā*, supports it with the well-known *ḥadīth* report according to which every infant is born in a state of *fiṭra*; he thus expresses his own position, namely, that children are innocent and non-accountable, and cannot be held responsible for their parents' actions.[43]

Emotional reactions to the death of infants and children

The severity of the problem of infant and child death in medieval Muslim society, particularly in the late Middle Ages, when so many children fell victim to the Black Death, together with the possibly growing awareness of the parents' difficulty in coping with that problem, seem to have been the main causes of the flourishing of the genre of consolation treatises for bereaved parents in Egypt and Syria between the end of the thirteenth and the sixteenth century.[44] The uniqueness of these treatises lies in their very existence as separate compilations dedicated exclusively to the religious and psychological problems connected with infant and child death.

As mentioned above, almost nothing was new in the content of the consolation treatises. They were composed of *ḥadīth* reports, narrations and anecdotes derived from earlier sources and generally lacking any concrete details concerning, for example, the causes of and reactions to children's death. This gives the treatises a somewhat impersonal character. Moreover, it may well be that the *ḥadīth* reports and the various narrations do not always reflect concrete events even from the times in which they appeared, namely, the first centuries of Islam. Nevertheless, they seem to represent types of adult response to infant and child mortality which existed in no small measure in medieval Muslim society. The earlier materials were therefore still relevant in the late Middle Ages. Formulas such as *'lā ya'īshu lahu* (or *lahā*) *walad'* ['none of his – or her – offspring survives'] or *'wa-anā raqūb la ya'īshu lī walad'* ['I am a woman of whom no offspring lives'] occur in *ḥadīth* reports and are cited by authors of consolation treatises to describe a tragic situation with which they and many people of their generations were familiar.[45] That is also apparently the case with a large number of reports including the prophetic promise that bereaved parents would be rewarded by entering Paradise – where they would meet their deceased children once again – or by being protected from the fires of Hell. Interestingly enough, the most common version of this *ḥadīth* report refers to parents who were bereaved of not fewer than three children:

> The Prophet – may Allāh bless him and grant him peace – said: 'Every Muslim who is bereaved of three of his children – those who have not committed any sin (that is, very young) – will be admitted by God to Paradise as an act of mercy on His part.'[46]

Moreover, according to another *ḥadīth* report, the Prophet hesitated whether parents who lost 'only' one of their children – apparently a very common occurrence – were entitled to such a reward or not; eventually he compromised and made the concession.[47]

The most interesting themes of the consolation treatises as well as a few lamentation poems written for or by bereaved fathers are the tension between the emotional–spontaneous type of reaction, on the one hand, and religious–'rational' one, on the other, and the efforts to harmonise them.[48] Among several types of parent–child relationship, these writings bring to light strong psychological links resulting in moving emotional reactions in cases of death. However, in contrast with this type of reaction – reflected in many ḥadīth reports and anecdotes cited in the consolation treatises – other reports which apparently represented the authors' view and supply the *raison d'être* of their compilations, call for restraint and control and even point out the religious 'advantages' of children's death. The latter motif appears also in lamentation poems. It thus seems clear that in a situation of total indifference to children's death the consolation treatises and the lamentation poems would not have had to be written at all. Their main task was not to deal with the theological problems involved in the death of innocent creatures but rather to cope with outbursts of emotions and with the psychological difficulties experienced by bereaved parents. As al-Manbijī puts it: 'The death of a child, which occurs to most of the people in our time, causes the parents anxiety and lack of forbearance and patience, all as a result of the too small number of religious exhortations.'[49]

Strong emotional reactions to the death of a person close to one were condemned from the religious point of view in general, not only in cases of children's death, since they implied a sceptical attitude towards the divine promise of eternal life in the Hereafter and a preference for earthly values.[50] In religious terms, the death of a child is one of the most difficult ordeals the Muslim is expected to endure in order to prove his belief and submission to the divine decree. This notion is mentioned by all the authors of the consolation treatises that we have checked.[51] Al-Qaysī, moreover, emphasises the suffering involved in this ordeal from the psychological and even physical points of view by describing it as a flame burning in the heart and the liver.[52] No wonder, then, that the traumatic reaction of bereaved parents ended in some rare cases with their own death.[53] The common spontaneous reaction, however, was less destructive, but still very sentimental. Many reports depict parents and other people bursting into tears and weeping as a reaction to the death of a child. In some cases it is clear that the deceased child was very young. The emotional behaviour of the Prophet Muḥammad at the funeral of his son Ibrāhīm, who died in his infancy, served as an example to validate such a reaction when control and restraint were in fact expected. The report reflects the two contradictory types of reaction – the emotional, on the one hand, and the religious–'rational' on the other, and subsequently their harmonisation. The first type: 'And the Prophet went in front of Ibrāhīm's coffin, then he sat on his grave. Then Ibrāhīm was brought down to his grave and the Prophet, seeing him laid in the grave, shed tears (*damaʿat ʿaynāhu*). When Muḥammad's companions saw him doing so they also started to weep and even to cry loudly (*bakau ḥattā irtafaʿat aṣwātuhum*).[54]

The opposite reaction, that of restraint and control, is represented here by Abū Bakr who asks the Prophet: 'Are you crying after having forbidden crying (at funerals)?!' The Prophet, in his reply, suggests a form of compromise based on a distinction between the emotional domain, symbolised by the eyes and the heart, being controlled, in a way, by the conscious domain symbolised by speech: '*Yā Abā Bakr, tadmaʿu al-ʿayn wa-yawjaʿu al-qalb fa-lā naqūlu mā yuskhitu Allāh* ['O Abū Bakr, the eyes shed tears and the heart hurts but we say nothing which irritates God'].[55] And in another version of this report: '*Inna al-ʿayn tadmaʿu wa-al-qalb yaḥzunu wa-lā naqūlu illā mā yurḍī rabbanā wa-innā bi-firāqika, yā Ibrāhīm, la-mahzūnūna*' ['the eyes shed tears and the heart is grieved but we say only what satisfies God (although) we grieve your departure, O Ibrāhīm'].[56] In yet another ḥadīth report relating the death of Ibrāhīm the human emotions are projected on to the natural surroundings; the sun is said to have been eclipsed on the very day on which the infant died.[57]

The pattern of the report described above occurs in other *aḥādith*, although sometimes the order in which the opposite types of reaction are introduced is reversed. In a *ḥadīth* report cited by al-Qaysi[58] it is told that one of the Prophet's daughters sent for him as her son was dying. The immediate response of Muḥammad was refusal. The only message he had for the grieving mother was one of forbearance and endurance (what we call the religious– 'rational' type of reaction). But the daughter, who might have been expecting a miracle, kept begging the Prophet to come. The Prophet's eventual encounter with his dying grandson brought about a dramatic change in his behaviour. Shaking, he took the boy in his arms and cried. Here too the harmonisation between the two types of response is presented by the explanation Muḥammad gives for his reaction. The shaking, he says, has been caused by Allāh and is to be interpreted as a sign of God's mercy on those believers who are themselves merciful. Thus, Muḥammad's response, although it could have been seen as too emotional from the religious point of view, was approved as religiously legitimate.

It is told that Rajā' b. Ḥaywa used the example of the Prophet to justify the emotional reaction of the Caliph Sulaymān on the death of his son Ayyūb in spite of the contradictory advice of 'Umar b. 'Abd al-'Azīz to remember God and to be patient. According to the narration, Sulaymān understood very well the psychological significance of crying. Without it, he says, his liver would have been torn.[59]

In addition to weeping, some other forms of emotional reaction are mentioned in the sources. A father is described as becoming distraught every time he saw the toys of his deceased son.[60] Another one refrains from eating and drinking as a result of his son's death.[61] And yet another father spends long nights without sleep, thinking of his dead son.[62] And indeed, Isḥq b. 'Imrān, a Muslim doctor of the ninth–tenth century observed that 'the loss of a beloved child . . . can release such sadness and dejection that melancholy is the result'.[63]

It can be argued that emotional responses to child mortality are not necessarily an indication of warm relationships between parents and living children, that, as DeMause puts it, 'expressions of tenderness toward children occur most often when the child is non-demanding, especially when the child is either asleep or dead'.[64] This might be true but, as far as our sources are concerned, not the whole truth. Many reports in the consolation treatises reflect parental love and tenderness towards living children and some understanding of their needs. In a narration, cited by al-Qaysī, there is a description of a father whose little son used to join him while he was sitting in the company of the Prophet and his companions. The vivid description implies an intimate relationship between father and son: '*Wa-fīhim rajul lahu ibn ya'tihi min khalaf ẓahrihi fa-yaq'udu bayna yadayhi*' ['there was a man among them whose little son used to approach him from behind and then sit in front of him'] as if they were playing together. No wonder, then, that the father could no longer attend these meetings after the child's death, fearing painful memories which would cause him sadness.[65] In another narration related by al-Manbijī, one of Muḥammad's companions who had been absent from their meetings is said to have been nursing his ailing son who eventually died.[66]

Close physical relations between parents and infants expressed by kissing (*taqbīl*), smelling (*shamm*), caressing (*mu'ānaqa*), and putting the infant on the parents' breast (*iḥtiḍān*) and the like are referred to in many reports. Some of them are included in special sections within the *ḥadīth* compilations entitled '*Mā jā'a fī ḥubb al-walad*' ['Prophetic traditions on loving children'],[67] '*Bāb raḥmat al-walad wa-taqbīlihi wa-mu'ānaqatihi*' ['A chapter on having pity on children, kissing and caressing them'][68] and the like. Children used to be called by pet-names such as '*Qurrat 'aynī*' ['he is my consolation'] and *thamarat fu'ādī* ['the fruit of my heart'].[69] Also children, especially when grown-up, are portrayed as arousing their parents' expectations, making their parents proud and other people envious. Children were expected to be energetic, brave and intelligent.[70]

Testimonies from anthropological researches carried out in contemporary Middle Eastern Muslim communities, with their traditional extended families, support the assumption that warm relationships between parents, particularly mothers, and children were not rare in medieval Muslim society although the opposite is also mentioned.[71] These relations find their expression, *inter alia,* in the parents' shock and bereavement in cases of infant and child death regardless of the frequency of events such as these.[72] To this, modern literary testimonies, such as Taha Ḥusain's *al-Ayyām*, should be added. In some extremely impressive passages the strong emotional reactions of the author's parents to the death of their little daughter and their son (no longer a child but rather a young man) are depicted.[73]

Certainly, the sources also reflect a socially pragmatic attitude towards children and the advocacy by religious teachers of marriage as primarily a means of procreation. A *ḥadīth* report appearing in many versions and cited in the consolation treatises mirrors a well-known socio-biological type of reaction to the loss of a child, namely, bearing another child as compensation for the deceased one,[74] but this does not necessarily contradict warm relationships with living children and feelings of bereavement when they die.

Al-Manbijī admits that the death of a grown-up child is a greater loss to his parents than that of an infant since, being endowed with intelligence and good character, he is much more helpful. But as Le Roy Ladurie observes with regard to Montaillou, although 'love for children was not . . . entirely disinterested' and 'a male child meant a strong right arm (to the peasants) . . . he also meant much more . . .'.[75] This seems to be the case with at least some Muslims as well. And indeed, al-Manbijī himself, in accord with other authors of consolation treatises, devotes much space in his work to reports intended to console not only parents who had lost young children and new-born infants but also those whose baby was still-born.[76]

The term 'children' in the *ḥadīth* reports and early anecdotes means almost exclusively males; and on the parental side, mothers are relatively rarely mentioned. Indeed, from birth females were discriminated against in medieval Middle Eastern society. As we have seen, efforts were made by Muslim scholars to denounce the rejection of new-born females which sometimes found expression in a father's wishes to see his daughter dead: '*Kunta tatamannā mawtahā*'.[77] On the other hand, there are no grounds for the common assumption that infanticide, especially as a family-planning device, was practised only on female infants in pre-Islamic Arabia and, as mentioned above [see original reading], there are some indications to the effect that, although forbidden by the Qur'ān, this practice did not disappear altogether in later periods.[78] The absence of female children from many reports in the consolation treatises was not therefore necessarily the result of lack of a spontaneous–emotional reaction to their death. However, the sensitivity of adults to the death of female children might have developed in later periods as reflected, for example, in the title of al-Ṣāliḥī's treatises,[79] and in the third chapter of al-Sakhāwī's *Irtiyāḥ al-akbād*, devoted, *inter alia,* to '*Mā qīla fī mawt al-walad wa-al-wālidayni wa-al-akh wa-al-zawja wa-al-ibna*' ['What was related concerning the death of a child, of parents, a brother, a wife and a daughter'].[80]

The psychological need for consolation expressed in the sources is further evidence of the distress caused by children's death. Abū Hurayra is asked by Khālid b. 'Allān to supply a *ḥadīth* report to comfort him on the death of his two sons: '*Innahu qad māta lī ibnāni fa-mā anta muḥaddithī 'an Rasūl Allāh ṣal'am biḥadīth yuṭayyibu anfusanā 'an mawtānā?*'[81] ['I lost two of my sons. What Prophetic reports can you narrate to comfort us?']. And a bereaved father thanks Ḥasan al-Baṣrī for alleviating his grief: '*Hawwanta 'alā wajī 'alā ibnī*'[82] ['You made my grief on (the death of) my son easier'].

Providing comfort for bereaved parents – '*Taṭyīb khāṭir alwālidayni 'alā al-awlād*'[83] – was one function of the consolation treatises. The other was to restrain excessive emotional reaction which was, as mentioned above, not acceptable from the religious point of view, especially in cases of children's death. *Ṣabr* (steadfastness) and *iḥtisāb* (the readiness to grant children to Allāh) are the ways of response most exalted in the treatises for which a great reward is promised in the Hereafter. Many reports – some examples are cited above – promise bereaved parents the protection from the fire of Hell and the admission to Paradise as consolation for their children's death.[84] Even an aborted foetus serves as his parents' advocate in the world to come and helps them enter the garden.[85] These motifs are elaborated fully in the reports emphasising the 'advantages' of bereavement of children: '*Faḍl man māta lahu walad*'.[86] Moreover, some reports portray the sorrow of those whose offspring did not precede them into the Hereafter: '*Ḥasra man lam yuqaddim walad^{an} fī al-ākhira*'.[87] The next step was to describe parents as wishing for the death of their children in their quest for eternal reward and delighted when that wish was fulfilled.[88]

On the one hand, there are descriptions of emotional reactions and, on the other, the religious ideal, namely, the readiness to entrust one's children to God and even delight at their death. However, many reports suggest a compromise, that is to say, permission to express restrained emotional responses along with acceptance of and resignation to the divine decree.

Notes

1 Ullmann, *Islamic Medicine*, p. 57; Demaitre, 'The idea of childhood', p. 465; McLaughlin, 'Survivors and surrogates', pp. 111, 112, 119; Wilson, 'The myth of motherhood', p. 186; Le Roy Ladurie, *Montaillou*, pp. 220–21; D.L. Ransel, *Mothers of Misery: Child Abandonment in Russia* (Princeton, 1988), pp. 266–74; Kottek, 'Childhood in medieval Jewry', pp. 378–79.

2 McLaughlin, ibid., p. 145 (note 37).

3 Al-Sarakhsī, *al-Mabsūt*, Vol. II, p. 57.

4 Ibid., and see also: al-Manbijī, *Tasliyat ahl al-maṣā'ib*, p. 115.

5 Ibn Qayyim al-Jawziyya, *Tufat al-mawdūd*, pp. 62–64.

6 Al-Manbijī, ibid., pp. 112–17.

7 Ibid., p. 113. And see also Jalāl al-Dīn al-Suyūṭī, *al-Ḥāwī li-al-fatāwā* (Cairo, 1959), part II, p. 189.

8 Al-Manbijī, ibid., p. 112.

9 Ibid., p. 113.

10 Ibid., p. 114.

11 Musallam, *Sex and Society in Islam*, pp. 57–59.

12 Al-Manbijī, ibid., pp. 114–15. Apparently for that reason al-Ghazālī (*Ihyā' 'ulūm al-dīn*, Vol. II, pp. 68–69) recommends giving an aborted foetus a name.

13 Al-Manbijī, ibid., p. 114.

14 Ibn Taghrī Birdī, *al-Nujūm al-zāhira* (Popper's translation), Vol. XVIII, pp. 71–72 (cited in Dols, *The Black Death*, pp. 241–42).

15 Mūsā b. Muḥammad Qutb al-Dīn al-Yūnīnī, *Dhayl mir'āt al-zamān* (MS. Topkapi Sarayi), AHMET 2907/E3, fol. 222b. My thanks to Dr 'Amalia Levanoni for drawing my attention to this reference.

16 See Kh. Moaz and S. Ory, *Inscriptions arabes de Damas, La stèles funeraires, I. Cimitière d'al-Bāb al-Sagīr* (Damascus, 1977) (out of 80 gravestones surveyed three were erected on tombs of youths but none on a child's); A. 'Abd al-Tawwāb and S. Ory, *Stèles Islamiques de la nécropole d'Assouan* (Cairo, 1977) (out of 400 gravestones surveyed not one is a child's).

17 Ibn Abī Ḥajala, *Sulwat al-ḥazīn*, fol. 30a, and cf. Ammar, *Growing Up in an Egyptian Village*, p. 93.

18 See above.

19 J. Idleman-Smith and Y. Yazbeck-Haddad, *The Islamic Understanding of Death and Resurrection* (Albany, 1981), p. 168; W.M. Watt, 'Suffering in Sunnite Islam', *Studia Islamica* 50 (1979), pp. 5–19.
On these questions as dealt with in Christian theology, see, for instance, the fascinating literary description by James Joyce in *A Portrait of the Artist as a Young Man* (London, 1986), p. 213.
On a theological discussion of children's death in medieval Jewish sources, see: S. Abramson, *Ba-Merkazim uba-tephusoth bi-tekuphath hageonim*, pp. 62–64.

20 Idleman-Smith and Yazbeck-Haddad, ibid., pp. 179–80.

21 Ibid., pp. 168–71.

22 Al-Manbijī, *Tasliyat ahl al-maṣā'ib*, p. 106; Idleman-Smith and Yazbeck-Haddad, ibid., p. 169.

23 Al-Manbijī, ibid., p. 107. The verses discussed are 38–42 in Sūra 74: 'Every soul is a pledge for its own deeds; save those who will stand on the right hand. In gardens they will ask one another

concerning the guilty: "What hath brought you to this burning?" ' [English translation: M. Pickthall, *The Meaning of the Glorious Koran* (New York and Toronto, n.d.)]. On the child's innocence as 'the symbol and model of perfect piety', especially among Muslim mystics, See: Rosenthal, 'Child psychology in Islam', p. 16.

24   Al-Manbijī, ibid., p. 106–7, 108–10. See also above, Chapter 4.

25   Al-Manbijī, ibid., pp.71, 93.

26   Ibid., p. 111. See also Idleman-Smith and Yazbeck-Haddad, ibid., p. 173.

27   See: al-Suyūtī, *al-ḥāwī li-al-fatāwā*, part II, pp. 311–16. On the questioning in the grave by the inter-
rogating angels, sometimes identified as Munkar wa-Nakīr, see Idleman-Smith and Yazbeck-Haddad,
ibid., pp. 41–42.

28   Muḥammad b. Abī Bakr Ibn Qayyim al-Jawziyya, *Kitāb al-rūḥ* (Cairo, 1957), p. 88, and see above,
Chapter 4.

29   Ibn Qayyim al-Jawziyya, ibid.; al-Suyūtī, ibid., pp. 312, 313. See also Idleman-Smith and Yazbeck-
Haddad, ibid., p. 174.

30   Ibn Qayyim al-Jawziyya, ibid.

31   Al-Suyūtī, ibid., pp. 313–14; Ibn Ḥajar al-Haytamī, *al-Fatāwā-fiqhiyya al-kubrā*, part II, p. 30.
Talqīn in this context sometimes means to prepare the dying believer by reciting to him the basic
articles of faith. Sometimes, however, *talqīn* was practised after the believer had died but before his
burial.

32   Ibn Qayyim al-Jawziyya, ibid., p. 87. See also: Rosenthal, 'Child psychology in Islam', p. 15.

33   See above, Chapter 4.

34   Ibn Qayyim al-Jawziyya, ibid., p. 88.

35   Taqī al-Dīn Muḥammad Ibn Taymiyya, *Majmū'at fatāwā* (Cairo, 1326/1908–9), Vol. II, p. 178.

36   The Zaydiyya, one of the Shī'a's branches, arose from the revolt of Zayd b. 'Alī, against the Umayyads
in 740. The Zaydis 'essentially retained the politically militant but religiously moderate attitude
predominant in the early Kūfan Shī'a.' See: W. Madelung, *Religious Trends in Early Islamic Iran*
(Albany, 1988), p. 86.

37   Al-Hādī ilā al-Ḥaqq Yaḥyā b. al-Ḥusayn, *Majmū' min kutub al-Imām al-Hādī ilā al-Ḥaqq* (MS. The
British library, London), Or. 3798, fol. 60a. See also Abū al-Ḥasan 'Alī b. Ismā'īl al-Ash'arī, *Maqālāt
al-Islāmiyyin* (ed. H. Ritter) (Leipzig and Istanbul, 1929–30), pp. 55, 201, 250, 254, and Rosenthal,
ibid., pp. 12–14.

38   'The name of the great theological school which created the speculative dogmatics of Islam'. See:
Shorter Encyclopaedia of Islam, p. 421 (s.v. 'al-Mu'tazila').

39   'The schismatic revolutionary movement arising out of the opposition in 'Alī's Kāfan army to his
arbitration agreement with Mu'āwiyya after the battle of Ṣiffīn (657)'. See Madelung, ibid., p. 54.

40   Al-Ash'arī, ibid., p. 89; Rosenthal, ibid., p. 11.

41   Al-Ash'arī, ibid., p. 111; Rosenthal, ibid., p. 12.

42   Al-Ghazālī, *Ihyā' 'ulūm al-dīn*, Vol. IV, pp. 38–39.

43   Ibn Taymiyya, ibid. For a similar theological dispute in Jewish circles in the tenth century (apparently
under Islamic influence) see: Abramson, *Ba-merkazim uba-tefusoth*, pp. 62–64.

44   See above, Introduction.

45   Abū 'Isā al-Tirmidhī, *Ṣaḥīḥ* (Bulaq, 1292/1875–76), part II, p. 181 (*Kitāb al-tafsīr*, sūra 7); al-Qaysi,
Bard al-akbād, fols. 169b–70a; al-Suyūtī, *al-Iḥtifāl*, fols 5b–6a; al-Manbijami, *Tasliyat ahl al-maṣa'ib*,
p. 70.

46   Al-Bukhārī, *Ṣaḥīḥ*, Vol. II, pp. 315–16, 347. See also al-Qaysï, ibid., fol. 167a; al-Suyūtī, *Fadl
al-jalad fi faqd al-walad* (MS. The Library of the University of Leiden) Or. 474(30) fol. 249b; id., *al-
Iḥtifāl*, fols 5a, 5b, 6a; al-Manbijī, ibid., pp. 67–73. See also versions with four children: ibid.,
pp. 73–77; Ibn al-Jawzī, *Aḥkām al-nisā'*, p. 385.

47   Ibn al-Jawzī, ibid., p. 380; al-Suyūtī, *al-Iḥtifāl*, fol. 6b.

48   See, for example, Abū al-Ḥasan 'Alī b. 'Abbās b. Jurayj Ibn al-Rūmī, *Dīwān* (Cairo, 1973–79), Vol.
I, p. 244, Vol. II, pp. 625, 626; Jamāl al-Dīn Ibn Nubāta, *Dīwān* (Cairo, 1905), pp. 156, 218, 347,
348, 546; L. Cheikho, *Kitāshu'arā' al-nasrāniyya*, part I: *'Fī shu'arā' al-jāhiliyya'* (Beirut, 1920),
pp. 271ff. (al-Ḥārith b. 'Ubād's elegy on his son Bujayr). This elegy is discussed by J.A. Bellamy in
'Some observations on the Arabic *rithā*", p. 48.

49   Al-Manbijī, *Tasliyat ahl al-maṣā'ib*, p. 91.

50   See, for instance, Mālik b. Anas, *al-Muwaṭṭā'*, p. 79; Abū Zakariyā Yaḥyā b. Sharaf al-Nawawī,
al-Masā'il al-manthūra — fatāwā al-Imām al-Nawawī (Beirut, 1972), p. 58; Taqī al-Dīn Ibn Taymiyya,
al-Ikhtiyārāal-fiqhiyya min fatāwāShaykh al-Islām Ibn Taymiyya (Beirut, n.d.), p. 90; al-Manbijī,
ibid., p. 115. Cf. Goitein, *A Mediterranean Society*, Vol. V (Berkeley, Los Angeles, London, 1988),
pp. 173, 174.

51   Suyūṭī, *Faḍl al-jalad*, fol. 248b; al-Qaysī, *Bard al-akbād*, fol. 165b; al-Manbijī, ibid., p. 87.

52   Al-Qaysī, ibid.

53   Al-Qaysī, ibid., fol. 180b; al-Manbijī, ibid., p. 88.

54   Al-Qaysī, ibid., fol. 188b. See also al-Bukhārī, *Ṣaḥīḥ*, Vol. II, p. 328.

55   Al-Qaysī, ibid., fols 188b–189a.

56   Al-Bukhārī, ibid.

57   Al-Bukhārī, *Ṣaḥīḥ, Kitāb al-adab, bāb* 109; Ibn Qayyim al-Jawziyya, *Tuḥfat al-mawdūd*, p. 64.

58   Al-Qaysī, *Bard al-akbād*, fol. 182b.

59   Al-Qaysī, ibid., fol. 189a.

60   Al-Qaysī, ibid., fol. 174a.

61   Al-Qaysī, ibid., fol. 184a.

62   Al-Manbijī, *Tasliyat ahl al-maṣā 'ib*, p. 87.

63   Ullmann, *Islamic Medicine*, p. 73.

64   DeMause, 'The evolution of childhood', p, 17.

65   Al-Qaysī, *Bard al-akbād*, fol. 169a; al-Manbijī, *Tasliyat ahl al-maṣā'ib*, p. 84.

66   Al-Manbijī, ibid., p. 86.

67   Al-Tirmidhī, *Ṣaḥīḥ, Abwāb al-birr, bāb* 11.

68   Al-Bukhārī, *Ṣaḥīḥ, Kitāb al-adab, bāb* 18, and see above, Chapter 4.

69   Al-Manbijī, *Tasliyat ahl al-maṣāib*, p. 82.

70   Al-Qaysī, *Bard al-akbād*, fol. 171b.

71   See, for instance, Ammar, *Growing Up in an Egyptian Village*, Chapter IV, esp. p. 105; Friedl, 'Parents and children', p. 201.

72   See, for instance, Granqvist, *Child Problems among the Arabs*, pp. 90–92.

73   Ṭaha Ḥusayn, *An Egyptian Childhood* (translated by E.H. Paxton) (London and Washington, DC, 1981), Chapter 18. See also Atiya, *Khul-Khaal*, pp. 4, 5, 7, 9, 10, 11, 26–27, 152–53.

74   See below, Chapter 7.

75   Al-Manbijī, *Tasliyat ahl al-maṣā'ib*, p. 90; Le Roy Ladurie, *Montaillou*, pp. 210–11.

76   Al-Manbijī, ibid., pp. 100–101.

77   Al-Qaysī, *Bard al-akbād*, fol. 166a.

78   See above and Chapter 8 below.

79   See above, Introduction.

80   For full details of the manuscript see above, Introduction.

81   Al-Manbijī, *Tasliyat ahl al-maṣā'ib*, p. 78; al-Suyūṭī, *al-Iḥtifāl*, fol. 6a; al-Qaysī, *Bard al-akbād*, fol. 168b.

82   Al-Manbijī, ibid., p. 89.

83   Ibid., p. 106.

84   See above notes 46, 47 and also al-Qaysī, *Bard al-akbād*, fols. 166b–167b, 169b–170a; al-Manbijī, *Tasliyat ahl al-maṣā'ib*, pp. 78, 83, 86, 98, 99, 100, 106.

85   Al-Qaysī, ibid., fols 168a, 168b.

86   Al-Bukhārī, *Ṣaḥīḥ, Kitāb al-janā'iz, bāb* 6.

87   Al-Suyūṭī, *al-Iḥtifāl*, fol. 7a.

88   See below. Chapter 8.

Martha Saxton

INTRODUCTION TO THE FIRST VOLUME OF THE *JOURNAL OF THE HISTORY OF CHILDHOOD AND YOUTH*

T HE EDITORS ARE EXTREMELY PLEASED to offer this first volume of the *Journal of the History of Childhood and Youth*, a publication that owes its existence to the vision and labors of the members of the Society for the History of Children and Youth. Beginning with the first conference in 2001, the Society has organized biennial conferences, published a newsletter, and been the source of innovative monographs and broad works in this important area of study. The Society's decision to launch a journal testifies to the rapidly increasingly richness of this field and, to use an apt figure of speech, how fast it has come of age.

The Society has led the effort to draw attention to the historical relevance and utility of age as a category of analysis. Importantly, the Society has insisted on studying childhood in a global, not western context. The scholars who contributed to this volume have laid out the multiple ways that studying childhood and children around the world gives us unique insights into the values and goals of our own society as well as others. States articulate their hopes and plans most clearly in their ideas about childhood and their programs for children. The discrepancy between a culture's ideals for childhood and its actual provisions, national compromises and failures, also provide significant insights into the particular shapes and forms that childhoods actually assume in addition to giving a measure of any single government's genuine commitment to its children. Our understandings of individual identity formation, the structure of the family, the relationship between the household and the state, as well as a wealth of cultural and social institutions are significantly altered once we focus on the experiences of childhood and youth. Childhood offers a unique perspective on our conceptions of autonomy and agency, since the rearing of children has done so much to shape the social meaning of dependency. International scholars of childhood have challenged very basic Western assumptions such as the idea that human development is inevitably linear and that social change must be based on modern notions of time. They have also called into question the inevitability of the western model of childhood as increasingly "precious," bound to parallel the advent of modernization and a middle class. Other scholars have pointed to the ways children in some societies pass through a variety of institutions and contexts, rather than having a continuous experience in a nuclear family.

Like other new fields, such as women's history and colonial history, the history of childhood and children destabilizes traditional assumptions about what counts as history and who gets counted in making that history. When historians take children and childhood into consideration, new questions and perspectives demand attention. Children's participation in the economy, long seen as exceptional or pre-modern takes on new significance in a comparative, global perspective. Even in the United States, working children were the norm, and only in the 1930s when the depression made jobs so scarce for adults was anti-child labor legislation truly general. Working from the perspective of childhood also gives scholars new ideas about how to think about children's agency, which, like the agency of women, often gets overlooked because of the everydayness of their activities. Additionally, age functions to describe expected processes of maturation and to allot legal statuses and categories of responsibility.

The editors and contributors are aware of the unique difficulties of doing childhood history. The overwhelming majority of children leave no records of themselves. Practitioners are called upon to devise new ways to open doors onto the experience and imaginations of children, and, in the words of one of our contributors, to "both enhance and shake up" history and childhood studies. The study of material culture can greatly aid scholars of childhood, and the *Journal* will include an Object Lesson in every issue, which will exemplify how paying attention to things can shed light on the experience of a child or youth. This issue we begin with Wendy Ewald's arresting portrait of a child refugee from the Democratic Republic of Congo photographed in the British seacoast town of Margate along with an image of his favorite objects.

Contemporary scholars of childhood and youth insist not only on studying children around the globe, but also on bringing multiple disciplines to bear on that study. This interdisciplinary approach, ideally including psychologists, neurobiologists, sociologists, legal experts, literary scholars, to name only a few, will produce a uniquely rich, multilayered knowledge. The editors believe that this cross-disciplinarity gives the field a special utility in providing information and analysis for policy makers. In this first issue of the journal, we have included several pieces that either discuss policy questions or provide information that would be significant in creating policy. We believe that the work of historians and other students of childhood and children is well-positioned to inform those who are creating programs that touch the young, and we will publish in each edition at least one essay that explicitly deals with a question or questions of policy.

The editors are delighted to welcome readers to the first number of the *Journal of the History of Childhood and Youth*. We are happy to be participants in the process of promoting scholarship on children, childhood, and youth, and we are most grateful for all the Society has done to support and encourage this effort.

Chapter 9

Irving E. Sigel

INTEGRATIVE SUMMARY

[...] IMAGE IS AN ELUSIVE CONCEPT that makes it difficult to present a coherent, precise definition. One reason for this difficulty is that the origins of the construct have different intellectual roots and different referents. There is an external image as in a photograph, a drawing, a sculpture. These images can be symbolic or representational. There are internal images, assumptions about the "picture" in the mind. The argument as to the reality of this notion is up for debate (see Barlow, Blakemore, & Weston-Smith, 1990), while other writers on the ontogenesis of the mind make no reference to images (e.g., Carey & Gelman, 1991). With all of this controversy and disagreement, why use the term *image*? Image provides an inclusive metaphor describing views of children who are depicted in many forms and representations. The construct *image* is used as a mental phenomena, such as representations, or perceptions, or as an external representation as in art, music, poetry. It is these different uses and different meanings that enable the observer of the cultural scene in its broadest sense (e.g., artistic, social, intellectual, historical, philosophical domains) to perhaps create an image of childhood. Concern for children's welfare and upbringing is a frequent topic of interest, but it is described or depicted in terms of the medium. The message in the medium is a reflection of the cultural context in which the medium is embedded. Consequently, examining the medium relative to its cultural roots communicates an image of childhood. For example, in many 18th-century English paintings children are depicted as little adults dressed in adult fashions, whereas in folk-art paintings done in the United States during the same period, children are portrayed as doll-like figures. I do not want to carry this analysis too far except to point out that art is one of the ways we, as observers, can infer the images people had of children at that time. Before detailing these observations, it is important to provide some perspective on imagery as a viable construct for analysis. My contention is that as an observer or as a participant in societies and cultures, it is possible to abstract an image of a conception of childhood that, however, may be taken for granted. The reason is that the way children are conceptualized reflects some basic realities.

The interest in image stems from the sense that it provides a useful overarching construct to examine how children are depicted in various knowledge domains. And then the further question: "So what if we know about these variations in perspective of children?" Does such an investigation have scientific or historical value?

As social scientists, understanding how cultures image their children provides a basis for understanding cultural practice and policies for dealing with children. Images of childhood, we argue, help us to define a host of child-related activities. As we begin this journey we ask, again and again, why do we want to use images? On the one hand it can be said to obfuscate issues in trying to understand how different knowledge systems use, or at least convey, a picture of childhood. The images are in fact statements interpreting the real object. Although presented in an external form, it is the viewer who, in the final analysis, makes the interpretation of the meaning of the representation. Not only is the viewer interpreting the representations from his or her own vantage point, but the creator of the image if also interpreting the reality. So we have two interpreters of the social scene of childhood—the creator of the form and its viewer. No representation of an object in any of the aforementioned ways of representing childhood is necessarily isomorphic with another reality. Each viewer constructs his or her own interpretation. My point is that the meaning of the construct *image* has to be ultimately shared so as to have some meaningful dialogue as well as shared cultural interpretations. It is in effect a metaphor which has a broader meaning base than the usual term *concept* that often arouses cognitive associations, whereas *image*, in common parlance, brings forth perception associations (e.g., pictures in the mind), and cognition as well because these pictures are interpreted in a cognitive context, usually the belief system of the observer.

Each of the writers [see original reading] has told his or her tale of images of childhood within a single discipline. Although there was no clear definition of the term in any of the sections, each did proceed to use the construct as a point of entry to examine the way the different disciplines do view childhood. So on a conceptual level we have a database to ask what these discussions contribute to our understanding of childhood.

Each of these fields of knowledge has revealed that conceptions of childhood are not as diverse as one might first imagine. The anthropologist and the psychologist come to understand childhood in the here and now. Each of them discusses the images of childhood in the contemporary scene, whereas in the religious views of childhood, we find descriptions that transcend time and they are embedded in texts. Sander shows how the different discourses by which these images can be approached yield a portrait of children embedded in a theological–moral universe in which children and childhood have a very special place. Religious beliefs have been institutionalized so that they have become one of the most powerful socialization forces. However, in the increasingly secular world of science, little attention is paid to the religious traditions as important socialization agents (Vandenberg, 1992). In fact, there has been little work done in psychology addressing this particular question.

Parents are viewed as the prime socialization agents. The source of the parents' practices are usually attributed to their social status, education, gender, and their personal characteristics. Even when psychologists address parental belief systems, the religious orientation of the parents is overlooked (Sigel, McGillicuddy-DeLisi, & Goodnow, 1992). Religion is not treated as an important source of influence. In the review by Kim and Sigel, no studies were found that investigated the religious conceptions of childhood that played an obvious role in the childrearing practices of adherents. This is not to say that religious imagery is irrelevant. There is minimal interest in the secular society in the western world, although in the United States there is an increase in Christian, and even Jewish, orthodoxy, both of which derive their images of childhood and rules regarding childrearing from religious texts—for Christians, the Christian Gospels as the basic text and for the Jews, the Torah and its derivatives, especially the Shulhan Aruch.

Whether religious imagery is or is not an important perspective is unclear, for it may well be the case that psychologists in particular have overlooked this set of beliefs as being important, at least in the early years. Sander points out which role the imagery of childhood plays in the moral realm as compared to later childhood as investigated in anthropology and psychology. In the religious texts, the messages are presented as narratives or parables reflecting ways children should be or as explicit rules for children's behavior because of the nature of the child or customs and rituals depicting something about children's growth and development. Psychologists present their images of childhood in the form of narratives or grand theories of childhood, as well as by the topics they study with empirical methods. However, the relations between these two components of the field are not necessarily one of mutual interest, but rather, are, at times, antagonistic. Evidence of what images psychologists have of children who carry out empirical, "scientific" studies can only be inferred from the theoretical basis of the research and the methods employed. This was discussed in the analysis of published research in two major journals representing the child development establishment and by referring to some of the major narratives and theories of child development.

In summary, images are manifestations of cultural beliefs and values that define virtually all childrearing practices and also lead to the development of institutions that participate in this process of childrearing. For some societies (mostly Western) governmental policies are usually derived from images of children as functioning and participating in the community. On the one hand, childrearing practices and philosophies reflect social values, expectations, and aspirations for children, whereas on the other hand, images also spark these practices, wishes, and desires for children.

How can it be that there is this twofold function that seems to be contradictory? It is as though we put images in double jeopardy in determining the practices, for example, while still manifesting the image on the other. This dilemma can be resolved when we invoke the notion of the ideal and the real. Images reflect family and social aspirations and appropriate social behavior for children. The efforts to achieve these goals are the instrumental actions that are the overt manifestations of the images of the parent. The degree to which these actions mirror the images of childhood depends on the parents' skill in creating the parental actions that are close to the image in question. My contention is that as an observer or a participant of societies and cultures, it is possible to abstract an image of a conception of childhood that, however, may be taken for granted. The reason is that the way children are conceptualized reflects some basic realities and alternatives are irrelevant, wrong, or unknown.

In the following, I discuss images of childhood from the perspective of religion, using Sander's section as a basis for the discussion, followed by the work of Harkness from anthropology, and finally Kim's report of psychological images as reflected in research journals. I then conclude with a discussion of the implications of their similar concerns and differences with attention to the implications of this state of affairs.

Images of childhood in religion

Sander points out that it is naive to assume one can speak of religion as a unitary belief system. It is more accurate to depict religion as a diverse set of theologies, each with its own belief system. Differences in point of view between these beliefs exist. However, analyses from a religious perspective shows sets of obligations of children that prescribe behaviors, such as "Honor Thy Father and Thy Mother." This becomes an obligation because if it were not commanded, children might not feel obligated to follow it.

The images that are sources of influence may be very explicit for example, the notion that children are born with original sin and only through training and entering into the religious community through baptism and communion can a child be saved from hell and damnation. Every society has some type of conception of the nature of childhood and development that serves the primary purpose of rearing children to conform to the statutes, customs, and practices of a particular society.

Sander states that he has had difficulty in finding explicit descriptions of images of child-hood in the usual reference books he has searched. Nevertheless, his further discussion reveals that every religious theology with a written set of sacred writings does have numerous statements referring to children and childrearing. It may well be a Western expectation that separate tracts should be devoted to children's nature and how to rear and educate them. In many religious tracts, however, there are numerous references, not only to children, but also to the origins of the group. The emergence of the ancestors defined not only their origins but also their relationship to the source, as exemplified by the Adam and Eve story in which this pair was created by a fatherlike figure—God. Embedded in all of these creation narratives is an explicit or implicit description of the relationship of the progenitors to their creator which is often in the form of a parent–child relationship with strictures as to how they should behave vis-à-vis each other as in Adam and Eve. Although no children are readily described in that story, once the spell of the innocence has been broken through Adam's eating from the tree of knowledge, attention is directed toward descendants and therefore, children. From this point on by direction and indirection, the Hebrew Bible and its Christian descend-ants have revealed images of childhood. These images are metaphors for how children and childrearing will be depicted with the avowed purpose of creating a continuity of the people. This developmental narrative, however, is not unique to Hebrews or Christians. Rather, it is a universal requirement of cultures to survive. The more explicit the "rules" are for childrearing, the greater the expectation that members of the group will have the guidance they need to carry out the mandates of the culture for survival. It seems reasonable to argue that explicating with authority the parental controls required for culturally appropriate childrearing and children's relationship to parents and elders in the society is a universal principle varying across societies in form but not in function.

For whatever historical reasons, societies have evolved, each in its own way, creating specific forms of behaviors and beliefs which ensure their survival. In the course of such historical development, it is very likely that the bases for parent–child relationships and methods of parental control and power over children resided initially in the religious belief system of that particular society. This can be documented in the Moslem, Judaic, and Christian traditions, particularly because they each refer to the God figure as Father and humans as their children. Other traditions also use the founding figure of Buddha or Confucius as the source and the authority for defining images of childhood through obligations placed on parents to children. Even though differences within and between these groups in types of imagery may exist, the simple fact is they have something to say about childhood and parenting. Chances are, the "images" of childhood are described in the context of religion because the authority for making pronouncements about social controls of all types, including childrearing resides in the consciousness of the Divine. Thus, the religious establishment, be it a priesthood, a sacred text, or education and training, is in a considerable position of power in establishing the moral bases of parenting. But, the specific rules that are enunciated are the manifestations of the "image of childhood" type of Divine overarching universal religious depictions of the nature of children and prescriptions of how they should be reared so that in their development they will become the embodiment of the culture. Essentially, children enable the culture to become eternal and everlasting if, and only if, they are truly indoctri-nated. This social goal is probably shared by each member of a society. Over and above the socially normal conceptions of children, similar processes are involved at the family level or some kinship unit, depending on the complexity and the homogeneity of the society. Irrespective of locus, concepts of the nature of children and children's development are universal characteristics for human groups and essential to their survival as a culture.

Throughout history, cultures have expressed in verse, song, dance, folktales, myths, and rites images of their origins in creation myths, images of their ancestors, and relationship with the physical and social environment. Ways of living with all of these visible and invisible forces provide images of childhood. The baptism, the first communion, the circumcision of the Moslem boy and the Bar Mitzvah of the Jewish male are each practices that define the child in terms of original sin (baptism), becoming a member of the group by some outward ceremony or educational ceremony depicting membership (circumcision, communion, Bar Mitzvah). Each of these ceremonies makes statements denoting cultural images of child. The infant is either born without sin as in the Moslem tradition, or with original sin as in the Roman Catholic tradition, or as an innocent needing to be educated before he or she can assume his or her rightful responsibility in the religious community, as in the Jewish tradition. At birth, Jewish children are innocents to be reared by their parents and educators as early as feasible. Age 3 was the Orthodox age for learning to read. Thus, we do have events that are not perceived as anything unusual, but that are expected as a natural state of affairs and are taken for granted. I doubt if there is any analysis of these activities by the mass of individuals; maybe philosophers and clergy have a perspective. For most laypeople these activities are just taken for granted like any other natural phenomena.

The scholar's interest in religious derived images stems from a search for a useful, overarching heuristic by which to examine how children are depicted in various knowledge domains. From this approach we come to the problem of validity and consensus. Every observer who comes to view religious texts or practices as representing his or her own theological vantage point, but the religious creator of the image is also interpreting the reality from his or her theological perspective. So we have, for example, a Roman Catholic priest and a Moslem Imam, two interpreters of the social scene of childhood coming from revealed religions that depict the nature of childhood. It is not the action of the child that expresses the image, but rather each of religious leader's view. There is little reason to expect either of the viewers to alter his or her images because each has truth about human nature and its development. My point is that the content of the image is not shared. This poses a problem regarding meaningful dialogue and shared cultural interpretations. There is a strong case for religious participants to disagree because of the differences in their choice.

Social science images: anthropology and psychology

These two disciplines are part of the knowledge domains that perceive themselves as falling within the realm of science. Where religion is a matter of belief based on theological concerns, anthropology and psychology are in the realm of the rational and the objective, wherein the investigators search for knowledge about the human condition with the conviction that their theories and methods will help to enlighten us about the effects of particular childrearing efforts. However, each of these investigators has an implicit image. When we examine the positions each of these fields takes on images of childhood, we find vast differences between anthropology and psychology. Harkness describes the process of observer perspective, not as a rational objective recording of the images various societies have of their children, but rather, of their own unwitting bias or metaphor that guides their observations and interpretations of the human condition they observe. For example, the section by Harkness clearly reveals how anthropologists changed their image of childhood from the 19th-century ethnographies where the child was viewed from the perspective of an abstraction to the current scene where the child is viewed as part of a developmental niche. The developmental niche construct described by Harkness is a broad approach to the study of children in the context of their social–cultural–emotional environment. Psychologists' "images" of childhood vary with their theoretical perspective. The images in some cases are developed in poetic, descriptive language where the whole child and his or her social environment are integrated into a unit. The early work of investigators such as

Barker and Wright (1951) has described children in their natural habitat allowing for a detailed, almost bird's eye view, of the child as he or she saunters through his or her hometown. This form of narrative is found in other studies such as those of Coles (1990) in the many volumes he has written about children (e.g., *The Spiritual Life of Children*). These volumes are one set of case studies of real children in a real world. They are admittedly not presented as scientific studies, but rather as sensitive descriptions of how different kinds of children live. It is a quasi-anthropological study. On the other extreme are scientific theories of children emphasizing a particular aspect of the whole child (e.g., Piaget on intellectual development, Damon on children's social world). In between these two perspectives are the fragmented views of children as described by Kim and Sigel where we found a highly fragmented set of studies (mostly experimental) with little attention paid to the sociocultural psychological world of children. The reader is to assume that the demographic and age-related variables indicate something about children. From these data the reader is left with the observation that he or she, the reader, is not confused; rather, the field of developmental psychology is confused. Even if all of the pieces are put together, the image of the child is like a Deschamps painting (e.g., the "Woman on the Descending Staircase"), rather than a vibrant, living being who has a life, interests, feelings, and who is a product of various kinds of experiences. However, the relation between these components of psychology produce a nonimage of childhood. Take your pick. In fact, the way to approach this diversity is to step back and reflect on the metaphors that members of these various professions and subprofessions use in constructing images of childhood. Harkness described these metaphors that are useful not only in evaluating ethnographic work but they can also be used to evaluate individual scientists. We find psychologists who fall into the mechanistic camp, for example, the behaviorists, or the contextualists (e.g., the social cultural Vygotsky types).

Some reflections on the significance of the study of images of childhood

Given the universality of interest in the child's survival and development, the next topic of interest is: what kind of children are acceptable? What are the requirements for the survival of the ones deemed acceptable? What are the cultural practices that reflect parents' beliefs about how every child develops and of course how their own child grows and develops in every facet of life?

These are the universal concerns of every society and every set of parents within those societies. However, cultures differ in their beliefs and practices vis-à-vis childrearing and assignments of responsibility for particular socialization practices. For example, in most Western countries educational institutions are responsible for intellectual development, whereas religious education may vary from schools to churches. Institutional arrangements may also vary among cultures so that common childrearing practices in general may be more culturally specific at the microlevel, such as literacy training, but at the macrolevel every society will socialize its children into some type of oral, written, or both forms of communications. That parents from many cultural groups hold beliefs on virtually every aspect of a child's physical, social, sexual, and intellectual development has been well documented among anthropologists (e.g., Harkness & Super, 1992; LeVine, 1988; Whiting & Child, 1953), among psychologists (Bornstein, 1991; Goodnow & Collins, 1990; Sigel et al., 1992), and among cultural historians (Ariès, 1962).

Our knowledge about parenting and childhood beyond our own personal experience comes from those disciplines in the social, biological, and behavioral sciences that have elected to focus on childhood as a major foci of study. Two major sources of influence may define how childhood is studied. One determinant is the disciplinary orientation of the investigator, the second is the related theme of the specific aspect of childhood that becomes a major subject of interest. Because children are complex multidimensional organisms living in many different cultures under a wide spectrum of environmental conditions, investigators studying children have an open field as to what and how to frame the research questions they wish to pursue. The choice of the research question will also influence the methods and procedures of study. Psychologists will select different types of issues for study than anthropologists, whereas historians will study questions dealing with social and cultural history. The philosopher of science will raise questions about the paradigms each of these groups study for example, and in so doing will raise questions about the validity and generalizability of the findings. In a way (and pardon the triteness of my analogy), we can think of childhood as the elephant and each of these theories of the human condition focuses on parts of the elephant, and so some never see the whole elephant, whereas others see the whole, but as an individual standing in isolated splendor. Still others see the elephant as an embodiment of a spiritual expression of Divine creation. These questions are addressed either as research questions or questions of dogma and given truths. Some will address the questions of behavior in the social setting, and others relationships between parents and children, whereas others will examine the child at one point in time, whereas still others will look at the course of development. To complicate the issue, the image of childhood then casts its shadow, not only on the larger questions as described earlier, but also on rather specific and narrow questions, such as development of IQ, or peer relations, or the significance of epochs of development.

In effect, there is no consistent image of childhood. To paraphrase Grotberg (1976a) in a prophetic volume she edited entitled, *Two Hundred Years of Children*, substituting the word *image* for her word *attitude*, she wrote:

> There are no attitudes [images] toward [of] children which are or even have been held by all the members of the society at the same time. In fact, there are attitudes [images] held by different groups which are almost totally opposite from each other at any given time. Whether children are inherently good or bad, whether children are chattels or have independent rights, whether children are economic resources or are economically dependent, whether all children are valuable or only those of social status, whether children should be trained or permitted to develop, whether children need restrictions or need advocacy— these conflicting beliefs shape conflicting attitudes [images]. However, there are dominant attitudes which may be identified over the centuries and which shaped many of the institutions or institutional changes over time.
>
> (p. 405)

Summary

Grotberg's description of childhood was presented in the context of the United States (Grotberg, 1976a). For example, when viewing images of child and childhood within various religious traditions, Sander (this volume [see original reading]) writes, "The sources from which we can, directly or indirectly, derive images of the child and childhood in the religious tradition of a people are as varied as they are numerous" (p. 15). Harkness comes to a similar conclusion although through a different analysis. She holds that "images of childhood in anthropology have been viewed through the lens of a primary preoccupation with understanding the phenomenon of culture and its manifestations in human life. Images of childhood, in this context, have both reflected and informed anthropology's changing conceptualization of culture itself" (p. 36). Developmental psychology as a field reflects considerable disarray as to its image of childhood. In contrast to the anthropologist, the psychologist focuses more in the individual, with little or no concept of childhood as a whole. Psychologists, using a physicalist model of science, approach the study of children from two vantage points: (a) children are studies as experimental subjects whose presumed simplistic status provides insight into basic human functions, especially learning; and (b) as providing a prelude to adulthood. As the study by Kim and Sigel shows, contemporary research in developmental psychology focuses on narrow and specific dimensions such as IQ, peer relationships, and so on, with little concern for the culture, the context, or even the setting in which psychological phenomena are studied.

Harkness suggests that these differences among the disciplines and even within disciplines can be explained by resorting to differences in world views, Using Pepper's (1942) concept of *World Hypotheses,* Harkness claims that this approach enables her to classify anthropological findings into each of the metaphors. By so doing, she offers us a way in which to understand the significance of the findings from anthropology. The Pepper metaphorical analysis is appropriate to every field of endeavor because it holds that the epistemological base of the investigator is at the "root" of the problem.

Let us return to the basic question before us, which is, "What accounts for the differences in images of childhood among diverse disciplines and professional groups?" We addressed this question earlier when we concluded that on the macrolevel the images share a common function; namely, that of endowing children with a value for societal and cultural continuity. Over and above that common aspiration, the microlevel of image differences are due to different epistemologies and the practices that these images influence.

References

Aries, P. (1962). *Centuries of childhood: A social history of family life*. New York: Knopf.

Barker, R. G., & Wright, H. F. (1951). *One boy's day: A specimen record of behavior*. New York: Harper & Row.

Barlow, H., Blakemore, C., & Weston-Smith, M. (Eds.), (1990). *Images and understandings*. New York: Cambridge University Press.

Bornstein, M. H. (1991). Approaches to parenting in culture. In M. H. Bornstein (Ed.), *Cultural approaches to parenting* (pp. 3–19). Hillsdale, NJ: Lawrence Erlbaum Associates.

Carey, S., & Gelman, R. (Eds.), (1991). *The epigenesis of mind: Essays on biology and cognition*. Hillsdale, NJ: Lawrence Erlbaum Associates.

Coles, R. (1990). *The spiritual life of children*. Boston: Houghton Mifflin.

Goodnow, J. J., & Collins, W. A. (1990). *Development according to parents: The nature, sources, and consequences of parents' ideas*. Hillsdale, NJ: Lawrence Erlbaum Associates.

Grotberg, E. H. (1976a). Child development. In E. H. Grotberg (Ed.), *Two hundred years of children* (pp. 391–420). Washington, DC: U.S. Department of Health, Education, and Welfare.

Grotberg, E. H. (Ed.). (1976b). *Two hundred years of children*. Washington, DC: U.S. Department of Health, Education, and Welfare.

Harkness, S., & Super, C. (1992). Parental ethnotheories in action. In I. E. Sigel, A. V. McGillicuddy-DeLisi, & J. J. Goodnow (Eds.), *Parental belief systems: The psychological consequences for children* (2nd ed., pp. 373–91). Hillsdale, NJ: Lawrence Erlbaum Associates.

LeVine, R. A. (1988). Human parental care: Universal goals, cultural strategies, individual behavior. In W. Damon (Series Ed.) & R. A. LeVine, P. M. Miller, & M. M. West (Vol. Eds.), *New Directions for child development: Parental behavior in diverse societies* (Vol. 40, pp. 3–11). San Francisco; Jossey-Bass.

Pepper, S. C. (1942). *Word hypotheses: A study of evidence*. Berkeley: University of California Press.

Sigel, I. E., McGillicuddy-DeLisi, A. V., & Goodnow, J. (Eds.), (1992). *Parental belief systems: The psychological consequences for children* (2nd ed.), Hillsdale, NJ: Lawrence Erlbaum Associates.

Vandenberg, B. (1992), Sacred text, secular history and human development. *Family Perspectives, 26*, 405–21.

Whiting, H. W. M., & Child, J. L. (1953). *Child training and personality*. New Haven, CT: Yale University Press.

PART 2

A social construct: Childhood in different times and places

AS ARTICULATED IN PART 1 OF THIS VOLUME, the theory in the 1990s that childhood is a social construct encouraged scholars to look at the multiple meanings of childhood. The goal of this section is to provide an overview of key historical scholarship that contributes to our understanding of how the modern model of childhood varies through time and space. Historical attention to particularism does not imply a focus on the lives of individual children. As historian Colin Heywood states in the introduction to his book on the history of childhood in the West, "What we will be looking for in various societies is some understanding at a theoretical level of what it is to be a child, rather than mere descriptions of individual children."[1]

Generally speaking, the trend in the modern era has been for adults to view children as innocent, in need of protection from adult society, and important for the future of the nation, as well as important in their own right. The years of childhood have extended in length, and, the number of children in families has decreased. This model originated in the West in conjunction with the establishment of systematic and mandatory education, the welfare state, family planning, and the field of pediatrics. Historically, the degree to which children universally experienced the modern model of childhood depends upon the intersectionality of gender, class, race, religious affiliation, disability status, location in international imperial hierarchies, and relation to forces of globalization. In most cases, the conception of childhood in non-western societies either evolved alongside or in the opposite direction of the modern western model of childhood. Even within parts of the West there were similar divergences.

Before introducing the historical scholarship on the variations in the modern model of childhood, let's first have an overview of the modern model's main components, many of which we take for granted today. The modern model evolved in the West. The idea that childhood should be spent in school apart from the world of adults developed largely as a result of the industrial revolution in the West, a growing middle class, Enlightenment thinkers, the Romantics, and competing nationalisms. With industrialization, many western children no longer spent their childhoods in the realm of agriculture learning the necessary skills for adulthood under the supervision of the family. In factories, the streets, and mines, children worked in harsh, unhealthy conditions, often as wage-earners. This reality stood in stark contrast to

Enlightenment thinkers' interest in molding certain children through education and the Romantics' notion of childhood as a carefree period in life.

By the end of the 1800s the humanitarian needs of children outstripped the philanthropic resources of public reformers and care passed to the state, which sought to save children from work in order to ensure future manpower. Hence began the process by which governments created universal, free, mandatory schooling and other institutions, like juvenile courts, geared exclusively for children's well-being. The goal of assisting children in order to create a future citizenry is captured in historian Hugh Cunningham's commentary on state concern for children's rights, "Compulsory schooling was not introduced simply or mainly to try to provide all children with an experience of childhood. It has to be understood in a context of state rivalry, and a worry about the effectiveness of the socialization of children in the reproduction of the social order."[2] Recent scholarship, notably that by historian Lydia Murdoch, emphasizes that private and public welfare institutions were not mutually exclusive, but influenced each other on a number of children's issues.[3]

The development of the field of pediatrics in the nineteenth century also shaped the modern model of childhood. Although medicine had always recognized a set of diseases particular to children, the professionalization of medicine for children meant an increase in institutions (like hospitals) uniquely for children as well as the ability to make professional assessments of children's mental and physical capacities. The latter opened up the door for advancing theories on the origins and causes of children's behavior, psychology, and sexuality. Furthermore, pediatric medicine (such as smallpox vaccines) contributed to a decrease in the mortality rates of children at the end of the nineteenth century. Changing patterns of health and disease have responded to and helped to form conceptions of childhood and adolescence as life stages.[4]

The history of global childhood reveals that the modern model of childhood has in fact multiple meanings. World historian of childhood Peter Stearns articulates, "Even as the modern model of childhood began to be formulated in Western society, in the eighteenth and nineteenth centuries, a quite different set of changes affected children in many other parts of the world."[5] The selection of scholarship presented in this part of the volume makes significant contributions to unmasking the fissures in the modern model of childhood.

Secret Gardens, Satanic Mills is one of the first books of its kind to rethink in terms of gender the traditional narrative of the concept of childhood in European history. The authors find that girls' childhood was conceived of and experienced differently than boys'.[6] While the modern model of childhood entailed increased separation of children from the adult world, adults saw girlhood as a phase in life that required more adult supervision (for reasons of protecting chastity and honor) than boyhood. At the turn of the last century nationalists justified protecting and educating girls not for the girls' future contribution to the nation as citizens or wage-earners, but rather for their centrality to reproduction and their roles as cultural emblems of national purity. The editors of *Secret Gardens: Satanic Mills* make clear that we cannot overlook girls' resistance to the gendering of the modern model of childhood. For example, some European upper-class girls used consumption and leisure practices to create a self-identity beyond that of mere reproducers.[7]

Afsaneh Najmabadi's piece in this part of the volume explores the role that gender played in Iran's early twentieth-century education movement. Iranian reformers valued girls' education so that girls could grow up to be educated mothers who would raise sophisticated citizens. Najmabadi's article presents an example of how cultural conceptions of girlhood in Iran evolved differently from those of boyhood in the turn of the last century. Reforms saw girls as subjects worthy of education because of their future role as educators of children. Najmabadi makes clear that this trend for girls should not be viewed as disciplinary or emancipatory, but rather as transformative.

The economic class in which a child is born plays a significant role in determining the degree to which he/she experiences the modern model of childhood. Jan Kociumbas' chapter about poor, convict children in Australia argues that they were used as cheap labor instead of being educated while incarcerated. She writes, " . . . the children of the poor might be innocent and malleable, but their work potential was far too valuable to be lost in costly, prolonged schooling or unproductive play."[8] Boy juvenile convicts sent to Australia in the 1800s were assigned to farm labor and girls were usually assigned to domestic service and expected to perform sexual services. Australian Aboriginal children under the care of Europeans were also not entitled to a prolonged childhood free from labor and devoted to learning through childish play.[9] These children were seen as a resource to be exploited.

Race is another factor that determines a child's opportunity to be educated and spend a childhood free of the burdens of adulthood. Joseph Illick's book *American Childhoods* interrogates the manifestation of race in shaping childhood in American history, making the point that white Americans used scientific evidence to justify the inferior status inflicted on African-American children. Illick's chapter explores how a child's race determined the type of childhood that society afforded him/her in American history. In the context of African-American children, society often viewed them as uneducable and they had to care for themselves since their parents were forced to work. The prolonging of childhood for learning, which was an essential component of the modern western model of childhood, did not apply to all children universally.

Childhood is addressed by every major religion in the world. The modern model of childhood does not resonate squarely with all the world's religions, which is significant regardless of whether or not a child grows up in a secular society. In the introduction to their edited volume *Children and Childhood in World Religions*, the editors write, "Even if children or their parents are not members of a specific religious community, religion nevertheless shapes them both directly and indirectly through its influence in many areas of cultural, social and political life."[10] The implications of religion on childhood are numerous, from determining rites of passage to setting attitudes towards child-rearing. The introduction to *Children and Childhood in World Religions* allows readers to try to relate the modern model of childhood with the traditions of Judaism, Christianity, Islam, Hinduism, Buddhism, and Confucianism. This selection explores not only the importance of studying how religion shapes childhoods, but also it offers some general points for comparison.

Whether or not a child has a disability impacts adult ideas about what to expect from and offer to a child. In western history, excluding disabled children was often done out of the belief that disabled children were incapable of benefiting from education or that they would transmit their deficiencies to the next generation and so had to be isolated to protect society. Not until the last couple of decades has the state integrated disabled children into institutions associated with the modern model, as is discussed in the case of twentieth-century America by Philip Safford and Elizabeth Safford. This chapter outlines the battle that disabled children in twentieth-century America have had to fight to be afforded the opportunities of the modern model of childhood. The belief that children with disabilities could not learn has meant that the history of these children has involved a disproportionate amount of neglect and abuse.

Colonization and imperialism often worked to move childhood for non-western children in opposite directions from the modern model. The chapter by Beverly Carolease Grier discusses how colonialism in Zimbabwe increased children's participation in the labor force. This was due to explicit recruiting techniques as well as growing rural poverty from whites' appropriation of peasant land. Colonialism actively sought to keep indigenous children out of school and in the labor force. By the end of the nineteenth century, working-class and poor children in England had progressively moved out of the workplace, while children in colonial Zimbabwe filled mining camps.

In the face of modern western imperial control over the world, people in the non-West sought to negotiate and change the confines placed on their societies. In some contexts, indigenous elites in non-western countries resisted European encroachment by embracing aspects of the western model of childhood. For example, in the face of an increasingly imperial world economy dominated by Europeans, Ottoman reformers molded western-style education to suit the Ottoman context, as articulated in the chapter by Benjamin Fortna. Reformers viewed children as surrogates for the nation and sought to make their nations more competitive with the West by reshaping children. The remaking of children's education often involved a delicate balance of making new western ideas compatible with authentic traditions.

Conditions of childhood today are governed not only by local conditions, but also by a world context. Research on globalization and childhood demonstrates that the shift in value (economic to emotional) experienced by western children in the twentieth century has not always occurred in the same way or to the same extent in non-western societies, and even some parts of western societies. In many parts of the world, child labor persists due to a lack of enforced compulsory schooling, a family's lack of resources to invest in schooling, and a will-ingness to accept child labor by the world's elite. Peter Stearns' chapter in this part of the volume looks at the role that globalization has played in shaping how non-western children have experienced the modern model of childhood. While the economic, political, and cultural forces of globalization have facilitated the spread of the western model of childhood, it also has had the impact of dividing the world's children.

The overall statement that global historians make about childhood in world history is that in the non-West the modern model of childhood developed alongside or in the opposite direction of that in the West. It is worth concluding the introduction to Part 2 by encouraging the reader to think about potential alternatives to the prevailing premise of the field. This raises questions about the modern model of childhood as a valid model for comparison. A number of factors have facilitated the ethnocentric tendency to focus on the impact of western trends in the rest of the world, and those factors include missionary education, colonial rule, the develop-ment of international law focusing on setting uniform standards for all children and the strate-gies of international agencies such as UNICEF, the World Bank, and others. At the end of this section, consider if there might be a new set of ideas — besides the tenets of the modern western model of childhood — which historians could use to compare childhoods in time and place.

Articles

10. Najmabadi, Afsaneh. "Crafting an Educated Housewife in Iran," in *Remaking Women: Feminism and Modernity in the Middle East,* ed. Lila Abu-Lughod (Princeton: Princeton University Press and Cairo: American University in Cairo Press), 1998, pp 91–125.

Gender

- What types of sources does Najmabadi use?
- How does Najmabadi show that gender shapes conceptions of childhood? Give examples.
- Why might Najmabadi not think the trend for education was emancipatory for girls?

11. Kociumbas, Jan. "Children in Chains: Juvenile Convicts" in *Australian Childhood.* Australia: Allen and Unwin, 1997, pp 21–37.

Class

- What link does the author show between juvenile labor and class?
- What were the justifications for denying convict children an education?
- How did reformers try to change this?
- How did reformers battle with the economic advantages of employing poor children?

12. Illick, Joseph. *American Childhoods.* Philadelphia, Pennsylvania: University of Pennsylvania Press, 2002, pp 36–54.

Race

- How did child-rearing practices from Africa change in early American life?
- What role did being enslaved play in the making of and the experience of some children?
- What were children's experiences like in the aftermath of slavery?
- In what ways did African-American families persevere despite the obstacles?

13. Browning, Don and Marcia Bunge, eds. *Children and Childhood in World Religions.* NJ: Rutgers Press, 2009, pp 1–14.

Religion

- Why is it important to understand the role of children in world religions?
- Why is it important to understand the social and geographical context of a religion when studying the role of children in that religion?

14. Safford, Elizabeth and Philip Safford. *A History of Childhood and Disability.* Teachers College Press, 1996, pp 286–300.

Disability

- Trace the different ways children have been sorted in school over the last century.
- What is full inclusion?
- How have the lives of children with disabilities changed over time?
- What is the "new history" to which the authors refer at the end of their article?

15. Grier, Beverly. *Invisible Hands: Child Labor and the State in Colonial Zimbabwe.* Praeger, 2005, pp 69–110.

Colonialism

- What challenges were posed to the construction of African childhood in the early decades of colonial rule?
- What were the characteristics of the new colonial construction of African childhood by the end of the First World War?
- How did the boys experience these changes differently than girls?

16. Fortna, Benjamin. "Emphasizing the Islamic: Modifying the Curriculum of Late Ottoman State Schools" in *Enfance et jeunesse dans le monde musulman* edited by Francois Georgeon and Flaus Kreiser. France: Maisonneuve & Larose, 2007, pp 193–209.

Imperialism

- Describe the coexistence of the Ottoman/Islamic mode of education with the western/secular mode.
- In what ways does the author show agency?
- In your opinion, what tenets beyond the western model of childhood might be helpful for comparing childhoods in time and place?

17. Stearns, Peter. *Childhood in World History*. New York: Routledge, 2010, second edition, pp 143–55.

Globalization

- How has globalization impacted conceptions of childhood?
- Do you think that globalization has had a favorable or unfavorable impact on children?

Suggestions for further reading

Bai, L. (2005) *Shaping the Ideal Child: Children and Their Primers in Late Imperial China*, Hong Kong: The Chinese University Press

Bass, L. (2004) *Child Labor in Sub-Saharan Africa*, Boulder, CO: Lynne Rienner Publishers

Briggs, L. (2002) *Reproducing Empire: Race, Sex, Science, and U.S. Imperialism in Puerto Rico*, Berkeley, CA: University of California Press

Campbell, G., Miers, S. and Miller, J. (eds.) (2009) *Children in Slavery Through the Ages*, Athens, OH: Ohio University Press/Swallow Press

Doumani, B. (2003) *Family History in the Middle East: Household, Property, and Gender*, Albany: State University of New York Press

Dwork, D., (1987) *War is Good for Babies and Other Young Children: A History of the Infant and Child Welfare Movement in England 1898–1918*, London: Tavistock Publications

Elman, B. and Woodside, A. (eds.) (1994) *Education and Society in Late Imperial China, 1600–1900*, Berkeley, CA: University of California Press

Evered, E. (2007) An Educational Prescription for the Sultan: Hüseyin Hilmi Pasa's Advice for the Maladies of Empire, *Middle Eastern Studies*, 43 (3), pp.439–59

Fonseca, C. (1989) Pais e filhos na familia popular (início do séc. XX), *Amor e familia no Brasil*, edited by d'Incao, M. and Londono, F. Sao Paulo, SP: Editora Contexto

Gonzalez, O. and Premo, B. (2007) *Raising an Empire: Children in Early Modern Iberia and Colonial Latin America*, Albuquerque, NM: University of New Mexico Press

Gottlieb, A. (2004) *The Afterlife Is Where We Come From: The Culture of Infancy in West Africa*, Chicago, IL: The University of Chicago Press

Helgren, J. and Vasconcellos, C. (eds.) (2010) *Girlhood: A Global History*, New Brunswick, NJ: Rutgers University Press

Hendrick, H. (2003) *Child Welfare: Historical Dimensions, Contemporary Debates*, Bristol: The Policy Press

Hsiung, P. (2005) *A Tender Voyage: Children and Childhood in Late Imperial China*, Stanford, CA: Stanford University Press

Humphries, S., Mack, J. and Perks, R. (1988) *A Century of Childhood*, London: Sidgwick & Jackson in association with Channel Four Television Co.

Jablonka, I. (2004) *Enfants en Exile*, Paris: Editions du Seuil

Klaus, A. (1993) *Every Child a Lion: The Origins of Maternal and Infant Health Policy in the United States and France, 1890–1920*, Ithaca, NY: Cornell University Press

Leinaweaver, J. (2008) On Moving Children: The Social Implications of Andean Child Circulation, *American Ethonologist*, 34 (1), pp.163–180

Markel, H. and Stern, A. (eds.) (2002) *Formative Years: Children's Health in the United States, 1880–2000*, Ann Arbor, MI: University of Michigan Press

Moses, A.D. (ed.) (2005) *Genocide and Settler Society: Frontier Violence and Stolen Indigenous Children in Australian History*, New York: Berghahn Books

Saada, E. (2007) *Les Enfants de la Colonie*, France: Editions de la Découverte

Seth, S. (2007) *Subject Lessons: The Western Education of Colonial India (Politics, History, and Culture)*, Durham, NC: Duke University Press

Wright, D. and Digby, A. (eds.) (1996) *From Idiocy to Mental Deficiency: Historical Perspectives on People with Learning Disabilities*, London: Routledge

Zembrzycki, S. (2007) 'There Were Always Men in our House': Gender and the Childhood Memories of Working-Class Ukrainians in Depression-Era Canada, *Labour/Le Travail*, Fall, 77 (31). Available online: www.historycooperative.org/journals/11t/60/zembrzycki.html

Notes

1   Heywood, C. (2001) *A History of Childhood: Children and Childhood in the West from Medieval to Modern Times (Themes in History)*, Cambridge: Polity Press, p.10.

2   Cunningham, H. (2005) *Children and Childhood in Western Society since 1500*, London: Longman, p.161.

3   Murdoch, L. (2006) *Imagined Orphans: Poor Families, Child Welfare, and Contested Citizenship in London*, New Brunswick, NJ: Rutgers University Press.

4   Goldman, J., Meckel, R. and Prescott, H. (2004) *Children and Youth in Sickness and in Health: A Historical Handbook and Guide*, Westport, CT: Greenwood Publishing Group, p.xiv.

5   Stearns, P. (2010) *Children in World History*, New York: Routledge.

6   Maynes, M. J., Soland, B. and Benninghaus, C. (eds.) (2004) *Secret Gardens, Satanic Mills: Placing Girls in European History, 1750–1960*, Bloomington, IN: Indiana University Press.

7   Maynes, M. J., Soland, B. and Benninghaus, C. (eds.) (2004) *Secret Gardens, Satanic Mills: Placing Girls in European History, 1750–1960*, Bloomington, IN: Indiana University Press.

8   Kociumbas, J. (1997) *Australian Childhood: A History*, Sydney: Allen & Unwin, p.28.

9   Kociumbas, J. (1997) *Australian Childhood: A History*, Sydney: Allen & Unwin, p.2.

10 Browning, D. and Bunge, M. (eds.) (2009) *Children and Childhood in World Religions: Primary Sources and Texts*, Piscataway, NJ: Rutgers University Press, p.3.

Chapter 10

Afsaneh Najmabadi

CRAFTING AN EDUCATED HOUSEWIFE IN IRAN

SEVERAL RECENT WRITINGS ON WOMEN in the turn-of-the-century Middle East have noted the centrality of motherhood and wifehood, particularly their regulation through textbooks of domestic sciences, to the discussions of the notion of "woman" in this period.[1] Whether it is argued that women themselves used this modernization and scientization to improve their status in society, or that the process contained and frustrated the possible feminist potentials of women's awakening, or even that the scientization was a disciplinary and regulatory process that crafted a modern womanhood in contradistinction to a traditional one, these arguments do not adequately deal with the significant shifts that concepts of motherhood and wifehood had gone through to produce this discourse in the first place.

If the well-known argument for women's education—that educated women made better mothers and wives—sounds very traditional and, given our late-twentieth-century sensibilities, reads as a reinforcement of women's old professions, this disappointment perhaps arises from lack of attention to what important shifts in "mother" and "wife" constituted the subtext of that argument.[2] In Persian texts, these shifts in meaning from premodern to modern normative concepts reconfigured woman from "house" (*manzil*) to "manager of the house" (*mudabbir-i manzil*). They were closely linked to the educational debates of the last decades of the nineteenth century and the first decades of the twentieth. The modern educational regimes, deeply gendered from the start, were central to the production of the woman of modernity through particular regulatory and emancipatory impulses that I will review in this essay. Moreover, I hope to demonstrate that these two seemingly conflictive impulses in fact enabled each other's work. For woman, the emancipatory possibilities of modernity and its disciplinary "technologies" were mutually productive.

From "house" to "manager of the house"

Premodern normative concepts of wife and mother can be read through Persian books of ethics that were aimed at producing a perfect Muslim man, as man of God, man of the household, and man of the polis.[3] Although these books vary, there are a number of common points that are at the center of my concern here: that the father, not his wife, was the manager of the household (*mudabbir-i manzil*) and in charge of the discipline and education of the children (sons, more specifically), and that the biological mother was not necessarily and at times not preferably the nurturer and caretaker of the child.[4] These texts were male-authored; moreover, the reader was assumed to be male, and in the section on discipline and management (*siasat va tadbir*) of the household, he was addressed as the head of the household, as the managing owner of property, wives, children, servants, and slaves. The first function (regulation of property) had not only textual priority over the other three; in fact, the other three seem to have been at the service of the first: "The motive for taking a wife should be twofold, the preservation of property and the quest of progeny; it should not be at the instigation of appetite or for any other purpose."[5] The man was given advice on who constituted a good wife ("The best of wives is the wife adorned with intelligence; piety, continence, shrewdness, modesty, tenderness, a loving disposition, control of her tongue, obedience to her husband, self-devotion in his service and a preference for his pleasure, gravity, and the respect of her own family").[6] He was also advised on how to regulate and rule his wives: "Once the bond of union is effected between husband and wife, the husband's procedure in ruling his wife should be along three lines: to inspire awe, to show favor, and to occupy her mind."[7]

Similarly, the section on children was directed to the man.[8] It was the father, not the mother, who was in charge of a child's upbringing. He was the one who named him, chose a wet nurse, and was responsible for his physical and mental development.[9]

Not a nurturer and an educator—like the later mother of late-nineteenth-century Persian texts on women and education of the nation—the motherhood depicted in these treatises resides in the first place in the womb. Although the mother is given a secondary nurturing role in much of the premodern literature on parenting, her primary contribution is to provide the vessel of the womb for conception and prebirth nurturing of the fetus.[10]

Indeed, some of the reformist critical literature of the nineteenth century continued to treat mothering in apparently similar terms. Mirza Aqa Khan Kirmani (1853/54–96), one of the most important critical intellectuals of nineteenth-century Iran, wrote in *Sad khatabah* (One hundred discourses) of five schools in which "every individual man gains his ethics and perfects his temperament and character. The first of these schools is the womb of the mother where the fetus gains the fundamentals of his ethics and acquires those character traits and attitudes that during the term of pregnancy were in the mother, innately or as acquired character. If, for instance, the mother is mean and jealous, whether she was innately so or became so, undoubtedly this character trait will inhere in that fetus."[11] If she was scared of something, had bad or good dreams, or became ill, this experience, Kirmani argued, would be transmitted to the fetus.

The second school was the family. Every suckling child was trained according to the manners and ethics of his family, the closest among them his mother.[12] This was the only place that Kirmani wrote of the mother as an educator for the child, after which he returned to emphasizing the influences of the womb. For instance, he argued that the reason Iranian children were ugly and ill-statured was because at the time of conception the father had not approached the mother with desire and happiness.[13]

Kirmani argued at great length that the first school, the womb of the mother, was the most important and most influential. What traits of temperament and manners entered into the fetus's blood was very difficult to change. It was for this reason that one had to be considerate toward women and have regard for their rights. He argued that when the time came for people to address their oppressors and complain, the son would seek his rights against the father who had failed to take him to school to learn sciences and skills and techniques and crafts and manners and ways of humanity. In contrast, the fetus in the mother's womb would ask why she had taken it to mourning sessions and cried so much for the dead *imams* and their relatives, instead of taking care of it in happiness and kindness.[14] Notably, Kirmani suggested that the wife would interrogate the husband about why he had not treated her as a companion and helpmeet, why he had made her dumb, deaf, and blind, deprived her of all rights of humanity, and buried her alive in a house, forcing her to take refuge in tricks and guile. The husband, on the other hand, would complain that the wife, instead of being a companion in life, had ruined his life with trickery.[15]

Despite some similarities between Kirmani's nineteenth-century *Sad khatabah* and a premodern text like Tusi's thirteenth-century *Akhlaq-i Nasiri*, these works differ vastly. Whereas Tusi wrote as a Muslim philosopher for other Muslims and was concerned with the production of the perfect Muslim man, the author of *Sad khatabah* spoke of himself as an Iranian (*man-i Irani*),[16] concerned with the sorry state of the Iranian nation (*millat-i Iran*). He considered his ideal reader to be not a Muslim man in search of this-worldly and other-worldly perfection but an Iranian man concerned with the fate of Iran.[17] The perfect man had changed from a Muslim believer to an Iranian citizen.

The continuities and discontinuities of Kirmani's concept of mother and wife with Tusi's are worth pointing out. To envisage the womb not simply as a vessel but as a school (*maktab*) imputed all the disciplinary and regulatory functions of school to the womb. Not only did the bearer of the womb regulate the character of the fetus, but now the regulatory process turned back upon the womb/woman. National formation began with the womb. If differently constructed Iranians were to be produced, woman as potential mother needed to be regulated and reconstructed. But the new notion of schooling also heralded new rights: because of the womb's central importance, "one needs to pay special attention to and care for women and their rights so that children will not become ill-tempered and bad-natured."[18] In Iran, however, Kirmani argued, "women are deprived of all rights of humanity and are forbidden the pleasures of life. . . . Iranian women are treated as lower than animals; nay, they are less valued than the dogs of Europe and the cats of cemeteries."[19]

Thus in Kirmani's rearticulation of premodern wisdom, the womb became the ground at once for regulatory practices toward women and for awarding women particular rights. This double movement, combining disciplinary techniques and emancipatory promises, becomes a general feature in the rethinking of gender in the Iranian modernist imagination. I will discuss its workings on several levels later in this essay, but here I want to point out the enabling dynamic of this double movement. It is by no means the case that the two strands of this movement simply contradicted and frustrated one another. Rather, the disciplinary and emancipatory movements enabled each other's work; in this particular case, a newly envisaged womb produced the regulatory and emancipatory drives at once in order to produce children worthy of modernity.

Woman was also reconfigured as wife: she was to be man's companion in life. Kirmani argued at length against gender segregation and against the veil, which in his opinion not only failed to guarantee a woman's chastity but constituted a severe hindrance to her belonging to humanity and her attainment of education and knowledge. It had reduced half of the Iranian people to a paralyzed, enchained state of ignorance with no ability to render any service to society. Rules of segregation also deprived men of the beneficial effects of socializing with women. Kirmani held these restrictions responsible for pederasty in Iran.[20] Moreover, he argued that men and women married without having known or even seen each other and thus began their married life, more often than not, with dislike—if not hatred—from the first night of marriage when they would finally set eyes upon each other.[21]

In another work, *Hasht bihisht*, most likely coauthored with Shaykh Ahmad Ruhi around 1892 as an explication of Babi religion, Kirmani had expressed similar but more radical views.[22] The authors of *Hasht bihisht* argued strongly against parents' forcing their children to particular choices of spouse, and for the need of men and women to choose their own mates willingly and get to know each other for several years during their engagement. They also spoke of the equality of women and men in the pleasures, benefits, and rights of marriage, and of the necessity that women be educated in all sciences, skills, crafts, and ethical matters. They argued for the removal of the veil, but at the same time, to prevent sin, evil, and fornication, they prohibited women from talking to men who were strangers to them.[23] They emphasized women's comprehensive equality with men and recommended that men include women as their left hand in all activities so that both hands could work equally. Furthermore, they linked the social lot of women, through motherhood, to the fate of humanity. In other words, motherhood became a mediating term between two concepts central to modernity: progress and women's rights. "Women's *hijab* (veil) and *tura* (laced face cover), their segregation from men, and their loss of all rights of humanity such that they are not even counted among human beings cause great corruption in the world of humanity, because this delicate kind constitutes children's early education. They are the teachers in the household and the fountainhead of all progress for humanity."[24]

This argument differentiates a modernist work such as *Hasht bihisht* from earlier books of advice and ethics. Instead of being part of the household—in fact, sometimes collapsed into the household and referred to as the household (*manzil*)—and subject to the man's management, woman has become the manager of household affairs and the educator of children.[25] Moreover, Kirmani and Ruhi continued to press their argument to full equality of men and women:

> Because of the ill ways men have treated them and have placed them outside the domain of humanity, half of the world of civilization and urbanity has remained unused and without effect. But the world of humanity cannot reach for perfection unless women become equals and partners with men in all affairs and rights; in fact, human traits are much more perfect in women compared to men. . . . in all rights including learning and education, government, inheritance, industries, and commerce women must be equal to men. . . . This decree is for the reform and education of women, to bring them out of the terror house of darkness and ignorance into the open field of the city of humanity and civility. Undoubtedly because of this decree the world of humanity and civility will double in size.[26]

Educational regimes

Few, if any, of the nineteenth-century reformers would call for such radical gender parity as Kirmani and Ruhi did. But by the first decade of the twentieth century, in articles in the constitutionalist press, the argument that women should be educated because they were educators of children, companions of men, and half of the nation had gained wide currency and was reiterated as a matter of obvious fact—"like the sun in the middle of the sky."

Hasht bihisht's concept of an ideal educational regime was exceptionally severe: "Children should be taken away from mothers upon birth and taken to a house of education to be brought up under the supervision of skilled teachers and clever women (*zanan-i shatir*) who, in appropriate schools, have studied especially the science of education and upbringing of children."[27] The authors drew on a manufacturing analogy to demonstrate their meaning. Such schools were like a factory that took in as raw material bits of wool and produced delicate fabric.[28] This became a common metaphor even in writings of reformers who did not advocate such a radical break. Schools were often referred to as human-making factories (*karkhanah-'i adam'sazi*), bringing the transformative and regulatory punctuations of modern production onto human beings. That many writers found this metaphor apt reflects how vastly the concept of education that they were advocating differed from what it sought to replace. The education of men and women in premodern institutional and informal settings of mosques, Qur'anic neighborhood schools, or in the home, could hardly be compared to an orderly regulated manufacturing process.[29]

Not only the educational regime and institutions but the very concept of knowledge was consciously formulated in contradistinction to older concepts of knowledge.[30] In *Sad khatabah*, Kirmani contrasted the concepts of science/knowledge (*'ilm*) of religious scholars (*'ulama'*) with that of chemistry, politics, law, political economy, and natural sciences, arguing that "any nation that is more civilized has higher sciences, vaster needs, and higher means."[31]

Whereas in premodern texts knowledge pertained to man's perception of God and his rules,[32] modern knowledge pertained to issues of civilization and progress. The nineteenth-century writers took pains to distinguish their concept from the older "order of things."[33] Zuka' al-Mulk, editor of *Tarbiat* (Education)[34] felt obliged to make this distinction explicit: "If in this newspaper we speak of the weakness of science and the lack of learned men, this has nothing to do with the science of religion and guiding learned men. . . . Undoubtedly religion and faith supersede all else . . . and our learned men . . . are suns in the heaven of truth and stars of the sky of guidance,"[35] He then went on to emphasize, however, that "the point is that the order of the day of Resurrection (*nizam-i kar-i mu'ad*) depends on the order of making a living (*intizam-i amr-i mu'ash*) . . . and of course the country, in order to put in order the affairs of this world, needs arithmetic and geometry and algebra and calculus and analysis and medicine and rules of agriculture and commerce and many other things. For instance, if we want to build a dam or construct a bridge or cure an ill person, would it be correct to go to a learned man of religion?"[36]

Another significant shift was the emergence of a concept of education that had become centered on literacy. The authors of *Hasht bihisht* considered "reading and writing . . . [as] self-evidently the basis for prosperity of any group of people and the key to all progress in the world."[37] Emphasizing literacy as central to the new education, Zuka' al-Mulk wrote, "Whoever cannot read, cannot know, and if he does not know, how can he be a capable person?"[38] This emphasis on reading and writing is related to the shift from a largely oral culture, supplemented with a calligraphic writing tradition, to a print culture.[39] Whereas in the old system of knowledge, it was conceivable that one might become knowledgeable without being literate if one had a powerful and well-trained memory—a cherished quality[40]—the new knowledge could be attained only through reading and writing.[41] Reading now became distinct from reciting—though in many languages such as Persian and Arabic the same word continues to be used for both. Zuka' al-Mulk referred to the ability to read and write as "the key to prosperity and happiness (*kalid-i sa'adat*); nay, it is its elixir (*kimia-yi sa'adat*)."[42] *Kimia-yi sa'adat*, once totally associated with the sciences of religion (the title of the Persian version of Ghazali's *Revival of Religious Sciences (Ihya al-'ulum al-din*) is *Kimia-yi sa'adat*), now had come to be defined as the skill of reading and writing.

It is noteworthy that the nineteenth-century educational treatises, though addressed to men, were not addressed to them as private men, as fathers of the household in their responsibility to educate their sons—as, for instance, *Akhlaq-i Nasiri* had been. Education was now a national concern. It was for the sake of national progress and as a public duty, rather than for individual perfection or as a religious obligation, that the new education was urgently needed. It was thus expected that *the government* would undertake the task. After prophets sent by God to educate people, one writer argued, the task of education fell upon "people in charge and the wise men and kings."[43] The educational duties of the government were to be supplemented by those of private persons of means, not as heads of households but as men of the nation, as citizens: "It is incumbent on any patriot of means and on all powerful lovers of the nation to spread as much as possible these good methods [of education] and to guard the means of universal education (*tarbiat-i 'ammah*)," Mirza Taqi Khan Kashani wrote.[44]

It was within these more general debates on education that girls began to creep in as subjects worthy of being educated. In a significant departure from premodern texts, Kashani's essay, for instance, ended with a section that was addressed to fathers and mothers and called for the education of girls as well as boys: "Teach your children, sons and daughters, science and obedience."[45]

The difference gender makes

In addition to their appearance as subjects worthy of education, girls also began to appear next to boys as characters in books designed for the education of the young. A book of parables from 1876 has as many female as male characters in its stories.[46] Designed to highlight good and bad character traits, the stories are thoroughly gendered: those with boys as central characters teach lessons about what character traits were desirable in little boys, and those with female characters construct the desirable character traits for girls. In one parable, Mas'ud's New Year's present to his parents is to demonstrate that he can read any text they choose.[47] A frivolous little girl, Kawkab, is disliked by everyone because she is undisciplined and shameless, laughs a great deal for no reason, opens her mouth in front of people and makes awful noises, runs around and pays no attention to others, does not greet people properly, talks nonsense, eavesdrops on others' conversations, and so forth. In contrast, the four-year-old exemplary girl, Khawrshid Khanum, is impeccably obedient and well-mannered. Everyone likes her; she gets up in the morning with her parents without a fuss, dresses herself up, cleans herself, performs her ablutions, and prays. She spends her whole day doing only good things, plays by herself contentedly, does not bother adults, does not meddle, is already in a Qur'anic school and can read the Qur'an and other texts, and does nothing without her mother's permission. The tale ends happily: Kawkab, despite her many defects, is a very smart girl and decides to become friends with Khawrshid Khanum and to learn everything from her. Kawkab reforms and becomes well-liked.[48]

This pattern of moral construction continues throughout the book. Desirable moral traits for boys include being content with life, generosity, not being prone to anger and cruelty, knowing one's manners, being God-fearing and charitable, honesty, and pursuit of sciences and higher education. For girls, they include tidiness, being obedient to one's mother, not hiding anything from one's parents, lack of arrogance, hard work, and learning womanly crafts. One girl, in addition to learning her knitting, sewing, needlework, and embroidery, learns reading, arithmetic, and "the prices of everything." This proves useful since she keeps account of her mother's little sewing and embroidery business. When she loses her mother at the age of eleven, she is already a competent businesswoman and brings one of her aunts to manage household affairs so that she can take care of the business with peace of mind.[49]

Unlike the bulk of the book, which according to the author was a translation/adaptation from Arabic of an originally French text, the epilogue concerns only young men.[50] It was written by the author himself and titled "On Manners of Talking, Movement, and Eating." In a remarkable cultural shift, the epilogue serves to buttress the gender hierarchies that might have been interrogated by the previous tales. Now the young man is advised to avoid, insofar as is possible, talking to commoners, children, women, and mad or drunk people.[51] He should not walk moving his arms and shoulders, as do women and hermaphrodites.[52] The famous wise man Luqman appears as an interlocutor, advising "his son" not to trust women, not to tell his secrets to women and children, and not to adorn himself as women do.[53]

Another figure of wisdom, Abuzarjumihr-i hakim, advises his pupil that what ruins greatness is meanness in rich people, arrogance in 'ulama', shamelessness in women, and deceit in men.[54] In answer to the question, "Could anyone become fortunate through another person?" he responds, "Man through God, child through father and mother, and wife through a good husband."[55] Thus, through a parallel construction, the wife is placed in the same relation of subordination to her husband as man to God and as children to parents. Despite the epilogue, however, the text is novel for its inclusion of girls as subjects of specific educational attention, unlike the corresponding chapters in *Akhlaq-i Nasiri*, for instance, where the child was evidently, if unstatedly at first, a son.

Other educational texts of the period similarly include girls while clearly marking gender distinctions and hierarchies within that inclusion. *Ta'lim al-atfal* (Teaching children), a teacher's manual on how to teach the alphabet more efficiently through new techniques, has drawings depicting both boys' schools and girls' schools, all pupils properly seated behind desks; however, whereas the boys are all sitting on chairs, the girls are squatting on the floor, behind low desks.[56] After instruction in the alphabet, numerals, and months and years of the zodiac system, a male character, Mirza Muhammad, is used to teach prayers, followed by a female character, Fatima Khanum, to teach fundamentals of religion and the names of the twelve Shi'i Imams.[57] Subsequently, Mirza Muhammad sets an example by becoming a prayer leader for his classmates. Fatima Khanum invites her classmates on a Friday to play with dolls and to sew and "thus they learn the science of housekeeping and the necessary arts."[58] In a second volume, the students are taught poetry, geography, and arithmetic. Notably, there are no girls in the second volume.

The encouragement to include girls in the new educational regime became less ambivalent by the turn of the century. In a cautious statement, Zuka' al-Mulk, after reiterating that the education of children was the key to everything else, noted that this had to start with fathers and sons, but he went on to say that, "God willing, the turn for mothers and daughters to be educated will also come, since experienced scientists and skilled educators have said that the bulk of the education of children is in the hands of mothers. . . . It is evident that daughters like sons need teachers . . . but for now we should pay attention to more urgent matters and reforms."[59] Following this brief remark on daughters' and mothers' education, the paper received and published a piece by no less a personage than Hajji Sadr al-Saltanah, the minister of general welfare (*favayid-i 'ammah*).[60] After a brief introduction, the author quotes Napoleon to the effect that one must try harder for girls' education than boys', since girls (as future mothers) aid our dear children and lay the foundation for children's education.[61] He continues, "In Europe, girls' schools are separate from and not mixed with boys'. In India, in one of the schools for girls that is built from the charitable deeds of Suhrabji Shahpurji, I saw Zoroastrian girls who shone like stars from the light of science. I went to another school built by Manikji Khawrshidji. Girls were learning crafts and were skilled in sewing." He then expounds on the bad conditions of Iranian women, because they have no literacy skills (*savad*) and are ignorant of any crafts and arts, whereas even ugly women of Europe are moons in the sky of perfection, because of the holy spirit (*ruh al-qudus*) of science.[62]

Comparison with Europe also provided an important subtext of Talibuf's *Kitab-i Ahmad*, one of the most influential books on education in late-nineteenth-century Iran.[63] In the preface, Talibuf speaks as a concerned citizen of Iran. In the book he takes on the voice of a father, tutoring his son, Ahmad. The triple position of citizen/father/tutor allowed Talibuf to write the book not only as a treatise on education but as a modernist text on Iran's sociopolitical problems and how to overcome them. The book was explicitly modeled after Rousseau's *Émile*. Yet the differences are significant. In the eighth chapter of the first book, the author notes that while in much of the introductory section Ahmad has been echoing

Émile's conversations, one must adapt the conditions of the Western Émile (*Imil-i maghribi*) to those of the Eastern Ahmad (*Ahmad-i mashriqi*).[64] The central problem informing the book is not how through a model education to resolve the conflicts between the natural and the social man; rather, it is how to overcome the disparity between the innate giftedness of Iranians and their current state of ignorance and idleness. In other words, how through a scientific education to produce a competent and patriotic citizen. Unlike the solitary Émile, Ahmad has two brothers and two sisters. Through comparison with the experience of the older brother, Mahmud, who has attended the old school system, Talibuf constructs the difference that his proposed educational methods represent: Ahmad is first tutored at home by his father—the narrator of the book—and later, in the second volume, he is sent to one of the new schools. In the third volume, he has already earned an engineering degree and has authored many books. He has become a model scientific citizen. The depiction of the two sisters, Zaynab and Mahrukh, constructs the gender difference. They are childish and playful; at times they are reprimanded by Ahmad for their unbecoming behavior or their ignorance; they are in awe of their smart brother's scope of knowledge. Yet as spectators to Ahmad's various experiments at home—through which he is learning scientific reasoning—they occasionally get to ask a question or offer him a helping hand, confirming his superior knowledge and status while making the point that girls are also eager to learn something. Surprisingly, although at several points Talibuf notes that in "civilized countries" both women and men are educated, there is nothing in these three volumes about the daughters' education.[65] In fact, by the third volume, where Ahmad speaks as an adult model citizen, Mahrukh and Zaynab have totally disappeared. This tension in Talibuf's text is worthy of further consideration. Talibuf presents rather negative judgments about European women and gender relations. He writes with disdain and disapproval of women's wearing low-cut dresses, putting on makeup, and going to dances.[66] The paradox of his noting women's education in "civilized countries" yet not advocating it for Iran perhaps stemmed from this moral anxiety.

Educating educators of the nation

The issue of women's education received its first full, detailed attention with the publication in 1900 of a partial translation/adaptation of Qasim Amin's book, *The Liberation of Women*, only a year after its Arabic publication in Cairo.[67] A number of chapters were translated by Yusuf Ashtiani (I'tisam al-Mulk) and published under a significantly different title, *Education of Women* (*Tarbiat-i nisvan*).[68] Amin's status as an Egyptian Muslim thinker served to authorize the publication of the first full-length book in Persian devoted to advocacy of women's education. In his preface, Ashtiani notes that not only had European thinkers composed books on the subject of women's education and its importance, but a group of famous Egyptian writers had also written extensively on women's rights and the necessity of their education.[69] But, he continues, there were still no books in Persian that would uncover the benefits and harms of women's education, and it was for this reason that he has translated a number of the chapters from *The Liberation of Women*. His selectivity is worth noting. Not only is the second chapter, "Women and the Veil," completely eliminated in Ashtiani's adaptation, but the final paragraph of the introductory chapter is changed. Amin wrote,

> Were women's socialization effected in accordance with religious and moral principles, and were the use of the veil terminated at limits familiar in most Islamic schools of belief, then these criticisms would be dropped and our country would benefit from the active participation of all its citizens, men and women, alike.[70]

Ashtiani changes it to the following,

> Provided education of women is carried out according to fundamentals of our solid religion and rules of morals and manners, and with due regard to conditions of *hijab*, we will reach our goal, bitter conditions will be behind us, and sweet days will emerge.[71]

Whether he modified Amin's proposition to avoid the kind of reception this book had received in Egypt, or because this reflected his own stance on the issues of veiling and gender segregation at this time, the selectivity and adaptation, as well as the change in the book's title, point to two important conclusions. First, for him and other Iranian reformers of this period, the central target of reform regarding women's status was women's education. On this there was a strong consensus. Second, no fixed connection existed between the issue of veiling and women's education. While some, such as Mirza Aqa Khan Kirmani, considered the veil and gender segregation as signs of backwardness and impediments to women's progress, other reformers, such as I'tisam al-Mulk and Talibuf, considered the veil and gender segregation customs worthy of respect and preservation.[72] Similarly, in the writings of women on education from the end of the nineteenth century onward, there was no single position on the issue of unveiling among the women who worked for education. Muzayyan al-Saltanah, a tireless educationalist, publisher and editor of one of the most important early women's journals, *Shu-kufah* (1914–18), vehemently opposed unveiling and wrote in her journal against women's abandonment of *hijab*. At the same time, she published essays and poetry by women such as Shams Kasma'i and Shahnaz Azad known for their alternative views.[73]

For Kirmani and Ashtiani, as much as for Amin, the central conviction was that the "evidence of history confirms and demonstrates that the status of women is inseparably tied to the status of a nation."[74] The progress of the nation was seen as dependent on the progress of women.[75] And if the country's backwardness as compared to Europe could be overcome through the acquisition of sciences and a new kind of education, then the conditions of women could also be improved in a similar move.[76] Women's education was now perceived as the most fundamental step in the nation's quest for civilization. As we come to the first years of the twentieth century, we encounter the argument that women's education should be given higher priority than men's, since from educated women would arise a whole educated nation.

From the very beginning, women's education was seen as distinct from men's education. Once the domain of the man of the polis had expanded into the national community, this man of the nation, unlike the man of *The Nasirean Ethics*, could no longer be expected to be in charge of both national politics (*siasat-i mudun* having become *siasat-i mamlikat*) and management of the household (*tadbir-i manzil*). Woman was now to become his helpmeet, to become the manager of the household (*mudabbir-i manzil*), instead of being subject to his management. Like the transformation of the womb from a vessel to a school, the transformation of woman from house to manager of the house was at once a regulating and an empowering moment. The regulatory and disciplinary regime of modern sciences was to come to bear on woman's daily life activities. Whereas the man was to be educated in the new sciences to be up to the tasks of national politics, economics, and modern industries, the woman was above all to be educated in the science of home management:

> [A] woman cannot run her household well unless she attains a certain amount of intellectual and cultural knowledge. She should learn at least what a man is required to learn up through the primary stage of education. . . . It is important

for a woman to be able to read and write, to be able to examine the basis of scientific information, to be familiar with the history of various countries, and to be able to acquire knowledge of the natural sciences and of politics. . . . [A] woman who lacks this upbringing will be unable adequately to carry out her role in society or in the family.[77]

Transformation of the wife from household to manager of the household required the breakup of female homosociality within that space. Whereas previously female homosociality was seen as a threat to male bonding, a disruption of the world of men, of the relation between men and between man and God, now it would pose a threat to the orderly management of the household, which required the wife to regulate her female servant instead of chatting, socializing, and solidarizing with her. This was explicated at some length in the literature that advised women on how to deal with their servants.[78]

Family itself was now reenvisaged. Socially, it became relocated in relation to the national community, rather than in relation to other kin groups and families: "[T]he family is the foundation of a country," and within the family, woman as mother was the foundation. As such "her intellectual development or underdevelopment becomes the primary factor in determining the development or underdevelopment of the country."[79] This reconfiguration gave new meanings to motherhood. A mother was no longer merely the vessel for the growth of the fetus; her nurturing and educating roles became more important and began to over-shadow her function as a womb. Mothering came to be defined as nurturing and educating. In fact, she was now to mother the country. Unlike the situation in the Nasirean household, in which the father was fully in charge of the children's upbringing, now the mother acquired the primary responsibility.[80] Maternal ignorance was now seen as the prime reason for troubles of all kinds.[81] Women's education was therefore oriented toward the upbringing of an educated (male) citizenship. This was not a call "for equality of education for men and women," but for "the possibility for boys and girls to have a comparable educational experience throughout the primary stage."[82]

The envisaging of the family as the foundation of the nation, as standing for a building block of the nation, also meant reenvisaging relationships within it. Ignorant women were not only unsuitable as mothers but also unfit as spouses: "An educated man likes order and a systematically arranged home. . . . When a man finds his wife in this ignorant condition, he quickly despises her."[83] In place of the Nasirean awe of wife for husband, in an evident hetero-sexualization of male homosociality, a sentiment comparable to friendship between men was proposed to constitute the right bond between husband and wife: "Friendship provides us with a good example of the power of true love between individuals."[84] This was yet one more reason for women's education: "A man and woman whose upbringing and education differ cannot experience this type of love."[85]

Unlike the original publication of the Arabic text in 1899, the translation and publication of Amin's book in Persian in 1900 did not become an occasion for public debate on the education and status of women. The publication was well received among reform-minded intellectuals but does not seem to have provoked counterarguments.[86] There were occasional articles that obliquely talked of women's education.[87] More explicitly, a serialized article in the Calcutta-published journal *Habl al-matin* argued extensively along the same lines as Amin's book. It emphasizes women's lack of education as the cause of a nation's decline and misfortune, expresses its regret that "we Muslims have neglected this important matter and have done nothing to educate our women," and asks, "How could any people hope for progress if their women who constitute the first teachers and educators of their children are captives in the realm of ignorance?"[88] A subsequent section gives four reasons why education of women would benefit men: (1) children's education would become perfect because both parents would be working on it, (2) children's gifts would become evident at an earlier stage of life, (3) today's men are educated, but they are stuck with uneducated wives; children thus receive contradictory training and education from their fathers and mothers, which produces problems in their education, and (4) every nation's civilization is dependent on women's and men's education, since men and women need to live and socialize together.[89]

Education of women is also linked in this article to the imperial power of Europeans: "But even in household management women of Europe and America have surpassed those of Asia. A European household gives cause for envy to an Asian king's palace. The good order of household objects and the pleasantness of the rooms . . . competes with the gardens of paradise. . . . Husband and wife, like body and soul, provide each other with comfort of life and happiness of soul. They assist and love each other. . . . Nations that have mothers like European women can conquer other lands and rule over other nations."[90] In the East, however, women are kept ignorant yet expected to fulfill three immense tasks: to keep their husbands happy, educate their children, and manage the house. This is beyond their ability. How can a woman who is ignorant of her tasks and her husband's rights manage to satisfy him, especially if the husband is a man of science and a master of an art? Their pairing is like putting a parrot and a crow in the same cage.[91] Most interestingly, women's role in the house is projected as paralleling that of men in social affairs and national politics. In fact, for man to be able to be the good citizen, woman must be a good household manager: "Woman's role in the management and order of the house and in supervising its income and expenditure is like that of a minister of the land. . . . The well-being of the family and supervision of rights of the people of the household and the general direction of the household belong to the mistress of the house. Men who are in charge of the big affairs of the world cannot spend their valuable time in these small matters."[92]

These discussions do not seem to have produced immediate results in terms of furthering women's education. Three and a half years later, another series of articles in the same journal, entitled "Rights and Liberties of Women," referred to Qasim Amin as a pioneer of women's education and reviewed the attacks against him and the debates of that time in the Egyptian press. It noted the translation of his book by Mirza Yusuf Khan I'tisam al-Mulk into Persian, its publication in Tabriz, and its favorable reception in Iran, expressing regret that in Iran, unlike other Islamic countries, nothing but talk had come of it all.[93]

As in Egypt, as Omnia Shakry shows (chapter 4 in this volume [see original reading]), the conceptual shifts in meaning of "wife" and "mother" found their more immediate effect in projections of a new kind of mother and wife in texts on child rearing. One such text was *Tarbiat-i atfal* (Rearing of children).[94] Whereas there were no assumptions in the premodern texts that the biological mother and the breast-feeder of the child should be one and the same person (in fact, the child was to be entrusted to a wet nurse upon birth), the author of *Tarbiat-i atfal* argues that "a mother who entrusts her child to someone else upon birth has taken away from herself half of the label 'mother' and should thus not be called a mother. What is better and lovelier and more suitable than a mother looking after her own children? But some mothers prefer to leave this job to others and engage in useless leisure activities. This is the result of bad education that these mothers have received from their forebears."[95] The author regrets that mothers are ignorant of motherly skills and promises that if "women, instead of learning useless arts, would spend their time learning how to look after their children, how to dress them with ease and handle them safely, how to feed them to ensure their health, how to exercise them," soon wonderful results would emerge.[96]

While the mother, rather than the father, is now the person addressed in a text on the upbringing of children, the child remains a male child. She is to mother sons of the homeland (*abna'-i vatan*). After some introductory remarks about the relationship between physical and mental health, the author, quoting Montaigne, recommends that children should be kept away from things that would make them female-tempered and turn them into beautiful youth. They should instead become strong young men; if children were brought up in comfort and ease, they would not become men.[97]

The book is composed of three parts: on physical upbringing, mental upbringing, and on (wet) nurses. In chapter 1, we are told that the health of a newborn depends on things prior to birth, such as the state of intercourse between husband and wife, the conditions of marriage, their age, manners, and other qualities. Subsequent chapters give advice to pregnant women on how they should dress, eat, move, wash, and bathe, on the state of their feeling, and on sexual intercourse during pregnancy. Other chapters cover in detail such topics as hygiene of the newborn, effects of cold and heat on the newborn, clothing of the newborn, how to put it to sleep, and feeding the baby (the differences between human milk and that of cow, goat, or donkey, the amount of milk and for how long the baby should be breast-fed, the effect on their milk of what mothers and wet nurses eat, the effect of their menstruation, the effect of sexual intercourse, of pregnancy, of anxiety and nervous conditions on milk, how to tell good and bad milk apart). Five chapters are devoted to arguing why, for the mother, the child, the family, and the nation—and on no less than physiological, emotional, and moral grounds—it is best for the child to be nursed by the mother. The next four chapters cover the qualities of a mother who wants to breast-feed her own baby. Mixed feeding receives a one-page chapter, poor mothers and difficulties of infants in suckling one each, before a concluding chapter brings this long subsection to a close.

Despite such detailed persuasions and exhortations, the author concedes that some mothers may not be able to breast-feed their own infants; in such cases hiring a wet nurse is preferable to artificial feeding. A wet nurse should be brought in, rather than the infant's being sent out. Other chapters cover artificial feeding (a very last resort), bowel movements, urination, perspiration, and monitoring the child's weight, teething, weaning the baby, walking, exercising, and taking the child outdoors, smallpox vaccination and other childhood diseases, and how to deal with a child's death.

Book 2 is devoted to the mental upbringing of the child (*tarbiat-i 'aqlani*). Reiterating the advantages of a child's growing up on mother's milk and father's kindness, instead of being sent away for a couple of years to a village wet nurse, the author emphasizes that even if the child is entrusted to a wet nurse for physical care, the mother must remain in charge of mental care and intellectual development.[98] Again unlike the *Nasirean Ethics*, which assumed that the father was in charge of the child's upbringing, this section of the book is addressed to the mother. A third book discusses the issue of whether children should be brought up with other children or individually. A chapter on crèches for working mothers has been omitted in the translation, the translator notes, since it was not seen as relevant to the conditions of Iran. The translator finally brings the book to a close by reminiscing about his own mother.[99]

The publication of a book of this genre marked an important moment: the moment of entry of the printed words of male authors (a European author mediated through the Iranian translator) and modernist reformers into a domain that had been largely oral and female. Previously, advice on child rearing had been passed orally among women, mothers and daughters, wet nurses and nannies, sisters, female friends, and neighbors. The entry of male-authored texts into this female domain began to regularize mothering practices toward the upbringing of new men, men of the nation.

These early themes, the crafting of a new kind of mother and of a new kind of wife, and the accompanying proposition that the progress of the nation depended on the education of women, were echoed in articles in the constitutionalist press of the first decade of the twentieth century. The following passage from the constitutionalist journal *'Adalat* combines many of the oft-repeated arguments in favor of women's education:

It is evident that the progress and prosperity of every country and nation are dependent in general on science and the knowledge of men and in particular on the education of women. . . . If our women [*pardagian*—the veiled ones] are not educated, how can they take proper care of our newborn who are the hope of our dear homeland? How can they know the correct rules of nursing the child, that is, the three ways of natural nursing, artificial feeding and the proper combination of both? How will they know how many times and how much daily they must feed the child and how to organize the child's sleep time, how to bathe it and keep it tidy and clean? And should it become necessary to entrust these fruits of our hearts to nannies, how will they know what the shape and face and hair and teeth and milk and age and breast of the nanny they choose should be like? How will they know when it is time to wean a child? What proper food to give it? . . . Doesn't a man who is sensitive and thinks dearly about his religion and homeland deserve a companion who shares his grief and comfort? . . . Also if our women continue to be ignorant, how can they manage the affairs of the household? . . . If they know nothing about hygiene, how can they nurse the sick?[100]

It was in the same period that the establishment of new schools for girls gained momentum.[101]

Mothers of the nation claiming citizenship

By the first decade of the century, women had taken charge of girls' education, wrote tirelessly in the press on female education, encouraged women of means to put their resources into this cause, organized fund-raising events, and provided free schooling for those who could not afford it. The early girls' schools were all established by women and often in their own residences. Many of them faced hostility. Memoirs and letters of some of the women involved provide us with moving accounts of the difficulties they faced in this pioneering work.[102] The issue of women's education became one of the bones of contention between pro- and anti-constitutionalist forces. Shaykh Fazl Allah Nuri (discussed in Sullivan's essay, chapter 6, this volume [see original reading]), a prominent anti-constitutionalist cleric, saw "the opening of schools for women's education and elementary schools for young girls," along with "spread of houses of prostitution," as one of the breaches in Islamic law perpetrated by constitutionalists.[103] This statement was construed as the Shaykh's fatwa against women's education and was used to agitate for the closing down of the new educational establishments. Women educationalists voiced the most articulate defenses of girls' schools in this debate. Addressing Shaykh Fazl Allah Nuri directly, one woman essayist took him to task on his religious credentials. She insisted that her God, unlike his, was just and had not created men and women of different essences such that one deserved the blessings of education and the other was to remain bestial; that the Prophet of her God had made it obligatory for all Muslim men and women to seek education, whereas his God had forbidden women to seek education. She challenged him to name a single woman close to the Prophet who was illiterate or ignorant, and interrogated his right to speak in the name of *shari'a* (Islamic law), going on to defend the structure and curriculum of modern schools over traditional *maktabs,* explaining the benefits of education for women, and eventually concluding that nothing in Islam opposed women's education. Unless he could answer all her arguments, he would have to admit that he had spoken thoughtlessly.[104]

In the women's writings of this period, both the general discourse of progress and civilization and the more particular notion of women's roles as educated mothers, wives, and household managers were employed not only to insist on their right to education but as a jumping-off point for demands for further equality with men: If the backward nation could catch up with European civilized nations through the acquiring of modern sciences and education, as the modernist discourse upheld, the backward woman could catch up with the modern man in a similar move, women authors argued. A female teacher of one of the new girls' schools wrote, "What is the difference between women of Iran and those of Europe except for science? Why is it that women of Europe are on a par with men or are even superior to them?"[105] Connecting the modernist theme of the centrality of science to the progress of nations, a female school principal similarly argued:

> The key to the treasure of prosperity in both worlds . . . is science alone. Through science alone humanity can succeed in satisfying its needs and pushing forward its civilization. Its principles of ethical purification, home management, and politics could be based only on science. And solely through science can it protect its honor, property, life, and religion. . . . It was through science that they [Europeans] took away Turkistan and the Caucasus from us;[106] it was through the force of science that India, with such glory and with some 260 million inhabitants . . . was separated from us. The same with Egypt, Greece, Crete, Sicily, Spain, etc. . . . Through science they have swallowed more than half of Iran, the true birthland of ourselves and our forefathers, and they intend to take away the rest . . .
>
> Perhaps some may think that the Europeans are not of our kind, and therefore to think of becoming their equal is impossible. First, this is utterly false. . . . Second, even if that were true, what do you say about the Japanese? At least we should follow our Asian sisters, the Japanese, . . . in pursuing sciences and acquiring industries. It must be emphasized that educating women is more important than educating men, since the education of men is dependent on education of women and their caretakers. Therefore, you respected women must seriously and with great effort seek sciences and spread knowledge . . . so that liberty, equality, and fraternity can be established in our homeland and we too can acquire that civilization and life that the Europeans have.[107]

Claiming oneself as a new kind of mother and wife was the crucial link in these arguments:

> Because of the duties of a woman to mother and educate humanity, the harms of ignorance are a hundredfold worse for them and the advantages of learning a thousand times greater. A learned woman will keep her house clean and orderly, thus making her spouse happy. A learned woman will educate her child according to rules of health and hygiene and wisdom. . . . A learned woman will protect her family relationship and will prevent discord and difference, which is the greatest cause of destruction of family and nation. . . . A learned woman can advise her spouse in some worldly affairs. . . . A learned woman can increase her spouse's happiness when he is happy and console him when he is sad.[108]

Daughters of Shams al-Ma'ali, founders of two schools for girls, explained in a letter to the journal *Iran-i naw* that they had decided to establish these schools so that "in the future, every household is headed by a learned lady who knows well household management, child rearing, sewing, cooking, and cleaning, and from whose breast milk love of homeland will be fed to the infants so that they shall be deserving of service and sacrifice."[109]

The trope of family was sometimes used analogically (the country is like a family), sometimes as a unit that went into the composition of the country ("the prosperity of every city and country is dependent on the order and prosperity of its homes. . . . if there is order and progress in every home, a city will progress and become civilized and wealthy"). Both were put to work in support of women's education: "Progress, prosperity, and the order of every home are dependent upon [a nation's] women. . . . Until women are educated, progress and civilization of the country are impossible."[110]

What has been subsequently categorized as a "discourse of domesticity"—that is, the vast literature on scientific housekeeping, child rearing, and husband keeping that was produced at the turn of the century by both male and female writers—and from a late-twentieth-century viewpoint may seem to have frustrated the perspectives of women's lives and contained their social advance, for women of the early twentieth century provided the very grounds upon which the male domain of modern education could be opened up to women: women needed to be educated in all these sciences of household management in order for families to prosper and for the country to become civilized.[111] Women's assuming the position of the learned (*mudabbir va mudir*) manager and head of the household (*manzil*)—instead of being part of the household subject to the management of the man—far from frustrating the dynamics of women's movement into public life and national recognition provided the empowering basis for it. That this move also produced the later containment of women's drive toward higher education became evident in the 1930s when the issue of university education for women was debated and those opposing it used these arguments against women's admission to universities.[112] But that is a much later episode of the story and for that reason, I would argue, that categorization of the literature which scripted a new concept of woman centered on notions of scientific household management, learned mothering, and educated husband keeping as a discourse of domesticity or cult of domesticity is a misnomer that prevents us from understanding why women embraced these notions in the first place.

The literature on scientific household management achieved its full development in the pages of the women's press. The first women's journal was in fact named *Danish* (Knowledge). Edited by Dr. Kahhal, a woman ophthalmologist with an active practice,[113] it began publication in September 1910, with a banner that read: "This is an ethical journal of the science of housekeeping, child rearing, husband keeping; useful for girls' and women's moral development, It will not say a word on national politics." Many articles were devoted to household management[114] (including discussion of how to manage servants—a topic that occupied an even more prominent place in the pages of Iran's second women's journal, *Shukufah*), husband management,[115] child rearing,[116] and children's health and hygiene.[117]

Though later issues began to run articles on how to look after one's clothes and hair, and information on cosmetics, the emphasis for sustaining one's marriage was put on education.[118] "A girl educated in Europe," praised the "new situation of women." In the old days, she argued, women had no education and had no status in their husband's eyes unless they were young and beautiful; now educated women had many good qualities. One good moral outcome of this situation was that husband and wife now lived together in affection and did not look at other people. What a big mistake it had been when women sought their place in their husband's heart through making up their faces and putting on fancy clothes, instead of paying attention to educating their children and housekeeping. It was in fact knowledge and good qualities that a husband never tired of, not good looks and fancy clothes. She exhorted her dear sisters who were already educated to continue seeking knowledge and not to waste their lives. She urged them to be equal to their husbands, at least in education. They should not think that having pleasant manners and a kind tongue could guarantee his love, A wife should be a friend and companion to her husband; that is, in every work and every matter she should be a help to him. But how could an uneducated wife give help to her husband?[119]

By this time both male and female authors placed higher national priority on girls' education than on boys' education, or even on the development of a body of new law, the issue that had occupied the center of modernist discourse a few decades earlier: "The progress, uplifting, and civilization of every nation, every country, is dependent on three things: first, the education of girls; second, science; third, law. . . . The education of girls, which is the first step for prosperity and the first step for uplifting, is far more important than the other two, since it is girls and women from whom sons and daughters come and by whom they are educated until they are of school age."[120]

As I have already indicated, discussion of these issues was used not to contain and frustrate women's activity but to effect it. For instance, women were told that "if a woman is illiterate, she should pursue literacy immediately, because only if she can read the newspapers will she know everything and be able to communicate effectively with her husband."[121]

Though earlier articles were sometimes addressed to both mothers and nannies the emphasis was decidedly on biological mothers' nurturing their children and using nannies only as a last resort. An article in the third issue of the journal was devoted to all the physical, moral, and political ills that ensue from entrusting one's child to a nanny.[122] Mothers were told to avoid giving their unique (*yiganah*) child to a stranger (*biganah*) nanny; the child must receive nourishment from the breast of mother's love.[123] Much was made of the goodness of the mother's milk and of the dirty/impure milk of a nanny who lived an unhygienic life. The author described a child whose eyes developed a twisted condition because the nanny had twisted eyes, a Persian prince who drank camel's milk and rode camels all his life because he had been entrusted to an Arab lady in childhood, an honorable lady who was incontinent all her life because her nanny had been so and she had inherited the disability from her,[124] and the foul language that children pick up from their nannies.[125] The article ended with a list of conditions to set and qualities to look for should one have no recourse but to entrust the child to a nanny.[126]

Perhaps even more than *Danish,* the journal *Shukufah,* begun in 1914, was oriented toward production of a new type of mother and envisaged new marital relationships. *Shukufah* was edited by Muzayyan al-Saltanah, herself an active educationalist who established three elementary schools and one vocational school for girls during the same period as she was publishing *Shukufah.* She also served as a kind of inspector ("investigative reporter") of girls' schools in Tehran in that period. She would visit schools and write reports in the pages of *Shukufah* about the students and the quality of teaching.

Article after article in the pages of *Shukufah* advised women to forget all the nonsense that their mothers and grandmothers had taught them about how to keep their husbands. To become a woman of modernity was a learning process that demanded an unlearning, a de-constitution, of womanhood.[127] Women were told that they should consider the house their kingdom to run. All the important qualities necessary for running the affairs of a country, such as the basics of humanity, honesty, trustworthiness, hygiene, working hard, valuing time, seeking knowledge, resistance in the face of hardship, avoiding bad manners, were learned in childhood, argued Maliktaj. If there was a woman who taught these to her children, then you knew for certain that the affairs of that country would fare well and the country would advance, and vice versa.[128] Muzayyan al-Saltanah also demonstrated a concern about regularization of schools' curriculum and put great emphasis on schools as the place for ethical and moral development of young girls.[129] Though the journal continued *Danish's* tradition of publishing series of articles on women's as well as children's health and hygiene, a growing number of articles were concerned with women's moral development, demonstrating a clear anxiety over the direction of changes that were becoming evident in women's social performance.[130]

The new schools were constituted as the social space for development of moral behavior, and for learning the sciences of cooking, sewing, child care and husband management. A special curriculum was thus developed for the scientization of household affairs (*umur-i baytiyah*); it included courses on home management, education of children, hygiene, fine arts and crafts, and cooking. Textbooks were also produced with this orientation in mind. *Tarbiat al-bunat* (The education of girls), for instance, one of the texts prepared for the new girls' schools, was translated from the French by Mirza 'Azizallah Khan, with the express intent of its becoming a second-grade textbook. It was published in 1905, and by 1911 it was already into its second printing. The book, subtitled "The Science of Home Management," is organized in six parts (twenty lessons). It begins with a definition of this science, "on which the happiness and prosperity of every family depends,"[131] and goes on to explain why, despite possible popular cynicism, home management is a science and ought to be taught and learned as such. The book ends with a dozen recipes for French soups and other food. It gives examples of positive and negative repercussions for the lives of families with learned versus illiterate housewives, defines the necessary characteristics of a competent housewife as order, competence, and cleanliness, and projects three female character types among housewives. The first is disorderly and careless. Named Lady Pleasure ('Ishrat Khanum), she is wasteful of her own efforts and her husband's property, and spends her time chatting away with other women of the neighborhood. The second, Lady Agreeable (Bihjat Khanum), strives to be a good housewife, draws upon her traditional know-how to do her best, but is disorderly because she has never properly learned how to run a household. The third, who is held up as an exemplar, knows how to categorize and to label things properly, to keep a budget book, and to organize her time efficiently, and thus is able to finish her chores before her husband and children return home, When they are back, she busies herself with some light sewing, or reading a book, or keeping her husband company. Unlike Lady Pleasure, who spends her time in idle conversation with other women—a disapproved female social activity—the exemplary woman is oriented toward companionship with her husband. Significantly, she is named Lady Chaste ('Ismat Khanum), transmitting chastity through the new science to the modern educated woman.[132]

Thus was crafted the new woman: the scientific mother and the companionate wife, the learned woman versed in the sciences of cooking, sewing, and breast-feeding. Of such woman, ministers, state scribes, doctors, and professors would be born, not porters and mean fortune-tellers.[133] She would not only produce better children; she would also prevent her man from behaving badly, "as American women have stopped their men from drinking and obstinacy."[134]

The school curriculum included, in addition to the science of homemaking, lessons on hygiene and the introduction of sports and gymnastics. The desirability of the latter now began to be linked to a critique of veiling. In a graduation address focused on the science of hygiene, Badr al-Dujá Khanum, graduating from the American College for Girls, expressed her regret that because of veiling Iranian women had been deprived in recent centuries of engaging in sports, and thus it was not surprising that most Iranian women were weak and unhealthy.[135]

Later, in the 1920s, we come across a new genre, the rules of etiquette (*adab-i mu'ashirat*): texts of initiation that were designed to teach women how to interact properly with unfamiliar men. Once these were learned, it was imagined that woman would be ready to step into a heterosocial arena without undermining the social and cultural order:

> The words *chastity* and *honor* are not in the vocabulary of creation. A woman is
> not born chaste; she becomes the protector and the policer of her chastity. Until
> women learn the duty of policing and guarding themselves, freedom will create
> irreparable damage for their womanly delicacy and feminine pride. Therefore
> we must teach self-policing. Freedom will follow. . . . In Europe and the free

countries, in parks and promenades, one rarely sees a man gazing at a woman or a woman paying any attention [to a man], unless they have made their chastity and honor their means of livelihood. . . . A good policer is a woman who does not allow those who are seeking to deceive and use her to utter a single impolite or improper word. . . . Once women are shown the ways of policing, that is, the rules and etiquette of women's socializing with men, then freedom and sharing life between women and men will follow without any hindrance.[136]

I want to emphasize here again the enabling work of two seemingly conflicting notions: one disciplinary, the other emancipatory. It was the moment of "freedom and sharing life" with men that made the self-policing not only a workable but a desirable project for women. And, conversely, the new disciplinary and regulatory practices and concepts defined the acceptable social space for freedom for the modern woman. The success of this double work made her place in the nation possible. She would be ready to become a citizen. In fact it was within the space of the girls' schools that women had already begun to constitute themselves as citizens from the time of the Constitutional Revolution. Following the then popular pattern of forming associations, women formed their own associations, held meetings, and gave fund-raising "garden parties" to raise funds for the government and for girls' schools.[137] Forming such associations had itself become an expression of citizenship. Girls' schools, often private residences of prominent women, were at once places of learning and venues for such meetings. Thus women were constituting at once a new individual self through literacy and a new social self through patriotic (*vatani*) political activities. As "managers of the house," they were beginning to transform "the house" into a social space of citizenship.

Women in these meetings spoke as citizens, as "we Iranians," addressed the general political problems facing the country, and often bemoaned the disadvantages that deprived them of the chance to be of more help to the homeland. Not only did women make a claim to the rights of citizenship, but they sometimes proved their concern as citizens by challenging the ability of men to run the Constitutional regime.[138]

In fact, the first cautious claims to equality made by women were formulated within the educational domain. "I take up the pen to complain greatly about fathers and husbands of Iranian girls. Why do they not know yet that woman and man in this world are like the two wheels of a carriage; they must be equal, neither having any privilege over the other. If one of the two wheels of a carriage is deficient, it will be impossible for it to move," wrote Shahnaz Azad. This precarious claim to equality was immediately modified in these terms: "It should be evident that by equality I mean equality in education and learning of sciences, not in any other matter."[139]

Another woman, Shams Kasma'i was more daring. In a poem sent to *Shukufah* from Ashkabad, she called upon her sisters to educate themselves in order to cure all their deficiencies, to use their power of speech, reason, and rationality to conquer the whole world, to set fire to all superstitions, to tear asunder the veil of oppression, and to prove the equality of their rights with men through their words, their deeds, and all their power.[140]

This poem could well be the first pronouncement of the language of equality of rights, of a new kind of modern feminism, in Iran. The new mother and wife had begun to make a different claim to womanhood. These new claims eventually came to clash with the limits set by the former discourse, as I have pointed out. This clash came to the fore in the context of the new round of "educational debates" of the 1930s. Did women need to go to higher education institutes? Was not the goal of their education to become better mothers and wives? What were they going to do with their higher diplomas then? These arguments were advanced against women's entry to upper grades of high school and later university education. Having been entrapped by the very discourse that had opened up education to them in the first place, women now opted to enlarge their notion of "domestic duties" to mean national service. The new home to whose management they now began to lay a claim was no longer their conjugal household but the national home, Iran. Women's embrace of Riza Shah's agenda in the 1930s can thus be seen as not a "selling out" of women's cause to the increasingly powerful state; rather, Riza Shah's program of constructing the citizen as a servant of the state—*nawkar-i dawlat*—provided the possibility for women to break out of the trap of what can now indeed be named domesticity. They could claim their right to higher education and to many professions in the name of service to the state. Having mothered the nation, they could now serve the state. Again, one can see both disciplinary and emancipatory dynamics in this scenario: appropriation of the notion of servant of the state enabled women to claim their right to higher education and professions while subjecting those rights to regulations, demands, and agendas of the state—a legacy that marked the Iranian women's movement during the Pahlavi era.

Notes

1   Beth Baron, *The Women's Awakening in Egypt: Culture, Society, and the Press* (New Haven: Yale University Press, 1994); Margot Badran, *Feminists, Islam, and Nation: Gender and the Making of Modern Egypt* (Princeton: Princeton University Press, 1995); Afsaneh Najmabadi, "Veiled Discourse—Unveiled Bodies," *Feminist Studies* 19, no. 3 (Fall 1993): 487–518.

2   See Baron, *Women's Awakening*, p. 67: "An ideology of womanhood emerged from the early women's press that reinforced women's roles as mother, wife, and homemaker." And Badran, *Feminists, Islam, and Nation*, p. 63: "Education for girls was quickly harnessed to the cult of domesticity; it was put to the service of elevating women's family roles, especially that of mother."

3   See, for instance, Nasir al-Din Tusi, *Akhlaq-i Nasiri*, ed. Mujtabá Minuvi and 'Aliriza Haydari (Tehran: Khwarazmi, 1978), a thirteenth-century C.E. text. English translation: Nasir ad-Din Tusi, *The Nasirean Ethics*, trans. G. M. Wickens (London: George Allen & Unwin, 1964); Jalal al-Din Dawwani, *Akhlaq-i Jalali*, a fifteenth-century C.E. text (Lucknow: n.p., 1957); Muhsin Fani Kashmiri, *Akhlaq-i 'alamara: akhlaq-i muhsini*, ed. Kh. Javidi (Islamabad: Pakistan and Iran Center for Persian Studies, 1983), a seventeenth-century C.E. text. For a discussion of ethics in Islamic premodern writings, see R. Walzer and H.A.R. Gibbs, "Akhlak," *Encyclopaedia of Islam*, 2d ed., pp. 325–29; and R. Rahman, "Aklaq," *Encyclopaedia Iranica*, pp. 719–23. See Avner Gil'adi, *Children of Islam: Concepts of Childhood in Medieval Muslim Society* (London: Macmillan, 1992), p. 4, on the Greek origins of some of the important ethical, psychological, and pedagogical notions in these texts.

4   A note of clarification is warranted here. Although the books of ethics that I draw upon range from the thirteenth to the seventeenth century, I am not presuming that the discourse on ethics remained unchanged in this period. A study of the historical transformations of the ethical discourse for this period is beyond the scope of this essay, and my arguments here do not depend on it. My use of *The Nasirean Ethics*, for instance, is a recognition that this text had acquired a "model for imitation" status. Later texts took a great deal, in many cases verbatim reproduction of large sections and arguments, from this text and modeled their rhetorical and formal structures upon it. This does not mean that the discourse, much less child-rearing practices, remained identical. Some of these differences I will note in the text. Beyond these differences, however, it is their common assumptions that concern me here.

5   Tusi, *The Nasirean Ethics*, p. 161, *Akhlaq-i Nasiri*, p. 215; see also Fani Kashmiri *Akhlaq-i 'alamara*, p. 127.

6   Tusi, *The Nasirean Ethics*, p. 161, *Akhlaq-i Nasiri*, pp. 215–16; see also Fani Kashmiri, *Akhlaq-i 'alamara*, p. 128.

7   Tusi, *The Nasirean Ethics*, p. 162; *Akhlaq-i Nasiri*, p. 217. We are also told that "[t]he philosophers have said that a worthy wife will take on the role of mother, friend and mistress." (Tusi, *The Nasirean Ethics*, p. 164; *Akhlaq-i Nasiri*, p. 219.) In *Akhlaq-i 'alamara*, the third point in the regulation of a wife is significantly different: that the husband should treat his wife's relatives with respect and that he should not, without good cause, hurt her by bringing in another wife: "The relation of man to *manzil* (household? wife?) is like that of heart to body. A man cannot be manager (*mudabbir*) of two *manzils*, in the same way that one heart cannot be source of life for two bodies" (Fani Kashmiri, *Akhlaq-i 'alamara*, p. 131.)

8   See Tusi, *The Nasirean Ethics*, pp. 166–67; *Akhlaq-i Nasiri*, p. 222; see also Fani Kashmiri, *Akhlaq-i 'alamara*, p. 136. Fani Kashmiri prefaced this section by emphasizing that the child was given in trust by God to father and mother and that God held both responsible for the child's upbringing (p. 135). Yet by the end of this paragraph the plural subject becomes singular and masculine (in his recitation of Arabic narratives). He also considered a wet nurse preferable to mother for the care of child (p. 136).

9   Persian does not have distinct pronouns for "he" and "she," and the words used for "child" in these writings, *farzand* and *kudak*, could refer to either a girl or a boy; that is, there is no linguistic sign to designate the child as a boy; I have followed the authors' own later textual disambiguation in using the pronoun "he" to designate the child, since at the end of this section, after all has been said about the child's tutoring, chastisement, encouragement, skills he needs to learn, qualities he needs to acquire, Tusi, for instance, concludes: "So much for the chastisement of children. In the case of daughters, one must employ, in the selfsame manner, whatever is appropriate and fitting to them. They should be brought up to keep close to the house and live in seclusion, cultivating gravity, continence, modesty and the other qualities we have enumerated in the chapter on Wives. They should be prevented from learning to read or write, but allowed to acquire such accomplishments as are commendable in women. When they reach the bounds of maturity they should be joined to one of equal standing." (Tusi, *The Nasirean Ethics*, p. 173; *Akhlaq-i Nasiri*, pp. 229–30.) For a similar close, see Fani Kashmni, *Akhlaq-i 'alamara*, p. 141. The textual place of this one paragraph displays the "supplementarity" of "daughter" to "child" in this ethical discourse.

10   Tusi, *The Nasirean Ethics*, p. 179; *Akhlaq-i Nasiri*, pp. 237–38.

11   Mirza Aqa Khan Kirmani, *Sad khatabah*, MS in Edward G. Browne Collection, Cambridge University Library. Sections of *Sad khatabah* concerned with Kirmani's views on women were published in *Nimeye Digar*, no. 9 (Spring 1989): 101–12. Quotation from *Sad khatabah*, p. 126b; in *Nimeye Digar*, p. 103. For Kirmani's life and an analytical survey of his writings, see Firaydun Adamiyat, *Andishah'ha-yi Mirza Aqa Khan Kirmani* (Mirza Aqa Khan Kirmani's thoughts) (Tehran: Payam, 1978).

12   Kirmani, *Sad khatabah*, p. 127b; in *Nimeye Digar*, p. 103.

13   Kirmani, *Sad khatabah*, p. 156b. The third school was the religion of the people, which explained why Jews, Christians, and Muslims were different in character. The fourth was the government; Kirmani argued that people under oppressive governments developed differently from those under just governments. And finally, the fifth school was the climate and natural circumstances of the land. (*Sad khatabah*, p. 128a; in *Nimeye Digar*, p. 103.)

14   The reference to "mourning sessions" concerns the many shi'ite rituals of mourning the tragic misfortunes of the eleven *imams*, 'Ali and his male descendants, the most important of which are the Muharram rituals commemorating the battle of Karbala in c.e. 680 in which Husayn and his followers were killed by Yazid's army.

15   Kirmani, *Sad khatabah*, pp. 149b, 150a and b, and 151a.

16   Ibid., p. 95b.

17   On the significance of this shift in self-constitution for the emergence of nineteenth-century Iranian modernism, see Mohamad Tavakoli-Targhi, "The Formation of Two Revolutionary Discourses in Modern Iran: The Constitutional Revolution of 1905–6 and the Islamic Revolution of 1978–79" (Ph.D. diss., University of Chicago, 1988).

18   Kirmani, *Sad khatabah*, p. 128b; in *Nimeye Digar*, p. 104.

19   Kirmani, *Sad khatabah*, pp. 128b and 129a; in *Nimeye Digar*, p. 104.

20   The modernist writings on gender also mark the heterosexualization of love. Love in classical Perso-Islamic literature is often male homoerotic. This is reflected not only in the celebration of male-male love couples, such as Mahmud and Ayaz, but also in books of advice with separate chapters on love and marriage, where in the former chapters the beloved is male, and issues of marriage and love, unlike the case in the later modernist discourse, are constructed as belonging to different domains. See, for instance, 'Unsur al-Ma'ali, *Qabusnamah*, ed. Ghulamhusayn Yusufi (Tehran: Jibi, 1974), chap. 14 (pp. 100–106), "On Love," and chap. 26 (pp. 144–46), "On Seeking a Wife." With the heterosexualization of love and the romanticization of marriage, homosexuality came to be viewed as a debased expression of sexual appetite that resulted from sexual segregation and the unavailability of women to men. On modernist judgment of premodern homoerotic love, see Nasrallah Purjavadi, "Badah-'i 'ishq," *Nashr-i danish* 12, no. 2 (February–March 1992): 6–15, where he speaks of the love of Mahmud for Ayaz as "morally the most filthy (*aludah'tarin*) of loves" (p. 8). On similar developments within Turkish modernity, see Deniz Kandiyoti, "Afterword," in this volume.

21   Kirmani, *Sad khatabah*, pp. 135a through 138a; in *Nimeye Digar*, pp. 109–12.

22   Mirza Aqa Khan Kirmani and Shaykh Ahmad Ruhi, *Hasht bihisht* (n.p., n.d.). On the significance of Babism for the emergence of Iranian modernity, see Mangol Bayat, *Mysticism and Dissent: Socioreligious Thought in Qajar Iran* (Syracuse: Syracuse University Press, 1982).

23   Kirmani and Ruhi, *Hasht bihisht*, p. 9. Later in the text, on p. 122, this prohibition is modified: women can talk to strange men, but no more than twenty-eight words, and only when matters of necessity arise.

24   Ibid., p. 121.

25   For a similar shift in turn-of-the-century Lebanon, within the context of the socioeconomic transformations there, see Akram Fouad Khater, " 'House' to 'Goddess of the House': Gender, Class, and Silk in Nineteenth-Century Mount Lebanon," *International Journal of Middle East Studies* 28, no. 3 (August 1996): 325–48.

26   Kirmani and Ruhi, *Hasht bihisht*, p. 122. The word "decree" (*hukm*), refers to Babi religious edicts.

27   Ibid., p. 144.

28   Ibid., p. 145.

29   On premodern educational institutions and concepts of knowledge, see Jonathan P. Berkey, *The Transmission of Knowledge in Medieval Cairo: A Social History of Islamic Education* (Princeton: Princeton University Press, 1992). See also his "Women and Islamic Education," in *Women in Middle Eastern History: Shifting Boundaries in Sex and Gender*, ed. Nikki Keddie and Beth Baron (New Haven: Yale University Press, 1991), pp. 143–57, for a discussion of premodern Islamic education of women.

30   My arguments in this essay are greatly influenced by the writings of Mohamad Tavakoli-Targhi. See "Refashioning Iran," *Iranian Studies* 23, nos. 1–4 (1990): 77–101, and "The Formation of Two Revolutionary Discourses." In particular, I take from his writings the importance and meaning of conceptual shifts in notions such as science knowledge, nation, and politics in nineteenth-century Iran.

31   Kirmani, *Sad khatabah*, pp. 94 through 98; quotation from 97a.

32   See, for instance, Zayn al-Din al-'Amili al-Jaba'i, *Munyat al-Murid* (a sixteenth-century C.E. text), trans. Muhammad Baqir Sa'idi Khurasani (n.p.: Intisharat-i 'ilmiyah Islamiyah, 1950), p. 30, on division of knowledgeable people (*danishmandan*) into three categories: *'alim bi-allah, 'alim bi amr-allah*, and *'alim bi-allah* and *amr-allah*.

33   On changes in concepts of *ta'lim* and *tarbiat* as pertains to Egypt, see Timothy Mitchell, *Colonising Egypt* (Cambridge: Cambridge University Press, 1988); Omnia Shakry, "Schooled Mothers and Structured Play: Child Rearing in Turn-of-the Century Egypt," chap. 4 in this volume. For Morocco, see Dale F. Eickelman, *Knowledge and Power in Morocco: The Education of a Twentieth-Century Notable* (Princeton: Princeton University Press, 1985). See also Margot Badron, "From Consciousness to Activism: Feminist Politics in Early Twentieth Century Egypt," in *Problems of the Middle East in Historical Perspective*, ed. John Spagnolo (London: Macmillan, 1992), pp. 27–48.

34   It began publication in 1896 and was devoted to the idea that the contemporary differences among nations had nothing to do with any innate differences but arose from different educational regimes. ("Opening Remarks [*Aghaz-i sukhan*]," *Tarbiat*, no. 1 [December 17, 1896]: 1–3.) It advocated that "[a]ny nation that sees itself behind any other nation is obligated by requirements of humanity . . . to race after education and to go with its head instead of its feet [that is, to move at top speed] on the path of civilization to catch up with the caravan that has gone ahead of it." (*Tarbiat*, untitled lead article in no. 2 [December 24, 1896]: 1–4; quotation from p. 1).

35   *Tarbiat*, lead article dubbed a parenthetical remark (*jumlah-'i mu'tarizah*) to clarify some points and avoid misunderstandings, in no. 4 (January 7, 1897): 1–4; quotation from p. 1.

36   Ibid., p. 2.

37   Kirmani and Ruhi, *Hasht bihisht*, p. 139.

38   *Tarbiat*, no. 42 (September 30, 1897): 3; in Persian it reads, "*har kah nakhwanad chah danad va har kah nadanad chah tavanad?*" This represents an extension of the chain between power and knowledge, as expressed in the well-known verse from Firdawsi—"whosoever is knowledgeable, he shall be a capable person" (*tavana buvad har kah dana buvad*)—to link knowledge and reading.

39   See Walter J. Ong, *Orality and Literacy: The Technologizing of the Word* (London: Routledge, 1982).

40   See Mary Carruthers, *Book of Memory: A Study of Memory in Medieval Culture* (Cambridge: Cambridge University Press, 1990).

41   I would like to thank Jonathan Berkey for helpful conversations about this point. Further confirmation appears in the entries in biographical dictionaries on blind scholars, some born blind. See Fedwa Malti-Douglas, "*Mentalités* and Marginality: Blindness and Mamluk Civilization," in *The Islamic World: From Classical to Modern Times*, ed. C. E. Bosworth, Charles Issawi, Roger Savory, and A. L. Udovitch (Princeton: The Darwin Press, 1989), pp. 211–37. See also Dale F. Eickelman, "The Art of Memory: Islamic Education and Its Social Reproduction," in *Comparing Muslim Societies: Knowledge and the State in a World Civilization*, ed. Juan R. I. Cole (Ann Arbor: University of Michigan Press, 1992), pp. 97–132.

42   "On Schools (*Makatib va madaris*)," no. 48 (November 11, 1897): 2.

43   Zhiniral Mirza Taqi Khan Kashani, *Tarbiat: namah'ist dar qava'id-i ta'lim va tarbiat-i atfal* (Education: An essay on rules of training and educating children) (Isfahan: Dar al-taba'ah-'i farhang, 1881), p. 47.

44   Ibid., p. 46.

45   Ibid., p. 61.

46   Mahmud ibn Yusuf, *Ta'dib al-atfal* (n.p., 1876).

47   Ibid., pp. 6–10.

48   Ibid., pp. 11–17.

49   Ibid., pp. 110–19.

50   Ibid., pp. 185–209. Much of the educational writing in Persian from this period on was closely linked with the French educational debates and texts of the time.

51   Ibid., p. 187.

52   Ibid., p. 188.

53   Ibid., pp. 195, 197, and 201.

54   Ibid., pp. 203–4.

55   Ibid., pp. 206–7.

56   Miftah al-Mulk Mahmud, *Ta'lim al-atfal* (Tehran: n.p., 1897), 1:5, 11, 21, 32, 42, and 96; 2:19, 32, 60, 105, and 117. In contrast, a depiction of a Qur'anic school has all the pupils sitting on the floor and the teacher in the act of caning a pupil (2:11).

57   Ibid., 1:68–80 and 95–101.

58   Ibid., pp. 81–94 and 102–6; quotation from p. 105.

59   Untitled lead article, *Tarbiat*, no. 36 (August 19, 1897): 1–4; quotation from pp. 1–2.

60   *Tarbiat*, no. 40 (September 16, 1897): 2–4.

61   Ibid., p. 3.

62   Ibid., pp. 3–4. Comparison between women of Europe and Iranian women, including mention of different educational practices regarding men and women, went back at least to the late eighteenth century, to the travelogues written by Persian-speaking voyagers from India and Iran to Europe, In fact, this "travel literature" constituted a central medium through which reconceptualizations of gender, including issues of women's education, took place. See Mohamad Tavakoli-Targhi, "Imagining Western Women: Occidentalism and Euro-eroticism," *Radical America* 24, no. 3 (July–September 1990): 73–87.

63   'Abd al-Rahim ibn Abu Talib Tabrizi (Talibuf), *Kitab-i Ahmad ya safinah Talibi* (Istanbul; n.p., 1893). A second volume was subsequently published in 1894 (Istanbul: Matba'ah-'i Khawrshid). A third volume was published under a different title. *Masa'il-i hayat* (Tiflis: Matba'ah-'i Ghayrat, 1906).

64   Talibuf, *Kitab-i Ahmad,* 1:81.

65   Ibid., p. 72; 2:4.

66   Talibuf, *Masa'il-i hayat,* p. 36.

67   For an English translation, see Qasim Amin, *The Liberation of Women*, trans. Samiha Sidhom Peterson (Cairo: American University in Cairo Press, 1992). There is a large critical literature on Amin's works in English. See, for instance, Leila Ahmed, *Women and Gender in Islam* (New Haven: Yale University Press, 1992); Baron, *Women's Awakening*; Badran, *Feminists, Islam, and Nation*; and essays by Lila Abu Lughod and Omnia Shakry in this volume (chaps. 4 and 7). Here I am concerned with Amin's text, through its Persian translation, as a document within the educational debates of this time in Iran.

68   Yusuf Ashtiani, trans., *Tarbiat-i nisvan* (Tabriz: Matba'ah-'i Ma'arif, 1900). A fuller translation was published later, translated by Muhazzib, "under instructions from the Ministry of Education," under the title *Zan va azadi* (Woman and liberty) (Tehran: Chapkhanah-'i markazi, 1937). Muhazzib also translated Amin's *al-Mar'at al-jadida* "under instructions from the Ministry of Education," under the title *Zan-i imruz* (Today's woman) (Tehran: Chapkhanah-'i markazi, n.d.).

69   Ashtiani, *Tarbiat-i nisvan*, unnumbered initial pages. The titles he lists are Amin's *Tahrir al-Mar'a, Falsafat al-zuwaj, al-Mar'a fi al-sharq* (Marqus Fahmi 1894), *al-Mar'a fi qarn al-'ashrin*, and *al-Mar'a fi al-'usra.*

70   Amin, *The Liberation of Women,* p. 10.

71   Ashtiani, *Tarbiat-i nisvan*, p. 14.

72   For Talibuf's position, see Talibuf, *Kitab-i Ahmad,* 2:11, where the unveiling of women is seen as one of the ill consequences of falling under foreign Christian rule; and p. 34, where he refers to "the good custom of our women's *hijab*" ('*adat-i mamduhdh-hijab-i 'unas-i ma*).

73   The dichotomous division between traditionalist and modernist positions was consolidated during the Pahlavi period. In the early 1930s, under Riza Shah, all Independent women's journals and organizations were replaced by a single state-sponsored organization, Ladies Center (*Kanun-i banuvan*,

established in 1935). This was followed by the unveiling order in early 1936. The Ladies Center was officially under the supervision of the Ministry of Education, and schools and Tehran University were the sites where many of the initial unveiling experiments were carried out. It was these later political and cultural developments that consolidated the identity between women's rights and unveiling in the domain of the modern.

74   Ashtiani, *Tarbiat-i nisvan*, p. 12 (Amin, *The Liberation of Women*, p. 6).

75   Ashtiani, *Tarbiat-i nisvan*, p. 69 (Amin, *The Liberation of Women*, p. 75).

76   Ashtiani, *Tarbiat-i nisvan*, p. 63 (Amin, *The Liberation of Women*, pp 63–64).

77   Ashtiani, *Tarbiat-i nisvan*, pp. 17–18 (Amin, *The Liberation of Women*, p 12).

78   See, as an example, "The Incurable Pain of Being in the Hands of Ignorant Servants (*Dard-i bi'darman-i giriftari dar dast-i khadamah-'i nadan*)," *Shukufah* 3, no. 9 (April 13, 1915): 2–3.

79   Ashtiani, *Tarbiat-i nisvan*, p. 69 (Amin, *The Liberation of Women*, p. 72).

80   Ashtiani, *Tarbiat-i nisvan*, p. 41 (Amin, *The Liberation of Women*, p. 23).

81   Ashtiani, *Tarbiat-i nisvan*, pp. 47–49 (Amin, *The Liberation of Women*, pp. 26–27).

82   Ashtiani, *Tarbiat-i nisvan*, p. 52 (Amin, *The Liberation of Women*, p. 28).

83   Ashtiani, *Tarbiat-i nisvan*, p. 29 (Amin, *The Liberation of Women*, p. 17).

84   Ashtiani, *Tarbiat-i nisvan*, p. 34 (Amin, *The Liberation of Women*, p. 20).

85   Ashtiani, *Tarbiat-i nisvan*, p. 35 (Amin, *The Liberation of Women*, p. 20).

86   See, for instance, the letter from Talibuf to I'tisam al-Mulk, dated 26 Sha'ban 1318 (December 15, 1900), reprinted in *Bahar*, nos. 9–10 (May–June 1911): 551–52.

87   See, for instance, "On Reforming the Condition of Schools in Iran (*Dar islah-i vaz'-i makatib-i Iran*)," *Parvarish* 1, no. 17 (October 15, 1900): 7–10; 'Abd al-Husayn, "Adventures in Europe (*Mukhatirat-i 'Urupa*)," *Parvarish* 1, no. 21 (November 16, 1900): 2–4; and the editorial essay (untitled) in *Ma'arif* 2, no. 34 (February 27, 1900): 3.

88   "An Essay Devoted to Education of Girls (*Maqalah-'i makhsus dar ta'lim-i 'awrat*)," *Habl al-matin* 9, no. 12 (January 6, 1902): 16.

89   "An Essay Devoted to Education of Girls (*Maqalah-'i makhsus dar ta'lim-i 'awrat*)," *Habl al-matin* 9, no. 16 (February 6, 1902): 5–7.

90   "An Essay Devoted to Education of Girls (*Maqalah-'i makhsus dar ta'lim-i 'awrat*)," *Habl al-matin* 9, no. 17 (February 10, 1902): 15–16; quotation from p. 15.

91   Ibid.

92   Ibid.

93   "Rights and Liberties of Women (*Huquq al-mar'a va hurriyat al-nisvan*)," *Habl al-matin* 12, no. 38 (June 26, 1905): 12–14; no. 39 (July 3, 1905): 20–22; no. 43 (July 31, 1905): 6–7; no. 44 (August 7, 1905): 10–11.

94   Muhammad Tahir ibn Iskandar Mirza ibn 'Abbas Mirza, *Tarbiat-i atfal* (n.p., 1891).

95   Ibid., pp. 5–6. The class implication of this argument is worth noting. Women "of leisured classes" are assumed to engage in giving their enfants to wet nurses. The practice, however, was much more widely in use. Though they did not hire professional wet nurses, women of other classes often breast-fed each other's infants, especially during the illness of a neighbor or a friend.

96   Ibid., pp. 7–8.

97   Ibid., pp. 12–13.

98   Ibid., pp. 234–35.

99   Ibid., p. 264.

100   "A Letter from the City (*Maktub-i shahri*)," *'Adalat* (formerly *Hadid*) 2, no. 19 (November 23, 1906): 5–8. See also Sayyid Husayn, "On the Duties of the Real Teachers of Men, That Is, Women (*Dar farayiz-i murabbian-i haqiqi-i mardan ya'ni nisvan*)," *Hadid* 1, no. 13 (September 21, 1905): 4–6; "The Ill Effects of Ignorance of Mothers (*Vakhamat-i nadani-i madaran*)," *Hadid* 1, no. 15 (October 4, 1905): 2–3; Zia'allah, untitled article, *Hadid* 1, no. 20 (October 10, 1905): 5–6; Muhammad Riza, "Seeking Knowledge Is Incumbent upon Every Muslim Man and Woman (*Talab al-'ilm faridatun 'ala kull muslim wa muslima*)," *Hadid* 2, no. 13 (September 12, 1906): 1–2; Na'mat'allah, "Family Life or Real Happiness (*Hayat-i 'a'ilah ya sa'adat-i haqiqi*)," *'Adalat* 2, no. 43 (April 15, 1907): 8 and no. 44 (April 24, 1907): 5–8; Mu'avin al-Tujjar, "Letter from a Wise Person (*Maktub-i yaki az khiradmandan*)" *'Adalat* 2, no. 46 (Rabi' al-awwal 1325; May 1907): 7–8; "School for Girls (*Madrasah-'i bunat*)," *Vatan* 1, no. 1 (January 6, 1906): 3–4; "Education of Girls Is the Most Important Pre-condition of Civilization and Improvement of Ethics (*Tarbiat-i bunat shart-i a'zam-i tamaddun va tahzib-i akhlaq ast*)," *Subh-i sadiq* 2, no. 27 (March 8, 1908): 1–2; Vasiq al-Saltanah, "Seeking Knowledge Is Incumbent upon Every Muslim Man and Woman (*Talab al-'ilm faridatun 'ala kull muslim wa muslima*)," *Iran-i naw* 1, no. 56 (November 1, 1909): 4; Munir Mazandarani, "Seeking Knowledge Is Incumbent upon Every Muslim Man and Woman (*Talab al-'ilm faridatun 'ala kull muslim wa muslima*)," *Iran-i naw* 1, no. 91 (December 17, 1909): 1–2.

101   American Presbyterian missionaries had established a girls' school in 'Urumiyah in 1838. Sisters of St. Vincent de Paul opened schools for girls in 1865 in 'Urumiyah, Salmas, Tabriz, and Isfahan, and one in Tehran in 1875. In 1895 the American School for Girls was established in Tehran. Schools for girls were established by various religious denominations of Iran in the last decades of the nineteenth century. Armenian schools for girls were established in Tehran in 1870, in Qazvin in 1889, in Sultanabad in 1900, and in Isfahan in 1903. The first Jewish school for girls in Tehran, *Ittihad (Alians)*, was established in 1898, and in Kirman Zoroastrians established *'Unas-i Jamshidi* in 1902. *Tarbiat-i bunat* was established in 1911 by Baha'is in Tehran. The first Muslim school for girls on the new model is reported to have been established in Chalias near Kirman in 1897, but we know nothing more about this school. This was followed by *Parvarish* in 1903 in the residence of Hasan Rushdiyah with Tubá Rushdiyah (his sister-in-law) as its principal. This school was forced to close down within a short time because of the open hostility it faced. More lasting efforts came on the eve of the Constitutional Revolution (1906–9). *Mukhaddarah* was established in 1905, *Dushizigan* (by Bibi Khanum Astarabadi) and *Hurmatiyah-'i sadat* in 1906, and in 1908 Tubá Azmudah opened *Namus*. The following years witnessed a rapid expansion of such schools in Tehran. Provincial capitals followed suit: *Bunat* was opened in Qazvin in 1908, *Bunat-i Islami* in Rasht in 1911, and *Fatimiyah* in Shiraz in 1920. The information on girls' schools has been extracted from newspaper reports of the period and from the following sources: Ministry of Education, Endowments, and Fine Arts (*Vizarat-i ma'arif va awqaf va sanayi'-i mustazrifah*), *Qavanin va nizam'namah'ha, ihsa'iyah-'i madaris va makatib, a'za'va mustakhdimin* (for 1927), pp. 62, 74, 110, 112, 124, 130, 132, 142, 158, 162; "Brief History of Education (*Tarikhchah-'i ma'arif*)," pt. 2, in *Ta'lim va tarbiat* 4, nos. 7–8 (October–November 1934): 459–64; Shams al-Din Rushdiyah, *Savanih-i 'umr* (Tehran: Nashr-i Tarikh-i Iran, 1983), p. 148; and Fakhri Qavimi, *Kar'namah-'i zanan-i mashhur-i Iran* (Tehran: Vizarat-i Amuzish va Parvarish, 1973), pp. 128, 131, 142. By 1911, there were 47 schools for girls in Tehran with 2,187 students (compared with 78 for boys with 8,344 students). See Mustafá Mansur al-Saltanah, *Rapurt-i salianah dar bab-i ma'arif va ta'limat-i 'umumi: sanah-'i 1328–29* (Tehran: Vizarat-i ma'arif va favayid-i 'ammah va awqaf, 1911), appended tables, no page number or table number. For more information on women's education and in particular the establishment of schools, see the forthcoming essays in *Encyclopaedia Iranica* on education.

102   See Qavimi, *Kar'namah*; Badr al-Muluk Bamdad, *Zan-i Irani az inqilab-i mashrutiyat ta inqilab-i sifid*, 2 vols. (Tehran: Ibn Sina, 1968, 1969) for some of these stories. For a contemporary account, see the letter by Bibi (Khanum Astarabadi), "Letter from a Woman (*Maktub-i yiki az nisvan*)," *Tamaddun* 1, no. 15 (May 7, 1907): 2–3. See also Mihrangiz Mallah and Afsaneh Najmabadi, eds., *Bibi Khanum Astarabadi and Khanum Afzal Vaziri* [in Persian] (New York and Bloomington, Ill.: Nigarish va nigarish-i zan, 1996).

103   Huma Rizvani, ed., *Lavayih-i Aqa Shaykh Fazl'allah Nuri* (Tehran: Nashr-i tarikh-i Iran, 1983), pp. 28, and 62. Many other religious leaders, however, such as Hajj Mirza Hadi Dawlatabadi, father of Sadiqah Dawlatabadi (discussed by Sullivan, chap. 6 in this volume), Shaykh Hadi Najmabadi, father of Agha Baygum and Bibi Naj-mabadi, and Shaykh Muhammad Husayn Yazdi, husband of Safiyah Yazdi, supported the establishment of new schools for girls, and their own female family members were active educationalists.

104   "Essay from a Lady (*Layihah'-i yaki az khavatin*)," *Habl al-matin* (Tehran) 1, no. 105 (September 1, 1907): 4–6. For another protest letter by a group of women, see "Grievance of Association of Women of Tehran to the Respected Association of Students (*Tazallum-i jama'at-i nisvan-i Tihran bah anjuman-i muhtaram-i ittihadiyah-'i tullab*)," *Musavat* 1, no. 18 (March 22, 1908): 5–6.

105   "On the Miseries of Women (*Dar bicharigi-yi zanan*)," *Iran-i naw* 3, no. 102 (July 26, 1911): 3.

106   This refers to the tzarist takeover of these provinces in northern Iran in various military campaigns in the first half of the nineteenth century, delineating the contemporary borders of Iran in the north.

107   *Iran-i naw* 1, no. 114 (January 18, 1910): 4.

108   From the speech of one of the students of the Hunar school, on the occasion of the examination of its students, *Iran-i naw* 3, no. 83 (July 3, 1910): 3.

109   *Iran-i naw* 1, no. 19 (September 15, 1909): 3. See also Tayirah, "Letter from an Iranian Lady (*Maktub-i yaki az khanumha-yi Irani*)," *Iran-i naw* 1, no. 17 (September 13, 1909): 2, and her long essay serialized in the same paper, in which she developed similar arguments for women's education: Tayirah, "Essay by a Knowledgeable Lady (*Layihah-'i khanum-i danishmand*)," *Iran-i naw* 1, no. 65 (November 13, 1909): 3; no. 69 (November 18, 1909): 3; no. 78 (November 30, 1909): 2–3; no. 84 (December 8, 1909): 3; no. 92 (December 18, 1909): 3–4.

110   All quotations from Tayirah, "Essay by a Knowledgeable Lady (*Layihah-'i khanum-i danishmand*)," *Iran-i naw* 1, no. 78 (November 30, 1909): 2–3.

111   It is significant that the Persian expressions, constructed in parallel, "house management," "husband management," and "child management" (*khanah'dari, shawhar'dari*, and *bachchah'dari*) were distinct

and remain largely so, indicating rather distinct tasks and preoccupations. In other words, a combined construct, such as "housewife" (*zan-i khanah'dar*), was not opted for until recently and even then largely as a statistical category.

112   See Camron Amin, "The Rise of the Professional Woman in the Iranian Press, 1910–46" (paper presented at the Berkshire Conference of Historians of Women, June 1996), and his "The Attentions of the Great Father: Reza Shah, 'The Woman Question,' and the Iranian Press, 1890–1946" (Ph.D. diss., University of Chicago, 1996).

113   She is often wrongly referred to as the wife of one Dr. Kahhal, based on a reading of *khanum duktur Kahhal* as *khanum-i duktur Kahhal*, perhaps an indication of historians' disbelief that a woman ophthalmologist could have existed.

114   "Household Management (*Khanah'dari*)," *Danish*, no. 1 (September 11, 1910): 4–5; no. 4 (October 22, 1910): 7–8; no. 6 (November 6, 1910): 4–6; no. 8 (November 28, 1910): 8.

115   "Husband Management (*Rasm-i shawhardari*)," *Danish*, no. 1 (September 11, 1910): 5–6; "Husband Management (*Shawhardari*)," no. 7 (November 13, 1910): 4–6.

116   "Child Management (*Bachchah'dari*)," *Danish*, no. 10 (December 17, 1910): 2–3.

117   "Children's Hygiene (*Hifz al-sihhah-'i atfal*)," *Danish*, no. 1 (September 11, 1910): 2–3; no. 3 (October 10, 1910): 4–6; no. 4 (October 22, 1910): 2–4; no. 5 (October 31, 1910): 8; no. 8 (November 28, 1910): 2–4; no. 17 (February 4, 1911): 2–3; no. 23 (March 25, 1911): 5–7; no. 25 (April 22, 1911): 5–7; no. 30 (July 20, 1911): 2–4.

118   *Danish*, no. 7 (November 13, 1910): 6–7; no. 8 (November 28, 1910): 7–8; no. 9 (December 10, 1910): 6–7; no, 10 (December 17, 1910): 5–8; no. 17 (February 4, 1911): 3–4; no. 25 (April 22, 1911): 8; no. 26 (May 8, 1911): 4–7.

119   "Letter from a Girl Educated in Europe (*Maktub-i yiki az dukhtarha-yi tarbiat'shudah-'i Yurup*)," *Danish*, no. 27 (May 23, 1911): 2–3.

120   'Ali Zanjani, "Education of Girls (*Tarbiat-i dukhtaran*)," *Danish*, no. 22 (March 12, 1911): 2–3; quotation from p. 2.

121   "Husband Management (*Rasm-i shawhardari*)," *Danish*, no. 1 (September 11, 1910), p. 6.

122   "Nanny Cannot Be Kinder Than Mother (*Dayah az madar mihraban'tar ni-mishavad*)," pt. 1, *Danish*, no. 3 (October 10, 1910): 2–4, pt. 2, no. 5 (October 31, 1910): 2–4. Recall that Fani Kashmiri had argued the opposite: that it was preferable to engage a nanny for the care of the child. *Akhlaq-i 'alamara*, p. 136.

123   "Nanny Cannot Be Kinder Than Mother," pt. 1, p. 2.

124   Ibid., pp. 3–4.

125   Ibid., pt. 2, p. 2.

126   Ibid., pp. 3–4.

127   See, for instance, R.H.M., "Iranian Women's Knowledge: One of the Origins of Our Misfortunes (*Ma'arif zanha-yi Iran: yiki az sarchashmah'ha-yi badbakhti-i ma*)," *Shukufah* 1, no. 9 (May 5, 1913): 1–2; no. 10 (May 26, 1913): 2–3; no. 11 (June 13, 1913): 3; no. 14 (August 27, 1913): 3. "On the Fundamentals of Respected Ladies' Lives (*Dar asas-i zindigi-i khanumha-yi muhtaram*)," *Shukufah* 1, no. 17 (November 4, 1913): 3; 2, no. 18 (November 21, 1913): 4; no. 19 (December 15, 1913): 3; no. 20 (December 25, 1913): 4; no. 23 (February 12, 1914): 3–4.

128   Maliktaj, Untitled article, *Shukufah* 1, no. 4 (February 14, 1913): 2–3; no. 5 (February 28, 1913): 2–3; no. 7 (April 2, 1913): 1; no. 7 (April 2, 1913): 1. For other articles on the importance of educated wives and scientific mothers for the political fate of the country, see N. R. (An Iranian girl), "Learning about the Truth of Matters (*Agahi ya haqiqat-i matlab*)," *Shukufah* 1, no. 6 (March 13, 1913): 2–3; article by principal of elementary school "Hurriyah-'i sadat," "The Green Grass Was Trampled upon by Discord (*Basat-i sabzah lagadkub shud bah pa-yi nifaq*)," *Shukufah* 1, no. 7 (April 2, 1913): 1–2.

129   "What Is a School and What Are Its Qualifications? (*Madrasah chah nam ast va sharayit-i 'u kudam ast?*)," *Shukufah* 1, no. 5 (February 28, 1913): 1–2; no. 7 (April 2, 1913): 2–3; no, 8 (April 20, 1913): 2–3; no, 9 (May 5, 1913): 3; no. 14 (August 27, 1913): 2–3. "Enter the House through Its Entrance (*Fa'idkhalu al-buyut min ab-wabiha*)," *Shukufah* 1, no. 12 (July 28, 1913): 2–3; no. 14 (August 27, 1913): 1.

130   "Bad Imitation (*Taqlid-i bad*)," article started in issue no. 1 (which I have not been able to find), continued in *Shukufah* 1, no. 5 (February 28, 1913): 3; no. 7 (April 2, 1913): 3. "Who Is a Good Girl? (*Dukhtar-i khub kudam ast?*)," *Shukufah* 1, no. 11 (June 13, 1913): 3. A more detailed analysis of *Shukufah* deserves a separate essay.

131   Mirza 'Azizallah Khan, *Tarbiat al-bunat* (Tehran: Matba'ah Khawrshid, 1905), p. 6.

132   Emphasizing the link between the acquisition of modern education and chastity, many of the earliest schools for girls were named appropriately: *Namus* (honor), *'Ifaf* (chastity), *'Ismatiyah* (place of

chastity/innocence), *'Iffatiyah* (place of chastity), and perhaps most tellingly *Hijab* (veil). In other words, education was constructed as a replacement of the physical veil, as protector of honor and chastity. For further discussion of this point, see Najmabadi, "Veiled Discourse."

133   See "On Children's Hygiene (*Dar hifz al-sihhah-'i atfal*)," *Shukufah* 1, no. 17 (November 4, 1913): 1.

134   "On Duties of Real Teachers of Men, That Is, Women (*Dar farayiz-i murab-bian-i haqiqi-i mardan ya'ni nisvan*)," *Hadid* 1, no. 13 (September 21, 1905): 4–6.

135   *Iran-i naw* 3, no. 81 (July 1, 1911), p. 3.

136   *Payk-i sa'adat-i nisvan* (a women's journal published in the northern provincial capital city Rasht, under the editorship of a woman, Rushanak Naw'dust) 1, no. 1 (October 7, 1927): 8. See also the article titled "Chastity," in the same journal, 1, no. 6 (September 1928): 168–74. Other journals of the same period, such as *Iranshahr, Farangistan*, and *Nahid* had similar articles in their women's columns.

137   For a discussion of these women's activities, see Janet Afary, "On the Origins of Feminism in Early Twentieth-Century Iran," *Journal of Women's History* 1, no. 2 (Fall 1989): 65–87; Bamdad, *Zan-i Irani*; Mangol Bayat-Philipp, "Women and Revolution in Iran, 1905–11," in *Women in the Muslim World*, ed. Lois Beck and Nikki Keddie (Cambridge: Harvard University Press, 1978), pp. 295–308; Rushanak Mansur, "Women's Images in the Constitutionalist Press (*Chihrah-'i zan dar jarayid-i mashrutiyat*)," *Nimeye Digar*, no. 1 (Spring 1984): 11–30; 'Abd al-Husayn Nahid, *Zanan-i Iran dar junbish-i mashrutah* (Saarbrucken: Nuvid, 1989); Afsaneh Najmabadi, "*Zanha-yi millat*: Women or Wives of the Nation?" *Iranian Studies* 26, nos. 1–2 (Winter-Spring 1993): 51–71; Homa Nategh, "The Woman Question in Some of the Writings of the Left from the Constitutional Movement to the Era of Riza Khan (*Mas'alah-'i zan dar barkhi az mudavvanat-i chap az nihzat-i mashrutah ta 'asf-i Riza Khan*)," *Zaman-i naw* 1 (November 1983): 8–17, 27; Eliz Sanasarian, *The Women's Rights Movement in Iran* (New York: Praeger, 1982).

138   For a discussion of these points, see Najmabadi, "*Zanha-yi millat*."

139   *Shukufah* 4, no. 4 (January 20, 1916): 2–3.

140   *Shukufah* 4, no. 8 (April 2, 1916): 8–9.

Chapter 11

Jan Kociumbas

CHILDREN IN CHAINS:
JUVENILE CONVICTS

Thomas Willetts No.1809
 tried 12 March 1833, arrd. V.D.L Aug. 1834.
  Trade: None   Height: 4 ft. 11 in.
  Complexn: Dark   Head: Small
  Hair: Brown   Whiskers: None
  Visage: Small   Forehead: M. Ht.
  Eyebrows: Brown   Eyes: Grey
  Nose: Small   Mouth: Med. Wide
  Chin: Small   Remarks: Pockmarked, scar on Rt. Arm
 Arrived in Van Diemen's Land August 1834.
 Convict. 7 Years' Transportation.
 Tried at Warwick, transported for stealing Stockings.
 Character—*Very Bad.*[1]

THOMAS WILLETTS, AGED SIXTEEN, was one of about 25,000 male and female convicts aged eighteen or under who were sent to Australia—that is, about 15% of all those transported between 1788 and 1868.[2] Thomas' destination was Point Puer, a new institution established in Van Diemen's Land specifically to deal with juvenile males. Here it was thought that they could be transformed into useful, law-abiding adults.

Owing to variations in official definitions of childhood, the exact number of juveniles transported to Australia will probably never be known. The children themselves were uncertain about their age. One of them, when asked, answered. 'I was so young when I was born that I cannot tell.' We do know, however, that there were at least five times as many boys as girls transported, and that the proportion of male and female transportees in their mid to late teens grew steadily as the transportation system matured. Of 900 convict males arriving in 1812–13, only 3% were under sixteen, whereas between 1837 and 1842 the numbers of juvenile boys were so great that 1,600 were dispatched to Van Diemen's Land alone, in nine ships specially devoted to transporting the young. At the same time, significant numbers of juveniles were also coming out on adult transports. In 1835, for example, the *Henry Porcher* brought to New South Wales 51 boys aged sixteen and under—almost 20% of its total human cargo. Though the transportation of juveniles to the eastern colonies peaked around 1840, shiploads were still sent to Western Australia until 1852.

By the 1830s officials were compiling increasingly detailed physiological descriptions of young offenders. These also provide a glimpse of the world from which they were being removed. It seems that even by contemporary standards, Thomas Willetts and his companions were short and perhaps underweight, though this depends on trusting their stated age. Four thirteen-year-olds on the *Lord Goderich* (one of the ships carrying exclusively convict boys), measured a mere 3ft 11in. In 1843 the Guardian of Juvenile Immigrants in Western Australia reported that many employers did not want such small, 'delicate' children and he doubted that their recorded age was accurate. The Governor of Parkhurst, however, said in 1847 that boys often declared they were older than their reported age. If the boys were right, then they were indeed remarkably short. From these descriptions, we also know that perhaps a fifth of the child convicts transported in the 1830s and 1840s were scarred by smallpox. Many had occupational injuries, such as the loss of fingers or a hand. About one-third of the boys and many convict women and girls had decorative tattoos.

Juvenile convicts at Port Jackson

During the first thirty years of the system, young offenders were few and did not attract special attention or debate. Of some 586 male and 192 female First Fleet convicts, only a sprinkling were juveniles. They included young Elizabeth Hayward, aged thirteen when convicted of stealing clothes in 1787; and John Wisehammer, aged sixteen, serving seven years' transportation for stealing a bladder of snuff. Much more desperate and certainly more hungry was seventeen-year-old John Bennett, hanged in Sydney in May 1788 for lifting three and a quarter pounds of biscuits and four pounds of sugar from the government stores. Transported for seven years for highway robbery, Bennett had received an 87-stroke flogging for 'breaking out of irons' within a fortnight of sailing for Botany Bay. He received a further 45 lashes 'at the cart's tail' soon after arrival for theft, and was the second person to be executed in the new penal colony.

In England, though the criminal law defined young people as children until fourteen, those aged from seven could be held criminally liable if it were proved that they knew they were doing wrong. Up until the 1820s, some of the younger children convicted of petty offences were released because the range of punishments seemed too harsh. Others, however, were hanged, gaoled or transported exactly as if they were adults. Since young offenders had been sent to the American colonies since the early seventeenth century, there was nothing to preclude transporting them to New South Wales as lively little adult labourers. Indeed, after a seven-year term, they would be the right age to fit into the formula for 30-acre family farming.

These early juveniles had not been transported on special ships, but had sailed with adult convicts and on arrival slept in tents or in the open air. The new penal settlements were labour camps rather than penitentiaries, where the boys were expected to assist with clearing land, planting crops, cutting timber and breaking stone for buildings, wharves and roads. The girls cooked, sewed, washed, harvested and served the general needs of officers and convict men. These children also shared the privations of the early years, when grain failed, cattle strayed and livestock died, and even the rabbits brought from the Cape by the First Fleet failed to adapt to the new environment. After the loss of the supply ship *Guardian* at the Cape in December 1789 and the wreck of the *Sirius* on Norfolk Island in March 1790, food was ever more carefully rationed according to gender and age, and most of it went to able-bodied, labouring men. By May 1792, when rations had been reduced to bare subsistence level, women and children over ten received a weekly ration of one and a half pounds of flour, two pounds of salt meat, and three pounds of maize. As Collins conceded, two pounds of salt pork, when boiled, shrank away to nothing, barely affording three or four morsels a day. Though colonists rapidly learned to supplement rations with local animals and plants, years of such a low-vitamin diet may have caused physical and mental deterioration, especially from the mid 1790s when rum was over-consumed.

Convict children in assignment

The labour potential of the juvenile convicts found a strong demand, especially after the development of an assigned labour system in 1793, when many civil and military officers settled in the colonies and took up land grants for farming. Since they disdained manual work, it became customary to assign to them up to ten convict workers at the state's expense, a service not generally available to ex-convict farmers. This practice allowed officers to acquire most of the profit (and sterling currency) derived from sales of food to the Government Store, and to monopolise the importation of vital commodities during the hungry years. Accordingly, they acquired much of the best farming land, often by forcing ex-convict farmers out of business.

Though the government still employed some convict boys, many of those arriving after the mid 1790s were assigned to the larger, private farms to the south and west of Sydney, where they became grooms, gardeners, labourers, or general servants. They were dependent on their employer for shelter, clothing and food and could be brought before a magistrate, usually another land-owner, for any misdemeanour. As the colony expanded, a few boys found their way into more skilled trades such as tailoring, hat-making or boat-building. Later they might earn a ticket-of-leave for good behaviour and work on their own account. Britain's changeover to mass production meant that apprenticeships in skilled trades were ever more closely guarded, because in return for a child's services artisans contracted to pay a small wage and to impart the skills of their trade. Craft workers were being transformed into a labour 'aristocracy', proud of their autonomy, workmanship and the family security which membership of a craft union or friendly society provided, guaranteeing insurance against accident, unemployment or death. In the colonies, however, competition from rising numbers of native-born children and from those arriving with free immigrant parents made it difficult for juvenile convicts to gain access to the few skilled apprenticeships available.

Convict girls, like the women, were usually assigned to domestic service, where they were also expected to perform sexual services, first for civil and military officials, later for a wide range of colonial men. Their humble origin and lack of protection from family and kin meant that few could evade this sexual exploitation, which commenced during the voyage. On many ships it became customary to permit the crew free access to the women and to prostitute the 'youngest and handsomest' to naval vessels at common ports of call. Ships' officers also subjected women and girls to harsh corporal punishments, often of a sadistic and sexual nature. This savage treatment was rationalised by the prevailing belief of educated male Europeans that working-class women, like indigenous ones, were sexually depraved and troublesome, but useful in colonisation for carnal pleasures, labour and as a demographic resource. After arrival, little non-sexual work was made available for convict women and no shelter. The fact that many had left husbands and children in Britain was of little account. They were expected to survive initially by becoming prostitutes or mistresses, later perhaps by marrying one of the convict or ex-convict males. Thus Mary Branham, convicted in 1784 at the age of thirteen for stealing clothes, by 1790 was the mistress of Lieutenant Ralph Clark, one of the officers administrating the Norfolk Island settlement. In 1791, when he returned to England to his wife, she was left with their child.

The assignment system promoted this sexual and reproductive role, for it became routine for prospective male employers to go on board newly arrived ships and select their servants personally. 'The cattle that were brought in the *Hunter*, and which were sold by auction at this time, were not greater objects of contest than were these females,' reported Judge-Advocate David Collins after ninety-four women convicts arrived on the *Britannia* in July 1798. Collins himself was the father of at least three illegitimate children, two by Sydney convict Ann Yeates and one by sixteen-year-old Margaret Eddington, daughter of a convict couple. Lieutenant King, sent to establish the Norfolk Island settlement in 1788, left two sons to convict Ann Innett. Since economic opportunities for independent women were scarce, most convict girls had no choice but to attempt to secure more permanent de facto relationships or marriage. In this many were successful, for the convict colonies remained male-dominated societies until the mid-nineteenth century and even later in rural areas. In New South Wales and Van Diemen's Land in the early 1830s, women comprised only 28% of the total European population of 93,500.

Increasing numbers of child convicts

In the period following the Napoleonic Wars this indifference towards the convict child changed considerably, partly due to a steady rise in the number of children being brought before the British courts. This reflected the rising unemployment of adult breadwinners and children alike. Not only were thousands of demobilised servicemen now in search of work; the drift to the cities fuelled earlier marriage and sexual activity, accelerating birth rates. Doubling between 1811 and 1821, the population continued to climb steeply over the next decade. The increasing birth rate itself focused attention on the young. In 1821, almost 50% of the people in England and Wales were aged nineteen or under. Family trauma was compounded by growing political protest, resulting in the hanging, imprisonment or transportation of breadwinners. By the 1830s some 10% of the English population and 25% of the Irish depended on parish charity. In 1834 a New Poor Law denied the traditional form of parish 'outdoor relief' to destitute rural families and made charity dependent upon entering a workhouse. Here family members were split up and conditions were made as punitive as possible, forcing the able-bodied poor to move to the cities. Older children often preferred this option, since workhouses now periodically cleared their floors of destitute children by arrangement with manufacturers who put them to work night and day, A Factory Act of 1819, forbidding the employment of children under nine in cotton mills and manufactories, was flagrantly contravened, while in less easily inspected industries juvenile 'sweated' labour reached new extremes. In rural areas, gangs of children aged from four upwards worked from dawn to dusk under overseers, pulling turnips and doing other onerous outdoor work: in domestic industries such as lace-making, they handled bobbins from the age of three or four and worked a twelve-hour day; in the mines they spent the entire day in darkness, some as 'trappers' in charge of the ventilation doors, older ones driving pit ponies or crawling through narrow passages hauling coal.

Rising numbers of child 'criminals' also arose from changes in policing. Although legislation such as the Vagrancy Act of 1824, the Malicious Trespassing Act of 1827 and the Metropolitan Police Act of 1829 put all the unemployed at greater risk of arrest, it fell most heavily on juveniles since it transformed formerly tolerated street behaviour and survival tactics into specific crimes. Statistics on juveniles collected by sociological 'experts' added to panic that respectable society was being swamped by a rising tide of young delinquents. It followed that the inception of special children's ships and penal institutions completely overcame magistrates' former reluctance to convict the young.

Changes in penal ideology and the convict system during the 1820s

Growing concern over juvenile offenders was not caused by sheer numbers alone. It was also prompted by calls for better methods of penal 'correction'. In tandem with their attack on convict labour as slavery, both the Utilitarian and evangelical wings of the liberal reform movement had been evolving ways of separating punishment from labour. Random transportation sentences were to be replaced by fixed terms of incarceration. Careful assessment of character and new educative techniques would transform each prisoner mentally and morally before release to swell the free labour force. Reformers advocated replacing flagellation and physical punishment with a more subtle, permanent colonisation of the mind. Some favoured rationalist theories of education such as the mechanistic pleasure-pain principle and the association of ideas. New sciences such as phrenology suggested that repetitive mental exercise might develop certain mental 'faculties' and shrink others. Religious reformers favoured Bible readings and catechal instruction, encouraging penitence by tasks of stupefying repetition, with round-the-clock surveillance of sexuality. Mechanical contrivances such as the treadwheel were invented, supposedly gauging the degree and appropriateness of chastisement. Also required were special buildings, preferably like Bentham's 'Panopticon' where all inmates could be classified and constantly observed. Particularly recalcitrant characters would undergo solitary confinement and personal torment in silent, dark cells. As for the missions, remote situations were favoured for these new penitentiaries. As for Aboriginal people, so for convicts, release would follow when mental modification was considered complete.

This agenda, however, was fraught with difficulties. Incarceration, though necessary for penance and re-education, clashed with employers' demands for cheap adult and child labour. This was a particular problem in the convict colonies where pastoralists, heavily dependent on the convict workforce, were just as opposed to reformist penal ideology as they were to missionary efforts to transform Aboriginal people into diligent 'free' labourers. These men were sufficiently influential in the 1820s to force a compromise. The assignment system was permitted to continue while a range of modern penitentiaries was built in the convict colonies and at home. Thus, colonial assigned labourers who committed secondary offences against their masters could be sent to one of these new, experimental institutions located, for example, at Norfolk Island and Moreton Bay.

The tension between the ideal of educative incarceration and the dependence on cheap assigned labour was especially acute when applied to the young. Philanthropists thought that Rousseau's concept of childhood innocence and education should be extended to include the convict child. In a rhetoric of 'rescue' and 'protection', they began to argue that perhaps even these children were essentially pliable and good, the victims of parental 'neglect'. They should be accommodated not with hardened adult criminals, to be 'schooled in vice and crime', but in separate institutions that gave them a godly education and useful trade. However, as Locke had long ago made clear, the children of the poor might be innocent and malleable, but their work potential was far too valuable to be lost in costly, prolonged schooling or unproductive play. Nor did the fruit of their labour belong to their parents—it was a resource to be exploited by employer or state. In Locke's view pauper children should be consigned to the workhouse from the age of three. Besides, a well-run factory or workhouse was itself a kind of school, imposing as much discipline as any schoolmaster could dole out.

A second impediment to schooling convict juveniles involved fears that incarceration might encourage homosexuality, especially among boys. Male juveniles herded together might also 'contaminate' each other by exchanging information of a criminal or political kind. Not until the 1840s were similar fears expressed about girls. Whereas this might have reflected their fewer numbers, it was also a measure of the fact that girls were considered less innocent than boys. Though this meant they were more easily corrupted and, once 'fallen', harder to reclaim, because most convict girls were of or close to marriageable age, doubts about incarcerating them usually focused on the fact that this interfered with early wedlock, where their dangerous sexuality could be disciplined *gratis* by their spouse. For boys, however, anxieties about homosexuality prompted constant experimentation in penal discipline. Pastoralists, critical of incarceration, argued with reformers obsessed with real and imagined threats to the purity of the young. For convict boys, these interventions on their behalf had as much value as they did for Aboriginal children incarcerated in missions. 'Rescue' often meant a more punitive regime and a future not necessarily happier than that of taking their chances in the outside world.

Separating the men from the boys: the Carters' Barracks

In Britain, interest in the protection and education of juveniles was accelerated by the interventions of Elizabeth Fry and the Prison Discipline Society, as well as by allegations by British men of property that the transportation system was failing to arrest the rise of 'crime'. In 1819 a British enquiry was told that juvenile gangs of up to 150 young boys were at loose in London, not only picking pockets and stealing from shops, but also sleeping promiscuously with each other and with girls. Accordingly, from 1817 separate special accommodation was arranged for boys on male convict ships and in 1819 an ambitious experiment in re-educating convict boys was developed at the Carters' Barracks.

Just out of Sydney along the Parramatta Road at Brickfields Hill, this institution for 'Government men' was the prototype of several penal innovations. In 1823 it became the first convict establishment to introduce the treadwheel. Part of this building was turned over to incarcerating young male offenders, housing over 100 by 1820. Here, as in the Native Institution, the boys received minimal school instruction (two hours) every morning, before instruction in a trade, which varied from 'gardener' to 'shoemaker', 'harnessmaker' to 'wheelwright'. Each day was rigidly divided into mechanistic, measurable units of time. On Sundays, religious instruction was provided. After a three-year programme, the boys were released to assignment. In Britain, a similar separation of juveniles from adult offenders was practised on the hulks from 1823 when first the *Bellerophon* and two years later the *Euryalus* were set aside for boys under sixteen.

Despite the rhetoric of reformers, the corporal punishment of boys found increasing favour, as documents from 1833 attest:

> 13. Edward Scandrake, Mangles, neglect of duty by feigning sickness, 25 lashes. He received 50 lashes last Monday week, but was never flogged before; his breech was sore from the last punishment: blood came at the first stroke: he screamed dreadfully at every lash: the blood running freely from the old wounds; he lost much blood: complained bitterly of the treatment at Carters' Barrack, and wished some one would examine into it; indeed all the Carters' boys invariably make the same complaint.

Adult criticism of the Barracks focused not on such savagery but on 'contamination' and costs. In 1832, Governor Arthur complained about the prolonged herding of boys on the hulks before transportation, arguing that after arrival the only solution was immediate assignment into 'secluded and compulsory employment with agricultural settlers in the interior of the colony'. In 1833 Governor Bourke, faced with growing numbers of juvenile convicts, reverted to this solution, assigning them straight from the ship into the service of colonists who had to reside at least twenty miles from Sydney. This practice continued in New South

Wales until the assignment system was phased out after 1838, by which time about another 1,000 boys had arrived there.

The result was that many newly arrived convict boys were sent to ever more remote, inland 'back runs' to work as shepherds. Known as 'crawling', this was an unskilled, lonely and despised task which, adult males avoided wherever possible. It involved following flocks all day on foot, and returning them at night to temporary yards constructed under the supervision of a hutkeeper. Here the sheep were watched till sunrise to prevent them from being 'rushed' by dingoes or straying should the wind blow the hurdles over. Some girls, black and white, were also employed as shepherds.

The more remote the area, the greater the risk of rape by older convict and ex-convict men. In 1838 James Rud, a 'New Chum' assigned as a shepherd to a pastoralist at Jerry's Plains, was watering sheep far inland at Currabubla Creek when an armed assigned servant of the Australian Agricultural Company approached him. Throwing the boy to the ground, the man threatened to blow his brains out, adding 'Now I will fuck you before I go'. That evening, when the boy had not returned, another man informed the hutkeeper that his 'New Chum' was still lying by the creek 'and he would like to fuck him' also. Eventually, when the sheep came home without the boy, the hutkeeper sent a second shepherd who found him 'in a dreadful state'. 'I felt seed come from his yard while it was in my fundament . . .' the boy told the court; '. . . he used great violence . . . I suffered so much from this act I was unable to turn in my bed for 10 days.'

As this savage assault interfered with the boy's ability to work, the other men reported it to the authorities. More often, employers brought child convicts before the courts to punish them for misdemeanours. The magistrate was the master's friend and almost certainly employed assigned servants himself.

[. . .]

The female factories

As ladies became more prominent among the evangelical reformers in Britain, more concern was expressed about the sexualised image of impoverished women. Female reformers believed that merely shipping out females, convict or free, as an antidote to male homosexuality or to the exploitation of Aboriginal women, was not sufficient. Home and family life must be made the basis of a new, more moral society, balancing the amoral world of the market and the rationalist rules of political economy by fostering the nurturing skills and refinement which, they believed, all women possessed. They believed that convict women were not all incorrigible prostitutes, but were reclaimable provided they were caught young and then educated. Then, rather than being disciplined by her husband, the reformed female convict might join her sisters as agents in *his* reform.

The fate of convict women and girls also interested male theorists relating penal reform to industrial efficiency and profits. Though some were committed to the rules of laissez-faire economics, which brooked no interference with female and child labour, others were aware that no society could continue dealing so harshly with its mothers and children without jeopardising its future labour supply. For one thing, industrial and sexual exploitation endangered female health and made far too many women and children dependent on charity. Furthermore, population had long been regarded as a valuable resource, part of the nation's 'treasure', and in the new industrialised economy profits depended on having a large reserve supply of workers to keep wages down. To these reformers, rising unemployment rates and rapid, haphazard population growth demonstrated the need for more efficient management of demographic capital, for greater encouragement of marriage and division of labour in the home, and for attention to factors such as the measurement of birth rates and mortality, health, sexuality and longevity. All these concerns forced attention to the 'protection' of girls.

In New South Wales an attempt had been made as early as 1804 to modify the treatment of female convicts as sexual commodities. Lieutenant King, back in the colony as governor and bringing with him a wife, assigned the upper floor of the new gaol at Parramatta as 'a secure place' to which 'delinquent' women could be consigned. It was a combination of workhouse, prison and nursery, where pregnant or nursing mothers and other unassignable women could be confined and put to work to produce linen, sailcloth and hemp. Known as the Female Factory, this institution had rapidly become far too small and most convict women had continued to fend for themselves. In 1821 a larger 'Factory' was completed at Parramatta; similar institutions were created in Hobart in 1821 and Georgetown in 1824. In 1827 the Hobart Factory was relocated at Cascades, and the Georgetown Factory was moved to Launceston in 1834. Newly arrived women and girls were now consigned here and those classified as assignable were dispatched to serve the employer class. As the ranks of wealthy merchants, pastoralists and their families expanded, the demand grew for a much more specialised range of female servants; seamstresses, cooks, kitchen and scullery hands, house-maids, nursemaids, ladies' maids, laundry workers and dairy hands. Assignment to one of these fields was in theory the first step by which the well-behaved could move towards freedom. Convict girls, however, were much more likely to be general servants. This meant being on call to all members of the household night and day for heavy tasks such as heaving hot water and firewood to every level of the house, stirring, squeezing, scrubbing, folding linen and clothes, moving heavy furniture and dusting and cleaning floors.

Consequently, for many convict girls the transportation experience was ever more likely to be entwined with the Factories. The proliferation of these institutions permitted magistrates to hand out secondary convictions with more abandon which in turn increased the disciplinary power of colonial masters and mistresses. As a group of convict women informed Charlotte Anley (an emissary of Fry) in 1836, in assignment they were worked 'like horses' and 'treated like dogs'. Young convict girls who committed a misdemeanour or became pregnant in service rapidly found themselves in a Factory 'Crime Class', such as the twelve-year-old sentenced in 1841 to 28 days labour at Launceston for impertinence to her mistress. Despite their name, these new institutions made less and less pretence of offering shelter or productive work for women and girls too refractory, ill or advanced in pregnancy to be assigned. To 'correct' them the factories resorted to solitary confinement on bread and water, head shaving, wearing an iron collar, breaking stones and picking oakum. All these measures were thought appropriate for women and girls who defied the best efforts of reformers and were becoming classified as a distinct criminal type.

Despite these innovative penal technologies, by the 1830s the Factories were attracting criticism. Far from erasing the stereotype of the sexualised, female convict, the Factories became notorious as alleged hotbeds of depravity. Sensational disclosures of inmates' deviance were partly triggered by practices like dances, songs, mock trials and other rituals ridi-culing authority, although these had long been a feature of convict solidarity in British prisons. The growing allegations of female misbehaviour were perhaps stimulated by new scientific theories about the sexual basis of female 'crime'. Juveniles, it was now said, were at the mercy of the 'Flash Mob', seasoned inmates who monopolised insider trade in comforts such as spirits or tobacco and engaged in homosexual liaisons or 'nailing', as it was called. The 'Mob' also encouraged girls to be insolent and disorderly in assignment or to run away.

Suggestions of the incidence of lesbianism in the women's institutions were alarming reformers mindful of the ideal of godly wives and prolific mothers. Since female institutions were overcrowded and there was a preponderance of single males, men were encouraged to visit the Factories and select a wife. Few women and girls opposed this outcome, even though marriage did not free them but assigned them to their husbands who could return them for a misdemeanour. Those who married from the Factory were likely to have met their suitor previously while in assignment (and indeed may have found themselves back in the Factory because of him). They thus had some opportunity to assess their chances of using marriage to escape at least from the penal system though not, of course, from unpaid household and sexual servitude. Even so. Sarah Bryant, aged eighteen when convicted in 1829, found that marriage in fact guaranteed neither of these outcomes. Extracted from the Parramatta Factory fifteen months after her arrival in the colony, the object of her affections was an ex-convict tailor. By 1835, however, he was a prisoner on the *Phoenix* hulk awaiting sentence for a property offence, while Sarah found herself again in assignment, this time further encumbered by an infant girl. Following numerous further convictions and punishment, she at length wrenched herself free of the system, gaining a conditional pardon is 1853.

The Artful Dodger defined

By the 1830s the growing numbers of children brought before the British courts convinced some reformers that urban street children were also a distinct criminal type. In the work of influential writers like Charles Dickens, younger urban boys figured as innocent objects who, though worthy of compassion, had been pushed out of the nest too early. Denied a childhood, they were in danger of being apprenticed into the tribes of stunted miniature adults thought to comprise the urban juvenile gangs. The detailed anatomical descriptions of convict boys like Thomas Willetts reflected this attitude. Apart from identifying individual absconders, the attention to measuring the body led to the efforts to locate, uproot and re-educate the potential offender before he or she hardened into a fully-fledged specimen of the deviant type. Despite growing concern about homosexuality, some authorities continued to see special juvenile institutions as the answer. In these places it was also easier to collect and collate information about the minds, bodies and moral values of the fledgling urban poor. By now, British magistrates appeared to be using the seven-year transportation sentence routinely for juvenile petty theft, even for first offenders, presumably in the belief that even if a sea-change made no difference, at least it helped disperse the juvenile gangs.

[. . .]

New institutions for boys: Point Puer

In the colonies, the debate between whether to educate convict boys upon arrival or put them to work had swung back firmly to the ideal of incarceration. In Van Diemen's Land, though older and stronger boys were consigned straight to labouring gangs such as those at Bridge Water or Saltwater Creek, most were sent to Point Puer, established by Governor Arthur in 1834. Here, though in barracks, they were in effect incarcerated in what was intended to embody a far more efficient, rational version of the reformers' ideal; than had been the case at Carters' Barracks. The site chosen was much more remote, 'a wretched, bleak, barren spot', quite unsuited to farming, and adjacent to the new adult penal station, Port Arthur, founded in 1830. Both these new institutions were separated from free society by a well-guarded, narrow neck of land.

At Point Puer, as at the Carters' Barracks, educative reformation entailed a minimum of formal instruction. Most of the boys' time was spent in semi-skilled work which helped to offset institution costs. The boys helped to construct an elaborate, Gothic church, and made wheelbarrows, coffins, school desks, garden gates, stocks and a pillory. Some helped to make bricks and nails, and sew the convicts' uniforms of yellow and grey wool. Others made Wellington boots which were sold at eleven shillings a pair, and even ladies' shoes, which fetched three shillings for the authorities. Moreover, the problem of a conflict between corrective education and productive labour was partly solved when transportation to New South Wales ceased in 1840 and the institution became part of the new 'Probation System'. All convicts would now follow a uniform course of punishment, either in a modern penitentiary or through a succession of work-gangs, passes and tickets-of-leave until eventually freed. Unprecedented attention was to be given to convicts' behaviour and character as they progressed through these phases of correction and work.

[. . .]

Parkhurst and 'exiles'

In the volatile debates about penal reform. Point Puer was no sooner founded than regarded obsolete, especially when contrasted with Parkhurst, the new British juvenile penitentiary that opened on the remote Isle of Wight in 1838. Intended to supersede the juvenile hulk *Euryalus*, Parkhurst offered superior facilities for classification, separation and surveillance, including separate cells in which every boy was to spend the first three or four months. Construction of a new juvenile penitentiary along similar lines commenced at Safety Cove near Port Arthur in 1844. This, however, was never completed, as the 'Probation system', almost from its inception, underwent further refinement. All convicts were now to be 'Exiles'—people who had already been schooled in a penitentiary in Britain. In 1842 the first 'Exiles' to arrive in Van Diemen's Land were hundreds of boys who had graduated from Parkhurst. Already in possession of a ticket-of-leave, their arrival hastened the decline of Point Puer, which closed by 1849.

Transportation to Van Diemen's Land ceased in 1853, but the colonial demand for juvenile labour continued. The image of the convict hulk persisted and was resurrected within a decade in nautical reformatories like the *Vernon*. In the interim, parties of Parkhurst boys were sent to New Zealand and Port Phillip, where over 500 had landed by 1846. A total of 334 were consigned to Western Australia where in 1844 one of their number, John Gavin, aged fifteen, was convicted of the murder of his mistress' son. He became the colony's first white person to be hanged.

In Britain, the transportation of children under fourteen years ceased in 1853. Transportation of Parkhurst boys to Western Australia ended in 1852, and of adult males in 1868. No female convicts were ever sent to Western Australia, due to the notion that since most women and girls were potential mothers and home-makers, the minority who continued to resist or fail in these roles were especially evil, transgressing not only the criminal code but nature itself. This view eventually promoted intervention to protect the 'innocence' of Aboriginal and working-class girls. In the penal colonies, the daughters of the convict women were already becoming acquainted with this unpleasant fact.

Notes

1   R. Hughes, *The Fatal Shore: A History of the Transportation of Convicts to Australia, 1787–1868*, Collins Harvill, London, 1987, p.412.

2   Humphery (1992), p.14. This chapter also draws heavily on Kyle (1988, 1992), plus Dow and Brand (1986), Buddee (1984), Hooper (1954, 1967), Brown (1972).
     See also general works on convicts, principally L.L. Robson, *The Convict Settlers of Australia*, MUP, Carlton, 1976, pp.38–39, 182, 187; S. Nicholas (ed.), *Convict Workers: Reinterpreting Australia's*

Past, CUP, Cambridge, 1988, p.52; C. Bateson, *The Convict Ships 1787–1868*, Library of Australian History, Sydney, 1983, p.79; A.G.L. Shaw, *Convicts and the Colonies*, MUP, Carlton, 1981; J. Hirst, *Convict Society and its Enemies*, Allen & Unwin, 1981; A.J. Gray, 'John Bennett of the *Friendship*', *JRAHS*, Vol.44, Pl.6, 1958, pp.399–409.

For the child too young to know his age, J. West, *The History of Tasmania*, Libraries Board of SA, Adelaide, 1966 [facsimile of 1st edn. Henry Dowling, Launceston, 1852], p.246; for the boys' heights and body marking, Humphery, p.14; B. Gandevia. 'A Comparison of the Heights of Boys Transported to Australia from England, Scotland and Ireland, c. 1840, with Later British and Australian Developments', *Aust. Paediatric Journal*, Vol.13, 1977, p.91; Buddee, pp.138, 157, 164; B. Gandevia, 'Some Physical Characteristics, Including Pock Marks, Tattoos and Disabilities of Convict Boys Transported to Australia from Britain c.1840', *Aust. Paediatric Journal*, Vol.12, 1976, pp.6–12; B. Smith, A Cargo of Women: Susanna Watson and the Convicts of the Princess Royal, UNSW Press, Kensington, 1988, p.176.

For the hungry years, J. Watt, 'The Colony's Health', in J. Hardy and A. Frost (eds), *Studies from Terra Australis to Australia*, Highland Press, Canberra, 1989, pp.142–45, 151.

For apprenticeship, E. Hobsbawm, *Worlds of Labour*, Weidenfeld & Nicolson, London, 1984, pp.252–72.

For the sexual exploitation of women and girls, see Collins (1975), Vol.2, p.87; Kociumbas (1992), pp.4–6, 19–20.

For early nineteenth-century Britain, P. Mathias, *The First Industrial Revolution: An Economic History of Britain 1700–1914*, Methuen, London, 1969, pp.191–93, 449; Thompson (1981), pp.339–41, 366–84; E. Hobsbawm, *Industry and Empire*, Penguin, Harmondsworth, 1981, pp.71, 73, 77; Pinchbeck and Hewill (1973), pp.390–405.

On penal ideology, see Magarey (1978), pp.11–25; M. Ignatieff, *A Just Measure of Pain: The Penitentiary in the Industrial Revolution*, Macmillan, London, 1978, pp.46–50, 61–63, 156–58, 183–87.

For London juvenile gangs, 1819, *BPP*, Report of Select Committee on Gaols, (Vol.7, No.579), Minutes of Evidence, pp.165, 169.

For Carters' Barracks, Earnshaw (1979): Return of Corporal punishments inflicted by sentence of the Hyde Park Barrack Bench, from the 4th to the 30th Sep. 1833, in the presence of E.A. Slade, J.P. Superintendent. Hyde Park Barrack, repr. In Appendix to Report from Select Committee on Transportation, 1837, *BPP*, (Vol.19, No.518) p.93. For rape of convict boy, AONSW, Bench Books, Muswellbrook 1838–43, Reel 671 (20 Apr. 1839); for Thomas Jackson, Spark (1976), pp.76, 92, 105, 112, 117.

For domestic service, Kingston (1975), pp.31–33; Dyster (1989), p.148. For Factories, Weatherburn (1979), pp.18–19; L. Heath, 'The Female Convict Factories of New South Wales and Van Diemen's Land . . . 1804–54', MA Thesis. Dept. of History, ANU, 1978, pp.171–72; Smith, pp.37, 39–40, 199; Daniels (1993), pp.133–49.

For 'Artful Dodger', C. Dickens, *Oliver Twist*, World's Classics, London, 1985, pp.58–59, 61–62, 140–45 [1st edn 1838]; *Fraser's Magazine*, Jun. 1832, pp.521–22, cited in J.J. Toblas, *Crime and Industrial Society in the Nineteenth Century*, Penguin, London, 1967, pp.52–54.

For Point Puer, Hughes, pp.412–14; R.C. Hooper, 'Some Observations on the Point Puer Experiment', *PTHRA* Vol.2, No.2, Mar. 1953, p.43; Kyle (1988), p.151; Shaw, p.244; D. Heard (ed.), *The Journal of Charles O'Hara Booth*. THRA, Hobart, 1981, pp.33, 61; Lempriere and Laplace both cited in Dow and Brand, pp.28, 30; Kyle (1992), pp.218–19.

For 'exiles', Shaw, p.286; Kyle (1988), p.151: Buddee, pp.98–104, 157–59, 164; Hetherington (1992), p.46.

References

Brown, Joan C., '*Poverty is not a Crime': The Development of Social Services in Tasmania 1803–1900*, THRA, Hobart, 1972

Buddee, Paul, *The Fate of the Artful Dodger: Parkhurst Boys Transported to Australia and New Zealand 1842–1852*, St George Books, Perth, 1984

Collins, David, *An Account of the English Colony in New South Wales* (ed. B. Fletcher), Reed, Sydney, 1975 [1st edn. 1798]

Daniels, Kay, 'The Flash Mob: Rebellion, Rough Culture and Sexuality in the Female Factories of Van Diemen's Land', *AFS*, Vol. 18, Summer 1993

Dow, Gwyneth and Brand, Ian, '"Cruel only to be kind"? Arthur's Point Puer', *History of Education Review*, Vol.15, No.1, 1986

Dyster, Barrie, *Servant and Master: Building and Running the Grand Houses of Sydney 1788–1850*, UNSW Press, Kensington, 1989

Earnshaw, Beverley, 'The Convict Apprentices, 1820–1838', *Push From the Bush*, No.5, Dec. 1979

Hetherington, Penelope, 'Child Labour in Swan River Colony, 1829–1850', *AHS*, Vol.25, No.98, Apr. 1992

Hooper, F.C., *Prison Boys of Port Arthur*, Cheshire, Melbourne, 1967

Humphery, Kim, 'Objects of Compassion: Young Male Convicts of Van Diemen's Land', *AHS*, Vol.25, No.98, Apr. 1992

Kingston, Beverley, *My Wife, My Daughter and Poor Mary Ann*, Nelson, Melbourne, 1975

Kociumbas, Jan, *Oxford History of Australia*, *Vol.2 Possessions*, OUP, Melbourne, 1992

Kyle, Avril, 'A Long Farewell': The British Experience and Colonial Fate of Juveniles Transported to Australia in the First Half of the Nineteenth Century', MA Thesis, Monash U., 1988

—— 'Little Depraved Felons', *AHS*, Vol.25, No.99, Oct. 1992

Magarey, Susan, 'The Invention of Juvenile Delinquency in Early Nineteenth-Century England', *Labour History*, No.34, May 1978

Pinchbeck, Ivy and Hewitt, Margaret, *Children in English Society, Vol.II, From the Eighteenth Century to the Children Act 1948*, Routledge & Kegan Paul, London, 1973

Spark, Alexander Brodie, *The Respectable Sydney Merchant: A.B. Spark of Tempe* (ed. G. Abbott and G. Little), SUP, Sydney, 1976

Weatherburn, Hilary, 'The Female Factory', in J. Mackinolty and H. Radi (eds), *In Pursuit of Justice* . . . Hale & Iremonger, Sydney, 1979

Chapter 12

Joseph E. Illick

AFRICAN AMERICAN CHILDHOOD

FREDERICK DOUGLASS WAS BORN IN 1818 in Talbot County, Eastern
Shore, Maryland, and there he spent his early years in the cabin of his grandparents,
Betsy (slave) and Isaac Baily (free), along with cousins and an infant uncle. His mother lived
nearby, though he did not see her during those years (later they were together several times)
and was never deeply attached to her, a situation he blamed on slavery. His father, whom he
may never have met, was white. "Slavery has no use for fathers or families," he later reflected,
but he claimed to have had a carefree and happy childhood with his grandmother, an intelligent woman who was physically powerful and skilled in fishing and farming.

She introduced six-year-old Frederick to his siblings at Wye House, a 12-mile-distant plantation managed by her master, Aaron Anthony (rumored to have been the boy's father), for the
wealthy and prestigious Lloyd family. She then slipped away, to the distress of her grandson,
who never again fully trusted anyone. At Wye House, the very bright and impressionable lad
experienced the indignities and cruelties of slavery, as well as the resentment of fellow slaves,
especially an auntie who bristled when Lucretia Anthony Auld—daughter of Aaron and wife of
Thomas (also rumored to be Frederick's father)—fed and cared for the boy. Lucretia took
Frederick to Baltimore, to live with Sophia and Hugh Auld, Thomas's brother and sister-in-law.

"I saw what I had never seen before; it was a white face beaming with the most kindly
emotions; it was the face of my new mistress, Sophia Auld." So Frederick wrote of his new
circumstances. "I had been treated as a *pig* on the plantation; in this new house, I was treated
as a *child*." About a year later Aaron Anthony died without a will, and the boy, now part of
an estate to be divided among Lucretia and her two brothers, was sent back to the place
where he had been born. Again he was rescued by Thomas Auld and returned to Baltimore,
where Sophia taught him to read, a subversive act which aroused her husband's wrath. But it
was too late. As Frederick wandered the city, and especially the docks, he improved his
reading, not to mention his listening, heard the word "abolition," talked with indentured and
free laborers, and got religion.

The Aulds recognized the rebellion brewing in his mind and, perhaps to protect the
15-year-old, shipped him to the run-down port of St. Michaels, back on the Eastern Shore.
But Thomas Auld would not allow Frederick to have a Sabbath school for other boys—shades
of Nat Turner! Rather, Auld hired him to Edward Covey, a pious "nigger-breaker" who

owned a farm nearby. Six months of beatings led the adolescent to fight back to a draw, an act for which he was not punished. In St. Michaels for the slack winter season, he organized youths again, this time for an escape. When it failed, Auld sent him back to Baltimore to be hired out as a skilled laborer. It was from this city, disguised as a seaman, that Frederick Douglass traveled by ferry, train, and steamer to Philadelphia and freedom.[1]

Most of the Africans brought to North America had come from west and west-central Africa. In the seventeenth century they arrived by way of the West Indies, while in the eighteenth century the vast majority came directly from Africa. Along the 3,500 miles of coastline from Senegal to Angola and its interior, there is considerable variation in climate, vegetation, and, consequently, ways of living. In this enormous area several hundred languages and myriad social customs flourished.

Nevertheless, there were elements of continuity within this vast region, linking its inhabitants to one another. The primary mode of identification for the African was the family and its descent groups. In west Africa, descent passed through the male, in west-central and central Africa, through the female. In either case, polygyny, the practice of a man possessing several wives or concubines, was a frequent if not universal practice.

Most Africans lived in small villages, although there were also large trading centers. Local economies were pastoral or agricultural, not based on hunting and gathering. Slavery among African peoples existed as an institution tied to the kinship system, with slaves employed as outsiders within the family but deprived of the protection that derived from belonging to the kinship group. Most slaves were women; enslavement of children and removal far from home was also a frequent practice. But the system in Africa, integrated as it was with kin and community, hardly resembled the North American chattel system, in which each slave was an individual commodity, legally salable.[2]

It was impossible to carry intact African customs of childbirth and child rearing to America, yet certain ones did survive in the New World, a fact largely unacknowledged until the middle of the twentieth century.[3] Childbirth in Africa was a women's affair, and not until the mother had spent six days lying with her child on a mat was a priest admitted to bathe (for the first time) and name the child, the name having been selected by the child's father in communication with spirits he encountered in a dream or while possessed. Childbirth in America drew to some extent on African folk beliefs, represented in such behavior as placing iron under the bed at parturition to ease birth pains and using cobwebs to stem hemorrhaging, as well as disposal of the placenta and treatment of the navel cord.[4]

The African practice of naming a child for the day, month, or season of his or her birth, as well as using the African rather than English designation, was evident among American blacks, slave and free. Often naming was delayed until it was reasonably certain the newborn would survive, since the necronymic pattern typical of European families, that is, bestowing the name of a deceased child on one newly born, was rejected in favor of recognizing the individual identity of the child. Finally, names were chosen to honor kin, showing the importance of the extended family.[5]

In west Africa, women nursed their children for two to three years and abstained from sexual intercourse until weaning was complete, yielding a birth interval of three to four years.[6] Across the Atlantic in the eighteenth century, when the slave population began to reproduce itself naturally in North America, nursing lasted a year or less, a situation probably brought about by the requirement that a mother return to work within a month of delivering. Indeed, immediately after delivery she was expected to do her own cooking and cleaning, activities that probably contributed to the high infant mortality rate.[7] She had either to take her infant into the fields or return to the slave quarters several times a day to feed it. (In Africa it was common practice for mothers to carry infants on their backs while they worked.)[8]

The relationship between work and infant survival, however, begins not after delivery but in the earliest months of pregnancy, at which time diet and the effects of disease are also critical factors. There is certainly evidence that many planters took the well-being of mother and child seriously. It is much less clear whether they understood the importance of early work release, even in times of illness. (Indeed, one slave mother related her work situation to her son's retardation.) Of course, many European Americans remained fatalistic about child death, black or white.[9]

The death rate among black infants was exceptionally high compared with that of their white counterparts, a fact attributed to nutritional liabilities, crib death, and poor postnatal care, as well as to neonatal tetanus, infanticide, worms, and overt sickle cell disease.[10] Once weaned, babes were under the care of children, usually siblings, only a few years older than themselves. (Babysitting chores ended at seven or eight.) This child care practice had roots in Africa. Among the Tiv of central Nigeria, for example, a six-month-old is assigned to an older sibling, usually of the same sex, who takes on the role of protector and accompanies the child everywhere.[11]

Anthropologists who have studied the Mandinka of Senegal argue that child caregivers not only "manage and shape the behavior" of their younger siblings but may also "facilitate the elaboration of certain values, attitudes, and beliefs that are subsequently critical elements of adult social behavior." These child caregivers are part of the village social structure and are able to articulate their responsibility.[12] But in America these caretakers were unsupervised unless an aged nonworker was available, and there appears to have been no village social structure to regulate their activities. While it is hard to believe that such care was trustworthy and easy to agree with the observer who sees child neglect as "inseparable from slavery and its work demands," some historians have judged that plantation nurseries resembled contemporary day care centers.[13]

But the basic psychological point is that for the African American child, the mother was frequently inaccessible (at least on the plantation—there were, of course, other living situations), having to return to work soon after she delivered.[14] One former slave explicitly recalled his "want of parental care and attention," noting that his parents were simply unable to tend him during the day.[15] It is not clear whether inaccessibility in itself raises fear in a child—or whether fear is aroused either by the distress an infant feels in the absence of someone who will soothe and feed it or by the greater intensity of response when an infant undergoes fear-inducing experiences (e.g., the presence of a stranger, a loud noise) alone. But separation inevitably engenders fear, although being left with a familiar companion/caretaker in a recognized place, as was the case with the young African American child, would mitigate the situation.[16]

Psychologist Lester Alston believes that the issue for the slave child was not bonding and attachment but satellization, the process which "permits children to develop sources of status and self-esteem around two years of age, once the 'inflated sense of self-worth' and the omnipotence of infancy are ended." In his view, owners were too powerful and parents too subjugated for slave children to look anywhere but toward the owner for status and self-esteem. Thus, a child could have developed an early autonomy, only to have it undermined during the satellization period.[17] Quite to the contrary, Wilma King asserts that slave parents were able to show their children "how to forge a balance between social courtesies to whites and their own self-esteem," while Marie Jenkins Schwartz argues that slave parents were always strong enough to negotiate with owners and taught their children through the example of their refusal to follow orders from owners. However, these two historians agree that parents had precious little time for their children.[18] It seems unlikely that fathers and mothers would have been able to instruct the young in lessons of self-esteem unless they were demonstrably powerful and/or the owner was weak and ineffectual.

In the Chesapeake in the eighteenth century, mothers usually were not separated by sale from their small children and so could expect to see them in the evenings; on large plantations, over half the fathers might also be present. Other fathers and older working children were likely to reside on nearby farms. With the emergence of a native-born slave population, a kinship network appeared, similar to that which existed in west Africa, allowing most children to live in the presence of familiars. A less positive scenario is that while planters valued the nuclear family—it was, after all, the unit of food and clothing distribution, the reproductive unit, and it served to attach potential runaways to the plantation—African Americans valued the whole extended family, which was seldom kept intact. The grim picture shows that the slave family, extended or nuclear, was always vulnerable and that most fathers did not live with their children.[19]

It would be only speculative to assert that children had, and at what age they had, the matter of their futures in mind. To some historians it appears that they played games which stemmed from their dawning recognition of their enslaved condition: "whipping" and "auction" perhaps provided ways of acting out so as to neutralize the real events. This interpretation is challenged by the observation that whipping games, for example, are universal. Certainly slave children saw their parents (but not their white peers) beaten, and their parents in turn beat them—whether because this was traditional practice or to prepare them for their adults lives. This violence must have assaulted any sense of autonomy they were developing.[20]

On the other hand, that black and white children played together on the plantation, usually boys with boys and girls with girls, probably made the future seem less portentous. Their games were influenced by the African past and the European American present. Nineteenth-century children, black and white, everywhere played the same games, though slave children transformed to their own uses the European games they learned from their white playmates. And white children, more than any other persons, taught their black peers how to read. Finally, white masters frequently petted black children, much in the patriarchal manner that they dealt with their own young.[21]

But the treatment, both positive and negative, was inconsistent. Meals, for example, were served to slave children in troughs, as if they were animals. The diet for children was exceedingly poor (meat was typically absent from their meals), as evidenced by the delayed growth of young slaves, at or below the rate of children of corresponding ages in the poorest populations of developing countries today. Diet did not improve until they entered the workforce, that is, until it was profitable to feed them well, after which time they showed remarkable powers of catching up in size.[22]

African American children were not usually required to do more than light work until the age of 10 or 12, when the harsh field life began.[23] This new situation marked the movement from childhood into adulthood. Sometimes it was accompanied by sale away from family.[24] Their parents, or at least their mothers, had trained them to be submissive workers, conforming (at least in appearance) to the demands of house mistresses, drivers, and owners who felt free to interfere in the child-rearing process. In Africa, children were taught their future tasks by imitating their parents of the same sex. African American parents did not have the luxury of teaching by example, and unlike European American parents they did not have firm control of their children.

The movement from childhood to adulthood in Africa was accomplished not by going to work or by separation from family but by initiation rites, much in the manner of American Indians.[25] The dramatic change in behavior and even in attachments must have had profound psychological meaning for the African American adolescent, perhaps intensifying early childhood fears of loss, a situation which served the interest of the slaveholder if only by investing the alternative to the hard labor of slavery—escape—with terror. If separation from family accompanied the new work regime, it would serve as an obstacle to the normal socialization of a young person. Simultaneously, the search of the newly separated adolescent for attach-ment probably reinforced the kinship system. It may also have contributed to the high rate of mental illness among slaves, a matter that has received little historical attention.[26]

The Emancipation Proclamation and the Thirteenth Amendment were intended to free African Americans from slavery. And, indeed, the institution disappeared—though immediately former slaveholders and other whites, as well, attempted to apprentice black children, even taking them from their parents who, the whites alleged, were unable to support them.[27] Yet black Southerners remained prisoners within a society controlled at every level by whites whose racial attitudes were unaltered by military defeat and proclamations of liberty. To them, blacks were inferior and must act appropriately. Until well into the twentieth century, the best African American parents could hope to do for their children was acquaint them with the demands of white domination and teach them the acquiescent behavior necessary for survival without sacrificing completely their sense of self-worth, their racial pride, and their hope.[28]

Parents could not, however, prepare children for the first humiliating racial insult. Even having white playmates was no insurance against it; indeed, under these circumstances it could be all the more hurtful. Robert Russa Morton never forgot the day when an eagerly awaited white playmate arrived home from prep school: not only was Robert's effusive greeting met with coldness but his childhood friend refused to shake hands; Robert was profoundly affected. And such insults were reified by continuing harassment—"The white children I knew grew meaner as they grew older," one black woman recalled—until a reser-voir of resentment and vindictiveness built up.[29]

Yet in no way could the flood gates containing these feelings be released on whites. Rather, black children had to master the mechanisms of control, even appear happy with their subordinate condition. Not surprisingly, young blacks became surreptitious students of their white enemies—the classroom of experience for African Americans whose schools were underfunded or nonexistent. (Blacks with white assistance had set up some public and private schools, but the poverty of the freed slaves and the resistance of Southern whites meant that funding was never close to adequate.)[30]

This was not a world parents could explain to children, much less justify except as the will of the Lord. Booker T. Washington, queried about "what sometimes seem hopelessly discouraging conditions," reminded his questioners "of the wilderness through which and out of which, a good Providence has already led us."[31] Indeed, because they too were the victims of white oppression, parents might well vent their anger and frustration on their offspring. Richard Wright described his boyhood in a household filled with sanctimony and violence; he was alternately preached to and beaten. Nor could whiteness be kept out of the black community, as skin hues, facial features, and hair texture created distinctions and hence divisions among African Americans.[32]

Despite these conflicts, the black family, both rural and urban, was a strong institution. Against great odds, African Americans had sought to cement slave marriages and families, simultaneously showing deep concern over their children's futures.[33] Herbert Gutman observes that in 1880 "between 66 percent and 75 percent of black children under the age of six everywhere lived with a mother and a father," while the so-called matrifocal family hardly existed. Between 1880 and 1900, however, the nuclear household declined in importance while the numbers of augmented and extended households increased. And intrafamily prob-lems, ranging from desertion to intergenrational battles, existed. Yet long marriages remained common, as did the attachment of parent to child.[34]

Family cohesiveness, however, only hints at child-rearing practices within the house-hold, though we can suppose continuity between the late nineteenth and the mid-twentieth century, about which we do have evidence. Illegitimate births were common before first marriages; mother and child almost always remained in the grandparental household, which served as a secure social setting for the child or children until the mother made a stable marriage. The first child was the most fondled and stimulated and often became the most self-confident and capable, illegitimate or not.

The greatest life pleasure of adults was found in relations with their young children. Hence, the infant's environment was fully human, virtually without baby furniture; it was held or carried most of the time, and even when bedded it was frequently accompanied. When the mother cradled it in her arms or held it in her lap, she also caressed it while her eyes explored its face. In the crowded household there were always others who wanted their turn, so that the infant was awake most of the day and slept a long night in its parents' bed. The giving and demanding of food was also an interactive routine. Bladder and bowel functions were quickly responded to, and training began early. Play most usually revolved around the pretense that the baby was aggressive, that it would bite and fight, and the mother in response was both indulgent and disciplinary but always involved.

With the revolution of walking, expectations changed. The former lap-baby, now knee-baby, was expected to use the chamber pot or excrete outside, but otherwise it could freely explore so long as it caused its mother no trouble. She began disciplining with a light switch, often playfully. The child world expanded to include the children's gang, whose members ranged from 15 months to a nurse-girl or boy of at least six, reminiscent of child care under slavery. But the mother remained engaged, enjoying the toddler's newfound independence. Thus the basis was laid for a healthy self-esteem, which made it possible for the parents to change their focus to the next sibling in line while expecting the almost three-year-old to transfer his allegiance to the children's gang, the core of which was the children of one family with some neighborhood hangers-on.

With these playmates the child ran, climbed, gossiped, seldom fought, and rarely saw toys. At 9 a boy might leave the group to range farther afield with his male age mates, unless he was the nurse, in which case he might remain until 14. Girls stayed on into adolescence, subdued and resigned, a mood foreshadowing the course of an adulthood lacking social status or material security but promising the pleasure of producing children. For girls and boys, the insular world of the black family was far safer than venturing into the larger society.[35]

African American childhood in the eighteenth and nineteenth centuries was profoundly affected by the social context of slavery and its aftermath. That context was accompanied by an ideology, a perception of the black minority, held by many white Americans. It was enunciated by George Wallace, a segregationist when he began his four terms (elected in 1962, 1970, 1974, 1982) as governor of Alabama, who reportedly gave barracks lectures during World War II defending his white supremacy position: "I don't hate them. The colored are fine in their place. But they're just like children and it's not something that's going to change. It's written in stone."[36] It did change, and Wallace recanted. Nevertheless, the idea of African Americans as children has had a history in America dating from the mid-nineteenth century.

Historian Thomas Webber argues that the planter class aimed to have slaves internalize values which would make them conscious of their own inferiority, "overflowing with awe, respect, and childlike affection for the planter and his family," happily aware of the rules of slave behavior, and convinced that slavery was not only right but the best of all possible worlds. Slaves were kept ignorant of the outside world and the written word, denied privacy, forbidden to recall their African past, and refused the very privileges that defined their white counterparts as adults.[37]

While Webber argues that most of the values, attitudes, and understandings taught by white masters were not accepted by black slaves, he concedes that one must look deep into the slave literature to reach this conclusion. In other words, even if slaves were not convinced by their masters, they had to disguise their true beliefs. How long this masquerade persisted, whether it still goes on, is a matter of debate.[38] But whichever side of the issue is taken, it seems that African Americans *eventually* fulfilled the expectations of European Americans who wanted to perceive them as perpetual children.

This was not the initial European perception of the African. Of course, blacks were subordinated in early American life, and probably they were believed to be inferior, although it was seldom argued before the 1830s that their inferiority was permanent.[39] However, the Abolitionist attack on slavery led to the Southern white defense that blacks were inherently suited to the institution and unfit for freedom, that they were in fact happy only under the guidance of white masters. While white servitude had naturally disintegrated, permanent black slavery was compatible with liberty and equality, as well as the biological inferiority of the African—by the 1840s, scientific evidence was marshaled to show that blacks constituted a separate species of person.

This sort of thinking could even be used by antislavery thinkers, such as the Unitarian pastor in New York who, on determining that the Negro's "nature is singularly childlike, affectionate, docile, and patient," concluded that it was un-Christian to oppress such a person. Indeed, were Negro characteristics not Christian virtues? Most white Northerners could not shake their racism, however, and when Republicans embraced the idea of Negro franchise after the Civil War, it was not as a consequence of believing in racial equality but, rather, the result of political expediency.[40]

White leaders in the postwar South adopted a paternalistic attitude toward blacks, expecting that these recently born citizens would turn as children to their political fathers. And, unsurprisingly, there were slaves who remained loyal to their former masters—and there were previous owners who insisted on retaining young blacks until they reached twenty-one.[41]

These leaders simply assumed segregation and, in fact, were essentially racist. As Darwinism became popular, they—and most others of European stock—accepted it as a newer justification for hierarchical assumptions. This was, in fact, a more benign point of view than another late nineteenth-century opinion: that blacks had degenerated since being freed from slavery.[42] The African-American-as-child was, at best, a permanent foster member of the American family.

This statement was graphically illustrated in D. W. Griffith's film *The Birth of a Nation* (1915), based on Negrophobe Thomas Dixon's novel *The Clansmen* (1905), in which book the African American is described as "half child, half animal." Griffith, whose father had fought for the Confederacy and later lost the family fortune, looked back fondly to a paternalistic South where all black slaves acted as children and, after the war, all freed blacks (save for a few "old faithful") behaved like animals, most notably the predatory males, until put in their place by the Ku Klux Klan.

This enormously popular movie, characterized by President Woodrow Wilson as "writing history with lightning," set the stage for the many films in which blacks, or rather black men, performed as inferiors, their characteristic depiction until World War II.[43] It was the stereotype promulgated even by whites who considered themselves friends of the African American, such as the prominent Atlantan who wrote in 1906: "The Negro race is a child race. We are a strong race, their guardians." In Walter Hines Page's novel *The Southerner* (1909), a character observes: "The Negro is a child in civilization. . . . Let us train him. . . . Let us teach him to do productive work, teach him to be a help, to support himself, to do useful things, to be a man, to build up his family life."[44]

The use of the male pronoun in this last passage, the admonition "to be a man," points to the assumption implicit in the white discussion of blacks since the word "child" had been introduced before the Civil War: not the African American but the African American *male* was the subject. This focus might be attributed to the exclusivity of male suffrage in defining an American citizen or to the fact that almost always men created the image of black-as-child (the important exception was *Uncle Tom's Cabin*).[45]

But deeper feelings also contributed to the focus on the male. The child/animal dichotomy suggests that a savage who is feared must be domesticated into a child who is either permanently immature (the Negrophobe viewpoint) or educable (the Negrophile perspective). And the dichotomy was perpetuated into the twentieth century. Donald Bogle titles his "interpretive history of blacks in American films" *Toms, Coons, Mulattoes, Mammies, and Bucks.* Toms are, of course, faithful and submissive, while coons are lazy and unreliable, but both exhibit childlike characteristics in contrast to the undesirable, animallike bucks.[46]

But the mammies and mullatoes? Both are women, the former portrayed as dark, fat, and competent, the latter light, curvaceous, and sexy. One raises boys, the other tempts men—the madonna and the whore. Historian Catherine Clinton asserts that the mammy is almost absent from the documents of antebellum America; she "was created by white Southerners to redeem the relationship between black women and white men. . .a counter-point to the octoroon concubine, the light-skinned product of a 'white man's lust' who was habitually victimized by slaveowners' sexual appetites."[47] Probably Clinton is guessing about the motive, but she is correct in pointing to the post-Civil War emergence of fond Southern white memories of the mammy as child rearer and household organizer.[48]

Indeed, it is undeniable that Southern white children in the prewar years were cared for by black women, just as white children had black playmates. Historian Eugene Genovese, who is convinced of the *real* presence of the mammy, captures both her strength and her weakness: "More than any other slave, she had absorbed the paternalist ethos and accepted her place in a system of reciprocal obligations defined from above." Strong because she operated resourcefully and responsibly within the system, she was weak because she could not pass her power to other blacks without making them even more dependent.[49] She was domesticated, though hardly made childlike, from the beginning and, hence, even more reassuring than a tom or a coon. Unlike the mulatto, she was neither a reminder of interracial sex nor a prod to the libido. That the most famous rendition of her character came from a white man in black-face—Al Jolson singing "My Mammy"—adds a bitter irony to the perspective.[50]

A turning point in the understanding of black male character came in 1941 when anthropologist Melville Herskovits published *The Myth of the Negro Past.* Herskovits accused scholars and policy makers of basing their work on myths that supported racial prejudice, the first one of which was "Negroes are naturally of a childlike character." Pointing to the sophistication of an African worldview, he concluded that "such maladjustments to the American scene as characterize Negro life are to be ascribed largely to the social and economic handicaps these folks have suffered, rather than to any inability to cope with the realities of life."[51]

World War II was a turning point in race relations in the United States, not because of white academic writing (American historians in the late 1950s were still fighting about whether the slave was actually a Sambo)[52] but because the determined action of African Americans, oftentimes lawyers, and the official response as seen in the desegregation of the armed forces in Korea and the *Brown v. Topeka Board of Education* decision of the Supreme Court.[53]

The courage demonstrated by African Americans during the ensuing civil rights struggle surprised most white Americans, as indeed it should have. The long and concerted effort to marginalize blacks and rationalize such treatment on the basis of their being essentially simple, weak, and vulnerable was confounded by their willingness to confront their enemies at lunch counters, schools, and courthouses, to create public demonstrations where sometimes their very lives were at stake. Ironically, in view of the perception of blacks as childlike, black youths played a leading role in the sit-in and voter registration movements, while both black children and youths desegregated the schools. What could have happened in their upbringing to encourage them to act so independently of white expectations?

It was a question all thoughtful Americans asked. Robert Coles, a white child psychiatrist from Boston, traveled to the South—"a region that considers them not merely children but (as Negroes) the children of children"—to find out, though he had to confess that it was "difficult to discover what prompted the initiative taken by these young people. A common charge is that they are 'brought out' by conspiring adults. Often it is quite the contrary; nervous parents have been afraid to allow their children's participation in the initially tense months of school desegregation, let alone the more volatile uncertainties of street demonstrations." Yet again and again, as he visited black families (and white as well), first in New Orleans and then Atlanta, he learned that black parents unfailingly prepared their children to survive in the intimidating white world.[54]

Ruby was one of the four little Negro girls who entered two white (and almost empty) elementary schools in New Orleans in 1960 to the accompaniment of mobs, threats of violence, television publicity and international attention, and intervening federal marshals. Coles had been studying stress in children created by severe physical illness and found that he could communicate better with young children through drawings than by talking. Ruby, six years old, never used the colors brown or black except to denote ground, and she consistently drew whites as larger and more lifelike than Negroes—until she realistically portrayed her maternal grandfather, who "has a farm that's his and no one else's." Although Ruby claimed to be happy living in New Orleans, she also wished for a farm, and her mother assured her the family could always stay with grandpa, who "can lick anyone and his brother together." (Ruby's father, who received a Purple Heart in Korea for risking his life to rescue a white soldier, was currently jobless—due to Ruby's school situation—and depressed.)[55]

Although temporarily suffering an eating problem, apparently brought on by a mob member who every day shouted she would poison and choke the child to death, Ruby was a healthy survivor. So were many other black children subjected to stress as a result of their roles in the racial struggle. Coles searched for an explanation. Yes, parents prepared their children, but they emphasized endurance (which certainly embraced nonviolence), not protest. The children wondered why they should face tyranny rather than danger; their parents were compromised by endurance. Yet even their peers were astonished. A white seventeen-year-old girl asked Coles: "Where did they ever learn to behave like that?" His answer (not to her) was that, compared with their age mates, "many of the youths taking part in racial demonstrations are better integrated psychologically as well as racially. They act out of deep moral convictions. . . . But for many of both groups [demonstrators and hecklers] the differences are less psychological than social or cultural."[56] History has the answer. This was not the first generation of African Americans to want freedom, nor the first generation of European Americans to resist granting it. But encouraged by federal action in the armed services and in the courts, not to mention the attention showered on these steps forward and their consequences on television, these black youths were able to act on beliefs long and deeply held.

Notes

1   William S. McFeely, *Frederick Douglass* (New York, 1991), 3–73; an explanation of Douglass's three autobiographies appears on 7–8.

2   These three paragraphs are derived from Donald R. Wright, *African Americans in the Colonial Era: From African Origins Through the American Revolution* (Arlington Heights, Ill., 1990). See also Matt Schaffer, *Mandinko: The Ethnography of a West African Holy Land* (New York, 1980); C. C. Robertson and M. A. Klein, "Women's Importance in African Slave Systems," in C. C. Robertson and M. A. Klein, eds., *Women and Slavery in Africa* (Madison, Wisc., 1983), 3–25; H. S. Klein, "African Women in the Atlantic Slave Trade," in ibid., 29–38; John Thornton, "Sexual Demography: The Impact of the Slave

Trade on Family Structure," in ibid., 39–48; G. I. Jones, ed., "The Early Travels of Olaudah Equiano [Gustavus Vasa]," in Philip D. Curtin, ed., *Africa Remembered* (Madison, Wisc., 1967), 60–98.

Contemporary accounts of child rearing include Margaret Read's *Children of Their Fathers: Growing Up among the Ngoni of Malawi* (New York, 1968) and R. D. Whittemore's "Child Caregiving and Socialization to the Mandinka Way: Toward an Ethnography of Childhood" (Ph.D. diss., UCLA, 1989).

3   Until the publication by Melville Herskovits of *The Myth of the Negro Past* (New York, 1941), the prevalent belief among European Americans was that the African American had no past and, therefore, no survivals could exist. Sterling Stuckey, in *Slave Culture: Nationalist Theory and the Foundations of Black America* (New York, 1987), maintains that "the depths of African culture in America have been greatly underestimated" (ix).

4   Elizabeth Anne Kuznesof, "Brazil," in Joseph M. Hawes and N. Ray Hiner, eds., *Children in Historical and Comparative Perspective* (Westport, Conn., 1991), 151. Also William Bosman, *A New and Accurate Description of the Coast of New Guinea* (1704; New York, 1987), 122–23, 208; R. E. Ellison, "Marriage and Child-Birth Among the Kanuri," *Africa* 9 (1936): 533–34; and Schaffer, *Mandinko*, 71, where it is observed that the "infant's naming ceremony of today is virtually identical to this one described . . . 180 years ago." Herskovits, *Myth*, 188–94.

5   Cheryll Ann Cody, "Naming, Kinship, and Estate Dispersal: Notes on Slave Family Life on a South Carolina Plantation, 1786–1833," *William and Mary Quarterly*, 3rd ser., 39 (1982): 202; Cody, "There Was No 'Absolom' on the Ball Plantations: Slave-Naming Practices in the South Carolina Low Country 1720–1865," *American Historical Review* 92 (1987): 563–96; Herbert G. Gutman, *The Black Family in Slavery and Freedom, 1750–1925* (New York, 1976), 185–204; Peter Wood, *Black Majority: Negroes in Colonial South Carolina from 1670 Through the Stono Rebellion* (New York, 1974), 181–86; Philip D. Morgan, "Slave Life in Piedmont Virginia, 1720–1800," in Lois Green Carr et al., eds., *Colonial Chesapeake Society* (Chapel Hill, N.C., 1988), 452.

6   Kuznesof, "Brazil," 151; Bosman, *Coast of Guinea*, 121; Russell R. Menard, "The Maryland Slave Population, 1658–1730: A Demographic Profile of Blacks in Four Counties," *William and Mary Quarterly*, 3rd ser., 32 (1975): 41.

7   Menard, 38–49. Herbert S. Klein and Stanley L. Engerman, "Fertility Differentials Between Slaves in the United States and the West Indies: A Note on Lactation Practices and Their Possible Implications," *William and Mary Quarterly* 3rd. ser., 35 (1978): 358; John Campbell, "Work, Pregnancy, and Infant Mortality among Southern Slaves," *Journal of Interdisciplinary History* 14 (1983/84): 793–812; L. H. Owens, *This Species of Property: Slave Life and Culture in the Old South* (New York, 1976), 40. In *Time on the Cross: The Economics of American Negro Slavery* (Boston, 1974), Robert Fogel and Stanley Engerman applaud health care for pregnant slave women and state that nursing mothers were kept on a light work schedule (122–23). Richard Dunn observes that on the Jamaican plantation of Mesopotamia, women with five or more children were allowed to stay home and raise them. "Caribbean Versus Old South Slavery," paper delivered at the University of Minnesota, April 29, 1994, 21.

8   Kuznesof, "Brazil," 151; Rev. Charles T. Dooley, "Child-Training Among the Wanguru. I. Physical Education," *Primitive Man* 7 (April 1934): 24–26.

9   Campbell, "Work, Pregnancy," 793–812; Brenda E. Stevenson, *Life in Black and White: Family and Community in the Slave South* (New York, 1996), 195; Owens, *This Species*, 40–41.

10   Kenneth F. Kiple and Virginia Himmelsteib King, *Another Dimension to the Black Diaspora: Diet, Disease, and Racism* (Cambridge, 1981), 96–116; Todd L. Savitt, *Medicine and Slavery: The Diseases and Health Care of Blacks in Antebellum Virginia* (Urbana, Ill., 1978), 120–29; Richard Dunn, "Caribbean versus Old South Slavery," 15; Richard Steckel, "A Dreadful Childhood: The Excess Mortality of American Slaves," *Social Science History* 10 (1986): 791. Cf. Fogel and Engerman, *Time on the Cross*, 124.

11   Eugene D. Genovese, *Roll, Jordan, Roll: The World the Slaves Made* (New York, 1974), 502; Paul Bohannan and Philip Curtin, *Africa and Africans*, rev. ed. (Garden City, N.Y., 1971), 115.

12   R. D. Whittemore and Elizabeth Beverly, "Trust in the Mandinka Way: The Cultural Context of Sibling Care," in P. G. Zukow, ed., *Sibling Interaction Across Cultures* (New York, 1989), 26–53. Photo in Schaffer, *Mandinko*, 100. See also Zukow, *Sibling Interaction*, chaps. 3 and 4.

13   Owens, *This Species*, 41–42, argues the case of child neglect while Fogel and Engerman, *Time on the Cross*, 206–7, present the other side.

14   Ira Berlin, in "Time, Space, and the Evolution of Afro-American Society on British Mainland North America," *American Historical Review* 85 (1980): 44–78, describes many different living situations, varying considerably by region and including households where there were but one or two slaves. Jean Butenhoff Lee, in "The Problem of Slave Community in the Eighteenth-Century Chesapeake," *William and Mary Quarterly*, 3rd ser., 43 (1986): 333–61, observes that 45 percent of the slaves in

Charles County, Maryland, lived in groups of ten or fewer. Obviously the issue of attachment would be different in these situations than on plantations.

Changes in African American ways of life during the late eighteenth century are the subject of essays by Gary B. Nash, Richard S. Dunn, Philip D. Morgan, and Allan Kulikoff in Ira Berlin and Ronald Hoffman, eds., *Slavery and Freedom in the Age of the American Revolution* (Charlottesville, Va., 1983).

15 J. W. C. Pennington, *The Fugitive Blacksmith* (London, 1850), 2, as quoted in Owens, *This Species*, 201.

16 "The situational feature of special interest to us in this work is, of course, being alone. Probably nothing increases the likelihood that fear will be aroused more than that." John Bowlby, *Attachment and Loss*, 3 vols. (London, 1969–80), II, 118. See also 142–43, 148, for the evolutionary explanation of the importance of companionship; 178–81 on fear.

17 Lester Alston, "Children as Chattel," in Elliott West and Paula Petrik, eds., *Small Worlds: Children and Adolescents in America, 1850–1950* (Lawrence, Kans., 1992), 210–15.

18 Wilma King, *Stolen Childhood: Slave Youth in Nineteenth-Century America* (Bloomington, Ill., 1995), 71; Marie Jenkins Schwartz, *Born to Bondage: Growing Up Enslaved in the Antebellum South* (Cambridge, 2000), 77–82. See also Mary Beth Norton et al., "The Afro-American Family in the Age of Revolution," in Berlin and Hoffman, eds., *Slavery and Freedom*, 180; John Blassingame, *The Slave Community: Plantation Life in the Antebellum South*, 2nd ed. (New York, 1979), 178.

19 Allan Kulikoff, "The Beginnings of the Afro-American Family in Maryland," in C. Aubrey Land et al., *Law, Society, and Politics in Early Maryland* (Baltimore, 1977), 176–82. The argument that most slaves lived in nuclear households and sustained monogamous marriages is challenged in Brenda E. Stevenson, "Black Family Structure in Colonial and Antebellum Virginia: Amending the Revisionist Perspective," in M. Belinda Tucker and Claudia Mitchell-Kerna, eds., *The Decline in Marriage Among African Americans* (New York, 1995), 27–56. On the contemporary African family, see A. R. Radcliffe-Brown and Daryll Forde, *African Systems of Kinship and Marriage* (London, 1950). On the extended family, see Cody, "Kinship and Estate Dispersal," 193. On vulnerability, see Stevenson, *Life in Black and White*, 179, 206–25; Lee, "The Problem of Slave Community," 361; Richard S. Dunn, "A Tale of Two Plantations: Slave Life at Mesopotamia and Mount Airy in Virginia," *William and Mary Quarterly*, 3rd ser., 34 (1977): 32–65.

Frederick Douglass, drawing on the authority of his own early years in bondage in early nineteenth-century Maryland, always denied the compatibility of slavery with the family. *My Bondage and My Freedom* (New York, 1855), chap. 3. In *Rituals of Blood: Consequences of Slavery in Two American Centuries* (New York, 1999), sociologist Orlando Patterson terms the idea of a stable slave family not only an "academic absurdity" but an "intellectual disgrace."

20 Genovese, *Roll, Jordan, Roll*, 505–6; David K. Wiggins, "The Play of Slave Children in the Plantation Communities of the Old South, 1820–60," *Journal of Sports History* 7, no. 2 (1980): 21–39. Bernard Mergen, *Play and Playthings: A Reference Guide* (Westport, Conn., 1982), strongly disputes the contention that slave children relieved anxieties and fears through play and thus more easily withstood bondage (42–43, 53 n. 1). Kuznesof says that in Africa "corporal punishment for children was rare"; see "Brazil," 151. But in Whittemore, "Child Caregiving," 173, 230, there are references to corporal punishment. And Herskovits views whipping as a survival from Africa, where it was and is "the outstanding method of correction." *Myth of the Negro Past*, 196. Genovese emphasizes beating as life preparation. *Roll, Jordan, Roll*, 509–12. Stevenson has evidence that white children were not whipped in front of blacks. *Life in Black and White*, 110.

21 Mergen, *Play*, 31, 39–41, 45. Dooley, "Child-Training," 26–31, treats games played by East African children today. C. M. Eastman's "NZW Swahili child's worldview," *Ethos* 14, no. 2 (summer 1986): 144–73, compares play in western and nonwestern societies. On reading and the petting of children, see Blassingame, *Slave Community*, 185; Genovese, *Roll, Jordan, Roll*, 512, 515–19; Wiggins, "Play of Slave Children," 25, 30–36. Though educating slaves was outlawed in some states, white owners might teach slaves to read the Bible, and of course house slaves and urban slaves might become literate simply by their proximity to the written word. And some ex-slaves claimed they were able to teach themselves. Janet Cornelius, " 'We Slipped and Learned to Read': Slave Accounts of the Literacy Process, 1830–65," *Phylon* 44 (1983): 171–85.

In *Deep like the Rivers: Education in the Slave Quarter Community, 1831–1865* (New York, 1968), Thomas Webber paints a benign picture of early African American life, arguing that "few slave children seem to have realized the significance of their slave status until their slave training began in earnest" between the ages of 10 and 14 (3–21).

22 Richard H. Steckel, "A Peculiar Population: The Nutrition, Health, and Mortality of American Slaves from Childhood to Maturity," *Journal of Economic History* 46 (1986): 721–41. Fogel and Engerman

judge slave diet to have been "quite substantial" (*Time on the Cross*, 113), while L. H. Owens assesses it as wholly inadequate (*This Species*, 50–69). In *Medicine and Slavery*, Todd L. Savitt, a medical student before he became a historian, questions the use of evidence by Fogel and Engerman as well as Owens on the matter of diet (86–87, nn. 8, 9). Savitt argues for the substantiality of diet (96). However, Steckel's work is the most convincing.

23   Alston sees this fact as possibly misleading, since children always had to perform *some* tasks, and thus "they may not have experienced changes in the work they did as mileposts in their lives." "Children as Chattel," 226–27.

24   On examining the records of a South Carolina planter, Cody found that no children under 10 were separated from their parents, few children between 10 and 19 were separated, but at the end of the 20–29 age span, only 40 percent of men were still with their mothers; daughters were twice as likely to stay with mothers. "Naming, Kinship, and Estate Dispersal," 207–8. Other evidence of keeping a family together appears in Daniel C. Littlefield, *Rice and Slaves* (Baton Rouge, La., 1981), 71. To the contrary, see Morgan, "Slave Life," 448–49.

25   Charles T. Dooley, "Child-Training Among the Wanguru. III. Moral Education," *Primitive Man* 9 (January 1936): 6; G. M. Culwick, "New Ways for Old in the Treatment of Adolescent African Girls," *Africa* 12 (1939), 425–27. On the circumcision ceremonies for boys and girls, see Schaffer, *Mandinko*, 95–101.

26   Owens, *This Species*, 44–46.

27   Gutman, *Black Family*, 402–12.

28   Leon F. Litwack, *Trouble in Mind: Black Southerners in the Age of Jim Crow* (New York, 1998), 3–76. Also John Dittmer, *Black Georgia in the Progressive Era, 1900–1920* (Urbana, 1977); Charles S. Johnson, *Growing Up in the Black Belt: Negro Youth in the Rural South* (Washington, D.C., 1941).

29   Litwack, *Trouble*, 8.

30   Donald G. Nieman, ed., *African Americans and Education in the South, 1865–1900* (New York, 1994), xi.

31   Booker T. Washington, *Up from Slavery* (1901; New York, 1965), 37.

32   Richard Wright, *Black Boy: A Record of Childhood and Youth* (New York, 1945). Half of this autobiography was expurgated to please the Book-of-the-Month Club, remaining unpublished until 1977. See Louis Menand, "The Hammer and the Nail," *New Yorker*, July 20, 1992, 79–84.

33   C. Peter Ripley, "The Black Family in Transition: Louisiana, 1860–65," *Journal of Southern History* 41 (1975): 369–80; Robert H. Abzug, "The Black Family During Reconstruction," in Nathan Huggins, ed., *Key Issues in the Afro-American Experience* (New York, 1971), 26–41; Leon Litwack, *Been in the Storm So Long: The Aftermath of Slavery* (New York, 1979), 229–47.

34   Gutman, *Black Family*, 443–50; Litwack, *Trouble*, 350–51, 420–22. For a good sense of rural family life, see Theodore Rosengarten, ed., *All God's Dangers: The Life of Nate Shaw* (New York, 1974).

35   Virginia Heyer Young, "Family and Childhood in a Southern Negro Community," *American Anthropologist* 72 (1970): 269–88.

36   *New York Times*, September 15, 1998.

37   Webber, *Deep like the Rivers*, 27–42.

38   Ibid., 157–250. That blacks accepted or rejected white values, attitudes, and understandings is not an issue with a single answer. Note the debate over slave personality, concisely summarized in Owens, *This Species*, 238, n. 8. Kenneth Stampp, in *The Peculiar Institution: Slavery in the Ante-Bellum South* (New York, 1956), made the case for extensive role playing. Stanley Elkins, in *Slavery: A Problem in American Institutional and Intellectual Life* (Chicago, 1959), argued that slaves became the role they played. Stampp conceded that some slaves became the role but most did not; see "Rebels and Sambos: The Search for the Negro's Personality in Slavery," *Journal of Southern History* 37 (1971): 367–92.

39   George M. Fredrickson, *The Black Image in the White Mind: The Debate on Afro-American Character and Destiny, 1817–1914* (New York, 1971), 43. This observation is born out in Winthrop D. Jordan, *White over Black: American Attitudes Toward the Negro, 1550–1812* (Baltimore, 1969). Europeans were concerned with issues such as complexion, religion, behavior (especially perceived sexuality), always viewing the Africans as alien but not depicting them as children.

40   Fredrickson, *Black Image*, 43–197.

41   Litwack, *Been in the Storm So Long*, 191–92.

42   Ibid., 198–282.

43   Actually, the first film about African Americans in which whites appear in blackface was *The Pickaninnies Doing a Dance* (1894). James R. Nesteby, *Black Images in American Films, 1896–1954* (Washington, D.C., 1982), 14. And despite the popularity of *The Birth of a Nation*, there was simultaneously a strong undercurrent of criticism, causing Hollywood to refrain from casting Negroes in

bad guy roles until *Sweet Sweetback's Baadasssss Son* (1971), save for the release of *Free and Equal* in the mid-1920s. Donald Bogle, *Toms, Coons, Mulattoes, Mammies, and Bucks*, 3rd ed. (New York, 1994), 16, 24–25.

44   Fredrickson, *Black Image*, 287, 295–96. A year before *The Southerner* was published, Jack Johnson became the world's first black heavyweight champion. The film of him kayoing white boxer Tommy Burns was burned to prevent race riots. Bogle, *Toms*, 17.

45   On Harriet Beecher Stowe's novel, as well as other pre-Civil War writings on slave childhood, see J. E. Illick, "African Americans: Childhood in Slavery, Childlike in Freedom—and Paul Robeson as Child and Parent," in William Pencak, ed., *Paul Robeson* (Jefferson, N.C., 2001).

46   Maybe the enormously popular radio show *Amos n Andy* would fit this interpretation. For a different point of view, see Gerald Nachman, *Raised on Radio* (New York, 1998), 272–95.

47   Catherine Clinton, *The Plantation Mistress: Woman's World in the Old South* (New York, 1982), 202.

48   Leon Litwack suggests that such memories were prompted by white repugnance at the assertiveness of the now-freed blacks. Conversation with author, January 13, 1999.

49   Genovese, *Roll, Jordan, Roll*, 360–61.

50   For an interpretation that Jews assimilated by appearing blackfaced in films, see Michael Rogin, *Blackface, White Noise: Jewish Immigrants in the Hollywood Melting Pot* (Berkeley, Calif., 1996).

51   Herskovits, *Myth*, I, 293.

52   Owens, *This Species of Property*, 238 n. 8.

53   Richard Kluger, *Simple Justice: The History of* Brown v. Board of Education *and Black America's Struggle for Equality* (New York, 1975).

54   Robert Coles, *Children of Crisis: A Study of Courage and Fear* (Boston, 1967), 319, 321, 337.

55   Ibid., 48–49, 76–82.

56   Ibid., 323, 331.

Chapter 13

Don Browning and Marcia Bunge

INTRODUCTION TO *CHILDREN AND CHILDHOOD IN WORLD RELIGIONS*

THIS VOLUME [SEE ORIGINAL READING] presents selected classic and formative texts on children and childhood from six major world religions—Judaism, Christianity, Islam, Hinduism, Buddhism, and Confucianism. As far as we can tell, no volume like this one currently exists. There has never before been an effort to bring together basic scriptures and documents that shaped the attitudes, practices, and teachings on childhood of these religions. The selections in this volume, although clearly not exhaustive, provide an introduction to central themes of children and childhood in these six world religions. By introducing and presenting classic texts on children from various traditions, the volume discloses a range of critical issues on relationships between children and religion and how these childhood traditions relate to their surrounding social contexts. Although this volume concentrates on texts that influenced a religious tradition's constructions of childhood and is not a social history, many of the chapters also provide valuable insights and bibliographical references to what is known about actual practices with children and their behaviors. In short, this book serves as a topography of the study of religion, children, and society; it fills a void in the current scholarship and functions as an indispensable guide to future research in the areas of religious studies and childhood studies.

The current volume is not only foundational for deepening our understanding of both children and religion and for strengthening research in a variety of academic disciplines; such a collection is also relevant to readers and audiences outside the academy, especially given our contemporary national and international situation. The texts assembled in this book are not just nice collections of interesting, perhaps curious, material; they are selections of readings vital to understanding aspects of contemporary social and political life in the United States and around the world. This is the case for several reasons.

First, because of the magnitude of impact that the major religions have had on culture and the life cycle of children and youth, it is important to understand them better. Religion shapes children through their socialization by parents and formal religious instruction, religious rituals in family and corporate settings, and religiously inspired views of marriage and gender. Even if children or their parents are not members of a specific religious community, religion nevertheless shapes them both directly and indirectly through its influence in many areas of cultural, social, and political life. Religious images and understandings of children are not confined to the inner life of a specific tradition; they spill over into the wider society, no matter how allegedly secular that society is thought to be.

Second, we must become more informed about relationships between religion and childhood because they are often a source of deep tension and heated debate here and abroad. Tensions surrounding the subject of children and religion can be found in the United States as well as in most countries where the forces of modernization and democracy have directly or indirectly challenged traditional religious beliefs and practices, raising questions about which authorities, institutions, and polities will shape the lives of children and families. On the one hand, some people are suspicious of what religions teach about childhood and whether or not religions benefit children in modern societies. Practices found within some strands of a tradition, such as the corporal punishment of children or child marriages, are often directly criticized. On the other hand, others perceive elements of modernization and contemporary culture as threats to children and their positive religious formation. Persons from a variety of religious traditions frequently express criticism of American culture, schools, media, and other institutions that influence their children. Such debates raise the important question of why some religious traditions feel that many aspects of modernization and democracy are threats to their children and others do not. There is no easy answer to this question, and responding to it is not the purpose of this book. Rather, our point is that even to begin to answer it, we must all know a great deal more about the childhood traditions of world religions.

Third, this volume is important because at the same time we are recognizing that the religion-childhood link may be a source of tension in the world, new social science research indicates that these religions may be sources of strength for children. Parents have historically tended to believe that passing on their particular religious tradition to their children positively influences them, and today there is a body of social-science studies suggesting that this intuition may be true, at least according to some measures of child well-being. Most of the research is still limited to the major religions in Western societies. For instance, Christian Smith and Melinda Denton in their exhaustive survey titled *Soul Searching: The Religious and Spiritual Lives of American Teenagers* (2005) showed that although most teens do not understand their religions deeply, those who are involved in religious life fare better in school, health, and job placement than the religiously unattached.[1] In 2003, a distinguished interdisciplinary panel of scholars released a report titled *Hardwired to Connect: The New Scientific Case for Authoritative Communities*. It argued that children, in order to attain psychological and physical well-being, need not only strong attachments to parents and families but also "deep connection to moral and spiritual meaning" of the kind generally provided by religious traditions.[2] The Search Institute has also found that involvement in a religious community is one of forty important "developmental assets" that strengthens child well-being.[3]

Fourth, since religious diversity is now the experience of every society and since all societies have children, many people want and need to know more about how the various religions relate to childhood. The great world religions are not just foreign realities in strange and distant countries. They are present everywhere—in the schools, marketplaces, neighborhoods, and voting booths of the United States as well as other countries around the globe. Thus, health experts, social workers, psychologists, and child advocates encounter this diversity when they meet in their practices individuals and families from different religious faiths. Teachers and professors at schools, colleges, and universities confront young people who were taught different faiths when children. Lawyers, doctors, and business people work with an increasingly diverse religious constituency and are often embarrassed by their lack of knowledge about religious traditions outside their own. Parents, too, desire to know more about what the world religions teach about childhood as their own children experience religious diversity in their schools and neighborhoods.

There have been efforts in recent years to compensate for this lack of knowledge and understanding. To remedy deficient knowledge in the medical and nursing professions, the Park Ridge Center published a book series titled *Health, Medicine, and the Faith Traditions.* These volumes examined several of the world religions from the perspective of what they taught about health, illness, aging, birth, and family. Childhood itself, however, was not a major theme.[4] There have been countless textbooks and sourcebooks assembled on the world religions, but children as such are generally neglected. A survey of introductory texts and sourcebooks over the last several decades found in their indexes only one reference to children, and this was to children as sources of "pollution" in Confucianism.[5] We can assure you that Confucianism has much more to say about children than this, as do all the major religions. Even one of the co-editors of this volume recently helped edit a major sourcebook titled *Sex, Marriage, and Family in the World Religions,* but it only addressed children as a category under marriage and family.[6]

Finally, this volume is also important within the context of mounting public concern about children and child well-being and the efforts of child advocates to address challenges facing children locally and globally. Across conservative and progressive lines, and both nationally and internationally, there is heightened awareness of the many challenges children face today. Many children here and abroad live in poverty and often are malnourished, receive inadequate educations, and lack proper health care.[7] These problems, in turn, often feed others, such as drug abuse, child labor, child soldiers, AIDS orphans, child-headed households, and sexually exploited children. Even children in affluent families often suffer neglect and abuse or struggle with addictions to drugs or alcohol. Scholars and child advocates also wonder about the effects of technology, the media, and global market pressures on rich and poor children alike. Child advocates around the world who represent both secular and faith-based nongovernmental organizations are taking increasing interest in religious traditions and beliefs because they shape a large part of the diverse social and cultural contexts in which child advocacy must be discussed and carried out, often determining the success or failure of child-focused programs. Furthermore, child advocates are seeking to learn more about varied religious responses to children's rights, particularly as these advocates participate in international debates surrounding the Millennium Development Goals and the ratification and implementation of the United Nations Convention on the Rights of the Child.[8]

For these reasons and others, *Children and Childhood in World Religions* is a valuable sourcebook for a variety of audiences and contexts in the academy and the public sphere both nationally and internationally.

Guiding themes and questions

As this volume shows, religions say a great deal about children, and each chapter explores some of the following central questions and themes. They are derived both from what these religions actually address and from our sense of the major concerns of the contemporary cultural conversation and debate about childhood and religion.

1.   *The nature and status of children.* What are a religion's core beliefs about a child's nature and status? What are its metaphysical or theological beliefs about children and their relation to what the religion holds as ultimate? What is a religion's understanding of birth, the moral status and agency of children, and a child's relation to good and evil?
2.   *Gender and sexuality of children.* How does a religion speak about differences between boys and girls? How does it interpret the sexuality of children and youth? Are there any normative views of children in the world religions that prescribe or proscribe certain

actions by children? What do these proscribed behaviors mean for issues of gender, sexuality, and impulse control?

3. *The role of children in central religious practices.* How do children participate in a religion's adult rituals? Are there special rituals for children? Does a religious community allow its children to participate in the secular rituals of the surrounding society?

4. *Obligations of parents and children.* How do religious traditions understand parental obligations to children and children's obligations to parents? How deep, long lasting, mutual, or asymmetrical are these obligations?

5. *Communal obligations to children.* How do religions speak about communal obligations to children and children's obligations to the community? Do particular religions have special institutions for children and youth, and how does the religion relate to external institutions dealing with children?

6. *Moral and spiritual formation of children.* How do the different traditions speak about the moral and spiritual formation of children? What practices and teachings are especially important in the process of spiritual formation? Who has responsibility for it? Is spiritual development forced or allowed to come freely?

The structure of the book

The selections have been chosen by leading scholars of six world religions. These scholars also have provided insightful introductions to the material they have assembled. The various editors have made no attempt to make parallel the periods from which the key texts have been chosen; the traditions develop in different ways and demand their own unique periodizations. Nor does every chapter give equal attention to the questions listed above; the religious traditions have different emphases and the editors were not always able to collect texts addressing in depth each of these issues. Editors have chosen selections representative of the history of the tradition, including some that reflect modern struggles to interpret—and perhaps reinterpret—a tradition. They have included selections that represent a variety of genres—legal, theological, poetic, and liturgical. However, not all traditions employ these genres to the same degree, and chapter editors have balanced their choices of texts on the basis of how each particular religion has communicated itself. Selections also have been chosen with an eye to their usefulness for comparison with texts from other religions.

Child, children, and childhood

A few sentences are needed about our use of the words child, children, and childhood. There is an important scholarly discussion as to whether it is possible to speak at all about "the child." Those on one side of this debate hold what has been called a "constructivist" view of childhood. They claim that there is no normative child or single cluster of characteristics pertaining to children. Hence, the best we can do is to speak of childhood—our cultural, historical, linguistic, and religious construal and constructions of children, and we should avoid references to "the child." Others hold what has been called an "essentialist" view of children. They believe there are characteristics common to all children, across history and cultures, and they sometimes use the term "child" to refer to these universal similarities.

   In this book we use all three terms—childhood, children, and the child. On the one hand, bringing into conversation the traditions of six highly diverse religions is almost by definition acknowledging that there is some validity to the so-called constructivist view. On the other hand, to use the term "child" is not in itself to essentialize the term; its meaning is qualified by the sentences, paragraphs, and entire text in which the term is used. Hence, we should not be too fearful of trying to discover some common characteristics about children that may be cross-cultural and interreligious. Such documents as the United Nations Convention on the Rights of the Child—and in fact the entire human rights project—suggest that seeing children through different religious and cultural eyes yields overlapping insights that will aid us in raising and protecting children with some common guarantees and supports regardless of the religion, society, and culture within which they reside.

The importance of form and context

Religious teachings and practices regarding children are shaped partially by the form and context of the religion. Judaism, Christianity, and Islam are religions with a sacred book: the Hebrew scriptures in the case of Judaism, both the Old and New Testaments in the case of Christianity, and the Qur'an in the case of Islam. The focus of these religions on their sacred book gives them a cohesion and compactness, even in the socialization of children, that arguably has not characterized Confucianism, Hinduism, and Buddhism. These latter three traditions each have multiple sacred texts that are variously honored in different strands and places but that do not constitute a single center of authority in quite the same way as the sacred books of Judaism, Christianity, and Islam.

In addition, although all of these traditions articulate norms and moral codes about children and childhood, they have distinctive ways of expressing them. For example, Judaism specifically represents itself as a religion based on law with identifiable legal teachings about children, education, and the duties of mothers and fathers. However, even though this law is seen as revealed by God, Judaism has not perceived it as static and unchanging. The interpretation of the law as it applies to children is a dynamically developing tradition. Islam is also a religion of the law—a body of law revealed in the Qur'an. Islamic law is also interpreted and codified in an evolving tradition, in this case the various traditions of law known as shari'a. Christianity, Confucianism, Hinduism, and Buddhism are not religions of the law in quite the same sense, even though they also evolved legal and moral codes. Their core is thought to lie elsewhere, for example the gospel (as in the case of Christianity), or meditative renunciation (as in the case of Hinduism and Buddhism), or family rituals (as in the case of Confucianism). Each one of these four religions, however, also has influenced the socialization of children and evolved rules, formal or informal, to guide this process. For example, Confucianism has developed powerful family traditions where children are taught to honor, if not worship, elders and ancestors in home-based rituals focused on the death and the remembrance of a parent or grandparent.

The social and geographical context of a religion makes a difference in its representations of children. No religion remains uninfluenced by its neighbors. For example, Christianity began as a movement within Judaism, and its attitudes to children were shaped by Jewish as well as Greek and Roman ideas and practices. In his chapter on Buddhism, Allen Cole shows how Buddhism unfolded differently in India and in China. In the Chinese context, Buddhism began to exhibit features of its Confucian host society. It gradually urged children to exhibit filial piety for elders, honor for the emperor, and interest in the fertility and the generational continuity of their extended families much the way these ideas were emphasized by the wider Confucian society. Such childhood emphases were less visible in the early days of the more world-renouncing teachings of Buddhism in India.

There often is tension within a religious tradition between what subeditors Marcia Bunge and John Wall have said could be called "low" versus "high" perspectives on childhood. By this distinction, they are pointing to whether a religion sees children as a source of wisdom and spirituality in their own right or whether their religious growth is viewed mainly as a matter of socialization from above or outside themselves by the authoritative teachings of an adult-transmitted truth or revelation. This tension can vary across and even within religions. For example, Yiqun Zhou in her chapter on Confucianism shows the tensions between Mencius (ca. 372–289 BCE) and Xunci (ca. 310–230 BCE). Although Mencius certainly believed that children needed to be socialized into Confucian teachings and ritual, he also saw them as potential symbols of moral perfection in themselves. Xunci, on the other hand, saw children as profoundly unruly and evil, and he believed that their spiritual perfection had to be cultivated entirely from above, that is, from the teachings and rituals adumbrated by the authoritative Confucius, his followers, and the extended Confucian family. This tension has continued in Confucianism throughout the centuries and exists even today as this tradition copes with the more child-centered cultures of Western societies.

Readers of the texts that follow should recall that all of these religions, in their ancient forms, saw children mainly through the eyes of adult men—fathers, grandfathers, and male religious leaders. This does not mean that we learn nothing of importance about children, mothers, or the relation of offspring to parents. It is rather that we do not gain these insights from the voice and perspective of children and women. However, in more modern times, all of these religions are beginning to acknowledge the independent angles of vision of children and their mothers. Furthermore, we are learning how to interpret ancient texts in ways that help us to see more deeply into the experience and agency of children.

Readers also should remember that, for the most part, we have very little direct knowledge of how children were actually raised in the formative periods of these traditions. It is difficult to construct on the basis of the texts alone the kind of social history that we value today which places religious teachings within the context of historical records about actual behaviors of children and their elders. Despite these difficulties, we welcome the work scholars are pursuing in this area.

Some general themes

Despite the varied forms and contexts of these religions and the limitations of our sources, the texts assembled here tell us much about the ideals and normative models of childhood that shaped their respective religious traditions. They also engage several common themes. We present a few of them below. There are more. But what follows will give the reader a taste of the possible conversations that can emerge in comparing these traditions.

Within the history of these religions, most of them have ways of speaking of children as a blessing. For example, Elisheva Baumgarten tells us that the Hebrew Scriptures represent children as a central blessing and that, as a sign of this blessing, the ancestors of the Jewish people were promised by God that their offspring would be plentiful. Christianity continued to see children as a blessing, although it put less emphasis on procreation as such. Children as blessings and the importance of procreation were both emphasized in Islam. Avner Giladi points out that although progeny and lineage are perceived as blessings in Islam, this was often stated more in terms of sons than daughters. Yiqun Zhou tells us that Confucian parents certainly loved their children and actively showed them affection, especially in their early years, but their sacred value was seen more as something achieved as they came to occupy their roles in household rituals honoring elders and ancestors. One might argue that Buddhism's doctrine of *samsara*, that is, stopping the cycle of birth and suffering, implied negative attitudes toward the birth of the child. However, Alan Cole believes that its view of the perfection of the Buddha's childhood and its gradual identification over time of all children with the Buddha had the long-term effect of elevating the status of children in Buddhist territories. In ancient Hindu texts, as Laurie Patton claims, the birth of a son is understood to be a critical part of a prosperous life.

These views of the sacred importance of children were often associated with an element of realism, if not utility. Judaism valued children as gifts from God, but it also believed that males were religiously obligated to have children for what they contributed to the survival and continuity of the covenant community. This is an accent also found in Islam. As Laurie Patton claims, ancient Hindu texts also view the birth of a son as a form of social security and continuation of the lineage. Alan Cole points out that although Buddhism in its early years had little to say directly about children, it gradually over the centuries became quite interested in their birth and growth. This was not so much to value procreation itself; rather procreation was valued as a requirement for the replenishment of the Buddhist tradition and its teachings.

Religious traditions also show interesting similarities and differences in the extent to which children in themselves are deemed as sources of religious inspiration. Bunge and Wall refer to the well-known words attributed to Jesus indicating that children are in some ways models for adults, "for it is to such as these that the kingdom of heaven belongs" (Matt. 19:14). Baumgarten cites Jewish sources that claim the fetus studies the Torah in the mother's womb, and learning its teachings in later life is actually a matter of recollecting what was earlier known in utero. Within Hinduism, Patton finds the idea of the child as closer to the divine, especially in classic myths of Krishna, which juxtapose childhood vulnerability with divine strength.

Some modern people are disturbed by what they believe the religions of the world teach about the evil or sinful nature of the child. Actually, the religions vary significantly on this issue within and across traditions. Furthermore, views of a child's sin and evil are often coupled with notions of their accountability and responsibility. Even those religions that hold strong doctrines of original sin, such as the parts of Christianity influenced by St. Augustine (354–430 CE), often balance this teaching by equally strong images of children born in the image of God. Baumgarten points out that Judaism has no understanding of the original sin of children and in fact sees the purity of the newborn child as a source for perfecting the wider society. Although Hinduism and Buddhism believe children at birth are contaminated through *samsara* by the evil deeds of their ancestors, this state of affairs is more a matter of the human condition in general than any special commentary on the special sinfulness of children. Confucianism, as Zhou mentions, is divided on the question of children's natural inclinations toward evil, with different points of view on this matter emerging repeatedly throughout its long history.

All of these religions have articulate understandings of parental and communal obligations to children. These traditions generally expect adults to address a child's basic needs of food, shelter, and affection; to provide spiritual, moral, and cognitive guidance; and to protect a child's property or inheritance. Religious traditions offer explicit guidelines for treatment and care of orphans or abandoned children. Initiating children into a faith tradition generally takes place through various ritual practices and study both in the home and the religious community. Particular religious ceremonies mark transitions from one stage of life to the next. Within Hinduism, for example, children are "ritually formed," as Patton suggests, through a variety of rituals that include cutting the umbilical cord to the accompaniment of Vedic mantras; naming and first feeding ceremonies; rites for the first time a child's hair is cut; and initiations into studying the Veda. In many religious traditions, schools external to the home also play a role in children's formation and education, such as in the Jewish rabbinic schools, the public and parochial schools of the Christian Protestant Reformation, or the *pesantren, kuttab*, and *madrasa* of Islam. Confucianism progressively institutionalized rigorous examination systems through state-run civil service systems for boys as one of the few ways to increase prestige and master the social space between filial duties to the family and service to the emperor.

Religious traditions also address children's obligations to their parents. Within Christianity and Judaism, the command to "honor your father and mother" extends to adulthood. Confucianism, and to some degree both Hinduism and Buddhism, have strong expectations that children will care for their elders, with obligations thought to last beyond the grave and even across eons of time. In his introduction to Buddhism, Alan Cole shows how a religion that appears to renounce the world, and hence the importance of children and families, also evolved complex patterns of reciprocity between celibate monks and their own mothers, fathers, brothers, and sisters. Teachings in Buddhism that at first glance appear to be world-denying and even neglectful of children in fact accompany very complicated ways of directly and indirectly supporting parents and their offspring as they struggle with the realities of finite life on earth.

Conclusion

The reader, however, would be wise not to press too far any of the above generalizations about children and childhood in world religions. Her or his immersion in the expert introductions and collections of texts that follow will bring clarification and nuance to everything we have suggested. Furthermore, religious traditions inevitably have different strands, tributaries, and divisions that also change over time. This means that almost every dominant characteristic of a religious tradition that scholarly observers might advance will be humbled by some exceptions lingering somewhere in its various nooks and crannies.

Each chapter and the volume as a whole provide the reader with an amazing array of possible attitudes toward and ideas about children and childhood both within and across traditions. The chapters also shed light on central religious beliefs and practices and the role children play in them. And they invite us to explore further the complex place of children in these and other religious traditions. Finally, the selections that follow prompt all readers— regardless of our religious and philosophical commitments—to reexamine our own preconceptions and beliefs about children and to reevaluate our responsibilities and obligations toward children themselves.

Notes

1   Christian Smith, *Soul Searching: The Religious and Spiritual Lives of American Teenagers* (Oxford: Oxford University Press, 2005).

2   *Hardwired to Connect: The New Scientific Case for Authoritative Communities,* a report released by the YMCA of the USA, Dartmouth Medical School, and the Institute for American Values (New York: Institute for American Values, 2003), 5.

3   For more information, see Search-Institute.org.

4   *Health, Medicine, and the Faith Traditions* included books such as David Feldman, *Health and Medicine in the Jewish Tradition* (New York: Crossroad, 1986), Fazlur Rahman, *Health and Medicine in the Islamic Tradition* (New York: Crossroad, 1987), and Kenneth Vaux, *Health and Medicine in the Reformed Tradition* (New York: Crossroad, 1984).

5   The children as pollution index entry is in Willard G. Oxtoby, ed., *World Religions: Eastern Traditions* (Oxford: Oxford University Press, 1996). Other texts that we consulted that did not reference children at all are listed below. It must be admitted that omission of the words child, children, or childhood in the index does not mean these books do not mention them, but it does suggest that the subject was not seen as important enough to merit inclusion in the index. See also Mircea Eliade, *From Primitives to Zen* (New York: Harper and Row, 1967); S. Vernon McCausland, Grace Cairns, and David Yu, *Religions of the World* (New York: Random House, 1969); Ward J. Fellows, *Religions East and West* (New York: Religions East and West, 1979); Niels Nielsen, Norvin Hein, Frank Reynolds, Alan Miller, Samuel Karff, Alice Cochran, and Paul McLean, eds., *Religions of the World* (New York:

St. Martins Press, 1983); Ninian Smart, *The Religious Experience of Mankind* (New York: Charles Scribner's Sons, 1964, 1976, 1984); Stewart Sutherland, Leslie Houlden, Peter Clarke, and Friedhelm Handy, eds., *The World's Religions* (Boston: G. K. Hall, 1988); Houston Smith, *The World's Religions* (San Francisco: Harper SanFrancisco, 1991); William Young, *The World's Religions: Worldviews and Contemporary Issues* (Englewood Cliffs, N.J.: Prentice Hall, 1995); John R. Hinneils, ed., *A New Handbook of Living Religions* (Oxford: Blackwell, 1997).

6   Don Browning, Christian Green, and John Witte, eds., *Sex, Marriage, and Family in the World Religions* (New York: Columbia University Press, 2006).

7   For more information about the situation of children, see the following Web sites: United States Census Bureau (census.gov); the Children's Defense Fund (childrensdefense.org); the United Nations Children's Fund (unicef.org); and the National Center for Children in Poverty (nccp.org).

8   The UNCRC was passed in 1989 by the UN General Assembly. Since then, it has been ratified by all but two nations: the United States and Somalia.

Chapter 14

Elizabeth Safford and Philip Safford

DIMENSIONS OF A "NEW HISTORY"

"The Century of the Child"

THE INDIVIDUALS WITH DISABILITIES EDUCATION ACT and the Americans with Disabilities Act suggest in their very titles how radically the context of human exceptionality has changed. England's Idiots Act of 1886 was repealed in 1913 by the Mental Deficiency Act, but terms like *deficiency* are no longer so readily applied to human beings. New language conventions acknowledge distinctions between disability and person, and between one's characteristics and barriers imposed by others; while some disabilities may be preventable, *all* associated handicaps can be ameliorated, if not eliminated. But even as barriers are removed, children remain inevitably handicapped by their very dependence and inability to choose the circumstances of their birth or nurture. The "Children's Century" had been envisioned as a time when the implications of that dependence would be fully recognized.

Thus, the First White House Conference on Children affirmed a societal commitment to *family*, a commitment maintained as President Wilson, declaring 1919 the Year of the Child, convened the second. The third produced the Children's Charter, which explicitly referenced exceptional children. With the United Nations' Declaration of the Rights of the Child, adopted in 1959, the idea of children's rights was presumably no longer a "minor enthusiasm" of a few reformers, but a worldwide cause. In its Third Declaration, in 1974, the U.N. Children's Fund affirmed that "the child who is physically, mentally or socially handicapped shall be given the special treatment, education and care required by his particular condition." But the gap between rhetoric and reality is nowhere more cruel than in society's tolerance of conditions that put children in harm's way. Today, more than half the incidence of childhood disability worldwide results from malnutrition, viral and bacterial infections, and communicable disease (Marfo, 1986). In America, one child in four is born into poverty, many go without immunization, most are affected by violence—physically or, given its ubiquitous nature, psychologically. These conditions, with prenatal exposure to drugs or toxic environmental elements, HIV-AIDS, exploitation in its many forms, and lack of hope for a better future—for many, for any future at all—describe not the beginning of the Century of the Child, but its end. Society creates disability in more than one sense.

"Services" have expanded dramatically, though not commensurate with their need, and while it would be gratifying to believe otherwise, we have seen that neither benevolence nor science has consistently served children with or at risk for disabilities well. Often, calamitous events like wars, devastating in their impact on children, have paradoxically stimulated action. Yet, though calls for children's rights have rung hollow and movements have faltered, they suggest a pattern of progress, expressed in social policy and in new paradigms for understanding both exceptionality and childhood. A comprehensive analysis of medical discoveries, technological advances, advocacy, and policy developments is beyond the scope of this final chapter. But among the lessons to be drawn from history are several overarching themes suggesting a foundation for a new history.

Diversity: the context of childhood exceptionality

The present "era" of services began with the century, but where children were concerned 1919—the Year of the Child—began a decade of paradox. Progressive reformers yet sought to improve the quality of life for children of the new European-Americans. Some, like Addams, Wald, and Florence Kelley, joined ranks with African-American leaders, in the NAACP and its forerunner Niagara Movement, in seeking racial justice in schooling as in other areas of American society. While white America's attitudes toward DuBois's "talented tenth" ranged from patronization to disbelief, feelings about the "submerged tenth" ranged from apathy to virulence (Lewis, 1993). Though progressive reforms continued, notably compulsory education and child labor legislation, the movement faded with its loss of social focus (Cremin, 1961). The idealism and national sense of mission President Wilson hoped to sustain seemed to evaporate with the Armistice; "normalcy" involved suppression of ideas and hostility toward all who were "different," thus a threat (Allen, 1931). Protectionism and eugenics converged with psychometrics in a scientific racism anything but celebratory with respect to human diversity, which impacted directly on children and their schooling.

Psychometric sorting and subsystems of "diversification"

As school enrollments swelled, so did the numbers of casualties. In 1909, in *Laggards in Our Schools*, Leonard P. Ayres had called for more economical alternatives to grade repetition for the 33.7% of elementary pupils he reported academically deficient. Estimating that more than half the pupils in large urban districts had mental and physical problems associated with poverty, and citing Connecticut's adoption of the Snellen chart in 1899, Wallin (1914) called for systematic screening to identify vision, health, and hearing problems. While recommending special "orthophrenic" classes for pupils who needed them, he also argued for a more flexible curriculum and organizational structures to accommodate remedial instruction. As we saw, progressivism's social-settlement facet was an important force in urging schools to provide both health services and special classes, perceived need for which grew in parallel fashion to increased pupil heterogeneity.

Tests seemed to offer an "objective" system of sorting to reduce this diversity to manageable proportions. Despite general enthusiasm about ability tests, concerns were raised, most famously by Walter Lippmann as noted in Chapter 6n [see original reading]. Nor were all educationists sanguine about the trend toward their wide adoption. Dewey (1916) believed that while tests might reveal talents of some pupils, they should not be used to close doors of opportunity for others. W. C. Bagley (1925), a prominent critic of progressivism, cautioned that tests could only suggest to the educator where to begin, not prescribe or limit goals;

improperly used, they were potential instruments of social Darwinism, a concern that subsequent educational tracking and exclusion have shown to be warranted. Such responses have often implied fear of contamination, rationalized with professions of concern for the presumptively less fortunate or less well-endowed, educationally defined as slow to learn, difficult to control, or likely to need special care. Or make others uncomfortable: the Wisconsin Supreme Court ruled in 1919 that "a mentally normal, blind child could be barred from school since his/her handicap had a depressing and nauseating effect on teachers and children" (Hensley, 1973, pp. 3).

While by 1918 all states had enacted compulsory education laws, exclusion policies soon followed; special education had come to mean "special place," but a more urgent concern was those children for whom schools provided no place at all. A half-century later, a Children's Defense Fund study (Washington Research Project, 1974), reported that, in addition to a "far greater number who are technically in school but who benefit little or not at all" (p. 2), nearly 2 million children and youth of school age, three-quarters of a million 13 or younger, were not enrolled in school. The investigators concluded

> that if a child is not white, or is white but not middle class, does not speak English, is poor, needs special help with seeing, hearing, walking, reading, learning, adjusting, growing up, is pregnant or married at age 15, is not smart enough or is too smart, then, in many places, school officials decide school is not the place for that child. In sum, out of school children share a common characteristic of *differentness* by virtue of race, income, physical, mental, or emotional "handicap," and age. They are, for the most part, out of school not by choice, but because they have been *excluded*. It is as if many school officials have decided that certain groups of children are beyond their responsibility and are expendable. Not only do they exclude these children, they frequently do so arbitrarily, discriminantly, and with impunity.
>
> (p. 4)

Schools had adopted policies of "conditional nurture," and as in medieval times what placed a child at risk was differentness. Disability, though not the only basis, provided one means of delineating who should be excluded and, ironically though not surprisingly, as compulsory education was mandated, states and local districts codified criteria for exclusion on the basis of "inability to benefit." Such policies, formulated in the 1920s, had by the early 1970s become, if anything, more firmly entrenched. Protypical was the explanation of Superintendent William J. O'Shea (1926) that New York's ungraded classes were not appropriate for all children with retardation. "Exclusion cases" included those with a measured IQ lower than 50, or higher in those who, "because of other special defects or physical disabilities can not profit by the type of instruction suitable to the majority of children in ungraded classes," who varied "as far from the typical ungraded-class pupil as the retarded child varies from the normal" (p. 38). Classes formed for those who "didn't fit" now excluded pupils who "didn't fit" those classes, with Wallin's and Farrell's belief that schools should serve all children a decidedly minority opinion.

New York's exclusion cases included children with epilepsy, postencephalitis, chorea, and "psychopathic personality or actual psychoses," as well as "deviant physical growth" patterns, like those with "mongolian features . . . unfortunate individuals who can be recognized by the physical stigmata . . . and small stocky build. They are always seriously retarded in intelligence, and it has been useless to attempt instruction except on the very lowest level. . . . Obviously, such training can at present be better provided in the homes of children or in institutions" (O'Shea, 1926, pp. 38–39). Elimination of exclusionary policies, often codified in legislation, culminated decades of advocacy by parents, sadly not always joined by special educators, excepting such rare leaders as Richard Hungerford, of the Detroit and then New York districts (Blatt, 1975). In Cuyahoga County, Ohio, where school officials had concluded that instruction of " 'low mentals' . . . does not lie within the sphere of 'education' " (Schmidt, 1970, p. 52), a group of parents formed "community classes," lobbied for state enabling legislation, and began a network that became the Association for Retarded Children (now Citizens) (Turnbull & Turnbull, 1990). By 1954, more than 30,000 people were active in groups advocating for persons with mental retardation (Stevens, 1954). Landmark court decisions—*PARC et al. v. Commonwealth of Pennsylvania* (1971) and *Mills v. Board of Education* (1972)—established precedent for Free Appropriate Public Education (FAPE), the cornerstone of P.L. 94-142, and *zero exclusion*.

Crucially, FAPE encompassed the principle of Least Restrictive Environment, for steadily increasing numbers of pupils had been placed in separate programs. Automotive transportation had contributed to schools' ability to provide alternatives to residential settings, but that capability, combined with growing psychometric expertise, contributed to the ascendancy of the segregated special class model. By the 1920s, about two-thirds of large American school districts had such classes (Abraham, 1972); with this enhanced diagnostic capability, the number placed grew from about 26,000 in 1922 to 357,000 in 1948, slightly more than 1.2% of all pupils. Over the next decade, that nearly doubled, and by 1968 it had reached 2.2 million, the most dramatic postwar increase being in classes for children identified as mentally retarded: from 87,000 in 1948 to 390,000 in 1963 (Farber, 1968).

While school psychology's purview and its practitioners' expertise have never been restricted to testing, the school psychologist's role became increasingly restricted to diagnostic evaluation to determine eligibility for special education (and for inclusion in school), often the basis for state funding allocations. While it ranges widely, depending on needs of the individual student, the average annual per-pupil cost for special education is today about twice that for regular education students, but about 13% of that cost is for assessment. In the 1985–86 school year, the number of pupils found eligible based on evaluation had reached 4.1 million, and 4.8 million in 1990–91, not including those in gifted programs. Since many more did not meet required criteria, the cost of simply determining which pupils were eligible had become staggering (Moore, 1988).

A third factor in the growth of special classes, though its impact was at first slight, was another critical outcome of the 1930 White House Conference: creation of a department of special education in the Office of Education, with Elise Martens appointed in 1931 senior officer. Though assisted only by a part-time secretary for most of the two decades she held this post, and though other priorities preoccupied government, Martens worked to sustain attention to the needs of exceptional children through her ubiquitous pamphlets and leadership in organizing conferences (Aiello, 1976). Addressing one such conference in 1934, in the depth of the Depression, First Lady Eleanor Roosevelt warned that the cost to society of appropriate, differential instruction for exceptional children was far less than the cost of not providing it. While that theme has since become familiar, the Depression slowed momentum in the growth of services.

The postwar "boom," amplified during the Kennedy and Johnson administrations, reflected in increasing prevalence of special classes, led to debate concerning two key issues: effectiveness of such arrangements, and soundness—and fairness—of placement decisions. The former gave rise to numerous efficacy studies, which yielded ambiguous results with regard to social adjustment: Rejection and isolation of exceptional pupils was often observed in mainstream situations, yet special placement was often associated with low self-esteem, stigma, and restriction of models. Further, lower expectancy was often linked with special class instruction, and generally, though not invariably, academic performance indices favored regular class placement. But many factors made such comparisons suspect, principally the fact that pupils were quite purposefully, not randomly, assigned to the respective "treatments" (Gallagher, 1994).

As the civil rights movement gathered force, of even more urgent concern was the question of which students were referred by teachers for "suspected handicaps" and subsequently placed, and which students were more or less likely to be identified as gifted. Dunn (1968) saw probable discrimination in schools' tendency to label and segregate disproportionate numbers of minority pupils, writing that 60 to 80% of the enrollments in classes for pupils with mild retardation were "children from low status backgrounds—including Afro-Americans, American Indians, Mexicans, and Puerto Rican Americans; those from nonstandard English speaking, broken, disorganized, and inadequate homes; and children from other non-middle class environments" (p. 6). Mercer (1973) pointed out that many children able to cope with everyday life were labeled retarded "because they have not had the opportunity to learn the cognitive skills necessary to pass Anglo oriented intelligence tests" (p. 44).

Students of the history of American culture cannot fail to see parallels in majority attitudes toward, and hence opportunities provided for, persons with disabilities and persons of color. Just as DuBois thought Booker Washington's vocationally oriented training a trap for African Americans and the route to continued subservence (Lewis, 1993), John Carlin and other leaders of the Deaf community criticized "the lack of encouragement for deaf people to advance beyond manual trades" (Leakey, 1993, p. 86). Lane (1992) has delineated other striking parallels between Anglo-colonialist beliefs and policies concerning people of color and majority (i.e., English-speaking) attitudes and policies concerning deaf persons as a linguistic minority. Cultural deafness represents a special case, where educational "integration" has often meant denial of equity; for many other children considered exceptional, separate placement has meant segregated, thus inherently *unequal*, education.

While diversity in American society is increasingly multifaceted and complex, the core "American Dilemma" has continued to be a matter of black and white. In his classic study, Gunnar Myrdal (1944) noted the paradox "that the official political creed of America denounced, in general but vigorous terms, all forms of suppression and discrimination, and affirmed human equality" (p. 50), yet suppression, discrimination, and inequality have in this instance been accepted and maintained. From the time of the Revolution to the Civil War, in the North where schooling was available at all for African-American children, it was available through separate schools, most philanthropic but some public, like the New York African Free Schools. Even Boston, the first city to offer public education for black children, maintained separate facilities until state legislation forbidding such distinctions was enacted in 1855 (Bullock, 1967). Teachers of both races dispatched by missionary societies to Freedmen's Schools formed during Reconstruction were greeted hostilely, often terrorized, by native whites, but found adults hungry to learn, and parents determined that their children have that opportunity (Litwack, 1979).

A century later the U.S. Supreme Court, reversing *Plessy v. Ferguson*, ruled that separate is *not* equal. But did special education provide a means to perpetuate educational, and hence societal, segregation both of children with disabilities and of those *judged* to be different, and accordingly *labeled* as having disabilities? Carrier (1986) argues that the *Brown* ruling led "a number of school systems . . . to find other ways of sorting pupils, and many introduced or expanded ability grouping and increased provision for the mildly retarded and to a lesser extent the emotionally disturbed" (p. 302). Despite P.L. 94-142's mandates for nonbiased, multifactored evaluation, conducted with informed parental consent, a report by the National Academy of Sciences Panel (Heller, Holtzman, & Messick, 1982) revealed continued disproportionate percentages of minority and disadvantaged children—especially boys—placed in special classes. More than twice as many minority and lower SES children as middle-class, nonminority children continued to be reported placed due to learning and behavior problems (Ysseldyke, Algozzine, Richey, & Graden, 1982). But issues of equity and justice transcend special education; as Artiles and Trent (1994) concluded, "we find ourselves still grappling with the issue of overrepresentation and the problem of serving, equitably and effectively, children whose problems, in some cases, are more complex and stressful than the problems of the children described by Dunn" (p. 432).

The question of special education's efficacy cannot be answered simply, but clearly problems have been identified. In its *Eleventh Annual Report to Congress on the Implementation of the Education of the Handicapped Act*, the U.S. Office (now Department) of Education (USDOE) (1989) reported that the number of residential placements of children, having dropped significantly following implementation of P.L. 94-142 and as a facet of general deinstitution-alization, had remained steady for a decade. But monitoring teams reported that removal of pupils based on category of disability and the local district's service system was common, often without evidence that a student's IEP could be implemented only in a separate facility. Moreover, despite the provision for FAPE through age 21, the dropout rate of special educa-tion students was higher than that of the general school population, with only 59.5% gradu-ating, and students with disabilities had inordinately high rates of unemployment on leaving school or graduating. The report indicated that the number referred because of suspected learning disabilities had increased, and USDOE's (1993) report for the 1991–92 school year revealed that this category comprised 5.2% of the public school enrollment, more than half the special education enrollment. Shifts in categorical prevalence suggest a certain arbitrari-ness, but for the considerable proportion of the pupils assigned this label who do not complete school—36% in 1991—outcomes of separate instruction as a strategy to manage diversity, irrespective of categorical label, appeared less than optimal.

From zero exclusion to full inclusion

The so-called judgment or non-normative categories make up the vast majority of pupils determined eligible for special education, not only in the United States but in other industri-alized nations (e.g., Brennan, 1985; McGee, 1990). Most versions of the so-called Regular Education Initiative (REI), proposed by former USOE Assistant Secretary Madeline Will (1986), have primarily concerned these pupils (e.g., Reynolds, Wang, & Walberg, 1987). Their rationale has included the considerable expenditure and arbitrariness entailed in determining eligibility, negative impact of labeling and segregation—social as well as instructional—of pupils found eligible, and the lack of provisions to address individual needs of pupils *not* found eligible, a broad group mainly comprising children of low-income and minority families often described as "at-risk." The concept entails a presumably more effec-tive use of resources to address the individual needs of a greater number of pupils, within the context of a broader curricular framework, in such a way as to minimize stigma associated with removal from the educational mainstream. It entails a "restructuring" (Reynolds, et al., 1987) of the whole educational enterprise, at the least operational changes in the ways schools are arranged and pupils and teachers assigned, if not a fundamental paradigm shift concerning the role of schooling itself (Skrtic, 1991).

Although much discussed (in the special education literature, at any rate), seemingly responsive to calls in the 1980s for broad educational reforms, and widely endorsed, at least in spirit, "the REI was a *special* education initiative" that, except in certain states, brought "little concomitant change in general education programs" (Fuchs & Fuchs, 1994, p. 299). Its limited impact was attributed, at least in part, to the lack of involvement in discussion on the part of general educators. By the mid-1990s, however, calls for *inclusion*, a far more dramatic response to pupil diversity, got the endorsement of policymakers (National Association of State Boards of Education, 1992), and the concerned attention of the organized teaching profession. To some, it appeared that, in "radicalizing" the REI, full inclusionists may have revitalized special education reform, but in their "extremist" rhetoric and "uncompromising" advocacy for "students with severe intellectual disabilities," they jeopardized special education and its relationship to the broader enterprise of schooling (Fuchs & Fuchs, 1994, p. 303–4).

P.L. 94-142's mandate for zero exclusion had meant a radical departure from past practice, but barely two decades later the idea that even children with the most severe forms of disability could learn and could benefit from schooling was no longer revolutionary. Children formerly categorized as "unable to benefit from education," who warranted bare mention in textbooks as "custodial cases," were now identified in school records, as well as journals and texts, as *students*. The designation "trainable," as distinct from "educable," though not totally erased, was no longer legally defensible; *all* children with disabilities must be provided a Free Appropriate Public Education (FAPE), based on an Individualized Education Program (IEP), in the Least Restrictive Environment (LRE). The federal legislation represented a triumph of advocacy, achieved through a series of key court rulings, for every child's right to education.

The advocates were, as always, parents, but in this instance joined by an unlikely collection of professionals, initially a preponderance of behavioral psychologists and lawyers, with a steadily expanding diversity of practitioners and scholars, as well as a steadily growing number of persons with disabilities. In 1975, the American Association for the Severely and Profoundly Handicapped (AAESPH), now the Association for Persons with Severe Handicaps (TASH), was formed in Kansas City, its members electing Norris G. Haring its first president. Begun as an informal network of about 30 applied researchers, some of whom had been enlisted as expert witnesses in right-to-education litigation, the organization grew within just two decades to more than 9,000 members. In the context of a growing societal belief in the compensatory powers of early education, TASH members have been among those with particular interest in the potential benefit of intervention early in life for children with cognitive and physical impairments.

Early intervention and the "new environmentalism"

While the decade of the 1920s was a time of protectivism and intolerance, it paradoxically saw growing attention to children's special needs, reflected in such developments as psycho-educational clinics and treatment programs for troubled children—indeed, the birth of yet another small "movement," focused on children's mental health. The attention of child study leaders, now informed by psychoanalytic discoveries, turned to the first five years of life. Between 1923 and 1927, Arnold Gesell, having himself initiated what he called a "Guidance Nursery School" in 1918, published 13 articles on "the nursery school movement" and the potential of nursery education to prevent later emotional and behavioral problems (Ames, 1989, p. 36). Dewey's famous laboratory school, established in 1896, had in fact included preschool children, but in the 1920s several nursery schools were developed as facilities for demonstration, training, and research. In addition to Gesell's, reestablished in 1926 as the Guidance Nursery of the Yale Psycho-clinic, others included the Merrill-Palmer School's (later Institute) in Detroit, Abigail Eliot's Ruggles Street Nursery School in Boston, and Harriet M. Johnson's nursery in New York, later called Bank Street (p. 134).

By the end of the decade, Gesell (1930) averred that nursery education had moved from "a 'no man's land' to an 'every man's land': Psychologists, psychiatrists, kindergartners, primary school teachers, home economics and social workers, public health leaders, mothers' clubs, and mental hygiene organizations have found themselves side by side in the new interest in the preschool child" (p. 143). With respect to diversity, the interest was in children's individuality, pursued through child study, with a dual aim of promoting each child's positive development and of identifying potential problems. Nursery education was a child-centered enterprise but, like the Infant School a century earlier, it was enlisted to serve societal needs. And like special education, its spread was halted by the Depression and renewed by war, the Lanham Act of 1940 providing nurseries for children of women employed in defense work. But as the nursery and the kindergarten ideas continued to evolve, they reflected a benign, nurturing attitude toward young children in their diversity, captured by James Hymes's (1955) phrase "the child development point of view."

In the 1960s, another perspective on the role of early education vis-à-vis child diversity emerged, heralded by publication of J. McV. Hunt's *Intelligence and Experience* (1961) and Benjamin Bloom's *Stability and Change in Human Characteristics* (1964): Effective intervention early in life could change the course of children's subsequent development. This new environmentalism had its beginnings in a classic study (Skeels & Dye, 1939), extended to a larger sample (Skeels, 1941), reporting striking IQ differences in children attributable to differences in early nurture. After two years, children in the experimental group showed an average gain of 27.5 IQ points, while controls, initially somewhat higher in IQ than their counterparts, showed a substantial loss. This suggested a revolutionary notion, and most authorities, considering intelligence innate and immutable, and consequently retardation irreversible and permanent, reacted with skepticism to these reports from the Iowa Child Welfare Station. Nevertheless, a few other reports suggested a degree of cautious optimism concerning environmental influences on early development, heightened by Kirk's (1958) demonstration of significant gains made by preschool children with IQs ranging from 45 to 80.

By the mid-1960s, when Skeels (1966) reported compelling evidence of long-term differences in the adult status of the original subjects, the potential of early intervention to change children seemed nearly limitless, giving rise to a "first generation" of efficacy research focused on measuring children's developmental gains (Guralnick & Bennet, 1992). Could early intervention solve the "problem" of diversity by eliminating it? Even if such a goal were desirable, certainly few, if any, thought the central nervous system infinitely malleable. And some leaders saw reason for concern that, in focusing narrowly on questionable measures of intellect, the "environmental mystique" (Zigler, 1970), reductionist in its view of children and families, might endanger the early intervention enterprise itself. Reports that IQ advantages of children in Head Start were not sustained (Cicerelli, Evans, & Schiller, 1969) suggested that such concerns were not unfounded; as the bureaucratic machinery of the War on Poverty was being effectively dismantled, Project Head Start was, in fact, at considerable risk. As we know, it survived and is generally considered a highly effective social program, the potential of which has yet to be fully exploited.

In any event, as a parallel development to these efforts to change the futures of young children at environmental risk, the late 1960s saw the birth of early intervention with infants, toddlers, and preschool age children with identified disabilities, furthered by creation of the Handicapped Children's Early Education Program (HCEEP) in 1968. While biologically based conditions, such as blindness and cerebral palsy, could not be "cured" through early educational and therapeutic intervention, model programs funded by HCEEP, through its First Chance network, led to new understanding of childhood diversity and the meaning of efficacy for children and families, and consequently to reconceptualization of an old idea.

Collaboration

In Chapter 3 [see original reading], we reflected on the relationship of teacher and exceptional pupil, epitomized by the joint achievement of Helen Keller, who was not "cured" but
liberated, and Anne Sullivan Macy. We have also traced a pattern of *integration* of persons
with disabilities into the broader society, which as a societal goal has important implications
for education and other services for children. In the United States, a succession of court
rulings stemming from the pivotal *Brown* decision accelerated the trend toward integration,
culminating in the judicial doctrine of Least Restrictive Alternative, operationalized under
P.L. 94-142 as Least Restrictive Environment. Presumably, the story of increasing, albeit
mandated, collaboration between general and special educators is familiar to readers, although
it is still unfolding. Other dimensions of collaboration that have emerged as key elements in
the short history of early intervention—about three decades—involve relationships among
professionals, service systems, certainly children themselves, and professionals with families.
This overarching concept appears to be a core facet of a new historical context in which
exceptional children will grow to adulthood.

That a team is something more than the collective expertise of its members is a truism;
yet as diverse specializations emerged to address specific needs of children with disabilities,
role identities and prerogatives often superseded other concerns. This specificity of role and
responsibility has extended to service systems, each of which—for example, educational,
medical, child protection and advocacy, mental health, juvenile justice—has operated in
accordance with its own particular mandates, ethical codes, and fiscal constraints and mechanisms. As in all areas of human affairs, things seem to have been simpler in the past; however,
the mandated *service coordination* and increasingly preferred *transdisciplinary-team* approach
that have emerged during the short history of early intervention would appear to offer better
models for empowering families to enhance their own, and their child's, quality of life. These
concepts indeed represented a departure from earlier conceptions of the relationship between
professionals and families:

> "Let's wait awhile" is freqently heard from the lips of a parent who realizes that
> the little deaf or blind child needs the education which the State School provides,
> but who is reluctant to part with him so young. He is still a baby—only six years
> old. In four or five years he will be better able to take care of himself and the
> separation may not be so hard. But remember, too, that in four or five years he
> will have lost the opportunity for the *early* training which is so important. The
> younger the child the easier it is for him to adapt himself to new ways of learning.
> Unless you can in your own home provide that which he needs in the prepara-
> tory stages of the work, then permit the State school to teach him as early as it
> will admit him.
>
> (Martens, 1932, p. 12)

The most striking contrast between past and present educational arrangements for children
with disabilities is that today most live at home with families (Turnbull & Turnbull, 1990).
Since the 1950s, parents have rarely been enjoined to give over responsibility for care and
instruction of their child, either to the state or to private agencies, nor is blame for the child's
difficulties—as in instances of autism and Attention Deficit Disorder—as commonly ascribed
to parents. Until quite recently, professionals hoped that parents would do as little harm as
possible in the early years of a child's life until their own ameliorative work could commence.
Some offered advice toward that end, notably Howe, who professed a family model to be
infinitely preferable to centralized institutions. But the "family model" that had taken root

was often one of subjugation and denial of human rights (Blatt, Ozolins, & McNally, 1979). The relationship between professionals and parents was, in any case, a one-sided one, predicated on the presumed superior knowledge of the former.

Over time, a succession of events cast the relationship in a different light. It will be recalled that, historically, instruction of children with impaired hearing emerged in response to efforts of their parents, well-to-do and influential ones, to be sure, whether it was a matter of finding and paying a tutor, lobbying for legislation, enlisting a respected advocate in their child's cause, even founding a school. Fathers like Cogswell and Hubbard were not to be patronized; they were the *patrons*. A century later, as American parents of children whose IQs excluded them from school formed community classes, similar developments occurred in other countries. In Ireland, "parents, friends, and professionals concerned with mental handicap formed themselves into voluntary associations and began to establish schools which were subsequently recognized by the Department of Education as special national schools" (McGee, 1990, p. 52). The pattern that emerged, spreading to a broader representation of families, was one of parents' seeking, and bringing about, services for children with disabilities where none had previously existed, or where provisions were seen as inadequate. The litany is long, as we have seen, involving children with speech impairments, retardation, cerebral palsy and other physical disabilities, emotional problems, severe and multiple disabilities, learning disabilities, and more recently autism, traumatic brain injury, Attention Deficit Disorder, Tourette syndrome, and specialized health care needs.

In advocating for their children, parents were redefining their relationship with professionals, as well as their child's needs. P.L. 94-142 attempted formally to define the relationship on the basis of parental rights but did little to bridge the distance between home and school. The parent who questions school recommendations, or requests services at variance with a district's standard arrangements (e.g., "supportive aids and services" for a child in a regular classroom), has often been branded a "problem." Professionals often express discouragement at their difficulty in getting parents to attend meetings, respond to requests, or sign the IEP, confirmed in successive USOE reports to Congress. With experience gained through early intervention, the relationship of professionals and families intended by the *Individualized Family Service Plan* may herald a new, collaborative context, and thus a "new history."

Coda

Among the challenging ideas emerging in connection with the philosophy of inclusion of children with disabilities within the context of societal, and educational, diversity, two in particular suggest that at the very core of a "new history," if such it will be, are exceptional children themselves. The first, *constructivism*, has been increasingly discussed in conjunction with inclusive early education for typical children and those with disabilities (e.g., Mallory & New, 1994), the second, often referred to as *interpretivism*, within the multidisciplinary field of "disability studies" (Ferguson, Ferguson, & Taylor, 1992). It may be that these represent fundamental paradigm shifts affecting all children, and adults, including those with disabilities.

Constructivist conceptions of children's learning as spontaneous, self-directed, and internally organized seem on the surface contradictory to the interventionist tradition of specialized instruction for children with disabilities. Indeed, such instruction has been intended for pupils whose needs were not met through conventional approaches, and the historical record is replete with references to "training"—to comply with adult wishes, to unlearn undesirable habits and acquire acceptable ones, to develop character and eschew vice through honest labor, to imitate the speech and social conventions favored by instructors, sometimes to learn a trade. Yet we have seen that such notions, in their time, did not differ markedly from expectations for the role of education for most other children. Moreover, history not only reveals common philosophical origins, anticipating the constructivist approaches now endorsed in early childhood education, at least through the primary years (Mallory & New, 1994), but striking instances of specialized pedagogy's embracing such practices prior to their adoption in general education. These have included early embracing of Pestalozzian methods and respect for children's inner nature and resources, in fact the "Quixotic" notion (Seguin, 1880, p. 3) that children be educated "for themselves," in recognition, as Burton Blatt (1981) expressed, that all can learn and all are worthy.

Interpretivist conceptions of disability, too, have striking resonance in Diderot's *Letter* (1749/1965) and as revealed in the emerging Deaf scholarship; the critiques by 19th-century Deaf leaders and by Thomas Cutsforth; Robert Scott's *The Making of Blind Men* (1969), Helen Keller's rich legacy, and many other accounts based on personal experience, written by persons with disabilities, or so labeled. As scholars continue to learn "insiders' perspectives," more exceptional individuals—notably Temple Grandin, Donna Williams, Kim Peek, and other persons with autism—tell their own stories, in their own voices. Two young men with Down syndrome, Jason Kingsley and Mitchell Levitz (1994), have recently shared their experiences, and their friendship, by sharing their conversations. Though also filtered through the lens of maturity, such accounts bring us closer to an understanding of how exceptionality was experienced during childhood, and, more importantly, of whose "history" it indeed is. To the extent that the work of future historians of exceptionality in children, informed by "insiders' views," can recount an end to "laws against the poor" and policies inimical to children, realization of every child's right to unconditional nurture, and society's recognition of the paradoxical inseparability of diversity and common humanity, it will describe a new history.

> I sit alone at night and look out into the night, and I wonder if I can make it in the world or if I will have a nice life. But for me I know that I have to do it for myself. For I am the only one who can make that come true. You see I feel like there is another person inside me, just waiting to get out.
>
> Some things are easier than others. Some things are harder than others for different people. Some people are good at one thing but not good at other things. . . . So I made up my mind the only way to beat this fear is to keep writing. It doesn't matter what I write but I have to keep trying over and over again.
>
> (Selections from *Student Journal*, Literacy Volunteers of Massachusetts)

References

Abraham, W. (1972). The early years: Prologue to tomorrow. In J. B. Jordan (Ed.), *Exceptional child education at the bicentennial: A parade of progress* (pp. 26–31). Reston, VA: Council for Exceptional Children.

Aiello, B. (1976). Especially for special educators: A sense of our own history. In J. B. Jordan (Ed.), *Exceptional child education at the bicentennial: A parade of progress* (pp. 16–25). Reston, VA: Council for Exceptional Children.

Allen, F.L. (1931). *Only yesterday: An informal history of the 1920s.* New York: Harper & Brothers.

Ames, L. B. (1989). *Arnold Gesell—Themes of his work.* New York: Plenum.

Artiles, A. J., & Trent, S. C. (1994). Overrepresentation of minority students in special education: A continuing debate. *Journal of Special Education, 27*(4), 410–437.

Ayres, L. P. (1909). *Laggards in our schools: A study of retardation and its elimination in city school systems*. New York: Charities Publications Committee.

Bagley, W. C. (1925). *Determinism in education*. New York: Nelson.

Blatt, B. (1975). Toward an understanding of people with special needs. In J. M. Kauffman & J. S. Payne (Eds.), *Mental retardation: Introduction and personal perspectives*. Columbus, OH: Merrill.

Blatt, B. (1981). *In and out of mental retardation: Essays on educability, disability, and human policy*. Baltimore: University Park Press.

Blatt, B., Ozolins, A., & McNally, J. (1979). *The family papers: A return to purgatory*. New York: Longman.

Bloom, B. S. (1964). *Stability and change in human characteristics*. New York: Wiley.

Brennan, W. K. (1985). *Curriculum for special needs*. Milton Keynes, U.K.: Open University Press.

Bullock, H. D. (1967). *A history of Negro education in the South: From 1619 to the present*. Cambridge, MA: Harvard University Press.

Carrier, J. G. (1986). *Learning disability: Social class and the construction of inequality in American education*. Westport, CT: Greenwood Press.

Cicerelli, V. G., Evans, J. W., & Schiller, J. S. (1969). *The impact of Head Start on children's cognitive and affective development: Preliminary report*. Washington, DC: Office of Economic Opportunity.

Cremin, L. A. (1961). *The transformation of the school: Progressivism in American education, 1876–1957*. New York: Random House.

Dewey, J. (1916). *Democracy and education*. New York: Macmillan.

Diderot, D. (1965). *Lettre sur les aveugles à l'usage de ceux qui voient*. In P. H. Meyer, *Diderot studies*. Geneva: Librarie Druz. (Original work published 1749)

Dunn, L. M. (1968). Special education for the mildly retarded: Is much of it justifiable? *Exceptional Children, 35*, 5–22.

Farber, B. (1968). *Mental retardation: Its social context and social consequences*. Boston: Houghton Mifflin.

Ferguson, P. M., Ferguson, D. L., & Taylor, S. J. (Eds.). (1992). *Interpreting disability: A qualitative reader*. New York: Teachers College Press.

Fuchs, D., & Fuchs, L. S. (1994). Inclusive schools movement and the radicalization of special education reform. *Exceptional Children, 60*, 294–309.

Gallagher, J. J. (1994). The pull of societal forces on special education. *Journal of Special Education, 27*(4), 521–530.

Gesell, A. (1930). A decade of progress in the mental hygiene of the preschool child. *Annals of the American Academy of Political and Social Sciences, 151*, 143–148.

Guralnick, M., & Bennett, F. C. (Eds.). (1992). *The effectiveness of early intervention*. Orlando, FL: Academic Press.

Heller, K. A., Holtzman, W. H., & Messick, S. (Eds.). (1982). *Placing children in special education: A strategy for equity*. Washington, DC: National Academy Press.

Hensley, G. (1973). Special education: No longer handicapped. *Compact, 7*, 3–5.

Hunt, J. M. (1961). *Intelligence and experience*. New York: Ronald Press.

Hymes, J. (1955). *The child development point of view*. Englewood Cliffs, NJ: Prentice-Hall.

Kingsley, J., & Levitz, M. (1994). *Count us in: Growing up with Down syndrome*. New York: Harcourt Brace Jovanovich.

Kirk, S. A. (1958). *Early education of the mentally retarded*. Urbana: University of Illinois Press.

Lane, H. (1992). *The mask of benevolence: Disabling the deaf community*. New York: Alfred A. Knopf.

Leakey, T. A. (1993). Vocational education in the Deaf American and African-American communities. In J. V. Van Cleve (Ed.), *Deaf history unveiled: Interpretations from the new scholarship* (pp. 74–91). Washington, DC: Gallaudet University Press.

Lewis, D. L. (1993). *W. E. B. DuBois: Biography of a race, 1868–1919*. New York: Henry Holt.

Literacy Volunteers of Massachusetts. (1994). *Student journal: A collection of writings by adult new readers*. Boston: Author.

Litwack, L. F. (1979). *Been in the storm so long: The aftermath of slavery*. New York: Alfred A. Knopf.

Mallory, B., & New, R. (1994). *Diversity and developmentally appropriate practices: Challenges for early childhood education*. New York: Teachers College Press.

Marfo, K. (1986). *Confronting childhood disability in developing countries*. New York: Praeger.

Martens, E. H. (1932). *Parents' problems with exceptional children* (Office of Education Pamphlet No. 14). Washington, DC: U.S. Government Printing Office.

McGee, P. (1990). Special education in Ireland. *European Journal of Special Education, 5*(1), 48–64.

Mercer, J. (1973). *Labeling the mentally retarded*. Berkeley: University of California Press.

Moore, M. (1988). *Patterns in special education service delivery and cost*. Washington, DC: Decision Resources Corporation. (ERIC No. ED303027)

Myrdal, G. (1944). *An American dilemma: The Negro problem and modern democracy* (Vols. 1 & 2). New York: Harper & Brothers.

National Association of State Boards of Education. (1992). *The report of the NASBE study group on special education*. Alexandria, VA: Author.

O'Shea, W. J. (1926). Mentally handicapped children. *Twenty-eighth annual report of the Superintendent of Schools*. New York: Board of Education.

Reynolds, M. C., Wang, M., & Walberg, H. (1987). The necessary restructuring of special and regular education. *Exceptional Children, 53*, 391–398.

Schmidt, S. N. (1970). *Out of the shadows*. Cleveland, OH: Council for the Retarded Child.

Scott, R. A. (1969). *The making of blind men: A study of adult socialization*. New York: Russell Sage Foundation.

Seguin, E. (1880). *Report on education (U.S. Commissioner on Education at the Vienna Universal Exhibition)*. Washington, DC: U.S. Government Printing Office.

Skeels, H. M. (1941). A study of the effects of differential stimulation on mentally retarded children: A follow-up report. *American Journal of Mental Deficiency, 46*, 340–350.

Skeels, H. M. (1966). Adult status of children with contrasting early life experiences. *Monographs of the Society for Research in Child Development, 31*(3), (Whole No. 105).

Skeels, H. M., & Dye, H. B. (1939). A study of the effects of differential stimulation on mentally retarded children. *Proceedings and Addresses of the Sixty-third Annual Session of the American Association on Mental Deficiency, 44*(1), 114–136.

Skrtic, T. M. (1991). The special education paradox: Equity as the way to excellence. *Harvard Educational Review, 61*(2), 148–206.

Stevens, G. D. (1954). Developments in the field of mental deficiency. *Exceptional Children, 21*, 58–62.

Turnbull, A. P., & Turnbull, H. R. (1990). *Families, professionals and exceptionality* (2nd ed.) Columbus, OH: Merrill.

U.S. Department of Education. (1989). *Eleventh annual report to Congress on the implementation of the Education of the Handicapped Act (PL 94–142)*. Washington, DC: U.S. Government Printing Office.

U.S. Department of Education. (1993). *Fifteenth annual report to Congress on the implementation of the Education of the Handicapped Act (PL 94–142)*. Washington, DC: U.S. Government Printing Office.

Wallin, J. E. W. (1914). *The mental health of the school child: The psychoeducational clinic in relation to child welfare*. New Haven, CT: Yale University Press.

Washington Research Project. (1974). *Children out of school in America*. Washington, DC: Children's Defense Fund.

Ysseldyke, J., Algozzine, B., Richey, L., & Graden, J. (1982). Declaring students eligible for learning disability services: Why bother with the data? *Learning Disability Quarterly*, *5*, 37–44.

Zigler, E. F. (1970). The environmental mystique: Training the intellect vs. development of the child. *Childhood Education*, *46*, 8.

Chapter 15

Beverly Carolease Grier

STRUGGLES OVER AFRICAN CHILDHOOD: CHILD AND ADOLESCENT LABOR, 1890–1920s

The towns and mines and other industrial centres have, ever since the occupation of Southern Rhodesia, attracted a large number of native lads of ages ranging from about 10 years to 14 years. European employers have readily taken them into service at low rates of pay. Some have left their homes with the consent of their parents; others again have run away to see the world, leaving the family flocks and herds unattended.[1]

WITH THE ADVENT OF COLONIAL RULE to Southern Rhodesia in 1890, children's labor became the focus not only of senior men, but also of white farmers, mine owners, town dwellers, missionaries, and the British South Africa Company (BSAC) state. Each sought to assert control over children's labor and construct or reconstruct a childhood for Africans that suited their particular needs. Senior African men sought to intensify the labor of children and other junior members of the homestead in order to expand the production and sale of grains, vegetables, stock, and beer. They also attempted to control and benefit from the earnings of boys and male adolescents and youths whom they sent or who left home on their own to work for wages. White farmers acquired much of their labor in the early years through senior African men who, in exchange for continuing access to farming and grazing land, agreed to make the labor of their wives, children, and other junior homestead members available to the farmers. Mine owners met their growing need for cheap labor, in part, by engaging migrant boys and adolescent males at the lowest rates of pay, while white housewives and single men (African and white) in the towns and mining camps of the colony found in boys and male adolescents and youths their most important source of domestic labor. Even missionaries developed an interest in African children's labor, making liberal use of the unpaid labor of their pupils to perform domestic work, grow food and make furniture for sale, and construct buildings and roads on mission-owned lands. And, through law and practice, the BSAC colonial state took steps to increase the number of male children and adolescents in the wage labor force and to control and discipline child workers. "The younger a boy leaves home the better labourer he becomes," J. W. Posselt, Native Commissioner (NC) Charter, Mashonaland told the South African Native Affairs Commission in 1904.[2]

Thus, conquest and settler colonial rule brought in their wake efforts to strengthen or adapt the precolonial or patriarchal construction of African childhood and junior status and to introduce a new colonial construction of childhood as well. In time, the contradictions would become apparent. As in the decades prior to conquest, African patriarchs looked upon their unmarried sons and daughters as sources of agricultural and herding labor, credit, and *lobola* cattle. Children owed obedience and deference to their male elders as well as assistance in all work around the homestead. This construction of African childhood did not necessarily preclude migrant labor or schooling, at least, for boys. Preexisting expectations about children's labor could be adapted to the colonial situation and used by senior men as new avenues for traditional accumulation.[3] However, from the start, male elders were ambivalent about schooling and soon grew to be wary of migrant labor. Though many saw mission education as an investment in the future earning capacity of sons, in particular, time spent away at school deprived them of their children's labor just when they were expanding agricultural production for the market. Schooling also threatened senior men's authority and control over young people, particularly girls, making them less compliant with their parents' wishes and demands.[4] They were aware that much of the keen interest that African children, adolescents, and youths expressed in mission education stemmed from a desire to break away from patriarchal control and assert some autonomy over their lives.

And, while the earnings of migrant boys and adolescent males helped to pay the taxes of senior males and purchase stock, ploughs, and clothing, boys' experiences living away from home and earning wages, however small, ended the monopoly senior males hitherto exercised over the homestead's resources and the male transition to senior status. Migrant labor threatened to undermine precolonial constructions of African childhood and, by extension, junior and senior status. Thus, in education and in migration, senior men had reason to be fearful, for many boys and adolescent males did indeed seize upon the new opportunities opened up by colonization to challenge power relations in the homestead and redefine childhood and junior status. Armed with passes and labor contracts, including "underage" passes and contracts, boys and adolescent males attempted to use new European chronologically based definitions of *child* and *adult* to their advantage. As one Legislative Assembly member told his colleagues, "I know that even before they become 14 years old these picannins wish to have a registration certificate [pass], so that they can call themselves men".[5]

[. . .]

African children and "the age of fortune hunters," 1890–97

It was in good measure the search for the "Second Rand"—gold in amounts equal, if not superior, to the goldfields on the Witwatersrand in the Transvaal—that prompted Cecil Rhodes and his BSAC to invade Mashonaland.[6] Bypassing a confrontation with the Ndebele, the Pioneer Column of 196 white men, mostly South Africans, and African recruits from the Cape marched into the goldfields of Mashonaland in 1890. Promised a "free farm of 1,500 morgen (3,175 acres) and 15 reef claims of 400 by 150 feet," the white pioneers quickly disbanded and began to search for gold. In their immediate party and in their wake came other "fortune hunters" and missionaries. However, it soon became clear that Mashonaland was not the Second Rand and "Rhodes turned his acquisitive eye towards Matabeleland, whose mineral resources, he hoped, would be greater than those of Mashonaland, and where the fertile, well-stocked *high veld* was an added inducement." Rhodes found in a recent Ndebele raid upon Fort Victoria a pretext for invasion in 1893. This time, each white volunteer was promised a free farm of 3,000 morgen (6,350 acres), 15 reef and 5 alluvial gold claims, "while the 'loot'—the Ndebele cattle—was to be shared, half going direct to the

Company, and the remaining half being divided equally among the officers and men."[7] The Ndebele were defeated and Lobengula fled north in the direction of the Zambesi River where he died shortly afterwards. With these events, the BSAC and the settlers believed that the Ndebele state had completely collapsed.

By the time of the Ndebele and Shona Risings in 1896, whites had laid claim to 15.8 million acres of land in the Mashonaland and Matabeleland Provinces (one-sixth of the colony) which was parceled out to prospectors, traders, mining and land speculation companies, missionary bodies, and individuals. Matabeleland was affected more than Mashonaland by these alienations, with nearly all of the land in the "fertile, well-stocked *high veld*" being claimed by whites. With the exception of the Melsetter area, which was settled by Afrikaner trekkers, most of the early settlers were interested in mining rather than farming. As a consequence, for the time being, at least, this large-scale alienation of land had little effect upon most African owners, who continued to occupy and farm their ancestral lands. What affected the Shona and the Ndebele most immediately were the "native" policies and practices of the BSAC and the settlers: taxation, the seizure of cattle, sheep, and goats, forced labor, the sexual abuse of women and girls, and what Terence Ranger calls "private justice," settler physical abuse of African laborers with impunity.[8] Between 100,000 and 200,000 Ndebele cattle—more than half of the entire Ndebele herd—was seized by BSAC officials and settlers between 1893 and 1896. The Shona faired only slightly better, with one-third of their cattle, sheep, and goats in some areas confiscated as private loot and as taxes in lieu of cash to the BSAC. Their hardships exacerbated by natural disasters (rinderpest cattle disease, an invasion of locusts, and drought), the Ndebele, followed by the Shona, rose up in 1896 against BSAC and settler rule.

After initial successes, the Ndebele Rising was brought under control. A political settlement was reached with Ndebele chiefs, but fighting continued in parts of Mashonaland into 1898. Starved into submission or dynamited out of the caves into which they retreated, resisting Shona chiefs and their people were defeated community by community. Thousands of African men, women, and children were killed during the Risings, along with about 300 white men, women, and children. The Risings instilled fear and hatred of Africans in most surviving whites, but they led to a number of seemingly critical reforms in the way the colony was administered, particularly its "native affairs" policies. Among the reforms were the vetting of officials from Assistant Native Commission on up by the imperial government in London, the prohibition of discriminatory legislation, except in the sale of arms, ammunition, and alcohol to Africans, and the setting aside of land for exclusive African occupation (reserves).[9] As radical as these reforms appeared to be, in subsequent years, they did little to stop whites from gaining even greater control over African land and labor than they had before the Risings. Though, as Ranger points out, the Risings forced whites to take Africans into account and prevented a repeat of the kinds of abuses that had been widespread in the years before, settlers reaped the greatest benefits in the years that followed. Neither local officials nor the imperial government in London did much of anything to alter this course.

How did African children experience these earliest years of settler rule? The picture that emerges from accounts left by European travelers, journalists, missionaries, and BSAC officials and by several Africans is one of young people affected by and involved in every aspect of the economic, political, and military changes that unfolded. Boys and male adolescents were engaged as personal servants, carriers, and miners. Adolescents girls and young women were the targets of sexual abuse and exploitation by settlers and by white and African BSAC police before and during the Risings. Along with women, children were deeply involved in preparing for the Risings. They also served as child soldiers and were killed and taken hostage in large numbers by BSAC forces.

By the time of the Risings, boys and adolescent males, though not girls, were already finding their place in the colonial economy as sources of cheap labor for whites. The jobs that were most often mentioned in connection with them before 1896 were those that they would be heavily engaged to do after that date as well—personal or domestic service, including cooking, cleaning, washing, tending horses, and carrying loads for white and African police and employees of the BSAC and for white and African individuals in the emerging towns. Harry C. Thomson, an American journalist who covered the colony during this period, came across numerous African boys in service to BSAC employees. While paying a visit to the famous spirit medium, Chirimba, near Inyanga, Mashonaland, he wrote, an African "messenger of one of the native commissioners . . . passed the farm . . . attended by a piccanin to carry his things."[10] The other "carrier boys" pictured in the photographs in Thomson's book are not adult men but boys—pubescent and possibly prepubescent males— even though Thomson liberally used the term "boy" to describe adult African men as well.

There was also "Pikenen," described by another journalist, South African David C. de Waal, as a youth of about 17 years of age. However, the name given to him suggests either his diminutive size or, what is more likely, the name he had been given when he began working for whites at a much younger age. Pikenen was recruited in Beira, Mozambique to work as carrier, cook, and horse boy for Rhodes during the trip into Mashonaland. According to de Waal, on several occasions he and the other servants received quite rough physical treatment at the hands of Rhodes for what Rhodes considered laziness and indifferent service.[11]

Though mine and BSAC records alter the Risings show that boys under fourteen were employed on a widespread basis on the mines, the records of individual prospectors and fledging companies were haphazardly kept, if at all, in the years before. It is known that there had long been "Shangaan" or Ndau migration from what was to become the Melsetter area of the Eastern Highlands of Southern Rhodesia and southwestern Mozambique to the mines at Kimberley and on the Rand.[12] Among the migrants was a substantial number of adolescent males who were prepubescent or barely beyond puberty. As noted in Chapter 1 [see original reading], boys who were believed to have been younger than 11 were employed in under-ground mining, using heavy drills, precisely because of their small size. While this migration was voluntary, recruiters to the area for the mines and for other employment inside Southern Rhodesia were known to take young males by force. So fearful of child kidnapping were Africans in the Melsetter District that, when the American Board of Commissioners (ABC) missionary, George A. Wilder, arrived in the area in 1894, he reported that "before we can expect to see the children come to school, we must disabuse the public mind of the latest false impression, namely that we missionaries are waiting now until we collect a lot of chil-dren then we will make off with them to the coast."[13] Perhaps these people had living memo-ries of child captivity and sales to Portuguese slave dealers on the Mozambican coast. Or, perhaps they had a more recent experience of the practice, at the hands of recruiters. Though "child stealing"—taking African children without their parents' permission for the purpose of turning them into laborers—was outlawed by the 1911 Native Labor Relations Act, as I show in a later chapter [see original reading], it was practiced by labor-short white farmers in the Melsetter (Chipinga) area as late as 1949.

Child stealing was very much on de Waal's mind when he accompanied Rhodes to Mashonaland in 1890 and 1891. Writing of his impressions while passing through the Msvingo area, he noted that "The little children of the Simbabwe Kaffirs are really pretty. I felt inclined to catch a couple, take them to Capetown, and bring them up." When the opportunity to take a boy later presented itself, de Waal was receptive. "There was a pretty boy of about twelve at the kraal on whom my eye had fallen, and whom I more than once treated with coffee and pieces of biscuit, and I was soon much attracted to him. He was very obedient to me; every time I told him to run for the horses and bring them nearer to us, he gladly did so, and when at last we were ready to leave, he stood ready for departure also." De Waal was told by the boy and by two older African attendants that the boy's parents would not mind if he went. When de Waal asked Rhodes if he should take the boy without his parents' permission, Rhodes, who was at the time not only head of the BSAC but also prime minister of the Cape Colony, replied: "if the boy earnestly wishes to go with you, take him! He seems a good and funny little fellow." The Afrikaner frontier practice of child stealing had been outlawed at the Cape Colony in 1857. As it turned out, de Waal later wrote, the "pretty boy" of 12 vanished during the night and, so, did not accompany him to the Cape, leading de Waal to conclude, "Perhaps this was best, after all."[14]

African children were involved in the Risings at several levels. Grain had been sown and stored in large quantities in anticipation of the war. As women and children were responsible for most of the tasks associated with food production, they were intimately involved in preparing for the war. In the previous chapter [see original reading], we saw that Ndebele and captive and incorporated Shona male adolescents were trained for military service in regiments from the age of puberty. This practice continued during the Risings when they were used as child soldiers. Vere Stent, a South African journalist who was present at the most important *indaba* (meeting) between Rhodes and Ndebele chiefs in 1896, found amongst the Ndebele prisoners taken in the storming of Thaba S'Amamba "a group of lads from fourteen to fifteen years old. There were no men prisoners. These lads were fastened together by strips of hide drawn round their wrists so tightly as to stop the flow of blood and, in some instances, to cause bleeding. It seemed to me an inhuman thing to treat with unnecessary cruelty those who were really children." Stent was very unpopular with Rhodes and his men because of his critical reporting of the treatment of the Ndebele during the invasion of 1893. On the occasion of the Risings, when he protested that "we were not making war upon children,"[15] Stent was threatened with arrest and punishment if he attempted to interfere.

A large number of women and children were taken as prisoners during the assault on Thaba S'Amamba, along with 10,000 head of cattle as loot, Stent reported. In Mashonaland, Schmidt found, women and children were the majority of the people taken as prisoners in fighting. Many were held as hostages to force their husbands and fathers to surrender. Women and adolescent girls were raped and sexually exploited by white and African Company forces, according to Stent, and as Olive Schreiner retold in her fictional account of the war. And, possibly forcibly, possibly with their consent, many Shona women were "married" to members of the Native Contingent and other men who sided with the BSAC, as a form of reward, recalling the pre-1890s pattern among both the Shona and Ndebele of capturing women and girls in raids and war and distributing them as wives among the soldiers.[16]

While the Ndebele came to terms with Rhodes after several months of fighting and were allowed to return to the land to plant, the Shona were suppressed in a war that raged for almost another two years in some parts. Homesteads were burned, animals were confiscated, and prisoners were taken in the fighting. The Shona method of retreating into caves for defensive and offensive purposes stymied BSAC troops until they happened upon the idea of using dynamite to force the people out. Women and children figured prominently in the number of Africans injured and killed by this method. Thomson recounted an instance in which Chief Chesumba's people were met with a shower of bullets when he refused to send the women and the children out of the cave. They were told they had two hours "in which to send out their women and children." When none were sent out, the commander, De Moleyns, "was reluctantly obliged to blow up the nearest caves, and a number of women and children then crawled out, and were sent to the camp to be looked after." For four days, caves were blown up, as De Moleyns tried to get the people to surrender. "At last they did so, and the caves were destroyed as far as possible. One hundred and eleven men gave themselves up, and *five hundred women and children*; the rest managed to get away. It is believed comparatively few were killed." However, the capture of Chief Makoni involved considerable loss of life. A key leader of the Risings, Makoni was executed in 1896. According to Thomson, after Makoni fled into a cave,

> every effort was made with dynamite to force him to surrender, and he was told repeatedly through Tom the Cape boy, who acted as interpreter, that if he came out his life would be spared. On the 3rd September Tom urged him to give himself up, and he decided to do so; but as he was coming out of the cave, one of the volunteer officers caught hold of him by the arm, and dragged him out, asserting that he had taken him prisoner. His people then gave in, and came straggling out of the caves. The effect produced by the dynamite had been terrible, and the stench from the dead bodies was overpowering.[17]

Lord Albert Grey, the BSAC Administrator during the Risings, predicted that the war would produce "a number of orphan children towards which the Administration may stand in loco parentis."[18] He suggested that such children be taken to missionary stations where they could be educated. It is not clear if large numbers of orphans were produced by the suppression of the Risings, though some children were orphaned. Two such orphans were Paris and Archer, the young sons of Chief Makoni. Rather than being educated, they followed the more traditional path of children orphaned by warfare in southern Africa: they were put into service, in this case, in the military. According to Thomson:

> After their father was executed, two of his sons, about eleven and twelve years old, took service with [Major] Harding, who at that time, was acting galloper to Major Watts. He took a fancy to the boys, and asked their mother if he might have them, and she consented willingly, merely stipulating that they should be allowed to come back to see her once a year. . . . the boys became greatly attached to Harding, and he to them. They accompanied him on all his patrols, and became the privileged pets of the camp. I don't know what their real names were, but they were always known as Archer and Paris.

Paris later died from wounds he sustained when Harding's regiment attacked an African homestead. Archer "felt his loss deeply, for the two boys had been inseparable. He is still with Major Harding and bids fair to turn out a smart, dependable boy. He is now the bugler in the Black Watch as the native contingent is generally called in Mashonaland."[19] As we will see in later chapters [see original reading], the idea that African boys should be taken from their homes to perform domestic and other services for settlers lingered well into the twentieth century.

During these early years, there were no indications that the patriarchal construction of African childhood was in jeopardy. Though a few boys were beginning to leave home and, in some cases, run away, to seek wage labor, the economic and political instability of the period did not lend itself to large-scale or regular migration and wage labor employment of boys or men. The "age of the fortune hunters" was largely an era of primitive accumulation in which most of the white settlers sought to grab African land, cattle, and labor as they could. However, in only a few short years after the Risings, this picture would begin to change and, along with it, the construction of African childhood, particularly for boys. The patriarchal construction of old would begin to fray and a new colonial construction would emerge, but so also would a separate notion of childhood fashioned by boys and adolescent males themselves. It is to these developments that the remainder of the chapter is devoted.

With "sleeping accommodation and food": migrant boys and the accumulation strategy of capital in the post-Rising era

In the decade and a half after the Risings, the white population of Southern Rhodesia more than doubled, increasing from approximately 11,000 in 1901 to nearly 24,000 in 1911. As the numbers of settlers grew, so did their economic activities and their demand for African labor. The "labor problem"—the demand for cheap, abundant, and regular supplies of workers—vexed mine owners and farmers and threatened their economic survival.[20] The settlers turned to the state for the resolution of this problem. How the policies that flowed from this pressure affected children and adolescents is explored in detail in the next section. This section examines the accumulation strategies of settlers in the post-Risings years, The primary reason for the labor shortage was the ability of most senior African men to meet their cash needs by increasing the production and sale of grains, vegetables, beer, and stock, which, ironically, they sold in large quantities to mine owners and to some white farmers to feed their workers. For the time being, at least, continuing access to good agricultural land (either on the African "reserves," especially in Mashonaland, or on rented Crown- or privately-owned land in Matabeleland) and proximity to markets or transportation lines made it possible for many peasant families not only to avoid wage labor but to prosper as well. As Schmidt has shown, it was the reliance upon the labor of women and children that made this explosion of peasant production possible. Thus senior men adapted patriarchal constructions of senior and junior status, including childhood, to pay their taxes, pay school fees, and purchase ploughs and other imported items.[21]

One of the ways in which the mines and white farmers sought to meet their growing demand for cheap labor after the Risings was by taking on and even actively recruiting *picaninnies*—prepubescent boys under the approximate age of 14. This accumulation strategy was evident by 1898, by which time such boys could be found employed in every segment of the settler economy. Though, during this period, most boys and adolescents remained in the peasant sector, a growing number was becoming, if not "inured to the habits of labour," at least familiar with labor migration and wage work. The colonial construction of African male childhood, at least, was getting into gear.

White employers did not keep precise records of their workers by age. For example, though mining companies employed boys, the Chief Native Commissioner (CNC) noted in 1916 that, on the mines, the "deaths of boys under fourteen and unmarried females are not usually reported."[22] This practice belied the fact that "boys under fourteen" were employed on a widespread basis. The routine way in which *picaninny* wages were cited by officials, posted by mining companies, and quoted by white farmers is evidence of the pervasive employment of boys and adolescent males in the years immediately following the Risings. For example, in 1898, the year in which the CNC Matabeleland began reporting wage rates for prepubescent boys, he wrote that "piccanins" were paid 6d. per day or 15s. per month on the mines in his province, while adult male workers, such as "rock drill boys," "hammer boys," "truck and shovel boys," "surface boys," "boss boys," and "ox drivers" were paid from 25s. to 80s. per month.[23] As noted in Chapter 1 [see original reading], though officials and settlers often referred to adult African males as boys, they nevertheless made a distinction between sexually mature and immature males, particularly in the wages they paid. In 1901, the CNC reported that the mines paid wage rates ranging from 10s. to 80s. per month, "according to age and ability," with "competent hammer men receiving from 50s. to 60s. per month, and in cases of exceptional merit 80s., surface men from 25s. to 40s., and 'piccan-nins' from 10s. to £1."[24]

All mine wages were based on thirty day "tickets" (all of which had to be marked by the mine boss before wages were paid), with food and accommodation included. In 1899, the BSAC and the mining companies jointly established two Labour Boards, one each for Mashonaland and Matabeleland, to recruit local or indigenous labor for the mines.[25] In his first *Report* in March 1900, the Chief Native Labour Agent for Matabeleland reproduced the "Tariff of Wages" that guided his agency's recruitment. This tariff listed only two categories of wages: "wages of able-bodied men" (25s. to 60s. per month, with rations) and "wages of piccaninnies" (5s. to 15s. per month, with rations).[26] Thus, state-sponsored recruiters were explicitly directed to seek out prepubescent boys for work on the mines, sign contracts with them (or their parents), and transport them, sometimes for considerable distances, to the mines that had requested them. There the boys and adolescent males worked a specified number of 30-day tickets while being housed and fed by the mine owner. A total of 10,787 workers were recruited by the Matabeleland Labour Board between January 1899 and the end of March 1900, many of whom, it is safe to assume, were boys and adolescents. Because the Masters and Servants Ordinance (MSO) of 1899 made it illegal for children under 16 years of age to sign their own labor contracts, it is not clear how these children were signed on. It is possible that, in some cases, parents signed, while in others, the boys were issued what came to be called "underage" contracts by officials. Technically, such contracts were not enforceable under the MSO. I will return to this issue in the next section of this chapter and in Chapter 4 [see original reading].

Labor was one of the central questions taken up by the South African Native Affairs Commission (SANAC), which in 1903–4 received written and oral evidence from officials, white farmers, miners, traders, and missionaries and from several African chiefs and pastors in Southern Rhodesia. It is clear from the evidence presented to the SANAC that early wage work was at the core of the settler notions of African male childhood. Witnesses were asked to survey their districts or businesses for the wage rates of various categories of labor. More than two-thirds of the NCs queried responded with lists of rates that included *picaninny* wages for jobs ranging from herd boys and general agricultural laborers on white farms, to cooks and surface workers on the mines, and store boys and domestic servants for whites in town. The Acting NC Mazoe, Mashonaland informed the Commission that "small boys" in his district were employed as herds at 5s. and 6s. per month and on the mines at 10s and 15s. per month, with "sleeping accommodation and food."[27] The NC Umtali and Inyanga in eastern Mashonaland, where gold was mined at Penhalonga and Rezende, wrote that "Boys of nine to eleven years old can readily get 10s. per month; while the wages of men go up from that to 60s., and after that the Natives who are specialists in any particular work get even more."[28] In neighboring Melsetter District, where farming was the main occupation of whites, the NC reported that "boys" received wages of 5s. to 20s. per month, while "adult Natives" were paid 10s. to 60s.[29] The NC Lomagundi, Mashonaland wrote that on the mines in his district, "Cooks (piccaninnies)" earned 5s. to 15s. per month on the mines in his district. "Each male Native, between the ages of ten and forty, if he keeps in regular employ, is able to earn wages varying from a minimum of £6 per annum to a maximum of about £40 per annum, exclusive of the value of his food."[30] The NC Selukwe, Matabeleland wrote that "ordinary boys (umfaans)" were employed as store and domestic servants for 15s. to 20s., including food.[31] The low wage rates the NC quoted for cooks on the Selukwe mines (5s. to 20s.) strongly suggests that *umfaans* (prepubescent boys in Ndebele and Zulu) were employed in this capacity, at least, on the gold and asbestos mines of his district. The Commission also heard from Rev. Douglas Wood of the South Africa General Mission at Risitu Valley, Melsetter who wrote that on the plot of land granted to his church by the BSAC there was not "a large body of Natives [tenants] under our control. All the labour we employ, which does not average more than four Natives at a time, mostly young boys, is purely voluntary, Natives coming to us from across the border [Mozambique] and elsewhere."[32]

The mines were the largest employers of African labor during this period, engaging more than 17,000 workers in 1906 and nearly 38,000 by 1910.[33] Only about one-third of these workers were local. The majority were migrant laborers from neighboring Northern Rhodesia, Nyasaland, and Mozambique, and included in their numbers were many boys and adolescent males. Many of these foreign migrants made the long journey to the colony's employment centers on their own, but many were *chibaro* or contract workers recruited by the Rhodesia Native Labour Board (RNLB), the successor to the Matabeleland and Mashonaland Labour Boards. The wages of *chibaro* workers were lower than the wages of voluntary or free labor and the contracts of these workers were longer. Reliance upon the ultra-cheap labor of *chibaro* workers during this period stemmed from the restructuring the mining industry underwent between 1903 and 1910 after the true extent of Southern Rhodesia's mineral wealth had become known. Though restructuring led to greater numbers of successful small workers and to rising profits for the industry as a whole, the mine owners had to keep production costs to a minimum in order to remain afloat and grow. Labor costs were pared to the bone by using *chibaro* workers and by minimizing expenditures on food, accommodation, medical facilities, and disability and death payments to African workers. The mining sector also minimized expenditures by employing child and adolescent workers who could do many adult tasks above ground and who could be paid even lower wages than adult *chibaro* workers. *Chibaro* child workers were the cheapest of all. Charles van Onselen notes that

> The use of child labour in certain sections of the Rhodesian [mining] industry has its roots in the years of reconstruction. From the earliest days of the R.N.L.B. young boys in the rural areas of central Africa were recruited by *chibaro*. To these children, bound by contract, fell the task of cooking for the adult workers making the long march to the mines. Once on the mines themselves, the boys earned their living through the relatively minor tasks of cleaning, sweeping or cooking in the compounds.[34]

Thus, as in the period after the Risings, boys and adolescents males, both local and foreign, were employed on a widespread basis on the mines as domestic servants, so much so that the NC Lomagundi, quoted earlier in evidence before the SANAC, equated "cooks" with *picaninnies* on the mines in his district. The government Compound Inspector reported in 1904 that "The average [wage] for adult labourers are: For surface work, 30s.; underground work, 50s.; special work, 65s. Boys employed on the mines as cooks and for cleaning up compounds, c., earn from 15s to 20s per month. All natives are paid on completion of 30 working days, and in addition to their pay receive rations."[35] Though van Onselen refers to the work these children performed as "relatively minor," it was work that was essential to mining operations and, hence, to accumulation. Large mines could employ as many as 500 to 700 workers, most of whom were housed in single-sex company-owned compounds. These workers had to be fed and their sleeping quarters maintained. By employing young boys at the lowest rates of pay, mine owners were able to lower their overall costs of production. On smaller mines and on most of the larger mines, longer-term single and married workers were allowed to build their own housing on the perimeter of the compound.[36] These mine workers directly engaged child and adolescent male domestics directly to clean, cook, wash clothing, and mind children. The low cost of the services provided by male child domestics (sometimes the pay took the form of the boy's food and shelter) subsidized the low wages the owners paid to the men who employed young domestics. Young male workers provided another "service" to adult mine workers that benefited capital on the mines of Southern Rhodesia and elsewhere in southern Africa. According to van Onselen,

> Unable to work underground because of their lack of strength . . . boys thus came to occupy, in compounds dominated by single male workers, a type of surrogate female role; their tasks were essentially those that were usually associated with women in traditional society. This, together with the structurally designed shortage of women in the compounds, partly explains the high incidence of sodomy involving young boys. Young and powerless in a new role [domestic servant in the mining compounds], these boys were vulnerable to the demands of adult men who were denied their normal sexual outlets by the compound system.[37]

More recent research on mine workers in southern Africa points to the complexity of what were in some cases "mine marriages" between older, more powerful mine workers and younger male workers in their teens: that such relationships had roots in some local cultures and, therefore, predated labor migration and work on the mines, and that they could induce older mine workers to remain longer on the mines. It is not clear if this research would apply to the boys considered here, who were much younger.[38]

Boys and adolescent males were also employed in the actual process of mining in Southern Rhodesia. Though the evidence collected thus far points to their use in above-ground work only, van Onselen's assertion that boys and adolescent males were not employed in underground work in the colony, due to their size, is open to question. Child labor use underground in neighboring South Africa and in Britain were important precedents for an industry that often took its cues from developments in those two countries. What is known, however, is that boys and adolescent males constituted the majority or a significant minority of the above-ground workers on certain mines in Southern Rhodesia. These were, as van Onselen has shown, the mines of the base metals industries, asbestos and mica, in particular: "if the limited physical abilities of boys protected children from the labour demands of mine managers on gold mines . . . in the base mineral industry on the other hand there were tasks which relied upon quickness of eye and agility of hand: work which mine owners and the Chief Native Commissioner considered eminently suited to children."[39]

The lower profit margins of the industry "made it impossible for the base minerals mines to compete even with the meager wages that were paid to black workers in the voracious gold mining industry."[40] As a consequence, these mine owners used the cheapest labor possible, which was the labor of children. For example, boys were put to work separating asbestos fibers from the rock matrix. One such mine, a Legislative Council member stated in 1910, "confined itself entirely to piccaninnies; that mine was in an exceptionally fortunate position in getting piccaninnies to do the work as well and at a cheaper rate than the ordinary mines had to pay."[41] In 1926, the Compound Inspector reported that 300 out of a total of 800 Africans employed on the mica mines in the northern part of the colony were boys between the ages of 10 and 15.[42] In this case, the majority were children of families that lived on the nearby Urungwe Reserve, Lomagundi District. Criticism from abroad, in the wake of the controversial Native Juveniles Employment Act, prompted the CNC to describe the children's working conditions somewhat defensively in 1926:

> Native juveniles who are voluntary employees are engaged on a monthly basis. They are paid four shillings per month and upwards according to their age, together with free food and quarters. Their ages range from 10 to 15 years. No

juveniles are employed in underground work or on work involving heavy
manual labour. Their work consists of cutting, splitting and sorting mica, a task
which is of the lightest nature and is eminently suited to juveniles. Juveniles sit
in open sheds and their work requires practically no physical effort. Conditions
under which they work are comfortable and hygienic.[43]

The young workers described at this mine, like at so many others, lived away from home and
family, in mine-owned housing. However, this was not always the case. Many child and
adolescent workers were the offspring of mine workers and their wives and partners or of
single women, including commercial sex workers, who were allowed by mine owners to live
on the mines and in the nearby locations. So essential did one mica mine owner find child and
adolescent labor from this source that he was said to have issued "mothers' rations, so that he
may keep the mothers on the mine, and every day the women in the compound are issued a
ration in order to keep their piccaninnies there."[44] Apart from commercial sex and the sale of
beer, cooked food, and other services for the poorly paid miners, there were no income-
earning opportunities for women and girls. "Mothers' rations" were clearly a form of payment
designed to encourage these women to remain on the mines and to make their children's
labor available to the owners.[45]

The ability of young boys to get jobs in town as domestic servants and even as mine
workers put pressure on farm wages. According to the CNC Matabeleland, "I may point out
here that the farmer, more particularly in the vicinity of Bulawayo, has an additional difficulty
to contend with, in the form of the high rate of wages paid to servants employed in town,
where the pay ranges from fifteen shillings to five pounds per mensem. An average of the pay
earned by one thousand natives in Bulawayo in the month of December [1910] shews a result
of one shilling per unit per diem. This is exclusive of the earning capacity of the 'piccaninny,'
who demands, and can obtain, from ten to fifteen shillings a month."[46] This would help
prompt white farmers to be at the forefront of efforts to make the BSAC state respond to
their labor needs.

The colonial construction of African childhood as a time of early wage labor pertained
largely, but not exclusively, to boys and adolescent males. This was so for two reasons. First,
as with the adult labor force, southern African capital preferred "single" male migrants who
could be paid as if they had no dependents. Theoretically, the women and (female) children
remained in the rural areas living off of subsistence crops, reproducing the labor force, and
absorbing the social welfare costs of the unemployment, illness, and old age of male migrants.
Second, African parents were resistant to allowing girls to leave home to work and, when girls
ran away, they were more likely to pursue them and return them to the homestead. Girls and
adolescent females continued to play a critical role in senior men's accumulation, through
their labor at home in the expansion of peasant production and through their value as sources
of bride wealth and grain or cattle in times of hardship. As Schmidt puts it, "Male elders feared
losing control over young women [i.e., daughters], their marriages, their bride wealth, and
their labor. It was assumed that any African female in urban areas would be 'ruined' by some
man—whether black or white, Hence, bride wealth, if it could be obtained at all, would be
reduced in value."[47] Older African women also opposed the migration and employment of
girls and young women (daughters and daughters-in-law) because they relied on their labor in
the homestead economy. Thus, if they worked outside the homestead at all, girls and adolescent females were more likely to work alongside parents or other relatives, as members of
labor tenant families and as seasonal piece and task workers on wage labor farms.

A few worked in domestic service. Early on, it was a matter of some concern to many
officials and white employers that domestic service in town was dominated by "youths from
14 to 18 years old."[48] Apart from the "black peril" myth—white fears of sexual assaults on

white women by black males—the primary concern about males employed as domestics was that they were not available for employers in other sectors of the economy. As the NAC put it, domestic service "could, and ought to be, placed in the hands of females. If this change could be brought about, a considerable number of men [and adolescent males] would be set free for vocations in which they could be more usefully employed. During 1910 an average of about 6,000 males were engaged in Salisbury and Bulawayo alone,"[49] A few years earlier, the CNC Matabeleland had proposed a boarding institution that would train African girls for domestic service and house them properly: "With a view to encouraging native girls [unmarried females] to enter domestic service a scheme is being considered for the purpose of establishing a training institute under proper control. Parents as a rule do not view with favour their daughters entering domestic service, but I feel sure such an institute would relieve them of any doubts they may entertain in regard to their children's welfare."[50]

In addition, officials proposed that hostels, under the charge of white matrons, be established in urban areas to house African females working as domestic servants so that they would not have to remain overnight in white households. To some extent, this was an acknowledgment of the potential for "white peril"—sexual assault and abuse of African females by settlers. Neither the boarding training institution nor the hostel system became a reality and domestic service continued to be dominated by male adolescents and youths. The CNC Mashonaland wrote in 1909: "I had hoped to have been able to report that native girls were beginning to enter service, but I find on enquiry that there are extremely few who work, and those only in the households of missionaries and Native Commissioners." He added, "I commend it to the earnest consideration of the missionaries whether they have not a great means of assisting in the solution of the labour problem, as well as of greatly improving the conditions in European households, by the careful and steady training of native girls for service."[51] The narrow range of whites for whom African "girls" were allowed to work also included white farmers, most likely landlords who could demand such labor from their tenants' daughters. The CNC Matabeleland wrote in 1908 that the "Matabele continue to shew a disinclination for their daughters to enter service in the towns, but in the country the number of girls employed in domestic service is steadily on the increase."[52]

African girls and adolescent females in town—those who fled without being pursued and the increasing number who were being born to African couples and commercial sex workers in town—faced a bleak wage employment picture. Apart from domestic service (which many white women actually opposed, out of fear of relationships between their husbands and the young servants), few jobs were open to them. Thus, they had to rely on the informal sector that catered to male African migrant workers. Many young girls accompanied their mothers from rural homesteads to town to sell grain, beer, and farm produce to Africans and whites from the early years of colonial rule. The NC Goromonzi reported in 1910 that dozens of girls, some below the age of 14, were in the mining camps of his district selling beer. With the help of their daughters and other girls, brewing and selling beer was an occupation of many of the women who resided permanently in town, with or without a husband or partner. Commercial sex work—a survival strategy of females in town—was not limited to sexually mature women. Van Onselen found it to have been the occupation of some adolescent girls as well."[53]

The state and the labor problem

The boys and adolescent males who sought wage work between 1890 and the First World War left home for one or more of a number of reasons: some were sent or given permission by their fathers to seek wage work; others, exercising agency, fled patriarchal authority and control; some fled the work of herding animals and farming, particularly as their families expanded the production of marketable output; still others, as officials were keen to emphasize, were lured by town life, with its freedom from parental control and its amusements and imported goods. There was another set of factors that influenced the departure from home. Officials did not often mention these factors but they were the consequences of the BSAC state's efforts to solve the colony's labor problem. They consisted of a series of legislative measures and official policies and practices put in place in the first decade of the twentieth century that had the direct effect of increasing the number of adolescent males who turned out to work for wages and the indirect effect of increasing the number of prepubescent boys who turned out. Through changes in the tax and pass laws, the recruitment of labor in neighboring territories, and the regularization of labor tenancies, the state sought to increase the number of African males as a whole who worked for whites, increase the length of the average employment period of the workers, reduce the high rates of desertion from the job, and stabilize the labor force on tenant farms. The legislation on labor tenancies had implications for the availability of girls as well as boys for work on white farms.

Though many scholars have examined these measures over the years, none have recognized that they were designed to affect African male adolescents and boys as well as adult men. In its drive to solve the labor problem, the state reinforced and strengthened the labor migration of boys. The state gave boys and adolescent males an additional push, in the form of taxation and recruitment. But it also gave them useful tools with which to challenge the patriarchal construction of childhood, in the form of passes, labor contracts, and possibly tax receipts they could acquire on par with sexually mature junior men and senior men. Encouraging boys and adolescents to take up wage labor and sign labor contracts was in keeping with the colonial construction of African male childhood as "a time for inurement to the habits of labour," when boys became accustomed to leaving home as young as possible and developed respect for white authority. However, by encouraging the exodus of boys from the homestead, the state faced a growing contradiction: on the one hand, these boys provided capital with much needed cheap labor; on the other hand, their growing assertiveness toward parental authority had implications not only for senior African men and the patriarchal construction of male childhood, but, in time, for white employers, officials, and the colonial construction of male childhood as well.

A 10s. hut tax introduced in 1894 held senior men liable for every "hut" within their homestead. Thus, polygamous men were responsible for paying a 10s. tax on the house occupied by each of their wives. Interpreted as a collective tax, however, senior men who were unable or unwilling to pay with resources on hand sent the junior male members of their homesteads out to work for wages. With the exception of the period of the Risings when collection of the tax was suspended, the hut tax served to stimulate some migrant labor among young men, adolescent males, and boys, but never in numbers sufficient to meet white demands. In 1901, the hut tax was converted to a head tax, payable by every African male "of the age of 18 years and upwards."[54] This new head tax was designed specifically to increase the number of men who turned out to work for wages. Polygamous men were required to pay 10s. for each additional wife after the first one. The CNC Mashonaland wrote in March 1902 that adolescents and boys younger than 18 responded to the new tax as well.

> The Hut Tax imposed under Ordinance No. 12 of 1901, which was called for in January last, has been paid up exceedingly well, and far beyond my expectations. The young men have come forward and paid their tax cheerfully, and it is with pleasure that I have to report that in various districts some young boys, under the age of eighteen, were very dissatisfied when their money was handed back to them, and informed that they were too young to pay.[55]

It is clear why the CNC reported "with pleasure" the eagerness of "young boys" to pay the head tax: their willingness to pay taxes bode well for their future as taxpayers and workers. What is less clear is why boys and adolescent males under the age of 18 came forward to pay a tax for which they were not liable. The tax was a very regressive one for boys who received only *picaninny* wages (5s. to 10s. a month at the time) for an average of two or three months' wage work a year. One possible explanation is the new notion of chronological age. Not yet reckoning age in this way, it is likely that many young males interpreted the individual head tax as applying to them, particularly if they had previously gone out to work to help pay the collective hut tax. Another possible (and related) explanation is that, as early as 1901, the payment of taxes by adolescent males and boys, as well as by young men, had become a symbol of changing notions of male childhood and junior status and that migrant labor and wage earning were key to bringing these changes about. Whether it was on the Rand or in the colony, migrant labor and wage work were rapidly coming to be a *rite de passage* in the reconstruction of male childhood and full male adulthood.[56]

Thus, many young males were attracted not merely by the adventure of leaving home, living in town or a mining camp, and buying imported goods, but also by the possibility of gaining some autonomy in their lives and some control over labor power, and most important, by the possibility of altering power relations within the homestead. For those boys and adolescent males whose fathers still possessed stock at this time, leaving home meant freedom from the long days of herding animals and from the harsh discipline that followed mistakes and lapses. For those boys and adolescents whose fathers had lost cattle to confiscation and rinderpest, migration and wage employment were gainful occupations of their labor time. The money earned and the goods purchased enhanced their status back in the homestead. Even if their fathers appropriated their earnings or part of their earnings for tax payments or for the purchase of stock and imported goods such as ploughs, the money earned by boys and adolescent males had the potential for undermining the monopoly senior males hitherto exercised over the homestead's resources. Young men might one day be able to pay their own bride wealth and, in this way, exercise more control over their own transition from junior to senior status. As we will see, there is evidence that some boys and adolescents even began objecting to paying their fathers' taxes during the early years of the head tax.

The 1904 Native Pass and Native Tax Ordinances gave further impetus to the migration of boys and adolescent males. Taken together, these two laws expanded the pool of male labor available to capital by lowering to puberty or 14 the age at which African males were required to register with officials, carry passes, and, by strong implication, pay taxes. The two laws reinforced the effort to introduce chronological age into the constructions of African childhood and adulthood, appropriating puberty, an important Shona and Ndebele life event in the transition from junior to senior status, for the purpose of capital accumulation. The Native Pass Ordinance required that all African males, upon reaching "the apparent age of fourteen,"[57] register with their local Pass Officer and obtain a registration certificate. Chiefs and headmen (who were beginning to receive government stipends) were required to ensure that all males within their jurisdiction were registered.

When leaving the district to search for work, African males 14 and older were required to obtain a "pass to seek work." Upon entering Southern Rhodesia from neighboring territories, all African males 14 years and older were also required to register with and obtain a pass from the closest magistrate or other official. The pass law sent the message that at 14 African males were expected to turn out to work. It incorporated adolescent males into the wage labor system in a systematic rather than haphazard way. It also sought to socialize them into respecting the sanctity of contracts and the authority of employers and the state, for one of the primary objectives of the pass system was to reduce desertion by tracking workers from one employer to the next. Workers whose registration certificates had not been properly signed off by their previous employer were presumed to be deserters, liable for arrest and imprisonment or fine, upon conviction under the Native Pass Ordinance and the MSO. As a device for reducing desertion rates, the pass system had a number of flaws that adult and child workers alike took advantage of. However, like paying taxes, the acquisition of a registration certificate became a symbol of adulthood for young African males. As noted earlier in this chapter, one settler member of the Legislative Assembly reported that "even before they reach the age of fourteen, these piccanins want a registration certificate so that they can call themselves men."[58]

Perhaps because most Africans did not yet reckon age in chronological terms, the Native Pass Ordinance applied to "natives" who had reached the apparent age of 14. Officials used puberty (physical exams, sometimes) to determine when an African male was liable to register. It also began using puberty to determine the age of tax liability, with the Native Tax Ordinance of 1904. Whereas previous tax laws specified 18 as the age of tax liability, significantly, the new law made no mention of a specific age for payment of the new tax, which was also doubled, from 10s. to £1. The new language on liability somewhat vaguely stated that "Every adult male native"[59] was liable, without defining who was an adult. This was a clear attempt to increase the labor force overall by turning out younger males. In correspondence on the subject of tax liability between 1905 and 1924, officials gave several explanations for using 14 or puberty as the age when African males should register, pay taxes, and, they bluntly added, go out to work for wages.

In a letter to the Magistrate of Gwelo in 1924, the Secretary of the Law Department summarized the state's approach, which he said had "withstood the test of time for nearly 20 years."[60] First, he noted, "according to Roman Dutch Law, a male native is considered to be an adult at the age of puberty—14 years." Second, "wage-earning capacity," combined with the age of puberty or 14 years of age, was "a fair basis on the assumption that a native above 14 years (when he is bound to obtain a registration certificate) generally demands and is given an adult's wages." Third, the Secretary argued, "As a result of exhaustive enquiries by Native Commissioners, it was established that, according to native custom, the youth is considered to attain the status of manhood and attendant civil rights on attaining the age of puberty." Finally, the Secretary wrote, in the opinion of the High Commissioner, which was circulated to NCs in 1905, "The words 'adult male native' in section 4 of the Native Tax Ordinance of 1904 shall be taken to mean a native who is physically capable of earning his livelihood."[61]

We saw in Chapter 2 [see original reading] that though puberty was an important life event in the progression of a Shona or Ndebele male from childhood to full male adulthood or senior status, it did not bring with it "the status of manhood and attendant civil rights," as the Secretary asserted. Indeed, as Jeff Guy and others point out, the age of sexual maturity for male youths or young men was an extremely frustrating (and politically dangerous) time precisely because they might remain juniors subordinate to their fathers, for another 10 or 20 years.[62] On the one hand, they were physically capable of becoming husbands and fathers, which, with a bride-wealth marriage, were necessary conditions for ascension to senior status or full adulthood. On the other hand, unmarried and dependent, sexually mature males were valuable to their fathers and to rulers, such as the Ndebele king, as sources of labor and as warriors. Fathers and rulers alike, therefore, had an interest in prolonging (up to a point) the young man's junior status. Thus, what NCs and officials in the Law Department were attempting to do was to alter the "customary" meaning of puberty for the purpose of systematically turning out male labor at a younger age.[63] Moreover, the Secretary was being disingenuous when he argued that males over the age of 14 could command an adult's wages, for white employers paid their wages according to age, ability, and experience. As we will see in the next chapter [see original reading], there was a continuous struggle between employers and adolescent males over the payment of "picaninny wages," employers seeking to pay them for as long as possible, while young workers sought ways to resist them.

Several missionaries protested the new registration and tax laws because they were said to draw boys away from school and into the wage labor force. For example, the Reverend Father M. Barthelemy, a Catholic missionary with experience in Victoria and Bulawayo, told the SANAC in 1904: "Our Native law here says that all 'adult' Natives shall pay the tax, but the law does not define what adults are. It seems that 'adult' means, according to the law, anybody above 14 years of age. . . . The interpretation seems to be those who have attained the age of puberty." He went on to complain: "This creates a great difficulty for us in our Mission Stations. Boys of 14 are just at the age when we can educate them, that is teach them to work and to farm—to work on the land—and if these school-boys—for we may call them so—are taxed, what are we to do?" When asked by a Commission member "Is not perhaps the design of those who have made the law and of those who are carrying it out that that is the age at which a young man can earn a man's wages?" Barthelemy replied, "Yes, but if they do not actually earn a man's wage, how can they pay that tax?"[64] Barthelemy did not receive an answer to his question, but he was justified in posing it: not every school age boy was in the work force, and when working school age boys were not paid "a man's wage." Officials did have the discretion to defer the tax for boys attending school, but the exemption had to be applied for on an individual basis.[65]

As mechanisms for expanding the pool of labor by incorporating younger African males, lowering the age of pass and tax liability and doubling of the tax from 10s. to £1 appear to have met with some success. The imprecision involved in determining age helps explain, in part, why the NC Gutu-Chilimzani could report in 1904 that not only did those who were made newly liable (14- to 18-year-olds) turn out to work in response, but boys younger than 14 as well.

> Owing to the New Tax Ordinance, many natives have already proceeded to the mines to earn the necessary money to meet the payment of the new tax in August next. Hitherto, the natives have always waited until the very last moment before going out to earn their tax. A fairly large number of youths from 12 to 17 years of age, proceeded with the men to the mines, to work for white men as house and horse boys."[66]

But it was not only imprecision, vagueness, or unfamiliarity with the notion of chronological age. Again, I would argue that obtaining a registration certificate, paying taxes, engaging in migrant wage labor, and living away from home were tools and experiences that boys and adolescent males could use to challenge patriarchal controls and notions of childhood. Boys and adolescents who obtained these documents and embarked upon these experiences were involved in constructing a new African (male) childhood and young adulthood that appeared to be engineered by settlers and the state. It was much more.

What about the prepubescent boys, those under the apparent age of 14, who turned out to work but who were not yet required to carry passes? Neither were such boys covered by the MSO, which prohibited boys (and girls) under the age 16 from signing their own contracts. Now boys between the ages of 14 and 16 were required to carry passes, but the law still forbade them to sign contracts without parental permission. Officials were faced with the problem of accommodating numerous such boys who turned up for work on their own and numerous white employers who wanted to—and did—engage them. How were they, particularly those under 14, to be disciplined and controlled, for the purposes of desertion and other violations of the pass law and the MSO? Perhaps as early as 1899, when the Labour Boards for Matabeleland and Mashonaland began recruiting and contracting prepubescent boys from neighboring colonies for work on Southern Rhodesia's mines, officials issued what were known as "underage" passes and "underage" labor contracts to boys under the age of 14. By 1920, the practice had become routine. In November of that year, for example, the Superintendent of Natives, Bulawayo noted that he had issued 392 contracts to "youths too young to be registered with certificates." The boys were carrying "under-age certificates or passes" issued to them by another official, possibly the pass officer in their home district.[67] These documents had no standing in the courts and would be the subject of some controversy after the First World War, when the tide of young boys leaving the rural areas in search of wage labor would rise considerably and young boy workers would be said to be out of control.

The labor tenancy system was the most important source of labor for the growing number of white farmers during the 1900s and 1910s. As Colonial William Napier, a white farmer who had lived in Matabeleland since 1891, told the SANAC in 1904, farmers only signed tenancy agreements with senior men or homestead heads. Only these kraal heads were in the position to command the labor of homestead members—wives and unmarried children and married children and their spouses and offspring, if they resided with the head. However, in calling out homestead members to work on the farm, he told the Committee, "I never call out of the old men. There are men who held more or less good positions at the time of Lobengula, and I always think it is *infra dig.* calling out these old chaps who are the owners of the kraals, and I only call out the young men."[68] Though he did not say so, Napier and other landlords also counted on the women and the children in their calculations of labor on tenant farms. The Private Locations Ordinance of 1910 sought to regularize the labor tenancies that had been established according to the post-Risings Proclamation 19 in Matabeleland. During the debate on the bill, William H. Brown, a Legislative Council member who was also a farmer, made it clear that the labor of young children was an integral component of the system. When the question of the maximum number of married males or family heads who should be allowed on each location or farm was under discussion, Brown reasoned that "40 male native adults to a 1,500 morgen farm means 80 to each 3,000 morgen farm. Supposing each represented a family of five, that would be 400 people whom [sic] a good number would be piccanins available for certain kinds of work for the farmer."[69]

Thus, for those white farmers who relied on labor tenancies, the accumulation of capital depended upon the patriarchal construction of African childhood as a time of work organized under the direction and control and for the benefit of senior males. However, labor tenancies rested on a contradiction between the interests of fathers and their children, particularly male children, when it came to the labor requirements and the forms of payment under agreements.[70] Many landlords preferred to keep the terms of their agreements vague so that they could make use of the tenants' labor as needed. This often prevented the tenant and his children from leaving the farm for a few months out of the year to earn cash. Attempts were made to use the registration certificate system and the MSO to tie males 14 and older to the farm. On many tenant farms, the tenant received only planting and grazing rights in exchange for the labor of his family members. When wages were paid, they were very low: 10s. per month in the Midlands, Salisbury, South Mazoe, and Umtali and 5s. in Melsetter.[71] Moreover, wages were often paid not to the individual wives and children and other family members who worked the farm but to the kraal head, who, as we have seen, did not usually work. Napier told the SANAC that he made the senior males "personally liable jointly and severally for all payments accruing"[72] under his agreements. This situation led to resistance and flight by young people, particularly males, from tenant farms. If enough children fled, the tenant was evicted for failing to fulfill the labor requirements of the agreement. The system left young unmarried males, in particular, facing the prospect of life-long junior status, as Michael

Morris points out in the case of neighboring South Africa where labor tenancies had a long history:

> for the younger sons the economic class struggle . . . had a double and contra-dictory effect. On the one hand, they were bound to provide most of the labour under conditions where they received none of the direct benefits (land, cattle, and corresponding status). Furthermore there seemed to be less and less possi-bilities, because of the general curtailment of land/grazing, for them to accumu-late stock when they would reach the status of forming their own contract with the farmer. The existence/perpetuation of the labour tenancy system in its disintegrating form therefore held little hope for them. On the other hand the existence of the system meant that they were deprived of any other benefits. Their wages were not high enough (supposing even that they were the ones who directly received them) precisely, as they perceived it, because of the land/grazing payment. Nor was the farmer able to (in any case he certainly was not willing to) pay them higher cash wages to become full time settled workers. The younger sons and daughters were therefore trapped in an impossible contradic-tion. They had either to struggle for land, or for increased full time wages, or to desert, leaving their unfinished contracts.[73]

As early as 1909, white farmers in Matopos, Matabeleland were reported to be "steadily clearing natives off their land, the given reasons being that the majority of youths and young men were attracted to the mines elsewhere by higher wages, leaving but few middle-aged and old persons available for the landowners' requirements."[74]

During the 1910s and 1920s, officials of the Native Department attempted to press landlords to sign written agreements that protected tenants from arbitrary eviction and fixed their wages and the period of time during which their labor would be needed.[75] In this way, tenants would know what was expected of them and when they would be free to leave the farm for part of the year to earn (extra) wages and landlords would be assured that their tenants' children would not permanently desert the farm. Well-capitalized farmers generally signed tenancy agreements that were in line with the ideas of the Native Department. Less capitalized farmers, such as those in Melsetter, continued to resist. However, by the end of the First World War, even many in Melsetter began to see the Native Department's point that securing written agreements could keep tenants from migrating to the mines.

From the 1930s, economic pressure increasingly made the labor tenancy system impos-sible. The capitalization of farming placed a premium on bringing under production land previously allocated to tenants. The Land Apportionment Act of 1930 sought to end African occupation of all land outside the reserves, including labor tenant farms and land owned by absentee landlords. Though Melsetter was exempted from the Land Apportionment Act for 10 years and the farmers there were allowed to make their own private agreements without wages, the larger trend in the colony was "to move towards a system of full-time wage labour, and to develop a rural proletariat."[76] In Chapter 5 [see original reading], I examine the consequences for children and adolescents of this phase in the history of capitalist develop-ment in agriculture, as it gave rise to a search by white farmers, large and small, for ways to attract and hold the wives and children of adult male farm laborers who could be called out of the farm compound for casual or seasonal farm work. Farm schools emerged as an impor-tant mechanism for achieving this goal. They tapped into the African thirst for education by providing "free" part-time elementary schools on white farms for the children of adult male farm workers. They would be opened and closed according to the farmers' need for child workers in their fields.

Peasant expansion, children's labor, and children's resistance: 1890–1920

In spite of the "large number of native lads" who left home to join the wage labor force during this period, the majority of boys and adolescent males, like the majority of their older counterparts, remained in the peasant economy where their labor was applied to expanding the production and marketing of farm produce and beer and to tending growing herds and flocks of cattle, sheep, and goats. And to the annoyance of officials, employers, and even missionaries, when boys went out to work for wages, they often returned home, after only two or three months of wage work, to help with weeding, scaring off pests, harvesting crops, and herding animals. The patriarchal construction of childhood and junior status was both reinforced and undermined during this period, for, though fathers and mothers relied, as of old, on children's labor in production, the broader context had radically changed. Boys and adolescent males and even girls and adolescent females had many more ways of successfully challenging patriarchal controls and, if necessary, surviving outside the homestead economy. Thus, during the era of peasant expansion, fathers simultaneously experienced greater benefits from their children's labor and the beginnings of uncertain control. The needs of senior men for labor, credit, and *lobola* cattle, which, in previous times were accessed through children, met with resistance, most often in the form of flight from the homestead.

[. . .]

The flight of children and adolescents from the homestead represented a challenge to the notion of African childhood as constructed by senior African men. While fathers (and mothers) sought to channel children's labor into increasing the production of crops and tending ever-growing herds and flocks and to use girls as sources of credit and cattle, many children rejected this construction of their childhood and youth. They used the towns, mines, and even mission schools as avenues through which to work out alternative constructions of African childhood. The NC Matobo, Matabeleland reported in 1907 that "About 400 native children are receiving instruction at the Matopo Mission and its two branch stations. . . . The younger generation of natives show an increasing desire for the advantages of education, which is not altogether shared by their parents, as the loss of the children's service is involved."[77] However, from the mid-1910s onward, their flight from rural homesteads and white farms would also be a flight from growing poverty.

The impoverishment of the peasantry and the mass rural exodus of boys

Officials viewed the expansion of peasant production with considerable ambivalence.[78] On the one hand, peasant farm produce supplied the mines, the towns, and even some white farms with much needed food at a time when there were few productive white farmers. On the other hand, peasant agricultural expansion deprived the mines and other employers of cheap and abundant supplies of labor, particularly on a year-round basis. Moreover, the use of family labor and labor-intensive technologies placed African producers in an advantageous cost position compared to the small but growing number of white farmers. The NC Selukwe, Matabeleland went to the core of the problem when he wrote in 1904: "The independence of the local natives in consequence of their ready means of acquisition of any quantity of land for tillage, and the good prices they can command by the sale of grain produced is accountable to a great extent for the comparatively small number who come in for work."[79]

Though the BSAC state had attempted to increase the supply of labor by changing tax and registration laws and by recruiting from neighboring territories, officials and white employers alike knew that the ultimate solution to their problems of labor and competition lay in depriving African peasants of access to good and well-situated agricultural land. As one white farmer, William H. Brown, forthrightly put it, the African peasant producer should be put into reserves "so far away from railways and markets that the white trader will not be able to buy from him and compete with the white farmers."[80] In 1908, the Company state embarked upon doing just that. Beginning around that time, a policy of "closing down peasant options outside of wage labour"[81] was vigorously pursued. It would have significant consequences for African children's labor availability and agency and, in turn, for white employers, the state, and the construction of African childhood.

Up to the late 1910s, the concerns of officials and settlers about migrating boys and adolescent males focused primarily on increasing their rate of wage labor-force participation. Some concern was expressed about their growing rebelliousness toward parents, elders, chiefs, and authority in general, but many officials actually saw this in positive terms. The CNC Mashonaland cautioned against interfering with the declining control of senior males and the growing individualism of young people, writing in 1912 that "Contact with civilisation is the cause of this, and though chiefs and others complain, no steps should be taken to prevent this gradual evolution. The increased powers granted to the Native Commissioners have materially assisted in breaking up these tribal methods of control, and I am glad that the results so far have been satisfactory."[82] In 1913 and 1914, the CNC reported that there was no labor problem in the towns because the younger generation was attracted to town life. Again, this was desirable, from a labor point of view. However, in the years immediately following the war, official views began to change. A number of officials began to write nervously about boys and adolescent males who left home in search of wage work in town, in particular. Some, including the CNC, went so far as to propose that the urban migration of juveniles—boys under the age of 14—should be blocked.

[. . .]

What was behind this mass rural exodus of prepubescent boys? Officials attributed it to the "disintegration of the tribal system and the consequent weakening of parental authority. Added to this is the novelty offered by town life, with its attractions and variety."[83] Though these might have been factors in the growing tendency of boys to leave home, the primary factor was of the state's and settlers' own making—the growing poverty of their families, particularly those who were forced to move onto or who already lived on the reserves, as the policy of "closing down peasant options outside wage labour" began to have its effect. While the years between 1890 and the First World War had been characterized by expansion for much of the African peasantry, the years during and after the war marked the beginning of contraction for many."[84] By the early 1920s, as Giovanni Arrighi's analysis has shown, the majority of adult males (defined as males over the age of 14) were in the wage labor force for part of the year earning wages that were essential to the reproduction of their rural households. The proletarianization of the African peasantry had begun. Hitherto invisible in studies of the twin processes of rural impoverishment and proletarianization were African children (boys). The outpouring of "native juveniles," their flight from worsening rural conditions, and their search for wage labor preceded by about four years the "sharp increase in African [adult male] participation in the labor market"[85] that is so critical to Arrighi's periodization of proletarianization in Southern Rhodesia.

The impoverishment and proletarianization of the peasantry were rooted in a decision taken by the BSAC in 1908 to promote white settlement.[86] The effects of this "white settlement policy" were, in turn, exacerbated by widespread and severe drought and famine in the colony between 1911 and 1914, a more geographically limited but nevertheless severe drought in 1915–16, post-war inflation, and a slump in farm prices and another drought in the early 1920s. Officials in and around Bulawayo were the first to sound the alarm about the influx of young boys, for the white settlement policy had its earliest and harshest effects on the peasants of Matabeleland. Seventy percent of Africans there lived on land that had been alienated to whites, including mining companies, land and mining speculators, absentee land-lords practicing "kaffir farming," bona fide white farmers, and the BSAC. As the number of whites taking up farming increased during the 1910s, so did the pressure on African peasants to move onto reserves, which were often remote and, in time, inadequate for them and their growing stock in cattle, sheep, and goats.

After a visit to the colony in 1907, the directors of the BSAC decided to diversify the economy away from mining by promoting white or capitalist farming. To ensure the success of the new policy, the BSAC took a number of steps: it established an Estates Department to promote white immigration and handle applications for resettlement in Southern Rhodesia; it opened information offices in London and Glasgow and placed agents in neighboring South Africa, to promote the colony's agricultural potential; it reorganized the Agricultural Department, brought in experts in several fields, opened experimental agricultural stations, and made extension services available to white farmers only; it established BSAC-owned tobacco, citrus, and ranching estates to serve as models for new white farmers; it established a Land Bank, which offered credit only to white farmers for "the purchase of farms, livestock, and agricultural equipment, and for improvements such as fencing and irrigation works"; and it lowered the sale prices of Company-owned land. The BSAC also acceded to white settlers the majority of unofficial seats in the colony's Legislative Council, thus giving settlers a powerful tool for shaping state policy in their interests.[87]

Finally, and perhaps most important, the BSAC launched a direct attack against the African peasantry, beginning with their land. In Matabeleland, the area set aside for African reserves constituted only 17 percent of the land in the province (7.7 million acres). The 16 million acres claimed by whites or set aside by the BSAC for future white occupation repre-sented not only the bulk of the land but the best land, "what the Ndebele called '*nga pakati kwe lizwe* (the midst of the land).' "[88] The reserves were largely waterless and located some distance from markets and transportation. In Mashonaland, 17 million acres, or 37 percent of the province, was set aside for African reserves. There, the reserves contained both good and poor soils. Nevertheless, "the great majority were situated in areas and on soils spurned by white farmers".[89]

Between 1908 and 1914, the Company reduced the African reserves by a further 500,000 acres and, in 1914–15, the Native Reserves Commission reduced them by another one million acres and redrew the boundaries of all the reserves "to exclude richer soils, higher rainfall and easy access to markets."[90] The attack on African land holdings did not end in 1915. More changes were in store with the Morris Carter Land Commission of 1925 and the Land Apportionment Act of 1930. In addition to these measures, the state and private landowners imposed a number of burdensome charges on African peasants living on white-owned land, in response to which many Africans chose to clear off and move onto the reserves: rent for every "adult male," in addition to taxes already paid to the BSAC; penalties on "kaffir farming" or the renting of land to Africans by white absentee landlords; grazing fees on cattle and other stock owned by African tenants; cattle dipping fees; and a 5s. tax on all unrestrained dogs.

The numbers of whites who were engaged in farming had been growing steadily since the reconstruction of the mining industry in about 1903, but, with the unfolding of the white settlement policy, their numbers grew much more rapidly. In 1898, there were only about 250 whites engaged in farming, occupying about 20,000 acres of land. The majority of indi-vidual white occupying landlords earned their living not by farming but by trading, trans-porting goods, supplying wood to the mines, and by collecting rents from their African tenants. In 1904, there were still only 425 white farmers, but by 1911, there were 1,324, about 2,040 in 1914, and 2,395 in 1920. These farmers cultivated 132,100 acres of land in 1911, about 183,400 acres in 1914, and 237,300 acres by 1920. They focused primarily on supplying the mines and urban areas with grain and meat, as African peasants had been doing, and secondarily, on maize and tobacco for export. The production of maize by white farmers rose from 45,800 (200-lb.) bags in 1904 to 634,100 bags in 1914. Tobacco production increased from 147,100 pounds in 1904 to more than 3 million pounds in 1914, after which time overproduction led to drastic declines until the tobacco boom of the mid-1920s. The number of settler-owned cattle soared as well, from about 30,400 head in 1904 to 341,900 head in 1914. A measure of the success of the white agricultural policy was that in 1912 white farmers supplanted African peasant farmers as the main suppliers of food to the mines.[91]

The general African response to these pressures was to move onto the reserves. It is estimated that between 1915 and 1925, some 60,000 Africans moved from white-owned land into the reserves. Another 60,000 moved to the reserves during the 1920s and close to that number relocated there between 1931 and 1941.[92] By the 1920s, many reserves were overcrowded with people and animals. The population shift was greatest in Matabeleland. As African families were forced to move onto the less fertile reserves, away from markets and rail and road links, they were less able to produce surplus crops or sell their surplus crops to markets. Less able to meet their cash needs through the sale of grain and other produce, they were compelled to send African males, including boys, into the wage labor force. Over the course of the 1910s, the CNC noted in his *Annual Report* a gradual but steady increase in the percentage of adult males who went out to work for wages and an increase in the length of time they remained in the wage labor force, from two to three months a year to four to six months or more a year.

As mentioned earlier, to these hardships were added drought, famine, and a steep rise in the post-war prices of the imported goods Africans most frequently consumed, followed by a slump in farm prices shortly afterward. Africans in the areas affected by drought coped in several ways. Those with cash or cattle purchased grain from traders and fellow Africans who were more fortunate than they. When the private system of grain relief broke down, the state intervened with loans of grain in exchange for promises to go out to work for wages. Many people survived the drought by eating wild fruits on the veld. Others (men) still preferred to "remain at home to look after their families and die with them if they cannot get food."[93] Finally, as officials and employers urged, many males left home to work for wages. According to John Ilife, "In Matabeleland and some higher regions of Mashonaland, food shortage swelled the labour supply,"[94]

It is within the context of these developments that we should place the mass exodus from the rural areas of boys, "many of them of tender age,"[95] the CNC reported in 1916. The movement onto the reserves, particularly those of Matabeleland, had specific consequences for boys, the primary herders of cattle, sheep, and goats. The two reserves that were set aside in the province by the 1894 Land Commission (Gwaai and Shangani) were particularly unsuitable for farming and stock raising, the Ndebele regarding them as "cemeteries not Homes."[96] They were without sufficient water resources for humans or animals and Shangani was in the tsetse fly zone. It is little wonder that the most pervasive theme running through official comments on the movement onto the reserves was the shortage of good pasturage for African stockholders and the lack of adequate water. These problems were only intensified by the droughts of the 1910s.

Most immediately, for boys and adolescent males, the move onto the reserves meant a tremendously increased burden to find adequate pasture and water for their fathers' animals. In their efforts to do so, they found themselves in competition with herd boys from other reserve homesteads. The droughts of the 1910s presented them with an impossible task. Weakened themselves by hunger and by a rise in some areas in diseases such as dysentery, chicken pox, measles, whooping cough, and cerebro-spinal meningitis, they were hard pressed to take animals further afield.[97] Their parents short of money or without money altogether, many boys fled, either to search for wages to send back to their families or "to escape the work of herding his father's cattle."[98] As for girls, they faced an intensification of their work in fetching water and firewood for the homestead and in cultivating poor soils. Some would try to flee the homestead for town, while others, along with their mothers, brothers, and fathers would turn increasingly to piece and task work on nearby white-owned farms.

[. . .]

Notes

1   Chief Native Commissioner to the Governor, "Memorandum Explanatory of the Bill to Provide for the Employment of Native Juveniles," April 12, 1926, No. 2, in Southern Rhodesia, *Papers Relative to the Southern Rhodesia Native Juveniles Employment Act, 1926, and the Southern Rhodesia Native Affairs Act, 1927.* Cmd. 3076 (London: H.M.S.O., 1928), 10. Hereafter *NJEA Papers.*

2   South Africa. *South African Native Affairs Commission, 1903–5,* vol. 5, *Minutes of Evidence,* Appendix D, *Written Replies to Circular Questions,* Cd. 2399 (Cape Town: Government Printers, 1905), 352. Hereafter, *SANAC Written Evidence.*

3   See Benjamin Davis and Wolfgang Dopcke, "Survival and Accumulation in Gutu: Class Formation and the Rise of the State in Colonial Zimbabwe, 1900–939," *Journal of Southern African Studies* 14, 1 (1987): 64–98.; Angela Cheater, *Idioms of Accumulation: Rural Development and Class Formation among Freeholders in Modern Zimbabwe* (Durham, NC: Duke University Press, 1984).

4   See Elizabeth Schmidt, *Peasants, Traders, and Wives: Shona Women in the History of Zimbabwe, 1870–1939* (Portsmouth, NH: Heinemann, 1992), 122–54.

5   Southern Rhodesia. *Legislative Assembly Debates,* November 2, 1926 (Salisbury: Government Printer, 1927), 20. Hereafter, *SRLAD.*

6   The following discussion is based on Ian Phimister, *An Economic and Social History of Zimbabwe, 1890–1948: Capital Accumulation and Class Struggle* (London: Longman, 1988), 4–36; Terence O. Ranger, *Revolt in Southern Rhodesia, 1896–97: A Study in African Resistance* (Evanston, IL: Northwestern University Press, 1967), 46–125; Robin Palmer, *Land and Racial Domination in Rhodesia* (Berkeley: University of California Press, 1977), 24–52.

7   Palmer, *Land and Racial Domination,* 24, 26, 28–29.

8   Ranger, *Revolt in Southern Rhodesia,* 57.

9   Ibid., 311–44. See also Phimister, *Economic and Social History,* 30–31.

10   Harry Craufuird Thomson, *Rhodesia and Its Government* (London: Smith, Elder, 1898), 75.

11   David Christiann de Waal, *With Rhodes in Mashonaland* (Cape Town: J. C. Juta, 1896), 211.

12   Patrick Harries, *Work, Culture, and Identity: Migrant Laborers in Mozambique and South Africa, c. 1860–1910* (Portsmouth, NH: Heinemann, 1994), 201.

13   George A. Wilder to Dr. Strong, April 27, 1897, American Board of Commissioners for Foreign Missions, Reel 194, Item 277 (Cambridge, MA: Houghton Library, Harvard University). Hereafter, ABC.

14   De Waal, *With Rhodes,* 284. 307–9. See also Cape Colony Act 22 of 1857 in Cape Colony, *Laws Regulating the Relative Rights and Duties of Masters, Servants, and Apprentices in the Cape Colony, Including the Workmen's Compensation Act of 1905,* comp. H. Tennant (London: J. C. Juta, 1906).

15   Vere Stent, *A Personal Record of Some Incidents in the Life of Cecil Rhodes* (Bulawayo, Rhodesia: Books of Bulawayo, 1970), 22, 27–29.

16   Schmidt, *Peasants, Traders, and Wives,* 39–42; Stent, *A Personal Record,* 45; Olive Schreiner, *Trooper Peter Halket of Mashonaland* (Parklands, Johannesburg: AD. Donker, 1992), 42–44.

17   Thomson, *Rhodesia and Its Government,* 109, 151–53. See also Schreiner, *Trooper Peter Halket,* 36; Ranger, *Revolt in Southern Rhodesia,* 268–310.

18   Quoted in Ranger, *Revolt in Southern Rhodesia,* 314.

19   Thomson, *Rhodesia and Its Government,* 144–46.

20   See John M Mackenzie, "African Labour in the Chartered Company Period," *Rhodesian History* 1 (1970): 43–58; John M. Mackenzie, "Colonial Labour Policy and Rhodesia," *The Rhodesian Journal of Economics* 8, No. 1 (1976): 1–15.

21   See Schmidt, *Peasants, Traders, and Wives,* 43–70; Phimister, *Economic and Social History,* 64–80.

22   Southern Rhodesia. *Report of the Chief Native Commissioner for the Year Ending 31st March 1916* (Salisbury: Government Printer, 1917), 6.

23   Southern Rhodesia, Native Department, I, Matabeleland, *Report of the Chief Native Commissioner for Year Ending 31st March, 1898* (Salisbury: Government Printer, 1898), 216.

24   Southern Rhodesia. *Report of the Chief Native Commissioner, Matabeleland, for the Year Ended 31st March, 1901* (Salisbury: Government Printer, 1901), 6. From 1898 to 1912, Matabeleland and Mashonaland were administered by separate CNCs. In 1913, the two positions were combined.

25   Phimister, *Economic and Social History,* 23.

26   "Report of the Chief Native Labour Agent (Mr. D.H. Moodie) for the Period Ended 31st March 1900," in Southern Rhodesia, *Report of the Chief Native Commissioner, Matabeleland, for the Year Ended 31st March, 1900* (Salisbury: Government Printer, 1900), 160.

27   SANAC *Written Evidence,* 311.

28   Ibid., 339.

29   Ibid., 350, 352.

30   Ibid., 368.

31   Ibid., 329.

32   Ibid., 375.

33   This paragraph draws on Phimister, *Economic and Social History,* 45–57. See also Charles van Onselen, *Chibaro: African Mine Labour in Southern, Rhodesia, 1900–1933* (London: Pluto Press, 1976), 17–28.

34   Van Onselen, *Chibaro,* 124.

35   "Reports by the Inspectors of Native Compounds, 31st March, 1903," in Southern Rhodesia, *Annual Report of the Chief Native Commissioner Matabeleland, for the Year Ended 31st March, 1904* (Salisbury: Government Printer, 1904), 30.

36   On the organization of housing on the mines, see van Onselen, *Chibaro* 34–38.

37   Ibid., 124. See also Charles Van Onselen, "Sex and Social Control in the Rhodesian Mine Compounds, 1900–933," *South African Labour Bulletin* 1, no. 7 (1994): 17–30.

38   On the practice of "mine marriage" elsewhere in the region, see Harries, *Work, Culture, and Identity,* 200–208; Patrick Harries, "Symbols and Sexuality: Culture and Identity on the Early Witwatersrand Gold Mines," *Gender and History* 2, no. 3 (Autumn, 1990); 318–36; T. Dunbar Moodie, "Migrancy and Male Sexuality on the South African Gold Mines," *Journal of Southern African Studies* 14, no. 2 (January 1988): 228–55.

39   Van Onselen, *Chibaro,* 124–25.

40   Ibid., 125.

41   Southern Rhodesia, *Legislative Council Debates,* June 2, 1910 (Salisbury: Government Printer, 1911), 73. Hereafter *SRLCD.*

42   Cited in Telegram from the Governor of Southern Rhodesia to the Secretary of State for Dominion Affairs, November 24, 1927, No. 18, *NJEA Papers,* 28.

43   Ibid., 28.

44   *SRLAD,* November 2, 1926, 20.

45   Van Onselen incorrectly interprets the large number of women and children on the mines as evidence of advanced proletarianization in the region. He argues that "The children at work on the mica mines reveals to what extent some African families had been proletarianised. The fact that mothers and fathers allowed their children to work on the mines at all indicated a desperate attempt to raise incomes that were themselves exceptionally low." *Chibaro,* 125.

46   Southern Rhodesia, *Annual Report of the Chief Native Commissioner, Matabeleland, for the Year Ended 31st March, 1910* (Salisbury: Government Printer, 1910), 4.

47   Schmidt, *Peasants, Traders, and Wives,* 157.

48   Southern Rhodesia, *Annual Report of the Chief Native Commissioner, Matabeleland, for the Year Ended 31st March 1903* (Salisbury: Government Printer, 1903), 3.

49   Southern Rhodesia, *Report of the Native Affairs Committee, 1910–11* (Salisbury: Government Printer, 1911), 4. Hereafter, *NAC Report.*

50   Southern Rhodesia, *Annual Report of the Chief Native Commissioner, Matabeleland, for the Year Ended 31st March, 1906* (Salisbury; Government Printer, 1906), 1.

51   Southern Rhodesia, *Annual Report of the Chief Native Commissioner, Mashonaland, for the Year Ended 31st December, 1909* (Salisbury: Government Printer, 1909), 5.

52   Southern Rhodesia, *Annual Report of the Chief Native Commissioner, Matabeleland, for the Year Ended 31st December, 1908* (Salisbury: Government Printer, 1908), 5.

53   Schmidt, *Peasants, Traders, and Wives,* 56–60, 157; van Onselen, "Sex and Social Control," 22.

54   Southern Rhodesia, *The Statute Law of Southern Rhodesia from 1st January to 31st December, 1901,* vol. 4 (Salisbury: Argus for Government Printer, 1902), 586.

55   Southern Rhodesia, *Annual Report of the Chief Native Commissioner, Mashonaland, for the Year Ended 31st March, 1902* (Salisbury: Government Printer, 1902), 6.

56   See Harries, *Work, Culture, and Identity.*

57   Southern Rhodesia, *The Statute Law of Southern Rhodesia. From 1st January to 31st December, 1904,* vol. 7 (Salisbury: Argus for Government Printers, 1905), 284.

58   *SRLAD*, November 2, 1926, 20.

59   Southern Rhodesia, *The Statute Law of Southern Rhodesia. From 1st January to 31st December, 1904,* vol. 7, 384.

60   Secretary, Law Department, to the Magistrate, Gwelo, March 20, 1924, 1. National Archives of Zimbabwe (NAZ), S235/367, S235/387. See also Circular No, 45/05, Taxable Age of Male Natives, C.N.C.'s Office, Salisbury, 28th December, 1905; No. 0.1069/617, Taxable Age of Natives, Chief Secretary's Office, Salisbury, 1st June 1906; Circular No. 34/06, C.N.C.'s Office, Salisbury, 7th June, 1906; Circular No. B. 42/10, Taxation of Native Youths at School, 22 August, 1910; Circular Letter No. 1395–1916, Chief Native Commissioner's Office, Salisbury, 27th June, 1916; Circular Letter No. R. 147/2162, Chief Native Commissioner's Office, Salisbury, 23rd January, 1918. NAZ S235/367, S235/387.

61   Secretary, Law Office, to Magistrate, Gwelo, 1, 2.

62   Jeff Guy, "Analysing Pre-Capitalist Societies in Southern Africa," *Journal of Southern African Studies* 14, no. 1 (1987), especially 30–37.

63   On the rewriting of "customary law" and the "fabrication" of "customs" during the colonial period, Martin Chanock, *Law, Custom and Social Order: The Colonial Experience in Malawi* (Portsmouth, NH: Heinemann, 1998); Kristen Mann and Richard Roberts, ed., *Law in Colonial Africa* (Portsmouth, NH: Heinemann, 1991); Sally Falk Moore, *Social Facts and Fabrications: "Customary" Law on Kilimanjaro, 1880–1980* (New York: Cambridge University Press, 1986).

64   South Africa, South African Native Affairs Commission, 1903–5, vol. 4, *Minutes of Evidence* (Cape Town: Cape Times for Government Printers, 1904), 193–94. Hereafter, SANAC *Oral Evidence.*

65   Secretary, Law Office, to Magistrate, Gwelo, 2, NAZ S235/367.

66   "Gutu-Chilimanzi District," Southern Rhodesia, *Reports of Native Commissioners, Mashonaland 31 March, 1904* (Salisbury: Government Printers 1904), 13.

67   Superintendent of Natives, Bulawayo, to Chief Native Commissioner, Salisbury, 8th November, 1920, No. 2, in *NJEA Papers,* 11.

68   SANAC *Oral Evidence,* 167–68.

69   *SRLCD,* June 22, 1908, 64. A morgen is equal to 2.116 acres.

70   Michael L. Morris, "The Development of Capitalism in South African Agriculture: Class Struggle in the Countryside," in *The Articulation of Modes of Production: Essays from Economy and Society,* ed. Harold Wolpe (London; Routledge and Kegan Paul, 1980), especially 229–40; Timothy J. Keegan, *Rural Transformations in Industrializing South Africa: The Southern Highveld to 1914* (London: Macmillan Press, 1987), 121–65.

71   John K. Rennie, "White Farmers, Black Tenants and Landlord Legislation: Southern Rhodesia, 1890–1930," *Journal of Southern African History* 5, no. 1 (1978): 91–97.

72   SANAC *Oral Evidence,* 169.

73   Morris, "The Development of Capitalism in South African Agriculture," 237.

74   Quoted in Phimister, *Economic and Social History,* p. 148

75   The following discussion is based largely on Rennie, "White Farmers, Black Tenants, and Landlord Legislation."

76   Ibid., 97.

77   "Matobo District," *Extracts of Reports of Native Commissioners in CNC Matabeleland Annual Report 1907,* 17.

78   On the emergence and decline of the African peasantry, see Arrighi, "Labor Supplies"; Palmer, *Land and Racial Domination;* Palmer, "Agricultural History of Rhodesia"; Phimister, *Economic and Social History,* 64–80.

79   "Selukwe District," in *Reports of Native Commissioners, Matabeleland, for the year ended 31st March 1904,* 18.

80   Quoted in Phimister, *Economic and Social History,* 65.

81   Phimister, *Economic and Social History,* 66.

82   Southern Rhodesia, *Annual Report of the Chief Native Commissioner, Mashonaland, for the Year Ended 31st March, 1912* (Salisbury: Government Printer, 1912), 1. See also *CNC Annual Report 1918,* 13.

83   CNC to Secretary, Department of Administrator, *NJEA Papers,* 12.

84   However, just as the rise of the peasantry had been uneven, so was its decline mediated by location and class, See Phimister, *Economic and Social History,* 64–80; Davis and Dopcke, "Survival and

Accumulation in Gutu." On the concepts of the rise and decline of peasantries in settler Africa, see Colin Bundy, *The Rise and Decline of the South African Peasantry* (London: James Currey, 1988).

85   Arrighi, "Labor Supplies," 206.

86   The discussion that follows is based on Arrighi, "Labor Supplies"; Palmer, "Agricultural History"; Palmer, *Land and Racial Domination*; Phimister, *Economic and Social History*, 64–91.

87   For discussion of these policies, see Palmer, *Land and Racial Domination,* 81–83. On famine in colonial Zimbabwe, see John Iliffe, *Famine in Zimbabwe, 1890–1960* (Gweru, Zimbabwe: Mambo Press, 1990).

88   Quoted in Phimister, *Economic and Social History*, 65.

89   Phimister, *Economic and Social History*, 66.

90   Ibid., 66.

91   Ibid., 61; van Onselen, *Chibaro*, 41–42.

92   Palmer, "Agricultural History," 238–43.

93   *CNC Mashonaland Annual Report 1912,* 2.

94   Iliffe, *Famine in Zimbabwe*, 44.

95   *CNC Annual Report 1916*, 10.

96   Quoted in Palmer, *Land and Racial Domination*, 33.

97   See Iliffe, *Famine in Zimbabwe,* 58.

98   Superintendent of Natives to CNC, No. 2 in *NJEA Papers*, 11.

Chapter 16

Benjamin C. Fortna

EMPHASIZING THE ISLAMIC: MODIFYING THE CURRICULUM OF LATE OTTOMAN STATE SCHOOLS[1]

L ITERATURE ON THE LATE Ottoman Empire has tended to treat education as responsible for a number of momentous, but essentially predetermined changes. One of the most critical is its putatively secularizing effect. The notion that Western-style education played a major role in severing the links between the empire's elite and their Ottoman and Islamic moorings has been central to our understanding of Ottoman demise and national "emergence". Even if state schools did have such an effect on many who passed through their classrooms, there is no reason to suppose it was anywhere near universal. In fact, there is considerable evidence that calls into question the secularizing nature of late Ottoman schooling. Although many have been quick to label education as an agent of secularization, among a host of other changes, few have actually looked at the way this "process" worked: at the thinking of the officials involved, at the curricula employed, at the teaching materials used, or at the schools themselves.

My approach has been to try to appreciate the various ways in which "Western" education, ranging from government policy to classroom life, was adapted to suit Ottoman circumstances.[2] The materials that I have consulted suggest that we should approach education not as a teleological "process", but rather as a series of exchanges, producing a range of potential consequences. For example, several disciplinary cases from state schools in the late Ottoman Empire offer narratives that allow us to appreciate the wide spectrum of possibilities on the "receiving end" of the educational exchange.[3]

In this work, I move through the presumptive chain of transmission to investigate the mechanics of educational adaptation in the late Ottoman period. I look at the way one feature of the Western-inspired educational apparatus — its centralized curriculum — was reformulated to align with an increasingly suspicious Ottoman view of Western encroachment. I begin with a discussion of some of the assumptions that have combined to obscure our view of educational change.

Two approaches have tended to color our understanding of education or specifically "modern-style" education which is usually deemed to be the only type that mattered in this period. Both view education, more or less, as a "delivery system". The first is the generally unqualified acceptance that education (including everything from epistemology to actual teaching materials) amounted to a wholesale importation from Western Europe.[4] The second assumption holds that this imported education was transmitted by the state directly to the populace. In neither case is there much room for mediation. While much of Ottoman state education did indeed depend upon Western principles of organization and content, Ottoman officialdom nevertheless selectively modified, appropriated and packaged them in ways that made sense in a changing Ottoman context. In the last decades of the nineteenth century, the official policy with respect to Western Europe assumed a more jaundiced, cynical stance; the more cozy relationship of the preceding Tanzimat period (1839–71/76) yielded to a more combative one as the Ottomans reassessed the manifold consequences – military, diplomatic, economic, intellectual, and cultural – of European hegemony.[5] Education is one area where this newly fashioned stance is easily seen. In this work, I argue that the re-formulations of Ottoman education were just as important in influencing the shape of educational exchange as their original, European form.

Crudely put, much of the literature treats education in the late Ottoman Empire as an imported commodity, delivered and received in remarkably functional fashion and as a "process" suffused with an unabashed linearity. The expansion of state education in the late nineteenth and early twentieth century is conceived as being composed of two rough segments: 1) importation, which is to say horizontal "borrowing" from West to East and 2) delivery, the vertical transmission of the imported material from the state to its student subjects.

Some of the most recent literature to address the question of social change through education continues to adopt this standard but, I think, troubled model. The importation of Western-style education, like Western ideas and commodities generally, has been character-ized by the "adoption" of epistemological systems and pedagogical methods and materials.[6] Since the main blueprint for Ottoman state education was heavily influenced by a memo-randum prepared by the French Education Ministry,[7] the schools are thought to have main-tained a largely foreign character (at least until they are somewhat miraculously transformed into more "natural" components of the consciously Westernizing post-Ottoman state). In the late Ottoman period, the western-inspired knowledge and apparatus are then said to have been transmitted directly to the students, who are treated as a "captive audience".[8] Happily, research into more geographically specific areas, such as Randi Deguilhem's recent work on Damascus, reveals the importance of the confessional nature and Islamic curriculum inherent in the late Ottoman educational package.[9] The appearance of "traditional" content in Ottoman schools on the local level points both to the reassessment of indigenous priorities and to the fact that this revised view was having a practical effect: the curriculum was becoming less foreign and more Ottoman.

The much more prevalent deterministic approach, however, admits little possibility of exchange, mediation or hybridization. Although Şerif Mardin's pathbreaking work called attention to late Ottoman attempts to bridge the gap between "traditional" and "scientific" understandings of society,[10] it has largely been taken as a given that there were two distinct paradigms, with little if any mixing. Not surprisingly, such failure to allow for Ottoman state education to be "Ottomanized" leads to a number of conclusions about the "process" in general, and what it engendered in the students upon whom it was inflicted. These poor souls are described as having been "polarized", the victims of "cultural dualism", even schizo-phrenia.[11] Granted the newness of the system, the multiplication of topics introduced through it, and the cultural dispersal of late Ottoman society, the process must have appeared shocking, perhaps even disorienting. But given also the extraordinary capacity of human beings to adapt to almost anything, particularly evident in our own era of globalization, this sort of analysis would appear to deny late Ottoman students the benefit of a doubt. As the disciplinary cases with which I have been working make clear, exchange was certainly possible on the individual level, even at the "receiving end": students could have a say in their life at school even when being taught, fed, housed, and disciplined by "the state". What is more, the Ottoman government was actively working at the systemic or institutional level to integrate the imported material with indigenous content, as we shall see in a moment.

Education "on paper"

First, let us mention some of the factors that have combined to produce this pre-determined view of late Ottoman education in the first place. Here, I should stress that the lack of detailed information about what took place inside the classroom and, more important, inside the minds of the vast majority of students, accentuates the prevailing assumptions about how education works and why it exists.

A constellation of factors, theoretical and logistical, has combined to shape what we might call the "mechanical engineering" approach to education. First, there has been a penchant for the quantifiable, a tendency to collect data (counting schools, students, teachers, etc.)[12] and for treating the entire question of education as a "problem" to be solved. Most accounts of education written in the 1960s and 1970s describe mechanical organizational diagrams of the Ottoman and Turkish Republican school systems.[13] One imagines faceless cadres of pupils passing along the organizational flowcharts from level to level. Underlying this structural approach is an overweening preference of the group over the individual, apparent in the wider literature on this period.[14] The broad range of potential human reactions to education is rapidly reduced to cohorts and treated as if they act and think alike.[15] Quite apart from the methodological problems associated with sources written in the dramatically altered post-Ottoman atmosphere in which criticism of the previous regime was encouraged, this collective approach is based on an extremely small number of memoirs written by former students.[16]

The prevailing approach has not equivocated when it comes to assessing the roles played by Islam and the state in late Ottoman education. The presence of anything Islamic in state schooling, to the extent that it was acknowledged at all, has been explained away as propaganda.[17] This flatly functional approach to Islam precludes any possible discussion about the multiple valences that the combination of Islam and "Western-style" schooling could have produced. While the role of Islam is thereby diminished, the role of the state is universally exaggerated. Such overemphasis stems from two different traditions. One sees the state as mainly positive, a source for effecting desired change, which is to say modernization. This view derived from the late Ottoman and Turkish Republican experience, in which the state was seen as the only viable agent of positive change.[18] Public education or, rather, its putatively secularizing aspect has thus received considerable attention for its role in the statist project of making the East more like the West. Conversely, there is a more recent tendency in the social sciences to see the state as equally powerful, but essentially negative. Attempting to apply the analysis of Michel Foucault to the Middle East, some have seen the state as quasi-monstrous. State schools are depicted more or less as prisons or as devices for controlling the population. Here, attention to official schooling regulations exaggerates state power.[19] Much as road manuals fail to prepare us for the stunts of our fellow motorists, such abstract normative texts do not foresee any of the nuanced exchanges and the bargaining that are part of the educational exchange. Moreover, what may have held for a country under direct colonial rule like Egypt does not necessarily work for the Ottoman Empire where European influence over state education, as strong as it may have been, was always mediated by the autonomous, indigenous government.

We need to make room for the complex and sometimes contradictory reactions (and interactions) that education engendered, at the individual as well as the group level. Following a lead proposed by Şerif Mardin,[20] I found Mikhail Bakhtin to be helpful here. Bakhtin's interest in the natural world led him to appreciate the different ways that organisms responded to stimuli. In human beings the complexity of the body's composition makes for a greater level of unpredictability. In fact, individual unpredictability lies at the core of Bakhtin's theory of answerability. Although present in seemingly simultaneous time and place, humans have different reactions to the "same" event because of differences in "placement". No two people can occupy the same place, and thus cannot observe an event or experience it the same way. For Bakhtin, answerability is directly related to the question of authorship, which is for him the chief difference separating humans from other species.[21] At the very least, Bakhtin's unbounded assumptions provide an interesting counterpoint to the much more restricted, deterministic approach of, say, Pierre Bourdieu's more recent work on education.[22] Ideally, perhaps, studies on educational effects would benefit from a productive tension between these two views, but my reading of what has been written about late Ottoman schools generally suggests that the less bounded approach needs a broader airing. For unless we wish to ascribe a sub-human status to students in late Ottoman schools (or any other for that matter), we must hold out the possibility, at the very least, that they just might have reacted in very different ways to the stimuli of state education.

Before we can appreciate the various possibilities in the Ottoman case, it is necessary to gauge the changing circumstances of the late nineteenth century. In what follows I describe the impact of foreign encroachment and the resulting change in the apparatus of late Ottoman education. This change subsequently alerts us to the possibility of a broad range of possible reactions.

Encroachment

Wariness of Western influence took two main forms. One appeared in response to the physical presence of foreign educators operating in Ottoman territory. Over the course of the nineteenth century both the numbers and types of foreign educational institutions increased dramatically in the Ottoman Empire. The options available expanded beyond the various indigenous schools operated by the religious establishments to include an array of foreign-run schooling. Depending upon where in the empire one lived, schools built by American, Austrian, British, Bulgarian, French, German, Italian, Russian and Serb groups, among others, were a possibility.[23] The expansion of foreign-run schools in the empire was so dramatic that the Ottoman government often had a difficult time merely keeping records on the various institutions.[24] But foreign educational encroachment caused more than bureaucratic problems. It produced a variety of responses ranging from the collective, *e.g.*, the state's attempt to counter with an increase in the capacity of its own institutions, to the individual, *e.g.*, the response of the Syrian *'âlim* Yûsuf al-Nabhâni.[25]

Just as foreign education operated as both a positive and negative spur to state activity, so did it act as a double-edged stimulus to alter what was taking place in Ottoman classrooms. On the one hand, the foreign schools were seen as potential objects of emulation. For example, in a memorandum written to Yıldız Palace in 1893, the Ottoman Education Minister Zühdü Paşa begrudgingly held up the example of the curriculum of the missionary schools as successful.[26] Zühdü singles out the teaching of three subjects that the Protestant missionary schools have used to great advantage in furthering their own political, religious, and cultural agenda. These are: religious principles, history, and English. The Education Minister explicitly links each of these subjects with its purported aim. Thus,

> The first of these three is for the purpose of spreading Protestantism; the second is to engender some political sentiments (*bir hissiyat-i siyasiye*) in the minds of the public and the Ottoman subjects in particular; and the third is for competition with France.[27]

According to Zühdü Paşa, these methods are responsible for the fact that young Ottoman subjects "have become accustomed to Frankish habits and customs due to the influence of their teachers and they remain subjects in name only, their minds having been changed." While Zühdü Paşa does not say so directly, the mention of these successful methods seems clearly intended to inspire their emulation by the Ottoman state school system.

On the other hand, the missionary schools produced a more defensive reaction. A common theme running through the memoranda submitted by provincially based civil servants to the capital was the need to combat the "dangers" inherent in the foreign educational presence on Ottoman territory. Building state-run alternatives figured as the first line of defense in Ottoman strategy, supported by complementary policies such as sending preachers throughout the countryside to warn against the dangers of foreign schooling and appointing teams of inspectors to monitor the foreign institutions. These were adjunct strategies; the main thrust of the state's response was building its own schools, institutions in which the state could have full control of how the students lived and what they learned.

As with the education endeavor generally, the European presence loomed large over the agenda of curricular modification. Correspondence dating from 1901 reveals the extent to which the Western presence made itself felt.[28] Initiated at the request of Abdülhamid II, the memoranda included in this file are responses to his request for remedies for a "situation that was a cause of regret to his Imperial Highness", namely, the fact that Ottoman subjects have sought to be educated in Europe or in foreign schools operating within the empire. Putting a stop to this practice was the overriding agenda at work. Although the recommendations were ultimately not validated by sultanic decree, the arguments behind them illustrate important facets of the logic at work in the curricular reform movement. In the thinking of the Hamidian bureaucracy, obviating the need for Ottoman students to study abroad could be effected by decree. The students could merely be ordered to return. But, by proposing certain changes to the domestic alternatives, the Ottomans were tacitly acknowledging the importance of the quality and relevance of their own educational offerings. In order to render Ottoman schooling a more realistic, not to mention palatable, option for the individuals involved, the state proposed several changes. These included streamlining the course load of students in most schools, which were deemed to suffer from a curriculum described as "crowded".[29] Attached to the file are lesson schedules that illustrate the proposed changes to reduce the number of classroom hours in the various schools. In the case of the preparatory (idadî) schools, these changes were predicated upon the proposed addition of one year to the idadî curriculum, a change that was not effected. The other recommendation was to devote more attention to lessons relating to "Islamic principles", as we shall see presently.

The political and economic interest of the state argued in favor of repatriating students who had been sent overseas to further their education. In fiscal terms, such substitution would save the Treasury both the cost of supporting the students living abroad and the costs associated with redundancy. The memorandum of the Meclis-i Mahsus includes the estimate that the state would save 300,000 kuruş annually by having them return.[30] But the main benefit for repatriating the students in Europe, some of whom were described as not actually studying but wandering about like vagabonds, was to render them dependent upon the state's own educational control.

Western influence can also be detected in another recurring theme in the correspondence relating to the commissions, namely the purging of European elements deemed to be detrimental to Ottoman society. This response seems to have been motivated by the growing trend toward European affectation in the empire as a whole, as evidenced in changing sartorial and literary tastes. More specifically, of course, the curricular refitting campaign was an attempt to temper the spate of cultural and ideological borrowing inherent in the Tanzimat era education plan.

This campaign sought to purge the detrimental elements and replace them with course content that would produce students both morally sound and politically loyal. According to a memorandum produced by the Meclis-i Mahsus in 1900, it was necessary to take action to ensure that:

> Those graduating from the established schools possess the attainments of science and knowledge (*müktessebat-i ilmiye ve fününiye*) that are necessary according to the progress of modern civilization, that they obtain intellectual incisiveness and religious firmness, that they be faithful to the sublime sultanate and endowed with sound morals.[31]

As this passage indicates, the Hamidian objective espoused neither a rush to imitate Western education nor its wholesale rejection. Rather, it sought what it repeatedly referred to as "modifications" (*ta'dilât*) that would draw on the attainments of both the Western and Eastern traditions.[32] It aspired to take the best of the European advances while attempting to hold the attendant dangers at bay. Inculcating sound, which is to say Islamic, morality was thus intended as a prophylaxis against the contagion implicit in the encroachment of the West.

What exactly was entailed in such an endeavor was never precisely articulated. Much in the way that the largely inchoate notion of "education" was so freely heralded as a general panacea for the empire's ills, moral instruction was advanced as the means of assuring that this new type of education conformed to official aspirations. Yet the changes made to the state school curriculum reveal the thrust of the Hamidian objective: making the schools more Islamic and more Ottoman.

Changing the curriculum

Hamidian curricular modification centered on the insertion of "Islamic" content into a "secular" curriculum. Sultan Abdülhamid II (r. 1876–1909) built an impressive number of state schools across the Ottoman Empire. But the schools he built had been planned during the reigns of his predecessors, and almost entirely along lines suggested by the French Ministry of Education. Abdülhamid's policy of reversing the comparatively open-armed embrace of the West is well known, earning for his period the labels "reactionary" and "despotic". Yet, the secondary literature on the subject assumes that the schools he built continued to act as agents of the Western agenda. My research has demonstrated that, on the contrary, Abdülhamid's educational policy was premised upon a more cynical attitude toward Western encroachment. The increased wariness toward and suspicion of foreign influence, especially that of Western missionaries and especially the Protestants among them, stemmed from the increasingly unshakable impression that the Great Powers were not keeping Ottoman interests to heart, particularly unavoidable after the occupation of Tunis by the French in 1881 and Egypt by the British the following year.

There was little that Istanbul could do to redress these usurpations, but education provided a means for Ottoman action on Ottoman soil. The chief weapon deployed to counter this impingement in the educational sphere was altering the curriculum Abdülhamid II had inherited from his predecessors by inserting "Islamic" content. To do so he empanelled numerous commissions to vet the pre-existing curricula, replacing courses such as Western "philosophy" with those on Islamic jurisprudence (*fıkıh*) and morals (*ahlâk*). In this way, his administrators sought to take advantage of the centralizing educational structure appropriated from the West, precisely to counter the West's own – and growing – influence in the empire.

Morals were thought to be "broken", a major source of the various problems afflicting the empire. A major campaign was launched to bolster morality – always treated in an exclusively Islamic manner. Changing the curriculum was only one component of this agenda, which included such measures as sending traveling *ulema* throughout the countryside in various provinces to warn against the dangers associated with foreign schooling, increasing the numbers of inspectors available to keep a watch on the various types of schools operating in the empire, and increasing the capacity of government schools to take on students as boarders so that their conduct could be more closely watched.

But altering the curriculum was by far the most efficient means with which to get the moral message across. In doing so, government bureaucrats took advantage of the highly centralized schooling system adapted from the French. A decision made in Istanbul to alter the lesson plan of the elementary schools, for example, would result in that same change being carried out in all institutions at that level throughout the provinces.

The Hamidian government exhibited a continual impulse to modify the school curriculum it had inherited. The raft of commissions created by the Sultan from 1885 onward and the correspondingly large number of reports they inevitably produced reveals the means by which Abdülhamid's bureaucracy attempted to inject moral education into what had initially been a much more secular system. As stipulated in the Education Regulation of 1869, the preparatory (*idadî*) schools were not intended to provide courses in morality or religion of any sort.[33] The first commission seems to have been instructed to adjust the schools' curriculum but not to address the subject of moral education. Its recommendations were limited to such subjects as the language of instruction. It suggested that Arabic replace Turkish as the chief language of instruction in schools in the Arab provinces and that French be abolished completely from the upper primary (*rüşdiye*) schools and be relegated to the status of an optional language in the *idadîs* and the *Mekteb-i Mülkiye*.[34] It also recommended the removal of several scientific courses from the crowded *idadî* curriculum. Although these changes appear not to have been adopted,[35] they represent the first evidence of an attempt to alter the school's curriculum on an empire-wide scale.

Within a year's time, Abdülhamid II created another curricular review commission. Starting a trend that would continue throughout his reign, the sultan charged the new commission with a more far-reaching brief. The imperial decree issued by the palace on 29 January 1887 ordained the creation of a commission to be chaired by the highest Muslim dignitary in the empire, the *şeyhülislam*.[36] This commission was charged with "reforming and correcting the curricula being studied in the *Mekteb-i Mülkiye* and the other Muslim schools" of the Empire. Appointing the *şeyhülislam* to head such a consultative body was just one of the signs portending the changes that Abdülhamid was to introduce into his school system. Moreover, the reference to the nominally ecumenical schools in the state system as being "Muslim schools" revealed the unofficial agenda behind educational expansion. Given the perceived preponderance of non-Muslim schools that had been opened in the empire, the state began to think of its *de jure* ecumenical schools as *de facto* Muslim institutions.

The change in education policy, however, went far beyond the level of personnel appointments and semantics. The very rationale for the impending changes spoke volumes about the new approach. The decree states that need for reform has been made clear by "signs of weakness in the religious principles of graduates of the *Mülkiye* and other Islamic schools". Placing this need for curricular reform in a larger context, the document explicitly referred to the enviable state of moral education as practiced in the non-Muslim schools of the Empire as a goad to change. Like other intragovernmental correspondence on educational competition which focused on the role of foreign and indigenous non-Muslim schools, which is to say both *millet* and missionary schools as a spur to the expansion of the Ottoman school system in the first place, this decree cites the non-Muslim schools "which are in every way preferable in this regard" as a major factor in its rationale for inserting morals into the state schools.[37]

The decree focused on the example of the non-Muslim schools as a source of emulation for their Ottoman counterparts. "By reorganizing their curricula, the non-Muslim schools have striven for excellence with respect to their students' morals and have produced results", the text of the decree announced. By contrast, in the Muslim schools, "the opposite situation is a source of regret to the Sultan". The culprit was identified as the "irregularity of the curricula of the Muslim schools" which had "predictably resulted in the heedlessness of the Muslim students".[38] The prescribed remedy was the reorganization of the curriculum. Not for the last time, the example of the non-Muslim schools served as a spur to reforming the counterparts in the state's own system.

Since the task of "reorganizing the curriculum" was not precisely defined, the selection of the individuals charged with carrying out that objective was significant. The choice of the şeyhülislam to head the commission was a clear indication of the increased role Abdülhamid II entrusted to the ulema in shaping educational policy. To be sure, the Sultan was not granting exclusive control of the process to the religious establishment; this commission, like almost all of its successors, was comprised of a roughly even balance of civil bureaucrats and ulema. But it was the şeyhülislam Üryanizâde Ahmed Esad Efendi who chaired the commission, assisted by the Assistant Director of the Mekteb-i Mülkiye, Hacı Recai Efendi. Their report is interesting for several reasons. First, because the report was produced by the şeyhülislam's office, it was penned in the Persianate Divanî script, a fact that makes it visually distinct from the normal correspondence concerning educational (and most other governmental) matters that appeared in rıka script. Secondly, the physical distinctiveness is indicative of the change in outlook represented by the commission's agenda. Invoking a phrase that would reappear frequently during the Hamidian era, the cover letter of the commission's report stressed the need to "strengthen the religious principles" of the students attending the state's schools.[39] The letter suggests two types of approaches aimed at accomplishing this goal. One was to "reorganize and reform" the curriculum. The other was to ensure that the students carried out their prescribed prayers. In other words, the schools were to oversee moral as well as intellectual development.

The full memorandum that the commission produced reveals the scope of the project it had undertaken. The curriculum of each type of school had been reviewed and a number of meetings had been convened at the Office of the şeyhülislam to discuss the changes to be made.[40] The commission's recommendations underscore the extent to which religion figured in the curricular reform effort. In his report the şeyhülislam suggested that Arabic, like French, be taught in every grade of the idadî schools and all of the higher institutions. Next, he recommended creating new "courses on the biographies and features of the Prophets, the historical deeds of the companions of the Prophet, and the biographies of the religious authorities and the famous ulema."[41] Furthermore, he proposed that the projected lessons in religious principles include "the instruction of the science of morals (ilm-i ahlâk) and of Islamic jurisprudence (fıkıh) in abridged form".

These specific changes conform to the strategy contained in the commission's memorandum and, more generally, to the overall tenets of Hamidian educational policy. This strategy consisted of several key points. First, it emphasized the importance of proper preadolescent education as a necessary condition for the religious basis of the entire religious community. "For a millet, the establishment of matters of belief truly depends on being led and guided on that path in the beginning stages of adolescence."[42] Secondly, it recommended augmenting the time allotted to religious instruction. "Since the instruction of both the religious sciences and the Arabic language in the primary (ibtidaî) and rüşdiye schools has been found to be insufficient," the memorandum continues, "it is necessary to expand their period

of instruction and to 'modify' their curriculum." "Modification" meant increasing the proportion of religious instruction, including "the teaching here also of treatises on belief sufficient
to fend off the danger" posed by students' "being occupied with Western works and writings
that are harmful to Islamic morals and to the exalted sultanate".[43] Thirdly, these curricular
efforts were to be supported by extra-curricular changes. The memorandum specifically
mentions the necessity of having the students perform their prayers as a congregation. "To
assure the proper functioning of the schools' instruction in this respect", the commission's
memorandum goes on to suggest the appointment of the 'alim Yahya Reşid Efendi, a madrasa
instructor and a member of the Council of Şeriat Investigation (*Meclis-i Tedkikat-i Şer'iye*), to
oversee inspection, that perennial stand-by of Hamidian state control.

Here is Hamidian education policy in microcosm: a moving away from the more overtly
secular aspects of the Tanzimat conception of Ottoman education toward a consciously
Islamic basis, and all of this being carried out against the backdrop of foreign encroachment
which renders the changes all the more pressing.

Conclusion

The scope of this work has not allowed for an examination of exactly what is meant by Islamic
content. Elsewhere I have analyzed texts used to teach morals produced as a result of the
Hamidian campaign to promote Islamic morality in the state schools.[44] On the basis of those
books and what can be gleaned from official memoranda on the need to bolster Islamic content
in the first place, several things seem clear. First, the state was trying to insert a basic, even boil-
erplate notion of Sunni Islam: It emphasized the unity of God, the role of the Prophet Muhammad,
the five pillars, all the while having recourse to Hadith and the Qur'an (cited in the original
Arabic). These characteristics mark the Hamidian agenda as distinct from the Tanzimat project;
the text I examined stands in contrast to an earlier analogue, the 1847 *Ahlâk Risalesi* of Sadık Rıfat
Paşa analyzed by Akşin Somel in his work in the present volume [see original reading].[45] In
contrast with the Tanzimat text, the Hamidian work is conspicuous for its overtly Islamic content.

I want to be very clear that I am not suggesting that the Hamidian regime was somehow
recreating the *kuttâb/medrese* system under the guise of public education. Neither was it
recreating the French *lycées* on Ottoman soil. The very *raison d'être* of each system was very
different; the schools run by the religious establishment were after all intended to train *ulema*
and save souls, while those of the state were built to fulfill a number of profane tasks, foremost among which was the training of capable – and loyal – bureaucrats. Yet as the perceived
threats to the empire loomed larger, the state increasingly looked to education to provide
more than just pedagogical functions. This is apparent in the extra-curricular arena; considerable time and money was spent on converting preparatory schools to house as well as teach
their students. Acting *in loco parentis* allowed the state to monitor and enforce right conduct,
in particular such religious duties as prayer and fasting. By emphasizing its Islamic nature,
state education was intended to act as a prophylaxis against the foreign contagion that was
seen to be eroding Ottoman and Muslim values.

The curricular changes discussed here allow us to glean a tangible sense of the objectives
of the late Ottoman state. Far more difficult is assessing the reactions such changes produced.
The newly assertive Islamic stance could prove to be quite powerful, affording the state the
opportunity to portray itself as taking the high moral ground.[46] On the other hand, the
strategy could easily backfire. The behavior of a few unscrupulous school officials could cast
doubt on the entire project.

Far from being a process with predetermined results, late Ottoman education was, like
the empire's own sense of itself and its relationship with the West, evolving, in flux. The

Hamidian state continually reshaped the educational blueprint it had inherited from the preceding period as it sought to redefine school content to its own liking. Given the impetus for adaptation, and not mere adoption, it is necessary to question the prevailing assumption that the Western educational mode, with its secular epistemology, necessarily transformed and "captured" the Ottoman/Islamic. It is more helpful, perhaps, to imagine scenarios in which the two coexisted or even in which the borrowed system was absorbed, captured by the borrower. What is important, I think, is not to preclude imagining any of the necessarily unpredictable individual responses that this quite untested amalgam of influences may have produced.

Notes

1   I thank Klaus Kreiser and Manuela Marin for organizing the stimulating seminar on *Education in the Mediterranean Muslim World* held in Salamanca in October 1998 and to Engin Akarlı and Hasan Kayalı and for their comments and constructive criticism on this paper.

2   See Benjamin Fortna, *Imperial Classroom. Islam, the State and Education in the Ottoman Empire*, Oxford, Oxford University Press, 2002.

3   A subject that I pursued in "The Training and Upbringing of Boys in Late Ottoman Schools", a paper presented at the Ertegün Conference on Gender and the Practice of Law in the Ottoman Empire, Princeton University, April, 1998.

4   A recent expression of this view can be found in Joseph Szyliowicz, "The Ottoman Educational Legacy: Myth or Reality", in L. Carl Brown, ed., *Imperial Legacy: The Ottoman Imprint on the Balkans and the Middle East*, New York, Columbia University Press, 1996, p. 293. Professor Szyliowicz states that, "The modern schools were largely transplants and foreign curricula were adopted wholesale."

5   See, for example, Engin Akarlı, " 'Abdülhamid II's Attempt to Integrate Arabs into the Ottoman System", *in* David Kushner, ed., *Palestine in the late Ottoman Period*, Jerusalem, Yad Izhak Ben Zvi, 1986, pp. 74–75, 85–86.

6   See F. Müge Göçek, *Rise of the Bourgeoisie, Demise of Empire: Ottoman Westernization and Social Change*, New York, Oxford University Press, 1996, pp. 68 ff.

7   Niyazi Berkes, *The Development of Secularism in Turkey*, Montreal, McGill University Press, 1964, p. 179.

8   Selim Deringil, *The Well-Protected Domains: Ideology and the Legitimation of Power in the Ottoman Empire, 1876–1909*, London, I. B. Tauris, 1998, p. 93.

9   Randi Deguilhem, "State Civil Education in Late Ottoman Damascus: A Unifying or a Separating Force?", in Thomas Philipp and Birgit Schaebler, ed., *The Syrian Land: Processes of Integration and Fragmentation*, Stuttgart, Franz Steiner, 1998, pp. 247 ff.

10   Şerif Mardin, *The Genesis of Young Ottoman Thought*, Princeton, Princeton University Press, 1962.

11   Göçek, *Rise of the Bourgeoisie*, pp. 73, 76; Berkes, *Development of Secularism*; Carter Vaughn Findley, *Ottoman Civil Officialdom: A Social History*, Princeton, Princeton University Press, 1989. For a critique of Göçek's approach, see Reşat Kasaba's review of her book in *New Perspective on Turkey*, Spring 1998 (18), p. 157.

12   See, for example, Bayram Kodaman, *Abdülhamid Devri Eğitim Sistemi*, Ankara, Türk Tarih Kurumu, 1988.

13   See Andreas Kazamias, *Education and the Quest for Modernity in Turkey*, Chicago, University of Chicago Press, 1966, pp. 268–69; Hasan Ali Koçer, *Türkiye'de Modern Eğitimin Doğuşu ve Gelişimi 1773–1923*, Istanbul, Millî Eğitim Basımevi, 1970, p. 163. There is undoubtedly a connection between the elevated status of the engineer in Republican Turkey and the mechanical approach to education that has pervaded most of the writing on the subject.

14   Şerif Mardin, "Projects as Methodology: Some Thoughts on Modern Turkish Social Science", in Sibel Bozdoğan and Reşat Kasaba, ed., *Rethinking Modernity and National Identity in Turkey*, Seattle, University of Washington Press, 1997; Engin Deniz Akarlı, "Modernity and State-Society Relations in Late Ottoman History and Historiography", paper presented at the University of Chicago, May 1998.

15   An exception to this trend can be found in Engin D. Akarlı, "Friction and Discord within the Ottoman Government of Abdülhamid II (1876–1909)", *Boğaziç Üniversitesi Dergisi – Humanities* 7 (1979), p. 20.

16   Göçek, *Rise of the Bourgeoisie*, p. 74.

17   Deringil, "The Invention of Tradition as Public Image in the Late Ottoman Empire, 1808–1908", *Comparative Studies in Society and History* 35, no. 1 (1993), pp. 3–29.

18   The development of this tradition is itself an interesting one. For a provocative account of counter-factual alternatives, see Çağlar Keyder's contribution in Karen Barkey and Mark von Hagen, ed., *After Empire: Multiethnic Societies and Nation-Building*, Boulder, Westview Press, 1997.

19   Timothy P. Mitchell, *Colonising Egypt*, Berkeley, University of California Press, 1991; Brinkley Messick, *The Calligraphic State: Textual Domination and History in a Muslim Society*, Berkeley, University of California Press, 1993. For a recent critique of Mitchell's approach, see Gregory Starrett, *Putting Islam to Work: Education, Politics, and Religious Transformation in Egypt*, Berkeley, University of California Press, 1998, pp. 24 ff.

20   Mardin, "Projects as Methodology", p. 77.

21   Katerina Clark and Michael Holquist, *Mikhail Bakhtin*, Cambridge (Mass.) Belknap, 1984, pp. 65 ff.

22   Pierre Bourdieu, *The State Nobility: Elite Schools in the Field of Power* (trans. Lauretta C. Clough), Cambridge, Polity Press, 1996.

23   The foreign schools have garnered a perhaps disproportionately large share of the scholarly attention devoted to education in the late Ottoman period. Among the many works to focus in whole or in part on missionary schooling in the Ottoman Empire are: Frank Stone, *Academies for Anatolia: A Study of the Rationale, Program and Impact of the Educational Institutions Sponsored by the American Board in Turkey: 1830–1980*, Lanham (Maryland), University Press of America, 1984; İlknur Polat Haydaroğlu, *Osmanlı İmparatorluğunda Yabancı Okullar* (Foreign schools in the Ottoman Empire), Ankara, Kültür Bakanlığı, 1990; Uygur Kocabaşoğlu, *Kendi Belgeleriyle Anadolu'da Amerika: 19. Yüzyılda Osmanlı İmparatorluğunda Amerikan Misyoner Okulları* (America in Anatolia through its own documents: American Missionary Schools in the Ottoman Empire in the nineteenth century), Istanbul, Arba, 1989; Abdul Latif Tibawi, *British Interests in Palestine, 1800–1901: A Study of Religious and Educational Enterprise*, Oxford, Oxford University Press, 1961 and *American Interests in Syria, 1800–1901: A Study of Educational, Literary and Religious Work*, Oxford, Clarendon Press, 1966; Derek Hopwood, *The Russian Presence in Syria and Palestine, 1834–1914; Church and Politics in the Near East*, Oxford, Clarendon Press, 1969; Aron Rodrigue, *French Jews, Turkish Jews: The Alliance Israélite Universelle and the Politics of Jewish Schooling in Turkey, 1860–1925*, Bloomington: Indiana University Press, 1990.

24   For further information on late Ottoman attempts to document foreign educational encroachment see Fortna, *Imperial Classroom*, pp. 75ff.

25   Amal Ghazal, "Sufism, Ijtihâd and Modernity: Yûuf al-Nabhâni in the Age of 'Abd al-Hamîd II", paper presented at the panel entitled *Redefining Islam in the Late Ottoman Empire*, Middle East Studies Association Meeting, Chicago, 1998.

26   Başbakanlık Osmanlı Arşivi (BOA), Yıldız Esas Evrâkı (YEE) 35/232. 19 Muharrem 1311/2 August 1893.

27   *Ibid.*

28   BOA, Sadâret Resmî Mâruzât Evrâkı (Y A Res.) 112/59. 22 Safer 1319/10 June 1901. It is inter-esting to note the involvement of the Ottoman military in the issue of curricular reform. This file includes a memorandum submitted by the "Tophane-i Amire Müşiri ve Umum Mekâtib-i Askeriye-i Şahane Nâzırı". Over the preceding decade, the Hamidian government had been actively involved in efforts to unify the curricula of all of the empire's civil and military schools. See BOA, Ayniyât Defterleri (AYN) 1428, 210.

29   The Ottoman attempt to streamline the crowded curriculum had parallels in Western Europe. In Germany, France, England, Scandinavia, and Russia fears abounded that students would be debilitat-ingly overburdened by the expanded curricula that they faced. The liveliest debate over the "overbur-dening question" raged in Wilhelmine Germany. See James C. Albisetti, *Secondary School Reform in Imperial Germany*, Princeton: Princeton University Press, 1983, pp. 119 ff.

30   Y A Res. 112/59. 2. lef.

31   Y A Res. 105/13. 3. lef. 13 Ramazan 1317/15 January 1900.

32   *Ibid.*

33   The Education Regulation (Maarif Nizamnamesi) of 1869 contains no courses in Morals in its *idadî* curriculum (p. 14). Students at the *rüşdiye* level were, however, to follow a course entitled the Principles of the Religious Sciences (*mebadi-yi ulûm-u diniye*), (p. 9). The copy of the Regulation referred to here is that found in BOA, YEE 37/330.

34   BOA, ŞD 209/54. 10 Cemaziyelahır 1303/ 16 March 1886. Increased attention paid to Arabic, the language of the Qur'ân, was critical to the moral element in the Hamidian educational agenda.

35   *Ibid.* Information about this commission comes from a document written by Münif Paşa. It refers to this commission, which was created during the term of Münif's predecessor in the Education

Ministry, Mustafa Paşa, in disparaging terms, stating that all it had to show for its work was a single protocol (*mazbata*) which he reproduces.

36   BOA, İrade Dah. 80409 4 Cemaziyelevvel 1304/ 29 January 1887.
37   *Ibid.*
38   *Ibid.*
39   BOA, Yıldız Mütenevvî Mâruzât Evrâkı (Y MTV) 25/52, 1. lef. 6 Cemaziyelahir 1304/2 March 1887. The Turkish term "*akaid*" is a plural form of the Arabic *'aqidah*, meaning article of faith, tenet, doctrine, etc. In late Ottoman parlance, the term "*akaid*" was synonymous with the study of the principles of the Islamic faith (*akaid-i islâmiye*). Şemseddin Sami, *Kamus-u Türkî* (Dersaadet [Istanbul]: lkdam Matbaası, 1317 [1899–1900]), 944.
40   Y MTV. 25/52, 2. lef 6 Cemaziyelahir 1304/2 March 1887.
41   *Ibid.*
42   *Ibid.*
43   *Ibid.*
44   See Fortna, "Islamic Morality in Ottoman 'Secular' Schools", *International Journal of Middle East Studies* 32/3, August 2000, pp. 369–93.
45   See his contribution to the present volume.
46   See Fortna, *Imperial Classroom*. pp. 202 ff.

Chapter 17

Peter Stearns

GLOBALIZATION AND CHILDHOODS

TWO DEVELOPMENTS IN THE LATER twentieth century ushered in a new era of globalization – an era of intensifying contacts and interactions among societies literally around the world. The most obvious development, and with direct impact on children and youth, was technological: satellite TV broadcasts facilitated global communications, including networks such as MTV, crucial in dispensing at least a version of international youth culture; and in 1990 the introduction of the Internet created an unprecedented means of contact, which many young people seized upon in societies otherwise as different as the United States and Iran. The second development was political: the decision of first China, then Russia to open to new kinds of international contacts. The Cold War ended; multinational companies expanded their outreach amid growing inducements to create market-based economies.

Globalization was not an entirely new process, and historians debate the chronology. Important influences from inter-regional contacts had affected childhood in earlier periods. More intense connections in the later nineteenth century, including Western imperialism, reshaped childhood in many areas and many ways. For Japan, for example, decisions about relationships to the external world brought global forces to bear on childhood from 1868 onward. There is no question, however, that globalization accelerated in the twentieth century, and particularly in the final decades, with a new variety of impacts on childhood.

Contemporary globalization was not a simple process. It was not entirely new, even in its impact on youth and childhood. The global spread of key sports such as soccer and base-ball, as part of the spectator life and athletic aspirations of young people from Latin America to Asia, had begun in the late nineteenth century. Another complexity: globalization provoked new kinds of resistance, some of them winning allegiance among groups of young people. Some Muslims, for example, feared the impact of globalization on their traditions, seeing it as a new means of Western dominance. Many Latin Americans feared the impact of American consumer culture on their offspring. On another front, groups of young people in the West and the Pacific Rim openly worried about globalization's impact on labor conditions and the environment. It was not certain that globalization would triumph over the various oppositions. In the West and Pacific Rim, polls showed that young people were more favorable to globalization, overall, than older adults were, priding themselves in their tolerance and openness to new ideas; but in Latin America, Africa, and other parts of Asia, young people and adults agreed on a certain wariness. Third complexity: globalization's emphasis on increasing international contacts did not point in a single direction, and this was of great importance to childhood. Economic globalization, for example, worsened the work situation of some children; but political globalization – that is, the growing outreach of international government and nongovernment organizations – moved toward increased advocacy of children's rights.

Globalization did not assume command of childhood; major regional patterns persisted, and the earlier trends embodied in the modern model of childhood, already well under way, largely persisted. Key aspects of globalization actually provided new support for this model, as we will see. Nevertheless, globalization deserves separate consideration as a new force in the history of childhood, creating additional kinds of change and resistance in the later twentieth and early twenty-first centuries. Four facets of globalization had particular impacts: new patterns of migration; the efforts of international political groups to provide international standards for the treatment of children; economic globalization, or the growing involvement of almost all regions of the world in a common process of production, along with the retreat of state-sponsored economies; and cultural globalization, or the spread of global consumerism.

Migration, of course, was not new, and it had always had consequences for children. Immigrant children in the United States around 1900, for example, had often played a special role as intermediaries between parents, whose English was often uncertain, and the new society in which they worked and, often, went to school. It was a challenging but sometimes invigorating experience, though frequently confusing to parents. At the same time, prejudices often surfaced that found targets among immigrant children; job opportunities might be limited thanks to ethnic bias, and gang activities embodied tensions among many urban youth in immigrant neighborhoods.

Two aspects of migration in the later twentieth century, loosely associated with globalization, added to this mix, along with familiar elements. First, migration occurred over unusually long distances and involved people of very different cultures. Pakistanis and West Indians poured into Britain; Turks and North Africans created large Muslim minorities in France, Germany and the Netherlands; Filipinos and Palestinians flocked to the oil-rich Persian Gulf states; Latinos and Asians created new diversity in the United States. In this situation, children's role as buffers between parents and the new society became if anything more important, but also more demanding. Opportunities for generational clashes within the immigrant community could increase, around issues such as dating or female dress. Opportunities for expression of prejudice could expand as well. Many immigrant youth in Britain faced growing hostility, punctuated by outright violence and race riots; gang activity could form in response, as in the rise of Latino youth gangs on both coasts in the United States by the early twenty-first century, or the emergence of (Asian) Indian gangs on Canada's west coast. Several riots by Muslim youth in France broke out in the early twenty-first century, reflecting high levels of joblessness and discriminatory treatment by police. Different kinds of youth music, such as the reggae styles brought from the West Indies, but also the sometimes racist punk rock, expressed creativity but also obvious tension in this intermixture of groups of young people in urban settings.

The second innovation, for some immigrant youth, involved the growing possibility of return visits to the home country, thanks to relatively cheap air travel or other facilities; Indians and Pakistanis often went home for vacations, preserving ties to extended families, and often providing occasion for marriage arrangements for young people themselves. The opportunity for many youth to become "bicultural" in this situation, conversant with two cultures and comfortable in switching back and forth, increased. This could involve young people who did not migrate, but whose contacts with cousins who did provided familiarity with the habits of other societies. Here was an obvious spur to globalization, though not to a single cultural model.

Efforts of international organizations to assist children and reshape childhood had begun in the aftermath of World War I – a sign of political globalization and the growing force of humanitarian world opinion. A variety of groups distributed food and other aid to children displaced in the war, including children in former enemy nations. While this applied mainly to Europe, the principle of special international charity for children gained ground steadily. After World War II, this would blossom into further efforts for refugees and for children in poor countries. Private organizations such as the Save the Children Fund, and political bodies deriving from the United Nations, both solicited philanthropy and distributed funds and products. The needs of poor children regularly outpaced donations, but the aid was significant, as were the new principles involved.

In the 1920s, also, the new International Labor Office, affiliated with the League of Nations, began to pass resolutions against child labor up to age 15. The goal was to extend the criteria now common in industrial societies to the world at large. This effort also broadened out under the United Nations after World War II. A host of conferences and resolutions attacked excessive work, while urging the right of every child to an education. The United Nations drafted formal statements on children's rights (the Convention on Rights of the Child was issued in 1989), and most nations signed on, at least in principle: the main goals were promotion of health, avoidance of abuse, access to education, plus more standard rights such as freedom of religion and expression – a familiar roster, but now conceived in terms of a global approach. A key focus by the 1990s was an effort to ban executions of children and youth for crimes and virtually all societies in the world accepted this agreement, with the United States one of the only holdouts (until 2005). The World Health Organization worked hard to promote children's survival and wellbeing, and a number of improvements occurred under its auspices – from inoculations that largely defeated some traditional killers, like polio, to educational programs designed to improve maternal care of infants. In the late 1970s, world opinion, as well as international organizations, became actively involved in attacking the Nestlé company for distributing infant milk formulas to regions where unsanitary water and parental ignorance led to higher death rates than occurred with breastfeeding; after initially resisting the international campaign, the giant company dramatically revised its approach in the 1980s. Other United Nations programs worked actively to promote some form of population control, in the interests of economic stability and children's wellbeing alike: a major conference in 1996 agreed on this goal, despite tensions with religious authorities in the Islamic world and in the Catholic Church; greater education for women was particularly recommended as a means of reducing population pressure. Finally, a variety of United Nations and private agencies worked to spread the most up-to-date principles of education and childrearing, often distributing materials urging parents to pay attention to their children as individuals.

The commitment of large numbers of well intentioned people, primarily from the more affluent countries, to a global vision of children's rights, health, and economic protection was an important part of globalization more generally. The idea of children's rights was novel in any society, but the notion of international agreement was at least as dramatic. It could have important effects, even aside from the resounding proclamations. In 2003, for example, the United Arab Emirates banned the use of children as jockeys in camel races: they had long been favored because of their light weight, strapped to the great beasts despite obvious terror. Here was an established pattern that had to be rethought by a nation eager for growing international contacts and a successful world role. The United States was affected as well. A Supreme Court ruling in 2005 held that minors could not be subjected to capital punishment, an area where the United States had, for several decades, differed from almost every other country in the world; international legal standards were cited as a key basis for the decision. More generally, along with imitation of the modern model of childhood by individual governments, the global movement on behalf of children helps explain the steady (if quite varied) decline of the birth rate and, even more, the decline of infant and child mortality; the same applies to the steady reduction of child labor in the final decades of the twentieth century, and the consistent increase in the percentage of children receiving at least some education.

There were, however, important limitations on the range of global action for children. In the first place, open disagreement flared on certain issues. A campaign in 1973 to win global agreement on a ban on child labor under age 16 failed, because not enough countries would sign on. Several poor countries believed that their economies depended to an extent on cheap child labor, and that many poor families had the same need; countries such as the United States refused to sign as well, both because of reliance on child labor among migrant agricultural workers, and because of a general resistance to international infringement on national freedom of action. A replacement agreement in 1989 was important, but more modest: extreme abuse of child labor was now outlawed in principle, with particular focus on sexual exploitation, sale of children to pay family debts, and use of children in military forces. Most countries did sign this document. There were also disagreements about birth control, with the United States, from the 1980s onward, withholding funds from international agencies that distributed birth control devices or in any way countenanced abortion. Catholic and some Islamic opposition added to disputes on this issue.

In addition to disagreements, many international political measures fell short because the problems were too severe, or because individual regions simply ignored the principles involved – sometimes even when they had signed the international convention in order to seem up-to-date and civilized. Many countries signed documents on children's rights to schooling, but because of lack of resources and family dependence on child labor, many children were left with no educational access at all. Other international standards provoked outright disagreement locally. Conflicts over birth control might pit wives against husbands, doctors against priests; and while the birth rate did drop overall, with major reductions in Latin America and in China, high rates persisted in Africa and in many Islamic regions. A huge gap opened, as discussed in Chapter 11 [see original reading], between ringing international rights statements and the actual treatment of children in cases of war and civil conflict: rights workers strove to mitigate the effects of war, with occasional success, but clearly they could not keep pace with the magnitude of the problem. Global influences on children were undeniable, but there was hardly a single, effective global voice.

Trends in child labor showed some of the limits of global standards efforts, and the modern model itself, while ultimately providing evidence of impact as well. The issue bridged between global politics and global economies. By the later twentieth century, rates of child labor were falling almost everywhere, with schooling on the rise, which did not negate the fact that a large minority of children still worked in some places, often amid extensive exploitation. But the case of South and Southeast Asia was particularly challenging because the region not only failed fully to comply with international efforts to curb the use of child workers, but actually experienced rising rates in the 1990s, bucking the global trend outright. Clearly some comparative regional analysis was essential, for even by 2008 United Nations' reports showed that up to 44 million children aged 5–14 were at work in the region, and while some decline was reported by this point, it was noticeably slower than in other areas. Explanations varied, in comparison with other regions where poverty was as, or even more, extensive. For India, the persistence of large rural populations was surely a factor, compared with societies such as Latin America, where poor families are more urbanized. A related point was the lack of a fully available school system, and some government hesitancy in pushing school requirements. Literacy rate gains lagged in consequence, which might also explain the tenacity of commitments to child labor. Within South Asia as a whole, localities in particular economic distress, or disrupted by civil war, as was the case until recently in Sri Lanka, saw more child labor simply as a function of families trying to make ends meet. A persistent claim was the strength of the long-standing view that children are simply supposed to work, and that they are ready to work at a young age.

Yet regional distinctiveness, and the incomplete hold of global standards, was not the end of the story. By 2008, after some lag, the South Asia region did seem to be pulling into the global trend of replacing work with schooling, particularly once some modest improvements in prosperity began to register. India had 17–20 million children working in 1999, but the figure had dropped to 12.6 million by 2008, a dramatic reduction. Global influence and the sheer impact of a more modern economy had a real, if gradual, effect.

Economic globalization added greatly to the complexity. Not only levels of trade, but also basic systems of production, shifted with this central development. Multinational companies, based in the United States, Western Europe, or the Pacific Rim, began setting up production facilities wherever they could find favorable labor costs, environmental regulations, and useful resources and transportation systems. Complex products such as automobiles were assembled from parts made in Asia, the Americas, and Europe. For simpler items such as textiles, giant sales companies such as Gap or Nike usually hired subcontractors who ran the actual factories in places such as Indonesia, Vietnam, or Lesotho.

Labor conditions in the multinationals were not always good – they were seeking low-wage areas, and they often skimped on safety equipment, while requiring long hours. They employed relatively little child labor, however – only about 5 percent of the children working by the early twenty-first century were in any sense directly working in the global economy. Economic globalization's impacts were more indirect, but they were huge. There were two major pressures. In the first place, global production often displaced more traditional manufacturing, in which children and young people had been employed. Along with continued population growth in places such as Africa and the Middle East, this led to massive rates of youth unemployment – figures of 30 percent or more in the cities were not uncommon. This became a key source, in turn, of various forms of unrest among young people, including participation in extremist religious and political movements. The second result of economic globalization involved a steady retrenchment of social programs by governments in societies such as Brazil or India. The reigning philosophy argued for freer market economies, rather than government spending, and agencies such as the International Monetary Fund and the World Bank, as conditions for development loans, often pressed for smaller welfare programs as well. Eager to advance economic growth, and hoping that growth would yield ultimate benefits to the poorer classes, governments pressed ahead, with very few exceptions. Family assistance dropped as a result.

Patterns were complex. Despite the pressures of globalization, the percentages of children working continued to drop steadily, as we have seen, from 6 percent of the total workforce in 1950 to 3 percent in 1990 – or from 28 percent of children under the age of 14 in 1950 to 15 percent in 1990. The declines accelerated during the 1980s and thereafter. By 2004, 88 percent of all children of the relevant ages, around the world, were attending primary school. Globalization was not, in sum, reversing the movement toward the more modern model. Nor were some of the horror stories straightforward. An Indian social scientist commented on newspaper reports lamenting the long hours and close confinement of child workers in fishery industries along the coast; the children had been recruited from other areas, often disputing with their parents, who wanted them closer to home. Yet the children themselves found work entirely normal, and rejoiced that they had escaped far poorer conditions in their villages of origin. They were pleased, as well, that they could send a bit of money to their families. Exploitation? Definitely, by many standards. But the key problem was grinding poverty. Globalization contributed to harsh child labor mainly insofar as it failed to resolve, and in some cases surely worsened, the economic constraints faced by so many families in the developing world.

Global competition and the reduction of social programs had a very clear result: an increase in the number of children in poverty. This occurred even in industrial countries such as the United States, and it had massive results in Africa, South and Southeast Asia, and parts of Latin America. The number of children dependent on activities in the street – begging, prostitution, occasional unskilled labor, petty theft – increased in many places. Outright child labor went up for a time, as we have seen, in South and Southeast Asia – mainly in small production shops and other outlets where the cheapest possible labor was essential to stay afloat. The increase was 50 percent in the late 1990s in this huge region, not counting those in family employment in agriculture, defying the larger global trends. Even more widely, many poor families, pressed by debt, sold children into labor. Purchase of young women for the sex trade almost certainly increased, with some transported to centers of sexual tourism, such as Thailand, from original homes in Eastern Europe or elsewhere. Some families even sold body organs for transplants, with adolescents a particular target. Whatever its other benefits – and there were strong arguments in favor of its good overall results for rapidly-growing economies in places such as China and India – globalization dramatically worsened the struggle for survival for many children and their families.

Global consumerism was the final major facet of globalization, affecting values and behaviors alike, and quickly embracing many children. We have seen the increasing association of childhood with consumerism in the West and Japan; it was not surprising that the relationship spilled over into other societies. Lebanese teenagers, in the cities, began to attend Western movies fairly regularly in the 1920s and 1930s. Enthusiasm for baseball gained ground among Japanese and Latin American youth, and the passion for soccer spread still more widely, But the full explosion of global consumerism for children awaited the later twentieth century, with its new technologies and market opportunities. Young people began to patronize fast food restaurants, often to the dismay of their parents – which was, of course, one of the purposes of these new tastes, McDonald's and similar outlets became havens for youth in Korea, China, and elsewhere, a place to see and be seen, and often to indulge other interests such as dating and romantic love. Television shows such as *Sesame Street*, translated into most major languages, promoted new standards for children, and MTV and global rock tours offered a common youth musical language and generated literally global fan clubs. Dress for urban young people began to standardize in many places, often against adult and traditional patterns, usually around the ubiquitous blue jeans. Patronage of theme parks provided new standards for parents to demonstrate their economic success and love for their children in a single consumerist swoop: taking the kids to Orlando became a ritual for caring, successful Latin American parents. This was the context in which Disney figures and Barbie dolls became part of the global children's play kit. This was the context in which many Chinese youth stayed up until daybreak to watch a European soccer tournament half a world away. With some plausibility, certain observers began to contend that a global youth culture had come into being.

In 2000, a young American Peace Corps teacher was working in an eastern Russian village that had never seen an American before, and that had no computer or Internet connection. Despite their isolation, her students reported a very precise notion of who the most beautiful woman in the world was, and their choice was Britney Spears. In the same year an anthropologist, working in Madagascar on teenagers and youth in an urban slum, realized that her subjects had a very definite idea of the beauty products young women should seek: those that would make them look more like Britney Spears.

Around 2000 also, television reached some of the more remote Pacific Islands. Seeing the new images, many girls became discontented with their bodies and traditional standards of plumpness. Rates of anorexia and bulimia went up markedly.

Global consumerism for children favored relatively prosperous regions and families. By 2000, increases in childhood obesity began to be noticed among middle-class children in China and India, not just in the West. Sedentary occupations and leisure activities, along with food abundance, began to have global consequences. Youth parties in Iran or Pakistan that featured Western music, Western cigarettes, and Scotch whisky were clearly signs of elite status, even as they defied local religious customs. But relatively poor children were not entirely excluded, particularly in the cities. Their earnings might go in part to new consumer products – fashionable clothing and cosmetics, for example, for participants in the sex trade in Madagascar.

It is also vital to recognize that the global youth culture was not based entirely on Western sources. Japan and a few other countries became creative centers as well, based on trends that, as we have seen, began as early as the 1920s. Japan gained worldwide prominence in promoting cute images and products for young children, playing on, but also spurring, a new conception of infancy: the craze for the Hello Kitty series was one manifestation. During the 1990s, a global passion for the Pokémon characters was another sign of Japanese influence. Japan also began to take the lead in various styles and products for youth cool, and cool exports topped Japan's list, in terms of earnings, by 2003. Japanese styles provided leading models of youth culture for East Asia and even around the Middle East. Japanese animation and electronic devices for young people figured prominently around the world. *Wired* magazine began to feature products adopted by young Japanese women as harbingers of larger global trends.

Youth consumerism was not as homogeneous as many people imagined, even when it clearly caught on. A passion for American rap music meant something different to young people whose command of English was limited. Playing with Japanese games or toys – some of the fads like Pokémon had roots in specific Japanese culture that did not travel readily – offered different meanings as well, depending on context. This kind of blending is a common result of new cultural contacts, and it certainly limited an ability to define a single youth culture.

Efforts to blend did not always work, of course. By the early twenty-first century, as cities and consumer opportunities grew in some parts of Africa, parents were offered opportunities to buy strollers for their infants, an obvious translation of global standards. But much resistance developed because of longstanding African traditions of carrying infants close, even while working. Mothers were reluctant to abandon a valued contact, and one that could benefit the child's emotional development. In Kerala, a state in southern India, conservatives tried to adapt the growing enthusiasm for beauty pageants among teenage girls. Their solution: a pageant in which contestants would demonstrate their knowledge of the local language and cultural styles, including dance. The problem: the types of young women interested in participating in the pageants had inadequate grasp of customary lore, while most traditional girls still shunned the pageants. It was hard to find a real winner, and the effort at combining failed, at least in the short term.

There were, however, some shared features. From global consumerism, youth and, to a lesser extent, children in many regions gained a sense of separate identity and belonging. A young man in Hong Kong, asked why he patronized McDonald's, noted that he actually didn't like the food much, compared with Chinese fare, but he gloried in seeing and being seen in such a cosmopolitan place. Clearly, new styles gave young people an alternative to accepting full parental control; consumerism in this sense could be a real weapon in a quiet power struggle in which the balance shifted toward youth. Children often had an unprecedented edge in leading larger societies, including adult family members, toward greater consumer familiarity and competence (including computer literacy), a dramatic new role. At the same time, consumerism also affected adults' conceptions of childhood and their responsibilities as parents. At some point in the later twentieth century, parents in most places began to believe that providing goods and good times for kids was a vital part of their role, and experienced real guilt when their capacity seemed inadequate. There are hosts of symbolic and practical examples. By the 1980s, many Mexican parents began to convert to American-style Halloween, complete with candy for the kids, in contrast to the solemn religious festival that had long marked the celebration; parents in Istanbul began to buy Christmas presents for their children even though they were not Christian; and the Muslim holiday of Ramadan, a time of renunciation, began to alter through the purchase of gifts and cards for the young ones. Few institutions involving children could totally resist global consumerism, aside from the starkest poverty or the most remote rural locations.

Globalization by the early twenty-first century did not include actual global youth movements directed toward protest or agitation. During the late 1960s and early 1970s, ironically just before full-bore globalization, a hint of an international youth protest movement did emerge. Based particularly in Western Europe and the United States, but with some echoes in Eastern Europe and elsewhere, student risings attacked the Vietnam war, racism, the constraints of crowded schools and lack of mobility, and the trappings of consumer society that, the most vocal leaders felt, had snared their parents in superficial, meaningless lives. Student groups seized schools and, in Paris in 1968, mounted a near-revolution that gave them control of parts of the city for a time. Many observers contended that youth would replace the working class as the source of contemporary unrest, as the bearers of a humane conscience.

The prediction proved untrue. Western youth protest trailed off after 1973, though a few violent groups persisted in Europe for another decade. The passing of the baby boom reduced school crowding; some reforms in university programs were introduced; and consumerism proved more attractive than repulsive to most young people. We have seen that young people often joined in unrest by the outset of the twenty-first century, but it was most commonly under regional banners, including religious movements, rather than global ones. Many young people did support global human rights campaigns, and even more were drawn to environmental causes, though participation came disproportionately from the industrial countries. Different traditions and circumstances, as well as different degrees of attraction to aspects of globalization, divided the world's youth, even as it experienced some common influences.

Globalization itself was divisive, as we have seen. Relatively affluent children, participating in new forms of consumerism, differed greatly from the children newly pressed into work roles in India or the street-savvy kids in Rio de Janeiro, even though they, too, might aspire to some consumer lures. Teenage skinheads in Britain or Germany, who fomented violence against racial minorities, shared with immigrant youth an interest in youth-based musical styles, but the styles clashed just as the gangs did, and there was no uniform result. And for many children and adults alike, globalization influenced, but did not transcend, local traditions of childhood. Lebanese parents might seek a Western-style education for their kids, and read a few modern childrearing manuals, but they did not really want their children to accept Western levels of individualism over more traditional family obligations. The worlds of children remained diverse.

Globalization also had a complex relationship with the modern model of childhood, quite apart from the fact that its influence was incomplete in many areas. New streams of migration introduced more families to schooling and much of the other apparatus of modern childhood, though racism and unequal opportunities might limit the effect for some. Political globalization worked unambiguously toward the modern model: the international agencies wanted better health, lower birth rates, legal protections for children, less or no work, and heightened access to schooling. Unfortunately, of all the strands of globalization, the political arm was weakest in terms of actual impact. And economic globalization, in its results for many children, reduced the availability of the modern model for children in the streets or those formally employed, making it harder to win much time for schooling and, in some cases, complicating health conditions as well. Consumerism, finally, was compatible with the modern model for those children who saw consumerism as a source of pleasure along with schooling; it could have some individualistic implications compatible with the modern model as well, and it also promoted other modern features such as peer groups and age-graded activities. But consumerism could also distract from schooling and might prove irrelevant to the central features of the modern model.

Some observers argued, in fact, that globalization was setting the framework for childhood in many parts of Africa, at the expense of the modern model. Growing unemployment made many youth more marginal and reduced the relevance of schooling. Youth who could earn money, such as female prostitutes serving wealthy clients, often devoted their profits to consumerism, which did not, however, reverse their marginalization in the wider society. Youth in these circumstances did not emerge as a protected category with education its primary ultimate function. Marginalization was not a pattern that embraced all Africans, as eagerness for education persisted, with more aspirants for secondary schooling than there were places available; and the zeal for education often related to a commitment to reduce birth rates as well — in other words, the modern model in an African incarnation. But for many, in Africa and elsewhere, globalization could distract from the modern model or undermine it outright, generating a new set of factors at the dawn of the twenty-first century.

Finally, and more predictably, globalization could also encourage resistance in the name of tradition. Many young people rallied to threatened regional identities, even as they participated in some aspects of globalization. Many young women in the Middle East, for example, voluntarily returned to more traditional styles of dress around 2000, as a means of asserting their independence from foreign-dominated globalization and pressures for greater homogeneity.

Globalization, in sum, was a real force, adding to the factors prompting change in childhood in the years around 2000. Combining with the longstanding push toward the modern model in some cases, creating some additional common influences, globalization did not erase forms of diversity both old and new. The global village embraced many different types of childhood.

PART 3

Children's experiences

THE GLOBAL HISTORY OF CHILDHOOD IS generally concerned with how adults think about children and what institutions adults develop to shape children's lives. It is also concerned with how children create and understand their own lives. Part 3 of this volume focuses on the actual experiences and feelings of being a child. In a retrospective article about some of the challenges facing the field of the history of childhood, historians Joseph M. Hawes and N. Ray Hiner warn that the focus of study must not drift away from children to adults. They compare this drift to the risk of African-American studies moving to whiteness and women's studies to masculinity.[1] Scholars of traditionally marginalized groups sometimes run the risk of focusing too much on the oppressor or powerholder, as opposed to the oppressed or powerless.

A body of theoretical literature on the bottom-up approach to writing children's history does not yet exist.[2] To write history from the "bottom up" means to write history from the perspective of the ordinary person, instead of from the perspective of institutions and "great men." Historians of childhood build on analytical frameworks from fields like subaltern studies and social history, particularly labor history and the history of everyday life. These fields make the point that we need to look at history not through the lenses of the power-holders and elite but through the lenses of the masses and people ranked lower in societies due to their race, class or sex. Historians of childhood add age to that equation. Children are traditionally subject to decisions made for them by adults.[3] Historians who adopt a hierarchal approach of prioritizing the adult's perspective over the child's do not depict a wholly accurate representation of history. Children are living, breathing agents in history, and not passive, invisible, pitiful subjects.

Changing the perspective of writing history from the eyes of an adult to the eyes of a child enriches our knowledge of the history of childhood in four ways. First, it adds nuances to our historical awareness of children. Second, we learn that exceptions abound in generalizations. Third, theory does not always coincide with practice. Fourth, emotions, not just economics and politics, are driving historical forces, and, complexity can be found in the mundane. The authors in Part 3 of this Reader capture the voice of the child in various historical case studies. The difficulties to finding sources that privilege the perspective of the child were discussed in Part 1.

There is not a one-size-fits-all explanation of historical events. Nowhere could this be truer than in the history of childhood during the era of colonialism. The time between the fifteenth and twentieth centuries, when people from Europe developed colonies in other lands, wrought havoc on the lives of many indigenous children worldwide. Westerners gained control of land by trying to eliminate, culturally, economically, politically, and sometimes literally, the next generation of indigenous inhabitants. This resulted in the mass marginalization of many indigenous children in places like Africa, Latin America, the Middle East, Asia, and North America; however, the impact was not always the same both within and between these regions. Colonialism negatively impacted the type of schooling many indigenous children in colonies received in comparison to their pre-colonial past and in comparison to their white counter-parts. There was also a difference in the amount and quality of education offered to children of elite indigenous families versus low class.

In "A Most Remarkable Phenomenon," Juliet Pollard looks at the experiences of mixed race fur traders' children in the Pacific Northwest and finds that exceptions abound in gener-alizations about the impact of imperialism on this group of children. These children were the offspring of white people and indigenous people. While fur traders' children faced racial and cultural discrimination, Pollard argues that there was not one resulting life course that these children followed. The children ended up in every rung of society from the highest political class and down. The children grew up to fight the prejudice they faced and did not always succumb to stereotypes of them. This does not mean that those children did not suffer. We cannot always apply our modern-day assumptions about injustice in the past to assume that colonialism had a monolithic impact on society. Hardships that may seem extreme to us may have been taken for granted by some children.

Historical theory does not always coincide with history in practice. Historians often present the late nineteenth century and early twentieth century as the time in which abstract Romantic notions of the innocent, dependent child solidified through new government laws and policy towards mandatory and free schooling. The impact of these reforms was not evenly experienced in Europe. Anna Davin's book *Growing Up Poor* looks at how poverty manifest itself realistically in London childrens' lives between 1870 and 1914. She reveals that reform played out differently for girls than boys, as well as across the classes. By looking at the reality of slum-life poverty in British children's lives, she finds that authorities were more likely to overlook a girl's time out of school than a boy's. She uncovers a gender double standard in European reforms to help children in need. There was an uneven impact of policies relating to mandatory schooling and decrease in work hours.

Most historians focus on institutional, political, and economic forces that drive the history of childhood. However, by looking at the experience of children in history, we can gain insight into the emotions that drive the changes in children's lives over time.[4] Catriona Kelly's article "Thank You for the Wonderful Book" provides an example of this. Kelly questions the assump-tion that under Soviet power, the state managed and controlled children's reading. While the state made every effort to turn children into their prototype of nationalist discourse, Kelly uses oral history and letters written by children to reveal that children's response to the texts were diverse. Kelly's article explores how personal reactions to large historical forces help drive the life course of children in society. People respond as individuals to the world around them, despite monopolizing political forces.

The routine nature of children's daily life can lead some historians to view children as a nameless block not worthy of historical research. Looking at history from the eyes of the child, however, reveals that children's lives were anything but mundane. Complexity abounds in the everyday. The selection from Jane Humphries' *Childhood and Child Labour in the British Industrial Revolution* illustrates this idea. Humphries looks at children's roles in the industrial revolution through the lens of more than 600 working-class autobiographies. In analyzing what these children had to say about their relationships with parents and siblings, she discovers that the causes behind children's participation in the workforce were not as simple as previous historians have documented. What went on inside the private realm of the home, such as fatherlessness and sibling rivalry, affected children's fate, as did the inter-workings of the national economy (such as the movement of raw materials and the delivering of goods to final consumers). By investigating family dynamics and the daily lives of working-class and poor children, Humphries uncovers new causes behind child labor during the industrial revolution.

Due to various cultural forces and children's relative economic helplessness, children historically have found themselves in a position of dependence and subordination to adults. This does not mean that children do not impact their surroundings. By looking at children's history from the bottom up, the historian debunks the idea that only adults make history. As the examples in Part 3 show, children were not always victims, but participated in their own making, decisions impacting them, and the construction of the society around them.

Articles

18. Pollard, Juliet. "A Most Remarkable Phenomenon: Growing Up Métis: Fur Traders' Children in the Pacific Northwest" in *Histories of Canadian Children and Youth* edited by Nancy Janovicek and Joy Parr (UK: Oxford University Press, 2003), pp 57–70.

Exceptions abound in generalizations

- Explain the various life experiences of mixed-race fur traders' children.
- Does the author effectively convince you that mixed-race children were not victims? Why or why not?

19. Davin, Anna. *Growing Up Poor: Home, Street, and School in London 1870–1914.* Rivers Oram Press, 1997, pp 97–111.

Theory does not always coincide with practice

- Who watched younger children when mothers worked? Why?
- What impact did being a girl have on her education?
- In what ways did school fulfill different uses for children?

20. Kelly, Catriona. "Thank You for the Wonderful Book: Soviet Child Readers and the Management of Children's Reading, 1950–75" in *Kritika* (Vol. 6, No. 4, Fall 2005), pp 717–53.

Emotions, not just economics and politics, are driving historical forces

- What sources does the author use to access the voice of the child?
- Explain with examples what the author means when she writes, "But teaching children about reading was not left purely to parents" (page 272).
- What does the author claim about readers' responses to texts?

21.   Humphries, Jane. *Childhood and Child Labour in the British Industrial Revolution.*
London: Cambridge University Press, 2010, pp 172–209.

Complexity can be found in the mundane

● What aspects of home life and family life impacted children's fate?
● What evidence do autobiographies of childhood bring to bear on patterns of child labor
during the industrial revolution?

Suggestions for further reading

Ambaras, D. (2006) *Bad Youth: Juvenile Delinquency and the Politics of Everyday Life in
Modern Japan*, Berkeley, CA: University of California Press

Chen, D. (2004) *China's Son: Growing Up in the Culture Revolution*, New York: Random
House

Fonseca, C. (2002) Inequality Near and Far: Adoption as Seen from the Brazilian Favelas,
Law & Society Review, 36 (2), pp.397–431

Gardiner, J. (2005) *The Children's War: The Second World War Through the Eyes of the
Children of Britain*, London: Portrait

Glasser, C. (2000) *Bo-Tsotsi: The Youth Gangs of Soweto, 1935–1976*, Portsmouth, NH:
Heinemann

Hecht, T. (1998) *At Home in the Street: Street Children of Northeast Brazil*, Cambridge:
Cambridge University Press

Jiang, J. (2008) *Red Scarf Girl: A Memoir of the Cultural Revolution*, New York: HarperCollins

Jiang, Y. and Ashler, D. (2000) *Mao's Children in the New China: Voices From the Red Guard
Generation*, London: Routledge

Niu-Niu (1995) *No Tears for Mao: Growing Up in the Cultural Revolution*, Chicago, IL:
Academy Chicago Publishers

Saari, J. (1990) *Legacies of Childhood: Growing up Chinese in a Time of Crisis, 1890–1920*,
Cambridge, MA: Harvard University Press

Stargardt, N. (2006) *Witnesses of War: Children's Lives Under the Nazis*, New York: Alfred
A. Knopf

Steedman, C. (1980) The Tidy House, *Feminist Review*, 6 (1), pp.1–24

Van Emden, R. (2007) *Boy Soldiers of the Great War: Their Own Stories for the First Time*,
London: Headline

Ward, C. (1978) *The Child in the City*, New York: Pantheon Books

Notes

1   Hawes, J. and Hiner, N. (2008) Hidden in Plain View: The History of Children (and
Childhood) in the Twenty-First Century, *Journal of the History of Childhood and Youth*, 1
(1), pp.43–49.

2   The challenges adults have in placing themselves in the shoes of a child are discussed in *New
Formations: The Ruins of Childhood*, (42), a special issue in 2001 (London: Lawrence &
Wishart). The editors write, for example, that it is difficult at times for adults to even see
themselves as once being children: "It is unusually self-evidently difficult for adults to
'believe' that they were once babies, which is in itself uncanny; but one's own childhood, in
which one acquired and developed a capacity for representation, can seem more like a dream
than a documentary . . . It is thought there is a childhood, but not for us; that much of our

so-called childhood was the experience of our parents, of the adults who looked after us" (p.16).

3   One could argue that most people, regardless of age, are subject to the decisions made for them by others. In the case of children, however, the powerlessness comes primarily because of their age.

4   In light of the theme of Part 3 of this Reader, the selected reading for this example focuses on the emotions of the child him/herself. There are other books that look at the role that the emotions of the parents have in shaping the history of childhood. For example, Lydia Murdoch's *Imagined Orphans* (New Brunswick, NJ: Rutgers University Press, 2006) puts in to question the assumption that poor parents in late-nineteenth century England were indifferent to the fate of their children at the hands of state-sponsored separation programs.

Chapter 18

Juliet Pollard

A MOST REMARKABLE PHENOMENON: GROWING UP MÉTIS: FUR TRADERS' CHILDREN IN THE PACIFIC NORTHWEST

THROUGHOUT THE NINETEENTH CENTURY fur trade children were 'guinea pigs' for scientific theories and speculations about species and races.[1] By the late 1870s 'scientists' working in the new field of anthropology travelled the Northwest under the auspices of such agencies as the Smithsonian Institution studying native and Indian–white mixed blood populations.[2] One member of this new school of 'science', Dr Victor Harvard, reported in 1879 that there were 32,921 mixed-bloods sprinkled in communities on both sides of the border stretching from the Great Lakes to the Pacific Ocean and he determined that the best name that could be applied to the French, and non-French mixed-bloods who associated with them, was the old French term, Métis.[3] He was aware that this word was traceable from the Spanish, 'mestizo', meaning mongrel, but like many of his colleagues whose views were heavily imbued with Darwinian concepts of race, this was not a racist slur, but a recognition of the mixed-bloods' position in the evolutionary scheme of mankind.[4]

The 'scientific' recognition of the Métis identified not only a new people, but also a new culture. While some attempts were made to describe the culture, more concern was given to the effects of inter-racial breeding. The British Association for the Advancement of Science instructed its investigative committee:

> Especial importance attaches to the examination of mixed races . . . the resemblances and differences between the offspring and the parent stock, the number of generations during which inherited race characteristics are distinguishable, and the tendency to revert to one or other of the ancestral types.[5]

It was generally held that hybrids approximated the lifestyle of one or other of their progenitors. Nevertheless, it was noted that between these two extremes of half-breeds who lived as whites, and those who lived as Indians, there was a large middle group of intermarried mixed-bloods who as 'the true representative of race' were especially noticeable in the territory of the Hudson's Bay Company where they assumed the status of independent tribes of farming-hunters, distinct in 'manner, habit and allegiance' from Indians and whites.[6] This 'most remarkable phenomena', [sic] as ethnologist Daniel Wilson termed it, might also be regarded as a huge educational process whereby fur trade youngsters acquired a value system and lifestyle uniquely their own.[7]

One Hudson's Bay Company area where Métis culture flourished in the first half of the nineteenth century was the Pacific Northwest. Close to present day Portland, Oregon, stood Fort Vancouver, headquarters for the region and gateway to the Willamette River Valley where retired company servants and American mountain men farmed and supplemented their incomes as free trappers and traders. By the time the fort was established in 1824, mixed-blood children, fathered by men of John Jacob Astor's abortive fur enterprise in the region, and later, Nor-Westers, many of whom were themselves mixed-blood, had rooted Métis families in the region.[8] The uniqueness of this culture arose from the intermarriage of traders with women whose native cultures were considerably different from Indian wives east of the Rocky Mountains, and in the politics of joint occupation with its mingling of American and British traders, and its mixture of paternalism, as practised by the Hudson's Bay Company, and individualism, as characteristic of the American fur trade.[9]

School began at Fort Vancouver in November 1832. During that month the first five students—David McLoughlin, Billy McKay, Ranald MacDonald, Louis Labonte, and Andrew Dominique Pambrun—were gathered in the cramped chambers of a New Hampshire school-master for their first taste of formal education.[10] By 1838, the school had its own building and an enrolment of 60 pupils between the ages of five and fourteen.[11] Education was no longer restricted to employees' sons but embraced all the girls and boys of school age living in the vicinity of the fort, as well as some pupils that boarded. The school was free, non-denominational, and appears to have been compulsory. The children's lessons were drawn from texts current in English and American classrooms of the time.[12]

With the exception of Louis Labonte, the son of a Hudson's Bay Company servant, the boys in the first class went on to more advanced education in eastern United States, Great Britain, or Red River. All returned home to what had become Oregon Territory. David McLoughlin was general manager of his father's milling operations in Oregon City.[13] Billy McKay, by then Doctor McKay, clerked and practised medicine.[14] Ranald MacDonald settled at old Fort Colville after teaching English in Japan before US relations were established with that country.[15] Louis Labonte worked for the Hudson's Bay Company, farmed and trapped.[16] Andrew Pambrun was variously a schoolmaster, businessman, and farmer.[17]

Judged by the 'white values' which came to dominate the region, these boys achieved varying degrees of success, but if that is the only criterion used then the more important values in these boys' lives are lost. For these first schoolboys in the Pacific Northwest were all desig-nated 'half-breed' by the incoming white society, even though Pambrun and McLoughlin were more white than native, McKay more native than white, and only MacDonald and Labonte could claim equal heritage from Indian and white parentage.[18] While their histories reveal an ability to make their way in white society, these boys increasingly rejected the opportunity to be identified as 'white' as they reached middle and old age. Although they would be closely associ-ated with native peoples at various times, two of them living out their lives on Indian reserva-tions, they did not consider themselves Indian.[19] The bonds which tied these boys and many other fur trade children together went far beyond being collectively labelled 'half-breeds'. Their identities were rooted in their childhood nurturing in the Métis culture which developed in the region. They shared in youth, as they would in old age, a Métis consciousness that tran-scended the class structure of the Hudson's Bay Company and the ethnic heritage of their parents—a sense of self that was neither white nor Indian.[20]

Children in the fur trade culture might struggle for existence from the time of their conception to their birth. Some were unwanted. Wives were an asset, children were a liability.[21] Wives provided sexual satisfaction and companionship, performed a wide range of domestic tasks, and furthered trade ties with native peoples.[22] In the wider Euro-American society where pregnancies were often also unwanted, children could be a source of labour on farms or of income in factories.[23] In the all-encompassing organization of the Hudson's Bay Company, however, where there was full employment and job security, where food, shelter, and clothing were largely provided, children had little economic value. According to Company policy, traders who fathered children had to 'make such provision for the same as circumstances called for and their means permit'.[24]

To the 200 native wives living at Fort Vancouver by the late 1830s, pregnancy could have more immediate concerns. The great variety of natural childbirth methods which served well among the thirty-eight different cultures they represented were not always as successful when the father was white or part-white.[25] The mixed-blood baby could be larger, labour could be prolonged, and the possibility of death of mother and/or child could be greater. When increased massage, the use of a girdle, and other external remedies did not work, the labouring woman was left to her fate.[26] One doctor wrote:

> We find abortion quite frequent; some tribes have a reason for it, on account of the difficult labour which endangers the life of the woman bearing a half-breed child, which is usually so large as to make its passage through the pelvis of the Indian mother almost an impossibility.[27]

During childbirth, fur trade wives were sometimes assisted by their husbands as was customary among some native people, women on the American frontier, and in rural areas in Great Britain.[28] When difficulties arose, however, fort doctors might attend and use their crude forceps as best they could.[29] At that time, caesarian sections were not yet performed, but a craniotomy, whereby a crochet hook was inserted, the skull perforated, the brain drained, and the dead fetus removed, may have been performed when the baby was regarded as too large for the mother to deliver.[30]

Compounding economic and childbirth considerations, the genetic inheritance of the child was not without meaning to expectant fur trade parents. Some wives came from tribes which held strong beliefs about racial purity and disapproved of or disowned women who engaged in inter-racial unions.[31] Such views equated with those of the traders who generally concurred in the widely held notion that character and culture were quite literally carried in the blood. The educated gentlemen of the Company were also familiar with the arguments of polygenists who contended half-breeds were 'faulty stock', and the pre-Darwinian evolutionary concepts of phrenologists who postulated, among other ideas, that intermarriage with inferior people would lead to long-term effects on character and hinder mental progress.[32]

When a child was born, however, maternal and paternal feelings appear to have superseded other considerations. Infanticide, the result of cultural confrontation between Chinook mothers who wished to flatten their child's skull, rather than have an 'ugly baby' ranked as a slave, and trade fathers who refused to allow their wives this liberty, had largely ended with the ascendancy of the Hudson's Bay Company in the region.[33] Parental views about race, however, were never fully eradicated. The child, more indulged than abused, was treated differently than the wholly Indian or white child.

In contrast to attitudes in both Euro-American and native cultures, girls appear to have been the preferred sex. In the absence of white women, mixed-blood daughters were the most desirable marriage partners. Females became a strategic resource, symbolizing property and status being joined together. They were the pride of their gentlemen fathers, who, in a kind of 'Eliza Dolittle' fashion, attempted to mold them into what they thought a lady should be. Through carefully arranged marriages with incoming gentlemen traders, these daughters assured continuation of family wealth and power in the region. The fort, if not quite a female prison, secluded officers' daughters from inter-class entanglements with seekers of status and power and from possible liaisons with Indian males. Increasingly, the virtues of modesty and chastity were stressed.[34] Eloise McLoughlin, daughter of the Chief Factor, noted in her recollections of girlhood at the fort:

> We lived separate and private entirely. Gentlemen who came to trade never saw the family. The first Americans we saw were a very strange sight . . . When the missionaries [sic] ladies came . . . we mingled more.[35]

Since every daughter represented a possible marital alliance, daughters of company servants could gain upward social mobility by marrying a gentleman or his son thus breaking the rigid rank and class structure of the company and linking fur trade families in tighter and tighter familial relationships over time.[36] As the 'trappings of civilization' expanded with the coming of missionaries and white settlers, the 'tutored' daughter could, and often did, replace the 'untutored' mother in 'white' social settings. While native mothers were respected and retained a large measure of their native lifestyles, daughters who were Christianized and educated were accepted as white women with Indian blood.[37]

Such thinking was seldom extended to their brothers who were generally regarded as Indians with white blood. With sons, gentlemen traders were less able to reconcile their racial biases with their paternal feelings. They might view their sons as heirs, but usually provided for all their children in equal proportions in their wills.[38] They loved their sons as they did their daughters, but the nub of their mental dilemma was their inability to see their sons as their 'second chance' as they might have done in their native lands.[39] Since they were 'white' and therefore, 'inherently superior', their sons as part-Indian were 'inherently inferior' and would be unable to surpass them in intellect or vocation. They held out little chance that they would be able to enter the 'white world' through marriage as their sisters were able to do. At best, they hoped their sons could receive a good education, preferably abroad, marry fur trade daughters of equal social standing and that positions could be secured for them with the company or through friends and relatives. Ranald MacDonald's father reflected this view about sons when he wrote a fellow parent:

> Much better to dream of less for them . . . and to endeavour to bring them up in habits of industry, economy and morality, than to aspire to all this visionary greatness for them. All the wealth of Rupert's Land will not make a half-breed either a good person, a shining lawyer, or an able physician, if left to his own discretion while young.[40]

Fathers cultivated 'macho' masculinity in their sons, but feared they would 'go Indian'. They did not want their boys stirring up Indian troubles or disrupting the fur trade. To avert such possibilities, David McLoughlin's father, Chief Factor Dr John McLoughlin opposed the company policy and established the retired servants' settlement in the Willamette. He wrote: 'As half-breeds are in general leaders among Indians, and they would be a thorn in the side of whites, I insisted they should go to the Willamette, where their children could be brought up as whites and Christians.'[41]

Both mixed-blood servants, who identified themselves as French or Canadians, and white gentlemen traders oriented their sons in varying degrees towards a 'white world'. The gentlemen strove the hardest to retain their Euro-American cultural heritage and pass it on to their mixed-blood youngsters by attempting to raise them as white. The servants, who were no less concerned with the preservation of their Quebec traditions, were more flexible in adopting native customs and allowing their children freer association with native peoples. Both classes sought to eradicate or curb their sons' 'Indian dispositions' through education.

Religion was given a prominent place in the process. 'The Canadians', wrote Father Blanchet, 'had not forgotten their religion.' They petitioned the Bishop of Montreal for a priest each year from 1834 to 1836. 'Our children', they wrote in their 1836 petition, 'are learning very fast which makes us very eager for your assistance.'[42]

By the time Catholic clergy arrived one year later, American Methodists were established in the Willamette, American Presbyterians were in the Walla Walla–Spokane area, and a lone English Anglican priest was about to disembark to minister at Fort Vancouver. Teachers at the fort school were drawn from the missionaries and it followed that classes were generously steeped in religion. Here the students were not only encouraged to digest an education befitting 'white' Euro-American youths, but they were also required to absorb agricultural training of the type used in mission schools to 'civilize and Christianize' native peoples. The mission school approach covered all possibilities. If sons showed promise they could be sent abroad for further education, but if they weren't capable of educational advancement, as judged by teacher and father, then digging in the fort garden every afternoon, it was believed, would serve them best in later life.[43]

Even in households where 'race' was never mentioned, Métis children soon learned they were regarded as inferior people. American missionaries who taught the children were the first to write Home Boards encouraging white immigration as a means of keeping the half-breed 'descendants of the Hudson's Bay Company' from achieving ascendancy in Oregon.[44] Textbooks like William Mavor's *The Elements of Natural History* first published in 1808, but still used in the fort classrooms in the 1840s, claimed that native peoples were 'diminutive and ill shaped, their aspects as forbidding as their manners are barbarous . . .'[45] In short, concepts of white superiority based on so-called scientific evidence were strengthened with each passing decade as the children grew. The immigrants had come in search of upward social mobility, but when they reached Oregon the established Métis population were the 'haves'—they were the 'have nots'. The newcomers had much to say about equality, but recognized a 'natural superiority' among men.

Against this backdrop, children acquired much of their value systems in the larger classroom of the fur trade itself. Contrary to popular belief that fur trade families were large, population figures for the servants' village outside Fort Vancouver indicate that the majority of families had only one child and few had more than two.[46] Even though families appear to have been small, there was also a chronic shortage of housing and extended households and multi-family living arrangements were the norm. Under such circumstances the only child was seldom the only child in the household. In addition, many Chinook-speaking wives who made up the largest proportion of women in the village retained their slaves after marriage and their numbers swelled the ranks of the household.[47] Single male boarders and visiting relatives of the wives were also common in fur trade homes. Although the practice was dying out, a child might be raised in a household where his father had more than one wife. A visitor to the Willamette settlement recalls:

> I boarded the first three months at J.B. Desportes, a halfbreed, whose family consisted of two wives, besides one absent, by all, seven children, four or five slaves and two or three hired Indians, besides cats and dogs without number. All inhabited one room in common.[48]

As the children grew, they increasingly came under the care of others. Accidents shortened the lives of fathers and many mothers died before they were forty. Remarriage made common child rearing with step-parents, half-brothers, and -sisters. Orphans were assigned to families for care.[49] Under such conditions the Euro-American middle-class concept of personal privacy had little meaning. The lifestyle tended to be co-operative, rather than competitive.

Communal living which required the acquisition of tolerance and compromise at an early age, became, in modified form, the preferred way of living for many of the children in adult life.[50]

Families were transient moving in and out of cramped quarters and from fort to fort or on fur trade brigades depending on the work assignment of the father. Children born at Fort Vancouver could expect to be living in a new environment by the time they reached their fourth birthday.[51] Gentlemen continued to teach their children wherever they were stationed, whereas servants' children, if they received any formal education, did so in haphazard fashion.[52] Their world, like that of their parents who were mainly illiterate, relied heavily on memory retention and oral presentation.[53]

On any given day the children at Fort Vancouver could expect to hear thirty or forty distinct languages being spoken. French was the lingua franca of the fort, but English was used for business. There were at least thirty native languages including that spoken by the Kanakas, Hawaiian Islanders who laboured for the Company, as well as Gaelic, the tongue of some fathers. Such diversity promoted the development of Chinook Jargon, a composite of languages which permitted communications between the fur trade population and their Indian trading partners. The jargon bridged national, ethnic, and racial differences of parents and gave their offspring a new language unique to the Métis culture in the Pacific Northwest.[54]

The fort school was taught in English. In the classroom, 'the scholars came in talking in their respective languages . . . Cree, Nez Perces, Chinook, etc., etc.,'—language indicative of the bonding between mother and child during infancy.[55] Children were breast fed on demand and were therefore the constant companions of their mothers who carried them in cradle boards on the horn of their saddles or in baskets slung on the side of their horses while travelling.[56] When weaned at age two or three, they would be securely tied to their own horses or ponies and would begin to acquire the equestrian skills Pacific Métis were famous for.[57] About this time fathers appear to have played an increasing role in their children's lives. From their mothers they learned to be consumers of the natural environment; from their fathers they learned the economics and technology of the fur trade, agriculture, and other Company enterprises. The school moved the child from the mother's culture where discipline was by shaming and learning by imitating, to their father's where 'spare the rod and spoil the child' was a concept applied to both discipline and learning.[58] The children grew up aware of both Indian and white values and were able to harmonize both systems in their own lifestyle.

In this culturation process, Fort Vancouver, the major institution of social organization and industry, was important. Within were the school, church, hospital, tradesmen's shops, and retail outlet; without, the dairy, ranch, and 1,000 acres under cultivation. The latter furnished a diet superior to other working class peoples, while the former provided care for the population from the cradle to the grave.[59] A bell, used like a factory whistle, punctuated the day into blocks of time for specific tasks. The workday began when the bell rang at 5 a.m. At 8 o'clock the bell signalled breakfast. Two one-half hour breaks for smoking clay pipes and an hour for mid-day dinner, noted by the bell, broke the remaining 9 to 6 p.m. day, five days a week. On Sunday the bell announced Sunday school and church services. Evenings were regulated by curfew.[60] The rhythm of the fort and the school, which stressed punctuality and regularity, taught the children time-thrift habits. The beating of furs, helping in the gardens, and other chores led the youngsters into the work-cycle. Full initiation into the routine of their parents took place around puberty when lads apprenticed in company labour and girls prepared for marriage which usually took place before their eighteenth birthday.[61]

Although social scientists have been debating theories of culture for the past hundred years, they have yet to arrive at a precise definition of the term. There seems to be some consensus, however, that whatever culture is, it is not as simple as 'one culture per society', nor it would seem, is there any restriction on individuals or groups operating in one or more cultures concurrently or at different periods of their lives.[62] The education of fur trade youngsters equipped them with what has been described as 'response-abilities'. These abilities allowed them to successfully adapt to the changing environment in the Pacific Northwest after the demise of the fur trade and function so well in both white and Indian cultures that their apparent disappearance led past historians to be 'culturally blind' and conclude they were 'Victims of higher civilizations'.[63] The individual genealogies of the children reveal the development of a bi-cultural pattern which continues to exist among descendants who have some family members living on reservations, while others live within the mainstream of white society. What the genealogies fail to note is that most of the fur trade children carried their Métis traditions into their new social environments and although they modified these traditions to some extent, they continued to adhere to them and organize their lives along traditional patterns. In the second half of the nineteenth century the children were able to retain a Métis consciousness through a complicated network of kinship relationships which stretched through the entire region. Such patterns refute the myth that fur trade children were forced to 'go Indian' in later life because of racial prejudice in the dominant society. They also belittle the underlying assumptions in this myth—namely, that native people readily accepted mixed-bloods, that racial prejudice was the prime factor in determining the children's lives, and that Métis had no free will in making decisions on their own behalf.

In the 1850 Census of Oregon fur trade children were classified as foreigners, Canadians, French (meaning French-Canadian), or Scottish. As such they were a privileged group within the mixed-blood group which had developed after the settling of the territory. Classification as whites entitled them to US citizenship and 320 acres under the Donation Land Act of the same year—rights denied other half-breed children because of Indian blood.[64]

Most of the children in this study settled in family groups on the fringes of the new society—here they founded new communities in British Columbia, Washington, Oregon, and Montana. Some of these settlements granted under the Donation Land Act squatted on Indian lands and fell within reservation boundaries established in later years. In such cases, Métis, by virtue of their prior settlement, were awarded special status on the reservations. Native people, however, could be hostile towards 'frenchies' joining them.[65] The development of French Prairie, St Paul, and other Métis communities in the Willamette which remained a nucleus for the culture was curtailed by incoming settlers who bought Métis farms and the California gold rush where more than 200 French-speaking Métis in the valley died of fever in the mining regions.[66] Attempts by retired Chief Factor McLoughlin and Métis leaders to establish half-breed reservations failed.[67] Those that lived with native tribes, did so in cultures which were so altered by white technology and foreign ideologies that they resembled the fur trade culture of decades before.

While racism in the society cannot be denied, the degree of racial bigotry, largely propagated by the elite, must be measured against racial tolerance evident in the reminiscences of ordinary citizens. It must be equated with the fact that immigrants were largely single white males, who like their predecessors in the fur trade, united with native and mixed-blood women and had a vested interest in the welfare of the children they fathered. It must be balanced against the lives of these children who were found not just at the lower rungs of the new social structure, but on every rung from the highest political offices on down.[68] The most important point, however, is neither the amount of Indian blood nor the biological reality, but that the children themselves understood the outside world's view of them and fought the image of themselves as inferior people where and how they could.[69] Racial prejudice threw them back upon themselves, reinforcing their culture, and strengthening their identities as Métis people.

One aspect of survival is to take on the protective coloration of the invading culture. Métis adaptation did not mean capitulation of mixed-blood identities. Rather than victims, the Métis offspring of the traders challenged the dominant culture and often consciously chose to reject white society in favour of perpetuating a cultural identity which they retain to this day. In the twilight of Métis culture, consciousness remains. But in the late 1870s when two fur trade daughters, Christina MacDonald and Amelia Douglas, wife of Sir James Douglas, first governor of British Columbia, met for the first time, Christina noted: 'We talked in our excitement in French, in Indian and in mixed English and Lady Douglas remarked how she liked to hear the old language again.'[70]

Notes

1   Nineteenth-century scientific interest in Indian–white mixed-blood populations stemmed from a larger interest in the origin and nature of species and races. From the debates over Comte de Buffon's 'definition of Species', *Histoire Naturelle* (1749), to those which arose over Charles Darwin's *Origin of Species* (1858), 'half-breeds' were cited as 'evidence' to prove or disprove various ideas about species. See: Bentley Glass, Owsei Temkin, William L. Strauss, Jr, eds. *Forerunners of Darwin: 1745–1859* (Baltimore: Johns Hopkins Press, 1968); Robert Bieder, 'Scientific Attitudes toward Indian Mixed-Bloods in Early Nineteenth Century America', *Journal of Ethnic Studies*, 8,2 (Summer 1980); Juliet Pollard, 'Fur Trade Children: The Making of the Métis in the Pacific Northwest' (PhD thesis, UBC).

2   Although the word 'anthropology' was much employed, few of the men who published under the title were 'professional' anthropologists. Although the main focus of Lewis Morgan's work, for example, was the study of native peoples, as a kind of 'spin-off' were discussions about Métis and 'half-breeds'. For example, after a visit to Red River, Morgan wrote: 'As far as my personal observation has extended among the American Indian nations, the half-breed is inferior both physically and mentally, to the pure Indian . . .' Lewis H. Morgan, *Systems of Consanguinity and Affinity of the Human Family* (Smithsonian Contributions of Knowledge, Vol. XVII, 1871, reprinted 1970) Fn. p. 207.

3   Victor Harvard's paper was first delivered to the Anthropological Society of Washington, DC, 20 May 1879. It was later published as 'The French Half-Breeds of the Northwest', *Annual Report of the Board of Regents of the Smithsonian Institution, 1879* (Washington, DC, 1880), pp. 309–27. Noting that 'Métis' referred to French mixed-bloods, while English mixed-bloods were known as 'half-breeds', Harvard found that classification via paternal ancestry (blood line) did not fit the culture he examined. See also John Reade, 'The Half Breed', *Proceedings and Transactions of the Royal Society of Canada*, Vol. 3, 1885, p. 11.

4   Research into the origin and meaning of the term Métis conducted by Jose Hatier, President of the Métis Indian Alliance of North America, indicates that the word has been applied to French-native mixed-blood populations throughout the world. For those engaged in 'scientific' studies in the latter part of the nineteenth century it seems clear that they intended it as a pejorative term meaning 'mongrel'—a term consistently used along with 'hybrid' in species debates throughout the century. For example, see 'Review of "Darwin on the Origin of the Species by Means of Natural Selection"', *Canadian Naturalist and Geologist*, Vol. V; Reade, 'The Half Breed', p. 11; Jennifer Brown, *Strangers in Blood: Fur Trade Company Families in Indian Country* (Vancouver: UBC Press, 1980), pp. 172–73; correspondence and discussions between Jose Hatier, President, Métis Indian Alliance of North America and author, May 1983–January 1984.

5   The committee members were: Dr E.B. Taylor, Dr G.M. Dawson, Gen. Sir J.H. LeFroy, Dr D. Wilson, H. Hale, R.G. Haliburton, and G.W. Bloxam, *British Association for the Advancement of Science: Committee on North Western Tribes of The Dominion of Canada Report, 1887*, (London, 1887), p. 2.

6   Harvard, 'The French Half-Breeds of the Northwest', p. 314; Daniel Wilson, 'Pre-Aryan American Man', *Proceedings and Transactions of the Royal Society of Canada*, Vol. I, 1882–83, p. 43; Reade, p. 11.

7   Ibid.

8   The term most frequently applied to the people under study was 'French', while individuals were known as 'half-breeds' or 'half-bloods'. Since the first term would be confusing, and the latter two derogatory, the term Métis (somewhat less derogatory and increasingly being applied to mixed-blood populations in North America by academics) is used throughout the paper. Nearly all histories of Oregon discuss the fur trade era in the region. In particular, see J.A. Hussey, *Champoeg: Place of Transition* (Portland, Oregon Historical Society, 1967).

9   A discussion on how these forces shaped the culture is given in Pollard, 'Fur Trade Children'.

10   Debbie Bond, 'How Public School Started', *Clark County History*, 1975, p. 56.

11   John Ball, *Autobiography of John Ball* (Grand Rapids: Dean Hicks Co., 1925), p. 93; Thomas Jessett (ed.). *Reports and Letters of Herbert Beaver* (Portland: Champoeg Press, 1959), p. 30.

12   John Hussey, *Fort Vancouver: Historic Structure Report*, Vol. II (Denver Service Center, National Park Service, US Department of the Interior, 1976), pp. 291–315.

13   William R. Sampson, (ed.), *John McLoughlin's Business Correspondence, 1847–48* (Seattle, University of Washington Press, 1973), pp. 139–42; H.K. Smith, *John McLoughlin and His Family* (Lake Oswego: Smith, Smith and Smith Publishing Co., 1976), pp. 8–9.

14   William Cameron McKay, 'Additional Light on the Whitman Matter', *Oregon Pioneer Association Transactions*, 1887, pp. 91–93; William C. McKay Papers, Ms. 413, Oregon Historical Society, Portland; 'Reminiscences of Leila McKay', *Oregon Journal*, October 1927; Keith and Donna Clark, 'William McKay's Journal, 1866–67; Indian Scouts, Part 1 and II', *Oregon Historical Quarterly* (here-after, OHQ) (Summer, Fall 1978).

15   William S. Lewis and Naojiro Murakami, eds, *Ranald MacDonald* (Spokane: Inland-American Printing Co., 1923), pp. 152–233; Maria Leona Nichols, *Ranald MacDonald, Adventurer* (Caldwell, Idaho: Caxton Printers, 1940), pp. 100–139; Ranald MacDonald to E.E. Dye, Ms. 1089, Oregon Historical Society, Portland.

16   H.S. Lyman, 'Reminiscences of Louis Labonte', *Oregon Historical Quarterly*, Vol. I, 1900, pp. 169–87.

17   Andrew Dominique Pambrun, *Sixty Years on the Frontier in the Pacific Northwest* (Fairfield: Ye Galleon Press, 1978).

18   See footnotes 13–17; Harriet Duncan Munnick, 'Annotations', *Catholic Church Records of the Pacific Northwest: St. Paul, Oregon, 1839–1898*, Vols. I, II, and III (Portland: Binford and Mort, 1979).

19   See footnotes 13–18 for biographical sketches.

20   For a fuller discussion of Métis culture and consciousness, see Pollard, 'Fur Trade Children'.

21   Ross Cox, *The Columbia River* (Norman: University of Oklahoma Press, 1955), p. 362.

22   For information on fur trade wives in general, see: Brown, *Strangers in Blood;* Sylvia Van Kirk, *'Many Tender Ties': Women in Fur Trade Society in Western Canada, 1670–1870* (Winnipeg: Watson and Dwyer, 1980).

23   For examples, see: William L. Langer, 'Infanticide: A Historical Survey', *History of Childhood Quarterly*, Vol. 1 (1973–74), pp. 353–65; Neil McKendrick, 'Home Demand and Economic Growth: A New View of the Role of Women and Children in the Industrial Revolution', in McKendrick, ed., *Historical Perspectives: Studies in English Thought and Society* (London: Europa Publications, 1974); Ivy Pinchbeck and Margaret Hewitt, *Children in English Society*, Vol. II (Toronto: University of Toronto Press, 1973).

24   E.E. Rich, *The History of the Hudson's Bay Company, 1670–1870*, Vol. II (London: The Hudson's Bay Record Society, 1959), p. 453.

25   Female population figures and tribal affiliations at Fort Vancouver are drawn from the figures compiled by Susan Kardas in 'The People Brought This and the Clatsop Became Rich: A View of Nineteenth Century Relations on the Lower Columbia Between Chinookian Speakers, Whites and Kanakas' (Ph.D. thesis, Bryn Mawr College, 1971), pp. 208–10.

26   George J. Engelmann, *Labor Among Primitive Peoples Showing the Development of the Obstetric Science of To-day from the Natural and Instinctive Customs of All Races, Civilized and Savage, Past and Present* (St Louis: J.H. Chambers and Co., 1883), pp. 2, 9–10, 196. Dr George Engelmann rationalized that since peasant and native women had shorter labours than their more 'refined' sisters (or so it was believed), there could be a connection between shorter labour and the positions they assumed during labour. Engelmann sent out letters to doctors asking for information, the information about difficult labour due to larger babies born to Indian–white parents came from their responses. In the early twentieth century biologists who had rediscovered Gregor Mendel's neglected laws of inherit-ance began applying them to human heredity and the phenomenon of 'increased size', known as F1 (first hybrid generation) was used as proof that inter-racial breeding produced inferior offspring—the larger baby being regarded as 'abnormal' and therefore inferior. Others argued that 'increased size' meant superiority. See W.E. Castle, 'Biological and Social Consequences of Race-Crossing', *American Journal of Physical Anthropology*, IX, 2 (April–June 1926, pp. 145–56). Such factors as birth rank, age of mother, maternal diet, and physical size of parents, known to be significant factors in 'overweight' births today were not observed in the period under study. See: Pollard, 'Fur Trade Children'.

27   Engelmann, *Labor Among Primitive People*, p. 2. See also Nellie B. Pipes, 'Indian Conditions in 1836–38', OHQ, Vol. 32 (1931), p. 335.

28   Records of husband-assisted births are found throughout *Labor Among Primitive People*.

29   O. Larsell, 'An Outline of the History of Medicine in the Pacific Northwest; *Northwest Medicine*, Vol. 31 (1932), p. 484.

30   Jane B. Donegan, *Women and Men Midwives: Medicine, Morality, and Misogyny in Early America* (Westport: Greenwood Press, 1978), pp. 42–43.

31   For example, see 'Nancy Winecoop', *Told by the Pioneers, Reminiscences of Pioneer Life in Washington*, Vol. I (1937), p. 114.

32   For the extent of phrenologist influence, see George B. Roberts, 'Letters to Mrs F.F. Victor, 1878–83', OHQ, Vol. 63 (June-Sept. 1962), pp. 202–34; William Fraser Tolmie, *Physician and Fur Trader* (Vancouver: Mitchell Press, 1963), pp. 333, 363; Bieder, 'Scientific Attitudes towards Indian Mixed-Bloods in Early Nineteenth Century America', p. 24; David De Giustino, *Conquest of Mind: Phrenology and Victorian Thought* (London: Croom Helm, 1975), pp. 139–40.

33   Frederick Merk, ed., *Fur Trade and Empire: George Simpson's Journal* (Cambridge: Harvard University Press, 1968), p. 101.

34   By educating their daughters at home, fur-trade fathers were following a pattern of female education in Euro-American society. Chinook Indians also attempted to keep daughters chaste in order to further trade ties through advantageous marriages with white traders. See Merk, *Fur Trade and Empire*, p. 99; Jessett, *Reports and Letters of Herbert Beaver*, pp. 67–68.

35   Mrs Daniel Harvey (nee Eloise McLoughlin), 'Life of John McLoughlin, Governor of the Hudson's Bay Company's Possessions on the Pacific Slope at Fort Vancouver', Portland, Oregon, June 20, 1878 (handwritten manuscript, Bancroft Library, Berkeley, California), p. 13.

36   Kin relationships which transcended rank and class in the company are evident in Harriet Duncan Munnick, ed., *Catholic Church Records of the Pacific Northwest: Vancouver*, Vol. I and II, and *St. Paul*, Vol. I, II, and III (Portland: Thomas Binford Publisher, 1979, 1980).

37   For example, see Angus MacDonald to Christina MacDonald, E.E. Dye Papers, Ms. 1089, Oregon Historical Society, Portland. MacDonald writes to his daughter: 'You see now the value of education and money, the ignorant is always kept down. I hope you will be rich enough to take me to Edinburgh and Paris before I be much grayer . . . Your mother made her trip to Nez Perce (her people) all right. She spent two months on the trip and lost a valuable colt . . .'

38   Hudson's Bay Company Wills, A36, Hudson's Bay Company Archives, Winnipeg, Manitoba; Annie Laurie Bird, 'The Will of Thomas McKay', OHQ, Vol. 40 (1938), pp. 15–18.

39   Examples of fatherly love for sons are sprinkled throughout fur trade sources. For example, F.N. Ainnoine to James Murray Yale, Oct. 17, 1832, Yale Family Papers, Vol. II, BC Provincial Archives, Victoria. For the growing view of sons as a 'second chance' see Daniel Beekman, *The Mechanical Baby: A Popular History of Theory and Practice of Child Raising* (New York: Meridian, New American Library, 1977), p. 104.

40   Lois Halliday McDonald, *Fur Trade Letters of Francis Ermatinger written to his brother Edward during his service with the Hudson's Bay Company: 1818–1853* (Glendale: Arthur H. Clark Company, 1980), p. 254.

41   'Copy of a Document found among the Private Papers of the late Dr John McLoughlin', *Oregon Pioneer Association Transactions*, 1880, p. 49.

42   Archbishop F.N. Blanchet, *The Catholic Missionaries of Oregon* (Portland, 1878), p. 3.

43   Ibid., Cyrus Shepard of the Methodist Mission of Oregon to the *Zion's Herald*, Boston, October 28, 1835; 'Mrs Whitman—The Diary', in C.M. Drury, ed., *First White Women over the Rockies: Diaries. Letters, and Biographical Sketches of the Six Women of the Oregon Mission who made the Overland Journey in 1836 and 1838* (Glendale: Arthur H. Clark Company, 1963), pp. 99–114; Jessett, *Reports and Letters of Herbert Beaver*; McDonald, *Fur Trade Letters of Francis Ermatinger*, pp. 185–204. Ermatinger instructed his brother in Upper Canada to 'make a farmer' of his son since he was considered 'dull' at the Fort Vancouver school.

44   Rev. Myron Eells, *Marcus Whitman Pathfinder and Patriot* (Seattle: Alice Harriman Company, 1909), pp. 136, 148.

45   William Mavor, *The Elements of Natural History, Chiefly Intended for the Use of Schools and Young Persons* (London: Richard Phillips, 1808), p. 13; Hussey, *Fort Vancouver*, p. 315.

46   Kardas, 'The People Brought This and Clatsop Became Rich', p. 209. While Kardas's figures may be questioned, they fall within the pattern of 'small family size' in the Euro-American community. See, for example, Michael Katz, 'Household, Family, and Social Structure', *The Canadian Social History Project*, Report No. 5, 1973–74 (Toronto: The Ontario Institute for Studies in Education, 1974). Indian families have traditionally been regarded as 'small'.

47   Elsie Francis Dennis, 'Indian Slavery in Pacific Northwest', OHQ, Vol. 31 (1930), pp. 194–95; Pipes, 'Indian Conditions in 1836–38', pp. 336–37.

48   John Ball, 'Across the Continent Seventy Years Ago', OHQ, Vol. 3 (1903), p. 103.

49   Munnick, *Catholic Church Records.*

50   For example, see Ranald MacDonald to E.E. Dye, Aug. 8. 1892, Ms. 1089, Oregon Historical Society.

51   Kardas, p. 170. See also Fn. 46.

52   In the latter days of the fur trade some chief traders engaged teachers and opened their kitchen classrooms to other pupils besides their own children. See *Told by the Pioneers*, pp. 87, 113, 114, 118.

53   Munnick, *Catholic Church Records*, Henry Buxton to E.E. Dye, Sept. 28, 1892, Ms. 1089, Oregon Historical Society.

54   Chinook jargon was in use prior to the arrival of the Hudson's Bay Company, but during their rule it developed more fully. One of the most interesting accounts of the jargon is given in *Notices and Voyages of the Famed Quebec Mission to the Pacific Northwest being the Correspondence, Notices, etc., of Fathers Blanchet and Demers together with those of Fathers Bolduc and Langlois* (Oregon Historical Society, Portland: Champoeg Press, 1956), pp. 12, 14, 18–19, 21, 80, 87, 90, 150, 169.

55   Hussey, *Fort Vancouver*, p. 291. Similarly, Lewis Morgan noted that Cree was the 'mother tongue' of many of the English speaking 'half-bloods' at Red River. Morgan, *Systems of Consanguinity and Affinity of the Human Family*, p. 206.

56   Ranald MacDonald to E.E. Dye, March 21, 1892, Ms. 1089, Oregon Historical Society, MacDonald discusses travelling in a basket in early childhood. Information on swaddling via the native cradleboard is given in C. Hudson and H. Phillips, 'Rousseau and the Disappearance of Swaddling among Western Europeans', *Essays on Medical Anthropology* (Athens: University of Georgia Press, 1968), p. 14.

57   'John Work Journal', Aug. 27, 1824 (BC Provincial Archives).

58   Examples of childhood disciplining are given in Hussey, p. 291; Pambrun, *Sixty Years on the Frontier*, pp. 27–37.

59   Information on the diet of the working class in England is contained in Charles Francatelli, *A Plain Cookery Book for the Working Class* (London: Scholar Press, 1977; copyright 1852). Pinchbeck and Hewitt, *Children in English Society*, pp. 407, 420, 428; E.P. Thompson, *The Making of the English Working Class* (New York: Penguin Books, 1979), pp. 220, 316, 319–20. For the diet of the Fort Vancouver worker, see Lester A. Ross, 'Early Nineteenth Century Euroamerican Technology within the Columbia River Drainage System' (Fort Vancouver National Historic Site Report, n.d.); Douglas Leechman, 'I sowed Garden Seeds', *The Beaver*, Winter 1970, p. 32.

60   Harvey, 'Life of John McLoughlin, pp. 6, 9; Thomas Roulstone, 'A Social History of Fort Vancouver: 1829–49', (MA Thesis, Utah State University, 1975), pp. 99, 134–35.

61   Some ages of marriage are given in Munnick, *Catholic Church Records;* others can be calculated from *Early Marriage Records: Clackamus County, Wasco County, Oregon* (Tualatin Chapter Daughters of the American Revolution, Oswego, Oregon, 1960).

62   Sidney W. Mintz. 'Culture: An Anthropological View', *The Yale Review*, 71, 4 (1982), pp. 499–527.

63   Duke Redbird, *We Are Métis* (Toronto: Ontario Métis and Non-Status Indian Association, 1980), pp. 6–7.

64   *United States Census of Oregon, 1850*. Oregon Historical Society; *Genealogical Material in Oregon Provisional Land Claims*, Vols. I–VIII, 1845–49 (Genealogical Forum of Portland, Oregon, 1982); *Oregon Donation Land Claims*, Vols. I–IV (Genealogical Forum of Portland, Oregon, 1967).

65   John P. Gaines, Alonzo A. Skinner, Beverly S. Alien to Hon. Luke Lea, Commissioner Indian Affairs, May 14, 1851, *Message From the President*, 1850–1851, pp. 468–72; Thomas Jessett, *Chief Spokan Garry: 1811–1892* (Minneapolis: T.S. Denison and Company, 1960), pp. 96–98, 108, 113, 119–20.

66   Willard Rees to Hubert Bancroft, Sept. 18, 1879 (Bancroft Papers, Bancroft Library, Berkeley). There were 48 Métis land claimants in 1842 in the Willamette Valley. See J.N. Barry, *The French Canadian* Pioneers (Portland, 1936).

67   Pambrun, pp. 134–38; Sampson, *John McLoughlin's Business Correspondence*, p. 69.

68   By 'elite' I mean scientists, academics, politicians, clergy—people who had access to media coverage. The reminiscences given here contain many examples of life in communities where white men and native women were the norm, and indicate a high degree of racial tolerance. See *Told By the Pioneers;* Fred Lockley, *Conversations with Pioneer Women; Conversations with All Sorts and Conditions of Men; Visionaries, Mountain Men and Empire Builders* (Eugene: Rainy Day Press, 1981, 1982). Many people who would later be well known in public life emerge from fur trade childhoods. Take as an example, Dr S.F. Tolmie, premier of British Columbia (1928–33), who was the seventh son of trader Dr W.F. Tolmie and his Métis wife Jane Work, daughter of Chief Trader John Work. See S.R. Tolmie, 'My Father William Fraser Tolmie', in Tolmie, *Physician and Fur Trader*, pp. 385–95.

69   By 'biological reality' I mean the present biological evidence which suggests there is no such thing as races. See: Richard H. Osborne, ed., *The Biological and Social Meaning of Race* (San Francisco:

W.H. Freeman and Company, 1971), pp. 3–13; Stephen Jay Gould, *Ever Since Darwin* (New York: W.W. Norton and Company, 1977), pp. 231–37. In their writings, fur trade children seemed compelled to prove that they were as good as white men. See McKay to E.E. Dye; Lewis and Murakami, *Ranald MacDonald;* Pambrun, *Sixty Years on the Frontier;* Robert Birnie, 'Life and Adventures of Robert Birnie born at Astoria, Oregon, Feb. 7, 1824', San Francisco, 1972, Ms. 65–33, Bancroft Library.

70   Christina MacDonald McKenzie Williams, 'The Daughter of Angus MacDonald', *Washington Historical Quarterly*, 13 (1922), p. 116.

Chapter 19

Anna Davin

NEEDED AT HOME

Minding the little ones

IF MOTHER OR OLDER CHILDREN could not care for infants during the day, and if there was no crèche to take them, what were the alternatives? The occasional father took charge if his wife was in work and he was not, or if his hours were different, or if she was ill.[1] Another member of household or family might be available: most likely someone whose age or poor health made it hard for them to get work—often a grandparent, if one was part of the household or lived nearby.[2] A sister just released from school might be kept at home rather than sent to work. Old and young might combine forces, as in a family of Drury Lane flower-sellers in 1889, where a forty-five-year-old mother of six cared for the babies of her two eldest daughters with the help of her youngest.[3] A child might go to a nearby relative, perhaps a married sister.[4] Of working mothers surveyed in a turn-of-the-century report, half regularly left children with relatives.[5] Sometimes—how often we cannot know—children were locked in for the day or, if older, locked out.

The more prosperous mother—a shopkeeper, for instance, or perhaps an artisan's wife—engaged a 'nurse', a girl who had just left school, to look after the baby during its waking hours. (Mrs Layton did this at ten, in Bethnal Green in 1865.)[6] Wage-earning mothers could not usually afford this arrangement. Sometimes neighbour or landlady obliged for the odd day, but for more she would have to be paid.[7] Sometimes there was a local child-minder, most often an older woman who kept herself by taking in infants for money.[8] Child care could consume a third or a half of the earnings of a woman who worked for wages. As a child-minder in 1885 observed, she did not make much out of her charge of sixpence a day for each of the three babies she looked after (supplying their milk and food), 'but the women only earn 1s. 6d. to 2s. themselves'.[9] Nearly thirty years later, in a case noted by Clementina Black, a woman who earned eleven shillings for four days' work was giving nearly half to a neighbour who charged 1s. 2d. a day to mind her two small children.[10]

The need was often an irregular one. Some women's employment was casual—now a day washing, now a day cleaning, now a few days in factory or workshop during a rush. Some women had regular part-time work, three or four days a week in a laundry, for instance. Or a woman doing homework needed time, perhaps several hours, to go two or three times a week to the warehouse with the finished trousers (or sacks or matchboxes or whatever) and to collect the next lot of work. Or the prospect of a heavy wash with toddlers underfoot loomed. So 'twopence or a cup of tea to some old woman or little girl to mind the baby for a few hours', was 'an item which you may find in the poorest budget'.[11]

Where the older children already looked after the younger ones outside school hours, it was tempting to save those coppers by keeping a child at home for the odd morning, or after-noon, or both. This, as we shall see, was the pattern of girls' absence from school. It was on girls that the burden of child care chiefly fell, and girls whose attendance was most affected by the lack of crèche facilities.

Under some circumstances, domestic need was officially recognized. It was possible, for instance, for an older child to become a half-timer, combining school and work like the child workers of the northern mill-towns.[12] In London in the 1870s this was in principle allowed only when a child was 'beneficially and necessarily at work', and she or he still had to attend for ten out of twenty-five hours a week changed in 1879 to five out of the ten weekly attend-ances.[13] Many half-timers were said to be employed in household work.[14] Others again did industrial work, usually in small workshops or domestic outwork, though Bryant and May's match factory used some half-timers in the 1870s.[15] Teachers disliked the arrangement.[16] For half-timers were often irregular even in the attendances they were supposed to make; they were unsettling in their effect on other pupils and harder to get through examinations. They also depressed the attendance rates to which government grants were keyed, and so, under the payment by results system, could lower the teachers' salaries.[17] In London official policy was to phase out half-time attendance, and half-timers dwindled from 2,417 in 1879, to 1,873 in 1889–90, to 693 in 1893, to 88 in 1899–1900.[18] After that it was formally abolished in London.

There were however informal arrangements about half-time attendance, such as would escape the official record. Harriet ('Mighty'), the sister of Arthur Harding, born in 1882, was the mainstay of her crippled mother long before she was permitted to leave school and start full-time work. She looked after her young brother and sister; she went to and from the Bryant and May depot to return the matchboxes her mother made and collect materials for new ones; she shopped; she foraged; she traded, she washed; she ran every kind of errand. To combine all this with full-time school was not possible. So three days a week, her brother recalled:

> Mighty, instead of going to school, would hop it. My mother came to some arrangement. . . . They didn't want to summon her, my mother being a cripple, so they made this special arrangement—twice a week she went to school and the other days she had off.[19]

This was probably not official. A later example can certainly not have been sanctioned: half-time had been formally ended in London when Mrs M., who was born the eldest of seventeen in Hoxton in 1896, was permitted at twelve to go half-time so as to help at home. Her mother had new twins, four babies needing bottles, and a broken arm; so her grandmother, who 'went to ask', presumably made a strong case.[20]

A child approaching the age of release and not behind with school work could sometimes get complete exemption from further attendance, if the authorities were persuaded that her services or her earnings were really needed. Such exemptions were ratified with phrases like: 'Children's earnings required owing to poverty of parents'; 'Required at home owing to special circumstances'; 'Wanted to go to work'; and so on. But poverty and special circum-stances had to be extreme for exemption to be granted, and the age and standard demanded rose steadily. In the school year 1894–95, 1,205 children were excused from attendance, most over twelve and in or above Standard Four. Next year the Board stopped exemption for children under thirteen, and allowed it between thirteen and fourteen only for those who had attended regularly for five of the six preceding years. Eight hundred and forty-six children were excused in 1896–97. They stiffened the requirements still further in 1898, and the total was down to 313 by the end of the decade.[21] The exceptional cases where exemption was granted show how desperate the need had to be; moreover, most of these girls had only two months to go before they could leave anyway, and often they were in the highest possible class, Standard Ex-Seven. Here are examples:

> Ellen Pearce, 13 years 10 months, Standard Five, mother widow . . . parish relief; one elder girl earns 7s., total income 12s. 6d., rent 5s., two children younger.
>   Florence Plummer, 13 years 10 months, Standard Seven, father deserted family, mother unable to work, eight children none over school age, rent in arrears, family living on charity and will probably go into the workhouse, two children invalids.
>   Ruth Card, 13 years 6 months, Standard ex-Seven. Father . . . ill . . . five younger children, girl has offer of situation in confectioner's shop at 3s. a week with board and lodging.
>   Nelly Kempton, 13 years 10 months, Standard ex-Seven, mother dying of cancer . . . required to attend to home.[22]

The threshold of desperate need set by the authorities bore no relation to the family's perception of need, especially as it was linked to age and formal attainment not to crisis. Parents were unwilling to cede priority to the demands of school. At a sitting of North London Police Court in 1891, the sixty parents summoned for not sending their children to school included:

> Several poor widows who complained of having to go out to work and keep six or seven children, without having the privilege of the services of the elder children 'nearly fourteen years of age' who might assist in the maintenance of the family.[23]

It was hard for parents to accept an edict which threatened the natural (often the only possible) resort in domestic emergency, that daughter should stand in for mother, or son earn a wage. The girl herself, or the boy, might also regard school as an irrelevancy to be escaped from as soon as possible, and want to play more part in the family economy. A Putney father in 1902, was found guilty of falsifying his daughter's birth certificate to justify her absence from school. He claimed the daughter had done it herself, which she confirmed, and that he had genuinely thought her fourteen anyway.[24] The magistrates, who fined him five pounds or a month in prison, presumably did not believe that a 'child' would have initiative or skill enough for the forgery, let alone that she could want to abandon childhood for an adult role so soon. (They might also have doubted his casual attitude to exact age, unthinkable by then among those more literate or more exposed to bureaucracy.)[25] It is quite possible, however, that father and daughter spoke the truth.

Older girls might well put home before school, and be backed up by parents, particularly mothers. Sometimes, it seems, they effectively left school before the permitted age. In the 1890s, Maidstone Street school, in Haggerston (a poor part of Hackney, bordering on Bethnal Green), suffered 'very irregular attendance, especially among the elder girls',[26] and one headmistress there made lists in the logbook of persistent absentees the school visitor was to pursue. These show that some children were not just irregular: they never came.[27] In one list of thirty-four girls (6 Sept. 1895), twenty names were starred, to indicate, according to the head, that 'the parents refuse to send, and in many of these cases the children are at work'. One had missed nineteen school weeks, another eighteen, two more seventeen. Others had showed up only sporadically over periods as long. Another list, of twenty-one names (3 March 1896), showed girls who in the previous eleven months had managed respectively fifty-two, fourteen, fifteen, ten, thirty, forty-seven, twenty-four, sixty, sixty-six and eighty out of a possible total of over 400 morning and afternoon sessions. Most of these, and those who had attended least, were from Standards Four and above, so probably between eleven and thirteen years old.[28] In the whole list, too, the majority were from standards above Four. (Other lists gave no indication of standard or age.)

Similar cases figure among the 'typical' absentees listed in School Board records, like these from Hackney in 1892:[29]

> Girl aged 12 in Standard Two. . . . Absent 12 months. . . . Parents say 'Old enough to leave school', 'Won't send any more'. They have removed five times since Christmas; when found they remove again before action can be taken. The last fine is still outstanding as the present address is not known.
> Girl 12 absent 13 weeks. There is no father, and the child is kept to mind the baby while the mother goes out to work. The child is the oldest of four.

'Typical cases', and occasional lists for one school (I have not found data as clear in other logbooks)[30] over five years, are of course no basis for statistical analysis. But annual school returns show that Maidstone Street school was not the worst girls' school in Hackney for attendance, and Hackney's average attendance rates were close to the average for London. In other poor schools too, then, there may well have been girls marked absent on the register more often than present.

Overall, however, the most common pattern for girls—in contrast with boys—was to turn up during most of the week but miss two or three mornings or afternoons.[31] This is suggested by a School Board return in 1899, where figures for the last quarter of 1898 were analysed to show the weekly attendance of boys, girls and infants.[32] In those three months only 17.5 per cent of girls managed ten out of ten attendances a week, while 23.9 per cent of boys did. Among boys, 59.2 per cent made nine or ten attendances, and 22.3 per cent made seven or eight. Among girls, 46.4 per cent made nine or ten, 35.6 per cent managed seven or eight, and 7.7 per cent (as opposed to 2.5 per cent of boys), only six. The infants' rate (influenced, of course, by still other factors)[33] was lowest for full attendance (13 per cent); for eight attendances and under, it was almost the same as the girls'. The most striking disproportion is in the figures for nine attendances out of ten, a level achieved by 35 per cent of boys, 33.5 per cent of infants, and only 28 per cent of girls.[34]

Girls, then, were more likely to miss attendances than boys, and more of them missed more. More boys would miss a single morning or afternoon; more girls would miss two, three, or more, but especially three. School logbooks confirm this. At a poor school newly opened in Upper Holloway, the headmistress deplored girls' irregularity.

> *17 Feb 1873* Numbers again small. . . . Parents say they would be glad to send but their girls' services at home cannot be dispensed with.
> *10 July 1873* It seems almost impossible to induce the parents to make an effort to send their girls regularly—they are kept at home for everything.[35]

Illness at home kept the girls away as nurses. When the head of Gainsborough Road school (Hackney) in 1885 asked the attendance officer why girls' attendance was more affected by a prevailing sickness than boys', she was told that the girls, being 'more useful in the house', were 'wanted to nurse the sick ones'.[36] If their mothers were ill themselves, or in childbed, girls not only nursed them but took on running the household.

Mothers engaged in homework, as many wives of unskilled men were at times, valued their children's help on the work, or as messengers with it once finished, or with the baby; and when under pressure they kept them home.[37] The girl was unlikely to protest, and indeed might make the decision herself: she knew as well as her mother what was needed.

Child care was often the immediate cause of girls' absence, to free the mother for other work, to replace her if she was ill, or to cope with emergency. Heads of girls' schools noted poor attendance on days when infants' schools were shut for vestry elections, as this 'necessitated many girls staying away to look after their younger brothers and sisters'.[38] When an epidemic closed the Stepney Crèche in 1880, the School Board visitor came daily to ask when it would reopen, 'almost beside himself as the children are staying at home to nurse babies'.[39] In Southwark in 1872 lower enrolment of girls was blamed on the insufficiency of school places for infants.[40]

Washing days were notoriously bad for attendance, and everyone understood why. As a settlement worker put it:

> One fully appreciates how tempting it is to keep Mary Jane at home, at least on washing day. Perhaps there are six little ones, one of them a small baby, and twins of eighteen months.[41]

At one school, lessons from Wednesday afternoon were moved mid-year as it was local washing day, and the many girls who regularly missed those lessons might fail their exams.[42] Elsewhere Monday posed the same problem, with the additional disadvantage of being the day when the week's fee was due.[43] Friday was bad too. ('It seems almost impossible to secure a satisfactory attendance on Friday afternoon', wrote a headmistress in 1874.)[44] It was the hardest day for homeworkers, when money had to be accumulated for the weekend. It was the day when casual cleaning work could most easily be had. And even mothers who did not do paid work were more likely to keep back their children on that day 'to tidy up the house'. By the 1890s a special effort was being made in some schools to make Friday afternoons attractive, with extra time for play, visiting lecturers, sometimes experimental science lectures (as a show, however: girls did not study science—see next chapter [see original reading]) and even a street organ engaged to play in the school yard for half an hour.[45]

The double standard

The pattern of girls' irregularity was a difficult one to deal with; but the authorities scarcely tried. They held that 'needed at home', as an excuse for absence, 'must, under the circumstances, be accepted as reasonable'.[46] Efforts to provide school-based child care had failed; legal enforcement was unrealistic if only two or three attendances a week were missed. It is not surprising to find a fatalistic tolerance of such absence.[47]

There was some attempt to keep absence for domestic reasons within limits, though enforcement varied in this respect as in others. In 1874 a School Board committee on attendance problems took evidence from the superintendents of visitors in each division of London. In Chelsea, the practice was 'occasionally [to] excuse the attendance of a child over ten for one day a week, where it appears that there is a large family to wash for, and a baby is to be cared for'. In the City, an elder child was sometimes allowed to stay and help if there was illness at home. In Hackney, up to fourteen days' absence was allowed if the father was out of work or the mother ill. In Lambeth, half-time was granted if there was 'great poverty' and the child had passed enough standards. In Marylebone, the mother's confinement was accepted as an excuse for absence, for girls.[48] Whatever the theoretical limits, they were probably applied with some flexibility. Florence H., in Bethnal Green in the 1890s was brought up by an elder sister because of her mother's death. She often took a note saying that she had 'had to stay at home and mind the baby'; this would be accepted, she later recalled, as long as she 'didn't stay away too much'.[49]

In general, for girls, 'the necessities of domestic life' held good as an excuse.[50] In 1900, Sir Charles Elliott of the London School Board, writing to *The Times* on the attendance question, divided reasons for absence into three groups: 'excusable', 'doubtful' and 'inexcusable'. In the first category he placed 'retention at home on account of illness of some member of the house whether for infectious disease or . . . confinement of mother, or accompanying mother or little brother or sister to hospital, etc.'; in the second, 'helping mother' (the excuse, he said, 'most frequent of all'), and in the last, being employed at home more than twice a week.[51]

Twice a week, that is, could be tolerated, even at the level of statistics and official pronouncements.[52] The individual teacher or attendance officer, knowing particular circumstances and seeing no alternative, might often condone a still higher level of absence. A Deptford teacher around 1900 regularly put up with losing one of her eight-year-olds: the harassed mother (a widowed washerwoman) would call through the classroom window at Frankham Street school, ' "Come on out, Liz, I need you", and the teacher would say, "All right, you'd better go then," and let her'.[53] In the same way, a teacher might tolerate lateness, and even try to cover it up, because she knew what a child had to do before school. Children who arrived after 9.30, when the registers closed, were supposed to be recorded as absent. But Board inspectors complained of inaccurate records of lateness: 'It is impossible to get some teachers to see that in registering facts, sentiment has no place'.[54] Self-interest may have played some part, however: teachers would be reluctant to inflate the number of 'absentees' by including late-comers, since this ultimately affected their pay. Heads, with less personal contact with the children and more stake in successful discipline, might be stricter. Some conducted real campaigns on punctuality.[55] Being unpunctual, like being irregular, was affected by home circumstances and the parents' attitude to school—both how much the child's help was needed, and how seriously the parents took the demands of education.[56] Again, as with irregular attendance, girls were affected the most.

Girls definitely found it harder to get to school on time. The question of punctuality was explored by a School Board inspector in a report in 1883. During a sample week, he calculated, 71 per cent of boys and only 51 per cent of girls were marked early (that is, arriving before nine o'clock, when classes started). In five girls' schools, he added, 'less than a third were marked early'.[57] When a system of rewards for regular and punctual attendance was set up in 1887, the number of reward cards given to boys was consistently about 30 per cent higher than that for girls (see Table 6.1 [see original reading]).[58] HMI Nickal's evidence to the Cross Commission confirmed the unpunctuality of girls, especially in poorer schools. He was asked whether in 'schools generally' many children missed the first lesson. (The question was prompted by concern about scriptural instruction, which always came first.)[59] He answered, 'Yes, in girls' schools'; and submitted as examples figures on punctuality at a range of schools. In two very rough and poor schools 31 per cent and 38 per cent of the girls arrived before the first lesson began, about 20 per cent missed it altogether, and the rest were present for some of it. At another school, poor but 'of a little better description', 51 per cent were on time, and 12 per cent too late for any scripture instruction. At a school with a slightly higher fee (twopence instead of a penny), long established but in 'a rather poor crowded neighbourhood', 52 per cent were on time, 23 per cent present for most of the lesson, and 10 per cent too late. Even at a 'comparatively new school in an outlying district', 4 per cent missed the lesson and 15 per cent were late. It was only in a few of the best schools that 90 to 95 per cent were on time and none missed scripture 'habitually'.[60]

The reward-card statistics, show that although rates varied between neighbourhoods, girls' punctuality was never up to boys'. Boys even in the poorest School Board divisions received more reward cards in 1887 than the girls of any division, with the exception of Greenwich, whose girls outdid the boys of Chelsea, Finsbury, Marylebone and Hackney.[61]

This difference was rooted in the division of domestic labour. Although both boys and girls ran early morning errands, boys' other work before breakfast mostly took the more regular form of delivering newspapers, milk or bread. These rounds made them tired for school but they were less likely to be late. Some witnesses before the 1902 Committee on children's employment maintained that children with regular employment were regular at school, neither absent nor late, whereas 'those who work at home are the worst'.[62] Girls' usual task to get younger children dressed and fed and take toddlers to infant school or crèche affected afternoon as well as morning punctuality. Small children are hard to hurry; and the task could be onerous. Workers at the Stepney crèche in 1895 noticed a child who every morning brought 'an infant she was hardly able to carry', and then went back to Whitechapel (perhaps a mile) for another child, old enough to walk much of the way, but whom she carried a good deal so as to get to school herself. (They provided 'an old perambulator, to ease the child's labours'.)[63] So the unpredictable last-minute demands of child care and domestic crisis contributed to making girls late more frequently than boys, as well as to keeping them away more often.[64]

But girls' lateness and absence for domestic reasons were not tolerated by the authorities simply because they could not be helped. Other factors were involved. Although in their notion of the family children were dependent, duty to the family and the authority of the father (and behind him the mother) were also central precepts. Legislative restriction of employment had already undermined the right of parents to their children's earnings. Further interference with parental prerogative was not acceptable to everyone.[65] In 1899, in a Parliamentary debate whether to raise to twelve the age at which half-time exemption was allowed, many expressed reluctance to impinge on parental rights.[66] One rural member (Mr Jeffreys, North Hampshire) thought the law should be left as it was.

> Why should not parents in the poorer classes of life treat their children as we do in our class of life? If the parents think that a girl, having passed her Fourth Standard, can leave school and help her mother in the house and attend to the smaller children, why not entitle them to do so? Why not have more confidence in the parents? In a similar way, if a boy passes the Fourth Standard, why should he not leave school to help his father in tending cattle or scaring birds?

The member for Birkenhead, Sir E. Lees, thought employment of a child of eleven was the lesser evil if the alternative was that the mother should go out to work. That the claims of family sometimes came before the claims of school was a view held even by some members of the London School Board: the system of awards for regular attendance was criticized at a committee meeting in 1900 because it meant that 'children have been sent to school or insisted on going when their highest duty was to their home'.[67] Such general sentiments had a long heritage. They survived most tenaciously, however, when combined with ideas about gender difference.

Girls were consistently absent more than boys (see Table 6.2 [see original reading]). Yet problems of attendance were discussed largely in terms of boys. In 1886–87, the average attendance rate for boys' schools under the London Board was 82 per cent; for girls' schools it was 76 per cent, a difference of six points. The difference varied with the fee charged by the school, and so, presumably, with the poverty of the families concerned. Table 6.3 [see original reading] shows the variation. The problem of improving attendance was initially presented by the school authorities as one of efficient scheduling and better enforcement. The need was for conscientious attendance officers to make sure no children went unrecorded and to pursue truants, and for co-operative magistrates to enforce the law even when it conflicted with 'their idea of what it should be'.[68] This approach dominated the 1870s and early 1880s. Other explanations did begin to be heard ('the poverty, the sickness, and the home needs of the parents. . . . I really do find scarcely an unreasonable excuse given'),[69] but the stern allegations about defiant truants, inadequate enforcement and irresponsible parents continued to be frequent.'[70]

At the same time, in the drive to improve the general average the lower attendance of girls was not much remarked. One inspector, Mr Ricks, reporting on 1875–76, observed that, 'In general the attendance of boys is better than that of the girls and infants', and without comment on the girls went on to explain the irregularity of infants.[71] Mr Noble, for South London in 1877, listed sixteen schools with 90 per cent attendance, and fourteen with attendance below 70 per cent. In his first list there were twelve boys' schools, two girls' and two infants'; his second comprised eleven girls', two infants', and one mixed.[72]

Inspector McWilliam's report on attendance and punctuality in his South London division in 1883 tabulated attendance rates for three years (see Table 6.4 [see original reading]). His accompanying comment was that:

> The fact that the regularity of the girls keeps steadily below that of the boys and infants, shows that it is home cares rather than indifference or defiance which is the cause of much of the irregularity.[73]

He offered no solution, and passed on to discuss at rather more length the problems of boys' absence.

The polarized assumptions (truancy versus domestic need) also influenced punishment. Albert and Olive, brother and sister whose father made chairs in a domestic workshop, had to take a barrow-load of chairs to the wholesaler twice a week in their dinner hour. When the delivery was from Bethnal Green to London Fields, a manageable mile, they were all right. But sometimes they had to go three miles to Bermondsey, with the risk, too, of delay if Tower Bridge was letting river traffic through. This made them late for afternoon classes. At Albert's school the head waited on the stairs and caned all late-comers without excuse or exception. Olive, in the girls' school, was never caned.[74]

Attempts to establish different causes of absence in different groups were made for a School Board committee set up in 1890 to investigate attendance. Its printed proceedings include a report from the Committee of Representative Managers of London Board Schools, whose chair, William Bousfield (himself previously a member of the School Board), argued that:

> everything really depended . . . upon the character of the parents. Where the parents were in steady employment and of steady habits themselves, regular attendance was as a rule secured. . . . The difficulty really existed with the children of parents who were of irregular habits, or who were constantly out of work.[75]

This distinction between regular and irregular work slipped easily into an assumption about moral regularity, both here ('steady employment and steady habits') and in the classification presented for the Committee by the School Managers. Children attending London elementary schools were divided by it into three categories, which are worth quoting at length:[76]

(a)   Those of parents fairly well off.
    (i)   These generally attend well . . . except:
    (ii)   Infants, who do not attend unless quite well and the weather is fair.
(b)   Those of parents who are poor, but in regular work and of regular habits.
    (i)   Infants are entered early and attend well.
    (ii)   Girls attend regularly as a rule, but are liable to be detained to take care of younger children, for home washing, in cases of illness, etc.
    (iii)   Boys attend regularly as a rule, but leave school early to get work.
(c)   Those of parents in irregular work, such as costermongers, dock labourers, etc, and of the idle and dissolute.
    (i)   Infants are often entered early and attend better than other children of same age, the school being regarded as caretaker.
    (ii)   Girls are often most irregular. The mother's earnings are frequently larger than the father's and the girls are kept at home to look after babies and children, or are sent to beg in the streets, sell flowers, etc.
    (iii)   Boys are generally very irregular. Parents of this class have often no control over their children, though they encourage their begging and getting odd employment. From this class comes the great bulk of truants, street arabs, crossing sweeper boys and young criminals. The whole of this class are more migratory in their habits than the others . . .

In their model, then, the children of the well-off attended well. The regularly employed were respectable, and their children attended well even if they were poor, except that sometimes the girls were needed at home—which was not incompatible with their being respectable. The irregularly employed were (actually or potentially) idle and dissolute, and their children, except the infants, were very irregular. Comparison of the model with attendance figures confirms some of their observations (such as the high attendance of the infants of the poorest class), but it also brings out important distinctions obscured by their concern with moral ordering.[77]

Detailed comparison is made possible by the attendance returns given each year for all Board schools in the reports of the School Management Committee. Individual schools often had a marked social character, established partly by the nature of the district they served, and partly also by the level of the fee charged. (The system of charging different fees at different schools was one way of reassuring better-off and respectable parents that their children could be accommodated in the Board system without being exposed to rougher ways.)[78] Such differences can be illustrated from the account given by Mrs Bartle (born in Poplar in 1882, her father a coastal seaman who became a mate) of the two schools she attended. The first, Thomas Street, charged sixpence, a very high fee.[79] She recalled it as:

> really very superior . . . some of the better-off children used to go to Thomas Street. And of course there were tradespeople's children as well . . .'

> When my mother went to register my sister there ('cause my sister went before I did) . . . the headmistress of course told her it was sixpence a week, and she asked mother what father's position was, and mother told her . . . and she says, I think you're a very ambitious woman.[80]

When they moved, the mother's sights had to be lowered, and the girl went to Sydney Road, Homerton: a 'terribly rough school', where pupils fought in the street with Irish children from a nearby Catholic school and the fee was twopence. School Board statistics record high attendance rates at Thomas Street and low at Sydney Road.[81]

Using school fees as a guide to the approximate social standing of the school, we can explore the classification offered by the School Managers through one year's average attendance rates for the boys, girls and infants of London Board schools, according to fees charged.[82] (See Table 6.5. [see original reading])

In 1886–87 the thirty-two schools with a fee of fourpence or above may be taken to represent category (a) in the Managers' list; the 114 threepenny schools and the 233 twopenny schools their category (b), and the fifty-seven penny schools their (c). It should be noted that nearly three-quarters of the children were in twopenny and threepenny schools. Table 6.5 confirms that attendance improved with prosperity, but it also shows that girls' attendance was always, at each level, lower, and that in poverty it deteriorated more than either boys' or infants'. The girls' rate drops by 11 points (from 83 to 72 per cent) between the fourpenny school average and the penny; while the boys' rate falls by only 8.4 points (from 86 to 78.3 per cent), and the infants' by a mere 2.3, from 79 to 76.8 per cent.

The difference between boys' and girls' attendance was least (3.6 per cent) in the schools which charged fourpence or more. (At sixpenny Thomas Street it was only 2.3.) In the other three groups it was 6.6, 6.0 and 6.2 per cent. It is significant that there was always some difference. It is also interesting that the School Managers' analysis did not take note of it: they made no distinction between girls and boys in their category (a); in (b) they implied girls' greater absence but did not dwell on it; while in (c) they gave reasons for boys' and girls' respective absence rates without remarking that girls were absent more. Yet the annual statistics of the Board make clear that it was a difference which could be seen everywhere.

The lower attendance rate of girls, if noted at all, was attributed to home cares, with no suggestions on how to improve it. Boys' absence continually drew comment; it was defined as truancy and attributed to indifference and defiance; and various ways to control it were tried. Special roving Street Visitors were assigned to search 'streets or open spaces, markets, railway stations' for truants. Girls' absence was not seen as truancy;[83] homes were not searched in the same way, and girls ('necessarily required at home more than boys') were relatively immune from pursuit.[84] More boys than girls were sent to mend their ways in Truant and Industrial Schools;[85] and probably the parents of absentee boys were more prosecuted and more punished than those of absentee girls.[86] The School Board's 1890 inquiry into attendance discussed the subject almost entirely in terms of truancy, and took evidence from thirty-nine headmasters and only three headmistresses.[87] (No children or parents were called.)

An 1880 case reported in *Social Notes* suggests that domestic responsibilities were also a less acceptable excuse for boys.

> A poor woman in the house I live in has three children, two are babies, and one a boy of eleven years. . . . The woman's husband gives her 12s. to pay rent and provide food and clothing with. To nurse the babies she keeps her boy from Board School now and then, when she has a chance of going out to earn a shilling or two. For this crime she was summoned before the Board-school Committee, who treated her explanation with contempt and would not allow the boy's absence for even half a day . . .[88]

'A boy ought never to miss an attendance, unless there was not an elder girl in the family', was the opinion of Mrs Hickman, School Visitor for the City and Westminster, in 1890.[89]

Girls' absence, by implication, was to be condoned. If, at each level of enforcement, tolerance was more likely for girls kept at home than for boys, then, where there was any choice, the tendency for domestic responsibilities to fall on girls would be confirmed.

By the end of the century attendance rates had generally improved. The gap between the girls' rate and the boys' had narrowed to 4.2 per cent but was still there,[90] and it continued to be obscured and excused by the double standard. Girls' lower attendance, Spalding explained in 1900, stemmed from their 'greater usefulness in the domestic economy'. In his summing up he effectively ignored the difference:

> It cannot be considered unsatisfactory that more than half the total roll (50.7 per cent) should make perfect, or almost perfect, attendances, having regard to the many hindrances to regular attendance. These arise from the impossibility that infants should not often fail, from circumstances beyond their control, to attend school; the need for occasional help in the household from the girls; the squalor and destitution of many of the homes from which the children come; and the unavoidable absences on account of illness, not only of the children actually suffering, but also of the children living in houses where there is infection.[91]

Again, girls' domestic duties are given as contributing to absence from school, but the extent is not remarked on. 'More than half the total roll (50.7 per cent) . . . make perfect or almost perfect attendance', so the composition of that 50.7 per cent is forgotten: 59.2 per cent boys plus 46.4 per cent girls plus 46.5 per cent infants equals 50.7 per cent children.

The usefulness of school, then, was perceived as different for girls and for boys by those concerned with the provision of elementary education, whether at the level of the individual or of social and national interest. Boys were to be workers and citizens, and needed schooling to discipline and educate them. If they came from 'irregular' families which were irresponsible about sending them to school, this was especially important. Girls' intended future was domestic. So the call of domestic obligation was more properly made to girls, and its fulfilment was more properly the responsibility of girls. If girls did not attend regularly it meant that family need was being put before education. But for girls this was ultimately as it should be: as women they would not be citizens, their work would be in the home, and they should indeed put the family first. Thus the double standard undermined the formal equality of educational provision.

Notes

1   Information on this is scanty, but c.f. Black, *Married Women's Work*, p.23 (laundry-worker's consumptive husband tended the two youngest and cooked dinner for all five children), p.29 (seasonally unemployed husband looked after the children; wife working as a paper-sorter), and p.90; also Toogood, 'Role of the Crèche', p.81. The father of Miss H. (born Kensington, 1902), a restaurant manager, cared for the children during the day when the mother was very ill: transcript, p.12.

2   George Lansbury told the 1895 *R.C. Aged Poor* (qq.13,824–25) that in Bow and Bromley many old people on outdoor relief minded the children of their daughters 'who go to work for Bryant and May's, and also shirt stitch, and that kind of work'. C.f. Black, *Married Women's Work*, p.19; and numerous examples: e.g. McCleary, *Infant Milk Depots*, p.35, case 12; Miss N. (born Shadwell, 1895), transcript, p.5, and Mrs K. (born Battersea, 1897), transcript, p.4.

3   [Harkness], *Toilers*, 1889, pp.21–23.

4   When Frank S. (born Hoxton, 1884) was out of work his wife did laundry-packing and he walked the pram from Battersea to Chelsea and back each day so that her sister could have the children; transcript, p.80.

5   Christian Social Union *Report*, quoted Malcolmson, 'Laundresses', p.457.

6   Davies, *Life*, pp.20–22 (and p.3 her elder sister); c.f. Bosanquet, *Rich and Poor*, p.834. Arlidge noted in 1892 (*Diseases*, p.557) that with 'the almost universal adoption of the perambulator', young nurses suffered less often from 'lateral curvature of the spine and general one-sidedness produced by 'carrying children on one arm'.

7   An Acton laundress supporting two children on her own paid the landlady 1s. a week to look after the baby, and 2s, 6d. a week rent; she earned about 12s. 6d, a week: *R.C. Labour*, PP 1893–94, 'Employment of Women', p.22, Witness 139.

8   A Poor Law Inspector reported that it was 'very common' for 'old women in receipt of relief [to] . . . mind their neighbour's child during the day while they are getting work'. As Poor Law Unions refused relief in such cases, it is not surprising that they could not confirm this: *S.C. Protection Infant Life*, PP 1871, evidence q.3,884 and Appendix 4. Behlmer (*Child Abuse*, p.40) cites an 1877 report of numerous unlicensed nurseries run in cramped Clerkenwell homes by widows and spinsters.

9   Coate, 'Some Phases of Poor Life'. Rates varied (and rose) from 2s. 6d. a week in 1858 (*Times*, 7 Jan, police reports, Eleanor Emmerson); to 3s. to 4s. 6d. a week or 3d. to 6d. a day in 1871 (*S.C. Protection Infant Life*, 1871, Appendix 4); to 6s. or 7s. in 1873 (SBL *Minutes*, 28 May, pp.552, 1,105); to 4d. to 8d. a day in the 1890s (*Crèche Annual*, 1893–94, pp.14–15 and *R.C. Labour*, PP 1893–94, 'Employment of Women', pp.22–23); while rates quoted in 1915 range from 6d. to 1s. 2d. a day, with one minder earning from 11s. to 14s. a week (Black, *Married Women's Work*, p.19; see also p.62; pp.111–12). Crèches never paid their way, but they were always too dear for some mothers (see previous chapter [see original reading]).

10   Black, *Married Women's Work*, p.19.

11   Bosanquet, *Rich and Poor*, p.83.

12   For northern half-timers, see Hicks, 'Education of the Half-Timer'; Robson, *Education of Children in Industry;* Frow, *Half-Time*, and Silver, 'Ideology and the Factory Child'.

13   SBL *Final Report*, p.196.

14   *R.C. Factory Acts*, PP 1876, evidence, Buxton and Croad (London School Board), q.3,112.

15   For a girl half-timer in domestic box-making in Shoreditch in 1883, see PRO, ED 14/19, 4 May 1883; and for one in a pipe-making workshop in Tabard Street (Borough), see GLRO A/RNY/86, ms. letter E. Beard to Mrs H. Selfe Leonard, 24 Nov. 1887.

16   C.f. *School Board Chronicle*, 13 March 1880, p.246; SBL *Minutes*, 20 March 1884, p.862.

17   Here my concern is with reasons for the difference between boys' and girls' attendance patterns— sickness and lack of shoes were common to both.

18   See SBL *School Accommodation and Attendance Committee, Reports*, Table D.

19   Samuel, *Underworld*, p.31.

20   Mrs M. (born Hoxton, 1896), my notes of tape played at Hackney People's Autobiography meeting 4 April 1974, p.1. C.f. William Nn (born Poplar, 1896), ms. memoir, pp.17, 42: when his father was missing work through ill-health, he stopped going to afternoon school to help his mother make rope or canvas fendoffs [fenders] for a nautical dealer. From eleven till fourteen, he was an unofficial half-timer; and he was not allowed to sit the scholarship exam for secondary school.

21   SBL *Byelaws Committee, Reports*, e.g. 1889–90; *School Accommodation and Attendance Committee, Reports*, 1894–1900, Appendix 5. See also Rubinstein, *Attendance*, pp.36–37.

22   LCC *Education Committee, Minutes*, 26 Oct. 1902, pp.1, 182.

23   *The Times*, 23 Sept. 1891, p.8.

24   *Daily Chronicle*, 13 Oct. 1902, p.9.

25   C.f. cartoon Irishwoman registering for the new old-age pension, who cannot give her date of birth and says 'Faith, yer honour, there was no such thing as dates when I was born': *Punch*, 28 Oct. 1908, reproduced in Quadagno, *Aging*. Booth thought labourers often did not know their exact age: *R.C. Aged Poor*, PP 1895, evidence, q.10,967.

26   *H.M. Inspector's Report*, 1893, copied into Logbook, Maidstone Street, 28 Aug. 1893.

27   Logbook, Maidstone Street, 6 Sept. 1895, 3 March 1896, 12 March 1898, 31 Oct. 1899, 9 May 1900. C.f. also NUT *Report on School Attendance*, Oct. 1891, p.3 (PRO ED 10/11); and Macnamara's 1900 claim that some 25,000 of the 755,940 children on the school rolls in London were so often away that 'practically the only education they get [is] . . . their names on the school rolls': 'Progressivism', p.795.

28   For average ages per standard, see Logbook, Maidstone Street, 19 Sept. 1902. On greater irregu- larity of older children, c.f. SBL *School Management Committee, Minutes*, 14 Dec. 1888 (on Morris Road school, Tower Hamlets).

29   SBL *School Accommodation and Attendance Committee, Report*, 1892, Appendix 8, pp.266–68.

30   The logbook for Bell Street school has similar entries, but without age or standard: see 8 and 15 Oct. 1894; 29 March, 3 May, 24 Aug., 29 Nov. 1895; 31 July 1896; 3 Feb. 1897. In slum schools 'a full

fourth of the children on the rolls are seldom seen in school', according to Tabor ('Education', p.501).

31   Attendance at Brunswick Road school, Hackney, was 'little over 70 per cent and many of the boys are confirmed truants . . . away from school for weeks together. In the girls' school the percentage is equally low but there is no truancy': SBL *Minutes*, 13 July 1888, p.1,220 (School Management Committee Report).

32   Quoted in Spalding, *School Board*, p.136.

33   If domestic arrangements allowed, infants were more often kept at home in bad weather or for minor illness; they also succumbed in greater numbers to the infectious diseases which regularly swept through schools.

34   This return was quoted by Macnamara at the School Attendance Officers' national conference in 1900 to show that one-fifth of the children on the rolls made half-time or less. Both in this speech (*School Attendance Officers' Gazette*, Jan. 1901, p.162), and in 'Progressivism' (1900), he ignored the differences between boys, girls and infants, and his definitions and comments relate entirely to boys.

35   Logbook, Cottenham Road, 17 Feb. 1873, 10 July 1873.

36   Logbook, Gainsborough Road, 12 June 1885.

37   See examples in Rubinstein, *Attendance*, pp.60–61. Outwork is discussed more fully below.

38   C.f. Logbooks, Bell Street, 14 Dec. 1894, 18 Jan. 1889, 17 May 1897; Garratt Lane, 23 Nov. 1894, 19 April 1897, 18 April 1898; Gainsborough Road, 14 May 1897, 6 May 1898; Anglers Gardens, 27 Nov. 1885; Randall Place, 4 March 1892.

39   *Crèche Annual, 1880–1*, p.10.

40   Letter from Southwark Divisional Inspector, 15 April 1872 (PRO ED 14/1). Only 4,772 girls were on the rolls, to 7,647 boys; and 5,531 infants between three and five were reported not at school.

41   Hodson, *Letters*, pp.38–40. C.f. Mrs Layton (quoted previous chapter [see original reading]), who like other local children always stayed away on washing day: Davies, *Life*, p.4.

42   Logbook, Anglers' Gardens, 30 Jan. 1888, 17 Sept. 1890.

43   It was claimed in 1890 that 'on Mondays children were often kept away from school because the mother had not been "to pawn"' and had no money yet for the fee: SBL *Special Subcommittee, Administration of Byelaws, Report*, p.82.

44   Logbook, Cottenham Road, 18 Sept. 1874; 10 May 1875; similar references abound in other logbooks.

45   See Spalding, *School Board*, p.186; SBL *School Management Committee, Report*, 1889–90, p.lxxv; Logbooks, Bell Street, 5 Dec. 1895, 24 Jan. 1896; Anglers Gardens, 17 March 1893; Randall Place, 9 Feb. 1900, 10 May 1895.

46   Memorial from SBL to Education Dept, 28 Feb. 1881, asking for help over Baby Rooms (PRO ED 14/1).

47   C.f. Rubinstein, *Attendance*, p.64: 'helping mother', along with working in theatres and fields, 'enjoyed a tolerated position in the eyes of the Board and the Government, if only because it seemed impossible to stop'.

48   SBL Byelaws Committee on . . . uniform enforcement, 1874, evidence, qq.587–88.

49   Florence H. (born Bethnal Green, 1892), transcript, pp.11–12.

50   Ernest Gray in House of Commons debate on Education Estimates, 17 June 1897, reported *Schoolmaster*, 26 June 1897, p.1,129. C.f. Rubinstein, *Attendance*, p.63.

51   Quoted *Education Report, 1899*, PP 1900, p.297.

52   C.f. Rubinstein, *Attendance*, p. 47: before 1901 prosecution was unlikely unless attendance fell below seven out of ten.

53   Mag Ayling, on her aunt (born 1891, Deptford), recorded in class at Goldsmiths' College, 15 June 1983.

54   SBL *School Management Committee, Report*, 1887–88, p.xlv.

55   For one head's punctuality campaign, see Logbook, Flint Street, 1877, 12 July (several sent home), 23 Aug. (over 20 turned away), 6 Sept., 13 Sept. (a great number sent home, 'next week I shall punish them with the cane'), 18 Sept., 19 Sept. ('I have punished the late children, but it seems to do little good'), 27 Sept. (more punctual), 9 Oct. ('again lost their mark through coming late'), 10 Oct. (kept in), 18 Oct. (sent home), 24 Oct. (more punctual, none sent home).

56   The logbooks show so many causes of lateness (as of absence) that it seems unnecessary to look beyond ill-health, inadequate clothing, domestic and other responsibilities and the rest. But defensive entries by heads do often blame the parents' lack of interest in education.

57   SBL *Minutes*, 20 Dec. 1883, pp. 184–86. Inspector McWilliam's district was north Lambeth and north Southwark (Neckinger to Kennington Oval, Thames to Camberwell Green) but for this report he included nine other schools, mainly East End.

58 The system was later criticized for improving only the punctuality of those already punctual: it made the regular child 'one who sacrifices everything for the sake of perfect punctuality', and offered no incentive to the child whose chance was already lost: Memo from chairman, SBL Subcommittee, Medal System, SBL *Minutes*, 30 March 1900.

59 C.f. SBL Chairman's lament in 1880 that unpunctuality interfered with scripture instruction: Reed, 'Ten Years', pp.674–75; and SBL *Management Committee Reports*, 1887–88, p.xlvi, and 1888–89, p.xiii (worse still, 'this loss occurs principally in those cases where there is least probability that home or Sunday school teaching will compensate').

60 *Cross Commission, 2nd Report*, PP 1887, evidence HMI Nickal, qq.39,874–79.

61 SBL *School Management Committee Reports*, School Returns, 1887–88 to 1893–94.

62 *Employment of Schoolchildren*, PP 1902, evidence Hetherington (Hackney), q.956; Bevan (Hackney), qq.2,691–98; Eves, Appendix 18.

63 *Crèche Annual, 1895–6*, pp.8–9.

64 Celia R. (born Waterloo, 1899) was regularly caned for being late because her mother sent her on last minute errands: notes from SE1 People's History Group, 4 Aug. 1981.

65 C.f. discussion in Rubinstein, *Attendance*, (pp.98–103, esp. p.102) of a ruling in 1884 that a twelve-year-old nursemaid was 'discharging the honourable duly of helping her parents': 'a reasonable excuse for her non-attendance at school'; and Lewis, 'School Fees and the School Board', p.292.

66 *Hansard* 1 March 1899, cols 962–63 and 972.

67 Memo from chairman, SBL *Subcommittee, Medal System*, 1900.

68 See, for instance, SBL *Minutes*, 8 Feb. 1884: in the Board's reply to an Education Department enquiry on obstacles to improved attendance all four points concern enforcement.

69 *Cross Commission, 2nd Report*, PP 1887, evidence Mrs Burgwin (head Orange Street, Southwark), qq.17,064–65. For extended discussion of social causes of poor attendance, and of attempts to deal with them, see Hurt, *Schooling*, chaps 5–8,

70 For example SBL *School Management Committee, Report 1887–8*, p.xliv (Inspectors' Reports); or Memorial from Metropolitan Board Teachers Association, 1889 (PRO ED/10 10). Lewis ('School Fees and the School Board') argues convincingly that arguments based on moral categorization were becoming less tenable.

71 SBL *Inspectors' Reports*, PP 1878, p.8.

72 SBL *Inspectors' Reports*, PP 1878, p.31.

73 SBL *Minutes*, 20 Dec. 1883, p.186.

74 Albert M. (born Hoxton, 1894), transcript, pp.A36–41.

75 SBL *Special Committee, Administration Byelaws*, 1890, Report, p.68.

76 As previous note, p.142.

77 The managers' moralizing reminds us that such questions occasioned continuing political struggle within the Board and school administration more generally: c.f. Lewis, 'School Fees and the School Board'.

78 C.f. Marsden, 'Residential Segregation'; 'Education and Urbanization', pp.88–90.

79 Only two other Board Schools in Tower Hamlets charged as much: SBL *School Management Committee, Report*, 1886–87, Table R, School Returns, Tower Hamlets.

80 Mrs Bartle, transcript, pp.16–17. The school's superiority was attested in inspectors' reports, which praised its achievements in examinations and also in drill.

81 The rates were 91.3 per cent for boys, 89 per cent for girls, and 80 per cent for infants at Thomas Street; 71.1 per cent, 75.8 per cent, and 71.7 per cent at Sydney Road: SBL *School Management Committee, Report*, 1886–87, Table R, School Returns, Tower Hamlets and Hackney.

82 See SBL *School Management Committee, Report*, 1886–87, School Returns, London. The few mixed schools are not included here; and calculations are made on the basic fee only (it was reduced for the brothers and sisters of a child already attending the school). Infants' fees were lower, but still preserved differences.

83 C.f. SBL *Special Subcommittee, Administration Byelaws, Minutes*, 24 Oct. 1889: heads' responses to the question, 'Do you have many cases of truancy among your scholars?' record from five to ten times as many truant boys as girls, despite a reverse ratio in attendance figures.

84 *Employment of Schoolchildren*, PP. 1902, p.9 (report of H.M. Inspector King).

85 In 1871 339 cases of boys and seventy of girls were dealt with by the School Board Industrial Schools Officers: most boys were remanded or sent to Industrial (i.e. Truant) Schools, and under half of the girls (SBL *Minutes*, 13 Dec. 1871, p.25). Subsequent reports suggest a similar pattern.

86 SBL *School Accommodation and Attendance Committee, Report*, 1892–93, Appendix xviii, gives details concerning nineteen boys and seven girls in Finsbury in 1892: four boys were sent to Truant Schools, and no girls; fines were higher for the boys. Spalding (*School Board*, pp. 143–45), in 1900, records

740 boys in the SBL's five residential Industrial Schools, and fifty girls. London children could be sent elsewhere, but the national sex ratio was similar; in 1895 there were 13,133 boys in such institutions to 4,241 girls: *H.M. Inspectors' Report*, 1895.

87   SBL *Special Committee, Administration Byelaws*, 1890, p.91.
88   *Social Notes* 1, 11 Sept. 1880, p.96.
89   SBL *Special Committee, Administration Byelaws*, 1890, p.91.
90   *Board of Education Report*, PP 1899, p.295 (Mr King's General Report on schools of the Metropolis). Boys' average attendance for 1898 was 85.3 per cent and for 1899 85.8 per cent; girls' was 81.1 per cent (1898) and 81.6 per cent (1899); infants' 78.2 per cent and 71.1 per cent.
91   Spalding, *School Board*, pp.136–37.

Chapter 20

Catriona Kelly

"THANK YOU FOR THE WONDERFUL BOOK": SOVIET CHILD READERS AND THE MANAGEMENT OF CHILDREN'S READING, 1950–75

ACCORDING TO A PATRIOTIC CLICHÉ of the post-Stalin era, the Soviet people was "the most given to reading in the entire world" (*samyi chitaiushchii narod v mire*). As a corollary, reading was, commentators argued, given a central place in the socialization of children by every Soviet family, however humble. A pronouncement by Lev Kassil' in 1964 is typical: "One can say with absolute confidence that throughout the extent of our motherland there is not a single dwelling with even one child in it where there is not also at least one children's book."[1] But teaching children about reading was not left purely to parents. Enormous efforts were expended by state institutions on circulating children's literature, and on making sure that this was read in the appropriate way. School syllabi dictated not only "set books," in the sense of those discussed in class, but also "extracurricular reading" (*vneklassnoe chtenie*), which might form the subject of debates organized by the "class supervisor" (grade-level teacher, whose duties included providing moral guidance to pupils and organizing "cultural work" such as theater visits and excursions).[2] Guides and magazines for parents provided recommendations on how to supervise children's reading, an activity held to require the exercise of great care and responsibility.[3] Libraries—as in earlier periods of Soviet history—worked as centers of the Soviet civilizing mission: children's tastes were monitored through the use of record cards, and staff members affirmed their tastes (if these seemed to be moving in the right direction) or, alternatively, tried to nudge them into reading material of different kinds (if the child were unduly fond of adventure stories or some other marginal genre).[4]

By the late 1960s, there was some criticism of excessive controlling behavior on the part of librarians.[5] But regulation continued by means of strategies such as the use of recommendatory bibliographies, posters, and personal advice. An article about children's reading of Pioneer newspapers published as late as 1983 still emphasized the need to develop "political thinking" above all, and to teach children to read systematically; it advocated methods such as circulating a memo with a list of Instructions ("Read every article carefully!" etc.), holding competitions and quizzes about the content of each issue, putting together a display board (*stend*) of related items, acting out the "plots" of specific stories, and so on.[6]

Alongside schools, libraries, and parents, Komsomol and Pioneer organizations had a role in regulating guidance. Officially speaking, they were *shefy* (guides and patrons) of the publishing houses for children's literature, issuing directives about major political themes that were supposed to be covered by the printed output of the house and in its outreach work.[7] By the post-Stalin era, however, the direction was rather "hands off": editors had a fair amount of leeway regarding the themes that they invoked beyond the Soviet political canon and issues deemed topical at the time ("communist education," the space race, etc.).[8] While Komsomol apparatchiks of the late 1920s and early 1930s had spent a great deal of energy micromanaging the circulation of literature (worrying that children liked adventure stories too much and this or that book was unsuitable and should be removed from the shelves), by the 1960s their efforts were concentrated in the specific field of "Pioneer" and "Komsomol" literature, as represented by, say, the official hagiographies of Pavlik Morozov, Zoia Kosmodem'ianskaia, and Pioneer war heroes such as Volodia Dubinin and Lenia Kotikov, which children were supposed to read as preparation for enrollment in the Pioneers.[9] Such material was made available in "Pioneer corners" in schools,[10] discussed at Pioneer and Komsomol meetings, and included at the "talks round the bonfire" that were held at Pioneer camps over the summer.

How effective, one might ask, was all this? To what extent did Soviet educators, ideologues, parents, and other "responsible adults" succeed in imposing their tastes on the younger generation? The present article attempts a preliminary answer to that question, based on two complementary sorts of evidence—oral history (which has all the usual disadvantages of retrospective commentary but allows access to status groups, such as the working class and peasantry, that have not generally left behind written memoirs), and letters written by children themselves to Soviet publishing houses in the 1950s, 1960s, and 1970s (which provide us with important evidence of actual children's response to books at the time when they were written but emanate from a self-selected and hence self-defining elite).[11] It argues that children's responses to texts were diverse, a diversity that may be correlated directly with the social background from which they came and the degree to which the values held there overlapped with those in the Soviet cultural establishment. At the same time, it emerges that even the children who were most adept in expressing "convergent" views often did this in ways that to a significant degree departed from adult conceptions of what the art of responding to a book should be about.

Children reading: problems and concepts

Reader-response is a notoriously difficult area of historical investigation, and, where the tastes of children in past generations are concerned, the classical evidence employed in "history of the book" studies, such as sales figures, is even more suspect than usual.[12] Children are not usually consumers of books in the elementary sense that they buy these themselves. Often, they stumble on volumes that are simply lying around. Even if books are specially bought, the purchases are often made by adults: parents, obviously, but also other relations (one sales niche is known by modern British book professionals as "grauntie" books, that is, books purchased by grannies and aunts for birthdays and so on). Often, too, these purchases are driven by factors not directly connected with the child's personal preferences, even as constructed from a distance—above all, the purchaser's own tastes as a child. The retrospective character of memoir sources is still more of a problem here than it is with memoirs recalling adulthood, since the gap between author and earlier self is psychological as well as temporal in nature.[13] Diaries and letters are not only scarce but also only dubious expressions of the personalities of those who wrote them, since often adults have had a hand in prompting their composition and in some cases in regulating the details of the material presented therein.

Perhaps, though, one should stop thinking in terms of "authentic" childhood reading experience as necessarily distinct from adult control. As linguistic anthropologists have been arguing for more than 20 years, adults play a direct role not just in showing children what to read, but in teaching children how to read as well. In the words of Shirley Brice Heath, "[w]ays of taking from books are just as much a part of learned behavior as are ways of eating, sitting, playing games, and building houses." She also notes, "[c]hildren have to learn to select, hold, and retrieve content from books and other written or printed texts in accordance with their community's rules or 'ways of taking,' and the children's learning follows community paths."[14] Heath makes concrete this abstract insight with reference to three alternative methods of socializing children to read, as practiced in "Maintown," "Roadville," and "Trackton," aliases for three different communities in North Carolina with dominant populations of, respectively, affluent middle-class, white working-class, and black working-class residents. In "Maintown," children learn very early from question-and-answer sessions with their parents that books are supposed to be talked about analytically, and both this basic procedure and the individual questions prepare them efficiently for the priorities of school education, where event recapitulation and content-retelling are less valued than are "reason-explanation" and "affective commentaries."[15] In "Roadville," on the other hand, a tremendous respect for books is allied to great wariness about the status of the book. Adult commentaries not only fail to draw any connection between the text and the wider world (so that a child will be told that a fantasy yellow image of a bird on a pond is a "duck," without being told how it relates to the living brown creature also so called that they feed bread to on a Sunday), but may also emphasize that "books" and "real life" are very far apart. Finally, in "Trackton," the book is an incidental object in a culture that is strongly shaped by oral tradition: here, children early learn to tell stories themselves, become accustomed to hearing stories that are shaped by rhetorical identifiers such as ring form, and grow up in a world where non-verbal communication is at least as important as verbal communication.

Clearly, Heath's representation is schematic, indeed verging on the stereotypical. But it does have some value in capturing basic differences between the status of the book in different communities and the impact of these on the socialization of reading. While testing out the model in terms of Soviet history is problematic, given that memoirs and oral history sources tend to be uncommunicative about how children were actually taught to read in an interpretive sense (the most that customarily gets remembered is which reading primers were used), peripheral references point to the existence of widely differing attitudes toward the book and to differing ways of bringing children into contact with it. Sources such as mothers' diaries representing life in intelligentsia families make clear the enormous weight laid on intellectual development in early childhood by such families and the importance accorded to rational, substantive discussion of philosophical and aesthetic issues. The care with which children's opinions about the world and about books are recorded suggests that the way children were taught about reading in this social group approximated that found in "Maintown."[16]

The official campaign to disseminate *kul'turnost'* gave "Maintown" attitudes toward reading a crusading flavor that they did not have in the America Heath was describing. Library work with children during the late Soviet era was considerably more interventionist than it was in the contemporary West. Libraries molded juvenile tastes not just by guiding individual readers but by excluding material that was considered "unsuitable" (a technique employed in the West as well, though censorship of material for children was more haphazard in British or American libraries, say, than it was in Soviet ones).[17] In addition, they organized outreach events, such as exhibitions, competitions, and "reader conferences," at which issues of the day and canonical texts were discussed. At these, children were taught not just what to read but how to read—what kind of things to say and think about the books that they consumed.[18]

The "book famine" (*knizhnyi golod*) of the late Soviet era made libraries a more likely venue for Russian child readers than libraries were for their Western contemporaries, so that this propaganda of "mainstream" methods of how to read had a better chance of reaching its target. The potential for mismatch between children's tastes and those of librarians lay in the possibility that highly recommended books would simply not be available in enough copies—that children would not be able to read what they were supposed to—rather than in the possibility that they would somehow get hold of "unsuitable" material.[19]

Reading outside "Maintown"

On the other hand, oral history reveals the existence of other models as well. There were, in Soviet Russia, "Roadville" households, where books were considered objects of great importance, but ones to be venerated rather than read. A woman from a working-class background in Moscow, born in 1941, remembered that her first contact with reading came through her grandfather:

> He had lots of books, old ones. I can remember a volume of Pushkin. Grandad rebound books and he used to treat them very carefully, everything was all glued. There was . . . this volume, volume 1, which I took out of his bookcase, when . . . when I started reading more or less. On the whole he didn't let you take the books. But I was a tidy girl, so he let me.[20]

Another woman, born in 1920 in Pskov province, lived in a family where reading was a ritual, rather than a process of gaining access to information: "My father was a party man, but illiterate, eh. He'd often make me read aloud . . . what's that book called? A party book, I've forgotten, forgotten what it was called. He'd often make me read a few of those aloud."[21]

In families of this kind, the few books were usually totemic choices—if not "party" books, then the works of classic writers or books about them, such as the "book about Pushkin" remembered by a woman born in Pskov province, 1932.[22] The standard idiom used was not "to read a book" but "to study a book" (*uchit' knigu*), as in phrases of the type, "You just sit there quietly and study that book!" (*Sidi spokoino, uchi knigu!*).[23]

Shockingly for the myth *of samyi chitaiushchii narod v mire*, there is evidence also for the existence of a "Trackton"-like culture in the society, where books did not come at the top of the value system. Oral history work in villages, particularly, indicates that books were scarce and, where present, scarcely treated as "books" at all. As a woman born in 1938, who spent most of her childhood in rural parts of Vologda and Leningrad provinces, remembered:

> *Informant:* We'd go through [the Bible] like a photo album.
> *Interviewer 2:* You didn't read it?
> *Informant:* Nay-nay. If there was a caption to the picture . . . "The Deluge" or something, we'd read that. Otherwise, we'd just look at the pictures.[24]

This household at least had a copy of one book, though not one that would have been approved by Soviet ideologues. Contrary to the assertions of Lev Kassil', there were Soviet homes where there were no books at all—even children's books. A teacher who worked during the late Soviet era in the southern Russian town of Taganrog recalled that many of the households where her pupils were brought up owned no reading material whatsoever.[25] As books became more widely available in the second half of the 20th century, the idea of the book as "sacred object" started to disperse, but indifference to books persisted: not everyone felt compelled to avail him- or herself of the opportunity to buy reading matter.

Parental socialization could, then, be at variance with official models of teaching children about reading, rather than (as was supposed to happen) reinforcing this. To be sure, children brought up in households where books were unfamiliar or outlandish objects could develop addictions to reading.[26] Thus the cultivation of leisure practices became at once the expression and the instrument of social mobility and of a burgeoning intelligentsia identity. Often, however, children assimilated the attitudes of the households from which they came. In the words of one Leningrad woman born in the late 1960s, and brought up in a truck-driver's family:

> Eh, if I'm really honest, I can't say I exactly . . . well, really liked reading. I read when I had to. [. . .] Though there were a couple of things that really got me going. That would be more like class seven or eight [i.e., age 14 or 15]. Well, *Shchit i mech* [Shield and Sword],[27] I really loved reading that book; I think I read it a few times, it's a nice fat one. Then there was some other book, can't remember what. But mostly, the other books. I read them because . . . so as to . . . well, we were going to do them in school in any case.[28]

One notes here the greater emphasis on the physical presence of the book—"a nice fat one"[29]—than on its contents; equally, one notes the sharp separation in the informant's mind between books to be "gone through for school" (*prokhodit'*) and those read for pleasure.

Among historical subjects of this kind, reading often made its way into the schedule of leisure activities at second hand, brought into a generally alien world through a link with another activity. Children might, for instance, read a book *after* having watched the film on which it was based (as in the case just mentioned—see note) or consult some practical guide related to a hobby activity that interested them.[30] In some minds, this led to a stark polarization between "interesting" books (practical ones) and "boring" books (imaginative literature, most particularly the literary classics). A working-class Leningrad man born in 1960, for example, remembered consuming with enthusiasm books from the series *V mire fantastiki i prikliuchenii* [The World of Fantasy and Adventure]: "Eh, we had a whole big cupboard full of the things [again, note the emphasis on physical substance]. I read them all. I was reading away at all that for several years. Right. Very interesting things they were. I really gulped them down [*Eto ia zapoem chital*]." He also enjoyed various kinds of scientific magazines ("I really gnawed away at those magazines [*Vot eto ia gryz eti zhurnaly*] [. . .] Right. *Iunyi naturalist* [Young Naturalist], *Iunyi tekhnik* [Young Technician], *Modelist-konstruktor* [Scale Model Maker]—all those things"). Belles-lettres, on the other hand, had less appeal: "I hated the literary classics. Couldn't stand that stuff. Well, other people's lives: what do I want to be messing round there for? [*Nu, chuzhie zhizni, chto wne koposhit'sia tam.*] But when I said I thought Tolstoi was boring, I fell right out of favor in class nine [aged 16] [. . .] and I don't like Pushkin either. So what's so big about him? The world goes on its sweet way without him [*solntse i bez nego svetit khorosho*]."[31]

Confessions of this kind should not be taken entirely at face value. The collapse of Soviet power has brought a collapse of the totalizing aesthetic standards imposed by that power: informants now relish the chance to exercise their taste in ways that would not have been permissible in the schoolroom and may well exaggerate the extent of their nonconformity in the past, particularly in speaking to an interviewer who is a member of the intelligentsia. At the same time, the concrete material provided about early reading and the way in which it is described (with references to books as objects with a physical presence, to be "gulped down" or kept from childish vandalism) reflects a very different set of attitudes from those found in households where books were taken as a given. The evidence suggests that, though "main-stream" reading patterns were often effectively disseminated to children who grew up in home environments that would not themselves have provided tutelage in analytical reading, there was also a significant proportion of children who did not absorb such patterns and retained traditional associations between reading and ingesting, in the most physical sense, rather than mental processing.[32] Children who read in "aberrant" ways tended to be regarded, once they reached school, as morally recalcitrant and intellectually deficient. Although a good many Soviet teachers—perhaps the majority—remained committed to multi-ability teaching after "special schools" were introduced in the 1960s, there is also evidence (in oral history, from the pupils' end) of institutionalized prejudice against working-class pupils. In one Leningrad model school, for example, the "best" teacher for the primary section was able to pick out her own class, "which she, of course, did on the basis of who their parents were [. . .] our class included the daughter of the director of [a major] factory, various party officials, and artists, too."[33] Seen from the other end, the situation often resembled being written off before you had begun. As a working-class Leningrader born in 1960 remembered his school years:

> Well, I got stuck with this teacher-training expert [*metodist*] in German. She was a real cow. That's the only word. You'd try hard to find one as bad as her wher-ever you looked. "You abortions! [*A, nedonoshennye!*] Only fit to end up in a technical college!"[34] [*Po vam vsem PTU plachet!*] [. . .] But she fawned on the prize pupils like she was going crazy. [. . .] If you were up for answering questions, she'd ask a trick one specially so she could give you three minus at most. You could cram that stuff in yourself all week, but she'd make sure you messed up, and you'd end up with egg on your face whatever you did.[35]

The situation was the more tragic in that many working-class parents' involvement with school was essentially limited to monitoring the quality of their children's marks: bringing home a "two" meant you got a thrashing.[36] Not surprisingly, children from this group also bore a fair amount of enmity toward high achievers, and their energy tended to go into conflicts with these, rather than into campaigns for self-improvement.[37] They tended—as is suggested both by oral history and evidence from work by Soviet sociologists during the post-Stalin era—to take their attitudes to reading into adulthood as well.[38]

Whatever one's doubts about the precise fit of Heath's tripartite schema to Soviet material, there certainly were significant status-related differences in the socialization of reading. The attitudes prevailing in the home and social group more widely were fundamental to the issue of which books got read and how. Indeed, family perhaps played a greater role in the late Soviet era than in the early Soviet decades, both because literate but non-reading parents were less likely to encourage their children to read than illiterate, book-worshiping ones, and because of the general "privatization" dynamic of the era, with its strong emphasis on the centrality of family life and on the importance of rational consumption (which included, but was not limited to, the consumption of books).[39]

It is instructive to bear these points in mind given the long history, under Soviet power, of emphasizing that childhood experience was homogeneous. The tendency to identify the welfare of children with the nation's very identity on the one hand, and the official under-standing of Soviet society as class-free that was introduced with the promulgation of the Soviet Constitution in 1936 on the other, blended together to create a situation where child-hood experience became living proof that Soviet society was classless. All Soviet children, irrespective of their parents' occupation, enjoyed—so the myth went—a perfectly happy childhood, while Western children were either pampered bourgeois brats or workers' sons and daughters groaning in poverty.[40]

If children's experience was unitary, it followed that "the child reader" was a universal figure, whose responses could be predicted in advance, and who would be suited by some types of literature and not by others. As is well known, during the first decade of Soviet power, the *skazka* (fairy tale) had been a controversial genre, with powerful figures in the education ministry, including Nadezhda Krupskaia, taking the view that writing about supernatural and counterfactual phenomena constituted a bourgeois form of escapism that was uncongenial to proletarian children.[41] At the 1934 First Congress of Soviet Writers, however, the *skazka* was returned to favor as the quintessential genre of children's writing: the idea was now that *all* children loved fantasies and should be provided with these in quantity.[42] In retrospective commentaries on the Stalin era, this shift is often regarded as progressive—a move away from the constrictive ideology and explicit didacticism of the 1920s and toward a recognition of children's essential nature as readers.[43] It is best interpreted, however, as the imposition of an alternative form of didacticism on children's writers and (indirectly) on child readers: one where the purpose of contact with literature was the development of the imagination.[44] Not all children were or are drawn to fantasy, or indeed to fiction. There was a proportion of children (its size is difficult to quantify, but "a substantial minority" would be a safe lower estimate) for whom nonfiction was the essential reading experience. In the period under discussion, children in this group gravitated toward journals such as *Iunyi tekhnik;* books about geography, science, and technology; and biographical series such as *Zhizn 'zamechatel' nykh liudei* (Lives of Remarkable People).[45]

The primary assumptions of this article are that the tenet of an inevitable or natural juvenile response to books has no analytical value (its importance as a legitimating strategy for commentators on children's literature notwithstanding); and that children's reading should be seen as dynamic and multifaceted, involving engagement not only with books but also with the process of being taught how to read. Children's response to reading and to being taught about reading is not purely passive, since they bring to these experiences a set of further perceptions and experiences, some of which may be based on participation in a full-scale children's subculture.[46] Adult input is, however, crucial both in providing material to read and in shaping how to read it.

How precisely did the process of "managing reading" work in Soviet Russia at the period of most interest here, the late Stalin and post-Stalin eras? Here the limits of oral history are reached. Informants usually remember rather vaguely what they were taught at a given point; they may also (consciously or unconsciously) suppress material that has a strong ideological coloration. Hence, contemporary documentation must be used to complement retrospective sources, as Nicholas Stargardt has argued in a recent book on children's war experience in Germany.[47]

Soviet assessments of children's reactions to books

The difficulty in assessing Soviet reality is the scarcity of sources recording children's perceptions, particularly for the post-Stalin era. A few children's diaries depicting the Stalin era, such as David Samoilov's "Dnevnik schastlivogo mal'chika" (Diary of a Happy Boy) or Nina Kosterina's posthumously published diary, have come to light, but such material is rare and not socially representative (both Samoilov and Kosterina came from Moscow families close to the top of the cultural elite).[48] In the absence of diaries, one needs to look elsewhere. One possible source for the study of children's reading as a process mediated by adult control would be school essays. The evidence that these provided would likely be rather one-sided, however, given that children exercised no influence on what the Soviet school program contained, even in the relatively liberal era of the late 1920s, let alone at later stages of history. More broadly, notions of what was interesting and appealing to children had little role in the content of the syllabus or the methods according to which it was taught.[49] By the late 1940s, schoolchildren's essays on literature tended to differ more in terms of an author's acuity in grasping what was expected from him or her by the teacher and in putting this into practice (or, conversely, lack of acumen in doing this) than they did in terms of idiosyncratic points of interpretation.[50]

A better source for understanding how the negotiation between children's responses to literature and adult direction of these functioned is the research on juvenile reading that was done by pedagogues outside the school system and librarians. Before the Revolution, and in the early days of Soviet power, such research—as with research on children's responses to the cinema and the theater—was generally conducted in questionnaire or interview form. In 1932–33, for example, the Nauchno-issledovatel'skii institut detskoi literatury i detskogo chteniia (Institute of Children's Literature and Children's Reading), a department of the People's Commissariat of Education (Narkompros), organized a large-scale survey, carried out in the form of interviews, of child readers in Moscow province. The survey established that books with a high profile among this audience included Furmanov's *Chapaev*, as well as such forgotten masterpieces as Vaisenberg's *Povest' o nefti* (Tale of Oil Production) and Matveev's *Komissar zolotogo poezda* (The Commissar of the Golden Train); most of the respondents had some idea of what a "shock-worker" was and of what Pioneers were supposed to be like ("activists"; "they have clean notebooks").[51] From the point when the condemnation of "pedological perversions" in July 1936 made questionnaire work, like IQ testing, ideologically suspect, different methods of measuring children's reactions were used. Central among these were studies of the fan mail that children sent to the Detgiz (later Detskaia literatura) publishing houses in Moscow and Leningrad.

Like the letters written by adult readers to Soviet newspapers, or the slush piles (*samotek*) of Soviet publishing houses, children's fan mail cannot be considered a spontaneous phenomenon. Its composition was, as we shall see, strongly encouraged by teachers and parents, as well as fostered by the publishing houses through the promise of prizes for the best letters. Writing fan mail was not obligatory, however, in the way that writing a school essay was. While attempts were made to program content in advance by suggesting topics to write about, the fact that critiques were not issued retrospectively and grades were not assigned gave those writing letters a bigger space for self-articulation than was allowed to the writers of school essays. Even in the filtered form in which such letters are now available—typed copies filed in annual reports on reader correspondence held in the archives of publishing houses—they convey significant insights into changing reader preferences and into fluctuating patterns of reading as interpretation.

Obviously, such materials do not constitute a representative sample of reactions from the child population as a whole. A child who wrote to a publishing house was likely to enjoy reading, to be eager to express a view, and to be reasonably articulate in doing so. But the social—and more particularly geographical—range of authors of such letters was wider than the social and geographical range of children who later went on to write their memoirs.[52] In any case, even if these letters tell us only about how some children read, the information that they give about this is significant; one might compare them to the workers' diaries, readers' letters, and official autobiographies that are currently popular sources for the study of adult history in the Soviet era. The remainder of this article is therefore devoted to a close study of children's letters, preceded by some information about the institutional context in which they were produced.

Readers' letters as documents: institutional management and genre rules

Like all Soviet publishing houses and journals, the central state children's press, Detskaia literatura (or Detizdat and Detgiz, as it was known in its earlier phases of existence), received many thousands of readers' letters a year, both at its Moscow and at its Leningrad premises. A high proportion of these contained comments about publications put out by the press. Within the publishing houses themselves, little seems to have been done with the letters. But for decades, the material was forwarded to, and processed by, the Dom detskoi knigi (DDK) in each city—a separate institution from Detskaia literatura, though with close connections to it, charged with doing outreach work with readers to promote Detskaia literatura publications and to give the publishing house some indication of how books were going down with their target audience. The DDK, then, acted both as a clearing house for reader opinion and as a place for shaping reader tastes; in between these objectives, a carefully controlled space for children's expressions of interest in books was allowed to flourish.

The Moscow DDK was set up early in 1950, and the Leningrad one in the autumn of that year. Institutionally, the DDK were subordinated to the city publications office (in the Leningrad case, the Leningradskoe otdelenie izdatel'stv), being classified as *tvorcheskie labora-torii* (creative laboratories) thereof. They were themselves divided into various departments, including, in the Leningrad case, a *kabinet massovoi raboty* ("office of work with the masses"—before 1962), and a *kabinet propagandy* and *kabinet izucheniia dets-koi literatury i chitatel' skogo vospriiatiia knig* (propaganda office, office for the study of children's literature and reader responses—after 1962). More concretely, the Leningrad facilities included a library with (until 1963) a reading room and exhibition halls, among them a "museum of the children's book." The on-site activities ranged from discussion sessions devoted to work in progress and to new publications, readings by writers of their work and opportunities for readers to meet them, an exhibition of books round which a variety of thematic guided tours were offered, lectures, and "reader conferences" devoted to specific books or topics. Additionally, staff at the DDK organized a variety of activities for schools and did outreach work with child readers generally: for instance, coordinating competitions in which children were encouraged to submit reviews of a Detgiz book that they had read recently (lists of recommended books were distributed along with the invitations to participate in the competition, though reviews dealing with books not included on these lists seem to have been accepted as well).[53]

Much of the outreach work was directed through libraries, the chain of command reaching down from the DDK to the Central Children's Library and finally to district libraries.[54] The most public event of the year was "Children's Book Week," a program of methodological talks and consultations for libraries, exhibitions, public readings, and reader conferences, held not only in the DDK itself but also in libraries, schools, and so on.[55]

The work of DDK, or certainly the Leningrad part of it, remained to a large extent stable throughout the late Stalin and early post-Stalin eras. Just as children's magazines and newspapers marked the onset of the new era essentially by omissions (the disappearance of hagiographical pieces about Stalin), rather than by the incursion of notable new topics,[56] so the DDK continued, in the 1960s, to have a mixed program of ideologically slanted, generally socially conscious, and purely "literary" events. In late 1950 and early 1951, for instance, it hosted discussions of Stalin's *Marksizm i iazykoznaniia* (Marxism and Linguistics), evenings devoted to "books about leaders and heroes," books about "the iron will and bravery of the Soviet people," and on the Soviet official peace movement.[57] But in the same season, the DDK also held puppet shows, a talk on prophylactic medicine, and a series of talks on "Your Favorite Books," which included not only predictable Stalinist classics such as Polevoi's *Povest' o nastoiashchem. cheloveke* (Tale of a Real Man), Fadeev's *Molodaia gvardiia* (The Young Guard), and Ostrovskii's *Kak zakalialas' stal'* (How the Steel Was Tempered) but also less sternly ideological works such as Kataev's *Beleet parus odinokii* (A White Sail Gleams), Gaidar's *Shkola* (The School), Kal'ma's *Deti gorchichnogo raia* (The Children of Mustard Heaven), and Kaverin's *Dva kapitana* (The Two Captains).[58]

Ten years later, in 1962, the program had not changed a great deal. Although various events were planned to commemorate the 40th anniversary of the Pioneer movement (for instance, conferences of writers, librarians, pedagogues, and Pioneer leaders on "The Pioneer Theme in Recent Children's Literature"), and the Lenin cult was given its predictable due, other themes included the outside world and book manufacture; and among books in the spotlight were Vil'iam Kozlov's adventure story *Na staroi mel'nitse* (The Old Mill) and Grigory Iagdfel'd's "comic fairy tale" (*smeshnaia skazka*) *Den' chudes* (Day of Miracles). Similarly, in 1972, alongside events connected with the 50th anniversaries of the Pioneer movement and of the founding of the USSR, there was an exhibition on the fairy tale (*V mire skazok*) and events dedicated to a variety of different books, not all with strong political links.[59]

There was comparable continuity in the themes offered at excursions for schoolchildren round the DDK. In the late 1950s, these contained a mixture of Soviet patriotism and celebration of official children's organizations, on the one hand, and information about children's classics and book history, on the other. For instance, topics addressed in September 1958 included "Books about Our Heroes," "Heroes of the Civil and Great Patriotic Wars," and "They Fought for the Motherland," but also "How the Book Was Made" and "An Exhibition of Children's Fairy Tales."[60] As we shall see, something of the same continuity was evident in children's reactions to literary works as well.

This general relationship is not surprising, given that children's letters to Detskaia literatura were not random expressions of juvenile opinion. Some of the volumes published by the press had a paragraph at the end encouraging readers to write in with comments; and, as mentioned above, the competitions for the best response to a book were a very public way of stimulating response to the Detskaia literatura product. Furthermore, some of Detskaia literatura's outreach work was aimed at helping librarians tutor children in more detailed, complex, and "appropriate" responses to books. This process should not, though, be seen exclusively, and perhaps not even primarily, as reflective of specifically Soviet political ideology. Nonetheless, the ways in which Soviet children were guided were not precisely analogous to intellectually ambitious American bourgeois culture as depicted by Heath, with its concentration on "reason-explanation" and "affective commentaries," rather than content recapitulation. Indeed, emotive responses were—according to official guidance—precisely to be avoided in favor of detached judgment. As a lecture given by N. Serova at the DDK on 24 November 1950 put it, "We are also aware of numerous successful discussions when the person leading the discussion and the pupils taking part feel that this is not simply an exchange of impressions and feelings but also of judgments."[61] Accompanying this maneuver from "emotion" to "judgment" (or from the dictates of the "heart" to those of "reason," as the tropes of Enlightenment literature would have named it) went another: as the child reader moved away from emotional spontaneity and toward analytical distance, so he or she also acquired sensitivity to the formal features of the text.[62] It was vital, Serova emphasized, "to teach pupils not only to share emotionally (*perezhivat'*) what is in the book but to tease out thoughts and the beauty of expression and of artistic form."[63]

Serova offered sample literary analyses together with this generalizing advice, of a kind on which children might be encouraged to model their own responses to literary texts (*otzyvy*). These analyses pulled in a slightly different direction from her overall strictures, concentrating mainly on sententious character analysis of the kind that was also the focus of work with texts in school literature lessons during the early 1950s (and at earlier and later periods of Soviet history, too).[64] At the same time, she emphasized the need to leave some room for children's expression of personal opinion even at this moralizing level, stressing that librarians should not "impose their own view" (*naviazyvat' mnenie*) about which character in a story was the most admirable.[65] In submissions for the reviewing competitions held in the early 1950s, children were also to some extent encouraged to express their own opinions of books, though here the points they were told to concentrate on were a little more "Soviet": "what is interesting and useful about this book, what the author's main purpose is"—with especial attention, once more, to characters and actions.[66] Yet at the same time, one has to bear in mind that "expressive reading" (*ekspressivnoe chtenie*, high-pathetic reading aloud) was, throughout the Soviet era, a skill taught in the classroom and one on which the pedagogical establishment placed considerable value. For example, in 1947 a group of inspectors from the Academy of Pedagogical Sciences in Moscow commended a teacher whose stirring account of Lermontov's patriotism had enabled her pupils to "emotionally and expressively recite" work by the poet. [67] In other words, it would be a mistake to see reading, in the eyes of Soviet child experts, as a purely analytical process; it was also supposed to be a profoundly sentimental (a term I use in the technical, rather than the denigratory, sense) activity.

From hero worship to fantasy: children's letters in the 1950s–60s

Examination of the propaganda efforts of the DDK, and its outreach work with children in particular, provides a clear picture of the type of child reader that the educators, publishers, and librarians aimed to produce. This child reader would have been familiar with "quality" literature (that is, the canonical Soviet texts for children), which he or she would have read with due attention to topical issues of the day, key themes, and genre and with analytical abilities in play. The question now to be asked is: how far did the raw material of children's letters reflect these pedagogical aims?

Children certainly showed an ability to respond to key themes in the literature that they read. For instance, the emphasis on character-building in texts by adults was strongly reflected in terms of the books child readers chose to respond to, both in the Stalin era and in later years. Among the books attracting the highest numbers of readers' letters in 1951–52 were Konstantin Simonov's *Podvig kapitana Saburova* (Captain Saburov's Feat) (33 letters), Pavel Zhurba's life of the World War II hero Aleksandr Matrosov (35 letters), Iurii German's *Rasskazy o Dzerzhinskom* (Stories about Dzerzhinskii) (26 letters), Antonina Golubeva's life of Sergei Kirov, *Mal'chik iz Urzhuma* (The Boy from Urzhum) (26 letters), and Emma Vygodskaia's patriotic tale *Opasnyi beglets* (A Dangerous Fugitive) (60 letters).

These books were all stirring tales of heroic endeavor in the face of deadly danger, sometimes with a "rags to righteousness" plot. For instance, Zhurba's life of Matrosov, originally published in 1949, showed the young Aleksandr ("Sashka") graduating to a children's home after life as a street waif. He at first wanted to run away but soon learned to be "firm in attaining his ends, orderly in his daily life and at work, sensitive with his comrades." Friendship was of vital importance: "He valued his friends and friendship and was rich in his friends; the other boys clung to him." As a young man he had an episode of (entirely innocent) romantic love but was quick to recognize his life's true aim: "His passionate wish was fulfilled: he was called up into the army." Here he relished Komsomol meetings almost as much as military work and, inspired by thoughts of his sweetheart, fought bravely with his unit. Finally, he found himself in desperate straits, with no ammunition left, and entirely surrounded. "Only his boundless spiritual force and sacred desire—to carry out his duty as quickly and fully as possible—remained." When his dead body was discovered, blood scarlet as poppies flowing into the soil, his captain took out the object that Aleksandr Matrosov had worn next to his heart: "his Komsomol card, emblazoned with the name of Lenin."[68]

Golubeva's life of the Leningrad party leader Sergei Kirov showed a rather more "normal" childhood, poor but cheerful (the young Sergei could not afford to buy toys but enjoyed having fun with bits of wood, and he had a story-telling, snuff-taking grandmother to look after him after his mother died). But then Sergei also ended up in an orphanage, this time a prerevolutionary one, offering vile Tatar stews (sic) and compulsory daily prayers in place of uplifting moral education. Faced with a library almost empty of interesting material, Sergei had made his way magnetically to quality books such as *Priroda i liudi* (Nature and People). He began his revolutionary activities young, while doing teaching practice after attending Kazan Trade School and Industrial School, and had soon found the true path.[69]

Iurii German's *Tales about Dzerzhinskii* was different from these first two, because it represented the adult Dzerzhinskii but was narrated in rattling, thrillerish style, turning Dzerzhinskii's revolutionary activities into exciting "outwitting the cops" stuff. Throughout, too, the hero's sympathy with children was emphasized: at one point, his attention was distracted from revolutionary work by the sight of an emaciated, rat-chewed boy; at another, he rescued a hungry boy at a station; and in a third scene, he tenderly watched two young boys asleep in a revolutionary lair:

> He stood by the bed and looked. The lamp was very dim. Dzerzhinskii turned up the wick and bent over the sleepers. Heavens! It was children, two children, lying under a school uniform coat. What a thing! They must have been 13, not more. Why were they hidden here? They were probably weeping from fear and calling for their mother!
>
> The boys slept on calmly. Dzerzhinskii sat down next to the table on a chair, propped his head on his hands, and drifted off into thought, looking at the sleepers. One of them smacked his lips in sleep. Some time passed, and he smiled. Why? What was he dreaming? Probably something very nice and cozy, like having tea with Mama and Papa at a round table. Nice tea with milk, and a roll and butter, and Mama and Papa, and the samovar grumbling and singing. A nice dream. But what would waking up be like?[70]

It is safe to say that the possible homoerotic connotations of this scene, such as might have perturbed an editor in an Anglophone children's publishing house during the early 21st century, were not intended to resonate with the original audience. Instead, Dzerzhinskii could be understood as imagining in advance the "happy childhood" that children would be guaranteed under Soviet power, which was, in reverse, the perspective that German's child reader was encouraged to adopt, regarding with awe the revolutionary sacrifices that had been made to ensure his or her happiness, as programmed by the prescient and philanthropic party leader.

These stories of heroes were explicitly didactic not simply because they showed how exciting it was to risk your life (or lose it) for the good of the cause, or because they represented "working on the self" as admirable and likely to help you win friends and influence people. They also—particularly in the case of Zhurba's book on Matrosov—showed the imitation of role models as an admirable quality in itself. Matrosov was portrayed reading with enthusiasm Maksim Gor'kii's stirring tale "Starukha Izergil'" (Old Woman Izergil'), which shows Dan'ko tearing out his own heart in order to light his oppressed people to freedom and self-determination: "He passionately wanted to know a lot and to be such as Dan'ko was." Matrosov was himself to become a role model even in life: "He learned from his elders, and the lads imitated him." Thus Matrosov became a vital force in mediating the philosophy of the earlier generation to his peers, a link in the great continuity of socialist tradition. He was a significantly different kind of hero from Pavlik Morozov, who had rudely challenged the authority of his (counterrevolutionary) father and grandfather.[71]

All this, to judge by the quantity of letters praising Matrosov, was enthusiastically received by many children. Individual letters also pointed to a strong tendency to identify the heroes of books of this kind as role models and to respond to them idealistically. For example, a girl from class two at a school in Gor'kii wrote: "I want to be like Dzerzhinskii, just as staunch and brave," while a boy from class ten in an unnamed city contributed a lengthy paean of praise to Aleksandr Matrosov:

> The description of how Matrosov worked on himself left a big impression on me. Orphaned early, he ended up living on the streets; he "traveled round" the whole country, moving from city to city. He was attracted by everything new he saw. [. . .] His curiosity knew no bounds. [. . .] Matrosov was also a good comrade; he valued friendship highly. But he wasn't friendly with just anyone; he picked his friends. Friendship in Matrosov's view meant that the friends didn't grudge one another anything. But that didn't mean they should cover up for one another's weaknesses. One has to help one's friend escape from that [i.e., weakness], to support him.[72]

Attitudes of this kind were expressed with regard to fictional characters as well. For instance, a boy from class five at a school in the town of Cheremkovo enthusiastically praised Vitalii Bianki's *Na velikom morskom puti* (On the Great Sea Route): "I liked the character called 'Sea Devil' best; he was a brave boy who never showed fear; he went out fishing on his own into the storm. I liked how he wanted to catch a sea devil and managed to."[73] Indeed, children— like adult readers in many generations, from Lermontov's contemporaries inclined to identify Pechorin with his creator, to the radicals inspired by Chernyshevskii's *Chto delat'*? (What Is to Be Done?), to Andrei Zhdanov's calumny of Anna Akhmatova as "half-nun, half-whore" because her poems represented secular love as a religious experience—appear to have found difficulty in drawing, or been reluctant to draw, a firm line between the fictional and the real. Confusion, or maybe just fusion, was fostered by the Soviet tradition of "poeticizing" the lives of real heroes (Morozov, Matrosov, Kirov, Dzerzhinskii), and of writing about fictional heroes as though they were real. Children were, for instance, regularly informed of what Timur, the imaginary hero of Arkadii Gaidar's very popular story *Timur i ego komanda* (Timur and His Team) might have done in a given situation; and in the 1960s, he was even used as a kind of advice columnist by the children's press.[74]

Obviously, the high proportion of readers' letters enthusing about heroes should not be seen as purely reflective of children's tastes. The vision of *druzhba* in the letter about Matrosov, for example, copies the kind of material being published in official youth magazines during the late 1940s, when "correct" friendship (a support to moral development, never threatening to integration in the wider *kollektiv*) was the subject of strings of propaganda texts.[75] Oral history, in contrast, reveals a rather different concept of *druzhba*, based on group solidarity above all. "Shadow" practices such as copying (*spisyvan'e*) and prompting of classmates called to the blackboard to regurgitate their homework (*podskazka*) flourished in Soviet class-rooms, notwithstanding official condemnation, and a friend who refused to help out by supplying information when needed would not have been regarded as a friend at all. Reporting of misdemeanors by classmates generally, let alone close friends, was regarded with deep disapproval.

At the same time, going by the same oral testimony, heroes had high recognition value, and hero-worship was a genuine and widespread emotion in the Stalin era. A Muscovite woman from the same generation as those who would have been writing to Detgiz in 1950 (she was born in 1936) remembered "swallowing whole" everything that she was taught about Soviet patriotism, from Pavlik Morozov onward, while a slightly older informant from Leningrad recalled that one of the books that most moved her in childhood was a life of Marx for the nursery age: "I read that he used to go all the time to the British Museum, to the library there; and he had no money and he had to take his suit to the pawn shop. He couldn't go to the library till Engels turned up and redeemed the suit, and then he could go to the library again; and when I heard that story read aloud, I always wept."[76]

In the post-Stalin years, the publishing landscape changed significantly. Lip service might still be paid to the leader cult, with the publication of books about Lenin and so on, but there was a marked shrinkage in the proportion of hagiography among the books put out by the publishing house.[77] Internal reviews for the house, particularly by younger reviewers, now appealed to an ideal of the "natural child" to justify their opinions. A review of Viktor Goliavkin's book for younger children, *My s Vovkoi druz'ia, vmeste igraem, vmeste rabotaem* (Vovka and I Are Friends, We Play and Work Together), written in March 1960, praised the "fresh, cheerful, mischievous, genuinely childlike manner" of the book, and continued:

> The secret of V. Goliavkin's charm as a writer lies in his unaffected, childlike intonation, naive and crafty at the same time. Goliavkin doesn't suck up to the reader, doesn't indulge in fake baby-talk, he conveys characteristically "childish" logic, children's sense of proportion and view of life absolutely naturally, through his language and intonation.[78]

This was in tune with a general move, in the post-Stalin era, toward "child-centered" aesthetics in literature for children. On the one hand, writing by children (like children's drawings) was championed by adults, as it had not been since the 1920s, as a true expression of talent, not to be adjusted by pedagogues.[79] On the other, there was now much more emphasis on children's tastes and on "childishness" (in a positive sense) as appropriate yardsticks for work by adult writers. A particularly important effect of this was the new rise to dominance of the adventure story, a genre espoused by some of the most prominent writers of the era, such as Viktor Goliavkin and Radii Pogodin. Also important was a new interpretation of the *skazka*, which now became a vision of a world of wonder and strangeness, to which older children, as well as younger ones, might have access. Sometimes the first genre could slide into the second. Iurii Koval's short novel *Prikliucheniia Viti Kurolesova* (The Adventures of Vitia Kurolesov), for instance, began with the narrator watching black swans swim in central Moscow and continued with the tale of a boy trying to buy a pig and ending up with a "tatty-looking ginger dog," which dog in time led the boy and the police to some beekeeping villains.[80] Such emphasis on fantasy and on the autonomy of the child's imagination had not been seen since the 1920s; and, appropriately enough, the 1960s also saw the republication of several books written during the 1920s that had been extremely popular at the time but had been suppressed during the Stalin era: a notable example was *Respublika Shkida* (The Republic of Shkid, the latter word an acronym for Shkola imeni Dostoevskogo, or Dostoevsky School), about a utopian children's home for young offenders in 1920s Leningrad, by two ex-inmates of such a home, L. Panteleev (whose real name was Aleksei Eremeev) and Grigorii Belykh.[81]

Children's tastes, as expressed in readers' letters, moved in harmony with the new publishing policy.[82] Books where fantasy predominated were very popular in terms of number of responses received. The "top hits" of 1965, in terms of letters received, were Vil'iam Kozlov's *Prezident kamennogo ostrova* (The President of Stone Island) (around 150 letters in the course of the year) and Iurii Tomin's *Shel po gorodu volshebnik* (A Wizard Was Walking through Town) (111 letters in the course of the year). Also extremely popular were the science-fiction stories of Georgii Martynov, which collectively produced 135 responses over the year. The overall number of letters with material about books sent had also risen strikingly since the early 1950s (4,171 were received in 1965 as against 1,282 in 1951–52), which was probably also an indication of greater interest in the list. At the same time, the number of letters received per author was rather more evenly spread, beyond the big hits, with quite a cluster coming in at 50–100 letters: for example, Radii Pogodin's adventure stories *Kirpichnye ostrova* (Brick Islands), *Ozhidanie* (Expectation), and *Utrennii bereg* (Summer Shore) (71 letters); various animal stories by Vitalii Bianki (a highly popular writer since the 1920s) at 55 letters; and *Republic of Shkid*, along with other works by Panteleev, at 95 letters.[83]

The new reader choices pointed to changed trends. Kozlov's *President of Stone Island*, for example, was a well-written, lively adventure story about a slightly oddball Soviet family (the regulation two children, but only a father, no mother) spending the summer out in the country, at a cottage where the father himself had stayed as a boy. The sister was getting to the stage where she was attracting interest from boys, to the disgust of her brother, from whose perspective the novel was related. The rather slight plot hinged round a meeting with a gang of boys from a local orphanage on a nearby island, the leader of whom had named himself "President of Stone Island" (hence the novel's title). Rivalry between the outsiders and insiders was quickly resolved, and the groups spent the summer having adventures together. The book was in the vein of classic children's stories such as Twain's *Tom Sawyer*, or Arthur Ransome's *Swallows and Amazons*, rather than appreciably "Soviet." The children involved did no Pioneer work, though they fantasized about perhaps discovering criminal activity on the basis of some mysterious tire-tracks. Both in terms of era and in terms of geographical setting, *President* refused to be pinned down; notions of political heroism and of public service were far away.[84]

Tomin's *Wizard Was Walking through Town*, a novel of considerable charm, focused on Tolik, a lazy and lively 11-year-old who was delighted to discover, while closeted in the police station after his arrest following a bout of outrageous lying, a magic box of matches that granted his every wish. Things went very well as he used it to get (finally) on the right side of his mother, to avert a failing grade from his teacher, to cheat at chess against his best friend, to win an ice-hockey standoff against a bullying group of older boys, and then to rescue one of the bullies from the lion's cage at the zoo, thus turning himself into a local hero. At this point, though, it turned out that the matches were the property of an ambitious and vindictive boy magician with bright blue eyes, who abducted Tolik and his best friend in an attempt to confine them in his upside-down world, where idleness and mischief-making spelled *bon ton*. After being able to trick his terrifying robot guard by relying on the latter's incapacity not to obey his original set of orders even when the situation clearly demanded a different response, Tolik was able to rescue his friend and the two made their way back to Leningrad and a life without the support, but also without the danger, provided by the matches. The moral undertones of Tomin's story were clear, but the book was in no sense a parable: it was typical of the fantasy-adventure genre of the early 1960s, not too far removed from a less elaborate version of J. K. Rowling's *Harry Potter*[85]

It was precisely the fantasy side of such novels that appealed to many child readers, who felt that they gained access to another world as they read: "I literally lived the life and the events that unfolded in this book," commented a Minsk girl from class five (i.e., about 12 years old) on *President of Stone Island*.[86] Emotional engagement with the characters was another common feature: "I'm a girl, yes, but not the kind you could call a cry-baby (*gde mozhno skazat'*, "*vsegda glaza na mokrom meste*"), but I still cried when I got to the end," one 14-year-old girl wrote from Togliatti in 1972, after having read a novel by, once again, V. Kozlov.[87] "I have read many interesting books. I have also read G. Belykh and L. Panteleev's *Respublika Shkida*," wrote a 12-year-old girl from L'vov in 1965. "I loved this book right from page one. I lived through all the sorrows and joys, the excitement and upheavals, experienced by the heroes. Along with them, I was present at all the events that happened in *Shkid*. I could go on and on writing, but I have no words to describe my delight at this book. I wish the writers would write many more books like it!"[88]

Not just emotional revelations of this kind, but confessionalism of a broader sort, some-times quite startling in effect, could be heard in some of the letters. For instance, an anony-mous letter-writer from Cheliabinsk province wrote: "Of course, it's wonderful to be upright and principled! But have our parents got the point? They keep telling us that in our [i.e., their] day everyone lived differently; they did what they were told! So don't we do what we're told, confide in them about everything? But they still don't get what we're about."[89] Such missives indicated how the "reader's letter" might offer an opportunity to pour out confidences that would otherwise have had to remain unvoiced in a culture without teen magazines and advice columnists; but they also pointed to a situation where virtue was no longer its own reward, where living subjects now expected "understanding" and emotional communication, as well as the satisfaction that came from being "honorable and principled." Some children's letters, in praising the sensitivity of children's authors, also recognized by implication that children had a special mental world, which not all adults necessarily viewed with sympathy and under-standing. "I especially liked the way that the author noticed certain details in children and in their lives that other writers don't notice for some reason, and described them very simply and convincingly," wrote a 14-year-old girl from Moscow province in 1965, with reference to Radii Pogodin's *Summer Shore*.[90]

Conformity or subversion? Glossing children's responses

It would, of course, be naive to see the rise in popularity of fantasy as signifying simply a resurgence of natural child behavior once the lid had been lifted. Spontaneous self-expression and interest in worlds beyond the mundane, in particular those in outer space, were qualities that post-Stalinist education and texts directed at children actively sought to produce.[91] When one looks in detail at the content of the children's letters, it emerges that straight escape into fantasy was not the only value that children sought in their reading. Poetry remained as marginal in the post-Stalin era as it had before 1953,[92] and lives of heroes still had a place in some hearts, to judge by Detskaia literatura's postbag. To be sure, books such as German's life of Dzerzhinskii no longer featured among the "chart-toppers" of the day. Of the 4,171 children's letters sent to Detskaia literatura in the course of 1965, only about 22 addressed German's *Tales about Dzerzhinskii*, for example.[93] But such books still inspired enthusiasm in some, particularly, to judge by the highlighted letters, child readers from provincial outposts. As a girl aged about 14 wrote from Tadzhikistan in 1965, with a request for more information about Dzerzhinskii: "How did Dzerzhinskii die? What was his child-hood like? Where can I get a book that would tell me more? About his childhood. Here in Dushanbe, I've never come across a book like that."[94] Similarly, in 1963, *Orliata* (Little Eagles), a book about Pioneer war heroes, produced 31 responses over the first six months of the year.[95]

Still greater endurance was shown by abstract ideals of heroism. In 1965, a schoolgirl wrote to tell Iurii Tomin, "Your books help one understand honesty and fairness."[96] So strong was this commitment to morally uplifting writing in some children that they went to the extent of rebuking new-generation writers for not providing enough of it: thus one child in a group discussion of Radii Pogodin's children's thriller *Murav'inoe maslo* (Ant Oil) in the early 1960s complained that the text did not place enough emphasis on the moral reform (*perevos-pitanie*) of the characters. Equally, what children liked in Pogodin's stories included not just the adventure elements but also the emphasis on altruism—helping one's mother and younger siblings, bringing criminals to justice.[97] They continued to identify strongly with heroes, expressing uncertainty about whether they were real or made up, and sometimes trying to behave as the heroes did, too.[98]

Interesting also, in the context of an era in which quite a lot of discussion was going on among adults about the appropriate style for children's literature, was the conservatism of child letter-writers where the literary language was concerned. A boy who wrote in 1963 to enthuse about Martynov's science-fiction story *Kalliosto* noted, "I liked this book because it was written in a simple, clear style."[99] Children were especially stern about this point when it came to their own patronage of even younger readers. In 1965, a group of 15-year-olds from Saratov wrote to protest against the style of a republication of stories by Mikhail Zoshchenko, which they had unwittingly purchased for first-graders they had taken under their wing. Phrases such as "don't be a fool" (*ne bud' dura*), "It's a trifle" (*eto meloch '*), "gobble" (*slopat'*), "do a nasty" (*podstroit' gadost'*) and "a whacking great dog" (*sobachishche*) were just not good enough, they thundered. "This book can't teach our little ones anything good. [. . .] Are we surprised when our little brothers and sisters learn expressions like this? It turns out, they don't need to hang out 'on the street' to learn them: they can get them from books for preschoolers."[100]

Conversely, in the early 1950s, the impeccably orthodox choice of themes among letter-writers did not necessarily mean that tension between adult expectation and child performance was avoided. For example, heroic themes could provide an excuse for self-praise, or indeed, blatant boasting. In the words of a female pupil from class three in a Gor'kii school: "I want to be like Iron Feliks. I'm a prize pupil. This year, I got my long-awaited Pioneer tie. I try to be an example to my sister. 'A Pioneer is an example to all' [*Pioner—vsem rebiatam primer*]."[101] On the one hand, this correspondent is like a living version of the model girls in propaganda from the postwar years, such as the annoying elder sister from Fedor Reshetnikov's painting *Opiat' dvoika!* (Two Again!) On the other, the girl's lack of capacity for self-criticism would not have been considered a virtue under high Stalinism.[102] The tendency for achieving children to become the victims of callow arrogance had been a widely expressed anxiety among politicians and pedagogues since the mid-1930s, when the child prodigy stopped being seen as a kind of infant freak and began to be regarded as an admirable phenomenon. Already in 1934, one commentator, writing in *Pravda*, expressed concern that children who were given too much attention as a result of their achievements (prizes for catching robbers and saboteurs and so on) might become "whiny and capricious" (*kichlivye*).[103]

Such views had a degree of substance. Congratulated by their teachers, held up as examples to other children, the beneficiaries of all sorts of "perks" (such as access to scarce books or ones considered unsuitable for other children), prize pupils sometimes also exploited their position in ways that adults found embarrassing. "Spoiled" behavior was probably the least socially dangerous version of this. Far more risky was when prize pupils employed the rhetoric that they had so efficiently internalized to challenge the adults from whom they had learned it. For example, in the late 1940s, a group of girls at a prestigious school in Moscow responded to the many lectures they had heard about "maidenly virtue" by denouncing their teacher to the headmistress for immoral behavior when they found she was having a relationship with a man.[104] While no dramatic confrontations of this kind emerge from the readers' letters processed by DDK, they still show us children behaving in an assertive manner—talking about themselves, not about their place in the collective or in the generational hierarchy—at the precise time when they appear most in thrall to the political orthodoxy of the day. In this respect, readers' letters are quite different from the apparently analogous genre of letters to political leaders, where reference to one's educational achievements was used as a legitimating strategy, a way of emphasizing that one had the right to approach the high being in question.[105]

If responses to heroic literature could sometimes be more socially radical than might seem on the surface, it was equally the case that responses to fantasy were in many cases perfectly "orthodox." Kozlov's *President of Stone Island*, for example, showed the younger generation spending their time in ways that imitated what their father had done at an earlier era, and coming to him for advice about how to behave. The "tuition/imitation" pattern was just as significant as in Zhurba's life of Matrosov, though now it was set out differently—the generational "chain of command" ran down through the family, rather than being embodied in institutions beyond the family (the father, a patriarch on a private scale, had much more authority than anyone in the orphanage). Like Gaidar's classic *Timur and His Team*, a book that was also about an adult-approved secret society, the book played on children's fantasies of independence while propounding the values of the older generation. To be sure, the "general good" was advocated in a less blatant way than in Gaidar's book, but this was in tune with the growing tolerance of individualism in Soviet society generally. In enjoying such books, then, children were reacting exactly as well-intentioned adults of the day supposed that they should react, not presenting a challenge to authority. Their engagement with such literature should therefore not be seen as straightforwardly liberating, any more than their engagement with hero-based narratives should be seen as unambiguously submissive. The bulk of those who wrote to publishers were early teenagers, or pre-teens, and their letters had greater complexity than the occasional letters by younger children that trickled in to the press, which generally fell into the "how lovely" category.[106]

At the same time, readers' letters do indicate some capacity by children to exercise leverage over adults, albeit at one remove. The staff of Detskaia literatura could hardly avoid being aware of the significant expansion in letters sent by children in the 1960s and 1970s, as compared with the early 1950s.[107] In addition, "meet the author" sessions were meant to provide writers with feedback that they were supposed to act on, as well as fulfilling a tutorial function. There is no doubt that, from the point of view of the predominantly urban, intellectually achieving readership who were the most assiduous group of letter-writers, children's literature was more "child-centered" in the 1960s than it had been before. In turn, such readers were likely to pass their tastes on to their own children, perpetuating the individualist, politically neutral values of the children's literature of the 1960s into the 1980s and beyond. As Omry Ronen has pointed out, children's literature of the 1930s retained a loyal readership, seldom making its way into the secondhand bookstores where the novels of the day for adults were abundantly displayed.[108] The same was true, in later generations, of writers such as Vil'iam Kozlov. Into the 21st century, to judge by postings on the Internet, texts by these writers enjoy a lively popularity of a kind long denied such once-influential texts as German's stories about "Iron Feliks."[109]

Conclusion

This article has addressed the hitherto largely neglected topic of the "management of children's reading" under Soviet power. Every effort was made to ensure that children read the right books, and in appropriate ways. The output of the state publishing house, Detskaia literatura, was controlled; the content of libraries, and the way that children used these, was regulated; the school syllabus imposed recommended lists of "extracurricular reading"; and children were encouraged to write considered responses to books as a voluntary, leisure-time activity, with strategies such as competitions used to provoke letters addressing particular books and particular topics. Everything was done to turn child readers into a Soviet version of the type named by Shirley Brice Heath, with reference to the United States, as "Maintown" readers—people who consume books in a rationalistic, self-conscious, exegetic manner.

The values embodied in the management of children's reading pretended to universalism. All children were supposed to read texts in the same way (for example, to dislike *skazki* during the 1920s and admire them once they had been declared appropriate reading in 1934). In fact, as with the Soviet direction of taste more generally, the direction of children's taste raised to the level of national dogma a set of appreciations and beliefs that were strongly linked to social status. The model of socializing children's reading that prevailed was hegemonic: just as in the American communities studied by Heath, it was educated and socially confident parents (in Soviet terms, members of the intelligentsia) who were most likely to provide their children with tuition in how to read books in the requisite analytical, rationalistic, yet at the same time emotionally involved, manner that was assumed to be the right way of reading. It was possible for working-class and peasant children to espouse the same model (as they might be helped to do by exposure to education and to outreach work, the effects of which should not be underestimated). But if they did not do so, their efforts as readers were likely to meet with incomprehension or contempt, with adverse impact on their educational prowess.

If the responses of these readers are retrievable only from oral history (according to official perceptions, the kind of reading that they were doing was not "reading" at all), another group of children, those who wrote letters of appreciation to publishing houses, on the face of it represented a quintessential illustration of "Maintown" socialization at work. As they proudly boasted in their letters, these children were often the successes of the school system—"top pupils" (*otlichnikt*) who knew exactly what they had to say to impress their teachers. Even so, the letters that children in fact wrote about books, however orthodox they may seem in some ways (even the surge of interest in fantasy from the late 1950s was a "licensed" phenomenon, reflecting a shift of emphasis in the pedagogy and cultural politics of the day) were also to at least some extent the expression of values which ran contrary to those in adult culture.

Although children's letters to publishers, then, came from a juvenile "elite" (and one whose members were in some cases rather arrogant about their status), they did not fully reproduce what children were being taught. Real-life child enthusiasts for literature were not the pure fantasists imagined by Chukovskii, lost in worlds of the imagination, but neither were they the dogmatic supporters of realism at all costs that Krupskaia had considered sensible children must be. Moreover, the critical procedures in which children engaged were seldom anywhere near even the primary stage of response to text (untutored but engaged and enthusiastic) that was envisaged in guides to work with child readers. Rather, the central purpose children had in writing to publishers was often, below the surface, to talk about themselves. This included boasting about one's status as a prize pupil or one's superior sense of moral values, but it was not limited to this. By the 1960s, children also used letters to set down their fascination with worlds beyond everyday reality, to record their hobbies and interests ("I like books about animals"; "I don't like children's books (but did enjoy this one)," and so on.[110] They also used them to speak about biographical issues, including the new theme of conflict with parents. Even in the multiply filtered and partial form in which they have come down to us in archives, readers' letters reflected at least some of the diversity of children's experience, as well as its susceptibility to local political factors.

The destinies of the children who wrote these letters were, one suspects, equally diverse. In some respects, the "prize pupils" who devotedly wrote to publishing houses seem like miniature versions of the *vydvizhentsy* of the 1930s, trotting out their expressions from the "speaking Bolshevik" phrase-book with a glibness seldom matched in the adult world.[111] At the same time, children's very fluency had the potential to generate conflicts with the system. The crucial model of identity in the early Soviet period had, after all, been expressed in a "conversion narrative," where the thinking subject progressed gradually to enlightenment from social deprivation and cultural backwardness.[112] In this model, the actual moment of being broken and remade, and the sense of humility and gratitude to higher authority that it inspired, held as much importance as adherence to political orthodoxy in itself.[113] In this context, the person who had been orthodox from childhood presented something of a problem: staunch political orthodoxy might not be accompanied by the requisite levels of humility, yet any "conversion" could only mean a turning away from political orthodoxy. Indeed, it is not hard to find cases where children who had happily turned out "Soviet" material in their pre-teen years and adolescence became articulate opponents of the system later on, graduating from *bien pensant* writings that resembled material printed in their textbooks to texts that struck directly at the beliefs they had once insouciantly celebrated.[114]

Notes

1   L. [A.] Kassil', *Delo vkusa: Zametki pisatelia*, 2nd ed. (Moscow: Iskusstvo, 1964), 115. (It was not characteristic of children's writers to use two initials in their bylines; when the second initial has been supplied, it is given in square brackets.) On myths of the Soviet reader, see particularly Stephen Lovell, *The Russian Reading Revolution: Print Culture in the Soviet and Post-Soviet Eras* (Basingstoke, UK: Macmillan, 2000), esp. chap. 2.

2   The concept of "out-of-class reading" (*vneshkol'noe chtenie*) was introduced as soon as a compulsory curriculum was. See *Programmy i metodicheskie zapiski edinoi trudovoi shkoly*, no. 3 (Moscow and Leningrad: Gosizdat, 1927), 36. There were 22 texts on the "optional" list, including Pushkin's *skazki*. Later syllabi, such as *Programmy nachal'noi shkoly na 1957–1958 god* (Moscow: Uchpedgiz, 1957), had longer lists. On the work of the "class supervisor," see N. I. Boldyrev, *Klassnyi rukovoditel': Posobie dlia klassnykh rukovoditelei srednikh shkol*, 2nd ed. (Moscow: Gosudarstvennoe uchebno-pedagogicheskoe izdatel'stvo, 1955), 195–200; appendix 18, 344–48. For a class discussion of such reading, cf. ibid., appendix 13, 325, which stipulates that the class supervisor should hold group sessions on "How to Handle a Book," and on "Gor'kii's Story 'How I Studied.'"

3   See, for example, "Detskoi knige—pochetnoe mesto v sem'e," *Sem'ia i shkola*, no. 7 (1953): 1–4, recommending Maiakovskii, Gaidar, and books about Lenin and Stalin by A. [Aleksandr T.] Kononov (i.e., *Rasskazy o Lenine* [Moscow and Leningrad: n.p., 1939]); M. [Manuel' V.] Bol'shintsov and M. [Mikhail E.] Chiaureli (i.e., *Rasskazy o velikikh dniakh* [Moscow and Leningrad: Detgiz, 1952]); Iu. [Iurii P.] German's *Rasskazy o Dzerzhinskom* (see below); and L. [Lev A.] Kassil', *Ulitsa mladshego syna* (Moscow and Leningrad: Detskaia literatura, 1951), co-authored with Mark L. Polianovskii. An example of guidance for parents is V. [Vladimir O.] Osipov, *Kniga v vashem dome* (Moscow: Kniga, 1967). Material of this kind goes back to before the Revolution: see, for example, "Tezisy po voprosam chteniia detei doshkol'nogo vozrasta, vyrabotannye Petrogradskim obshchestvom sodeistviia doshkol'nogo vospitaniia," *Doshkol'noe vospitanie*, no. 3–4 (1917): 247–48.

4   Felicity O'Dell, *Socialisation through Children's Literature: The Soviet Example* (Cambridge: Cambridge University Press, 1978), 61–70; and Elaine C. Miller, *Reading Guidance in Soviet Children's Libraries* (Birmingham, UK: Birmingham Library School Co-Operative, 1978). O. Vasil'eva, "Kniga i chitatel'," *Nedelia*, no. 47 (1962): 11, is a journalist's enthusiastic firsthand account of a day spent doing library work with children. For the attitude in the early Soviet period, see E. Uvarova, "Novye puti bor'by s detskoi besprizornost'iu i beznadzornost'iu," *Detskii dom*, no. 3 (1928): 12: "At the present time, the children's library is not a mere book repository with the function of doling out loan volumes, but a living pedagogical institution."

5   See, for example, an article published in 1983, arguing that children should be encouraged to read adventure stories because these developed their emotional and imaginative capacities (I. A. Svirskaia, E. L. Ogurtsova, and L. N. Asinovskaia, "Prikliuchencheskaia literatura v sovremennoi detskoi biblioteke," in *Differentsial'noe rukovodstvo chteniem detei: Sbornik nauchnykh trudov* [Leningrad: Tsentral'naia detskaia biblioteka, 1983], 37–50).

6   See L. A. Anishchenko, "Pionerskaia gazeta i ee iunyi chitatel'," in ibid., 121–33.

7   See, for example, "O provedenii nedeli detskoi i iunosheskoi knigi (Kopii postanovlenii Sekretariata Tsentral'nogo Komiteta VLKSM po pionerskoi i shkol'noi rabote, za 1970–71)," typescript held in the reading room of the Center for the Preservation of Youth Organization Documents (Tsentr khraneniia dokumentov molodezhnykh organizatsii, TsKhDMO), Moscow, a branch of the Russian State Archive of Socio-Political History (Rossiiskii gosudarstvennyi arkhiv sotsial'no-politicheskoi istorii, RGASPI). This document sets out themes for "Children's Reading Week" in 1970, which were to include the life of Lenin and his associates (*soratniki*), the Communist Party, the Komsomol, the "heroic achievements of Soviet people at work and on the fields of battle" (*trudovye i boevye podvigi sovetskikh liudei*), and the "Friendship of Peoples."

8   Publishing houses, journals, and newspapers for children and young people were under the super-vision of the Central Committee of the Komsomol, to whose Department of Agitation and Propaganda they submitted reports on what they published. See, for example, the unsigned and undated report on the contents of *Molodaia gvardiia* for 1968, which criticizes the journal for not publishing enough fiction and lively reportage, as opposed to dry lists of biographical events, for the upcoming Lenin anniversary in 1969, and demands more political content in future issues. The report does not make statements about the aesthetic or intellectual value of anything published, however, simply referring in an abstract way to the need for high literary quality (TsKhDMO f. 1, op. 34, d. 447, ll. 234–37). Conversely, there were efforts in the post-Stalin era to improve the literary quality of what was published in the Komsomol's own journals and papers: cf. the holding of a "creative seminar" in 1982 to try and attract young authors and prepare them for what was needed ("Materialy po podgotovke k provedeniiu tvorcheskogo seminara rukovoditelei detskikh izdanii / Otchet o provedenii programmy, spiski uchastnikov i t.d.," TsKhDMO f. 1, op. 95, d. 207, ll. 1–13).

9   On hero literature, see Catriona Kelly, *Comrade Pavlik: The Rise and Fall of a Soviet Boy Hero* (London: Granta, 2005).

10   For instance, in 1961–62, the magazine for Pioneer leaders, *Vozhatyi*, published a pull-out section entitled *Sputnik*, containing lives of young heroes.

11   An elite that was also, it would seem, skewed in terms of age and gender. As noted below, the key age for letter-writing was the pre-teen and early teen years, and it would seem that girls also outnum-bered boys in this activity. Such observations have to be made hesitantly, however, because letters are available in the form of published digests, including only the letters that the staff of the Children's Literature publishing house found most interesting: it is possible that older children and girls were better at producing the responses that their audience found appropriate.

12   For a study based on this kind of material, see S. P. Luppov, ed., *Frantsuzskaia kniga v Rossii XVIII veka: Ocherki istorii* (Leningrad: Nauka, 1986).

13   This does not mean that memoirs are useless in reconstructing childhood reading. Even the highly official collection of autobiographies, *Sovetskie pisateli: Avtobiografii* (Moscow: Khudozhestvennaia literatura, 1969–87) contains valuable information, indicating above all the eclecticism of juvenile tastes.

14   Shirley Brice Heath, "What No Bedtime Story Means: Narrative Skills at Home and School," *Language in Society* 11, 1 (1982): 49–76: repr. in *Linguistic Anthropology: A Reader*, ed. Alessandro Duranti (Oxford: Blackwell, 2001), 318–2, citations 318, 336.

15   Ibid., 322.

16   For an example of such a "mother's diary" from the 1920s, see Esfir' I. Stanchinskaia, *Dnevnik materi* (Moscow: Novaia Moskva, 1924); from the 1930s, Irina R. Kliuchareva, *Iz dnevnika materi: O nekoto-rykh voprosakh vospitaniia* (Moscow: Gosudarstvennoe uchebnopedagogicheskoe izdatel'stvo, 1951); and from the 1960s, Valeriia S. Mukhina, *Bliznetsy* (Moscow: Prosveshchenie, 1969).

17   On library censorship in the early Soviet era (which set the pattern for what was done later), see Evgeny Dobrenko, *The Making of the State Reader: Social and Aesthetic Contexts of the Reception of Soviet Literature*, trans. Jesse M. Savage (Stanford, CA: Stanford University Press, 1997), esp. 190–91. Herman Ermolaev, *Censorship in Soviet Literature, 1917–1991* (Lanham, MD: Rowman and Littlefield, 1997), 7, describes the removal of Charskaia in 1923. Cf. Maksim Gor'kii's assertion in 1933 that far less of prerevolutionary children's literature was retrievable for Soviet readers than prerevolutionary adult literature ("Literatura—detiam," *Pravda*, 11 June 1933). Library censorship in the United States tends to have a "voluntarist" character, resulting from pressures by individuals (especially parents), lobby groups from the "moral majority," and educational authorities. See the pamphlet *Censorship in the Schools: What Is It? How Do You Cope?* posted on the website of the American Library Association; and Peter Hunt, "Judy Blume," in *Censorship: A World Encyclopedia*, ed. Derek Jones, 4 vols. (London: Fitzroy Dearborn, 2001), vol. 1, 253–54. In Britain, on the other hand, censorship has also been exercised by staff in libraries directly; a famous case was the removal of work by Enid Blyton in the 1970s. See Hunt, "Enid Blyton," ibid., 254–55. For general accounts of censorship and children's books, see Hunt, "Children's Literature," ibid., 461–64; and Susan Lehr, *Battling Dragons: Issues and Controversy in Children's Literature* (Portsmouth, NH: Heinemann, 1995).

18   On a visit to the Leningrad Province Children's Library, St. Petersburg, in September 2002, I was shown folders of work created by schoolchildren in the 1970s and 1980s for exhibitions and festivals, including the 40th anniversary of the end of the Great Patriotic War in 1945, contributions to the official peace movement, and so on.

19   As recorded, e.g., in Oxf/Lev M–03 PF22B, 12, where a woman born in Iaroslavl' in 1951 remem-bers: "My love of reading always gave me trouble. I was signed up at a library, but there was always a waiting list for good books there; you had to put your name down. Well, you'd get them in the end,

but then you couldn't keep them hidden [i.e., stop someone else grabbing them] when you were all living in the same room. So I read them in bed, under the blankets, with a flashlight."

20 Oxf/Lev M–03 PF3A, 4.

21 Oxf/Lev V–04 PF4A, 28.

22 Oxf/Lev V–04 PF15A, 11.

23 My thanks to Natal'ia Dvortsina for pointing this out.

24 Oxf/Lev V–04 PF6B, 53.

25 Oxf/Lev T–04 PF2B, 12.

26 An example from the early Soviet era is CKQ-M–04 PF5A, 8 (man b. 1918, small town, Tula province), whose stepmother's strictures against excessive reading (she told him he would turn into a "bookworm") did not discourage him. A late Soviet example is the informant in CKQ-Ox–03 PF8–9, whose parents were both village teachers from a peasant background, with a library of Russian classics and Marxism-Leninism, but who herself had much more catholic tastes, and especially a keen interest in the history of art.

27 A thriller by Vadim [M.] Kozhevnikov, with a base situation similar to Iulian [S.] Semenov's much better-known *Semnadtsat' mgnovenii vesny* (17 Moments of Spring)—a Soviet agent is posted to Hitler's Germany to pose as a German. It was made into an East German–Soviet co-produced film in 1968, directed by Vladimir Basov.

28 Oxf/Lev SPb–03 14 B, 29 (female informant, b. Leningrad, 1969).

29 Cf. another working-class informant from a similar generation (male, b. Leningrad 1960), Oxf/Lev SPb–03 PF17B, 18: "There was this Kotovskii book, *Staraia krepost'* [The Old Fortress: the book is in fact by Vladimir P. Beliaev and was first published by Detizdat in 1937; it had over 40 editions between then and the early 1990s], a nice fat book that, yes, that's the one, I remember it now."

30 For an example of reading inspired by watching films, see Oxf/Lev SPb—03 14B, 29, when the informant, asked if *Shchit i mech*, remembered as her favorite book, was on the school program, responds: "I reckon not, I reckon not. Least, don't remember it. I just wished it had been. I liked it [the film]; I wanted to read it [the book]. Then it turned out my auntie had a copy of the book."

31 Oxf/Lev SPb–03 PF 24A, 9–10. Cf. Oxf/Lev M–04 PF 24B, 17 (male informant, b. 1968, Moscow region): "The hassle . . . the hassle started back in secondary school, when a subject like literature turned up. [*Laughs*]. See, I don't like reading much. All you had to do in literature was read books, then talk about them, where someone . . . what he did and why. Some books I didn't read at all, some I read bits of, and some I read between the lines [skimmed]. So what could I answer? I'd mumble something—and from class eight [age 15], the threes [the lowest regular mark, equivalent to a C grade] started to flood in."

32 The reading and ingestion association (*chitat' zapoem*, "to binge-read," as with vodka) perpetuates a traditional appreciation of the word as a physical entity, expressed in practices such as writing the words of a spell down on paper and then ingesting it. See Albert Baiburin, "The Word in Traditional Russian Culture," *Forum for Anthropology and Culture/Antropologicheskii forum*, no. 2 (forthcoming in 2006).

33 Female informant, b. Leningrad, 1967, "Vospominaniia o shkol'noi zhizni" (unpub. typescript memoir, 2003), 2.

34 Professional'no-tekhnicheskoe uchilishche, a form of tertiary vocational education that, while in official terms equivalent in value to study at a university or institute, was considered a very inferior alternative by the teachers of ten-year schools.

35 Oxf/Lev SPb–03 PF 25B, 40.

36 Oxf/Lev SPb–03 PF 24B, 22. Cf. the recollection by a Moscow schoolteacher who began work in 1958 that a Tatar boy had run away from home after she, as a young and inexperienced teacher, gave him a two. She was warned by the school authorities never to give lower than a three again (Oxf/Lev M–04 PF35B, 12).

37 Oxf/Lev SPb–03 PF 15B, 55.

38 There is a notable overlap between the marginality of books in the culture of working-class children in the 1960s and 1970s and their marginality in the culture of working-class young adults, as one would expect. A small-scale questionnaire carried out at an Astrakhan' factory in 1964 indicated that nearly half the informants (22 out of 50) visited the cinema 6–10 times a month but only 7 read more than 7 books in 2 months. Not all the respondents gave precise details of their employment, but the majority among those who did were manual workers (27 as against 7 engineers). The list of favorite films (including *Ia shagaiu po Moskve*, but more particularly *Parizhskaia taina, Razvod po-ital'ianski, Vse ostaetsia liudiam*, and *Tishina*) was significantly longer than the list of favorite books, with many respondents simply naming genres ("adventure stories," "science fiction," "literary books"). Among favorite magazines and newspapers, the only *tolstye zhurnaly* to be named were *Volga* and

Iunost', alongside a range of other publications including *Sovetskii sport, Futbol*, and *Za rulem*. See "Ankety ucheta kul'turnykh zaprosov naseleniia, zapolnennye rabotnikami Astrakhanskogo teplov-ozremontnogo zavoda (iiul' 1964)," TsKhDMO f. 1, op. 32, d. 1175, ll. 1–152.

39   On which, see Catriona Kelly, *Refining Russia: Advice Literature, Polite Culture, and Gender from Catherine to Yeltsin* (Oxford: Oxford University Press, 2001), chap. 5.

40   See K. Kelli [Catriona Kelly], "Malen 'kie grazhdane bol'shoi strany: Detstvo, internatsionalizm i sovetskaia propaganda," *Novoe literaturnoe obozrenie*, no. 60 (2003): 214–51.

41   Most famously in her attacks on Kornei Chukovskii: see an internal review of 1926, N. K. Krupskaia, *Pedagogicheskie sochineniia*, 10 vols. (Moscow: Izdatel'stvo Akademii pedagogicheskikh nauk RSFSR, 1957–62), vol. 10, 220–21; and an article published in *Pravda* on 21 February 1928 (ibid., 252–56).

42   For a more detailed discussion, see my forthcoming article, "Riding the Magic Carpet: Children and the Stalin Cult," *Slavic and East European Journal* 49, 2 (2005).

43   See Omri [Omry] Ronen, "Detskaia literatura i sotsialisticheskii realizm," in *Sotsrealisticheskii kanon*, ed. Evgenii [Evgeny] Dobrenko and Khans Giunter [Hans Günther] (St. Petersburg: Akademicheskii proekt, 2000), 969–79.

44   See the excellent discussion in Karen Lesnik-Oberstein, *Children's Literature: Criticism and the Fictional Child* (Oxford: Clarendon Press, 1994).

45   The views of such children are clear in the significant proportion of letters in the files of the Dom detskoi knigi dealing with nonfiction and in work with informants: compare an unsolicited comment from an assistant in the Russian State Library, Moscow, who, as I ploughed my way through yet another run of *Koster* and *Pioner* for the late 1950s and early 1960s, expressed her commiserations that I would have to struggle through anything so uninteresting. When I asked her what she herself had read as a child, she replied immediately, "*Iunyi tekhnik.*"

46   As I have indicated elsewhere ("Opisyvaia istoriiu detstva v Rossii dvadtsatogo veka: Mify, predstav-leniia, teksty," in *Mir russkikh detei*, ed. L. P. Repina [forthcoming 2005]). I avoid the use of the term *detskaia subkul'tura* in a generalizing sense. A child who has little or no access to peer-group activities outside the home and the schoolroom may not participate in a *detskaia subkul'tura* at all; even children who do participate in one (e.g., spend time with a *kompaniia* in the courtyard of their apartment block or school, or in the city or village street) have an existence that goes beyond participation in this subculture. Furthermore, a wide variety of non-adult controlled peer-group activities exists, and any one child may participate in numerous different, even contradictory ones. The importance of peer-group attitudes in developing reading tastes should not be underestimated, however: oral history work points both to the importance of shared tastes in consolidating friendships and to the influence of siblings, friends, and others in steering reading tastes. See, e.g., T–04 PF3A, 11, female informant, b. 1954, who remembers her brothers bringing home adventure stories such as *The Count of Monte Cristo* and *The Last of the Mohicans* during the late 1960s.

47   Nicholas Stargardt, *Witnesses of War: Children's Lives under the Nazis* (London: Jonathan Cape, 2005), 16.

48   David [S.] Samoilov, "Dnevnik schastlivogo mal'chika," *Znamia*, no. 8 (1999): 148–67; and *The Diary of Nina Kosterina*, trans. Mirra Ginsburg (London: Valentine, Mitchell, 1968).

49   To be sure, in the first decade or so after the Revolution, between the abolition of the old *gimnaziia* program and the publication of the first mandatory new programs in 1927, children were allowed some input into what was taught in at least some classrooms. For example, in the experimental railway school run by N. I. Popova in Moscow, children did not merely learn their letters from alphabet books but designed and made their own alphabet books, and they were allowed a good deal of room to decide on their own activities (N. I. Popova, *Shkola zhizni* [Moscow: Novaia Moskva, 1924], 110, 34). But as Larry E. Holmes has convincingly argued in *The Kremlin and the Schoolhouse: Reforming Education in Soviet Russia, 1917–1931* (Bloomington: Indiana University Press, 1991), the tenor of classroom practice in many classrooms remained teacher-centered and regimented.

50   As indicated by inspectors' reports: see, e.g., "Spravki o sostoianii ideino-politicheskogo vospitaniia v shkolakh goroda Moskvy, sostavlennye po rezul'tatam obsledovaniia shkol v period s 20–30.04.48," Rossiiskaia akademiia obrazovaniia: Nauchnyi arkhiv (RAO NA) f. 32, op. l, d. 160, ll. 2–25.

51   RAO NA f. 6, op. 1, ed. kh. 42, l. 1 is the instruction on using the questionnaire, which was supposed to be gone through in a relaxed way (in the manner of a *zhivoi razgovor*); ed. kh. 5, ll. 58–103, is a selection of the completed questionnaires: on Chapaev, see ll. 58 ob., 61; on Matveev, l. 58; and on Vaisenberg, l. 61. For examples of prerevolutionary questionnaire work, see N. A. Rybnikov, *Derevenskii shkol'nik i ego idealy* (Moscow: Zadruga, 1916); and Rybnikov, *Idealy gimnazistok: Ocherki po psikhologii iunosti* (Moscow: Prakticheskie znaniia, [1916]).

52   Both individual published memoirs of childhood and collections of these (e.g., B. M. Bim-Bad and O. E. Kosheleva, *Priroda rebenka v zerkale avtobiografii* [Moscow: Izdatel'stvo URAO, 1998]) generally

have a strong metropolitan and intellectual bias. Some material about childhood in other circumstances, however, is available in testimony on specialized subjects—for example, collectivization, the Great Purges, and World War II. See, for example, S. S. Vilenskii, A. I. Kokurin, G. V. Atmashkina, and I. Iu. Novichenko, eds., *Deti Gulaga 1918–1956* (Moscow: Demokratiia, 2002). Memoir sources of all kinds also thin out dramatically when one reaches the 1950s, 1960s, and 1970s, so that letters to writers represent, alongside oral history, an essential source for work on this particular period.

53   This information is based on holdings in Tsentral'nyi gosudarstvennyi arkhiv literatury i iskusstva Sankt-Peterburga (TsGALI-SPb) f. 64. See anon., "Predislovie," to f. 64, op. 5, ll. 4–5; the publicity brochure for the Dom detskoi knigi in Leningrad (1953) in f. 64, op. 5, d. 6, ll. 7–8; and *Luchshii otzyv o prochitannoi knige sovetskoi detskoi i iunosheskoi literatury III tur* (Leningrad: Dom detskoi knigi Detgiza, 1950), ibid., l. 3. The likeliest exact date for the founding of the DDK seems to be 15 September 1950, given that this is the starting point of an engagement book held in TsGALI-SPb f. 64, op. 5, d. 7, passim.

54   On this, see the materials in TsGALI-SPb f. 64, op. 3, and ibid., f. 64, op. 2.

55   See the program for the 1953 event in ibid., op. 5, d. 38, ll. 1–3; and "Otchet o provedenii Nedeli detskoi knigi v Leningradskom filiale Dom detskoi knigi," ibid., ll. 4–28.

56   See, for example, *Pioner* and *Pionerskaia pravda* for 1956 and 1962. In a similar "disappearance" vein, note the item in the Detskaia literatura accounts for 1962, "Likvidirovany portrety (Stalina) na summu Rb. 314–04 (s iznosom Rb. 78–50)": "LO izdatel'stva 'Detskaia literatura': Otchet ob izdatel'skoi i finansovoi deiatel'nosti za 1962," TsGALI f. 64, op. 1, d. 166, l. 11.

57   "Kniga zapisei predpriiatii Doma detskoi knigi n[achalo] 15 sentiabria 1950 o[konchanie] 28 dekabria 1951," TsGALI-SPb f. 64, op. 5, d. 7, ll. 1 ob., 13, 16 ob.–17, 25. Similarly, "Children's Book Week" in 1953 gave considerable prominence to the "cult of personality" and to other patriotic and ideological topics such as the Stalinist plan for the transformation of nature and to books about Soviet heroes: "Glavnym obrazom propagandirovalis' knigi o velikikh vozhdiakh Vladimire Il'iche Lenine i Iosife Vissarionoviche Staline, knigi o Rodine, o Stalinskom plane preobrazovaniia prirody, o velikikh stroikakh kommunizma, o bor'be za mir, o pionerakh i Komsomole, o trudovykh uspekhakh sovetskikh liudei i t.d." See "Otchet o provedenii," ibid., d. 38,1. 4.

58   Ibid., d. 7, ll. 5 ob.–7 (puppet shows); 20 ob.–21 (Tvoia liubimaia kniga). The full list of books for this series included, besides those already mentioned, Kassil's *Ulitsa mladshego syna*, Liubov' T. Kosmodem'ianskaia's hagiographical life of her children, *Povest' o Zoe i Shure* (ghost-written by Frida A. Vigdorova), and Aleksei I. Musatov's *Stozhary* (a eulogistic account of life in the labor reserves, first published in 1948). Of all the book talks, that on *Deti gorchichnogo raia* got the largest turnout— 130 people (l. 29 ob.). Attendance was also high for a "meet the writer" series aimed at 13- to 15-year-old schoolchildren in October 1951—between 138 and 320 people came to the different events (ll. 46 ob., 47). By comparison, 80 people at the "peace" evening or 20 at the evening dedicated to "Marxism and linguistics" seems quite modest.

59   Ibid., d. 136, ll. 3–19, 21–32; d. 168, ll. 2–10, 12–21.

60   See "Gos[udarstvennoe] izd[atel'stvo] detskoi literatury 'Detgiz': Leningradskoe otdelenie. Dom detskoi knigi: Leningradskii filial. Kniga otzyvov i pozhelanii, n[achalo] 22 sentiabria 1958 ok[onchanie] 26 dekabria 1961," ibid., d. 122, ll. 2, 4, 18.

61   "Stenogramma lektsii N. Serovoi, 'Kak rabotat' s chitatel'skimi otzyvami' (24 noiabria 1950)," ibid., d. 3, l. 3. Serova's advice was in tune with a general high-Stalinist stress on the dangers of extreme emotion: the official life of Zoia and Shura Kosmodem'ianskaia by their mother emphasized that these model children had never let themselves go (L. Kosmodem'ianskaia [literaturnaia zapis' F. (A.) Vigdorovoi], *Povest' o Zoe i Shure* [Leningrad: Leningradskoe gazetno-zhurnal'noe izdatel'stvo, 1951], 113–14).

62   On the link between Stalinist attitudes toward appropriate behavior and those of the 18th century, see chap. 4 of Kelly, *Refining Russia*.

63   TsGALI-SPb f. 64, op. 5, d. 3, l. 6.

64   Cf. the observations in a report by inspectors from the Academy of Pedagogical Sciences on literature teaching in Moscow schools ("Spravki o sostoianii ideino-politicheskogo vospitaniia v shkolakh goroda Moskvy, sostavlennye po rezul'tatam obsledovaniia shkol v period s 20–30.04.48," RAO NA f. 32, op. l, d. 160, l. 6), which indicates that a typical topic for this date was "Pochemu ia ne mogu i ne khochu byt' pokhozhei [this was a girls' school] na Belinova" (in Chekhov's story "Chelovek v futliare"). For observations of this kind from a later period, see N. Mart'ianova, "Ia—repetitor," *Nedelia*, no. 13 (1984): 6, which indicates that paraphrase rather than analysis was required.

65   TsGALI-SPb f. 64, op. 5, d. 3, l. 19.

66   "Luchshii otzyv," ibid., f. 65, op. 5, d. 6, l. 5.

67   RAO NA f. 32, op. 1, d. 120, l. 22.

68   P. [Pavel T.] Zhurba, *Geroi Sovetskogo Soiuza Aleksandr Matrosov* (Moscow: Voennoe izdatel'stvo, 1949), quotations 14 (attainment of goal), 18 (friendship), 20 (romantic love), 21 (call-up), 27 (Komsomol meetings), 31 (thoughts of sweetheart), 41 (death scene), 44 (discovery of his body).

69   A. [G.] Golubeva, *Mal'chik iz Urzhuma: Povest' o detstve i iunosti S. M. Kirova*, 4th ed. (Moscow and Leningrad: Detskaia literatura, 1946), 13 (toys), 25–30 (grandmother), 52 (orphanage food), 92 (prayers), 97 (library), 176 ff. (teaching and revolutionary activities). There was also an abridged and simplified version of this book, *Rasskazy o Sergee Kostrikove* (Moscow and Leningrad: Detskaia literatura, 1951), labeled "for the primary school." The print run of the long version was 30,000, of the latter 400,000.

70   Iu. [P.] German, *Rasskazy o Felikse Dzerzhinskom* (Moscow and Leningrad: Detskaia literatura, 1947), 134–37 (emaciated boy), 163 (hungry boy), 117 (sleeping boys).

71   Zhurba, *Geroi Sovetskogo Soiuza*, 13 (Dan'ko), 18 (learning and imitation).

72   TsGALI-SPb f. 64, op. 5, d. 5, ll. 9, 31.

73   Ibid., l. 8.

74   "Chto posovetuesh', Timur?" *Pionerskaia pravda*, 29 June 1962: 1. Several items of this kind appeared around the time of the Pioneer rally in late June 1962.

75   See Catriona Kelly, " 'Is That Really Friendship?' The Management of Children's Affective Relationships in Soviet Russia," forthcoming.

76   CKQ-Oxf–03 PF OB, 3; CKQ-Oxf–03 PF 6B, 14.

77   For the proportions of lives of heroes in Detgiz/Detskaia literatura's output, compare *Plan izdanii gosudarstvennogo izdatel'stva Detskoi literatury Ministerstva prosveshcheniia RSFSR na 1952 god* (TsGALI-SPb f. 64, op. 1, d. 65), where the list is dominated by *skazki* and books about heroes, such as S. Karnaukhova, *Skazki o geroiakh*, Z. Komenkova, *S. M. Kirov i deti* (1. 16), or N. Zabila, *Pro vsekh: Stikhi o liubvi detei k tovarishchu Stalinu* (1. 4 ob.); *Plan izdanii . . . izd. Detskoi literatury . . . na 1956 god* (TsGALI-SPb f. 64, op. 1, d. 94); and *Plan izdanii . . . Gos. izd. Detskoi literatury . . . na 1957 god* (TsGALI-SPb f. 64, op. 1, d. 104), wherein heroic lives have a proportionately lesser role, and where the weight of "how to" books and of literature by non-Russian Soviet writers is boosted.

78   T. Khmel'nitskaia, untitled in-house review of Viktor Goliavkin, *My s Vovkoi druz'ia*, TSGALI-SPb f. 64, op. 3, d. 42, 1. 181.

79   See especially Vladimir [I.] Glotser, *Deti pishut stikhi* (Moscow: Prosveshchenie, 1964).

80   Iurii Koval', *Prikliucheniia Viti Kurolesova* (Moscow: Detskaia literatura, 1971).

81   L. Panteleev [A. I. Eremeev] and G. [Grigorii G.] Belykh, *Respublika Shkida* (Leningrad: Detskaia literatura, 1961).

82   Work with informants confirms the picture of very different reading patterns in people brought up in the 1930s–40s and in the 1950s–60s. For example, informants brought up in the 1930s express much more positive views about the cult of Pavlik Morozov than informants brought up in the 1950s or 1960s (see Kelly, *Comrade Pavlik*, chaps. 5–7). Informants brought up in the 1930s and 1940s recall playing "scenario games" on the basis of, say, *Chapaev*, or Fadeev's *Molodaia gvardiia*, while informants brought up in the 1950s and 1960s are more likely to remember Stirlitz or Dumas's *Three Musketeers*.

83   "Obzory chitatel'skikh pisem za 1965 god," TsGALI-SPb f. 64, op. 5, d. 151, ll. 2–8, 74–78, 145–48, 188. The approximation of "around 150" for Kozlov's *Prezident* was dictated by the fact that the figures for the last quarter aggregate letters about this book with other works by Kozlov (81 letters). The relationship between letters about *Prezident* and about other texts during the first three quarters, however, suggests that at least two-thirds would have invoked this particular novel, making the estimate a safe one. To put the thousands of letters received by the DDK in perspective, note that *Pionerskaia pravda* received over 200 times more missives in 1972: a staggering 288,763 letters ("Spravka o rabote s pis'mami redaktsii gazety *Pionerskaia pravda* za 1972 god," TsKhDMO f. 1, op. 34, d. 649, l. 4).

84   V. [Vil'iam F.] Kozlov, *Prezident Kamennogo ostrova* (Leningrad: Detskaia literatura, 1964).

85   Iu. [Iurii G.] Tomin, *Shel po gorodu volshebnik* (Leningrad: Detskaia literatura, 1963).

86   "Obzory chitatel'skikh pisem za 1972 god," TsGALI-SPb f. 64, op. 4, d. 170, l. 4. This motif of being transported to a different world is quite frequent in the letters. Cf. "Obzory chitatel'skikh pisem za 1963," ibid., d. 143, ll. 37–38, where a Russian girl from the Kazakh Republic enthuses over G. S. Martynov's *Kalliosto*: "to be frank, I almost started believing this society existed." In this case, she also emphasized how similar the society was to her own, though the aliens had black skins instead of white (on the motif of outer space as a realm of Soviet colonial domination, see Catriona Kelly, *The Little Citizens of a Big Country: Children and Soviet International Relations* [Trondheim: Program for East European Cultural Studies, 2002]).

87 "Obzory chitatel'skikh pisem za 1972 god," TsGALI-SPb f. 64, op. 5, d. 170, l. 8.

88 "Obzory chitatel'skikh pisem za 1965 god," ibid., d. 151, l. 99.

89 "Obzory chitatel'skikh pisem za 1972 god,"TsGALI-SPb f. 64, op. 5, d. 170, l. 8.

90 "Obzory chitatel'skikh pisem za 1965 god," ibid., d. 151, l. 102.

91 See above; and cf. the many articles on "arts education" (*tvorcheskoe vospitanie*) published in *Sovetskaia pedagogika* at this time, such as O. A. Apraksina and N. A. Vetlugina, "Sostoianie i zadachi muzykal'nogo vospitaniia v shkole," *Sovetskaia pedagogika*, no. 9 (1956): 46–58; and the surge of discussion within the Pioneer movement on the importance of artistic activities (e.g., A. Mazurova, "Zametki k zasedaniiu Soveta Vsesoiuznoi Pionerskoi Organizatsii po imeni V. I. Lenina po voprosu 'O dal'neishem razvitii initsiativy i samodeiatel'nosti vo vsesoiuznoi pionerskoi organizatsii imeni V. I. Lenina'" [1960], TsKhDMO f. 2, op. 1, d. 148, l. 41).

92 Here one should sound a note of caution. The Leningrad branch of Detizdat monitored letters that dealt with Leningrad-published books. The most popular poets working for children—Samuil Marshak and Kornei Chukovskii—had relocated to Moscow, and hence to the Moscow branch of Detizdat, in the late 1930s. Therefore, the standing of poetry among children has to be regarded as "not proven" from this material. Yet it does still seem that the key age span for letter-writing— around 10 to 14—was not one at which poetry was terribly popular. One notes that the three enthusiastic letters about Vadim Shefner's collection *Riadom s nebom* (Next to the Sky) that were received in 1963 all came from children in class ten (17-year-olds) ("Obzory chitatel'skikh pisem za 1963 god," TsGALI-SPb f. 64, op. 5, d. 143, ll. 62–63).

93 "Obzory chitatel'skikh pisem za 1965 god," ibid., d. 151, ll. 2–8, 74–78, 145–48. German is not listed in the final quarter (l. 188), but the number of letters for the year is unlikely to have exceeded 30. In the same year, Golubeva's *Mal'chik iz Uzhruma* clocked up around five letters, her *Rasskazy o Sergee Kostriakove* seven letters, and Zhurba's *Aleksandr Matrosov* around seven (again, in all cases the final quarter is unspecified) (ibid.).

94 "Obzory chitatel'skikh pisem za 1965 god," ibid., l. 85. Punctuation follows original. Cf. ibid., l. 154 (letter from girl aged seven, Amurskaia region); "Obzory chitatel'skikh pisem za 1963 god," ibid., d. 143, l. 98.

95 "Obzory chitatel'skikh pisem za 1963 god," ibid., l. 40.

96 "Obzory chitatel'skikh pisem za 1965 god," ibid., d. 151, l. 192.

97 "Protokol vstrechi shkol'nikov s pisatelem R. Pogodinym po obsuzhdeniiu knigi 'Murav'inoe maslo' i otzyvy chitatelei na knigu," undated typescript, ibid., d. 6, ll. 12, 11, 2.

98 For the difficulty in separating fiction and reality, see a girl from class seven in Astrakhan', writing in 1965 about Pogodin's *Kirpichnye ostrova*: "I liked it a lot. I really wondered: is it the truth written down in this book or inventions?" (ibid., d. 151, l. 101); for imitating heroes, cf. the boy from class eight in Ugritsk stating proudly that he is now mending his own trousers and repairing the shed, just as the boys in Ia. Mavr's 1959 novel *TVT* were doing (ibid., d. 131, l. 42).

99 "Obzory chitatel'skikh pisem za 1963 god," ibid., d. 143, l. 36.

100 "Obzory chitatel'skikh pisem za 1965 god," ibid., d. 151, l. 161. For controversy among adults, cf. the letter from a father in Kiev complaining that he was afraid to give Vil'iam Kozlov's book *Valerka-predsedatel'* to his daughter, because it contained such awful phrases as "to hell with you" (*chert s toboi*) and "chatterbox" (*trepach*) (ibid., d. 131, l. 38).

101 "Obzory chitatel'skikh pisem za 1952 god," ibid., d. 5, l. 10.

102 Cf. the experience of an informant in our oral history project who was refused entry to the Komsomol in the late 1940s when she answered the question, "How would you assess your work for the wall newspaper?" with the word "Magnificent" (CKQ-Ox–03 PF5B, 13).

103 V. Liadov, "O geroiakh v detskoi literature," *Pravda*, 25 February 1934.

104 See CKQ-Ox–03 PF1, l.

105 See my "Riding the Magic Carpet" for details of this strategy.

106 See the letter dictated to her elder sister by a five-year-old girl from Aktiubinsk in 1963 about a story by Vitalii Bianki: "Dear editors, I'm five. I go to nursery school. I have a sister. She attends class five. My sister read me the book about a school. I liked the book a lot. I asked her to write a letter. I can't write yet. If I'd been that little mouse, I wouldn't have been able to live without my ma, like he can. I wouldn't have been able to get myself food. My name is Ira" (TsGALI-SPbf. 64, op. 5, d. 143, ll. 15–16).

107 In 1951, there were 1,873 letters to Lendetgiz (ibid., d. 5, l. 4); in 1965, 4,171 for the year (ibid., d. 51, ll. 2–8).

108 See Ronen, "Detskaia literatura i sotsialisticheskii realizm," 970.

109 See, for example, www.fictionbook.ru (accessed 17 November 2004), inviting reader feedback, where Kozlov appears, but German does not.

110   For the first reaction, see "Obzory chitatel 'skikh knig za 1972 god," TsGALI-SPb f. 64, op. 5, d. 170, l. 98 (14-year-old girl, Yalta); for the second, ibid., l. 62 (19-year-old conscript, place not given: the author in question was Kozlov).

111   Influential studies of this social group include Sheila Fitzpatrick, *Education and Social Mobility in the Soviet Union, 1921–1934* (Cambridge: Cambridge University Press, 1979); Stephen Kotkin, *Magnetic Mountain: Stalinism as a Civilization* (Berkeley: University of California Press, 1995), from which the notion of "speaking Bolshevik" derives; and Jochen Hellbeck, "Fashioning the Stalinist Soul: The Diary of Stepan Podlubnyi, 1931–39," *Jahrbucher für Geschichte Osteuropas* 55, 3 (1996): 344–73.

112   See particularly Igal Halfin, *From, Darkness to Light: Class, Consciousness, and Salvation in Revolutionary Russia* (Pittsburgh: University of Pittsburgh Press, 2000).

113   As argued in particular by Oleg Kharkhordin, *The Collective and the Individual in Soviet Culture* (Berkeley: University of California Press, 1999).

114   A case in point was the poet Ol'ga Sedakova (b. 1949), who contributed thoroughly orthodox work to *Koster* as a girl in the 1960s but eschewed, on principle, publication in the Soviet Union once she had reached adulthood (in any case her dense, thoroughly cerebral, poetry, shot through with references to Christian belief and to philosophers such as Heidegger, was not the sort of material considered suitable for the public domain even in the late Soviet era). Oral history suggests that nostalgia for the Soviet era, among subjects born from the late 1940s onward, is rare to the vanishing point, though some informants will admit to regretting the days when it was possible to take pride in one's country: "Well, really, when there were festivals and we'd say, 'Long live the revolution!' we'd all have tears in our eyes. [. . .] The attitude Americans have [toward their country], that's the attitude we had. [. . .] All those years ago, we had lots of respect. And now everyone says all that was bad. I don't agree, I think youth should be different" (Woman b. 1950 in working-class area of Moscow, both parents factory workers, Oxf/Lev M–04 PF36B, 15).

Chapter 21

Jane Humphries

STARTING WORK

Introduction

THE **GREAT VIRTUE OF APPROACHING CHILD** labour through auto-
biography is the ability to see the issue in context, to be able to trace the labour supply to
its origins in family and community. Chapter 2 [see original reading] suggested a number of
interconnections between child labour and the economic and social changes of the eighteenth
and nineteenth centuries and concluded that the industrial revolution, as now understood, may
well have both unleashed a boom in children's work and itself been fed by children's work. The
current chapter explores this hypothesis at the micro-level in terms of factors that likely
promoted or retarded entry into the labour force such as social norms, a child's family circumstances and local employment opportunities. In so doing, it builds on key findings from earlier
chapters [see original reading]: first, an apparent precocious dependence on men and men's
earnings, manifest in attitudes to mothers and fathers and perceptions of their duties; and,
second, the extent of fatherlessness, and particularly de facto fatherlessness, in the eighteenth
and early nineteenth centuries. Together these two features imply a 'breadwinner frailty'.
Dependence on men's earnings meant that the loss or interruption of male support, an all too
common experience in these years, jeopardized families' survival. Like its close relation 'nuclear
hardship', the precocious adoption of this particular family form left individuals vulnerable
when families failed. Unless the authorities were prepared to let mothers and children perish
(and they were not) an alternative system of support was needed. Breadwinner frailty came to
complement nuclear hardship in prompting the spread and evolution of poor relief. Moreover,
it established the context in which children became families' second line of defence when men's
support was inadequate or interrupted; it set the scene for the upsurge in child labour.

Starting work

Most autobiographers describe starting work in some detail. They report their age at starting
work and the circumstances which lay behind it, especially if precipitate.[1] The authors' attention to this occasion is fortuitous. It provides an escape from the necessity of defining work,

hard even in the modern context, and in a world where the boundaries of the workplace and the home were permeable and where not all work was remunerated individually or in cash, likely insurmountable. The problem is passed back to the autobiographers themselves. What did they see as work, and how did they recognize starting work?

The autobiographers had no difficulty in identifying this milestone even when it was far away in time and space. Writing a lifetime later and from another continent, the Unitarian Minister Robert Collyer recalled clearly: '72 years ago last summer the bell tapped for me to go to work in the factory where my father and mother had served their time' (Collyer, 1908, p. 15). John Harris said simply 'At nine years of age I was taken from school and put to work in the fields' (1882, p. 32). John Clare predictably was more poetic: 'I believe I was not older than 10 when my father took me to seek the scanty rewards of industry' (1986, p. 3). William Arnold anticipated the astonishment of a later generation and the violence done to modern notions of childhood by his age at starting work. 'When I was six years and two months old I was sent off to work. Fancy that, only just over six years of age! This was at the end of February, or early March, and I do not think I shall ever forget those long and hungry days in the fields' (Arnold, 1915, p. 13).

The autobiographers drew clear lines. They distinguished between help with domestic tasks and childcare, which though boys they were often called upon to perform (see above, p. 115 [see original reading]), and *working*. Chester Armstrong was both playmate and guardian for his little sister, but work for him began when the manager of the local pit found him a job 'about the heapstead' (Armstrong, 1938, p. 53). Thomas Barclay was often called upon to be 'nurse' when his mother accompanied his rag and bone man father on his peregrinations, 'and often have I put my tongue into baby's mouth to be sucked in lieu of "titty" to stop her cries' (Barclay, 1934, p. 9). However, aged eight, he 'went to work, turning the wheel at Browett's rope walk' (Barclay, 1934, p. 14). Childcare could be work. For Bill H – the 'first work ever I did was to mind two little lads for a farmer', for which he got his breakfast and a penny (1861–62, p. 141). Tommy Mitchell (born 1833) also looked after children and for a similar reward, 'a good meal and, sometimes a penny and a thank you', A man passing by expressed disapproval of Tommy's nursing: 'Your father ought to find you something else to do, not to nurse children' (Mitchell, n.d., p. 2). Soon enough Tommy progressed to more manly work, cleaning shoes at a boarding school and then grinding coffee. Joseph Havelock Wilson (born 1858) remembered no embarrassment in looking after his first employer's 'beautiful baby boy', and recorded childcare along with sweeping and cleaning the ironmonger's shop as his first employment, for which he was paid 2s 6d per week (Wilson, 1925, p. 11). It was not the type of task but the social relations within which it occurred that signalled *work*.

The autobiographers distinguished too between part-time work done before school, or in the summer, and work proper. James Dunn ran errands to earn coppers after school and did harvest work to 'to help with the home-board' but started work aged eight when he went down the pit (Dunn, 1910, p. 7). Joseph Ashby (born 1859) scared crows for the local farmers part-time from age nine but work began for him 'in earnest' two years later (Ashby, 1974). Involvement in domestic manufacturing winding bobbins, carding wool or 'assisting' was definitely seen as work, as was becoming a half-timer in a factory. In the latter case, age at starting work was often associated with a birthday that propelled a boy over a legal hurdle, implying protective legislation's partial effectiveness. Joseph Burgess had started working punching cards for Jacquard looms when three months short of his seventh birthday, but it was not until he was eight that he could gain employment half-time as a piecer (Burgess, 1927; see also Brooks, 1950/1?). Four years later in search of full-time employment Joe represented himself as being the legal minimum age of 13. 'The certifying surgeon, however, had a word to say about that, and when he came to the mill, a fortnight after I had begun full time, he examined my teeth and promptly turned me down': a dismissal that was perhaps etched on Joe's memory by the surgeon simultaneously pulling one of his teeth (Burgess, 1927, p. 38). Alas, Joe simply sought work in the unregulated sector. James Turner (born 1857?) started work as a short-timer aged eight but 'then the Doctor refused to pass me; he said I was too little' (Turner, 1981, p. 1). In this case, withdrawal from work lasted longer. A collier looking for a boy to assist him took George Lloyd from the workhouse when he was aged 11. However, regulations prevented children younger than 12 from working underground, and so he was passed on to be apprenticed to a shoemaker (Lloyd, n.d.). Raymond Preston broke the Factory Act by working overtime when he was under 13 in order to increase the earnings he gave to his blind and widowed mother (Preston, 1930, p. 25). Robert Collyer initially worked a crippling 13 hours a day on weekdays and 11 hours on Saturday, but in 1833 'the burden was lifted' by a Factory Act which barred children under 9 and limited the hours of those aged 9–11 to 9 a day. Collyer had no doubt about the benefits that he secured from this seemingly paltry protection. 'This gave me a fine breathing space of about two years, and then I took the full stint with no harm; for the foundations were strong' (Collyer, 1908, p. 16). Later the provisions of the various Education Acts regulated the ages at which children could start work, though again these could be circumvented (Rubinstein, 1977). George Acorn was withdrawn from school and sent out to find a job aged 12, but the school board interfered. In his late nineteenth-century generation, boys had to be 14 to leave school, though aged 13 it was possible to get a labour certificate by passing an examination. George passed and was duly graduated into the world of work (Acorn, 1911).

The majority of autobiographers pinpointed age at starting work, and, in a number of additional cases, it could be identified from context. In only 97 cases was age at starting work indeterminate. But even here autobiographers often suggested precocity, stating that they began work at 'at a very young age' or 'as soon as able'. Abraham Holroyd does not tell his readers how old he was when he started handloom weaving, only that it was 'as soon as my legs were long enough to reach the treadles' (Holroyd, 1892, p. 10). Similarly, his contemporary, George Jacob Holyoake, could not remember his age when his father took him to the Eagle Foundry in Birmingham but only that he 'must have been very young' since his father held his hand as they walked along (Holyoake, 1906, p. 19). James Hillocks omits the age at which he was set to wind, 'the dreary lot of the weaver's children', but noted that he was so little and frail that the feet of the pirn-wheel had to be cut so that he could reach the spokes to drive it (Hillocks, 1862, pp. 12–13). In these cases contextual evidence fixes Holyoake's age at starting work as around nine and Hillocks's as six.[2] Thus, it is not clear that those who reported age at starting work were particularly young and that missing observations are systematically skewed towards older entry into work.

Age at starting work and the industrial revolution

Looking only by birth cohort, age at starting work first fell then rose, as shown in Table 7.1 [see original reading].[3] Formal testing suggests that this variation is unlikely to have occurred by chance.[4] Nor is the U shape the product of the particular chronological subdivision adopted. Regressing age at starting work on date of birth, a number of curve-fitting exercises confirm that a quadratic equation provides the best fit, with age at starting work falling until around 1800, when it began slowly to increase.[5]

The second and third cohorts of children that lived through the industrial revolution were more likely to be at work than were children of the same age in the previous generation. Only for the cohort born after 1850 was there a clear increase in the age at starting work, as the clustered bars in Figure 7.1 show [see original reading].

Does this increasing likelihood of early working during the late eighteenth and early nineteenth centuries capture a real trend or simply reflect other differences across the cohorts? If the middle cohorts systematically over-represent boys whose likelihood of early working was elevated, then the apparent variation over time would simply be an artifact of the surviving records.[6] On the other hand, chapters 3 and 4 [see original reading] established that the autobiographers' circumstances were demographically and economically representative. Their family structures and fathers' occupational affiliation and nominal earnings within those occupations were shown to vary, but more or less in line with the changes known to have affected the population overall. Moreover, based on different sources, Horrell and Humphries (1995a) concluded that the 1820s and 30s saw an increase in child participation rates and younger children at work. Judging whether the autobiographies support this story requires further investigation of the proximate causes of children's work, but a simple cohort analysis is consistent with the argument that child labour was no anachronism inherited from a more brutal past. Instead, it looks to have been reinvented and propagated in the crucible of industrialization, as hypothesized in chapter 2, above [see original reading]. To understand why this is so involves a closer look at how the economic changes of the era translated into labour market conditions and family strategies associated with younger working.

Causes of starting work

The autobiographers not only remembered starting work but also offered insight into the surrounding circumstances. Descriptions of entry into the labour market do not immediately invoke the choice theoretic framework of orthodox economics. There is little evidence of a conscious weighing of costs and benefits in the light of full information. Instead, the impotence of the boys and their families, their inability to resist what seemed like inexorable forces, is communicated in text after text. The authors lapse into an atypical passive voice. 'I was taken from school, at the age of nine, and never had the privilege of returning afterwards', recalled Robert Lowery (born 1809) (Lowery, 1979, p. 49; see also Harris, above, p. 173 [see original reading]). 'Found necessary' is Edward Rymer's phrase (Rymer, 1976, p. 3).[7] Behind the passive voice was a general desire to exonerate parents from blame. Few children supported the charge of parental exploitation made by contemporary social commentators or saw themselves as sent out to work to support shiftless or lazy guardians. The majority of parents were kind and caring, in short altruistic (see above, pp. 128–29 [see original reading]). What then explains parental compliance?

Social norms

Custom and practice, the conventions of the community and their own experience guided some parents. Alfred Marshall observed that 'Most parents are willing enough to do for their children what their own parents did for them; and perhaps even to go a little beyond it if they find themselves among neighbours who happen to have a higher standard' (1969, p. 180). To go further required not merely unselfishness and affection, but also resistance to the forces of habit and a vision of a differently ordered future. Some parents rose to the challenge. Timothy Claxton (born 1790) had uneducated parents who 'much to their credit' saw 'the importance of giving their children a better chance than they themselves had enjoyed' (Claxton, 1839, p. 2). In contrast, Thomas Okey was economically secure, and his grandparents could well have afforded to send him to the boarding school for which he yearned, but it was not to be. 'My appointed station in life *was* that of a basket-maker, and straightway I was set to work'

(Okey, 1930, p. 25). Even if mothers and fathers had aspirations for their children that bucked the social trend, friends and neighbours had ways of signalling community disapproval. 'It was quite the custom in those days for quite baby boys to get regular employment if not the mothers were charged with pampering them' (Bell, 1926, p. 36; see also Cooper, 1971, pp. 39–40). Limited imagination probably played a part in decisions to send children to work, and inter-generational transmission of social norms, as in Okey's case, above, may well help explain the resilience of child labour, but even when parents had ambitions, economic constraints overrode them.

David Barr's mother was resolved to 'improve the circumstances in which we were placed' and expressly had her children's 'future welfare' in mind (Barr, 1910, p. 19). On leaving Fillongley School aged 12, David had a great desire for further education. His mother, whose economic circumstances had improved during David's schooldays (he was her youngest or next-to-youngest child), took him to see a Dr Sheepshanks, the principal of Coventry Grammar School. Alas, the fees were beyond her means. David was 'compelled to return home to earn my living', though, note, with several years of education already under his belt and at the relatively advanced age of 12 (Barr, 1910, p. 24). When Samuel Gompers (born 1850) was removed from school and sent to work his father was scolded by the schoolmaster, who said that 'it was wrong to rob me of an education', but Samuel felt no resentment towards his father, who 'could not do otherwise' (Gompers, 1984, p. 4).

The autobiographers' world was not one where families could borrow against the future earnings of children and so withhold them from the labour market, even if there had been some way of making the associated inter-generational contracts stick and ensuring that more productive, higher-earning children recompensed parents who had borrowed (see above, p. 4 [see original reading]). Options were constrained by current levels of income, even if the benefits obtainable from education and training were recognized and the future welfare of children desired. For example, Thomas Catling (born 1838) had the chance to attend a college in Canterbury while defraying some of the costs by working as a missionary printer. But despite this offset, 'the demands were greater than my father could possibly meet' and the opportunity was lost (Catling, 1911, p. 28).

The idea that children should be useful as soon as they were able and that work was better than idleness was certainly widespread in both eighteenth- and nineteenth-century autobiographies. However, there is no evidence of any exogenous shift in standards in the late eighteenth century, and it would be hard to explain the boom in children's work associated with industrialization in terms of some kind of cultural bootstraps. What appears more likely is that other factors promoted child labour, and attitudes were reassessed in the light of the reality. As in the cases of Barr, Gompers and Catling, in explaining the circumstances that led to their early employment, autobiographer after autobiographer came back to the same theme: the inadequacy of family incomes relative to needs. The dominant factor in the child labour of the era appears to have been the cold, gray force of poverty, 'the narrowness of our circumstances', as Joseph Mayett termed it (Mayett, 1986, p. 1).

Incomes and needs

While chapter 4 [see original reading] found the economic circumstances of the autobiographers' families to be representative of the population, many families appear to have been in chronic need and many others only just able to keep the proverbial wolf from the door. The extent of distress is not surprising given that the classic surveys of the late nineteenth century, when conditions must have improved, still found about one third of working-class families in poverty (Booth, 1902; Rowntree, 2000; Gazeley, 2003). Neither the autobiographies nor any other source provide the information necessary to establish a poverty standard and chart the proportion of the population that fell short for this earlier era, but as suggested in chapter 4 [see original reading], they do provide some direct and indirect evidence on deprivation, which might explain age at starting work. Such evidence has to cover all sources of income and the various pressures on it, but given the primary importance of fathers' contributions, it is with their earnings that the investigation begins.

Fathers' earnings

Chapter 4 [see original reading] showed that the autobiographers' fathers followed a representative sample of eighteenth- and nineteenth-century occupations and earned typical nominal amounts within these jobs. On average then these families must have lived the trends charted by historians of men's real wages: a slow and unsteady improvement over the eighteenth century, a distinct pause between 1790 and 1830 and faster growth thereafter (Allen, 2007). Of course, average wages do not tell the whole story; structural and technological changes meant that some workers gained while others lost; and cyclical oscillations disrupted progress even for those ahead of the curve. What is astounding is that the plateau from 1790 to 1830 appears clearly reflected in the decline in age at starting work for the middle two cohorts of autobiographers. Can the relationship between men's wages and child labour be identified at a more disaggregate level in the autobiographies?

Although occasional autobiographers recorded their father's earnings (indeed chapter 4 used this information to check the authenticity of economic standards [see original reading]), the evidence is too scattered to use as an explanatory variable in the analysis of child labour. On the other hand, writers almost universally recorded a father's broad occupational group, and this provides a first approximation for his earning power. Table 7.2 [see original reading] shows the variation in age at starting work by fathers' occupational group.

Although the occupational classifications are not identical, the ranking of groups by ages at which sons started work follows the ranking by full-time money wages computed by Charles Feinstein (1998b).[8] Men in trades, clerical and service occupations were an aristocracy of labour who earned more than agricultural labourers or domestic manufacturers. Moreover men in these categories often worked on their own account and owned property, albeit on a small scale. Predictably, they were able to withhold their children from the labour market for longer than were men in other groups. More surprisingly, boys whose fathers were sailors also appear relatively advantaged. The category includes able seamen and master mariners who could earn significant amounts of money as well as naval recruits whose position was more ambiguous. But even in the Merchant Service, Ralph Davis concluded: 'taking everything into account ... Only in London was a man who had not been apprenticed to a skilled craft likely to earn as much' (Davis, 1962, p. 152; see also Rodger, 1986).[9]

Figure 7.2 [see original reading] shows the mean age at starting work by both fathers' occupational group and by cohort, to include the time dimension. The occupational groups replicate the U-shaped relationship between age at starting work and cohort. In four occupational groups (agriculture, mining, casual and clerical), the cohort born after 1850 started work later than did the cohorts born earlier, and if the comparison is with the two middle cohorts this is true for all occupations except the sea. In six occupational groups (agriculture, mining, factory, outwork, trades and services) the cohort born before 1791 started work later than did those born in the crucible of industrialization. However, although replicated within groups, the U-shaped variation in age at starting work by cohort is dominated by the across-group differences linked above to men's relative earnings. For example, the sons of tradesmen, seamen and service workers in all cohorts started work later than did manufacturing outworkers' and casual workers' sons even in the final cohort.

The ranking of the occupational groups was not static over time. Shifts in the occupational hierarchy are detectible in the relative ages at which sons began work. Domestic manufacturers, for example, were once part of the working-class elite, but deskilling associated with a more detailed division of labour and competition from factory-produced goods wore down their living standards. Their sons experienced a dramatic decline in age at starting work in the second cohort consistent with this loss of economic status. Soldiers' sons in the first and second cohorts started work later than did the sons of casual workers, but this advantage looks to have been eroded as soldiers' relative pay deteriorated.[10] In contrast, seamen's sons did not manifest the decline in age at starting work for the middle cohorts. Sailors' apparent ability to support dependent children through this period reflects the effects of the French and Napoleonic wars, when wages were pushed to extraordinary levels (Davis, 1962, pp. 123 ff.).[11]

Thus, while fathers' earning capacity clearly played a major role in families' economic circumstances and so conditioned children's age at starting work, it does not tell the whole story. Fathers who were factory workers, for example, were often relatively well paid, yet their children were some of the youngest workers in all phases of industrialization. The demand for child labour may well be part of the explanation here correlated with fathers' occupation and pulling in a direction opposite to relative earnings.

Moreover the level of earnings when fathers were in employment does not capture the economic security of the household and so its ability to dispense with children's earnings. The regularity of fathers' employment also played a role.

Availability of adult work

As described in the autobiographies, most parents were not only kind they were also hard-working: 'poor but industrious' is a recurring phrase. But industriousness went to waste if there was no work available. The process of industrialization itself involved the rise and fall of sectors, technological change, shifts in the location of work and an intensification of the business cycle. Falling relative wages and pools of unemployment were signals in a changing labour market, but it took time to read these signals, to distinguish a temporary situation from something more permanent and to decide upon an accommodation. A radical response was often expensive, involving migration or retraining and so blocked by imperfect capital markets. A holding strategy involved adding workers, putting more family members to work, finding jobs for children. This is exactly the behavioural response behind the backward-bending supply curve, central to the basic model of a labour market with child labour (see above, p. 26–29 [see original reading]), here observed at the micro-level.

A slump in the shipping trade, which obliged his father to join the Navy as a carpenter, led to W.C. Steadman entering the labour force as an errand boy aged eight (Steadman, 1906). George Lloyd, another shipwright's son, also saw his family slide into poverty and eventually disintegrate when his father was thrown out of work on the closure of Deptford Dock, leaving George to work in the South Wales pits (Lloyd, n.d.). In both these cases, the men and their dependants had moved away from their extended families and friends in search of work, so that when the axe fell they were some distance from traditional sources of support. Unemployment did not need to be of this sharp, cyclical kind to pinch working families. Seasonal under- and unemployment in agriculture created pressures to put children to earn that matched those in the cyclically unemployed industrial districts. Bill H—'s father earned 9s a week 'at the best of times' but often 'his wages were reduced to seven shillings' (H—, 1861–62, p. 140).

If conditions thought a passing problem persisted, a temporary expedient became permanent. Child labour then became a standard practice emulated by other desperate families and soon entrenched in community norms. Moreover if the generation of children sent to work early in response to shifts in the demand for labour had less opportunity to accumulate human capital, it grew up to be less productive and so less able, when the time came, to support its own children. In this way, demand shocks in the labour market could have echo effects that held the economy at low levels of productivity and high rates of child labour (see chapter 2 [see original reading]).

Such family-based 'added-worker effects' characterized the prolonged competition between hand trades and first workshop and later factory production, promoting and intensifying child labour. Here the problem was not just a lack of work but the falling prices of commodities hitherto produced using traditional methods and hand skills as they came into competition with similar goods now produced in workshops using a detailed division of labour and later in factories using water- and then steam-powered machinery and child labour. Given living memories of the earnings premia that their skills had secured, the changes crept up slowly on male domestic manufacturers. Prices had oscillated in the past so it was difficult to read their decline as the death-knell for hand production. In the long term, faith rested in industrial recovery and the power of skill to restore competitiveness. In the short term, domestic producers increased output to maintain incomes in the face of falling prices. Fathers worked longer and harder, but this was complemented by and not a substitute for their wives' and children's work. Thus Thomas Wood (born 1822) wound bobbins and then aged eight was sent to the mill to supplement the family's slender means, while his father clung to the 'doomed trade' of handloom weaving (Wood, 1994, p. 314). William Carnegie, a handloom weaver, did not display the market acumen of his son Andrew, for with the advent of steam power he 'did not recognize the impending revolution and was struggling under the old system' (Carnegie, 1920, p. 12). Even after emigrating to the United States, Carnegie senior clung to his trade. Only after the humiliation of hawking goods door-to-door did he bow to the inevitable and enter a mill.

Handloom weavers and their families were not the only group caught up in this dismal process, nor was competition only from factory production, aided as it was by machinery and steam power. Frank Galton, whose father was a saddler, a highly skilled trade that had called for a substantial apprenticeship premium, provided a description of the effects of competition from workshops using a more detailed division of cheaper labour on once-skilled workers and their standard of living. When Frank was born Galton senior had regularly been able to earn 70s a week, which at that time meant 'comfort and even some luxury' (Galton, n.d., p. 1). Ominously, a new system of production had begun to invade saddle making and 'there were springing up at Walsall and Wolverhampton large workshops where saddles were made on the principle of subdivided labour in which many parts were performed by boys and girls' (Galton, n.d., p. 5). The increased supply forced down the price and reduced wages for the London saddlers, Galton senior included. Moving several times to decreasingly salubrious surroundings, the family hit rock bottom when Galton senior became unemployed. Although in this case the father eventually found work, which enabled the family to survive albeit without restoring its previous prosperity, by then both elder boys, aged 13 and 11, were at work and Mrs Galton too had sought paid employment both within and outside the home.

Boot- and shoemaking was another among the many trades reorganized in this way, creating a fertile environment for the inclusion of child workers. An anonymous Master Shoemaker (born 180?) who had been apprenticed in London was appalled by the effects of the reorganization of his trade in Northampton, which he visited in the 1820s. Boots and shoes continued to be produced in a domestic setting but both methods and tools had been redesigned to accommodate women's and children's labour.

Factory Acts and School Boards were then unknown, and the detestable custom
of compelling women to do men's labour, and taking children from their pap to

work like niggers was in full swing. Too small to use the clams in ordinary use, clams of a smaller size were introduced for these child-workers. A feeling of horror used to creep over me whenever I passed over a threshold where this kind of labour was indulged in.

(Master Shoemaker, 1879, p. 376, see also Arnold, 1915)

As a result of these organizational initiatives, the prices for closing shoes were much lower in Northampton than in London, and according to the anonymous author the only ways a single workman could survive without the help of a wife and children were to 'scamp' it or work 16 hours a day. Competition from family labour involved either compromising quality or working longer hours. In this case, organizational initiatives rather than machinery and steam power had engineered the local economy to a bad equilibrium with child labour, as described in chapter 2 [see original reading].

War and postwar dislocations

The French wars superimposed additional booms and busts on various segments of the labour market (Bowen, 1998). Recruitment had mopped up substantial amounts of adult male unemployment at the end of the eighteenth century, and war production had boosted employment in arsenals, docks, foundries, furnaces and mines. Unsatisfied requirements spilled over into demand for child workers, while the supply of child labour probably increased, since much wartime employment instead of boosting family incomes disrupted male support. Thus Thomas Sanderson, a soldier's son, grew up in a household dependent on the washtub earnings of his mother and aunt supplemented by poor relief, his father's pay rarely seeming to reach them. Not surprisingly under these circumstances he was only eight when 'taken away from school to assist in making a fend for myself' (Sanderson, 1873, p. 7).

With peace, demobilization came quickly. Although the slaughter permanently removed a large number of prime-age males from the labour force (Greenwood, 1942), between 1814 and 1817, 200,000 common soldiers and sailors were released into an economy that was contracting and readjusting to peacetime conditions (Emsley, 1979). The father and uncles of Joseph Gutteridge had left their ancestral trade as fell mongers when Yorkshire capitalists absorbed the wool trade on the borders of Leicestershire and wiped out the hand trade of Coventry by the aid of steam, water power and improved machinery. These brothers adapted their skills to the silk trade, 'a new branch of commerce then just beginning to be established in Coventry'. Having made this adjustment their progress faltered as a result of the 'fearful drafts made upon the country to sustain our forces in the peninsula and America where they were struggling for their independence' (Gutteridge, 1969, p. 82). Five of six brothers were compelled to serve in either the regular Army or the militia. After the peace, they returned to find their native city in 'a most fearful state of collapse, provisions at famine prices, the various trades at a complete standstill, their former comfortable homes a wreck, and their wives and children in great poverty and distress ... The brothers worked as journeymen at the trades in which at one time they had hoped to have been masters' (Gutteridge, 1969, p. 83) Although eventually trade resumed, the stage was set for the next generation's slide into poverty and deprivation. Elsewhere in the country, Andrew Carnegie's maternal grandfather, a leather merchant and tanner, was ruined by the peace that followed Waterloo, stripping his descendants of any financial cushion against future economic shocks (Carnegie, 1920), as was James Saunders's (born 1844) grandfather, at one time a substantial farmer (Saunders, 1938?, p. 23, see also Bonwick, 1902).

War disrupted household economies in other, less obvious ways. George Sanger was descended from good Wiltshire stock, his father being the youngest son of a prosperous farmer, apprenticed to the respectable trade of edge-tool maker. However, aged 18, while visiting friends in London, he was press-ganged into the Navy and after various adventures eventually served on Nelson's flagship the *Victory* at the battle of Trafalgar. During the battle, Sanger senior was badly injured and lost several fingers. He was pensioned off and rejected by his surviving brothers (see above, p. 132 [see original reading]). Sanger senior responded with a 'little plain speaking the faculty for which among other accomplishments, he had acquired in his seafaring life' and thereafter earned a precarious living for himself and his growing family as a circus showman (Sanger, 1910, p. 12). Perhaps Sanger senior, like several other fathers who had seen active service in the many wars of the period, found it hard to settle back into civilian life and was pulled as well as pushed into his travelling existence. While life on the road was not dull, it involved dangers and deprivations for George and his eventual nine brothers and sisters.

John Bennett provides a different perspective on families' problems attempting to re-absorb men who had served in the armed forces. His ex-soldier uncles made periodic demands for employment on his carpenter and wheelwright father, straining the family business and prompting John's removal from school to work by his father's side (Bennett, n.d.). War, although now moving forward in time, had a more direct and dramatic impact on the economic fate of George Edwards (born 1850). His father was another man who, having fought for his country with an exemplary record, appeared to have had difficulties readjusting to civilian life. Somehow denied the £9 bounty promised on completion of 10 years' service, he could not obtain work in his native village. Disaffected, he spoke at a meeting of the unemployed, which sealed his fate with the farmers. Plagued by unemployment thereafter, Edwards senior received 14 days' hard labour for stealing turnips to feed his family He was now marked out as an ex-con as well as a rabble-rouser. This episode closed with a sojourn in the workhouse. On re-emergence aged not yet six, George went to work as a crow scarer for 1s a week (Edwards, 1998).

Mothers' contributions

Autobiographers saw not only fathers but also mothers as trying theirs best to keep their families afloat. They testify to the enormous, indeed even unhealthy, self-sacrifice character-istic of working-class mothers and to the devotion it inculcated in their sons (see chapter 5) Mothers' contributions were not primarily economic, as demonstrated in chapter 4 [see original reading]. Even with a very generous definition of economic participation, which counted a married woman as economically active if her son made any reference whatsoever to her augmentation of family resources, only between a third and a half of all mothers participated. Moreover, even when mothers were economically active, they were limited in what they could do, the time they could spend and the regularity of their employment. Outside the textile factory districts, married women's work was crowded into a ghetto of sweated trades and badly paid per unit of effort. The result was that even enterprising and hard-working mothers could add little to family income.

The question that chapter 4 left hanging was whether mothers' employment outside the home could substitute for their sons' labour. Although a systematic comparison is not possible because mothers' earnings were only patchily reported, cases quoted in chapter 4 (pp. 116–17) demonstrated that these were likely lower than those of even pre-adolescent sons, which suggests that mothers could not have substituted for working sons even if they had wanted to do so. Moreover, mothers' work, far from releasing sons to take advantage of educational opportunities, seems instead to have encumbered them with childcare and work in the home, from which they were certainly not exempt. Daniel Chater reported that because of his mother's home-working, he was never a regular attendant at school: 'it was often necessary that I should do the housework while my mother made the button-holes' (Chater, n.d., p. 6). But, however hard boys tried, it is difficult to imagine them able to compensate for a mother's absence or distraction. Boys had a comparative advantage in the labour force and mothers in domestic and caring work. This explains why many families appear to have preferred to send their boys out to work rather than have their mothers working away from home, and many mothers seem to have been strangely hesitant about seeking waged work even when there was no man supporting the household.

The preferences suggested in the autobiographical accounts are consistent with analyses of census enumeration which show mothers with working children to have had lower activity rates, ceteris paribus (Anderson, 1999). However, in quantitative analysis of the autobiographical evidence income effects hide such substitution. Rather than mothers and sons being substitutes for each other in paid work, employed mothers and young child workers are found in the same families, families marked by extreme poverty and in many cases by the absence of a male breadwinner. Certainly, autobiographers who recalled their mothers as economically active started work younger than those whose mothers were home-makers, though the relationship is not statistically significant.[12] Whether this result survives in a multivariate analysis remains to be seen.

Family size

In addition to exogenous economic factors like the levels of wages or piece-rates, and the availability of work, parents faced another problem in trying to make ends meet: the number of dependent children. The rising dependency rate of the period fed through into large numbers of children per family. Autobiographers were clear about the implications: a big family was a millstone around the necks of working men and women. '[T]hose that had large families were run pretty close', recalled Joe Robinson, who also remembered allowances being paid by the parish for every child after the first (Robinson, n.d., p.14). Small families were a boon, even if child mortality had reduced the burden in the cruellest possible way. John Clare said of his parents, who lost two children in infancy, that they had 'the good fate to have but a small family' (Clare, 1986, p. 3). Mothers especially were burdened by large families: 'My mother had many children, she reared eleven; but I soon came to see how much better it would have been for her – how much more enjoyment, peace, repose and freedom from anxiety would have fallen to her – had her family been limited to three or four children' (Holyoake, 1906, p. 15). Nor were boys backward in recognizing the negative effect that additional siblings had on their own standard of living. When a neighbour inquired after the health of his recently delivered mother, Nathaniel Dale (born 1805) responded, 'I wished the baby had not come, as I had heard my mother say she could not make the sugar and butter hold out from week to week, and I thought I should not get any now' (Dale, 1871?, p. 4; and see above, p. 127 [see original reading]). As babies grew, so did demand on resources. G.J. Wardle (born 1865) was the second in a family of eight, and as his father rarely earned more than 23s a week, 'it will readily be understood that times were often hard with us' (Wardle, 1906, p. 597) For older children particularly the need to support brothers and sisters often put paid to childhood ambitions and prompted early working. Abraham Holroyd's only schooling was paid for by his grandfather, as his parents were 'too poor to do anything, as they had four little ones all younger than myself' (Holroyd, 1892, p. 10).

Perceptions of competition for resources were not false. Among boys for whom both ages at starting work and total numbers of siblings are known, only children appear to have had a signal advantage. The 31 only children started work aged 11.76, while the 369 boys who had one or more siblings started work aged 10.60, a big enough difference to be historically as well as statistically significant.[13] Advantage is also apparent comparing boys with only one sibling and boys with two or more, but the difference is smaller and not statistically significant. However, the advantages of smaller sibling groups for age at starting work become larger and statistically significant comparing boys with three or more siblings and boys with fewer than three and persist until comparison is between boys with fewer than five and boys with five or more siblings. Even then the means continue to suggest earlier working for boys in larger sibling groups, but the differences between them are small and not statistically significant (see Humphries, 2007).

Birth order appears to have had ambiguous implications. Eldest children sometimes obtained a head start, enjoying some education and establishing strong ties with parents, before additional siblings arrived to strain the family exchequer and distract fathers and mothers. On the other hand, younger children often benefited from the contributions of older working siblings. Often children were marched into the labour force in rank order. Robert Watchorn went to work just as he turned 11. 'At that time there were six other children in our family, only one being senior to me and the youngest being about a year old.' His coal-miner father's wages were 'not enough to produce affluence', and his elder brother's additional wage while 'helpful' meant earnings still fell short of providing comforts for the family. It was time for Robert to volunteer for work (Watchorn, 1958, p. 15 see also Somerville, 1951). In fact, middle children seem anecdotally to have been at greatest risk, a view enunciated by Harry Carter (born 1749).'My oldest and my youngest brothers were brought up to good country scolars [sic], but the rest of my brothers with myself, as soon as we was able, were obliged to work in order to contribute a little to help to support a large family' (Carter, 1900, p. 3).

Unfortunately, birth order was less frequently recorded than family size,[14] but based on the 304 boys whose age at starting work and family position is known, it appears that age at starting work first fell and then rose with rank, confirming the suggestion that it was middle children, and especially middle children in large families, who were most disadvantaged. However, the differences were small and not statistically significant.

Family dysfunction and break-up

Although in general the autobiographers argued that parents did their best and were not responsible for their poverty, families, precociously nuclear and prematurely dependent on men and their earnings, could easily be damaged and even destroyed in these socially and economically insecure times. When this happened, the children were in a perilous position. The children most clearly at risk of brutal treatment, including early employment, were not children in families with avaricious parents but children in unstable families and children without parents or kin.

As earlier chapters have shown [see original reading], the dangers to family integrity were numerous and various. Mothers and fathers died while sons were under age and fathers disappeared, becoming detached from their children by work and military service as well as intentionally deserting them both before and after birth. Although the deaths and disappearances of mothers and fathers had different implications, in both instances the children in the attenuated families risked poor treatment and were liable to suffer early working.

Losing a mother at a young age was a psychological blow, but losing a father was economically catastrophic. Mothers could not substitute for the earning power of lost fathers, and if they tried to do so ended up neglecting their children's domestic well-being. Replacing a husband's economic support was not easy. Remarriage was a common reaction; often prompted by consideration of the children's welfare (Ashby, 1974). However, stepparents could be cruel; instrumental in abandonment or driving children to early work (see Marcroft, 1886; Price, 1904?; Freer, 1929) Moreover the autobiographies hint that widowers found it easier to remarry than did widows, especially those with children (see Freer, 1929), and if husbands had merely absconded and not died then remarriage was not an option unless a woman was prepared to be bigamous. The male-breadwinner family structure meant that female kin, however sympathetic, could rarely provide sustained support; only male kin could be of substantial help, and the supply of those willing as well as able was limited. The longer-term survival of these battered families depended on the efforts of the women and children themselves.

As already seen (chapter 4, above [see original reading]), mothers in families without male heads participated in the economy at higher rates than did mothers who had husbands or partners present.[15] This gap is not surprising. What is perhaps surprising is that the difference is so small and that the activity rate of lone mothers so low. Even more intriguing is the finding that the gap itself is almost entirely the product of the higher activity rate of unmarried, deserted and abandoned mothers. Widows participated at about the same rate, perhaps even less, than did mothers with husbands or partners present. Thus, even families without male heads appear to have been reluctant or unable to mobilize married women's labour time. How then did these families seek to survive?

Consistent with the idea that breadwinner frailty was one of the factors that promoted non-kin-based welfare, poor relief was a lifeline to many lone mothers and their children. On the death of her husband, after various trials and tribulations, the parish gave John Castle's mother 7s a week to raise her three boys (Castle, 1871). Other women too obtained outdoor relief (see Sanderson, 1873; Meek, 1910; Thorne, 1925?; Ashby, 1974; Bezer, 1977). Lone mothers were expected to contribute to their family's survival; so Mrs Castle, also, 'to get a living, went out as a nurse' (Castle, 1871, n.p.). The self-help demanded was within a framework that gave mothers time to care for their children. Some historians have suggested that support for lone mothers was relatively generous compared with what was available to other working families of the time and even compared with poor welfare-dependent families today and that this was particularly true for widows, who were treated more magnanimously than deserted wives or unmarried mothers (Snell and Millar, 1987; Humphries, 1998). This might help to explain the low participation rates of widows compared with other lone mothers

The New Poor Law was probably harsher than the Old, and levels of support diminished (Thane, 1978; Humphries, 1998), but, as historians have often observed, even after 1834 the pragmatism of local Guardians could soften the operation of the law. Thus, the New Poor Law, under which 'relief must be made painful and even disgraceful' provided support to Joseph Ashby's mother, Elizabeth Townsend, an unmarried mother, a wife and then a widow with three children. However, as the author of the family history recalled, it took longer in Tysoe for the widowed and the fatherless to regard help with shame, and the memory that the family's forebears had once themselves been Overseers, distributing not receiving relief, helped to maintain self-respect. That the family was part of the long-settled poor in the village also perhaps contributed to its relatively decent treatment (see Nash, 2006). Its low ebb reflected the insecurity of the age. The ubiquitous threat of downward mobility, the recognition that once solid respectable families could be cast down by accidents or bad luck as well as occasional rotten apples, softened the administration of poor relief. Moreover, and crucial for the discussion here, the weekly dole of 6 or 7s was not much below the average income in the village. Some men earned only 7 or 8s as agricultural labourers and had many more children than Elizabeth's three, low earnings and large families operating to put the Ashby-Townsends in the same boat as other local families, but it was a miserable and leaky boat! 'A life of great poverty' was the prospect (Ashby, 1974, p. 13) and, not surprisingly, Elizabeth Townsend sought employment to supplement her dole.

Whether or not relief was conditional on lone mothers' economic activity, it would be surprising if the Poor Law authorities had been willing to shield pauper children from the labour market for longer than the independent poor were able to withhold their children. The New Poor Law propounded the principle of 'less eligibility': poor relief was not to enhance the life chances or comforts of paupers beyond what was attainable by the least well-off among the self-supporting. For children, life chances depended on age at starting work, schooling and training. Parents and Poor Law authorities clashed over what was considered an appropriate age to require children to contribute to family income and what jobs were suitable (Carter, 1995; Honeyman, 2007). In particular, parents balked at sending children to work at a distance, which threatened family ties. Poor Law officials on the other hand may have had reasons to promote employment outside the home parish, since it carried the possibility at least of acquiring a settlement elsewhere. With settlement went responsibility for upkeep in time of need. Regardless of whether parish officials actively sought to export their poor in this way, there is ample evidence of pressure on poor families to employ their children at young ages, including the withholding of relief until children were so employed (Carter, 1995). Similar pressures are detectable in some autobiographical accounts; for example, the poor relief available to John James Bezer and his mother was at least partly contingent on their cotton winding.[16]

Even if families were in receipt of poor relief, in the absence of a male head, especially if there were younger siblings to support, it must have been difficult to forgo the earnings of older boys. Not surprisingly then the death, desertion, absence, unemployment or incapacity of fathers was one of the main factors precipitating boys' entry into the workforce. When James Sexton's father died prematurely at the age of 43, his mother was left 'to face the battle of life with a brood of six children'. James was 'the only one who could help her to meet the expenses of the slum dwelling which was our home', though in this case he had long been at work contributing to the family income (Sexton, 1936, p. 18). The mother of Edward Rymer, deserted by her husband, could not afford to dispense with Edward's and his brother John's contributions to family income, even though it was clear that their work in the coal pits was undermining their health (Rymer, 1976). Frank Forrest's idyllic life was rudely shattered when his father was transported for 'culpable homicide' and he had to go to work in a factory aged seven (Forrest, 1850, p. 6). Robert Lowery's father's serious illness was the cause of his removal from school and employment about the local slag heaps (Lowery, 1979).

On average, boys whose fathers were dead or had disappeared started work about seven months younger than did their peers. Thus, the 129 fatherless boys in the sample whose ages at starting work are known began work on average aged 10.34 years, while the 368 boys whose fathers were present when they began work started aged 10.90.[17] The difference is mainly the product of early working by boys from families which had never had a male head or whose male head had disappeared. Boys whose fathers had died did not experience a significant age penalty; just as widows participated in the economy at about the same rate as married mothers with husbands present, so their sons joined the labour force at about the same age as children with fathers present. However, the children of men who had never recognized them, or who had abandoned them in childhood, began work on average aged 9.40 years old, a full 18 months younger than peers with fathers.[18] These boys emerge as the most disadvantaged.

These ages at starting work imply very high participation rates for fatherless boys by age 10 or 11, especially for the illegitimate or abandoned. These boys shared with partial orphans the loss of a male breadwinner and the need to support younger siblings. Perhaps too their kin were less generous and poor relief more conditional. Nonetheless, bearing in mind the participation rates of lone mothers, reported above; it looks as if these families, like their counterparts headed by adult men, preferred their boys to work than for mothers to seek employment. Even in the final cohort when child labour was beginning to wane, by the time fatherless boys were 11 years old, they were more likely to be at work than were their mothers.

Chapter 5 [see original reading] established the greater resilience of lone-mother than lone-father households. The greater support lone mothers likely received from kin, charity and poor relief, alongside perhaps greater commitment to their children, enabled such battered families to survive. The dark side of survival was their reliance on the labour of their children, and particularly their older boys. Indeed other sources of assistance, whether from kin or poor relief, were often conditional on children's work: kin and Poor Law as well as God helping those who helped themselves! Did children left in families headed by lone fathers fare any better? Unable to access the same levels of kin and community support as lone mothers, less able then to combine childcare and breadwinning, and perhaps less doggedly attached to children, lone fathers frequently gave up the struggle and surrendered their children to relatives or the parish. Remarriage was one way in which widowers could remain living with their children, a consideration, which clearly tempted some fathers down this route (see chapter 5, above [see original reading]). Second marriages were not always hospitable to children left over from the first, as Ben Tillett discovered; his second stepmother was 'a good mother to her own four children, but I was the odd one out' (Tillett, 1931, p. 280). Thus, children in reconstituted families faced a different set of realities from those struggling to maintain the autonomy of lone-mother households, but often they were hardly less harsh.

Children outside family structures

Children who lacked both parents, whether abandoned or orphaned; were even more vulnerable than the fatherless. Such children, as shown in chapter 3 [see original reading], were common among the autobiographers, just as they were in the population from which the autobiographers were drawn. Many in this category had the classic outcast pedigree: illegitimacy. One common source of shelter for such children, as chapter 6 demonstrated [see original reading], was the extended family. Here their fates were about as varied as the patchworks of support that kept them from the streets or the workhouse. Frank Bullen (born 1857), a member of what he terms 'the ignoble company of the unwanted', like many other boys without parents was begrudgingly raised by relatives, sent to work at an early age (nine in his case) and signed on board a merchantman aged 12, where he felt life could be no worse than ashore (Bullen, 1899, pp. 1–2). In contrast, George Meek, blinded in one eye when a baby and left behind when his parents emigrated, had a happy childhood in the care of grandparents who also took in and raised a cousin (see also Price, 1904?). Alas, such networks of extended kin were insecure. When receiving families themselves faced stress, adopted boys were sometimes abandoned for a second time. Some families used the Poor Law as a temporary expedient in such circumstances. Meek's cousin was placed temporarily in the workhouse when his grandfather changed jobs, only to be reclaimed when the family was re-established. Henry Price lost his home when his grandparents emigrated and was discarded for a second time by his mother when she moved to Wales with her new family. One way or another, these boys had the habit of running out of kin. Grandparents in particular were inclined to die (Milne, 1901; Stanley, 1909). The Poor Law was then the only option. Even before this ultimate refuge, and even with the best-intended kin, adopted boys were likely to have had to show willing and work at earlier ages and certainly no later than those residing in their families of origin.

The fate of children who ended up in the care of the state depended on the particular Poor Law regime and even on the individual characters of local officials. Not only did the quality of care vary but also the official attitude to children's work and particularly the age at which it was appropriate to require them to start varied over time and across institutions.[19] Within the patchwork of care and diversity of policies, it would be surprising if poor relief saved wards of the state from early employment. In fact, historians have argued that the primitive welfare system of early industrial England operated to deliver children at relatively young ages into the labour force. Pauper apprentices, for example, were bound at younger ages than non-pauper apprentices (Snell, 1985; Sharpe, 1991; Lane, 1996). Indeed, for some historians, by the end of the eighteenth century pauper apprenticeship had degenerated under financial pressures and become little more than an institution for channelling children from poor families into whatever jobs were available, with little attention to training for their future and no attention to the wishes of their friends and families.

Fifty-seven boys received either outdoor relief in the context of some kind of family structure or were relieved within the workhouse during their childhood or youth.[20] These boys started work on average aged 9.55. The 459 boys who did not recall such assistance started work aged 10.88, a difference that is unlikely to have occurred by chance.[21] Thus, the involvement of the Poor Law did not protect impoverished children from early working, and sometimes appears to have provided the machinery and networks through which poor children were found work. At least 12 boys were employed or apprenticed directly from the workhouse: Anon, (born 1805), Bell (born 1846), Blincoe (born 1792), Burdett (born 1800?), Ince (born 1850), Lloyd (born 1865), Luck (born 1846), Price (born 1824), Reilly (born 1860?), Saville (born 1759), Shipp (born 1783?) and Walsh (born 1859). These span both the Old and New Poor Law. In addition, three other boys started work with a parish placement.

Several stories testify to the traffic in children from large urban workhouses to the early water-powered mills. Robert Blincoe's narrative is well known but corroborated here by the recollections of an anonymous parish apprentice (born 1805) who was taken from Bethnal Green Workhouse to work in a Derbyshire mill (Anon., 1849; see also Collyer, 1908, and below, p. 200 [see original reading]). Recently revisionist accounts have emphasized that the Poor Law did not only provide children from metropolitan workhouses to work in northern factories (Honeyman, 2007; Levene, 2009). The traffic was more widespread, with children from all parts of Britain placed in both traditional and new employments, both locally and at distance: a cheap and docile form of labour that fed the traditional small-scale manufacturing sector, the mining industry, the burgeoning transport and dealing trades, the merchant and Royal Navies, and even the Army and the oldest occupation, agricultural husbandry, as well as the new textile factories.

The dramatic and strategically important long-distance movement of batches of children has to be seen in a context where the Poor Law authorities routinely placed destitute children with whatever potential employers were available. Parish apprenticeship had a long history, originally providing poor children's upkeep as well as some modicum of training. Traditional examples occur among the autobiographers. John Stradley (born 1757), a foundling at Thomas Coram's hospital, was put out to nurse in a labouring family in Kent and then apprenticed to a blacksmith, almost certainly by the parish authorities. John's age at this time (eight) suggests that early on at least his apprenticeship was meant to secure him food and shelter while training was to follow (Stradley, n.d.). The autobiographers remind readers that agriculture too participated in the system. Bickers (born 1809) was a farmer's parish apprentice and Buckley a boy labourer in the roundsman system (Bickers, 1881?; Buckley, 1897).

Pauper apprenticeship also ensured a flow of young workers into the multitude of workshops and unmechanized but centralized production units of early industrial Britain, thereby contributing to Smithian growth, as Joseph Burdett's story illustrates. Burdett did not come from a broken home, but his circumstances and relationship with his (step?) father were such that he decided to ask the Overseers of the Poor to find him an apprenticeship, suggesting yet another way in which the working poor used the Poor Law to assist them with life transitions. On entry to Newark Workhouse, Burdett was required to work with the other boys at a factory bleach yard. Workhouses the length and breadth of Britain probably defrayed the expenses of relief by providing local employers with individually casual but collectively secure labour of this kind. Although the work was hard, Burdett found compensation in Sunday schooling and workhouse life. He judged his situation 'never so comfortable before' and refused to return to his family and be bound apprentice to his (step?) father (Burdett, 1985, p. 4). Instead, with his agreement, the Overseers apprenticed Burdett to a master stockinger who had lobbied the workhouse youth with what retrospectively appeared 'a very flattering account of the trade prospects' (Burdett, 1985, pp. 4–5). Burdett quickly learned his trade. As an apprentice, he had to earn a certain sum each week for his master, exposing his role as cheap and captive labour shoring up a trade in decline. As a journeyman, Burdett found it hard to get work, exposing pauper apprenticeship's tendency to channel the vulnerable into trades where reorganization and changing technology had undermined barriers to entry. So before apprenticeship as unskilled labour in the bleach yards, during apprenticeship as tied labour to a master stockinger and after apprenticeship as a peripatetic journeyman, Burdett constituted cheap labour in trades undergoing Smithian growth. Nonetheless, later in life Burdett continued to work as a stockinger and to describe his memoirs as those of a 'Stockinger and Sometime Apprentice'. Although his trade was less exclusive than he had originally hoped, it continued to offer greater rewards than unskilled labour, and, in this sense, his pauper apprenticeship was of real value.

The New Poor Law operated in a similar way, albeit within a modified legal framework. 'In those years, when tradesmen or miners wanted a strong lad who could do the work of a man … they applied to the Guardians. These were never loath to part with their charges to make room for the stream of newcomers constantly arriving' (Reilly, 1931, p. 10). Reilly was handed over, aged about 10 in 1870, to a Rotherham tradesman to whom he 'belonged' though there is no mention of indentures. John Ince and George Lloyd were both placed in service with colliers under the New Poor Law, even though the underground work for which Lloyd at least had been destined was by then against the law (Ince, 1888; Lloyd, n.d.).

The more casual and less formal placements of the later period may have involved greater numbers of children. Lucy Luck and her brother were both sent from the workhouse to a local silk factory when they were not yet nine years old, without the protection and support that an apprenticeship (even a pauper apprenticeship) provided. Lucy's complaint was not about the work she was required to do but the disreputable lodging found for her by the relieving officer and the potent threat to her well-being that such residence entailed (Luck, 1994). If children of an earlier era were vulnerable to abuse by being bound to a particular employer, children of a later one were threatened by being cast adrift without structure or support in a frightening and dangerous world.

Henry Price's reminiscences of the relationship between the workhouse and the labour market are particularly interesting for catching the system as it changed from the Old to the New Poor Law and for hinting at the possibilities for corruption embedded in this interface. Boys from Warminster Poorhouse, where Price was resident from 1832, were sent to work at an old factory where they manufactured chair seating. Henry was put to work making horsehair seating aged about eight. The work was dull and monotonous and the boys received no wages, but the employment appears to have been irregular and, at least in Henry's case, left time for schooling. Later a carpenter 'in want of an apprentice' came to the House and selected Henry. Terms were agreed. There was to be a two-month trial during which time Henry was to live with the family, subsidized by the parish to the tune of 18d per week. Henry fared well under these arrangements, though not learning much carpentry. Alas eventually the subsidy stopped and Henry was returned to the workhouse (Price, 1904?). Whether this was a New Poor Law economy measure or marked a prearranged milestone by which Henry was supposed to have become so productive that the subsidy was no longer needed, a transition he did not manage, remains unknown.

Interesting for the insight it provides into the origins of pauper apprentices in the early factories, the spread of the system beyond the London and Liverpool workhouses and the range of treatment that pauper children received, is the story of Robert Collyer's parents. Collyer senior's sailor father was lost overboard in a storm. The grandmother died within the year, leaving a family of some five children who were taken to an asylum in the City of London for shelter. Collyer's mother's father, also a sailor, but whose port was Yarmouth, was also lost at sea around the same time, leaving a similar family of four children who were taken to Norwich for relief. These personal tragedies then mesh with national developments, in terms of the wartime shortage of labour felt particularly sharply in the factory districts (see above, p. 154 [see original reading]). As Collyer tells it:

> Very early in the last century there was an urgent need for children to work in the factories they were building there on all the streams they could find fit for their purpose in the West Riding of Yorkshire. The local supply of 'help' could not begin to meet with the demand; and so the owners of the factories went or sent south to scour the asylums where children were to be found in swarms, to bring them north and set them to work as apprentices who must be duly housed, fed and clothed until the girls were eighteen and the boys twenty one.
>
> (Collyer, 1908, p. 2)

In the case of Collyer's parents, the apprentices were also to be taught 'the three R's and the boys some craft by which they might earn their living when they were free' (Collyer, 1908, p. 2). Agents for the factory owners found both Collyer's mother and father and brought them to work in a factory on a stream called the Washburn in the parish of Fewston. The children themselves participated in this decision but it hardly amounted to rational decision-making with complete information. 'He [Collyer's father] told me they gave him free choice to go or stay and wanted him to stay; but he said, "I will go". And so it was he went out, not knowing whither he went, was bound apprentice, and served his time first at the spinning frames and then in the forge, for it was his choice of a handicraft' (Collyer, 1908, p. 13). Collyer's father worked at Fewston, man and boy, for 32 years.

Not only did the Poor Law authorities recruit pauper children for batch employment in factories, but they also at times of national need recruited boys for the Army and Navy. The case of boy soldiers has received much less attention than that of boy sailors, but both reflect the belief that children could be used to plug gaps in national needs and yoked in semi-compulsion to maintain and defend national wealth. In 1797, three experimental regiments were formed partly to relieve the recruiting problems of the British Army and partly to relieve parishes of the burden of pauper boys (Cookson, 1997). Each regiment was composed of 1,000 boys. One such boy has left his story. John Shipp, an orphan who had been placed by the Overseers with a local farmer but was obsessed with soldiering from an early age, was recruited under this scheme. With a new suit of clothes as the cost to his parish, at the age of 10, John embarked on what was to be a fine career in the Army (Shipp, 1890).

Naval recruitment of poor boys has received more attention. As early as 1756, Lord Harry Powlett took poor boys from the streets of London and clothed them at his own expense to add to his crew (Rodger, 1986). This recruiting innovation allegedly inspired Jonas Hanway to found the Marine Society, a practical charity which took destitute (but not criminal) London boys, provided clothing and some rudimentary training and sent them to sea in either the Navy or the Merchant Service. During the Seven Years war the Society sent

10,625 boys and men into the Navy, at least 5 per cent of its total recruitment from 1755 to 1763 (Rodger, 1986, p. 162). Admiral Boscawen held that no other scheme for manning the Navy had the success of the Marine Society, though reformers, such as Berkeley, Lord of the Admiralty concerned with the task of manning during the Crimean war, had reservations about the quality of the pauper recruits and clashed with 'the anxiety of Parish Officers and Magistrates – to send into the Navy – all the sweepings of the Unions – and the troublesome boys of the Neighbourhood' (quoted in Bartlett, 1963, p. 314). Nor did sea placements of pauper boys disappear with the cessation of hostilities. Ongoing problems with manning meant that workhouse boys could not be passed up, and thousands continued to be recruited even at mid-century (Bartlett, 1963), while in the fishing fleets such as Grimsby, for example, pauper apprenticeship persisted into the twentieth century (Boswell, 1974). While no participant in schemes to recruit boy paupers into either the Merchant Service or Royal Navy has left an autobiographical account, there are boys who were driven by poverty to go to sea. Orphan Frank Bullen did not 'clamor for a sea life', as did other boys. He was 'under no delusion whatever as to the prospect [ahead]'. What lured him to enlist as a cabin boy aged 12 was the prospect of 'food and shelter' (Bullen, 1899, p. 2).

Access to productive resources

Although most of the autobiographers' families were wage dependent, a significant minority was self-employed or operated small-scale businesses, including family farms, consistent with the continuing importance of small-scale proprietorship in the British economy through the industrial revolution (Hudson, 1986, 2004; Berg, 1994). Growing up in a petit-bourgeois environment had contradictory effects on children's work. The availability of complementary inputs into production made children productive at young ages and promoted early working. The operation of a small farm or shop involved a myriad of small tasks suited to children. On the other hand, the ownership of wealth, even on such a small scale, meant income effects that could shield children from employment.[22]

Both types of effect can be observed in the autobiographies. William Stout belonged to a small-scale landowning family in Lancashire and was sent to school from an early age. However, from the age of 10 he was 'very much taken off the schoole, espetialy in the spring and summer season, plowtime, turfe time, hay time and harvest, in looking after the sheep, helping at plough, going to the moss with carts, making hay and shearing in harvest' to the extent that he 'made small progress in Latin, for what we got in winter we forgot in summer' (Stout, 1967, p. 70). James Croll's schooling was cut short by the demands of his parent's smallholding. 'The cause of my having to leave school so soon was this. My father, having one or two acres of ground, kept a cow, and as he was away from home during the greater part of the year following his duties as a stonemason, I had to be taken from school to assist my mother' (Croll, 1896, p. 12). Even more humble ownership rights could compromise a boy's schooling. John Bethune (born 1812) was sent to work aged about eight to herd two cows, which his father as a forester on a local estate was allowed to keep (Bethune, 1841, p. 22). Whether Stout, Croll and Bethune would have fared better if born into wage-labouring families of the same time and place is doubtful.

Boys could also be called upon to work in other types of family business if the need arose. John Bennett was taken away from school when his elder brother Stephen died 'to supply his place' alongside their jobbing carpenter father (Bennett, n.d., p. 2). Bethune apart, these boys belonged to relatively prosperous families and their ages at starting work do not seem out of line with the sample means. Thus although small-scale proprietorship influenced the kind of work boys did, and often precipitated employment, it also provided a context of sufficient relative prosperity to ensure that this rarely cast boys into hazardous work at relatively young ages. The overall effects of small business proprietorship are tracked in the multivariate analysis below.

Determinants of age at starting work

The various factors proposed as determinants of age at starting work are combined in a descriptive model estimated by multivariate regression analysis. The analysis identifies the effect of each factor holding all others constant.

Age at starting work is related to:

- a constant term which reflects the normal standards within the sample;
- three dummy variables which capture the cohort to which the boy belonged. The omitted cohort is the third (1821–50) so the cohort effects are relative to the influence on age at starting work of being born in this time period;
- a series of dummy variables which stand for the occupational group to which the father belonged. As explained above, the father's broad occupational affiliation captures relative earnings potential but is also likely to reflect local labour market opportunities and occupationally distinct social conventions governing respectable ages for children to start work. The omitted occupational marker is agriculture, so the occupational effects are all relative to the influence on age at starting work of a father in the agricultural sector;
- a dummy variable which reflects whether the mother was economically active in the form of working for wages, being self-employed, running a small business or self-provisioning as defined in chapter 4 [see original reading], definition 1;
- a continuous variable which measures the total number of children in the family;
- a dummy variable which captures whether or not the father had died before the time of starting work;
- a dummy variable which captures whether the father was absent for reasons other than death or had never been present during childhood;
- a dummy variable which registers whether the boy or his family received poor relief either in the workhouse or as outdoor relief during his childhood;
- a dummy variable which captures whether the family of origin had a small business such as a small landholding, a shop or a workshop of some kind.

The results are reported in column 1 of Table 7.3 [see original reading].

Age at starting work varied in a predictable way with the explanatory factors. When a boy was born continued to have an effect even when other factors were included in the analysis. There was no statistically significant difference in the mean age at starting work for children born between 1791 and 1820 or between 1821 and 1850, but the cohort born before 1791 or after 1850 were on average older when they began working. The dip in the age at starting work coincided with the pause in the growth of real wages from 1790 to 1830, the strains and stresses of industrialization and the problems created for many families by the French wars and the recruitment of adult men into the Army or Navy. On the other hand, age at starting work had clearly begun to rise for children born after mid-century. By this time child labour in the form of very young working was in retreat (see Cunningham, 2000).

Fathers' broad occupational group also influenced age at starting work. The sons of miners, clerical workers, soldiers, seafaring men and men whose occupations were unknown even at this broad level started work, other things being equal, at roughly the same ages as the sons of agricultural labourers. There are differences between these groupings that make some historical sense, for example the sons of sailors and clerical workers started work about six months older and the sons of miners and soldiers about six months younger, but numbers are small in some of these groups and so the differences are not statistically significant.

On the other hand, the sons of artisans were more than a year older and the sons of service providers almost a year older than were agricultural workers' sons, and these differences were statistically significant. In addition, the sons of factory workers, domestic manufacturers and casual labourers were all more than a year younger than were the sons of agricultural labourers when they began work. These differences are also statistically significant. The variation in the age at starting work with fathers' occupational group in part reflects the relative economic strengths of the different occupations. The regression results also register the influence of the demand side of the market for child labour. Adult male factory workers were relatively well paid, especially early in industrialization, yet holding all other things constant their sons started work at about the same age as the sons of men without trades or skills.

Mothers' economic activity was negatively associated with sons' ages at starting work, as it was in bivariate analysis. Mothers could not substitute for their sons in supporting families; rather economically active mothers and early work for children characterized the same families: the very poor and those without male breadwinners. There again this effect was not statistically significant. Family size also continued to be important in the multivariate analysis. The size of the coefficient suggests that having upwards of six siblings could swamp the effect of having a father who belonged to the labour aristocracy in terms of the age at which boys began work. Being fatherless also brought forward entry into the labour force, though there is an important distinction to be drawn between boys whose fathers had died, in which case the effect is small and statistically insignificant, and boys whose fathers had abandoned them or never recognized their existence, in which case the effect is large and significant. Boys deserted by their fathers started work almost 18 months younger than did boys whose fathers were present: a surely important insult to their life chances. Children in families unfortunate enough to have to appeal to the Overseers or Guardians, ceteris paribus, started work eight months younger than did their peers, the Poor Law unable or unwilling to offset poverty's prompts to early work.[23] Finally, children whose parents had a small business started work about 14 months older than did similarly placed children whose parents were employees. According to this source at least, the wealth effects of small-scale proprietorship outweighed the incentive to childhood employment embedded in the ownership of productive resources.[24]

These results remain robust to variations in modelling. For example, if a quadratic trend is used to model changes over time instead of the arbitrary demarcation of cohorts, the size and significance of the coefficients remain very close, as can be seen from column 2 of Table 7.3 [see original reading]. Similarly, as expected, conflating orphanage and absence of fathers into a composite variable produces an effect that is negative and significant at the 10 per cent level, but there are no other substantial changes to signs or significance levels.[25]

Conclusion

Did child labour increase during the first industrial revolution? The unique evidence from the autobiographies is unequivocal. Industrialization appears to have exercised a direct effect on child labour reducing age at starting work, an effect picked up in the positive and statistically significant effect of the cohort dummy for children born before 1791 even when controlling for a number of other exogenous variables. Part of this effect probably derived from an increased demand for children's labour associated with changes in technology: the standard interpretation of the child-intensive industrial revolution. Other independent variables implicated in the determination of age at starting work introduce new considerations. The autobiographical evidence allows children to be located within their family setting and so exposes the supply conditions of child labour. These conditions themselves likely varied to engineer an upsurge during the industrial revolution. Fathers' broad occupational group, reflecting both earnings capacity and local demand for child labour, family income, the lop-sided sourcing of family subsistence and men's likelihood of becoming separated from their wives and children, the conditionality of poor relief, mothers' inability to substitute for chil-dren in the labour force, family size and the possession of small-scale property are all shown to have influenced age at starting work, and all also shifted in this period so as to contribute to the increase in child labour.

Consistent with other evidence, the autobiographies also suggest that child labour declined from the mid nineteenth-century. Ceteris paribus, boys born after 1850 started work 18 months later than did boys born in the crucible of industrialization. This cohort effect embodies the increased earnings of adult males from mid-century, increasingly effec-tive protective labour legislation, more and better schools and changing social norms, which came to associate the schooled child and later working with working-class respectability. Independent trends in some of the other explanatory factors also played a role, though now in reducing child labour. For example, occupational structure now shifted to augment groups associated with later working; numbers of children in families began to decline; and perhaps families without fathers became less numerous.

The pressures laid bare and calibrated from the sample of autobiographies have begun to fill gaps in the historical record. The evidence suggests that the industrial revolution was indeed associated with an upsurge in child labour caused by a unique conjuncture of circum-stances. Britain industrialized early and at a relatively low level of average income. Economic growth disproportionately benefited the owners of property and land, and for several decades at the end of the eighteenth century real earnings on average remained flat. Prevailing social norms that favoured children's general usefulness were adapted to their employment in capi-talist enterprise. Organizational initiatives that involved a more detailed division of labour, specialization and greater discipline in the workplace meant that traditional manufacturing was able to utilize smaller, less physically competent and less skilled workers. Precocious develop-ment of wage labour produced an early dependence on men and male wages and undermined women's ability to contribute to family income, leaving children as a family's second line of economic defence. The coincidence of a wartime draft on the adult male population with a new kind of demand in isolated rural factories, the subsequent competition between domestic manufacturers and the developing factory system and the effects of population growth on the numbers dependent on male wages all played a role in pushing down the age at which children started work. The micro-manifestations of these aggregate forces enmeshed the autobiogra-phers. Sooner rather than later, they were called upon to contribute. With a remarkable lack of bitterness towards their families and communities, if not always towards the economic and social arrangements which seemed to make their work inevitable, they answered the call.

Notes

1   Jobs and remuneration are investigated in chapter 8, below [see original reading].
2   Holroyd's age at starting work remains indeterminate, and so his case is lost to the quantitative analysis.
3   Missing values for age at starting work leave the distribution of the autobiographies by cohort practically unchanged from that reported in chapter 2 (17.3 per cent, 23.8 per cent, 27.7 per cent and 30.8 per cent) [see original reading].

4   ANOVA rejects the hypothesis that the sub-groups are drawn from the same population (F = 11.836; sig. = .000).

5   Linear and logarithmic time trends were estimated for comparison.

6   One particular concern is whether the small number of autobiographies from the seventeenth century, which are likely written by men from a superior echelon within the working class, biases the first cohort towards the relatively prosperous whose age at starting work would be delayed. Exclusion of these cases from the analysis still suggests a U-shaped pattern in age at starting work by cohort or date of birth.

7   The use of the passive voice represents an attempt to put perspective on stressful events and is parallel with the finding of modern psychology that retelling painful episodes in the third person allowed narrators of life stories to reflect positively on difficult episodes (http://nytimes.com/2007/05/22/health/psychology/22narr.html?8dpc=&_r = 1&xml).

8   Feinstein's 'Transport and storage' category overlaps with the casual grouping used in this study and his 'Army and Navy' with 'Soldiering' and 'Sea', though the latter includes private fishermen and sailors who sometimes owned their own vessels and were a cut above the average naval recruit. At the other end of the scale Feinstein's 'Building' sector undoubtedly includes many of the artisans assigned to trades in the classification adopted in the analysis of the autobiographies. Unfortunately Feinstein conflates 'Mining' and 'Manufacturing' and within the latter group fails to distinguish between factory workers and domestic manufacturers. Moreover he has no categories analogous to services or clerical. But even though the comparison is necessarily limited it does suggest that the highest relative earners (e.g. building workers/tradesmen) had sons who delayed work longest (see Feinstein, 1998b).

9   Davis admitted that seamen had to work seven days a week, but in his view this was more than offset by the relatively good prospects of promotion compared with, say, farm labourers and artisans.

10   Improvements in soldiers' pay and the extension of opportunities for them to engage in supplementary work to boost incomes had improved their status relative to unskilled civilian labourers in the 1790s (Cookson, 1997). But soldiers' pay was static throughout the first half of the nineteenth century, the Army becoming increasingly less competitive in the labour market (Spiers, 1980). Moreover the true rate of pay was less than the shilling a day promised by the recruiting sergeant as it was surcharged for 'messing', laundry and sundry additional expenses (Spiers, 1980). It was not until the second half of the nineteenth century, prompted by the need to enhance recruitment at the time of the Crimean war, that net pay began to improve (Bartlett, 1963).

11   Peacetime wages were very stable, as therefore was their position in the inter-group ranking (Davis, 1962).

12   Age at starting work was lower for sons whose mothers were economically active for both definitions of economic activity and both samples used in chapter 4, though in all cases the relationship was not statistically significant.

13   The difference between these means is 1.16 years (t-stat. = 2.35; sig. =. 019).

14   It is also very difficult to disentangle the effects of family size and birth order.

15   Thus of the 151 boys whose fathers were not present in the households of their childhood 55 had mothers who were economically active, a participation rate of around 37 per cent or 44 per cent if cases where mothers died or disappeared during the autobiographer's boyhood are excluded. In comparison, and using the same definition of participation, some 29–36 per cent of mothers who lived in families headed by an adult male were economically active.

16   This family's experience also indicates the way in which relief was fine-tuned quickly in response to changing family circumstances. Initially granted when Bezer senior retired to a hospital for disabled sailors, their parish pension was stopped immediately the old man was discharged (Bezer, 1977, p. 164).

17   The difference is statistically significant (t-stat. = 2.136; sig. =. 033).

18   The difference is statistically significant (t-stat. = 3.71; sig. =. 000).

19   Alysa Levene (2009) has used the apprenticeship records for 10 London parishes to demonstrate the different practices and apparent policies with respect to placement.

20   Unfortunately it is not always possible to separate the cases where relief was given according to the form of relief (pauper apprenticeship, relief within the workhouse, outdoor relief), so the decision was taken to amalgamate the different kinds of relief.

21   The difference between means is 1.33 years (t-stat. = 3.675; sig. =. 000).

22   The contradictory effects of petty proprietorship and the often counter-intuitive results of land reforms that establish a class of small-scale farmers have been detected in child participation rates in today's poor countries, as Bhalotra and Heady have shown (2003).

23   It remains possible that without the Poor Law boys in this category might have begun work earlier still.

24   The effects operate in clusters to push boys into precocious work or afford them space for schooling and physical development. Thus boys whose fathers had abandoned their families were in many cases dependent on poor relief, while fathers who owned or operated small businesses were also in elite occupational groupings.

25   Similarly adding the CAMSIS ranking score of father's detailed occupation produces few changes, although the greater data demands reduce the sample size (for example, all cases where father's occupation is unknown have to be dropped). In this model father's CAMSIS score is positive but insignificant (although it does improve the R^2).

References

Acorn, George (1911), *One of the Multitude* (London: William Heinemann).

Anderson, M. (1999), 'What Can the Mid-Victorian Censuses Tell Us about Variations in Married Women's Employment?', *Local Population Studies* 62: 9–30.

Armstrong, Chester (1938), *Pilgrimage from Nenthead. An Autobiography* (London: Methuen & Co. Ltd).

Arnold, William (1915), *Recollections of William Arnold*, with a preface by Henry Pickett and an introductory note by James Saxton (Northampton: Privately printed).

Ashby, M.K. (1974), *Joseph Ashby of Tysoe, 1859–1919: A Study of English Village Life*, with an introduction by E.P. Thompson (London: Merlin Press).

Barclay, Thomas Patrick (1934), *Memoirs and Medleys. The Autobiography of a Bottle-Washer*, edited by James K. Kelly and with a foreword by Sydney A. Gimson (Leicester: Edgar Backus).

Barr, David (1910), *Climbing the Ladder: the Struggles and Successes of a Village Lad* (London: Robert Culley).

Bartlett, C.J. (1963), *Great Britain and Sea Power, 1815–1853* (Oxford: Clarendon Press).

Bell, Joseph (1926), 'Chapters from the Autobiography of a Village Lad. Showing the hardships and superstitions of Village Life in England in the first half of the last Century. From 1846 to 1858', TS and MS, Bedfordshire and Luton Archives and Record Service, Bedford.

Bennett, John (n.d.), Untitled, MS and TS, Bristol Record Office.

Berg, M. (1994), *The Age of Manufactures: Industry, Innovation and Work in Britain 1700–1820* (London: Routledge).

Bethune, John (1841), *Poems by the late John Bethune with a sketch of the Author's Life. By his Brother* (London: Hamilton, Adams and Co.).

[Bezer, John James] (1977), 'The Autobiography of One of the Chartist Rebels of 1848', reprinted in David Vincent (ed.), *Testaments of Radicalism. Memoirs of Working Class Politicians 1790–1885* (London: Europa Publications).

Bhalotra, S., and Heady, C. (2003), 'Child Farm Labor: The Wealth Paradox', *World Bank Economic Review* 17(2): 197–228.

Bickers, George (1881?), *Interesting Incidents Connected with the Life of George Bickers, Originally a Farmer's Parish Apprentice at Laxfield in Suffolk, but now Residing in Oulton, In the Same County, Being an Autobiography Of the Above, From 1809 to 1881, Inclusive* (Lowestoft: G.S. Cook).

Bonwick, James (1902), *An Octogenarian's Reminiscences* (London: James Nichols), extracted in J. Burnett (ed.), *Destiny Obscure: Autobiographies of Childhood, Education and the Family from the 1820s to the 1920s* (London: Allen Lane, 1982).

Booth, C. (1902), *Life and Labour of the People in London*, first series: *Poverty* (London: Macmillan).

Bowen, H. (1998), *War and British Society, 1688–1815* (Cambridge University Press).

Boswell, D. (1974), *Sea Fishing Apprentices of Grimsby* (Grimsby: Grimsby Public Libraries and Museum).

Brooks, Joseph Barlow (1950/1?), *Lancashire Bred. An Autobiography. Life in a Cotton Town from '75 to '95; From Ranmoor College to Oxford's 'dreaming spires'* (Oxford: Printed by the author, Church Army Press).

Buckley, John [pseud. of John Charles Buckmaster] (1897), *A Village Politician: The Life Story of John Buckley*, edited by J.C. Buckmaster with an introduction by the Rt. Hon. A.J. Mundella (London: T. Fisher Unwin).

Bullen, Frank Thomas (1899), *The Log of a Sea Waif, Being Recollections of the First Four Years of My Sea Life* (London: Smith, Elder & Co.).

Burdett, Joseph (1985), 'The Memoirs of Joseph Burdett, Stockinger and Sometime Apprentice to Mr. Kirk of Lambley in Nottinghamshire 1813 to 1817', typed from photocopies and edited by J. Bugg, TS, Nottinghamshire Archives, Nottingham.

Burgess, Joseph (1927), *A Potential Poet? His Autobiography and Verse* (Ilford: Burgess Publications).

Carnegie, Andrew (1920), *Autobiography of Andrew Carnegie*, with a preface by John C. Van Dyke (London: Constable & Co. Ltd).

Carter, Harry (1900), *The Autobiography of a Cornish Smuggler (Captain Harry Carter, of Prussia Cove), 1749–1809*, edited with an introduction and notes by John B. Cornish (London: Gibbings and Co.).

Carter, P. (1995), 'Poor Relief Strategies – Women, Children and Enclosure in Hanwell, Middlesex, 1780–1816', *Local Historian* 25: 164–77.

Castle, John (1871), 'The Diary of John Castle', TS, Brunel University Library, Uxbridge.

Catling, Thomas Thurgood (1911), *My Life's Pilgrimage*, with an introduction by the Rt. Hon. Lord Burnham (London: John Murray).

Chater, Daniel (n.d.), 'Autobiography of Daniel Chater', TS, Brynmor Jones Library, University of Hull.

Clare, John (1986), *John Clare's Autobiographical Writings*, edited by Eric Robinson, with wood engravings by John Lawrence (Oxford University Press, 1986).

Claxton, Timothy (1839), 'Memoirs', in his *Hints to Mechanics on Self-Education and Mutual Instruction* (London: Taylor and Walton).

Collyer, Robert (1908), *Some Memories* (Boston: American Unitarian Association).

Cookson, J.E. (1997), *The British Armed Nation* (Oxford: Clarendon Press).

Cooper, Thomas (1971), *The Life of Thomas Cooper. Written by Himself*, with an introduction by John Saville (Leicester University Press).

Croll, James (1896), 'Autobiographical Sketch', in *Autobiographical Sketch of James Croll, LL.D., F.R.S., Etc.*, with Memoir of His Life and Work, by James Campbell Irons, MA (London: Edward Stanford).

Cunningham, H. (2000), 'The Decline of Child Labor Markets and Family Economies in Europe and North America since 1830', *Economic History Review* **53**: 409–28.

Dale, Nathaniel (1871?), *The Eventful life of Nathaniel Dale, with Recollections & Anecdotes containing A great variety of Business Matters, &c., as occurred in the life of the author* (Kimbolton: Printed for the author).

Davis, R. (1962), *The Rise of the English Shipping Industry in the 17th and 18th Centuries* (London: Macmillan).

Edwards, Noel George (1998), *Ploughboy's Progress. The Life of Sir George Edwards*, foreword by Bert Hazell, edited and with an introduction by Alun Howkins (Norwich: University of East Anglia).

Emsley, C. (1979), *British Society and the French Wars, 1793–1815* (London: Macmillan).

Feinstein, C.H. (1998b), 'Wage-Earnings in Great Britain during the Industrial Revolution', in I. Begg and S.G.B. Henry (eds.), *Applied Economics and Public Policy* (Cambridge University Press).

[Forrest, Frank] (1850), *Chapters in the Life of a Dundee Factory Boy. An Autobiography*, edited by James Myles (Edinburgh: Adam and Charles Black).

Freer, Walter (1929), *My Life and Memories* (Glasgow: Civic Press Ltd).

Galton, Frank Wallis (n.d.), 'Autobiography', MS, Department of Manuscripts, British Library of Political and Economic Science, London.

Gazeley, I. (2003), *Poverty in Britain 1900–1965* (Basingstoke: Palgrave Macmillan).

Gompers, Samuel (1984), *Seventy Years of Life and Labor. An Autobiography*, edited and with an introduction by Nick Salvatore (Ithaca, NY: ILR Press, Cornell University).

Greenwood, M. (1942), 'British Loss of Life in the Wars of 1794–1815 and in 1914–18', *Journal of the Royal Statistical Society* **105**: 1–11.

Gutteridge, Joseph (1969), *The Autobiography of Joseph Gutteridge*, edited and with an introduction by Valerie E. Chancellor (London: Evelyn, Adams and MacKay).

[H——, Bill] (1861–2), 'Autobiography of a Navvy', Macmillans Magazine 5, November 1861–April 1862.

Harris, John (1882), *My Autobiography* (London: Hamilton, Adams and Co.).

Hillocks, James Inches (1862), *Life Story. A Prize Autobiography* (London: Houlston & Wright W. Tweedie).

Holroyd, Abraham (1892), 'Life of Abraham Holroyd', by William Scruton, from a manuscript provided by Mr Holroyd to Mr Scruton, in *Holroyd's Collection of Yorkshire Ballads*, edited by Charles F. Forshaw (London: George Bell and Sons, Ltd).

Holyoake, George Jacob (1906), *Sixty Years of an Agitator's Life* (London: T. Fisher Unwin).

Honeyman, K. (2007), *Child Workers in England, 1780–1820: Parish Apprentices and the Making of the Early Industrial Labour Force* (Aldershot: Ashgate).

Horrell, S., and Humphries, J. (1995a), 'The Exploitation of Little Children: Children's Work and the Family Economy in the British Industrial Revolution', *Explorations in Economic History* **32**: 849–80.

Hudson, P. (1986), *The Genesis of Industrial Capital: A Study of the West Riding Wool Textile Industry c. 1750–1850* (Cambridge University Press).

—— (2004), 'Industrial Organisation and Structure', in R. Floud and P. Johnson (eds.), *The Cambridge Economic History of Modern Britain, vol. I, Industrialisation, 1700–1860* (Cambridge University Press).

Humphries, J. (1998), 'Female-Headed Households in Early Industrial Britain: The Vanguard of the Proletariat?', *Labour History Review* 63: 31–65.

—— (2007), ' "Because they are too Menny . . ." Children, Mothers, and Fertility Decline: The Evidence from Working-Class Autobiographies of the Eighteenth and Nineteenth Centuries', in A. Janssens (ed.), *Gendering the Fertility Decline in the Western World* (Berne: Peter Lang).

Ince, Thomas (1888), *Beggar Manuscripts: an Original Miscellany in Verse and Prose* (Blackburn: North-East Lancashire Printing and Publishing Company Limited).

Lane, J. (1996), *Apprenticeship in England, 1600–1914* (London: UCL Press).

Levene, A. (2009), 'Parish Apprenticeship and the Old Poor Law in London', *Economic History Review* (in press).

Lloyd, George (n.d.), 'The Autobiography of "George Brawd"', MS, Brunel University Library, Uxbridge.

[Lowery, Robert] (1979), 'Passages in the Life of a Temperance Lecturer, Connected with the Public Movements of the Working Classes for the last Twenty Years. By One of their Order', reprinted in Brian Harrison and Patricia Hollis (eds.), *Robert Lowery, Radical and Chartist* (London: Europa Publications).

Luck, Lucy (1994), 'Straw-Plait Worker', in John Burnett (ed.), *Useful Toil. Autobiographies of Working People from the 1820s to the 1920s* (London: Routledge).

Marcroft, William (1886), *The Marcroft Family* (Manchester: John Heywood).

Marshall, A. (1969), *Principles of Economics* (London: Macmillan).

[Master Shoemaker] (1879), 'My Life and Adventures, by a Master Shoemaker', *The Boot and Shoemaker*, 14 June–6 September.

Mayett, Joseph (1986), *The Autobiography of Joseph Mayett of Quainton, 1783–1839*, edited by Ann Kussmaul, Buckinghamshire Record Society, XXIII.

Meek, George (1910), *George Meek, Bath Chair-Man. By Himself*, with an introduction by H.G. Wells (London: Constable & Co. Ltd).

Milne, William J. (1901), *Reminiscences of an Old Boy: being Autobiographical Sketches of Scottish Rural Life from 1826 to 1856*, with an introduction by Alexander Lowson (Forfar: John Macdonald).

Mitchell, Thomas Buller (n.d.), 'Tommy's Book', TS, Reference Library, Bristol.

Nash, J. (2006), 'Aspects of a Town in Decline: A Population Study of Burford, Oxfordshire, 1851–1901', unpublished D.Phil. dissertation, University of Oxford.

Okey, Thomas (1930), *A Basketful of Memories. An Autobiographical Sketch* (London: J.M. Dent & Sons Ltd).

Preston, Raymond (1930), *Raymond Preston, British and Australian Evangelist: Life Story and Personal Reminiscences*, edited by W. Kingscote Greenland, and with a foreword by Samuel Chadwick (London: Epworth Press).

Price, Henry Edward (1904?), 'My Diary', MS, Islington Public Library.

Reilly, Sarah A. (1931) *I Walk with the King: The Life Story of John Edward Reilly* (London: Epworth Press).

Robinson, Joseph (n.d.), 'Joseph Robinson's Reminiscences', TS, West Sussex Record Office, Chichester.

Rodger, N.A.M. (1986), *The Wooden World: An Anatomy of the Georgian Navy* (London: Fontana).

Rowntree, B.S. (2000), *Poverty. A Study of Town Life* (Bristol: Policy Press and the Joseph Rowntree Charitable Trust).

Rubinstein, D. (1977), 'Socialization and the London School Board 1870–1904: Aims, Methods and Public Opinion', in P. McCann (ed.), *Popular Education and Socialization in the Nineteenth Century* (London: Methuen).

Rymer, Edward Allen (1976), 'The Martyrdom of the Mine, or, A 60 Years' Struggle for Life', facsimile reprint in two parts, edited and with an introduction by Robert G. Neville, *History Workshop Journal* 1, Spring; 2, Autumn.

Sanderson, Thomas (1873), 'The Life and Adventures of Thomas Sanderson, As written by himself, in 1861, in the 53rd year of his age', in *Chips and shavings of an Old Shipwright; or, the Life, Poems, & Adventures of Thomas Sanderson; Author of 'Freaks of Fancy', &c* (Darlington: Bragg, Machine Printer).

Sanger, 'Lord' George (1910), *Seventy Years a Showman* (London: C. Arthur Pearson Ltd).

Saunders, James Edwin (1938?), *The Reflections and Rhymes of an Old Miller*, edited by W. Ridley Chesterton (London: Hodder and Stoughton).

Sexton, Sir James (1936), *Agitator. The Life of the Dockers' M.P. An Autobiography*, with a preface by the Rt. Hon. David Lloyd George, MP (London: Faber and Faber).

Sharpe, P. (1991), 'Poor Children as Apprentices in Colyton, 1598–1830', *Continuity and Change* 6: 253–70.

Shipp, John (1890), *Memoirs of the Extraordinary Military Career of John Shipp, late a Lieutenant in His Majesty's 87th Regiment. Written by Himself*, with an introduction by H. Manners Chichester (London: T. Fisher Unwin).

Snell, K.D.M. (1985), *Annals of the Labouring Poor: Social Change and Agrarian England, 1660–1900* (Cambridge University Press).

Snell, K.D.M., and Millar, J. (1987), 'Lone Parent Families and the Welfare State: Past and Present', *Continuity and Change* 2: 387–422.

Somerville, Alexander (1951), *The Autobiography of a Working Man, by 'One who has whistled at the plough'*, edited and with an introduction by John Carswell (London: Turnstile Press).

Spiers, E.M. (1980), *The Army and Society, 1815–1914* (London: Longman).

Stanley, Sir Henry Morton (1909), *The Autobiography of Sir Henry Morton Stanley*, edited and with a preface by Dorothy Stanley (Boston and New York: Houghton Mifflin Co.).

Steadman, William Charles (1906), 'How I Got On', *Pearson's Weekly*, 8 February.

Stout, William (1967), *The Autobiography of William Stout of Lancaster*, edited by J.D. Marshall (Manchester University Press).

Stradley, John (n.d.), 'Memoirs of John Stradley, 1757–1825', TS, Local History Library, Blackheath, as précised in John Burnett, David Vincent and David Mayall (eds.), *The Autobiography of the Working Class: An Annotated Critical Bibliography* (Brighton: Harvester, 1984–9).

Thane, P. (1978), 'Women and the Poor Law in Victorian and Edwardian England', *History Workshop Journal* 6: 29–51.

Thorne, Will (1925?), *My Life's Battles*, with a foreword by the Rt. Hon. J.R. Clynes, MP (London: George Newnes Ltd).

Tillett, Benjamin (1931), *Memoirs and Reflections*, with a foreword by the Rt. Hon. Philip Snowdon (London: John Long Limited).

Turner, James (1981), *Hard Up Husband. James Turner's Diary, Halifax, 1881/2* (Orwell, Cambs.: Ellisons' Editions).

Wardle, G.J. (1906), 'How I Got On', *Pearson's Weekly*, 22 February.

Watchorn, Robert (1958), *The Autobiography of Robert Watchorn*, edited by Herbert Faulkner West (Oklahoma City: The Robert Watchorn Charities Ltd).

Wilson, Joseph Havelock (1925), *My Stormy Voyage Through Life*, with a foreword by Sir Walter Runciman (Newcastle: Co-operative Printing Society Limited).

Wood, Thomas (1994), 'Engineer', in John Burnett (ed.), *Useful Toil. Autobiographies of Working People from the 1820s to the 1920s* (London: Routledge).

PART 4

Use of the past to articulate solutions to problems facing children today

THE MAJORITY OF THE WORLD'S CHILDREN live in poverty. Part 2 of the Reader contained many articles that showed that roots of injustice toward children lay in such historical forces as colonialism, patriarchy, and globalization. On a tangible level one need only think of the contemporary impact on children of dormant landmines to know that children are living embodiments of history. The goal of Part 4 is to think about how knowledge of the evolving conception of childhood equips us to work for positive change for contemporary children.

Part 4 explores how the global history of childhood is relevant to our world now. Many problems, such as child labor, facing some non-western children today were once pervasive among western children. The articles in this section provide historical parallels to some critical children's rights issues today, such as violence, labor, and illiteracy. A look at how western societies obtained such triumphs as near-universal literacy can provide tools for solving modern-day societal ills. The global history of childhood is a relatively new field and more work needs to be done on comparing children's situations in different historical moments and locations. As discussed before, the western model of childhood should not be seen as the only model for all the world's children.

The articles in this section should not be read through the lens of viewing western attitudes towards childhood as "advanced" and non-western as "backward." As Part 2 of the Reader pointed out, the "advances" achieved for some western children often came at the expense of their non-western peers. And, the type of childhood a person has depends on the intersectionality of class, gender, and race, regardless of country of birth. Historian Colin Heywood points out the need to see intersectionality in the past, when he writes,

> The problem for historians in this area is to avoid an air of triumphalism. One can point to a series of impressive advances for young people in the long term, such as improvements in infant and child mortality, average heights, literacy and school attendance rates. At the same time, the 'meaningless mean' risks masking huge inequalities within societies, the general progressive drift to improvement was interrupted by numerous whirls and eddies, and even in the twenty-first century there is little room in the West for complacency on child welfare among the poor.[1]

What are children's rights?

The Convention on the Rights of the Child (CRC) provides the framework for children's rights today. A copy of the CRC is included in this section. The CRC provides a framework for the aspirations that exist today for children's well-being around the world. The CRC broke new ground in matters relating to adoption, survival and development, protection of children's identity, sexual exploitation, neglect and drug abuse. It is the most comprehensive treaty for the protection and support of children in history.

The UN General Assembly adopted the CRC in 1989 on the basis that the scattered provisions relevant to children in existing human rights conventions did not take children's special needs into consideration. All but two countries, the United States and Somalia, have ratified the CRC. The convention applies to any human under the age of 18 and is guided by four fundamental principles: 1) a child must not suffer discrimination of any form; 2) a child's best interests should be taken into consideration in all decisions affecting him/her; 3) the child has the right to survive and develop, mentally and physically; 4) a child should be free to express his/her views and these views should be taken into account in all matters affecting him/her.

The international movement for children's rights evolved out of a turn to public action for children that occurred in the West in the nineteenth century. The Romantic notion of childhood innocence and the industrial revolution's placing of children in dangerous and unhealthy conditions fostered the development of charity and social welfare programs. Another contributing factor to these efforts was the growing competition between nations to produce a skilled and educated future workforce. The article by Hugh Cunningham outlines the key children's rights issues in western countries to which philanthropists and state governments responded between c.1830 and c.1920. Cunningham examines the period in western history in which child labor was critically curbed. He attributes the evolution of the western middle-class ideology of childhood to legal changes as well as a fundamental change in how society valued the child.

It was not until the jolt of the First World War that the effort began to draw up a declaration of children's rights that spanned beyond the nation-state. Children's rights activists argued that children should not suffer just because they were in a defeated country and that children's problems did not end with the war. The Englishwoman Eglantyne Jebb, founder of the Save the Children Fund, drew up a simple declaration of children's rights that was adopted by the League of Nations in 1924. The "League of Nations Declaration on the Rights of the Child" was only five paragraphs long and it consisted of duties that adults owed to children. The UN created in 1946 an emergency fund for children that in 1956 was renamed UNICEF. The 1948 Universal Declaration of Human Rights (UDHR) only contained brief references to the well-being of children and in 1959 the UN adopted the Declaration of the Rights of the Child. Unlike the 1924 declaration, it mentioned work and education and was ten principles in length.

The CRC differed from the two previous declarations in that it treated children as the subject of rights (rather than the object of concern) and it created a Committee on the Rights of the Child to supervise and implement its aspirations. Weeks after the CRC entered into force, there was a World Summit for Children in 1990 which laid out promises for children to be achieved by 2000. The decade-end review, entitled "We the Children," found only modest achievement. In 2000, the UN General Assembly adopted two Optional Protocols to the Convention to inhibit the involvement of children in armed conflict and to protect children from sale into prostitution and pornography. The same year, the International Labour Organization's (ILO) Convention No. 182 came in to force to protect children from the worst forms of child labor. In 2002 the UN reconfirmed its commitment to children by adopting a document called "A World Fit for Children," which created targets for achieving the Millennium Development Goals directly related to children by 2015.

The international children's rights framework sets a standard by which all childhoods around the world can be evaluated. Childhood, however, is a social construct and relative to time and place, as discussed in prior chapters in this Reader. This raises a much-debated question in the field of childhood studies: should there be (or can there be) a universal standard for childhood? Discourses that purport a universalist, timeless nature of childhood can be problematic. Equally problematic are discourses that construct childhood as region-specific and free from global, capitalist normalizing forces.

The selection by Sharon Stephens outlines critical points in the debates surrounding cultural relativity and conceptions of childhoods. She asks if children's rights activists base their universal conception of childhood on an imagined, monolithic western model of childhood. Stephens argues that there is no blanket model of childhood that can be applied to the world's children. However, the process of trying to find that model is what is important, according to Stephens.

The very language scholars use to assess children's rights is contestable. For example, the term "at risk" – so often applied to children today – has different meanings in different contexts. The article by Ingrid Lohmann and Christine Mayer unpacks the definitions of "at risk" in European history and gives an overview of how people often use the term to create a normative model of childhood across the globe. In order to properly assess and help children in need, scholars must pay heed to a society's specific terminology and definitions that relate to children.

In the debate on the universality of children's rights, it should be understood that certain ideas labeled as "western" do not necessarily preclude them from having a potential worth for non-western children. Also, non-western countries did not sit by helplessly as the children's rights movement evolved in its earliest stages. Numerous countries were engaged in processes of their own to respond to the needs of children. The article by Kathleen Uno looks at the process by which the late nineteenth-century Japanese government meshed local cultural ideas about child-rearing with new ideas about institutionalized, mandatory schooling. The modern phenomenon of day-care institutions and age-graded schools has meant that children are required to spend an increasing amount of time in the care of non-kin. This phenomenon has often been driven by the state and policy-makers seeking to reshape society.

Using the history of childhood to help children today

Taking the CRC as a viable guide to evaluating children's rights issues today, the rest of the articles in Part 4 use knowledge from the global history of childhood to understand aspects of the world today. Historians of childhood are motivated in large part by the concerns of the world in which they live. The wide acceptance of the CRC can give the misleading impression that children's rights are universally recognized.

According to the standards set by the CRC, quality education remains an elusive goal for millions of children. UNICEF finds that many of the world's children have potentials and dreams that may never be realized due to sub-par education and/or financial barriers (such as the need to work to contribute to a family income or the inability to pay school-related fees). UNICEF estimates that there are 93 million out-of-school children, which is equal to more than the entire population of the Philippines. The majority of these children are girls and they live in sub-Saharan Africa and South Asia. Studies find that education of girls can have a larger impact on a country's overall development. Whether in times of crisis or peace, in cities or remote villages, the CRC stipulates that every child is entitled to have access to quality education. The mere presence of a school is not sufficient to satisfy this non-negotiable right.

Quality education means that learning is child-centered, relevant to the reality of the pupils, tailored to different age groups, gender sensitive, rights-based, and safe. Children must not only enroll in school, but they must complete the required years of schooling. Primary education is absolutely essential, but it is not enough. Learning starts at birth, and the first few years of a child's life is critical to a child's cognitive skills. Post-primary education is also a basic right.

The enormous education deficits in many regions of the world today were once widely prevalent in Scandinavia. Ellen Schrumpf's article traces the evolution of how Norwegian children went from being industrial laborers in the late 1800s to school-children. Schrumpf details the change in character and social function of child labor in Norway. Many important lessons can be ascertained from the article about how to effectively implement the right to education. Schrumpf's article points to the importance of educational legislation, as well as the importance of understanding the social and cultural conditions and attitudes that foster child labor. The article highlights how achieving full-time attendance in school did not happen overnight. Although most Norwegian children no longer worked full-time by the beginning of the First World War, child labor existed in the form of part-time jobs, primarily done after school hours. An important point to consider in Schrumpf's article is that children are historical agents and their relationship with their surroundings impacts them each in their own way.

Another critical issue facing many children in the world today is the right to protection. The CRC stipulates that this includes war and also other forms of exploitation and cruelty, such as arbitrary separation from family, sale into prostitution, and abuses in the criminal justice system. The twentieth and twenty-first centuries have been the most violent for children in the world's past, particularly in regards to gender violence. In 2008, the UN officially declared rape to be a weapon of war because it destroys not only individuals but also whole communities. Today, girls suffer from some of the worst forms of sexual violence in the Democratic Republic of the Congo (DRC). The country has been in a series of civil wars over control of its abundant natural resources since gaining its independence in 1960. Known as the rape capital of the world, the majority of the victims are adolescent girls and 10 percent of the victims are under 10 years of age.

Set in a very different time and place than the modern DRC, the chapter from Mary Odem's book discusses statutory rape in late nineteenth- and early twentieth-century America. The historical parallel is intended to encourage readers to use the history of childhood to flesh out strategies for countering the problem of gender violence that continues to occur against children in all parts of the world today. Odem's article considers the role that the rule of law and activism played in curbing gender violence in American history. She finds that even with the passing of an Age of Consent Law, legal officers in California did not enforce it because they viewed female offenders as immoral. Societal attitudes favored white males and did not embody a single standard for sexual morality. Women reformers fought judges by arranging for groups to be at trials and petitioning for trials to include female jurors. Reformers could not rely on the state alone to show concern for protection of young women.

Children in western countries today are not exempt from human rights abuses. For example, in the USA, exploitive child labor exists in some rural farm areas, and living conditions in some urban areas are not much different than outright war zones. Additionally, many mainstream western children are facing a phenomenon called adultification. In his classic work *The Disappearance of Childhood*, cultural critic Neil Postman makes the argument that the dividing line between childhood and adulthood is rapidly eroding. One of the biggest contributions of Postman's book is not so much that childhood is disappearing, but his theory for why this is happening. Postman says that the printing press created childhood, while the electronic media is making it disappear. The printing press expelled the child from the adult world because books created a private world for the child. The child had to earn his/her way in to adulthood by learning to read. Children and adults no longer shared the same information environment. In the chapter included here, Postman illustrates his evidence for how modern media erodes the hierarchy between adults and children. Modern media does not exclude the child from the adult world of violence, sex, and drugs. Postman argues that childhood is disappearing in America due to the barrage of television that corrodes the divide between adulthood and childhood.

Counter-arguments to Postman's theory are of two types. Some critics say the new electronic media will create children's liberation because it allows children to participate in the society around them. Media is democratic and allows the child to escape from adult control. Other critics say that the negative impacts of the media do not have to imply an end to childhood. Educational institutions can play a role in developing children's ability to protect themselves. Media companies can engage children in participating in the production of programs themselves.

Academia cannot be separated from advocacy. The articles in Part 4 show that recognizing historical context and linkages is important for coming up with solutions to modern-day problems. Such recognition is important for cultivating a culture of children's rights. Children's rights are not just a set of legal procedures. Children's rights constitute a framework for viewing the world. The CRC holds that children are rights-holders by the mere fact of being alive. Fostering awareness and support for this idea is a key component to creating a world in which the theory of children's rights is practiced.

Understanding what leads to situations of injustice in children's lives is critical for fostering a culture of children's rights. Contextual awareness dissuades the onlooker from blaming disadvantaged and marginalized children for their own plight. Causes for children's suffering today are not ahistorical. There comes a point in which some children and their families are powerless to forces – be they historical, political, cultural, and/or economic – working against them. Hugh Cunningham describes this phenomenon in the case of working children during the industrial revolution. He writes,

> The phrase 'family strategy' conveys a sense of a family rationally, if perhaps hard-heartedly, considering a range of options open to it: of a family in control of its own destiny and making a choice ... In truth there comes a point where the 'parameters,' 'constraints' and 'delimiting factors' affecting 'choice' are so paramount that the notion of 'choice' becomes meaningless.[2]

In resolving issues such as child labor, the interests of the child, parents, and family must often be weighed against one another.

Making historical parallels between past and present children's rights issues can foster a culture of children's rights. Recognizing similarities across time and place cultivates a sense of a shared humanity. It dissuades the onlooker from taking a detached view of other people's suffering. The comforts that most of the people in the western world enjoy today can blind them to seeing other people's reality. The global history of childhood reminds us that all children are equally vulnerable. As Paula Fass writes, "At birth, all children are members of a world community, still unmarked by most social, national, and cultural boundaries."[3]

Articles

22.   The UN Convention on the Rights of the Child (CRC). 1989.

Children's rights

- Summarize the fundamental guarantees of the CRC.
- How does the preamble manifest itself in the content of the CRC?
- In what ways do some articles overlap with one another? Why might this occur?

23.   Cunningham, Hugh. *Children and Childhood in Western Society Since 1500.* Great Britain: Pearson, 2005, pp 137–70.

Origins of children's rights in the West

- Trace the evolution of the movement to curb child labor.
- In what ways did philanthropy draw the groundwork for state intervention in the lives of children?
- What are the weaknesses to relying on philanthropy alone to deal with children's issues?
- In what ways can the intervention of the state in the lives of children be seen as a way of policing social life? Make an argument for why you agree or disagree with this idea.

24.   Stephens, Sharon. Introduction to *Children and the Politics of Culture*, edited by Sharon Stephens. New Jersey: Princeton University Press, 1995, pp 3–24.

Debates on the universality of children's rights

- What is meant by children's cultural rights?
- Do you think that a universal common conception of childhood can be deciphered amongst all the cultures of the world? Why or why not?
- Could a universal conception of childhood be important to helping children worldwide have more equitable lives? In what ways yes and in what ways no?
- Do you expect frameworks of childhood to become more similar from one region to another over the next few decades? Why or why not?

25.   Lohmann, Ingrid and Christine Mayer. "Lessons from the History of Education for a 'Century of the Child at Risk'" in *Paedagogica Historica*. Vol 45, No. 1/2, pp 4–11. February 2009.

Cultural relativity

- What does it mean to say that childhood is a historical construct?
- Summarize the different definitions of "at risk".
- What influence did the medical profession have on defining the meaning of a "normal" child over the last few centuries?

26.   Uno, Kathleen. *Passages to Modernity: Motherhood, Childhood and Social Reform in Early Twentieth Century Japan.* Hawaii: University of Hawaii Press, 1999, pp 19–46.

The non-West actively engaged in the process of change related to modern-day children

- Describe household care in late nineteenth- and early twentieth-century Japanese households. What changes occurred?
- What does the author mean when she writes, " ... the modern Japanese state promoted the creation of new social institutions to consolidate its authority and to strengthen the nation"? (page 419) Give examples to illustrate.
- Why is it important to understand that the non-West actively engaged in the process related to the development of the modern model of childhood?

27.   Schrumpf, Ellen. "From Full-Time to Part-Time: Working Children in Norway from the Nineteenth to the Twentieth Century" in *Industrious Children: Work & Childhood in the Nordic Countries* edited by Ning de Coninck-Smith, Bengt Sandin, and Ellen Schrumpf. Denmark: Odense University Press, 1997, pp 47–78.

Curbing child labor

- What arguments justified child labor?
- What arguments were used to wage a campaign against child labor?
- How was changing ideas about childhood linked to the process of modernization in Norway during the turn of the last century?
- What lessons can be drawn from the past regarding curbing child labor? In what ways are the lessons not applicable to modern-day issues of child labor?

28.   Odem, Mary E. "Statutory Rape Prosecutions in California" in *Delinquent Daughters* (North Carolina: The University of North Carolina Press, 1995), pp 63–81.

Curbing gender violence

- Why, despite the age of consent law, did law officers not enforce it?
- What result did age of consent laws actually have on girls initially?
- What were some of the experiences girls had while under the examination of judges?
- How did feminists fight the judges?
- In what ways must the sexual reform and regulation in the United States during the late nineteenth and early twentieth century be understood as specific to gender, class, and race?
- How can looking at past examples of reforming gender violence help and not help in today's battles against gender violence?

29.   Postman, Neil. "The Disappearing Child" in *The Disappearance of Childhood*. New York: Vintage Books, 1994, pp 120–42.

The end of childhood

- Evaluate Postman's use of evidence to make his argument.
- Do you agree or disagree that childhood is disappearing? Why or why not?
- What should be done, if anything, about the problem outlined by Postman?
- What impact did the internet and media have on your childhood?

Suggestions for further reading

Alston, P., Parker, S. and Seymour, J. (eds.) (1992) *Children, Rights and the Law*, Oxford: Clarendon Press

Bakan, J. (2011) *Childhood Under Siege: How Big Business Targets Children*, New York: Simon & Schuster

Boyden, J. and de Berry, J. (eds.) (2005) *Children and Youth on the Front Line: Ethnography, Armed Conflict and Displacement*, New York: Berghahn Books

Carton, B. (2000) *Blood from Your Children: The Colonial Origins of Generational Conflict in South Africa*, Charlottesville, VA: University of Virginia Press

Dennis, J. (2007) *We Boys Together: Teenagers in Love Before Girl-Craziness*, Nashville, TN: Vanderbilt University Press

Greenhalgh, S. (2008) *Just One Child: Science and Policy in Deng's China*, Berkeley, CA: University of California Press

Mehran, G. (2002) The Presentation of the "Self" and the "Other" in Postrevolutionary Iranian School Textbooks in Keddie, N. and Matthee, R. (eds.) *Iran and the Surrounding World: Interactions in Culture and Cultural Politics.* Seattle, WA: University of Washington Press

Myers, T. (2005) Embodying Delinquency: Boys' Bodies, Sexuality, and Juvenile Justice History in Early Twentieth-Century Quebec, *Journal of the History of Sexuality*, 14 (4), pp.383–414

Van Bueren, G. (1999) Combating Child Poverty – Human Rights Approaches, *Human Rights Quarterly*, 21 (3), pp.680–706

Weiner, M. (1991) *The Child and the State in India: Child Labor and Education Policy in Comparative Perspective*, Princeton, NJ: Princeton University Press

Weston, B. (2005) *Child Labor and Human Rights: Making Children Matter*, Boulder, CO: Lynne Rienner Publishers

Notes

1   Heywood, C. (2001) *A History of Childhood: Children and Childhood in the West from Medieval to Modern Times (Themes in History)*, Cambridge: Polity Press, p.145.
2   Cunningham, H. (2005) *Children and Childhood in Western Society since 1500*, London: Longman, p.88.
3   Fass, P. (2006) *Children of a New World*, New York: New York University Press, p.11.

Chapter 22

THE UN CONVENTION ON THE RIGHTS OF THE CHILD

THE CONVENTION ON THE RIGHTS OF THE CHILD was adopted and opened for signature, ratification and accession by General Assembly resolution 44/25 of 20 November 1989. It entered into force 2 September 1990, in accordance with article 49.

Preamble

The States Parties to the present Convention,

Considering that, in accordance with the principles proclaimed in the Charter of the United Nations, recognition of the inherent dignity and of the equal and inalienable rights of all members of the human family is the foundation of freedom, justice and peace in the world,

Bearing in mind that the peoples of the United Nations have, in the Charter, reaffirmed their faith in fundamental human rights and in the dignity and worth of the human person and have determined to promote social progress and better standards of life in larger freedom,

Recognizing that the United Nations has, in the Universal Declaration of Human Rights and in the International Covenants on Human Rights, proclaimed and agreed that everyone is entitled to all the rights and freedoms set forth therein, without distinction of any kind, such as race, colour, sex, language, religion, political or other opinion, national or social origin, property, birth or other status,

Recalling that, in the Universal Declaration of Human Rights, the United Nations has proclaimed that childhood is entitled to special care and assistance,

Convinced that the family, as the fundamental group of society and the natural environment for the growth and well-being of all its members and particularly children, should be afforded the necessary protection and assistance so that it can fully assume its responsibilities within the community,

Recognizing that the child, for the full and harmonious development of his or her personality, should grow up in a family environment, in an atmosphere of happiness, love and understanding,

Considering that the child should be fully prepared to live an individual life in society and brought up in the spirit of the ideals proclaimed in the Charter of the United Nations and in particular in the spirit of peace, dignity, tolerance, freedom, equality and solidarity,

Bearing in mind that the need to extend particular care to the child has been stated in the Geneva Declaration of the Rights of the Child of 1924 and in the Declaration of the Rights of the Child adopted by the General Assembly on 20 November 1959 and recognized in the Universal Declaration of Human Rights, in the International Covenant on Civil and Political Rights (in particular in articles 23 and 24), in the International Covenant on Economic, Social and Cultural Rights (in particular in article 10) and in the statutes and relevant instruments of specialized agencies and international organizations concerned with the welfare of children,

Bearing in mind that, as indicated in the Declaration of the Rights of the Child, "the child, by reason of his physical and mental immaturity, needs special safeguards and care, including appropriate legal protection, before as well as after birth",

Recalling the provisions of the Declaration on Social and Legal Principles relating to the Protection and Welfare of Children, with Special Reference to Foster Placement and Adoption Nationally and Internationally; the United Nations Standard Minimum Rules for the Administration of Juvenile Justice (The Beijing Rules); and the Declaration on the Protection of Women and Children in Emergency and Armed Conflict,

Recognizing that, in all countries in the world, there are children living in exceptionally difficult conditions and that such children need special consideration,

Taking due account of the importance of the traditions and cultural values of each people for the protection and harmonious development of the child,

Recognizing the importance of international co-operation for improving the living conditions of children in every country, in particular in the developing countries,

Have agreed as follows:

Part I

Article 1

For the purposes of the present Convention, a child means every human being below the age of eighteen years unless under the law applicable to the child, majority is attained earlier.

Article 2

1.   States Parties shall respect and ensure the rights set forth in the present Convention to each child within their jurisdiction without discrimination of any kind, irrespective of the child's or his or her parent's or legal guardian's race, colour, sex, language, religion, political or other opinion, national, ethnic or social origin, property, disability, birth or other status.
2.   States Parties shall take all appropriate measures to ensure that the child is protected against all forms of discrimination or punishment on the basis of the status, activities, expressed opinions, or beliefs of the child's parents, legal guardians, or family members.

Article 3

1. In all actions concerning children, whether undertaken by public or private social welfare institutions, courts of law, administrative authorities or legislative bodies, the best interests of the child shall be a primary consideration.
2. States Parties undertake to ensure the child such protection and care as is necessary for his or her well-being, taking into account the rights and duties of his or her parents, legal guardians, or other individuals legally responsible for him or her, and, to this end, shall take all appropriate legislative and administrative measures.
3. States Parties shall ensure that the institutions, services and facilities responsible for the care or protection of children shall conform with the standards established by competent authorities, particularly in the areas of safety, health, in the number and suitability of their staff, as well as competent supervision.

Article 4

States Parties shall undertake all appropriate legislative, administrative and other measures for the implementation of the rights recognized in the present Convention. With regard to economic, social and cultural rights, States Parties shall undertake such measures to the maximum extent of their available resources and, where needed, within the framework of international co-operation.

Article 5

States Parties shall respect the responsibilities, rights and duties of parents or, where applicable, the members of the extended family or community as provided for by local custom, legal guardians or other persons legally responsible for the child, to provide, in a manner consistent with the evolving capacities of the child, appropriate direction and guidance in the exercise by the child of the rights recognized in the present Convention.

Article 6

1. States Parties recognize that every child has the inherent right to life.
2. States Parties shall ensure to the maximum extent possible the survival and development of the child.

Article 7

1. The child shall be registered immediately after birth and shall have the right from birth to a name, the right to acquire a nationality and, as far as possible, the right to know and be cared for by his or her parents.
2. States Parties shall ensure the implementation of these rights in accordance with their national law and their obligations under the relevant international instruments in this field, in particular where the child would otherwise be stateless.

Article 8

1.   States Parties undertake to respect the right of the child to preserve his or her identity, including nationality, name and family relations as recognized by law without unlawful interference.
2.   Where a child is illegally deprived of some or all of the elements of his or her identity, States Parties shall provide appropriate assistance and protection, with a view to re-establishing speedily his or her identity.

Article 9

1.   States Parties shall ensure that a child shall not be separated from his or her parents against their will, except when competent authorities subject to judicial review determine, in accordance with applicable law and procedures, that such separation is necessary for the best interests of the child. Such determination may be necessary in a particular case such as one involving abuse or neglect of the child by the parents, or one where the parents are living separately and a decision must be made as to the child's place of residence.
2.   In any proceedings pursuant to paragraph 1 of the present article, all interested parties shall be given an opportunity to participate in the proceedings and make their views known.
3.   States Parties shall respect the right of the child who is separated from one or both parents to maintain personal relations and direct contact with both parents on a regular basis, except if it is contrary to the child's best interests.
4.   Where such separation results from any action initiated by a State Party, such as the detention, imprisonment, exile, deportation or death (including death arising from any cause while the person is in the custody of the State) of one or both parents or of the child, that State Party shall, upon request, provide the parents, the child or, if appropriate, another member of the family with the essential information concerning the whereabouts of the absent member(s) of the family unless the provision of the information would be detrimental to the well-being of the child. States Parties shall further ensure that the submission of such a request shall of itself entail no adverse consequences for the person(s) concerned.

Article 10

1.   In accordance with the obligation of States Parties under article 9, paragraph 1, applications by a child or his or her parents to enter or leave a State Party for the purpose of family reunification shall be dealt with by States Parties in a positive, humane and expeditious manner. States Parties shall further ensure that the submission of such a request shall entail no adverse consequences for the applicants and for the members of their family.
2.   A child whose parents reside in different States shall have the right to maintain on a regular basis, save in exceptional circumstances personal relations and direct contacts with both parents. Towards that end and in accordance with the obligation of States Parties under article 9, paragraph 1, States Parties shall respect the right of the child and his or her parents to leave any country, including their own and to enter their own

country. The right to leave any country shall be subject only to such restrictions as are prescribed by law and which are necessary to protect the national security, public order (ordre public), public health or morals or the rights and freedoms of others and are consistent with the other rights recognized in the present Convention.

Article 11

1. States Parties shall take measures to combat the illicit transfer and non-return of children abroad.
2. To this end, States Parties shall promote the conclusion of bilateral or multilateral agreements or accession to existing agreements.

Article 12

1. States Parties shall assure to the child who is capable of forming his or her own views the right to express those views freely in all matters affecting the child, the views of the child being given due weight in accordance with the age and maturity of the child.
2. For this purpose, the child shall in particular be provided the opportunity to be heard in any judicial and administrative proceedings affecting the child, either directly, or through a representative or an appropriate body, in a manner consistent with the procedural rules of national law.

Article 13

1. The child shall have the right to freedom of expression; this right shall include freedom to seek, receive and impart information and ideas of all kinds, regardless of frontiers, either orally, in writing or in print, in the form of art, or through any other media of the child's choice.
2. The exercise of this right may be subject to certain restrictions, but these shall only be such as are provided by law and are necessary:
    (a)   For respect of the rights or reputations of others; or
    (b)   For the protection of national security or of public order (ordre public), or of public health or morals.

Article 14

1. States Parties shall respect the right of the child to freedom of thought, conscience and religion.
2. States Parties shall respect the rights and duties of the parents and, when applicable, legal guardians, to provide direction to the child in the exercise of his or her right in a manner consistent with the evolving capacities of the child.
3. Freedom to manifest one's religion or beliefs may be subject only to such limitations as are prescribed by law and are necessary to protect public safety, order, health or morals, or the fundamental rights and freedoms of others.

Article 15

1.   States Parties recognize the rights of the child to freedom of association and to freedom of peaceful assembly.
2.   No restrictions may be placed on the exercise of these rights other than those imposed in conformity with the law and which are necessary in a democratic society in the interests of national security or public safety, public order (ordre public), the protection of public health or morals or the protection of the rights and freedoms of others.

Article 16

1.   No child shall be subjected to arbitrary or unlawful interference with his or her privacy, family, home or correspondence, nor to unlawful attacks on his or her honour and reputation.
2.   The child has the right to the protection of the law against such interference or attacks.

Article 17

States Parties recognize the important function performed by the mass media and shall ensure that the child has access to information and material from a diversity of national and international sources, especially those aimed at the promotion of his or her social, spiritual and moral well-being and physical and mental health. To this end, States Parties shall:

(a)   Encourage the mass media to disseminate information and material of social and cultural benefit to the child and in accordance with the spirit of article 29;
(b)   Encourage international co-operation in the production, exchange and dissemination of such information and material from a diversity of cultural, national and international sources;
(c)   Encourage the production and dissemination of children's books;
(d)   Encourage the mass media to have particular regard to the linguistic needs of the child who belongs to a minority group or who is indigenous;
(e)   Encourage the development of appropriate guidelines for the protection of the child from information and material injurious to his or her well-being, bearing in mind the provisions of articles 13 and 18.

Article 18

1.   States Parties shall use their best efforts to ensure recognition of the principle that both parents have common responsibilities for the upbringing and development of the child. Parents or, as the case may be, legal guardians, have the primary responsibility for the upbringing and development of the child. The best interests of the child will be their basic concern.
2.   For the purpose of guaranteeing and promoting the rights set forth in the present Convention, States Parties shall render appropriate assistance to parents and legal guardians in the performance of their child-rearing responsibilities and shall ensure the development of institutions, facilities and services for the care of children.

3. States Parties shall take all appropriate measures to ensure that children of working parents have the right to benefit from child-care services and facilities for which they are eligible.

Article 19

1. States Parties shall take all appropriate legislative, administrative, social and educational measures to protect the child from all forms of physical or mental violence, injury or abuse, neglect or negligent treatment, maltreatment or exploitation, including sexual abuse, while in the care of parent(s), legal guardian(s) or any other person who has the care of the child.
2. Such protective measures should, as appropriate, include effective procedures for the establishment of social programmes to provide necessary support for the child and for those who have the care of the child, as well as for other forms of prevention and for identification, reporting, referral, investigation, treatment and follow-up of instances of child maltreatment described heretofore, and, as appropriate, for judicial involvement.

Article 20

1. A child temporarily or permanently deprived of his or her family environment, or in whose own best interests cannot be allowed to remain in that environment, shall be entitled to special protection and assistance provided by the State.
2. States Parties shall in accordance with their national laws ensure alternative care for such a child.
3. Such care could include, inter alia, foster placement, kafalah of Islamic law, adoption or if necessary placement in suitable institutions for the care of children. When considering solutions, due regard shall be paid to the desirability of continuity in a child's upbringing and to the child's ethnic, religious, cultural and linguistic background.

Article 21

States Parties that recognize and/or permit the system of adoption shall ensure that the best interests of the child shall be the paramount consideration and they shall:

(a) Ensure that the adoption of a child is authorized only by competent authorities who determine, in accordance with applicable law and procedures and on the basis of all pertinent and reliable information, that the adoption is permissible in view of the child's status concerning parents, relatives and legal guardians and that, if required, the persons concerned have given their informed consent to the adoption on the basis of such counselling as may be necessary;
(b) Recognize that inter-country adoption may be considered as an alternative means of child's care, if the child cannot be placed in a foster or an adoptive family or cannot in any suitable manner be cared for in the child's country of origin;
(c) Ensure that the child concerned by inter-country adoption enjoys safeguards and standards equivalent to those existing in the case of national adoption;

(d)   Take all appropriate measures to ensure that, in inter-country adoption, the placement does not result in improper financial gain for those involved in it;

(e)   Promote, where appropriate, the objectives of the present article by concluding bilateral or multilateral arrangements or agreements and endeavour, within this framework, to ensure that the placement of the child in another country is carried out by competent authorities or organs.

Article 22

1.   States Parties shall take appropriate measures to ensure that a child who is seeking refugee status or who is considered a refugee in accordance with applicable international or domestic law and procedures shall, whether unaccompanied or accompanied by his or her parents or by any other person, receive appropriate protection and humanitarian assistance in the enjoyment of applicable rights set forth in the present Convention and in other international human rights or humanitarian instruments to which the said States are Parties.

2.   For this purpose, States Parties shall provide, as they consider appropriate, co-operation in any efforts by the United Nations and other competent intergovernmental organizations or non-governmental organizations co-operating with the United Nations to protect and assist such a child and to trace the parents or other members of the family of any refugee child in order to obtain information necessary for reunification with his or her family. In cases where no parents or other members of the family can be found, the child shall be accorded the same protection as any other child permanently or temporarily deprived of his or her family environment for any reason, as set forth in the present Convention.

Article 23

1.   States Parties recognize that a mentally or physically disabled child should enjoy a full and decent life, in conditions which ensure dignity, promote self-reliance and facilitate the child's active participation in the community.

2.   States Parties recognize the right of the disabled child to special care and shall encourage and ensure the extension, subject to available resources, to the eligible child and those responsible for his or her care, of assistance for which application is made and which is appropriate to the child's condition and to the circumstances of the parents or others caring for the child.

3.   Recognizing the special needs of a disabled child, assistance extended in accordance with paragraph 2 of the present article shall be provided free of charge, whenever possible, taking into account the financial resources of the parents or others caring for the child, and shall be designed to ensure that the disabled child has effective access to and receives education, training, health care services, rehabilitation services, preparation for employment and recreation opportunities in a manner conducive to the child's achieving the fullest possible social integration and individual development, including his or her cultural and spiritual development

4.   States Parties shall promote, in the spirit of international cooperation, the exchange of appropriate information in the field of preventive health care and of medical, psychological and functional treatment of disabled children, including dissemination of and

access to information concerning methods of rehabilitation, education and vocational services, with the aim of enabling States Parties to improve their capabilities and skills and to widen their experience in these areas. In this regard, particular account shall be taken of the needs of developing countries.

Article 24

1.   States Parties recognize the right of the child to the enjoyment of the highest attainable standard of health and to facilities for the treatment of illness and rehabilitation of health. States Parties shall strive to ensure that no child is deprived of his or her right of access to such health care services.

2.   States Parties shall pursue full implementation of this right and, in particular, shall take appropriate measures:

    (a)   To diminish infant and child mortality;

    (b)   To ensure the provision of necessary medical assistance and health care to all children with emphasis on the development of primary health care;

    (c)   To combat disease and malnutrition, including within the framework of primary health care, through, inter alia, the application of readily available technology and through the provision of adequate nutritious foods and clean drinking-water, taking into consideration the dangers and risks of environmental pollution;

    (d)   To ensure appropriate pre-natal and post-natal health care for mothers;

    (e)   To ensure that all segments of society, in particular parents and children, are informed, have access to education and are supported in the use of basic knowledge of child health and nutrition, the advantages of breastfeeding, hygiene and environmental sanitation and the prevention of accidents;

    (f)   To develop preventive health care, guidance for parents and family planning education and services.

3.   States Parties shall take all effective and appropriate measures with a view to abolishing traditional practices prejudicial to the health of children.

4.   States Parties undertake to promote and encourage international co-operation with a view to achieving progressively the full realization of the right recognized in the present article. In this regard, particular account shall be taken of the needs of developing countries.

Article 25

States Parties recognize the right of a child who has been placed by the competent authorities for the purposes of care, protection or treatment of his or her physical or mental health, to a periodic review of the treatment provided to the child and all other circumstances relevant to his or her placement.

Article 26

1.   States Parties shall recognize for every child the right to benefit from social security, including social insurance, and shall take the necessary measures to achieve the full realization of this right in accordance with their national law.

2.   The benefits should, where appropriate, be granted, taking into account the resources and the circumstances of the child and persons having responsibility for the maintenance of the child, as well as any other consideration relevant to an application for benefits made by or on behalf of the child.

Article 27

1.   States Parties recognize the right of every child to a standard of living adequate for the child's physical, mental, spiritual, moral and social development.

2.   The parent(s) or others responsible for the child have the primary responsibility to secure, within their abilities and financial capacities, the conditions of living necessary for the child's development.

3.   States Parties, in accordance with national conditions and within their means, shall take appropriate measures to assist parents and others responsible for the child to implement this right and shall in case of need provide material assistance and support programmes, particularly with regard to nutrition, clothing and housing.

4.   States Parties shall take all appropriate measures to secure the recovery of maintenance for the child from the parents or other persons having financial responsibility for the child, both within the State Party and from abroad. In particular, where the person having financial responsibility for the child lives in a State different from that of the child, States Parties shall promote the accession to international agreements or the conclusion of such agreements, as well as the making of other appropriate arrangements.

Article 28

1.   States Parties recognize the right of the child to education and with a view to achieving this right progressively and on the basis of equal opportunity, they shall, in particular:
    (a)   Make primary education compulsory and available free to all;
    (b)   Encourage the development of different forms of secondary education, including general and vocational education, make them available and accessible to every child and take appropriate measures such as the introduction of free education and offering financial assistance in case of need;
    (c)   Make higher education accessible to all on the basis of capacity by every appropriate means;
    (d)   Make educational and vocational information and guidance available and accessible to all children;
    (e)   Take measures to encourage regular attendance at schools and the reduction of drop-out rates.

2.   States Parties shall take all appropriate measures to ensure that school discipline is administered in a manner consistent with the child's human dignity and in conformity with the present Convention.

3.   States Parties shall promote and encourage international cooperation in matters relating to education, in particular with a view to contributing to the elimination of ignorance and illiteracy throughout the world and facilitating access to scientific and technical knowledge and modern teaching methods. In this regard, particular account shall be taken of the needs of developing countries.

Article 29

1. States Parties agree that the education of the child shall be directed to:
   (a) The development of the child's personality, talents and mental and physical abilities to their fullest potential;
   (b) The development of respect for human rights and fundamental freedoms, and for the principles enshrined in the Charter of the United Nations;
   (c) The development of respect for the child's parents, his or her own cultural identity, language and values, for the national values of the country in which the child is living, the country from which he or she may originate, and for civilizations different from his or her own;
   (d) The preparation of the child for responsible life in a free society, in the spirit of understanding, peace, tolerance, equality of sexes, and friendship among all peoples, ethnic, national and religious groups and persons of indigenous origin;
   (e) The development of respect for the natural environment.
2. No part of the present article or article 28 shall be construed so as to interfere with the liberty of individuals and bodies to establish and direct educational institutions, subject always to the observance of the principle set forth in paragraph 1 of the present article and to the requirements that the education given in such institutions shall conform to such minimum standards as may be laid down by the State.

Article 30

In those States in which ethnic, religious or linguistic minorities or persons of indigenous origin exist, a child belonging to such a minority or who is indigenous shall not be denied the right, in community with other members of his or her group, to enjoy his or her own culture, to profess and practise his or her own religion, or to use his or her own language.

Article 31

1. States Parties recognize the right of the child to rest and leisure, to engage in play and recreational activities appropriate to the age of the child and to participate freely in cultural life and the arts.
2. States Parties shall respect and promote the right of the child to participate fully in cultural and artistic life and shall encourage the provision of appropriate and equal opportunities for cultural, artistic, recreational and leisure activity.

Article 32

1. States Parties recognize the right of the child to be protected from economic exploitation and from performing any work that is likely to be hazardous or to interfere with the child's education, or to be harmful to the child's health or physical, mental, spiritual, moral or social development.
2. States Parties shall take legislative, administrative, social and educational measures to ensure the implementation of the present article. To this end and having regard to the relevant provisions of other international instruments, States Parties shall in particular:

(a)   Provide for a minimum age or minimum ages for admission to employment;
(b)   Provide for appropriate regulation of the hours and conditions of employment;
(c)   Provide for appropriate penalties or other sanctions to ensure the effective enforcement of the present article.

Article 33

States Parties shall take all appropriate measures, including legislative, administrative, social and educational measures, to protect children from the illicit use of narcotic drugs and psychotropic substances as defined in the relevant international treaties and to prevent the use of children in the illicit production and trafficking of such substances.

Article 34

States Parties undertake to protect the child from all forms of sexual exploitation and sexual abuse. For these purposes, States Parties shall in particular take all appropriate national, bilateral and multilateral measures to prevent:

(a)   The inducement or coercion of a child to engage in any unlawful sexual activity;
(b)   The exploitative use of children in prostitution or other unlawful sexual practices;
(c)   The exploitative use of children in pornographic performances and materials.

Article 35

States Parties shall take all appropriate national, bilateral and multilateral measures to prevent the abduction of, the sale of or traffic in children for any purpose or in any form.

Article 36

States Parties shall protect the child against all other forms of exploitation prejudicial to any aspects of the child's welfare.

Article 37

States Parties shall ensure that:

(a)   No child shall be subjected to torture or other cruel, inhuman or degrading treatment or punishment. Neither capital punishment nor life imprisonment without possibility of release shall be imposed for offences committed by persons below eighteen years of age;
(b)   No child shall be deprived of his or her liberty unlawfully or arbitrarily. The arrest, detention or imprisonment of a child shall be in conformity with the law and shall be used only as a measure of last resort and for the shortest appropriate period of time;

(c) Every child deprived of liberty shall be treated with humanity and respect for the inherent dignity of the human person and in a manner which takes into account the needs of persons of his or her age. In particular, every child deprived of liberty shall be separated from adults unless it is considered in the child's best interest not to do so and shall have the right to maintain contact with his or her family through correspondence and visits, save in exceptional circumstances;

(d) Every child deprived of his or her liberty shall have the right to prompt access to legal and other appropriate assistance, as well as the right to challenge the legality of the deprivation of his or her liberty before a court or other competent, independent and impartial authority and to a prompt decision on any such action.

Article 38

1. States Parties undertake to respect and to ensure respect for rules of international humanitarian law applicable to them in armed conflicts which are relevant to the child.

2. States Parties shall take all feasible measures to ensure that persons who have not attained the age of fifteen years do not take a direct part in hostilities.

3. States Parties shall refrain from recruiting any person who has not attained the age of fifteen years into their armed forces. In recruiting among those persons who have attained the age of fifteen years but who have not attained the age of eighteen years, States Parties shall endeavour to give priority to those who are oldest.

4. In accordance with their obligations under international humanitarian law to protect the civilian population in armed conflicts, States Parties shall take all feasible measures to ensure protection and care of children who are affected by an armed conflict.

Article 39

States Parties shall take all appropriate measures to promote physical and psychological recovery and social reintegration of a child victim of: any form of neglect, exploitation, or abuse; torture or any other form of cruel, inhuman or degrading treatment or punishment; or armed conflicts. Such recovery and reintegration shall take place in an environment which fosters the health, self-respect and dignity of the child.

Article 40

1. States Parties recognize the right of every child alleged as, accused of, or recognized as having infringed the penal law to be treated in a manner consistent with the promotion of the child's sense of dignity and worth, which reinforces the child's respect for the human rights and fundamental freedoms of others and which takes into account the child's age and the desirability of promoting the child's reintegration and the child's assuming a constructive role in society.

2. To this end and having regard to the relevant provisions of international instruments, States Parties shall, in particular, ensure that:

(a)   No child shall be alleged as, be accused of, or recognized as having infringed the penal law by reason of acts or omissions that were not prohibited by national or international law at the time they were committed;

(b)   Every child alleged as or accused of having infringed the penal law has at least the following guarantees:

    (i)   To be presumed innocent until proven guilty according to law;

    (ii)   To be informed promptly and directly of the charges against him or her, and, if appropriate, through his or her parents or legal guardians and to have legal or other appropriate assistance in the preparation and presentation of his or her defence;

    (iii)   To have the matter determined without delay by a competent, independent and impartial authority or judicial body in a fair hearing according to law, in the presence of legal or other appropriate assistance and, unless it is considered not to be in the best interest of the child, in particular, taking into account his or her age or situation, his or her parents or legal guardians;

    (iv)   Not to be compelled to give testimony or to confess guilt; to examine or have examined adverse witnesses and to obtain the participation and examination of witnesses on his or her behalf under conditions of equality;

    (v)   If considered to have infringed the penal law, to have this decision and any measures imposed in consequence thereof reviewed by a higher competent, independent and impartial authority or judicial body according to law;

    (vi)   To have the free assistance of an interpreter if the child cannot understand or speak the language used;

    (vii)   To have his or her privacy fully respected at all stages of the proceedings.

3.   States Parties shall seek to promote the establishment of laws, procedures, authorities and institutions specifically applicable to children alleged as, accused of, or recognized as having infringed the penal law, and, in particular:

(a)   The establishment of a minimum age below which children shall be presumed not to have the capacity to infringe the penal law;

(b)   Whenever appropriate and desirable, measures for dealing with such children without resorting to judicial proceedings, providing that human rights and legal safeguards are fully respected.

4.   A variety of dispositions, such as care, guidance and supervision orders; counselling; probation; foster care; education and vocational training programmes and other alternatives to institutional care shall be available to ensure that children are dealt with in a manner appropriate to their well-being and proportionate both to their circumstances and the offence.

Article 41

Nothing in the present Convention shall affect any provisions which are more conducive to the realization of the rights of the child and which may be contained in:

(a)   The law of a State party; or

(b)   International law in force for that State.

Part II

Article 42

States Parties undertake to make the principles and provisions of the Convention widely known, by appropriate and active means, to adults and children alike.

Article 43

1. For the purpose of examining the progress made by States Parties in achieving the realization of the obligations undertaken in the present Convention, there shall be established a Committee on the Rights of the Child, which shall carry out the functions hereinafter provided.
2. The Committee shall consist of ten experts of high moral standing and recognized competence in the field covered by this Convention. The members of the Committee shall be elected by States Parties from among their nationals and shall serve in their personal capacity, consideration being given to equitable geographical distribution, as well as to the principal legal systems.
3. The members of the Committee shall be elected by secret ballot from a list of persons nominated by States Parties. Each State Party may nominate one person from among its own nationals.
4. The initial election to the Committee shall be held no later than six months after the date of the entry into force of the present Convention and thereafter every second year. At least four months before the date of each election, the Secretary-General of the United Nations shall address a letter to States Parties inviting them to submit their nominations within two months. The Secretary-General shall subsequently prepare a list in alphabetical order of all persons thus nominated, indicating States Parties which have nominated them and shall submit it to the States Parties to the present Convention.
5. The elections shall be held at meetings of States Parties convened by the Secretary-General at United Nations Headquarters. At those meetings, for which two thirds of States Parties shall constitute a quorum, the persons elected to the Committee shall be those who obtain the largest number of votes and an absolute majority of the votes of the representatives of States Parties present and voting.
6. The members of the Committee shall be elected for a term of four years. They shall be eligible for re-election if renominated. The term of five of the members elected at the first election shall expire at the end of two years; immediately after the first election, the names of these five members shall be chosen by lot by the Chairman of the meeting.
7. If a member of the Committee dies or resigns or declares that for any other cause he or she can no longer perform the duties of the Committee, the State Party which nominated the member shall appoint another expert from among its nationals to serve for the remainder of the term, subject to the approval of the Committee.
8. The Committee shall establish its own rules of procedure.
9. The Committee shall elect its officers for a period of two years.
10. The meetings of the Committee shall normally be held at United Nations Headquarters or at any other convenient place as determined by the Committee. The Committee shall normally meet annually. The duration of the meetings of the Committee shall be determined and reviewed, if necessary, by a meeting of the States Parties to the present Convention, subject to the approval of the General Assembly.

11.   The Secretary-General of the United Nations shall provide the necessary staff and facilities for the effective performance of the functions of the Committee under the present Convention.

12.   With the approval of the General Assembly, the members of the Committee established under the present Convention shall receive emoluments from United Nations resources on such terms and conditions as the Assembly may decide.

Article 44

1.   States Parties undertake to submit to the Committee, through the Secretary-General of the United Nations, reports on the measures they have adopted which give effect to the rights recognized herein and on the progress made on the enjoyment of those rights:
   (a)   Within two years of the entry into force of the Convention for the State Party concerned;
   (b)   Thereafter every five years.

2.   Reports made under the present article shall indicate factors and difficulties, if any, affecting the degree of fulfilment of the obligations under the present Convention. Reports shall also contain sufficient information to provide the Committee with a comprehensive understanding of the implementation of the Convention in the country concerned.

3.   A State Party which has submitted a comprehensive initial report to the Committee need not, in its subsequent reports submitted in accordance with paragraph 1 (b) of the present article, repeat basic information previously provided.

4.   The Committee may request from States Parties further information relevant to the implementation of the Convention.

5.   The Committee shall submit to the General Assembly, through the Economic and Social Council, every two years, reports on its activities.

6.   States Parties shall make their reports widely available to the public in their own countries.

Article 45

In order to foster the effective implementation of the Convention and to encourage international co-operation in the field covered by the Convention:

(a)   The specialized agencies, the United Nations Children's Fund and other United Nations organs shall be entitled to be represented at the consideration of the implementation of such provisions of the present Convention as fall within the scope of their mandate. The Committee may invite the specialized agencies, the United Nations Children's Fund and other competent bodies as it may consider appropriate to provide expert advice on the implementation of the Convention in areas falling within the scope of their respective mandates. The Committee may invite the specialized agencies, the United Nations Children's Fund and other United Nations organs to submit reports on the implementation of the Convention in areas falling within the scope of their activities;

(b)   The Committee shall transmit, as it may consider appropriate, to the specialized agencies, the United Nations Children's Fund and other competent bodies, any reports from States Parties that contain a request, or indicate a need, for technical advice or assistance, along with the Committee's observations and suggestions, if any, on these requests or indications;

(c)   The Committee may recommend to the General Assembly to request the Secretary-General to undertake on its behalf studies on specific issues relating to the rights of the child;

(d)   The Committee may make suggestions and general recommendations based on information received pursuant to articles 44 and 45 of the present Convention. Such suggestions and general recommendations shall be transmitted to any State Party concerned and reported to the General Assembly, together with comments, if any, from States Parties.

Part III

Article 46

The present Convention shall be open for signature by all States.

Article 47

The present Convention is subject to ratification. Instruments of ratification shall be deposited with the Secretary-General of the United Nations.

Article 48

The present Convention shall remain open for accession by any State. The instruments of accession shall be deposited with the Secretary-General of the United Nations.

Article 49

1.   The present Convention shall enter into force on the thirtieth day following the date of deposit with the Secretary-General of the United Nations of the twentieth instrument of ratification or accession.

2.   For each State ratifying or acceding to the Convention after the deposit of the twentieth instrument of ratification or accession, the Convention shall enter into force on the thirtieth day after the deposit by such State of its instrument of ratification or accession.

Article 50

1.   Any State Party may propose an amendment and file it with the Secretary-General of the United Nations. The Secretary-General shall thereupon communicate the proposed amendment to States Parties, with a request that they indicate whether they favour a conference of States Parties for the purpose of considering and voting upon the

proposals. In the event that, within four months from the date of such communication, at least one third of the States Parties favour such a conference, the Secretary-General shall convene the conference under the auspices of the United Nations. Any amendment adopted by a majority of States Parties present and voting at the conference shall be submitted to the General Assembly for approval.

2.   An amendment adopted in accordance with paragraph 1 of the present article shall enter into force when it has been approved by the General Assembly of the United Nations and accepted by a two-thirds majority of States Parties.

3.   When an amendment enters into force, it shall be binding on those States Parties which have accepted it, other States Parties still being bound by the provisions of the present Convention and any earlier amendments which they have accepted.

Article 51

1.   The Secretary-General of the United Nations shall receive and circulate to all States the text of reservations made by States at the time of ratification or accession.

2.   A reservation incompatible with the object and purpose of the present Convention shall not be permitted.

3.   Reservations may be withdrawn at any time by notification to that effect addressed to the Secretary-General of the United Nations, who shall then inform all States. Such notification shall take effect on the date on which it is received by the Secretary-General.

Article 52

A State Party may denounce the present Convention by written notification to the Secretary-General of the United Nations. Denunciation becomes effective one year after the date of receipt of the notification by the Secretary-General.

Article 53

The Secretary-General of the United Nations is designated as the depositary of the present Convention.

Article 54

The original of the present Convention, of which the Arabic, Chinese, English, French, Russian and Spanish texts are equally authentic, shall be deposited with the Secretary-General of the United Nations.

In witness thereof the undersigned plenipotentiaries, being duly authorized thereto by their respective governments, have signed the present Convention.

Chapter 23

Hugh Cunningham

SAVING THE CHILDREN, c.1830–c.1920

GOVERNMENTS AND PHILANTHROPISTS, as we have seen, had for centuries formulated and operated policies towards children. Why should the period between 1830 and 1920 be marked out for separate treatment? The answer is that for a significant number of reformers the purpose of a policy towards children was lifted clear of its old moorings: until the nineteenth century policies had been drawn up with a concern either for the child's soul or for the future manpower needs of the state. Both of these concerns remained in place in the nineteenth and early twentieth centuries, but they were joined by a new one, a concern to save children for the enjoyment of childhood. The ideology of childhood, the emergence of which was traced in Chapter 3 [see original reading], now began to influence public action.

Philanthropy was central to this child-saving activity. Philanthropists opened and ran homes for orphans and other neglected children, they organised schemes of emigration, they set up kindergartens and schools, they founded societies for the prevention of cruelty to children, and they had numerous programmes for visiting the poor. Although these things are not susceptible to measurement, there can be little doubt that this was on a scale greater than in the eighteenth century, and, outside some urban communities, than in the sixteenth or seventeenth centuries. It stands indeed in marked contrast to that decline of charity observable at least in France in the eighteenth century.

Who were these philanthropists and what impelled them to action? They certainly differed from those moved to charitable activity in earlier centuries who believed that the giving of gifts to the poor was a vital contribution to their own salvation. And yet the vast majority of them were Christian, normally quite explicitly so, both in their own lives and in the organisations which they established. Denominational rivalry had a part to play in impelling them to action, but no more than a part. Much more important was a missionary zeal to reach out to people who, in the slums of the new big cities of an industrialising world, seemed as heathen as the 'savages' of Africa or Polynesia. Of course this missionary zeal had its limits: a rank fear of 'the dangerous classes' sometimes surfaced alarmingly; Shaftesbury in 1840 saw 'the two great demons in morals and politics, Socialism and Chartism ... stalking through the land', and urged as a preventative that the neglect of children be ended. Leading Christian philanthropists in Europe, W.H. Suringar in the Netherlands and J.H. Wichern in

Germany, both at the forefront of efforts to reclaim neglected children, invoked similar fears.[1] The voicing of these anxieties about revolution was perhaps as much a rhetorical device to stir up the apathetic as a motivating force for the active philanthropist, but the latter certainly had no desire to upset the existing social order, rather to re-enforce it. Philanthropists were not utopians or revolutionaries, and they worked with the grain of the economic, social and political structures of their times. It was this which gave them power and leverage. From time to time, of course, they exposed themselves to criticism: Henry Mayhew could argue that the Ragged Schools of nineteenth-century London contributed to rather than diminished the crime rate; more powerful critics could raise questions over the policies and practices of philanthropists in transporting children to Canada; both Barnardo's and the British National Society for the Prevention of Cruelty to Children were subject to serious criticisms of the scope and direction of their activities.[2] But by and large philanthropic organisations concerned with children received a favourable press, and were accepted both in the communities in which they worked and in society at large.

Children were not the only people to be on the receiving end of nineteenth-century philanthropy, but they featured largely in philanthropic plans. Children were thought to be unformed enough to be savable. They represented the future. Their 'plastic natures', thought the Boston Children's Friend Society, 'may be molded into images of perfect beauty, or as perfect repulsiveness'.[3] And it was relatively easy to tap the pockets of the public by a senti-mental appeal on their behalf. Moreover, women played an increasingly important role in philanthropy in the nineteenth century, and it seemed both natural and politically safe that they should focus their work on charity towards children. In England in 1893 it was estimated that there were 500,000 women working 'continuously and semi-professionally' in philan-thropy, and many of them were involved in charities for children.[4]

In the philanthropic/missionary discourse we can often sense shock at the distance between the actuality and ideals of childhood as experienced within the middle and upper classes, and what they observed within the mission field. They saw 'children without child-hood'. The essentially romantic rather than Christian view of childhood as properly protected and dependent, and separate from adulthood, which had become dominant in the first half of the nineteenth century, provided a motivating reference point for any philanthropist. 'The ideal we place before us', wrote an American Progressive, Edward T. Devine, in 1910, 'is a protected childhood.' We can see this ideal in action in Florence Davenport-Hill's response to children in workhouses: 'It is painful to set aside our ideal of a childhood of innocence and bright playfulness, and to realise that there are among us thousands of children familiar with shocking vice ... '; her remedy, of course, was to try to place these children in an environ-ment where 'innocence and bright playfulness' could flourish.[5]

This view of childhood can be seen as a motivating influence in many countries from about the 1830s. In their study of charity for children in nineteenth-century British North America Patricia Rooke and R.L. Schnell argue that most of the ingredients of what we think of as a modern concept of childhood were present before the 1880s. There were in place policies which emphasised the need for protection and segregation of children and for making them dependent. All that was lacking was delaying the responsibilities of these children, for they were indeed expected to contribute to the economy at an early age. If this was true of Canada, it was even more the case for Britain which provided a number of models for policies towards children taken over by the Canadians.[6]

In trying to promote this view of childhood philanthropists aimed to immerse children in 'networks of good influence'.[7] Put another way, many working-class children came under some sort of surveillance or control by philanthropic organisations. Philanthropy had opened up huge areas for public intervention into working-class life – for, though its work rarely involved the state, it was emphatically public rather than private.

Philanthropists, however, were not the only people acting in the public sphere with a concern for children. Sometimes a distinction is drawn between a period of child rescue lasting from about the middle of the nineteenth century for some thirty years, and a more ambitious and far-reaching child-saving period from the 1880s onwards. Linked to this is the view that child rescue was primarily a task for philanthropists and voluntary agencies, and that in child-saving there was a more pronounced role for government and for a growing body of professionals concerned with childhood. Certainly in the period beginning in the 1880s there was a tipping of the balance in action on behalf of children from philanthropy to the state, and a growing involvement of professionals and experts in the task of saving the children. By the end of the century it was coming to be felt that only state action could secure a childhood for all children, and states began to take over from philanthropy the key role in so doing. In giving their impetus to 'saving the child', states had a variety of motivations, besides those which could be called child-oriented: concern about population levels; worry about the level of 'civilisation' of the masses; desire to breed a race capable of competing in the twentieth century. 'Saving the children' involved moving them somewhere close to the centre of the political agenda of the modern state.

Child labour

Child labour in Britain in the new conditions of the industrial revolution first brought the new ideology of childhood into play as a factor in policy-making. The regulation and control of child labour dates back centuries with an assumption that most children's first experience as full-time workers would be as servants or apprentices – that is to say, they would be living outside the parental home. Regulations defining the responsibilities of both masters and servants or apprentices had the full force of law. In addition the state had a responsibility to find apprenticeships for the children brought up in its care. What is sometimes seen as the first Factory Act in Britain in 1802 is better described as one of a long series of apprenticeship acts, seeking in this instance to protect pauper apprentices in the cotton mills. It was not therefore the principle of state intervention in the child labour market which was the novelty of the period beginning in 1830; that principle was well established. The novelty was the first voicing of the assertion that children had a right not to work at all.

That assertion had a long gestation period of some fifty years. From about 1780 we can begin to hear people questioning the prevalent assumption that children in poverty should be inured to work from an early age. In 1766 Jonas Hanway, in (significant title) *An Earnest Appeal for Mercy to the Children of the Poor*, had urged that when poor children were apprenticed out, 'it should be considered how to make labor as pleasant, or to speak more to the heart, as little *irksome* as possible, and with a tender regard to the measure of a young person's strength of body or mind'.[8] Hanway was a mercantilist, fully alive to the importance of training young people for the future service of the state, but he clearly doubted the sense of Locke's view, still being cited as authoritative, that poor children should be put to work at the age of three, with a 'bellyful of bread daily' supplemented by, in cold weather, 'if it be thought needful, a little warm water-gruel'.[9] Hanway also took up the cause of the boys and the occasional girl who were employed cleaning chimneys. Thanks very largely to Hanway, the cruelty inflicted on the children began to be recognized: they had to be induced up the chimneys by pin pricks on their feet or by a fire lit in the grate; and if they avoided death by suffocation they were peculiarly liable to cancer of the scrotum. Hanway's *A Sentimental History of Chimney Sweepers* of 1785 did more than simply set forth these cruelties; it embellished them in a rhetoric in which Hanway worked on people's sentiments, appealing to humanity, to Christianity, to pity, to compassion, to reason, to passion, and to national honour and traditions. Climbing boys were 'as children', he wrote, 'objects of our mercy and tenderest kindness'. Hanway was the initiator of a genre of literature which marked out the climbing boys as the epitome of exploitation, stolen and sold like slaves, all the more scandalous because, as a Sheffield campaigner wrote in the 1830s, '*They* are, of all human beings, the most lovely, the most engaging, the most of all others claiming protection, comfort, and love. They are CHILDREN.'[10]

Initially it was the damage to children's physique which attracted attention to the work of children in cotton factories. Alerted by an outbreak of fever in a cotton works, doctors in Lancashire in the 1780s laid down as an axiom that for children under fourteen 'the active recreations of childhood and youth are necessary to the growth, the vigour and the right conformation of the human body'. Childhood was being seen as at least in part a time for play. Without it children would not develop the bodily strength necessary for a successful adulthood, and in the cotton factories they were not receiving it. But over and above this utilitarian attitude there was an admixture of the sentimentalism which Hanway and the Romantic poets had legitimated. People began to be moved in curious ways by the sight of children at work; for most of the eighteenth century the response had been one of admiration for those who had organised such work, but by the end of the century people like Mrs Trimmer, an Evangelical who was not notably soft-hearted, found themselves unable to 'think of little children, who work in Manufactories, without the utmost commiseration'. Like the climbing boys, they began to be thought of as slaves, 'our poor little White-Slaves, the children in our cotton Factories', as S.T. Coleridge expressed it.[11]

Coleridge himself campaigned for an Act of Parliament to control the work of children. The 1802 Act had been largely concerned with pauper apprentices, but it soon became necessary to widen the focus to consider the so-called 'free labour' of children, that is the labour of children who were living in their families rather than being in the care of the state. The factories had begun to recruit such children. Critics poured scorn on the idea that this labour was in any sense 'free': 'If the labor were indeed free', wrote Coleridge, 'the contract would approach, on the one side, too near to suicide, on the other to manslaughter.' The Act of 1819, the first to address this 'free' labour, was something of a disappointment to reformers, but the campaign to improve conditions had a momentum which was not easily halted. It came to a head in the early 1830s, coinciding precisely with the campaigns for the emancipation of slaves in British colonies, part of its emotive force stemming from the claim that the British government seemed more concerned for the black than for the white slave, 'It is notorious', wrote Richard Oastler in 1833, 'that the health of the negro slave, of the adult felon, of the horse, of the ass, of the hare, of the rabbit, of the partridge, of the pheasant, of the cabbage, and of the strawberry, is protected by law; but at the same time, the Children of the Poor are unprotected by the law...'[12]

The government conceded that something had to be done, but was determined not to give in to the demands of the campaigners for a ten-hour day, for this would have had the effect of limiting the hours worked not only by children but also by adults; instead it focused on the children, banning work in factories by children under nine, and restricting the hours to eight a day for children up to the age of fourteen. Backing up the Act with an inspectorate, the government was effectively defining childhood as a period in which people needed protection by the law; and the period of childhood was carefully marked out by the utilitarian Royal Commission which had advised the government. The Commission argued that at the beginning of the fourteenth year 'the period of childhood, properly so called, ceases, and that of puberty is established, when the body becomes more capable of enduring protracted labour...' This physiological change coincided with a change in social status for

> in general at or about the fourteenth year young persons are no longer treated as children; they are not usually chastised by corporal punishment, and at the same

time an important change takes place in what may be termed their domestic condition. For the most part they cease to be under the complete control of their parents and guardians. They begin to retain a part of their wages. They frequently pay for their own lodging, board, and clothing. They usually make their own contracts, and are, in the proper sense of the words, free agents.

A child was becoming defined as someone who was not a 'free agent', who was dependent, and therefore in need of protection by law.[13] No children seemed more in need of protection than those who worked underground, hauling and pushing the coal wagons to the mine shaft. Another Royal Commission in 1842 not only described what happened, but included drawings of the children at work (Plate 4 [see original reading]), shocking contemporaries and standing ever since as an encapsulation of the conditions of child labour in the industrial revolution.

Government action was aimed in part against unscrupulous parents who would put their children to early and harmful work. Leonard Horner, the factory inspector, set the blame for what was going wrong in the factories at the feet of parents, and had little truck with paternal rights; 'If the father has his natural rights', he wrote, 'so has the child; and if the father robs him of these, the State must become his guardian, and restore them to him.' But alongside this willingness to contemplate an invasion of long-established parental rights went a recognition that economic forces were operating to the disadvantage of children; there was a strong demand for child labour. The Royal Commission saw that demand increasing 'in consequence of the tendency of improvements in machinery to throw more and more of the work upon children, to the displacement of adult labour'. That tendency, some thought, had causes 'as steady in their operation as a physical law'. Manufacturers, in competition with one another, would seek to reduce labour costs, and one way of doing that was to introduce machinery which could be operated by the cheapest labour, that of children. Defenders of the factory system pointed out how this was solving the problem which had been endemic for centuries, that of finding sufficient employment for children. But others, including the utilitarians, who had considerable influence on official thinking in Britain in the 1830s and 1840s, were forced to recognise that the hidden hand of capitalism might not always work to the benefit of all, and that there was a need for a corpus of law, reinforced by inspection, to prevent market forces from progressively employing more children and fewer adults.[14]

The extent to which market forces were already doing this needs emphasis. The young were crucial to the profitability of late eighteenth- and early nineteenth-century industry. In the British cotton industry in 1835 43 per cent of the workers were under eighteen. In the north-eastern United States the percentage of women and children in the manufacturing labour force rose from 10 per cent to 40 per cent from the early nineteenth century up to 1832. In 1852 in Manchester and Salford, 76 per cent of all fourteen-year-old girls and 61 per cent of all fourteen-year-old boys were employed in mills. In the words of a foreman in a wool mill in 1833, 'factories cannot be carried on without children … One effect of the present system is that children come to do the same work instead of the fathers; boys are worked in place of men.'[15] Nor was this process confined to the textile industry. When Henry Mayhew investigated the London artisan trades at mid-century, he found that the point put to him by the tailors and the boot and shoe makers and the woodworkers was not that machinery or technological innovation was leading to the substitution of child for adult labour: the cause lay rather in competition and the division of labour. Masters were driven to reduce their costs in order to survive. 'Twenty years ago', a small master in the woodworking trades told Mayhew, 'I don't think there was a young child at work in our business.' Now, 'our trade's come to such a pass that unless a man has children to help him he can't live at all'.[16] There seemed to be a process whereby competition drove down the cost of labour by the increasing use of child labour.

The utilitarians did not object to child labour in principle, only to its excess. Time in childhood, they argued, must be set aside for schooling and physical growth. But beyond that, and beyond a certain minimum age, there was no reason why children should not go to work and contribute to the family economy. Children therefore should be half-timers, half at work and half at school, a solution to the problem of factory work which won wide support in the middle decades of the nineteenth century. It was acceptable to Evangelicals like Lord Shaftesbury, one of the most passionate advocates of a Ten Hour Act, for his chief concern, as he never ceased to reiterate, was to ensure that children went to school.[17]

But for those touched by Romanticism a childhood in which children did any work at all was beginning to be seen as unnatural. The romantic view of childhood was widely disseminated and elaborated upon, and became embedded in the rhetoric of the factory movement of the 1830s and 1840s. Thus Philip Gaskell in his survey of factory conditions in his book *Artisans and Machinery* (1836) referred directly to Wordsworth's 'Intimations of Immortality from Recollections of Early Childhood' in writing that:

> It has been truly observed, and not less beautifully than truly, that 'heaven is around us in our infancy'. This might have been extended and said, that 'heaven is around and within us in our infancy', for the happiness of childhood springs full as much from an internal consciousness of delight, as from the novelty of its impressions from without. Its mind, providing the passions are properly guided, is indeed a fountain of all that is beautiful – all that is amiable – overflowing with joy and tenderness; and its young heart is a living laboratory of love, formed to be profusely scattered on all around.

Childhood here was a fountain irrigating the arid soils of adulthood. It came indeed to be seen as some recompense to mankind for the loss of Eden. It was, or should be, 'the weary life's long happy holyday', the archaic spelling of holiday emphasising the place which childhood had in God's plan for mankind.[18]

Armed with this kind of vision, the assertion of the rights of childhood became imbued with an emotional quality lacking in the utilitarian and evangelical perspectives. Reason gave precedence to feelings, and those feelings were brought to bear on children in the factories and mines and up the chimneys. Parental rights became as nothing in conflict with the rights of children. Indeed, the issue became not children versus parents, but children versus 'the factory system', a new and unnatural mode of production. Whereas in nature the young devoted their time to growing and playing, in human society, or at least in the factory system, the young were put to work. As Elizabeth Barrett Browning put it in 'The Cry of the Children',

> The young lambs are bleating in the meadows,
> The young birds are chirping in the nest,
> The young fawns are playing with the shadows,
> The young flowers are blowing toward the west –
> But the young, young children, O my brothers,
> They are weeping bitterly!
> They are weeping in the playtime of the others,
> In the country of the free.

To the English the offence against childhood was compounded by the fact that it was occurring in 'the country of the free' – in England. But in essence what Browning and others influenced by Romanticism were demanding was a childhood for all children everywhere which was in harmony with nature, and in which manual labour had no part. 'Ever a toiling *Child* doth make us sad', wrote Samuel Roberts of Sheffield in 1837. Three years later Douglas Jerrold, one of the founders of *Punch*, was to write of factory children that they were 'children without childhood'.[19] He did not need to elaborate: the romantics had helped to fix in the British mind an idea of what childhood should be.

Until the mid-nineteenth century the debates on child labour under industrialisation were concentrated in Britain. But as they industrialised, other countries also began to legislate to protect children. In France the 1841 Child Labour Law 'marked the emergence of a serious state concern with the supervision and protection of childhood'. Although this law was not very effectively implemented, it was followed up in the mid–late 1860s by 'a dramatic intensification of concern over child labor', which is partly explained by the historian of these events as stemming from the fact that a 'new understanding of childhood as a period to be prolonged and devoted to nurturing and education was a normative feature of the mentality of the comfortable classes in France by the late 1860s'.[20] The momentum of reform was only briefly interrupted by the events of 1870–71, and in 1874 France passed a Child Labour Law which set twelve as a minimum age for work. In Prussia the law of 1853 established twelve as the minimum age for employment in industry, with consistent enforcement only after a further act of 1878. In industrialised New England it was in the period from the 1840s that child labour laws were passed.[21] In industrialising countries, it may be asserted with some confidence, the crucial steps to control child labour were taken prior to the 1880s, and although utilitarian and evangelical arguments often helped shape the legislation, competing with them and influencing them was a growing belief that children should not work. When Progressives in the United States rather belatedly in the early twentieth century sought to move beyond a state to a federal response to child labour, they did so because, in the words of one spokesman, 'The term child labor is a paradox for when labor begins ... the child ceases to be'; and in the words of another, 'a child is industrially taboo' and 'to violate its rights is to touch profanely a holy thing'.[22] The magnitude of the shift that had been made needs emphasis; for most of the eighteenth century philanthropists and governments tried to create work opportunities for children from about the age when in the later nineteenth century they would be sent to school; for by that date few people could be found who would publicly deny that children should be saved from work.

[...]

Philanthropy, the state and children

The Societies for the Prevention of Cruelty to Children were in some sense privately-organised and funded agents of the state. The New York SPCC, for example, was a private corporation, but its agents were 'duly constituted officers of the law'. It was as though the state itself hesitated to be seen to be interfering too heavily in the daily lives of the people, and preferred to allow a private agency to act on its behalf. In contrast to many other SPCCs in the United States, the New York SPCC held to a policy of institutional care for children, and brought on its head considerable criticism both for this policy in itself, and for its general lack of accountability.[23] The relationship between philanthropy and the state in the care for children was fraught with difficulties.

In one perspective philanthropy had prepared the ground for later state intervention, with an easy transition from one to the other as the scale of the task outstripped philanthropic resources. But in another and more realistic one, philanthropists can be seen resisting state intervention in the fields which they had mapped out as their own. In the early twentieth century there was a growing critique of philanthropy as an agency for dealing with issues to do with childhood. Despite its own insistence on careful casework and on a separation out of the deserving and undeserving, or the helpable and unhelpable, philanthropy was condemned for indiscriminacy of another kind: it simply did not cover the whole population; there night be pockets of good coverage by philanthropic agencies next to areas without any.[24] There was still a good deal of support, perhaps majority support, within governments for what may be called the philanthropic solution to social problems, but in the first decade of the twentieth century there began to be voiced open criticism of philanthropy normally combined with condescending recognition of the philanthropists' good intentions.[25] It began to be argued that the state must act as the central and co-ordinating agency on behalf of children. In the United States and in Britain the phrase 'the children of the state', once used to refer exclusively to children in the direct care of the state, began to be used to refer to all children by advocates of a wider state role. 'All children are children of the state, or none are', declared Rev. Lloyd Jenkins Jones of Illinois in 1898.[26]

The identification of childhood as an area for state policy was accompanied and to some extent caused by a declining confidence in the family, some argued that if families were doing their jobs properly, there would be to call for a state policy for children; the solution was not to resort to state policies, but to force families to face up to their responsibilities. Others argued that many families were unable to look after their children properly, and that the state ought positively to intervene on behalf of children while at the same time enabling families to function more effectively. The provision of school meals by local authorities could thus be seen either as the removal from the family of a proper and valued role, or as a welcome relief to families who could concentrate their inadequate resources on other matters. But in both cases the family was in some kind of interrogation from philanthropists or the state; it was certainly no longer assumed that the rearing of children could simply be left to families with the state or voluntary organisations picking up the casualties.

The rate of infant mortality, which in many countries remained as high in the late nineteenth century as at its outset, provided the most obvious arena for intervention. By the early twentieth century there was in existence 'an international infant welfare movement of truly immense dimensions', with national organisations in Denmark, Germany, Italy, Luxemburg, the Netherlands, Norway, Rumania, Russia, Spain, Switzerland, the United Kingdom and the United States.[27] Although there were some differences in emphasis from country to country in the policies recommended for bringing about a reduction in infant mortality, what was more remarkable was the speed with which solutions initiated in one country were adopted in others. Thus the French *Gouttes de Lait* – milk depots – were tried out in Canada, the Netherlands, Sweden, the United Kingdom, the United States, and doubtless elsewhere, the message being spread by international conferences in Paris in 1905 and in Brussels in 1907.

The essence of the international infant welfare movement was the constitution of babyhood as a medical problem in which mothers were the front-line defence against germs.[28] Doctors asserted for themselves a new role in promoting the gospel of hygiene. 'The future of the race', claimed the *British Medical Journal* in 1904, ' ... rests largely with the medical profession.'[29] Mothers, it was said, too often careless and indifferent, were responsible for the high rate of infant mortality, and it was the task of doctors, with their ancillary staff of nurses and health visitors, to bring home to them their duties, not only to their own offspring but also to the future of the race.

This task was embarked on with enthusiasm, and accompanied by pronounced social action. There were determined efforts both to encourage breastfeeding, backed up by such statistics as those produced by the Children's Bureau in the United States showing infant mortality rates three to four times higher for those not breastfed;[30] and to improve the quality of milk supply for those mothers who were not breastfeeding, This was accompanied by campaigns to teach mothers or potential mothers lessons in hygiene and in childminding. Instinct was not enough. The National Congress of Mothers in the United States in 1912 was determined to 'battle down the old wall of belief that mother instinct teaches a woman all she needs to know about child nurture'.[31] Motherhood, it was insisted, carried with it heavy responsibilities, amongst them the duty to exit from the labour market unless there were very strong countervailing reasons why this should not happen. Schools for Mothers began to proliferate. Nurses gained access to working-class homes where they could try to enforce the gospel of hygiene.[32] Girls at elementary school were taught how to look after babies. In France, under the flag of *puériculture*, they were prepared for their biological destiny. In the United States, Little Mothers' Leagues for girls aged twelve and upwards, were designed so that the girls could pass on the message of hygiene to their immigrant parents; there were 239 of them in New York City alone in 1911, and by 1915 there were branches in forty-four American cities.[33]

Publicity was a key part of these campaigns. Better Baby contests in the United States in 1912 and 1913 were replaced by non-commercial but extremely successful Baby Weeks from 1916; Britain had its first National Baby Week in July 1917.[34] Few mothers can have escaped entirely the barrage of advice directed at them. In 1929 the United States Children's Bureau estimated that half of American babies had benefited from the government's child-rearing information. In Britain in 1918 there were 700 municipal and 578 voluntary maternity and child welfare centres, the number having nearly doubled since the beginning of the war in 1914.[35]

Concern about infant mortality was international and the solutions proposed differed only at the margin; and yet the motivations for action, and the structures of campaigns differed quite substantially from one country to another. Thus in France the campaigns had a strong pronatalist flavour, being designed to increase French population, while in the United States the concern was much more to Americanise recent immigrants and to promote economic efficiency. Doctors played a key role in all countries, but whereas in France their authority was recognised from the outset, elsewhere, in the United States and in the Netherlands for example, they were in some sense using the concern about infant mortality to promote their own status, and were anxious, as one American doctor expressed it in 1913, not to open the 'portals of this important field of preventive medicine to social workers and philanthropists'.[36] The latter were in fact already within the portals, some of them accepting medical leadership, but others campaigning for policies which not only taught hygiene but provided material support for mothers. Little, however, was likely to be achieved unless the state, often for reasons of its own, thought it fit to provide support for mothers.

The state's role was certainly more conspicuous in the spread of compulsory schooling. Many states had introduced schooling laws before the 1880s which were designed to provide a network of schools for all children. Some of these, as we have seen, date from the eighteenth century. Yet what marked nearly every school law prior to the 1880s was the gap between the intention and the reality. Take, for example, the Guizot law passed in France in 1833. Every commune or group of communes was to have at least one elementary school which had to be officially certified, and there were provisions made for training school teachers. On one level the law was an enormous success; there was a substantial increase in both the number of schools and the number of enrolments in the 1830s and 1840s, though it needs to be noted that the upturn began before 1833. By 1850, it is claimed, 'the principle of universal schooling, if not its practice can be said to have been established', and over the next quarter of a century 'the practice of full enrolment became the accepted norm'.[37] Nevertheless, in 1876 nearly 800,000 out of 4.5 million children of school age (18 per cent) were not registered in any school. Moreover, the schools and their teachers left much to be desired. 'Dark, humid, crowded, unventilated, unfurnished, unlit, unheated or smelly and smoky when a fire or stove was lit, drafty, unwelcoming, and ugly, such was the great majority of schools right through the end of the 1870s', writes Eugen Weber. Teachers were part-time, supplementing their inadequate salaries with other jobs.[38] Many rural schools opened in winter only, knowing that children would be required for agricultural work in the summer; summer attendance remained at less than three-quarters of winter attendance into the twentieth century. Furthermore, distance from school, bad roads, and lack of footwear meant that many children did not attend, or at least not with any regularity even when the school was open.[39] It is certainly possible to be too negative; the vast majority of children did attend a school before the 1880s, and there is evidence that they did so because their parents and their communities wanted and expected them to, rather than because central government tried to enforce attendance. Moreover, the system had an inbuilt mechanism for growth. Nevertheless, even if it was mainly at the level of the quality of provision rather than the quantity, the reforms of the 1880s had a marked impact.[40] In 1881 fees were abolished in public elementary schools; in 1882 enrolment in a school was made compulsory; in 1883 every village or hamlet with more than twenty children of school age was required to maintain a public elementary school; in 1885 the budget for the building and maintenance of schools and for the pay of teachers was substantially increased; and in 1886 there was put into place an elaborate system of inspection and control.[41] In the aftermath of defeat by Germany in 1870–71, the French schools may be seen as a national investment in a system which would make the French language universal (something by no means the case prior to the 1880s), and instil in the population a sense of pride in being French. But at the same time, and for different reasons, they began to be accepted by the people. The elementary skills of reading and writing and arithmetic were becoming more obviously a necessity for daily life, and the possession of the prized certificate could open up possibilities of economic and social advancement.[42]

In England and Wales the chronology was very similar. It was in 1833 that there was the first public grant of money for elementary schooling – though it was on a much smaller scale than in France. But a combination of church schools, Sunday schools and cheap private schools meant that a considerable majority of all children were receiving some schooling before the larger state interventions from the 1870s. The Act of 1870 was designed to ensure that there was a school in every neighbourhood, but it was only in 1880 that attendance was made compulsory for those aged five to ten, followed up in 1891 by the abolition of fees. The state's purpose in making schooling compulsory went beyond a desire to ensure that every child was taught the three Rs; it wanted to instil morality, and patriotism, and to train children in regular habits. Schools were designed to become a reference point for order; in the 1870s in London, it was 'like planting a fort in an enemy's country ... the symbol of tyranny and oppression'. The more neighbourly private schools were harried out of existence.[43]

In many countries it was in the last quarter of the nineteenth century that the way was opened to a major transformation in both the experience and the conceptualisation of childhood, the shift from a situation where children were thought of as members of the labour force to one where they were schoolchildren. Figures for numbers in school are notoriously difficult to interpret, for they sometimes refer to registrations and sometimes to attendances, but some leave no doubt of the extent of the change which was occurring. Thus in England and Wales the proportion of children aged five to fourteen who were in school rose from 24 per cent in 1870 to 48 per cent in 1880 to 70 per cent in 1900. In Austria the rise was less dramatic but significant nevertheless, from 43 per cent in 1870 to 53 per cent in 1880 to 66 per cent in 1900. Elsewhere, it is true, the figures lend no support to the proposition that it was in this period that a transformation occurred. In the Netherlands and in Norway the proportion of children in the age range at school was at or only slightly below two-thirds throughout the period 1870–1900; and on the other side in Italy the percentage of children at school was still only 39 in 1900. But this low figure for Italy must not be interpreted as implying that only 39 per cent of children in Italy received any schooling; if, say, the school leaving age was ten or eleven, then one would not expect very high percentages of those aged five to fourteen to be at school.[44] Moreover, even if, as in France, the figures for the proportion of children at school do not show any significant increase in this period, other measures suggest the importance of what was happening: illiteracy amongst bridegrooms and military recruits, which had been about 25 per cent in the late 1860s had dropped to 5 or 6 per cent by 1900.[45]

What was probably more important than the proportion at school was the fact that nearly all countries were making schooling compulsory. In the United States, for example, although in some areas child labour continued to vie with schooling, twenty-eight states passed compulsory schooling laws in the post Civil War period, and school attendance figures rose steadily.[46] Furthermore, states were putting in place measures to enforce that compulsion, and this undoubtedly changed the experience of schooling for children and for working-class parents who now came under a form of control which led to numerous conflicts with the state. In England and Wales there were nearly 100,000 prosecutions a year for truancy in the 1880s, and, although the number had dropped to 37,000 by 1910, the offence was second only to drunkenness out of all those brought before the courts.[47]

Attendance at school was not the only way in which working-class children and their parents found their lives to a novel extent shaped by the state. The schools themselves often placed a priority on the inculcation of 'the habits of order and obedience'. This frequently involved corporal punishment, and attitudes towards it could sharply divide families and schools. It also involved what Stephen Heathorn, with respect to England, has called 'a near-systematic process of national-identity construction ... initiated ... between 1880 and 1914'. In the stories of the nation which children learned there were different roles for boys and girls, and this was reinforced by the emphasis in the syllabus on needlework, cookery and laundry for girls, preparing them for lives as servants or housewives. In some ways this fitted working-class expectations, for girls were more likely than boys to be kept back at home to help their mothers, and the schools quietly sanctioned this.[48]

Compulsory attendance was not achieved without a struggle, but the bitter phase of that struggle was over by the 1920s, if not before. Parents and children had come to accept regular schooling as a norm. Despite the emphasis on national uniformity and regulation from above, there were many differences at local level in the experience of schooling, and while some children looked back on their schooling with what seems justified outrage, and took the very earliest opportunity to leave, for others it was a largely positive experience, and one which they would have wished to have prolonged.[49]

From the state's point of view, compulsory schooling provided opportunities for surveillance beyond anything that could be hoped for in the home. As the French psychiatrist Georges Heuyer put it in 1914, school was 'a laboratory for the observation of antisocial tendencies'.[50] From a rather different perspective, the evidence from schooling over a period of time provided ammunition for those concerned about the possible deterioration of the race in the urban civilisation of the nineteenth and early twentieth centuries. Dr Alfred Eicholz, an inspector of schools in Britain, presented photographs of children at a school in south London to an Interdepartmental Committee on Physical Deterioration, seeing improvement (Plate 5 [see original reading]). In the 1902 photograph there was, he said, 'a more civilised intelligent look about the children. They are better filled out and straighter.'[51] School was both the site of improvement and the provider of evidence for it.

The forty years between 1880 and 1920 were not in any simple sense a period when governments suddenly moved into surveillance and policing of areas of social life previously unknown territory to them. There is a long history of state concern with childhood, in some countries highly visible at national level, in others more obscure but nonetheless a presence at local level. Industrialisation, in Britain first and then in other countries, led governments into closer control than previously of child labour. A mixture of motives, including child unemployment, led them to impose compulsory schooling, which vastly increased the range and scope of the state's activities. Meanwhile philanthropic projects of the nineteenth century, on a scale and with a scope beyond the imagination of previous centuries, had attempted to deal with the social problems associated above all with urbanization. By the early twentieth century there was increasing feeling that the task was beyond the scope of philanthropy on its own, and that the state must take a more active role. There ensued battles between philanthropy and the state, not all of which ended up with a victory for more state involvement – for the philanthropists had powerful bodies of support. But there can be no doubt that the state's role was increasing, and that it was taking over from philanthropy the key role in 'saving the children'.

State concerns and children's rights

Compulsory schooling was not introduced simply or mainly to try to provide all children with an experience of childhood. It has to be understood in a context of state rivalry, and a worry about the effectiveness of the socialisation of children in the reproduction of the social order. The same context underlay schemes for the emigration of children or for their care within institutions in their own countries. How far, then, were policies which affected children in fact child-centred, how far was 'child-saving' actually about providing a childhood for children? The answer may lie in a consideration of the movement to enshrine 'the rights of the child'.

Reformers and philanthropists were deeply imbued with the romantic belief that childhood should be happy, the best time of life. 'God made childhood to be happy' wrote a Scottish Evangelical in the 1840s. It was something to which one would look back later both with nostalgia and for inspiration. 'A happy childhood', wrote Kate Wiggin in 1892, 'is an unspeakably precious memory. We look back upon it and refresh our tired hearts with the vision when experience has cast a shadow over the full joy of living.'[52] If these happy childhoods were to be achieved, childhood had to be sharply separated from adulthood, and its characteristics and needs had to be recognised. Childhood and adulthood, in this thinking, became almost opposites of one another. If adults were burdened with responsibilities, children should be carefree. If adults worked, children should play: 'play is the highest phase of child development', wrote Froebel.[53] If sex was part of the life of adults, it should play no part in that of children: in England and Wales the age of consent for girls was raised from twelve to sixteen. And if adults had to live in towns, children were entitled to contact with nature.

Philanthropists who had so wholeheartedly embraced the ideology of childhood and who were confronted with the realities of actual childhoods on city streets, began to formulate theories of the rights which properly belonged to children. We have seen how the idea of the rights of the child as against its parents or employers began to be set out in the 1830s in England. Towards the end of the century these rights came to be seen as more than rights to maintenance, education and protection, but as very specifically the rights to childhood. 'The rights of a child', wrote Benjamin Waugh, 'are its birthrights. The Magna Carta of them, is a child's nature. The Author, is its Creator.' God and nature between them laid out a plan for childhood which adults interfered with at their peril. A child, wrote Kate Wiggin, has an 'inalienable ... right to his childhood'[54] These rights were precisely the opposite of the rights which adults might claim to independence or freedom. As the Board of Public Charities in

Illinois put it, 'Dependence is a child's natural condition.[55] In 1913 Alexander McKelway, a leader in the campaign to restrict child labour in the United States, drew up a 'Declaration of Dependence by the Children of America in Mines and Factories and Workshops Assembled' in which the children 'declare ourselves to be helpless and dependent; that we are and of right ought to be dependent, and that we hereby present the appeal of our helplessness that we may be protected in the enjoyment of the rights of childhood'.[56] Children's rights therefore were the right to be protected, a theory which fitted well with the thrust of child-saving efforts.

Children themselves, the evidence suggests, on balance did not feel themselves to be beneficiaries of this discourse of rights. In its name, some of them were removed from their families, incarcerated in institutions, and transported across oceans. Some undoubtedly felt that it had been the saving of them. But most who were rescued found it difficult to come to terms with the institutional norms and practices which now shaped their lives. The girls who had been sexually abused found that they were regarded as polluted and potentially polluting, and were hidden away. Children sent to institutions to be saved, many without having committed any offence, saw it 'as a punishment'. Fostered and emigrated children were often mistreated, and adjusted with difficulty to the communities and rural environments which it was hoped would be the saving of them. Their sense of personal identity, derived from their families, was systematically undermined by discouraging the maintenance of any links with their past lives.[57]

There was nevertheless, in the early twentieth century, a growing international body of adult opinion campaigning for the right of children to protection. Swiss officials wrote in 1912 that 'In many ... states the powerful idea of protecting children and youth is becoming more and more the dominant preoccupation, not only of official spheres, but also of all the classes of the population', and they hoped for the creation of an *office international de protection de l'enfance*. It required the jolt of the First World War and its aftermath to bring to a head the disparate efforts of those thinking about drawing up a declaration of children's rights. Competing organisations lobbied the newly-formed League of Nations for the central role in co-ordinating children's rights. The successful initiative lay with an Englishwoman, Eglantyne Jebb, who had taken up the cause of children in the defeated countries; as children, she argued, they could hardly be blamed for and therefore should not suffer as a consequence of defeat. The Save the Children Fund was the outcome. Rather than winding down the organisation as the immediate crisis passed, Jebb found herself confronted with a succession of new situations where the children needed to be saved, and she was moved to draw up a simple declaration of children's rights which was adopted by the League of Nations in 1924. These rights were in fact duties of adults, it being formally recognised that 'mankind owes to the Child the best that it has to give'.[58]

Important as international organisations were in setting the tone of discussions, it was at the level of the state that laws were passed and action taken. In the thinking of the late nineteenth and early twentieth centuries the rights of children were entirely consonant with an increased role for the state in the lives of children. For it was the state alone which could enforce those rights. If, as was claimed, a first consequence of employing children was 'that they cease almost at once to be children', then it was the state's responsibility to prevent that too-early employment.[59] If home and school were the only two proper environments for children, then the state must ensure that children were indeed in homes which deserved the name or in school. And all this protection of the newly-defined children's rights was in harmony with the larger purposes of the state in securing the reproduction of a society capable of competing in the harsh conditions of the twentieth century. In the phrasing of the time, the interests of the child and the interests of the state were one and the same. A child-centred policy was one from which the state could only gain. Families might be the losers.

They sometimes took the initiative in handing over their children to the care of the state, but, as Donzelot noted, the more that children's rights are proclaimed, 'the more the strangle hold of a tutelary authority tightens around the poor family'.[60] Child-saving aimed both to provide the child with what was thought of as a childhood, and to ensure the future of society. The two aims were thought to be entirely consonant with one another.

Notes

1   H. Cunningham, *The Children of the Poor: Representations of Childhood since the Seventeenth Century* (Oxford, 1991), p. 86; J. Dekker, *The Will to Change the Child: Re-education Homes for Children at Risk in Nineteenth Century Western Europe* (Frankfurt am Main, 2001), p. 69.

2   *The Morning Chronicle Survey of Labour and the Poor: The Metropolitan District*, Vol. 4 (Horsham, 1981), pp. 34–78, 131–53; G. Wagner, *Barnardo* (London, 1979), pp. 86–172; G.K. Behlmer, *Child Abuse and Moral Reform in England, 1870–1908* (Stanford, 1982), pp. 119–60.

3   Quoted in D.J. Rothman, *The Discovery of the Asylum Social Order and Disorder in the New Republic* (Boston and Toronto, 1971), p. 213.

4   F.K. Prochaska, *Women and Philanthropy in Nineteenth-Century England* (Oxford, 1980), pp. 30–32, 224–25.

5   Devine quoted in R.A. Meckel, *Save the Babies: American Public Health Reform and the Prevention of Infant Mortality 1850–1929* (Baltimore and London, 1990), p. 103; F. Davenport-Hill, *Children of the State* (2nd edn, London, 1889), p. 22.

6   P.T. Rooke and R.L. Schnell, 'Childhood and charity in nineteenth-century British North America', *Histoire Sociale–Social History*, XV (1982), pp. 157–79.

7   B. Finkelstein, 'Casting networks of good influence: the reconstruction of childhood in the United States, 1790–1870', in J.M. Hawes and N.R. Hinter (eds), *American Childhood: A Research Guide and Historical Handbook* (Westport, Conn. and London, 1985), pp. 111–52.

8   Quoted in Cunningham, *Children of the Poor*, p. 31.

9   H. Cunningham, 'The employment and unemployment of children in England c.1680–1851', *Past and Present*, 126 (1990), pp. 129–30.

10 Cunningham, *Children of the Poor*, pp. 53–64.

11 Ibid., pp. 64–76.

12 Ibid., pp. 70–83.

13 Ibid., pp. 94–95.

14 Ibid., pp. 83–95; on the demand for child labour, see C. Tuttle, *Hard at Work in Factories and Mines: The Economics of Child Labor During the British Industrial Revolution* (Boulder, 1999).

15 C. Nardinelli, *Child Labor and the Industrial Revolution* (Bloomington and Indianapolis, 1989), p. 109; C. Goldin and K. Sokoloff, 'Women, children, and industrialization in the early Republic: evidence from the manufacturing censuses', *Journal of Economic History*, XLII (1982), p. 743; British Parliamentary Papers, *Industrial Revolution: Children's Employment* (Shannon, 1968), Vol. 3, C1, p. 96.

16 E.P. Thompson and E. Yeo (eds), *The Unknown Mayhew* (Harmondsworth, 1973), pp. 477–78.

17 H. Silver, 'Ideology and the factory child: attitudes to half-time education', in P. McCann (ed.), *Popular Education and Socialization in the Nineteenth Century* (London, 1977), pp. 141–66. For similar concerns in Sweden, see B. Sandin, ' "In the large factory town": child labour legislation, child labour and school compulsion', in N. de Coninck-Smith, B. Sandin and E. Schrumpf (eds), *Industrious Children: Work and Childhood in the Nordic Countries 1850–1990* (Odense, 1997), pp. 17–46.

18 Cunningham, *Children of the Poor*, pp. 88–94.

19 Ibid., pp. 51, 83–96.

20 L.S. Weissbach, *Child Labor Reform in Nineteenth-Century France* (Baton Rouge and London, 1989), pp. 84, 140, xiii.

21 Nardinelli, *Child Labor and the Industrial Revolution*, pp. 127–29.

22 V.A. Zelizer, *Pricing the Priceless Child: The Changing Social Value of Children* (New York, 1985), p. 55; R.H. Bremner (ed.), *Children and Youth in America: A Documentary History*, 2 vols (Cambridge, Mass., 1971), Vol. 2, p. 653.

23 Bremner, *Children and Youth in America*, Vol. 2, pp. 117–18, 185–222.

24 S. Tiffin, *In Whose Best Interest? Child Welfare Reform in the Progressive Era* (Westport, Conn. and London, 1982), pp. 187–214; B. Harrison, *Peaceable Kingdom* (Oxford, 1982), pp. 240–59.

25   J.E. Gorst, *The Children of the Nation; How their Health and Vigour should be promoted by the State* (London, 1906), pp. 12–14.

26   Cunningham, *Children of the Poor*, p. 211; Tiffin, *In Whose Best Interest?*, p. 218.

27   Meckel, *Save the Babies*, pp. 101–9.

28   P. Wright, 'The social construction of babyhood: the definition of infant care as a medical problem', in A. Bryman, B. Bytheway, P. Allatt and T. Keil (eds), *Rethinking the Life-Cycle* (London, 1987), pp. 103–21.

29   Quoted in D. Dwork, *War is Good for Babies and Other Young Children: A History of the Infant and Child Welfare Movement in England 1898–1918* (London, 1987), p. 21.

30   S.H. Preston and M.R. Haines, *Fatal Years: Child Mortality in Late Nineteenth-Century America* (Princeton, 1991), p. 27.

31   Quoted in A. Klaus, *Every Child a Lion: The Origins of Maternal and Infant Health Policy in the United States and France, 1890–1920* (Ithaca and London, 1993), pp. 142–43.

32   J. Lewis, *The Politics of Motherhood: Child and Maternal Welfare in England, 1900–1939* (London, 1980), pp. 27–113; C. Dyhouse, 'Working-class mothers and infant mortality in England 1895–1914', *Journal of Social History*, 12 (1978), pp. 248–67; Dwork, *War is Good for Babies and Other Young Children*.

33   Meckel, *Save the Babies*, pp. 144–45; Klaus, *Every Child a Lion*, p. 77–80.

34   Klaus, *Every Child a Lion*, pp, 144–54; Dwork, *War is Good for Babies and Other Young Children*, p. 211.

35   T. Skocpol, *Protecting Soldiers and Mothers: The Political Origins of Social Policy in the United States* (Cambridge, Mass, and London, 1992), p. 481; Dwork, *War is Good for Babies and Other Young Children*, p. 211.

36   Klaus, *Every Child a Lion*, passim, quoting p. 88; H. Marland, 'The medicalization of motherhood: doctors and infant welfare in the Netherlands, 1901–30', in V. Fildes, L. Marks and H. Marland (eds), *Women and Children First: International Maternal and Infant Welfare, 1870–1945* (London, 1992), pp. 74–96.

37   R. Grew and P.J. Harrigan, *School, State, and Society: The Growth of Elementary Schooling in Nineteenth-Century France: A Quantitative Analysis* (Ann Arbor, 1991), pp. 31–89, quoting pp. 78–79.

38   E. Weber, *Peasants into Frenchmen: The Modernization of Rural France 1870–1914* (London, 1977), pp. 304–8.

39   Ibid., pp. 318–23; Grew and Harrigan, *School, State, and Society*, pp. 67,

40   Grew and Harrigan, *School, State, and Society*.

41   Weber, *Peasants into Frenchmen*, pp. 308–9.

42   Ibid., pp. 328–38.

43   D. Rubinstein, 'Socialization and the London School Board 1870–1904: aims, methods and public opinion', in McCann (ed.), *Popular Education and Socialization in the Nineteenth Century*, pp. 231–64; J.S. Hurt, *Elementary Schooling and the Working Classes 1860–1918* (London, 1979); P. Gardner, *The Lost Elementary Schools of Victorian England: The People's Education* (London, 1984).

44   Calculated from B.R. Mitchell, *European Historical Statistics* (2nd edn, London, 1981), pp. 38–66, 785–806.

45   C.M. Cipolla, *Literacy and Development in the West* (Harmondsworth, 1969), p. 119.

46   J.P. Felt, *Hostages of Fortune: Child Labor Reform in New York State* (Syracuse, 1965), p. 7; W.I. Trattner, *Crusade for the Children: A History of the National Child Labor Committee and Child Labor Reform in America* (Chicago, 1970); D.I. Macleod, *The Age of the Child: Children in America, 1890–1920* (New York, 1998), p. 76.

47   Hurt, *Elementary Schooling and the Working Classes*, p. 203.

48   A. Davin, *Growing Up Poor: Home, School and Street in London 1870–1914* (London, 1996), pp. 85–153, quoting p. 134; S. Heathorn, *For Home, Country, and Race: Constructing Gender, Class, and Englishness in the Elementary School, 1880–1914* (Toronto, 2000), quoting p. ix; N. de Coninck-Smith, 'Copenhagen children's lives and the impact of institutions, c.1840–1920', *History Workshop*, 33 (1992), pp. 57–72.

49   Rubinstein, 'Socialization and the London School Board', pp. 250–58; J. Rose, 'Willingly to school: the working-class response to elementary education in Britain, 1875–1918', *Journal of British Studies*, 32 (1993), pp. 114–38.

50   Donzelot, *Policing of Families*, p. 132.

51   Interdepartmental Committee on Physical Deterioration, British Parliamentary Papers, 1904, vol. xxxii, p. 179.

52   T. Guthrie, *Seed-Time and Harvest of Ragged Schools* (Edinburgh, 1860), pp. 7–8; K.D. Wiggin, *Children's Rights: A Book of Nursery Logic* (London, n.d., c.1892), p. 31; cf. R. Bray, 'The children of the town', in C.F.G. Masterman (ed.), *The Heart of the Empire* (1901; Brighton, 1973), p. 127.

53   F. Froebel, *The Education of Man* (New York and London, 1887), p. 54.

54   Waugh, *Life of Benjamin Waugh*, p. 296; Wiggin, *Children's Rights*, p. 10.

55   Platt, *Child Savers*, p. 135.

56   Trattner, *Crusade for the Children*, frontispiece.

57   Jackson, *Child Sexual Abuse in Victorian England*, pp. 86–89, 135; L. Mahood, *Policing Gender, Class and Family: Britain, 1850–1940* (London, 1995), p. 148; Abrams, *Orphan Country*, pp. 35–77, 122–61, 251–54.

58   D. Marshall, 'The construction of children as an object of international relations: the Declaration of Children's Rights and the Child Welfare Committee of League of Nations, 1900–924', *The International Journal of Children's Rights*, 7 (1999), pp. 103–47, quoting p. 115; F.M. Wilson, *Rebel Daughter of a Country House: The Life of Eglantyne Jebb, Founder of the Save the Children Fund* (London, 1967), *passim*, quoting p. 224.

59   Bremner, *Children and Youth in America*, Vol. 2, p. 658.

60   Mahood, *Policing Gender*, pp. 141, 143; Donzelot, *Policing of Families*, p. 103.

Chapter 24

Sharon Stephens

CHILDREN AND THE POLITICS OF CULTURE IN "LATE CAPITALISM"

MANY ATTEMPTS HAVE BEEN MADE in recent years to map the "postmodern/postcolonial" world, characterized by transnational flows of commodities and people; by vast numbers of refugees, migrants, and stateless groups; by state projects to redefine the threatened boundaries of national cultures; and by a proliferation of ethnic groups, subcultures, and multicultural mixtures that challenge notions of stable, homogeneous identities. What emerges at the end of the twentieth century is an international process of production and exchange, together with a multitude of localized groups struggling to define themselves in relation to decentered global forces. The concept of culture has been central to these struggles. States and national elites, minority populations, and new social movements represent themselves as acting to protect traditional culture or to develop new forms of cultural identity.

In light of such debates about the nature of culture, what does it mean to talk about "children's rights to culture," along with rights to food, shelter, and health care? In *The Political Life of Children*, Robert Coles (1986) argues that a nation's politics becomes a child's everyday psychology. How do new forms of international and local politics of culture affect children? And how do children themselves experience, understand, and perhaps resist or reshape the complex, frequently contradictory cultural politics that inform their daily lives?

What sorts of social visions and notions of culture underlie assertions within international-rights discourses that every child has a right to a cultural identity? To what extent is this identity conceived as singular and exclusive, and what sorts of priorities are asserted in cases where various forms of cultural identity—regional, national, ethnic minority, or indigenous—come up against one another?

It is important to ask how international children's cultural-rights claims differ, for example, from the vision of South African state officials who used a language of people's rights to distinct cultures to justify apartheid. We need to examine more critically what it means to talk about a child's right to a cultural identity in a world where more and more children are growing up in complex multicultural settings, demanding that they move in and out of diverse social roles and create identities that bewilder and trouble their parents. What sorts of hybrid cultures might the children of Turkish "guest workers" in Berlin or Mexican migrant laborers in Los Angeles lay claim to? How do children in war-torn areas of the

Middle East, Southeast Asia, or American inner cities experience their relation to "traditional cultures" far removed from everyday realities?

While many argue that international cultural-rights discourses further the best interests of children themselves, in some contexts these discourses may be linked to significant risks to the physical, psychological and social well-being of children. Insofar as we accept the legitimacy of international-rights language, it might be argued that children also have rights not to be constrained within exclusionary cultural identities and not to have their bodies and minds appropriated as the unprotected terrain upon which cultural battles are fought.

The authors of papers in this volume [see original reading] explore various aspects of the current global politics of culture, in relation to changing discourses on childhood and to changing conditions and experiences of children in diverse world regions and social contexts. Especially exciting are the theoretical insights and practical implications that emerge when these papers—each an important work in its own right—are read together. My aim in this introduction is to suggest ways of reading the papers that push us toward new understandings—and even more significantly, toward new questions—about articulations among the ethnographic area and themes explored by individual authors.

There are good reasons a combined focus on children and the politics of culture, at this moment in the formation and transformation of a new world order, is important for exploring the shape and significance of contemporary global processes. In order to frame my discussions of individual papers, I begin with discussions of childhood as a social and historical construction, culture as a theoretically and politically contested term, and reasons childhood and culture are both being challenged and reconfigured in fundamental ways today. Discussion of the collected papers then provides a foundation for assessing current affirmations of children's rights to cultural identity and international discourses on the rights of the child more generally.

Childhood as a cultural construction

While Philippe Ariès's *Centuries of Childhood* (1962) was not the first social history to suggest a radical critique of universalistic notions of childhood, Ariès's challenge to naturalistic orthodoxies had a major impact on the social sciences. Ariès's work is striking, both for its impressive scholarly documentation and the boldness of its basic assertion: "[I]n medieval society the idea of childhood did not exist" (Ariès 1962:125). Ariès's work quickly became a foundational text for social-constructionist investigations into the profound "variability of human societies, all the more useful because it looked not to the 'exotic' or 'primitive' but to a familiar western European past" (Prout and James 1990:17).

Ariès argued that the modern conception of childhood as a separate life stage emerged in Europe between the fifteenth and eighteenth centuries, together with bourgeois notions of family, home, privacy, and individuality. Basing his argument in part on an extensive analysis of medieval paintings, Ariès asserted that before the fifteenth century, children past the dependent stage of infancy were conceived and depicted simply as miniature adults. By the eighteenth century, however, special conventions in artistic and literary representation clearly marked children as a distinct group and childhood as a separate domain, set apart from the everyday life of adult society. Notions of children's special nature and needs called for special attention to the child's emotional development in the home and for a protracted formal education in the school aimed at preparing children for the transition to an adult world.

Though the luxury of childhood was initially available only to the upper classes, notions and practices characterizing this new domain came to be propagated—not without significant resistance—throughout society. In time, a vast network of institutions—ranging from the nuclear family to school, health, and legal systems—contributed to the generalization of childhood, at least as an ideal, throughout Western society.

Ariès's work inspired a wide range of historical and sociological studies of private life, childhood, and the family, conceived not as naturally given containers for culturally specific content, but as themselves socially constructed domains. Ariès's claims for the uniqueness of childhood as an historically limited Western European creation also generated vigorous debates and critiques (for example, DeMause 1976, Hanawalt 1993).

But even if we modify Ariès's bold thesis and acknowledge that every known society has concepts and practices that in some respects mark off children from adults in order to assure physical care and socialization for biologically immature human beings, the originality and generativity of Ariès's claim remain. The *particular* form of modern childhood is socially and historically specific.

While all cultures have given meaning to physical differences of sex and age, it can be argued that the social worlds in which these physical signs become significant are so profoundly different that we are already doing analytical violence to complex constellations of meanings and practices when we single out notions of male and female or childhood and adulthood and attempt to compare them cross-culturally. These terms already presuppose a world of *Western* cultural assumptions—for example, that sexual or age differences are self-evidently dichotomous and that they define the parameters for exclusive identities.

There is a growing body of literature on Western childhood suggesting that the "hardening" of the modern dichotomy of child/adult, like the modern distinction female/male, was crucial to setting up hierarchical relations between distinct domains of social life—the private and public, consumption and production, objective need and subjective desire—upon which modern capitalism and the modern nation-state depended (see Boyden 1990; Qvortrup 1985).

As Barrett and McIntosh (1982:35) observe, "[T]he ideological construction of the family as the antithesis to the cash-nexus could *only* refer to a capitalist society." Similarly, the ideological construction of childhood as the privileged domain of spontaneity, play, freedom, and emotion could only refer to a society that contained and drew upon this private domain as the ground for public culture, discipline, work, constraint, and rationality.

In recent decades, there has been a proliferation of important works exploring the centrality of historically specific gender constructions within articulated structures of capital, nation-state, urban life, cultural forms, and subjective orientations characterizing modern Western capitalist society.[1] Compared to this extensive literature on gender, explorations of "the child" and its structural role in modern society are still relatively undeveloped.[2] In what respects are children—as foci of gender-specific roles in the family, as objects of regulation and development in the school, and as symbols of the future and of what is at stake in contests over cultural identity—pivotal in the structuring of modernity? How does the temporal move from child to adult correlate with the synchronic relation between female and male, or the construction of other cultures as our innocent, but immature and undeveloped, past? And if we are now witnessing wide-ranging restructurings of modernity, what implications might these changes have for the concept of childhood and the life conditions of children?

Prout and James, representative of a growing number of researchers arguing for culturalist perspectives on diverse childhoods, emphasize over and over again that "the immaturity of children is a biological fact of life, but the ways in which this immaturity is understood and made meaningful is a fact of culture" (1990:7). They celebrate an "emergent paradigm" in the sociology of childhood that is based on the "assumption that a child is socialized by belonging to a particular culture at a certain stage in its history" (15). Thus, comparative work on childhood should aim at "the analysis of how different discursive practices produce different childhoods, each and all of which are 'real' within their own regime of truth" (27).

But how and where are we to locate in the contemporary world distinct cultures, to be analyzed each "in their own terms"? The culturalization of childhood should not be bought at the cost of an awareness of the complexities of cultural definition in a postmodern world. Rather than merely explicating Western constructions of childhood, to be filled out in terms of gender, race, and class differences and to be compared with the childhoods of other cultures, we need also to explore the global processes that are currently transforming gender, race, class, culture—and, by no means least of all, childhood itself.

A contemporary crisis in the study of childhood: what is a child?

James and Prout (1990:2) note a contemporary crisis in the study of childhood, characterized by a sense of the inadequacy of previous frameworks. While the modern concept of childhood as a distinct stage in the human life cycle crystallized in nineteenth-century Western thought, the twentieth century has been characterized by a great elaboration of that conceptual space. Various technologies of knowledge (psychological experiments, ethnographic descriptions, medicalized analyses) have been applied to children, while ideologies of child-centered society give "the child" and "the interests of the child" a central place in the practices of legal, welfare, medical, and educational institutions. "But despite this rhetoric," James and Prout assert (1990:1), "any complacency about children and their place in society is misplaced, for the very concept of childhood has become problematic during the last decade."

At the heart of current debates, they suggest, lies the question: what is a child? In 1979, the International Year of the Child was launched, accompanied by internationally televised accounts of children whose lives were devastated by famine, war, and poverty. The concept of "the world's children" emerged in official discourses of international agencies such as UNICEF (the United Nations Children's Fund) and the World Health Organization. At the same time, however, affluent groups in Western society confronted a chasm between their idealized concepts of childhood and the realities of many children's lives, both in the Third World and in the heart of First World urban centers.

A decade later, an explosion of media coverage of child abuse, and particularly child sexual abuse, again challenged traditional beliefs about childhood and made public the private lives of children with no access to the mythic "walled garden" of "Happy, Safe, Protected, Innocent Childhood" (Holt 1975:22–23).

Thus, James and Prout argue, it is the past decade's consciousness of profound differences in the realities of children's lives—a consciousness facilitated by the global media—that has precipitated a crisis in the sociology of childhood and spurred the recognition that each culture defines childhood in terms of its own set of meanings and practices. While I agree with the observations of James and Prout, I would like to suggest a more radical explanation for the current crisis in the study of childhood. A historical perspective on "the world's children" suggests complex globalizations of once localized Western constructions of childhood. Current crises—in notions of childhood, the experiences of children, and the sociology of childhood—are related to profound changes in a now globalized modernity in which "the child" was previously located.

There is a rapidly proliferating literature theorizing the changing shape of the world system. Whether this new historical situation is framed as "late capitalism," "disorganized capitalism," "a global regime of flexible capital accumulation," or "postindustrial society" (see, for example, Mandel 1975; Lash and Urry 1987; Harvey 1989; and Bell 1974), analyses of childhood, gender, and the family have been largely neglected in these writings. Many of the authors exploring the world system, I would argue, are still operating in terms of distinctions between political economy and culture, the public and the private, that are themselves in the process of profound transformation. These shifting boundaries need to be theorized if we wish to explore emergent global processes, spaces, and identities.

A focus on childhood—and on other domains previously differentiated from the realm of political economy—is thus important, insofar as it breaks the frame of dominant models of transformations in the world system. It is also crucial for child researchers to rethink their own studies in the light of social and historical macroperspectives if they wish to understand the explosion of concern about children's rights and to anticipate new risks to children and childhood that would otherwise go unrecognized.

Children and childhoods at risk

As signs of a growing concern in recent decades with assaults on the space of childhood, consider the following book titles: *Children without Childhood* (Winn 1984), *Stolen Childhood: In Search of the Rights of the Child* (Vittachi 1989), *There Are No Children Here: The Story of Two Boys Growing Up in the Other America* (Kotlowitz 1991), *The Disappearance of Childhood* (Postman 1982), *Innocent Victims* (Gilmour 1988), *Broken Promise: The World of Endangered Children* (Allsebrook and Swift 1989), *The Rise and Fall of Childhood* (Sommerville 1982), *Pricing the Priceless Child: The Changing Social Value of Children* (Zelizer 1985), and *Children in Danger* (Garbarino et al. 1992—an exploration of the everyday experiences of American children in urban "war zones").

The list could be greatly extended, but the message here is clear. It was amplified at the May 1992 "Children at Risk" conference in Bergen. Discourses of lost, stolen, and disappearing childhoods and of abandoned, abused, exploited, and "disappeared" children run through the papers in this volume [see original reading].

The dominant theme is of children as innocent and vulnerable victims of adult mistreatment, greed, and neglect. Researchers cite the literal disappearance of children's bodies from the streets of Brazil and the prisons of South Africa and Namibia. The Chinese government's violent response to student demonstrations in Tiananmen Square was deplored in the international media as a nation opening fire on its own children. The Argentinian military regime was responsible for an unknown number of young people abducted by "security forces" and officially proclaimed as "disappeared." International media present child victims of famine disappearing more gradually: we are shown the starving bodies of glassy-eyed children with swollen bellies and emaciated limbs, literally wasting away.

The theme of lost childhoods includes not only physical assaults on and threats to children's bodies, but also the threatened spaces of an ideally safe, innocent, and carefree domain of childhood. Postman argues, for example, in *The Disappearance of Childhood* (1982) that the decline of American childhood as a protected space within the family began in 1950, as an "age of literacy" began to give way to an "electronic revolution." The inculcation of family values in the home and community values in the school gave way to an uncontrolled invasion of children's minds by market-driven media images and globally circulating signs. With this invasion came a loss of childhood innocence, and especially of sexual innocence.

It is, of course, questionable whether this protected space of familial and community harmony and of sexual innocence ever existed in the ways it is imagined. What I wish to draw attention to is a growing concern in recent decades with the domain of childhood as threatened, invaded, and "polluted" by adult worlds. At stake here are notions not only of innocence, but of nature, individual freedom, social values of enduring love and care (as opposed to temporally restricted economic and bureaucratic transactions), the family as basic unit of society, the bounded local community as the site of value definition and transmission, and the possibility of noncommodified social domains outside the realm of the market and market-driven politics.

The politics of the "nonpolitical"

Discourses of vanishing children and disappearing childhoods challenge us to explore the nature of current assaults on modern notions of childhood and on the bodies and minds of children who exist in complexly mediated relations to these ideals. Such assaults, I believe, must be considered in relation to current challenges to and refashionings of other domains previously conceived as largely *outside* the realm of politics and the market. Thus, we observe in recent decades a proliferation of works on the politics of social domains previously regarded as nonpolitical: naturalized spaces such as the self, the body, the family, childhood, and everyday life; a naturalized realm of the physical environment; and the archetypically cultural spaces of "pure" science, art, religion, and culture itself.[3] It is as though the realm of the political, the discursively negotiable and historically transformable, has moved out from its previous postion as a sort of historical buffer between nature and culture, to invade the "timeless" realms of natural law and intellectual purity.[4]

Habermas (1987) explores the progressive colonization of the "life-world" by the "systems world" in late modernity, as the taken-for-granted spaces of everyday life are restructured to accord with shifting political and economic demands. A defining characteristic of postmodernity is often said to be the denaturalization of objects, identities, and structures of social classification. Previously essentialized, naturalized categories come to be seen as transparently—and arbitrarily—organized by symbolic discourse.

While some authors celebrate new freedoms opened up by the dissolution of previously naturalized spaces, others take a more critical stance to the postmodern. The erosion and colonization of social domains previously seen as organized by their own distinctive logics can be seen as threatening an emerging new world order with the loss of any socially protected spaces *outside* the realm of globally circulating signs, goods, labor, and capital. The child—as a crucial modern symbol of nature and the object of protection and enculturation—is at risk of being written off as yet another postmodern discursive fiction.

What are the implications for society as a whole, if there are no longer social spaces conceived as at least partially autonomous from the market and market-driven politics? Where are we to find the sites of difference, the terrain of social witness, critical leverage, and utopian vision, insofar as the domain of childhood—or of everyday life or of a semi-autonomous realm of culture—is increasingly shot through with the values of the marketplace and the discursive politics of postmodern global culture? And what happens to the bodies and minds of children in the process?[5]

Children at risk—and as risks

This sense of the disappearance of childhood as a stable, natural foundation for social life is connected not only to laments for the lost innocence of childhood, but also to many examples of a growing fear of and anger at children. Consider, for example, the newly identified sociological phenomenon of *Kinderfeindlichkeit* (hostility to children) in Germany. In a December 1992 article in the *International Herald Tribune*, Marc Fisher comments on a bill proposed to the German parliament barring German parents from "spanking, boxing ears, withholding affection, constant nagging or threatening children with the bogeyman." Aggressive public policies are required, the argument goes, to inject love and affection for children into German society.

> Government analysts and psychologists say that despite wide-spread affluence, the success of postwar democracy and the best efforts of professionals, *kinder-feindlichkeit*, the German term for antipathy to children, has grown roots in a society suffering from excessive angst about the future. "The lost war and total destruction we suffered stripped away our certainty about basic values," said Ingrid Hoffman, spokesman for the German League for the Child. "The relations between generations were poisoned for a time."[6]

In a world of shifting values and challenged boundaries, we also observe an increasing obsession with the guarding of boundaries of the body, sex roles, the family, ethnic purity, and national identity—and, I would argue, increasing anger at children who cannot or will not fulfill their expected roles in the transmission of "traditional values." In an earlier period of modern society, noncompliant children could be categorized as "going through a stage" (as Prout and James [1990:12] note, "a biological explanation for a breakdown in social relationships") or, in more extreme cases, as "juvenile delinquents," in need of social correction and rehabilitation.

But what can we say about social worlds, such as those inhabited by the escalating numbers of "street children," regarded as largely *outside* the normative socializing control of adult society? From certain perspectives, of course, street children can be seen as *integral* parts of an emerging order of global capitalism. Moreover, there is much evidence that children living on the streets develop their own social organizations, relatively stable attachments to territories, and support networks linked to the sharing of food and goods (Boyden 1990:190ff.). Nevertheless, popular conceptions of street children frequently portray them as unsocialized or antisocial dangers to the established order and as primary *causes* of escalating social problems, such as increasing crime rates, drug trafficking, prostitution, and inner-city decay.

Notions of street children as non- or antisocial beings, presumably without families or values of their own, have been used to legitimate radical programs to eliminate the menace of street children in the interests of the general social good. Systematic assaults on Brazilian street children by organized "death squads," funded by the business community, frequently manned by off-duty policemen, and tacitly condoned by at least some government officials (see Henriques 1986; Larmer and Margolis 1992) are a particularly egregious example, but street children are a prime focus of fear and demands for more severe social controls in virtually every major urban center around the world (Boyden 1990:205).

The category of street children is a slippery one, shading into notions of only partially socialized young people living increasingly outside the regulatory spheres of family and school.

> In cities as disparate as Abidjan, Bogota, Cairo, Manila and Seoul, children playing in the streets and other public spaces and young teenagers congregating on street corners, outside cinemas or bars, have become synonymous in the mind of the general public with delinquent gangs.
>
> (Boyden 1990:188)

Frequently detained for the nebulous crimes of loitering and vagrancy, these assemblies of young people are most guilty of not conforming to socialization models according to which children are compliant vehicles for the transmission of stable social worlds.

In *Purity and Danger*, Mary Douglas (1985 [1966]) observes that dirt is "matter out of place"—and that objects in the interstices of conceptual structures are often regarded as profoundly dangerous and mysteriously powerful. Children on the streets are "people out of place."[7] They live in spaces people are supposed to pass through in their movements between socially sanctioned nodes of urban life; they are associated with illicit drug use and promiscuous sexuality, all the more reprehensible in children, who are supposed to be non- or presexual; and they represent a dangerous mixing of languages and cultural backgrounds. As children, they are even *more* out of place in the streets than adults. Street children are also endowed with the power to cause major urban disorders. They elicit violent reactions from those in power—far out of proportion, many have argued, to the numbers or strength of these children.[8]

Just as idle bands of youth and street children are seen as the cause of urban crime and decay, so also are hordes of hungry Third World children often seen as a major *cause* of global environmental problems. The cover of the *Economist*'s special issue on the 1992 UN Conference on Environment and Development depicts a mass of black children, whose images fill the cover frame and and blur together in the distance. Inside we learn that uncontrolled Third World population growth and poverty are the root causes of advancing deserts, vanishing forests, failing crops, and disappearing species ("Question Rio Forgets" 1992:11). The solution to global environmental problems, such perspectives suggest, is population control programs aimed at drastically reducing "excess populations"—people filling spaces and making demands on natural resources outside socially legitimated channels of ownership, exchange, and distribution. It is significant that in the popular media, these excess populations are often represented by crowds of hungry *children*, consuming whatever resources are available, but supposedly unable to participate in the global economy as producers (see Stephens 1992).

In the darkest scenarios of the disappearance of childhood, the theme of lost innocence takes on a negative valence. Children on the streets of Rio de Janeiro or in the ghettos of Los Angeles are not only killed. They also kill. Unrestrained and undeveloped by the ameliorating institutions of childhood, the innocence of children is perverted and twisted. In these stories, children are represented as malicious predators, the embodiment of dangerous natural forces, unharnessed to social ends.

There is a growing consciousness of children *at risk*. But the point I want to make here is that there is also a growing sense of children themselves as *the risk*—and thus of some children as people out of place and excess populations to be eliminated, while others must be controlled, reshaped, and harnessed to changing social ends. Hence, the centrality of children, both as symbolic figures and as objects of contested forms of socialization, in the contemporary politics of culture.

Widespread discourses of the loss and disappearance of childhood alert us to social processes that are currently reshaping the institutional and experiential frameworks of modern childhood. As Norma Field notes in her contribution to this volume [see original reading], the insight that the modern domain of childhood is a social and historical artifact, not a universal biological necessity, "has made possible the conceptualization (rather than the impressionistic bewailing) of the erosion of this institution in our own day."

The crucial task for researchers now, I would argue, is to develop more powerful understandings of the role of the child in the structures of modernity, the historical processes by which these once localized Western constructions have been exported around the world, and the global political, economic, and cultural transformations that are currently rendering children so dangerous, contested, and pivotal in the formation of new sorts of social persons, groups, and institutions. The challenge is to grasp the specificity of childhood and children's experiences in different world regions, national frameworks, and social contexts, while also seeking to illuminate the historical processes that not only link particular social worlds but are also crucially important in shaping and transforming them.

Conceptualizing the role of the child in modernity

Modern children are supposed to be segregated from the harsh realities of the adult world and to inhabit a safe, protected world of play, fantasy and innocence.

> Adult nostalgia for youthful innocence is symbolized by the whimsy of London's Museum of Childhood, with its display cabinets full of mechanical toys, china dolls, hand-painted dolls' houses, tin soldiers, electric train sets and Dinky cars. There is no place in this kind of childhood for labour in the factory or mine.
>
> (Boyden 1990:185)

Properly loved children should ideally be protected from the arduous tasks and instrumentalized relationships of the productive sphere. In the modern industrial world, "[T]he instrumental value of children has been largely replaced by their expressive value. Children have become relatively worthless (economically) to their parents, but priceless in terms of their psychological worth" (Scheper-Hughes 1989:12).

Boyden (1990:186) observes that "the norms and values upon which this ideal of a safe, happy and protected childhood are built are culturally and historically bound to the social preoccupations and priorities of the capitalist countries [and bourgeois classes] of Europe and the United States." The "needs of the child" figure prominently as grounds for the bounded and naturalized domestic space of modernity and for a marked sexual division of labor associated with differentiated spheres of reproduction/consumption and production.

Here we need not fall back on a notion of capitalism "calling for" or "bringing into being" a certain type of childhood—an unproductively reflectionist model of objective political economic processes simply calling forth new forms of subjectivity and everyday life. While children (especially males in earlier periods) eventually have to enter the workforce, the relation between the needs of the modern industrial economy and the socialization and education of children in home and school has never been simple. Modern children and childhood have always occupied more complex and critically important positions in the construction of modernity than a model of children simply as the raw materials of the capitalist marketplace would suggest.

David Harvey (1985, 1989) offers a more productive model for the analysis of changing constructions of childhood in the history of capitalist society. Harvey's aim is to theorize the structural and historical foundations for successive eras of capitalism, characterized by what he terms "structured coherences" of capital, political institutions, cultural forms, urban structures, and subjective orientations and punctuated by periods of wide-ranging disorganization and restructuring. Harvey posits an emerging modern period associated with free-market liberal capitalism (from roughly the 1890s to the 1930s); a period of high modernity linked to imperialist, state monopoly forms of capitalism (the 1940s through the 1960s); and an emerging late or postmodernist period linked to globalized structures of capital (from the 1970s to the present).

There is much important historical work to be done in conceptualizing the role of the child in modernity, for example, in relation to the modern nation-state and the development of child-focused institutions, such as the state-supported compulsory school.[9] In his pioneering work on the modern nation-state as a particular kind of "imagined community," Benedict Anderson (1983:16) asserts that "in the modern world everyone can, should, will 'have' a nationality, as he or she 'has' a gender." And, he might have added, as he or she "has" a childhood.

The creation of a modern state and national culture is integrally related to the creation of new sorts of gendered and age-graded subjects and spaces and the establishment of institutions variously engaged in spreading these constructions throughout society. As conceptions of a proper modern childhood developed within the European bourgeoisie, there was also increasing concern about deviant, wayward, and dangerous classes of children and about abnormal and indigent families.[10] In the early periods of industrialization, there was special concern about children on the streets—street traders, newspaper vendors, match and flower sellers, and messengers (Boyden 1990: 187–88). Urban street life in northern Europe, especially in working-class districts, became associated in bourgeois consciousness with notions of physical danger, immorality, and social disorder. The appropriate places for children were considered to be the home, the school, and designated play areas, while children were acceptable in public spaces only at restricted times and under adult supervision (for example, watching parades on national holidays). An English commentator on the British school system remarked in 1912, "[T]he whole system of national education has been reared on the foundation of the Ragged Schools, whose avowed object it was to draw children away from the fascinating misery of the streets" (Phillips 1912:206).

Within the provisionally structured coherence of modernity, notion of deviant childhoods have been a way of acknowledging differences in children's lives, while also legitimizing universalized notions of an ideal childhood. "Juvenile offenders" are thus marked for rehabilitation, while poor black children growing up in extended matrifocal families as seen as in need of compensatory social-welfare programs.

The globalization and export of modern childhood

And it is not only modern European national citizens who should have a particular sort of childhood, but populations around the world, in need of "civilization" and "development." Colonial projects were dependent not just on the establishment of new political and economic organizations, but also on the formation of social actors able and willing to function in complementary ways within them.

In recent years, historians and anthropologists have given increasing attention to the export of modern European domestic life as a critical site for producing new sorts of colonial laborers and imperial subjects (see Comaroff and Comaroff 1991). The export of modern notions of childhood, socialization, and education is inextricably connected to the export of modern constructions of gender, individuality, and the family.

Mala de Alwis (1991) explores, for example, the central importance that early-nineteenth-century British and American missionaries placed on refashioning Ceylonese women, so that they could in turn reshape the domestic world and provide appropriate socialization for children, before they became enmeshed within traditional structures of belief.

Missionary-sponsored boarding schools were also concerned with creating new identities for children. It was common practice for young girls to receive a new name, often that of a designated benefactress abroad, to mark this radical shift. "Thus Annamah could become Mary Walton overnight." She was taught Christian Scripture and prayer, together with needlework, orderliness, thrift, cleanliness, and accounting—all encompassed under the title of "Domestic Science" (de Alwis 1991:14).

We get a sense of the complexity of global exports of modern childhood and gender constructions when we consider how early Sri Lankan nationalists both drew upon and selectively refashioned these imported notions to define and protect visions of their nation's essential difference from the West. Late-nineteenth-century nationalists were concerned with asserting a non-Western native spirituality *within* the internationally legitimated framework of the nation. They wanted to appropriate the Western technologies and political strategies that had allowed the West to colonize and dominate the East, while also maintaining and reinforcing Eastern superiority in the spiritual realm.

Therefore, great effort was taken to protect this distinctive spiritual essence of culture which the nationalists believed could be contained and nurtured within the home by the women, while men waged the battle for Independence on the treacherous terrain of the profane, materialist outer world.

(de Alwis 1991:8)

The ideal female was to stand opposed both to the dangerously Europeanized upper-class woman (who wore European dress, drank alcohol, and smoked and was not sufficiently attentive to men and the home) *and* to the traditional native woman (coarse, immoral, and unable to understand the sacrifices necessary to construct a new nation). In constructing the ideal postcolonial woman, Sri Lankan nationalists negotiated a distinctive space between what they regarded as parochial tradition and uncritical modernity.[11]

And it was by means of this complex division between East and West, private and public, female and male that a distinctive boundary and relation between *child and adult* was made possible. The child, primarily socialized within the spiritual female realm and ideally educated in Buddhist schools, could later move out into the compromised adult world and, the proponents of nationalism affirmed, still retain the purity of timeless spiritual essence at the core of being.

Clearly, the social construction of modern forms of gender and childhood in Sri Lanka is different in important ways from gender and childhood in Europe and in other world regions. Clearly, also, the social spaces and subjective experiences of male and female, child and adult in these diverse contexts are related in integral ways.

In "Africa Observed: Discourses of the Imperial Imagination" (1991), Comaroff and Comaroff explore the complex significance that intersecting notions of children, women, animals, and nature had for diverse European colonial visions of Africans—and particularly black South Africans, considered to be among the most primitive groups on the "dark continent." In late-eighteenth-century Europe, "[T]he non-European was to be made as peripheral to the global axes of reason and production as women had become at home. Both were vital to the material and imaginative order of modern Europe. Yet both were deprived of access to its highest values." This stratified order was to be legitimized in nature, through biological differences between the sexes and races (Comaroff and Comaroff 1991:105). Just as Africans were feminized, in terms of their ostensibly uncontrolled passions and irrationality, so also were they infantilized and viewed in terms of their lack of qualities characterizing adult white European males—a vision that legitimized the civilizing process of issuing African "boys" into "moral manhood."

The Comaroffs also note, however, that "if degenerate nature was the foil to post-Enlightenment self-confidence, idealized nature was the trope of its critics and visionaries" (109). The naturalized differentiation of children, women, and peasants from civilized urban males made the former groups, together with "savage" non-Europeans, critical sites for the indictment of the "jarring and dissonant thing" that civilization had made of man (Coleridge, quoted in Comaroff and Comaroff 1991:110).

For our purposes here, it is important to note that early modern notions of childhood—as well as of gender, race, and nature—were both significant for and profoundly influenced by European colonialist experiences. If Africans were conceived as feminized and childlike, so also were notions of European women and children affected by the symbolic roles they played in both legitimizing and criticizing the European imperial project and civilizing mission.

Early modern notions of childhood were marked by stark tensions and contradictions, inasmuch as childhood was one of the key sites for the production of a newly emerging and widely contested liberal capitalist order. To what extent does a contemporary consciousness of burgeoning deviations from, as well as tensions and contradictions within, modern childhoods represent the transformation of a modern capitalist world in which these childhoods arose?

"Deviations" from modern childhood: a challenge to modernity?

A crucial part of describing the distinctive shape of modernity in different world regions and social contexts is exploration of the pivotal figure of the child and of the relation of this ideal construct to the diverse lives of children. As previously noted, James and Prout (1990:2) link a crisis in the sociology of childhood since the 1970s with increasing international media coverage of children's lives strikingly divergent from idealized Western concepts of child-hood. But child researchers certainly recognized differences among the world's children before this time. The point here is that *within* the provisionally structured coherence of high modernity, the "deviant childhoods" of Third World children could be interpreted as local particularities and instances of backwardness and underdevelopment, thus justifying expanded efforts to export modern childhood around the world.

A crucial question is whether contemporary notions of proliferating deviations from modern childhood—differences that are frequently glossed as "loss" and "contamination"—represent significant transformations in the nature of childhood and, more generally, in the social and historical project of modernity. My argument here is that we should at least take very seriously the possibility that we are now witnessing a profound restructuring of the child within the context of a movement from state to global capitalism, modernity to postmodernity.

A comprehensive theoretical discussion of how this global transformation might be framed is obviously far beyond the scope of this introduction.[12] One model I have found useful for thinking about contemporary children and childhoods at risk is the previously mentioned work of David Harvey. Harvey argues that the postwar Fordist-Keynesian order of production/consumption, big business/organized labor, and Keynesian welfare state was only a relatively stable aggregate of diverse practices and perspectives, whose organization became increasingly tenuous as gathering crises of capital overaccumulation transformed existing structures into obstacles to, rather than facilitators of, continued growth. Harvey sees these crises as coming to a head in the early 1970s, precipitating moves to smaller-scale, more flexible systems of production, marketing, and labor organization; geographical mobility of capital; and revivals of entrepeneurialism and political neoconservatism.

A newly emerging globalized "regime of flexible accumulation"—involving the increasing centralization and concentration of capital in multinational firms, as well as the failure of many older businesses and the proliferation of new sorts of local forms of produc-tion and marketing—has wide-ranging implications for the nature of local communities, national frameworks, and regional structures. The erosion of "self-evident" identities makes way for proliferating identity claims, from "traditional" ethnic groups challenging the capacity of national cultures to encompass ethnic differences to affirmations of new sorts of regional and global identities, such as the European Union and the Nation of Islam.

Harvey describes how an emerging global regime of flexible accumulation contributes to a widening gap in the First World between the very rich and the swelling ranks of the down-wardly mobile middle classes and poor, as well as to increasing conflicts between the North and South.[13] "Leaner," more flexible firms have little use for large numbers of unskilled laborers engaged in large-scale standardized production. Shifts away from mass production and marketing mean that the First World has less use for Third World laborers and that the primary movement of capital occurs between the wealthy nations of the North. Development programs in the Third World are being scaled down, in favor of "structural adjustment programs" to facilitate the repayment of national debts, with disastrous consequences for the everyday lives of Third World populations (see George 1989).

The implications of these changes for children are legion. As the Third World "comes home" to industrial nations, widespread economic uncertainty, unemployment, and decreased public services (such as health care, child care, and unemployment benefits) drastically affect the lives of children. In debt-ridden Third World countries, "austerity adjustments" and export-based national economies mean cuts in social-welfare programs and disruptions in local support networks. Increasing numbers of children live and work in conditions of poverty, while media representations of ideal childhoods sharpen the experience of material poverty as inner deprivation.

The materially privileged are affected too, as the conditions for economic well-being appear ever more tenuous and the future well-being of children ever more uncertain. Radical changes are called for in educational systems, in order to prepare children for participation in a rapidly changing adult world and to insure a sufficiently flexible body of "human capital" to society.

Add to these pressures on children the ethnic, religious, and racial conflicts set free and refashioned by the restructuring of national frameworks, as well as massive disruptions of local social networks associated with escalating numbers of refugees and migrant laborers, and we begin to see why children and the protected space of modern childhood are so profoundly at risk in a newly emerging world order.

[…]

The politics of culture

If a crucial dimension of late capitalism is a shift in the location and nature of boundaries between the material and the symbolic, nature and culture, then we should be surprised neither by current challenges to the naturalized domain of the modern child, nor by challenges to reigning notions of culture, the privileged realm of the symbolic.

In a review article on anthropological approaches to national and transnational cultures, Robert Foster argues that what is at stake in theorizing the emergent global order is not only "the prospects for conceptualizing cultural differences in world historical terms," but also "the concept of culture itself." There have been fundamental shifts over the past two decades in the ways anthropologists—and, of course, many others—formulate the concept of culture.

> Questions about social agents and agencies, rather than about the structural logic or functional coherence of normative and symbolic systems, now orient cultural inquiry. More and more often culture is treated as the changing outcome of "practice"—interested activity not reducible to rational calculation.
>
> (Foster 1991:235)

More and more often, the work of "making culture"—of producing and reproducing collectively held dispositions and understandings—is taken to be problematic. Culture is conceived as "the site of multiple contests informed by a diversity of historically specific actions and intentions" (Foster 1991:235).

In an article entitled "Invoking Culture: The Messy Side of Cultural Politics" (1992), Virginia Dominguez argues that we should be asking much more contextually specific questions about what is being accomplished socially, politically, and discursively when different notions of culture are invoked by different groups—nation builders, minority populations, local communities, academics—to describe, analyze, argue, justify, and theorize.

Like the modern notion of childhood, culture is an "historically situated discursive object with a particular European origin and Eurocentric history" (Dominguez 1992:22). Dominguez recounts a history of the anthropological concept of culture, wrested from elitist Euro-American culture in the late nineteenth and early twentieth centuries and transformed into pluralized, relativist, organically integrated cultures. In important respects, however, these two notions of culture have persisted side by side, with minority or peripheral populations described holistically and organically, while elite populations retain the term *culture*—as opposed to *politics* or *economy*—to refer to refined, aesthetic, intellectual pursuits, such as literature, dance, theater, and the visual arts.

Western culturalist discourses have come to occupy an increasingly global space. In order to make internationally legitimated claims to political autonomy, subject peoples must frame their resistance in national cultural terms. To be a nation means to have a distinctive cultural identity *and* to have the capacity to produce culture in the aesthetic and intellectual sense. Postcolonial populations are concerned with setting up their own museums, writing their own histories, and celebrating their own cultural traditions. Thus, Dominguez asserts, even when non-European peoples seek to resist Eurocentric constructions of their social worlds and to affirm their own distinctive identities, they must now do so at least partially in terms of a world system language of cultural identity and nationhood.

The past several decades have been marked by an increasing concern, both in anthropology and other disciplines and in state agencies, with "the politics of culture"—almost a catchphrase now, suggesting widespread challenges to the self-evident referentiality of the term culture. Within anthropology, for example, there is increasing concern about the ways a relativist, holistic concept of culture has been bought at the cost of a complex awareness of historical negotiation and conflict at the social frontiers within and between designated cultures.[14]

National ministries of culture are concerned with defining official cultural policies. Although the modernist notion of art (and culture more generally) stresses innovation and a certain degree of deviance, discussions of national cultural policies frequently revolve around what sorts of deviance can be accepted within state-funded cultural projects. Should state funds be given to artists whose work offends general public morality? More generally, what is deemed worthy of social reproduction by national cultural policies aimed at orienting cultural activities in schools and other public arenas?

As representatives of the contested future and subjects of cultural policies, children stand at the crossroads of divergent cultural projects. Their minds and bodies are at stake in debates about the transmission of fundamental cultural values in the schools. The very nature of their senses, language, social networks, worldviews, and material futures are at stake in debates about ethnic purity, national identity, minority self-expression, and self-rule.

In recent years, researchers have "discovered" that children are not empty vessels, waiting to be filled with adult values, but rather active, creative participants in society (see Gullestad 1991). The phrase "children's own culture" is meant to foreground children's agency, as well as to emphasize the importance of other children in the process of socialization.

In some of its manifestations, a notion of children's culture is grounded in a universalizing vision of children as naturally creative, playful, and spontaneous. This perspective is often combined with an archival approach to children's culture: the project for researchers becomes one of collecting children's games, rhymes, and songs—of documenting the manifold content of children's common cultural proclivities.

But the notion of children's culture is also important within less universalizing approaches to the study of young people as social actors in their own right, engaged in making sense of and recreating the social worlds they inherit. As several of the papers in this volume [see original reading] strikingly illustrate, children creatively live from the inside complex mixtures of languages and social domains that are external structures for many adults.

[...]

Notes

1   Important insights into modern gender constructions can be found in Mosse 1985; Enloe 1989; Parker et al. 1992; and Butler and Scott 1980.

2   Crucial foundations for this work include Donzelot 1980; Kessel and Siegel 1983; Steedman et al. 1985; Richards and Light 1986; and James and Prout 1990.

3   In "The End of the Body," for example, Emily Martin (1992) asks why the body has become the focus of such intense social and cultural attention today. Following Lévi-Strauss (1973 [1955]), Martin suggests that phenomena become the focus of attention in the academy when they are in the process of ending. While Lévi-Strauss was speaking of "the primitive," a world disappearing with the development of global modernity, Martin suggests that one of the reasons so many researchers are energetically studying the body today is because "we are undergoing fundamental changes in how our bodies are organized and experienced" (121). Some have claimed that under the impact of commodification and social fragmentation we are witnessing the end of the body as a coherently bounded social entity. Martin argues that "we are seeing not the end of the body, but rather the end of one kind of body and the beginning of another kind": "people in the United States (and perhaps elsewhere) are now experiencing a dramatic transition in body percept and practice, from bodies suited for and conceived in the terms of the era of Fordist mass production to bodies suited for and conceived in the terms of the era of flexible accumulation." My own perspectives on the current "end of modern childhood" have been profoundly influenced by Martin's important work. (See also Martin 1994.)

4   There is, of course, a long history of social scientific research exploring interpenetrations between domains of the market economy, artistic practices, religious beliefs, the family and everyday life, in contrast to popular conceptions of "art for art's sake" or of the family as a bounded "haven in a heartless world." I would argue, however, that in the past several decades an explosion of works on the politics of virtually every social domain represents a more radical perspective on the constructedness of social domains than was evident in mainstream social scientific writing in the 1950s and 1960s.

5   Per Olav Tiller has suggested to me that the tendency in academic circles, following Ariès, to see childhood as a historically unique discursive phenomenon existing only within its own socially and historically limited regime of truth, can itself be interpreted as a new sort of risk to children and to society as a whole. This claim can be used to dismiss or undermine the legitimacy of perspectives and values critical of dominant market-driven and politically instrumental practices and beliefs. Children's bodies and minds are thus laid bare as flexible "national resources" and "human capital" to be reshaped, without resistance, as changing economic and political circumstances dictate.

6   It might be argued that hostility to children begins even before their birth. The March of Dimes, an American national foundation focusing on maternal- and child-health issues, has concluded that battering of women during pregnancy causes more birth defects than all the diseases put together for which children are usually immunized (Gibbs 1993b:42).

7   I am grateful to Marianne Gullestad for suggesting the relevance of Douglas's work for the understanding of popular notions of street children.

8   Darcy Ribeiro, a Brazilian senator and anthropologist (cited in Larmer and Margolis 1992:17), observes that ten years of economic crisis and two decades of dictatorship are insufficient grounds for explaining how so many Brazilians have come to accept the idea that large groups of young people are to be treated as disposable goods, or for explaining the nature and level of violence against street children. Such violence and neglect need to be understood in the broader context of systemic violence to children. "While 1,000 children were murdered in 1991 [the official number of murdered street children—the actual number is certainly much higher], more than 150,000 Brazilian infants died before their first birthday from lack of proper nutrition, sanitation and health care."

9   In May 1994, the Norwegian Centre for Child Research hosted an international, interdisciplinary conference on the topic "Children and Nationalism" in Trondheim, Norway, which will eventually result in an edited collection of articles (Stephens, ed.).

10   Foucault's *Discipline and Punish* (1977) has already become a classic exploration of the links between the development of the modern school, the juvenile-welfare system, and the modern penal system.

11   See Partha Chatterjee (1989) for an important discussion of "colonialism, nationalism and colonized women" in the case of India.
12   A discussion of various perspectives on the theoretical framing of late capitalism or postmodernism and of contributions to this project that might come out of the ethnographically grounded field of social-cultural anthropology are the subject of my manuscript in progress, provisionally entitled *Postmodern Anthropology: A Question of Difference* (n.d.).
13   The designations First and Third World, North and South are, of course, only rough markers of geopolitical inequalities and are themselves increasingly problematic in an era of global capitalism, involving fundamental shifts and reconfigurations in national and world regional structures.
14   See Clifford 1988; Appadurai 1990; Gilroy 1987; Hannerz 1989; and Moore 1989.

References

Allsebrook, A. and A. Swift, 1989, *Broken Promise: The World of Endangered Children*, London, Hodder and Stoughton.

Anderson, Benedict, 1983, *Imagined Communities: Reflections on the Origin and Spread of Nationalism*, London, Verso.

Appadurai, Arjun, 1990, "Disjuncture and Difference in the Global Cultural Economy," *Public Culture* 2(2):1–24.

Ariès, Philippe, 1962, *Centuries of Childhood*, trans. Robert Baldick, London, Jonathan Cape.

Barrett, Michele and Mary McIntosh, 1982, *The Anti-Social Family*, London, Verso.

Bell, Daniel, 1974, *The Coming of Post-Industrial Society: A Venture in Social Forecasting*, London, Heinemann.

Boyden, Jo, 1990, "Childhood and the Policy Makers: A Comparative Perspective on the Globalization of Childhood," in Allison James and Alan Prout, eds., *Constructing and Reconstructing Childhood*, London, Falmer Press, 184–216.

Butler, Judith and Joan W. Scott, eds., 1992, *Feminists Theorize the Political*, Routledge, New York.

Cantwell, N., 1989, "A Tool for the Implementation of the UN Convention," in Radda Barnen, ed., *Making Reality of Children's Rights*, International Conference on the Rights of the Child, 36–41.

Chatterjee, Partha, 1989, "Colonialism, Nationalism, and Colonialized Women: The Contest in India," *American Ethnologist* 16 (4): 622–33.

Clifford, James, 1988, *The Predicament of Culture: Twentieth Century Ethnography, Literature, and Art*, Cambridge, Mass., Harvard University Press.

Coles, Robert, 1986, *The Political Life of Children*, Boston, Atlantic Monthly Press.

Comaroff, Jean, 1985, *Body of Power, Spirit of Resistance: The Culture and History of a South African People*, Chicago, University of Chicago Press.

Comaroff, Jean and John Comaroff, 1991, "Africa Observed: Discourses of the Imperial Imagination," in Comaroff and Comaroff, eds., *Of Revelation and Revolution: Christianity, Colonialism, and Consciousness in South Africa*, vol. 1, Chicago, University of Chicago Press, 86–126.

de Alwis, Mala, 1991, "Seductive Scripts and Subversive Practices: 'Motherhood,' Nationalism, and the State in Sri Lanka," proposal for doctoral dissertation research, Department of Anthropology, University of Chicago.

DeMause, Lloyd, ed., 1976, *The History of Childhood*, London, Souvenir Press.

Dominguez, Virginia R., 1992, "Invoking Culture: The Messy Side of 'Cultural Politics,' " *South Atlantic Quarterly* 91 (1): 20–41.

Donzelot, Jacques, 1980, *The Policing of Families*, London, Hutchinson.

Douglas, Mary, 1985 [1966], *Purity and Danger: An Analysis of the Concepts of Pollution and Taboo*, London, Ark Paperbacks.

Enloe, Cynthia, 1989, *Bananas, Beaches, and Bases: Making Feminist Sense of International Politics*, Berkeley and Los Angeles, University of California Press.

Ennew, Judith, 1986, *The Sexual Exploitation of Children*, Cambridge, Polity Press.

Epstein, Julia and Kristina Straub, 1991, *Body Guards: The Cultural Politics of Gender Ambiguity*, Routledge, New York.

Fisher, Marc, 1992, "If Bonn Spares Rod, Will it Spoil the Child?", *International Herald Tribune*, December 3, p. 1 (cont. p. 4).

Foster, Robert J., 1991, "Making National Cultures in the Global Ecumene," *Annual Review of Anthropology* 20:235–60.

Foucault, Michel, 1977, *Discipline and Punish*, London, Allen Lane.

Franklin, B., ed., 1986, *The Rights of Children*, Oxford, Basil Blackwell.

Freeman, Michael D.A., 1983, *The Rights and Wrongs of Children*, London, Francis Pinter Publishers.

Fyfe, Alec, 1989, *Child Labour*, Cambridge, Polity Press.

Garbarino, James, Nancy Dubrow, Kathleen Kostelny, and Carole Pardo, 1992, *Children in Danger: Coping with the Consequences of Community Violence*, San Francisco, Jossey-Bass Publishers.

George, Susan, 1989, *A Fate Worse Than Debt*, Harmondsworth, Penguin Books.

Gibbs, Nancy, 1993a, "Home Alone, Dead: As Two Tragedies Testify, Unattended Children Are a National Problem," *Time*, 1 March, 11.

——, 1993b, " 'Til Death Do Us Part," *Time* January 25, 42–44.

Gilmour, A., 1988, *Innocent Victims*, Michael Joseph.

Gilroy, Paul, 1987, *There Ain't No Black in the Union Jack*, London, Unwin Hyman.

Gullestad, Marianne, 1991, "Barnas egen kultur—finnes den? Tanker om barns aktive samfunnsdeltakelse" (Children's own culture—can it be found? Thoughts about children's active participation in society) *Samtiden* 4:41–49.

Habermas, Jürgen, 1987, *The Theory of Communicative Action*, trans. Thomas McCarthy, vol. 2, London, Heinemann.

Hanawalt, Barbara A., 1993, *Growing Up in Medieval London: The Experience of Childhood in History*, Oxford, Oxford University Press.

Hannerz, Ulf, 1989, "Notes on the Global Ecumene," *Public Culture* 1(2): 66–75.

Harvey, David, 1985, *Consciousness and the Urban Experience*, Baltimore, Johns Hopkins University Press.

—— 1989, *The Condition of Postmodernity: An Enquiry into the Origins of Cultural Change*, Oxford, Basil Blackwell.

Henriques, J., 1986, "Where Little Children Suffer," *Observer Colour Supplement Special Report*, 24 June.

Holt, John, 1975, *Escape from Childhood*, Harmondsworth, Penguin.

"In a 'Moral Vacuum': Britain Agonizes over the Murder of a Child—Perhaps by Other Children," 1993, *Time*, 1 March, 13.

Ingleby, D., 1985, "Professionals as Socializers: The 'Psy Complex,' " in S. Spitzer and A. T. Scull, eds., *Research in the Law, Deviance, and Social Control: A Research Annual*, vol. 7, London, JAI Press.

James, Allison and Alan Prout, eds., 1990, *Constructing and Reconstructing Childhood: Contemporary Issues in the Sociological Study of Childhood*, London, Falmer Press.

Jasper, James M. and Dorothy Nelkin, 1992, *The Animal Rights Crusade: The Growth of a Moral Protest*, New York, Free Press.

Katz, Cindi, 1994, "The Textures of Global Change: Eroding Ecologies of Childhood in New York and Sudan," in Sharon Stephens, ed., *Children and Environment: Local Worlds and Global Connections*, special issue of *Childhood* vol. 1, No. 1–2, 103–10.

——, 1991, "Sow What You Know: The Struggle for Social Reproduction in Rural Sudan," *Annals of American Geographers* 81(3): 488–514.

Kessel, F. S. and A. W. Siegel, eds., 1983, *The Child and Other Cultural Inventions*, New York, Praeger.

Kotlowitz, Alex, 1991, *There Are No Children Here: The Story of Two Boys Growing Up in the Other America*, New York, Doubleday.

Larmer, Brook and Mac Margolis, 1992, "The Dead End Kids: Who Is Killing Brazil's Street Children?" *Newsweek*, 25 May, 12–19.

Lash, Scott and John Urry, 1987, *The End of Organised Capitalism*, London, Oxford University Press.

Lévi-Strauss, Claude, 1973 [1955], *Tristes Tropiques,* trans. John Weightman and Doreen Weightman, New York, Atheneum.

Mandel, Ernest, 1975, *Late Capitalism*, Verso, London.

Martin, Emily, 1992, "The End of the Body?" *American Ethnologist* 19(1):121–41.

——, 1994, *Flexible Bodies: Tracking Immunity in American Culture—from the Days of Polio to the Age of AIDS*, Boston, Beacon Press.

Moore, Sally Falk, 1989, "The Production of Cultural Pluralism as a Process," *Public Culture* 1(2):26–48.

Mosse, George L., 1985, *Nationalism and Sexuality: Respectability and Abnormal Sexuality in Modern Europe*, New York, Howard Freitag.

Nash, Roderick F., 1989, *The Rights of Nature: A History of Environmental Ethics*, Madison, University of Wisconsin Press.

Newman-Black, M., 1989, "How Can the Convention Be Implemented in Developing Countries?" in Report from Radda Barnen, UNICEF seminar on the UN Draft Convention on the Rights of the Child, Stockholm, October, 36–41.

Parker, Andrew, Mary Russo, Doris Sommer, and Patricia Yaeger, eds., 1992, *Nationalisms and Sexualities*, New York, Routledge.

Phillips, M., 1912, "The School as a Means of Social Betterment," in Whitehouse, J. H., ed., *The Problems of Boy Life*, London, King, 206–27.

Postman, Neil, 1982, *The Disappearance of Childhood*, New York, Delacorte Press.

Postone, Moishe, 1993, *Time, Labor, and Social Domination: A Reinterpretation of Marx's Critical Theory*, Cambridge, Cambridge University Press.

Prout, Alan and Allison James, 1990, "A New Paradigm for the Sociology of Childhood? Provenance, Promise, and Problems," in James and Prout, eds., 1990, *Constructing and Reconstructing Childhood*, London, Falmer Press, 7–35.

"The Question Rio Forgets," 1992, *Economist*, May 30, 11–12.

Qvortrup, Jens, 1985, "Placing Children in the Division of Labour," in Paul Close and Rosemary Collins, eds., *Family and Economy in Modern Society*, London, Macmillan, 129–45.

Regan, Tom, 1983, *The Case for Animal Rights*, Berkeley and Los Angeles, University of California Press.

Richards, Martin and Paul Light, eds., 1986, *Children of Social Worlds: Development in a Social Context*, Cambridge, Polity Press.

Scheper-Hughes, Nancy, 1989, *Child Survival: Anthropological Perspectives on the Treatment and Maltreatment of Children*, Dordrecht, Reidel.

Singer, Peter, 1990 [1975], *Animal Liberation*, New York, Avon Books.

Sommerville, C. John, 1982, *The Rise and Fall of Childhood*, Beverly Hills, Calif., Sage Publications.

Steedman, Carolyn, Cathy Urwin and Valerie Walkerdine, eds., 1985, *Language, Gender, and Childhood*, London, Routledge and Kegan Paul.

Stephens, Sharon, 1992, "Children and the UN Conference on Environment and Development: Participants and Media Symbols," *Barn/Research on Children in Norway* 2–3:44–52.

——, 1993, "Children at Risk: Constructing Social Problems and Policies," *Childhood* 1(4): 246–51.

——, 1994, "Children and Environment: Local Worlds and Global Connections," in Stephens, Sharon, ed., special issue of *Childhood* on "Children and Environment," 1(1–2):1–21.

Stephens, Sharon, n.d., *Postmodern Anthropology: A Question of Difference*, book manuscript.

Vittachi, Anuradha, 1989, *Stolen Childhood: In Search of the Rights of the Child*, Cambridge, Polity Press.

Winn, Marie, 1984, *Children without Childhood*, Harmondsworth, Penguin.

Zelizer, Viviana A., 1985, *Pricing the Priceless Child: The Changing Social Value of Children*, New York, Basic Books.

Chapter 25

Ingrid Lohmann and Christine Mayer

LESSONS FROM THE HISTORY OF EDUCATION FOR A "CENTURY OF THE CHILD AT RISK"

THIS INTRODUCTORY ARTICLE PROVIDES the conceptual framework to integrate the following international contributions and their various historical, regional, institutional and cultural contexts. It does so by focusing mainly on three aspects: (1) Childhood and youth as social constructs, the varying classifications of these life phases, their concomitant ambivalences, tensions and social expectations, and the potential for conflict and risk these create. (2) The history and usage of the term, 'at risk' – a designation currently in widespread use despite (or because of) its excessively broad and fuzzy connotations. (3) The reconfiguration of childhood triggered by the normative construction of bourgeois childhood development, especially with a view to the procedures of normalisation and conceptions of normality that emerged in Western thought on this field.

The issue of children and youth at risk does not seem to need the support of history of education to justify its relevance and importance. Nonetheless, the discipline can offer an important contribution by demonstrating, reflecting and disseminating awareness of the fact that threats to children and youth do not simply constitute an ahistorical constant, but take on different shapes under different social conditions. Circumstances which one society would not even perceive as dangerous may be viewed as a significant threat in another. In short, the perception of "risk" is predicated on cultural, social and historical factors. Therefore, the articles collected here [see original reading] will show the reader that there is no innocent use of the term "at risk" in history and are liable to strengthen the conviction that the same applies to the present.

Recent studies on the history of socialisation, childhood and youth have shown that our very understanding of these concepts is historically and culturally constructed.[1] The realisation that childhood and youth are mutable and changing social constructs and "are and remain social reality, of which only a specific historical expression could disappear", as Christa Berg states, is universal today.[2] Berg also points to a second consideration that, *mutatis mutandis,* also applies to children and youth at risk: all academic study must reflect on the question whether its subject "is the world *of* children or perhaps rather a world preformed by adults *for* children".[3]

Defining childhood and youth

Philippe Ariès's study on the history of *mentalité* – *L'enfant et la Vie familiale sous L'Ancien Régime* (1960, Engl. 1962, Ger. 1975[4]) – has done more than any other publication to stimulate public and academic interest in the historical discovery of childhood as a phenomenon. Though his conclusions have been criticised and some refuted in detailed analyses,[5] the study nonetheless highlights an aspect that is central to the historicisation of childhood: the shift in consciousness and attitudes towards children, their situation and position that took place in the bourgeoisie and eventually coalesced into a new, universally applied interpretation of childhood.[6] At the same time, Ariès's study played a decisive role in stimulating the rising interest in childhood as a phase of life in social and historical sciences and its exploration as a sociocultural phenomenon. As a consequence of the resulting international efforts in childhood research and under the influence of social constructivist concepts since the 1980s and 1990s, thought about childhood has undergone another crucial change.[7] According to Helga Kelle, the new perspective is expressed mainly in analyses of the governmental, legal, institutional or discursive constructions of childhood and, on the other hand, the emerging view of children as actors in their own right and operating within their own reality.[8] It is characterised by (1) understanding childhood as a social construct that emerges as a social and historical unit embedded in a generational order; (2) perceiving childhood as a variable of social analysis that can never be entirely separated from other variables such as class, gender or race and ethnicity; (3) viewing childhood and children's social relationships and culture as "worthy of study in their own right, and not just in respect to their social construction by adults".[9] Thus also (4) regarding the active participation of children in designing and determining their own lives is necessary.[10] This new perspective also forms the interpretive context of the studies assembled in this issue.

That youth, too, is a historical, social and cultural construct as much as childhood becomes evident not least from the difficulties we experience when trying to pin down this elusive phase between childhood and adulthood. Its beginning and end are determined according to very different criteria in different social, cultural and historical contexts and even the seemingly unequivocally biological onset of sexual maturity has been shown to vary between cultures and historical eras.[11] Classical Antiquity already had developed a differentiated system of age groups which used three or four discrete classes. Medieval Europe assumed the existence of six age groups. The classification undertaken by Isidore of Seville (560–636) would become fundamental to much of the later academic and clerical discourse on the matter. He distinguished the six stages of (1) *infantia* up to the age of 7, (2) *pueritia* up to age 14, (3) *adolescentia* from 15 to 28, (4) *iuventus* from 28 to 49, (5) *senectus* from 50 to 77 and (6) *senium* on to death.[12] Thus, youth comprised two phases of life – *adolescentia* and *iuventus* – that spanned the ages from 15 to 49. These divisions were not, however, applied universally but rather varied in connection with social status distinctions. We can certainly state, though, that the medieval concept of *iuventus* does not match the modern idea of youth at all. As late as 1900, the definition of childhood and youth remains unclear, with physiological and anthropological categories forming the most influential criteria for dividing life stages. Thus the Brockhaus's *Konversationslexikon* (a popular German encyclopaedia) of 1902 defines a child (*Kind, Infans*) as "the human individual from birth to the onset of sexual development",[13] though it also refers to "childhood proper" as the time between "the first teething and the loss of the milk teeth", which would be the ages from one to seven. The entry for youth (*Jugend*) makes reference to age – both in the physiological and chronological sense – without any further explanation. The age development of the human was divided into the six stages: fetal, infancy, childhood (from age one to the loss of the last milk teeth around age 13 to 14), youth (from the loss of the last milk teeth to complete sexual maturity, i.e. around ages 13 or 14 to 20), manhood (mostly divided again into a youthful and mature stage) and old age (beginning at age 60).[14] Like its historical antecedents, this division addresses the male sex almost exclusively. Passing mention is made of a "female period of regression" between ages 40 and 50.

Comparable modern patterns of perception are still highly relevant for the subject of our discussion of children and youth at risk, since such age classifications determine, among other things, the criminal liability of children and youths under the law,[15] the age limits placed on child labour, and specific limitations on the working conditions of youths. In eighteenth-century Hamburg, the demand that children from the age of six onwards should earn part of their keep, as made by the *Allgemeine Armenanstalt* (a poor relief institution), received general consensus.[16] Rebecca Bates in this volume [see original reading] identifies a different classification of child-hood in the late nineteenth century: through prolonging the phase of childhood, philanthropic projects were able to classify adolescents as children beyond the age of 20 and thus include them in their charity programmes. This idea of extensive aid and support measures still underlies the United Nations' *Convention on the Rights of the Child* (1989/90) whose definition of childhood extends up to age 18 (which disregards any distinction between childhood and youth entirely).[17]

These very different definitions of the various stages of life show, for one thing, that child-hood and youth are very much social constructs. At the same time they also indicate the fact that the traditional conception of youth has mainly been male, not least evident in the fact that the focus of most fundamental studies of the history of youth is the male youth.[18] The idea that youth as a life stage is a modern invention needs to be corrected as well. Older classifications show clearly that premodern conceptions of a life phase analogous to it existed, though they did, of course, differ in terminology and definition. The invention of youth as a stage of life in its own right derives from the realisation that the stages of human development each have a specific importance for the reproduction of human society: Youth is constructed "as a stage of separation from society at large during which the individuals undergoing it have certain social tasks placed upon them under pedagogical guidance."[19] The modern construction of youth, much like childhood, as a transitory phase also shows ambivalences in the tension between protection and control, independence and submission, involvement and exclusion. Though differing in their specific historical and cultural reality, the expectations that societies have of their youth always hold the potential for conflict and risk.

Defining "at risk"

Various authors, among them Juliane Jacobi in her present contribution, have pointed out that the general term "at risk" does not occur in educational contexts before the twentieth century. Instead, we find a terminology that is specific to a number of assumed or actual dangers. In a leading German-language encyclopaedia from the early nineteenth century, the entry for "risk" (*Risico*, lat. *Periculum*, fr. *Peril, Danger, Hazard*, or *Risque*) explores two dimen-sions of meaning. On the one hand, it defines a state in which "one is not safe of one's life and limb, or even just one's possessions, but is placed in a state of fear of losing them". On the other hand, the term in its economic connotations refers to the limitation of entrepreneurial risk through insurance.[20] The verb "to risk" (*riskieren*) – in the sense of running a risk or placing something at risk – was already in colloquial use in the eighteenth century according to the Grimm dictionary, e.g. in the expression "*er risquirt sein ganzes Vermögen zu verlieren*" (he risks losing his entire fortune) or "*sein leben riskieren; seine ehre, seinen guten ruf riskieren*" (to risk one's life, one's honour, one's reputation)[21] The noun is established in German usage by 1900 at the latest, defined as a "danger, venture, especially in the macroeconomic sense, the danger of failure in an endeavour designed to generate a profit", (*Risiko (ital.), Gefahr, Wagnis, besonders in volks-wirtschaftlichem Sinne die Gefahr des Mißlingens einer mit der Absicht auf Gewinn ins*

Werk gesetzten Thätigkeit oder Unternehmung).[22] In English usage, the word risk, borrowed from French or Italian, may already have been used in a broader range of connotations. As early as the seventeenth century, it had the meaning of "Hazard, danger; exposure to mischance or peril", used in the expression *"to run a"* or *"the* (also *one's) risk",* or was used to mean a "venturous course".[23] Alongside these connotations, the word is used in an economic sense in England from the mid-eighteenth century at the latest, analogous to German usage mainly in the sense of "the chance or hazard of commercial loss, spec. in the case of insured property and goods".[24] The expression "at risk" meaning "in danger, subject to hazard", on the other hand, only surfaces in Anglo-American usage in the 1960s, where it is used in the context of child care and "'at risk' families" in phrases such as "[w]omen who were at high risk of bearing retarded infants" or "the baby was considered to be at high risk".[25] In past decades, the expression has developed into a handy formula to encompass the potential dangers in the environment of children and youths. Its frequent use not only by the multilateral international organs of cooperation and governance of the capitalist world such as the OECD[26] but also in academic circles is evidenced by the prevalence of publications, conferences and networks on the subject.[27] In other words, the term is enjoying a surge in popularity even though the connotative boundaries of what "at risk" describes seem to be broad and fuzzy and definitely warrant a critical discourse analysis.

As a definition that can be used in historical research, Hugh Cunningham suggests a perspective shift towards a conscious contrasting with the category of "not at risk": Thus, "the 'not at risk' children were those who enjoyed the protection of what came to be defined as 'the rights of children'. And those who asserted the 'rights of the child' were in fact engaged in a process of defining childhood itself."[28] He regards analysing the emergence of the "rights of children" as a way to specifically determine the dangers associated with childhood at a given time. The rights of children, in the sense of state measures to avert certain dangers, are also no invention of the nineteenth century. In the German lands, e.g. in the Prussian Code (*Allgemeines Landrecht für die Preußischen Staaten,* ALR, 1794), we find specific statutes forbidding child neglect,[29] regulations on compensating a child whose father and breadwinner had been killed,[30] and even a stipulation that accords the full human and civil rights as established in the French revolution (*allgemeine Menschen-und Bürgerrechte*) to the unborn child.[31] Comparable laws regarding parental duties of education and maintenance or the introduction of mandatory schooling are likely to be found in all European countries. They emerged as part of the developing modern nation-state and the process of secularisation which placed the responsibility for future generations on secular institutions (parents, the school and the state).

Even though the expression "at risk" has only lately been used in educational contexts, the very beginnings of modern pedagogics already show that alongside the phenomenon of growing up as such and the intergenerational obligations that it imposed, specific dangers and threats that young people could either be subject to or themselves pose were taken into consideration from the start. We need only recall the numerous admonitions and recommendations, laced with suggestions for prevention or mediation, that John Locke (1692) addresses to the father of the young gentleman and future heir: warnings against the wrong diet and clothes, against pampering and effeminacy, against the bad habits acquired in the company of schoolboys, or the deformation of the young gentleman's character by careless servants sowing the seeds of lifelong superstitious fears.[32] Or think of the statement on which Jean-Jacques Rousseau bases the fundamental text of modern pedagogy, *Emile* (1762), that the entirety of human society, particularly in urban environments, was morally rotten and endangered a child's development into a free, autonomous human being. These examples may suffice to demonstrate that the very earliest modern pedagogical thought already viewed growing up in connection with its potential dangers in some way or another. Indeed, their inclusion appears to be the foil against which pedagogical discourse came to flourish at all.

What is defined as a danger and what measures are taken to avert it depends on the specific historical context. Thus, Juliane Jacobi (in this issue [see orginal reading]) draws a differentiated image of the institutional approach to orphans and foundlings in her study of early modern orphanages. Similarly, the study by Maria João Mogarro and Silvia Alicia Martinez shows that the historical development of asylums and orphanages cannot be viewed solely – and probably not even mainly – in the context of social discipline, but that these institutions offered their charges the educational opportunities that enabled them to success-fully integrate into society. Less questionable of course are risks and dangers for children at war, as Christian Roith (in this issue [see original reading]) shows with the example of chil-dren's drawings from the Spanish Civil War which forebode the traumata of war the children experienced. And Sîan Roberts's article exemplifies that already after the First World War international networks were initiated which collected funds for child protection by means of exhibitions of children's art.

That not only empirically proven dangers but also those created by and within a discourse were used for labelling children "at risk" is demonstrated by Luca Godenzi and Norbert Grube. The "at risk" narrative thus frequently can be shown to be a construction by educators to stress their own merits. Geert Thyssen's case study, too, shows the degree to which the perception of "at risk" can be in the eye of the beholder or is only constructed by that party in the first place. Indeed, as Jeroen Dekker puts it in his contribution, the history of children at risk appears as a story of expansion that not only continues to produce new categories of risk, but also gives birth to the new measures and institutions to tackle them.

Undoubtedly, the horizon against which the problems of children and youth at risk have been perceived since the ending of the *Century of the Child* has once again widened and the awareness of the "diversity of childhood" increased in the process. Our perception today includes not only national and international, but increasingly global contexts. Thus, we now *know* that it is mostly children and youths who recycle our high-tech waste in African coun-tries and suffer extreme health hazards in the process.[33] We know that expensive carpets for sale in the first world are still widely made by child labourers in Asian low-wage countries. We know of Afghan children and youths living in rich cities like Hamburg, their residence permits perpetually at risk of revocation; of the refusal of multinational pharmaceutical companies to provide AIDS drugs to patients in poor countries – among them many children and youths – free of charge; of East European girls being trafficked into prostitution in Western Europe and North America; of sex tourism to Thailand, where boys are also avail-able cheaply, and so forth. When reviewing the old and new risks, we must come to the conclusion that even in wealthy Western countries, the situation of the young people so vari-ously addressed by children's rights and school reform nonetheless can hardly be said to have universally improved in the early twenty-first century. According to a recent representative survey (2008), 60% of parents in Germany fear "that their children may be worse off than themselves".[34] They do not feel overtaxed with the pedagogical challenges of bringing up children, but burdened by their financial situation, and despite rising expenditures on welfare, figures on dropping personal incomes prove them right.[35] In his study of neoliber-alism, privatisation and civil rights, Lawrence Grossberg points to negative developments in the USA. There, the percentage of young people living in poverty and without health insur-ance is especially high. Cuts in public education and the deteriorating legal situation of chil-dren are contributing to this problem.[36] While the benefits of economic growth go to the wealthy, the overall economic situation well into the ranks of the middle class has been declining, putting growing numbers of children and youths at risk.[37] Some 75% of all under-18-year-olds being murdered every year are killed by adults, according to Grossberg, and while the number of murders committed by children dropped by 46% between 1990 and 2000, reported crimes by youths overall rose by 100% in the same period.

Defining the "normal" child

Conceptions of childhood and, in connection with them, ideas of how a child should be have long existed in Western culture. Bourgeois morality and codes of conduct especially make claims to universality whose negative aspects become particularly visible when they are projected into missionary and civilising work in colonial – and sometimes no less in domestic – contexts. The contributions (in this issue [see orginal reading]) by Larry Prochner, Helen May and Baljit Kaur as well as Joost Coté on one hand and Wayne J. Urban on the other demonstrate this amply. The bourgeois normative definition of the development of the child began a "reconfiguration of childhood" (Turmel) with the active participation of academe. This brought forth "normalism" with its agenda of "normalisation".[38] The term "normality" itself derives from the Latin word *norma* (the geometric measure of the right angle). In nineteenth-century German usage, it meant a "regulation, rule or guideline".[39] The *Grimm'sche Wörterbuch* also has an entry for "*normal*" which broadly meant "serving as or according to a norm, regular: normal size, normal state, procedure etc.", "(*als norm dienend oder ihr gemäsz, regelmäszig: normale grösze, normaler zustand, verlauf u.s.w.*)".[40] Interestingly, this entry was not yet contained in the *Krünitz'sche Enzyklopädie* (1806), even though terms such as *Normalmaß* or *Normalkraft* were already in use at that time.[41] If we follow Jürgen Link's study on normalism, we first find the "normal" in the context of modern mass production and normalist procedures of data generation and statistical analysis. In his view, the "normal" is a closely interlocking complex of discursive concepts, models and practical procedures that is of the greatest importance for modern Western societies.[42] "Normal" therefore does not mean "an arbitrarily chosen, ahistorically imagined, more or less invariably spontaneously available 'everyday state', but only the result of specific processes of *normalisation*".[43] In education, the concept of a *Normalschule* – a school "which is organised so as to serve others as an example" ("*welche so eingerichtet ist, dass sie andern zum Muster dient*") was used since the last third of the eighteenth century.[44] Norm here still meant a design provided *de ex ante,* a prototype, as opposed to a serially produced norm derived *ex post* from averages.[45] The normalisation debate received a decisive impulse from the symmetrical distribution model of the bell curve, developed by the mathematician Carl Friedrich Gauss (1777–1855) in 1795 on the basis of astronomical data. It became a cornerstone of normalisation discourse with its strict limits of normality.[46] These limits of the normal are structurally important in that they serve to define it against the abnormal and create fear of denormalisation. Thus, the narrative of "concern for the child" not only centres on the quest for normality, but also on the prevention of divergence and abnormality founded on the fear of failing to meet the "normal".[47]

Detailed observations of adolescent development were made as early as the eighteenth century. However, these beginnings were still relatively harmless compared with the furious collection of data on children that was to follow – with surveys and records on their lives, bodies, studies of their physical growth that led to tables and norms to establish normal heights and weights used by physicians to judge their patients etc. The systematic and professional observation of children, paired with research into childhood life in terms of categorisation, classification, phases and stages, followed a specific idea of correct development which it ultimately both produced and reinforced.[48] The Enlightenment view of childhood and the nature of the child was transformed into a statistically derived model of normal development.[49] This development initially arose out of European endeavours, but through the child study movement a similar field of study emerged in the United States as well.[50]

Around the turn of the twentieth century, attention also turned to the study of the child's deficiencies.[51] The diagnostic method to gauge intelligence developed by Alfred Binet in 1905 played a central role here, introducing a scale of measurements that considerably refined Francis Galton's (1822–1911) designs.[52] The Binet-Simon test was introduced as the first intelligence test that psychometrically measured the mental development of a child in comparison with its age. This not only allowed comparisons between the mental faculties of children, but also differentiations between children of normal and subnormal aptitude for their ages. As Hilda Amsing and Fedor de Beer (in this issue [see orginal reading]) show, this intelligence test became a vital tool of scholastic selection and classification of children with mental disabilities and not only in the Netherlands. New scientific methods and measures not only brought forth new perspectives, but also generated new professions to service the field of normalisation endeavours. In the course of modernising the German educational system in the late nineteenth century, for example, the profession of school physician (*Schularzt*) was institutionalised to cover the newly introduced systematic physical examinations of school entrants.[53] The new, medicalised perspectives, methods and practices often clashed with established thoughts and approaches from a pedagogical paradigm, a situation that led to conflict and occasional power struggles.

In the early twentieth century the practices of observation, classification, grading and placing into the complex medical-social-bureaucratic network of interconnected agencies became far more prevalent, as Ian Grosvenor (in this issue [see orginal reading]) shows for the example of Birmingham. The body of data on the children and the families that the "centres of calculation" collected documented and evaluated for "the good of the child" and its future development from the 1930s onwards is truly staggering. Normality became a yardstick in almost all fields of life; groups that deviated from the norm were increasingly seen as a threat to public order. This applied especially to deviant behaviour by children and youths, as the inflationary use of the term *Verwahrlosung* (broadly describing the feral physical and psychological state resulting from neglect) illustrates: defined as "a perversion of the entirety of childish impressionableness" (*Entartung des Gesamtzustandes der kindlichen Bildsamkeit*), it became one of the most common topics of the public and academic educational discourse in early twentieth-century Germany.[54] Given the dominant position of normalistic concepts it almost goes without saying that lower-class children were invariably felt to be a public menace. The state sought to counter this through a range of educational measures up to and including institutionalising deviant youths.

The medical and psychological discourse on normal and abnormal was also reflected in scholastic practices as Catarina S. Martins (in this issue [see orginal reading]) shows in her discourse-analytical study of the education of the deaf pupils at *Casa Pia de Lisboa*, a Portuguese boarding school. Early twentieth-century deaf education, following contemporary scientific discourse, viewed deafness as an abnormality which was to be corrected through pedagogic normalising procedures and physical and mental techniques. The degree to which medical-pathological discourses influenced common perception is demonstrated by Catherine Kudlick (in this issue [see orginal reading]) by showing the images and constructions of adolescents with disabilities that entered literary narratives and thus shape our perception of the normal and abnormal to this day. The production of normality and deviance in child development remains an important subject of historical research, not least in view of the increasing popularity of applying standardised tests to children and youths.[55] Medical examinations today have become an obligatory part of a lifelong process of data collation that continues through school admission checkups and national and international scholastic performance tests – with no limit to the fury of collation and standardisation in sight.

Children and youth at risk: facets of a history of expansion

The international contributions assembled here address different historical, regional, institutional and cultural contexts through different methods and sources.[56] Their order in this issue is mainly chronological even though, as may be seen above, different categories are easily imaginable. They show facets of a history of children and youth at risk that Jeroen Dekker calls a history of expansion. Deliberately limiting his study to the Western world, he has shown that – beginning with the first children's Acts in France in 1889 through the international movement of children's rights to the UN *Convention on the Rights of the Child* one hundred years later – the group of children defined as maltreated was expanded, and with it the scope of various, often contradictory governmental, political, private and professional interests. On the whole it appears, if we follow Dekker, that risk experts were the group to profit most from this development. In a continuation of their success story, the century of the child at risk, as he has called the twenty-first century, is now introducing into social reality aspects of a totalitarian system that George Orwell foreshadowed in his writings 60 years ago. It is not only in the Netherlands that the introduction of electronic dossiers of youths is prepared with the help of educators, psychologists and doctors: they are to accompany adolescents defined as "at risk" – those with divorced parents, with a migration background, the unemployed etc. – to the age of 23, without the knowledge or consent of the families in question and accessible only to government-appointed experts.

Catherine Kudlick's contribution questions the links we naturally draw between youth at risk and disability. Disability in this context is regarded as a social category much like race, gender, class and sexual orientation, though it is not simply added to this list of social difference.[57] Rather, the question here is the role "disability has played in a broader set of scholarly concerns". On the basis of *Critical Disability Studies*, Kudlick shows in two literary stories that centre upon blind characters, *The Blind Man* by Guy de Maupassant (1882) and *The Blind Lark* by Louisa May Alcott (1886), what new perspectives of thought and interpretation emerge from a viewpoint centred on the "social or minority group model" and what understanding this can open compared with one wedded to the "medical or deficit/pathology model". Kudlick uses the two paradigms to show what (young) readers take away from the story: While the "pathology/deficit model" helps readers maintain a static image of disabled persons as passive, helpless, and pathetic victims, the other paradigm casts doubts on this construction and interpretation of disability and – as Kudlick puts it – forces the reader to confront the possibility that factors other than blindness itself (like prejudice, exclusion, lack of financial resources and cruelty) make the blind person's life so unbearable.

Juliane Jacobi addresses the question of how different European societies treated the problem of poverty. In the sixteenth century, an era defined by mass poverty as a result of social and economic crises, a sharp distinction between the good poor and evil poor emerged. However, the image she draws is more nuanced than many social history studies that, following Foucault, regard all state policy towards the poor as tainted with the brush of social disciplining. Institutions like the workhouse mainly benefited the "deserving poor" who went there voluntarily. It was mostly the "undeserving poor" (beggars and the work-shy) who found themselves incarcerated in the course of poverty policy. The deserving poor (widows, orphans, foundlings etc.) were considered members of the community who merited support – a view that especially benefited women (whose honour needed to be preserved). Based on comparative microhistorical analyses focusing mainly on the seventeenth and eighteenth centuries, Jacobi traces the efforts in orphanages in different parts of Europe to train and educate their charges. Many of them succeeded as adults in integrating into the life and occupational structure of the community.

To Luca Godenzi and Norbert Grube, "youth at risk" represents a narrative that allows them to uncover constructions and analyse and interpret threats. In a study of the early years of Pestalozzi's *Knabenschule* (boys' school) in Yverdon in the first decade of the nineteenth century, Godenzi and Grube microhistorically unearth the differences between pedagogical expectations, experiences and ideals which they read as symptoms in the perception of a crisis in education. Their analysis of life at the institution shows how deviations from socio-cultural and pedagogical norms were regarded as threats. The narrative of "youth at risk" created a dual dynamic between educational practice and the expectations of (mostly wealthy) parents in which, on the one hand, the possibility of improvements through long institutional education was presented while, on the other hand, any degree to which expectations were not met could be explained by the dangers and risks of youth.

To the naive eye, educational and missionary endeavours bearing the blessings of civilisation out into the British Empire might appear to be as purely humanitarian as their proponents long painted them. It was only in postcolonial discourse, which aims to overcome the binary contrast between coloniser and colonised, that modern Western history began to look behind this image. From the perspective of this discourse, Larry Prochner, Helen May and Baljit Kaur take this look, showing how the founding of infant schools for "heathen children" in the course of missionary work accompanied the creation of the Empire in very different colonial contexts from British India to Canada to New Zealand and even shaded domestic perceptions of poor children as "domestic heathens". In their study, Prochner, May and Kaur trace the methods used by Bell and Lancaster in their monitorial schools and the thoughts of Robert Owen – also adapted by missionary educators – that children should be schooled as early as possible in order to minimise the negative influence of their families and that care must be taken to make lessons fun so as to more surely anchor the civilising influence of school in them, by alienating them from their parents.

Catarina S. Martins ties her study to Foucault's writings in a discourse analysis of the education of the deaf pupils at *Casa Pia de Lisboa*. She addresses the question of how the medical and psychological discourse on normal and abnormal inscribed itself in pedagogical practices and technologies of schooling and which implications of this knowledge–power complex concerned the individuation process of the deaf child. Using analyses of discursive devices that were built around deafness and through which the deaf pupil was represented and classified in the educational arena she shows how abnormality was fabricated through the corrective practices and exercises for the normalisation of the deaf or, to put another spin on it, how the invention of abnormality created the norm. Her contribution gives us detailed insight into the complex discursive concept of normalism and demonstrates the role education could play in the process.

Maria João Mogarro and Silvia Alicia Martínez in their essay show how, in the course of the modernisation of the Portuguese education system, the growing perception of the importance of school education in all segments of society, and the attendant need for qualified primary teachers, opportunities were created for girls from asylums to be trained as teachers in the first *escola normal* (teacher training school), the *Escola do Calvário* in Lisbon (1866). For destitute girls whose future employment prospects had previously been those of domestic maids, seamstresses or embroiderers, this opportunity offered not only greater financial security, but also social advancement. On the basis of applications and the letters accompanying them between 1866 and 1882, Mogarro and Martínez trace the causes and complexities of this development. They show how asylums, orphanages, refuges and similar institutions in all their forms require a differentiated and historically contextualised task if their role is to be understood not only as creators of social discipline, but also as support for the poor's ability to help themselves.

While Prochner, May and Kaur see significant differences between the contexts they study and stress the importance of not treating one colony like another, Joost Coté focuses more strongly on the similarities of educational and scholastic colonial discourses, especially in view of the underlying racism. This approach, too, is methodologically fully justifiable, especially since the author shows that in the second half of the nineteenth and the early twentieth century, categories of racial threat increasingly dominated thinking in these fields and came to influence colonial education and school policies especially. The representatives of European civilisation in the regions studied by Coté – the Dutch East Indies, British India and Australia – feared for the whiteness and cultural solidarity of settlements where poor settlers mingled with natives. These communities, in the view of the European policy-makers, needed intervention in order to preserve the purity of European culture, the prestige of the white race and its economic predominance by any means necessary. Mixed-race families were regarded a particular risk as they combined the terrifying moral characters of two perceived political and economic threats: lower (working) class and race. Coté shows that a systematic segregation of schools along racial lines was implemented and light-skinned children were forcibly removed from "full-blood" communities.

Rebecca Bates's article looks into the common philanthropic practice in nineteenth-century Britain of reforming the poor by locating children to the New World. By studying the voluntary organisations *Barnardo's* and the *National Children's Home* (NCH), she traces the philanthropists' understanding of working-class childhood and vocational education, paying particular attention to the question of how philanthropists between 1874 and 1900 increasingly divided children into two cohorts defined by age and work responsibilities. Bates's analysis shows how the category of childhood could be expanded beyond the customary age of 14 – at which poor law assistance to children ended – to well beyond the age of 20 for philanthropic purposes in order to accommodate youths in programmes of education and supervision. In the process, childhood was increasingly seen as having distinct phases in which children needed to be treated in different ways, though. For young people who were targeted for assisted emigration, a vocational training was viewed as the close of their educational progress.

While Grosvenor profitably applies the spatial turn to his analysis, Geert Thyssen uses the analytical category of the field. He underscores the ambivalence underlying the designation of children and youths as subject to certain dangers and exemplifies discursive fields that spread this rhetoric. His example is the anti-tuberculosis movement that arose in Italy in the early twentieth century and survived through much of the century (beyond its country of origin). This movement and the open-air schools it created regarded a type of Locke–Rousseauean natural method combining fresh air, not too exciting nutrition and similar approaches as a panacea that would not only prevent deviancy but also turn at risk children into good citizens. Thyssen shows among other aspects how teachers served as willing foot-soldiers for governments and experts in defining children and youths at risk. In a return to current social and cultural analyses of the at-risk discourse,[58] he emphasises its two-edged nature. The discourse not only – ideally – allows for actual threats to be neutralised, but also generates stigmatisations and vertical differentiations.

Sîan Roberts looks into how non-governmental organisations and influential educators, artists and architects as well as political and humanitarian activists cooperated after the First World War to raise public awareness and financial support for issues of child protection through an exhibition of children's art. She explains how the exhibition of children's art by the pupils of Franz Cizek's Viennese Juvenile Art Class, opened in London in 1920 to international acclaim, founded a tradition of using exhibitions as educational, political and humanitarian interventions. Roberts's analysis demonstrates that later exhibitions of children's art, e.g. during the Spanish Civil War or during the Second World War, show a number of shared characteristics with the 1920 exhibition. Nonetheless, they differ from the earlier model in that children's drawings now were viewed more strongly as psychological effects of conflict and as impressions of war. The contribution draws our attention to the fact that children's drawings, exhibitions of children's art and exhibition catalogues are a productive but hitherto largely underused field of study for historians of education.

Christian Roith's contribution is thematically linked with Roberts's study. He focuses on drawings by children from the Spanish Civil War which were created in school colonies where the children and their teachers were housed following their evacuation from the war zone and separation from their parents. Though such drawings had already been of pedagogical and psychological interest at the beginning of the century, their application as a therapeutic method to deal with the trauma of war only began with the Spanish Civil War. Roith states that they were also used to inform the international community about the situation of these children in order to raise economic aid and political support for the Republic. Exhibitions of selected drawings from the school colonies were organised for this purpose. Like the drawings produced by children in Theresienstadt concentration camp under the guidance of Friedl Dicker-Brandeis between 1942 and 1944,[59] these drawings from the Civil War can be regarded as historical documents which have so far found too little resonance in history of education and childhood. Roith shows that they not only allow us to identify the individual and collective experience patterns of a generation, but give the children themselves a voice.

Linking to Dekker, Ian Grosvenor reconstructs the formation of networks of professionals created in the 1930s and 1940s for the example of Birmingham. These regional "centres of calculation" regarded it as their task to initially define the risks, then to calculate them, collecting data on children and youths, and finally to disseminate their results in a quest to create public consensus on action. Even at this time, part of the attitudes that constituted the position of expert was the belief that the parents concerned need neither consent nor be given access to the data collected on their children. Grosvenor's suggestion to expand historical analysis by a spatial dimension expands our perspective on the effects of the knowledge–power complex within a specific location in space and time and the manner in which – naturally, in the best interests of the child – unfolded its Foucauldian technologies of governance in the interplay of experts and the public. This approach to analysis specifically not only shows up the shifts in the respective technologies of governance, but also illuminates the manner in which the authority of a speaker's position is created and supported.

Hilda Amsing and Fedor de Beer use the example of the Dutch city of Groningen in the 1950s to show how entrance tests for schools for children with mental disabilities gave rise to conflicts over the demarcation of expertise between educators, medical doctors and psychologists and how the ensuing debates, which mainly revolved around the competence of testing intelligence, prioritised either the concept of pedagogisation or that of medicalisation. Even though the creation of the position of the Dutch school psychologist and the strong pedagogical influence on this particular sub-discipline of psychology appeared to have ended this conflict, Amsing and de Beer show that debates on the testing of intelligence and the question as to who holds the authority to define intelligence for the scholastic arena have not been resolved.

By means of critical document analysis, Wayne J. Urban also casts what you might call a postcolonial eye on the recent history of schooling and education in the United States and its development. Urban's comparative reading of two types of texts draws on an old, but nonetheless still productive realisation in history of education: that it can be interesting and illuminating to look not only at official documents, but also at their predecessors (in the shape of grey literature and archive materials). In this case, this applied to the 1962 *Education and the Disadvantaged American* report along with the documented discussions that preceded its publication. Following Barry M. Franklin's study of the hidden semantics of "backwardness" and "at risk" in the US education system,[60] Urban identifies the explicitly ethnocentric, not to say racist positions that underlay the creation of the report and were visible in its predecessors, but entirely purged from its final version. A Supreme Court decision against racial discrimination in school had been in force since 1954, and an according shift in school administration and curricula would have been required. The means by which a core problem of the US education system in the 1960s was turned into one that the 1962 report no longer even addresses are clearly and illuminatingly traced by Urban.

Notes

1   On the development since Antiquity see e.g. Egle Becchi and Dominique Julia, *Histoire de l'enfance en Occident*, tome 1: *De l'antiquité au XVIIe siècle*, tome 2: *Du XVIIIe siècle à nos jours* (Paris: Éditions du

Seuil, 1998 [ital. ed. 1996]); *Encyclopedia of Children and Childhood in History and Society*, ed. Paula S. Fass, 3 vols (New York: Macmillan Reference USA, 2004), since early modern times cf. e.g. Hugh Cunningham, *Children and Childhood in Western Society Since 1500* (1995), 2nd ed. (London and New York: Longman, 2005).

2   Christa Berg, "Das Thema," in *Kinderwelten*, ed. C. Berg (Frankfurt a.M.: Suhrkamp, 1991), 9.

3   Ibid., 7.

4   Philippe Ariès, *Geschichte der Kindheit* (Centuries of Childhood) (Munich and Vienna: Hanser, 1975) (16th ed., June 2007).

5   Cf. e.g. Klaus Arnold, *Kind und Gesellschaft in Mittelalter und Renaissance. Beiträge und Texte zur Geschichte der Kindheit* (Paderborn: Schöningh, 1980), 10–16; Becchi and Julia, *Histoire de l'enfance*, tome 1, 16–25; Christin Sager, "Die "Geschichte der Kindheit". Internationale und disziplinäre Unterschiede in der Rezeption von Philippe Ariès," *Zeitschrift für pädagogische Historiographie* 14, no. 2 (2008): 71–75.

6   Neumann, Karl. "Zum Wandel der Kindheit vom Ausgang des Mittelalters bis an die Schwelle des 20. Jahrhunderts," in *Handbuch der Kindheitsforschung*, ed. Manfred Markefka and Bernhard Nauck (Neuwied: Luchterhand, 1993), 192.

7   Cf. especially: Allison James and Alan Prout, eds, *Constructing and Reconstructing Childhood: Contemporary Issues in the Sociological Study of Childhood*, 2nd ed. (London: Falmer Press, 1997); Allison James, Chris Jenks and Alan Prout, *Theorizing Childhood* (Cambridge: Polity Press, 1998), Barrie Thorne, "Sociology and Anthropology of Childhood," in Fass, *Encyclopedia of Children*, 771–76.

8   Helga Kelle, "Kinder in der Schule. Zum Zusammenhang von Schulpädagogik und Kindheitsforschung," in *Schulforschung und Kindheitsforschung – ein Gegensatz?*, ed. Georg Breidenstein and Annedore Prengel (Wiesbaden: VS Verlag, 2005), 139–60, 145.

9   Prout Alan and Allison James, "A New Paradigm for the Sociology of Childhood? Provenance, Promise and Problems," in James and Prout, *Constructing*, 7–33, 8.

10   Jens Qvortrup, "Die soziale Definition von Kindheit," in *Handbuch der Kindheitsforschung*, 109–24; Michael-Sebastian Honig, *Entwurf einer Theorie der Kindheit* (Frankfurt a.M.: Suhrkamp, 1999). The approach is developed further in Alan Prout, *The Future of Childhood: Towards the Interdisciplinary Study of Children* (London and New York: RoutledgeFalmer, 2005).

11   *Jugend in der Vormoderne*, ed. Klaus-Peter Horn, Johannes Christes and Michael Parmentier (Köln: Böhlau, 1998), VII.

12   Edmund Hermsen, "Jugendleben im Hoch-und Mittelalter," in Horn et al., *Jugend*, 123–25; Arnold, *Kind und Gesellschaft*, 17f; Klaus-Peter Horn, "Was ist denn eigentlich Jugend? Moderne Fragen und vormoderne Antworten," in Horn et al., *Jugend*, 1–20, 11ff.

13   "Kind," in *Brockhaus' Konversations-Lexikon*. Neue revidierte Jubiläumsausgabe, 14th ed., vol. 10 (Berlin and Wien: J. A. Brockhaus, 1902), 333.

14   "Jugend," in *Brockhaus' Konversations-Lexikon*, vol. 9, 1030.

15   See Bernard Stiegler, *Die Logik der Sorge. Verlust der Aufklärung durch Technik und neue Medien* (Frankfurt a.M.: Suhrkamp, 2008). [*Prendre Soin. De la jeunesse et des générations*. Paris: Flammarion, 2008]

16   Christine Mayer, "Kinderarbeit und pädagogische Reform an der Wende vom 18. zum 19. Jahrhundert," in *Straßenkinder – arbeitende Kinder. Sozialisationstheoretische, historische und kulturvergleichende Aspekte*, ed. Christel Adick (Frankfurt a.M.: IKO-Verlag, 1997), 55–72.

17   Some articles, however, specify lower age limits or leave decisions up to the legislation of the signatory states; cf. Volker Lenhart, "Kindheit in der Dritten Welt – gegen die Marginalisierung der Mehrheit in der Theorie der Kindheit," in *Kinder, Kindheiten, Konstruktionen. Erziehungswissenschaftliche Perspektiven und sozialpädagogische Verortungen*, ed. Sabine Andresen and Isabell Diehm (Wiesbaden: VS Verlag, 2006), 201–12, 210f.

18   Cf. e.g. Walter Hornstein, *Vom "Jungen Herrn" zum "Hoffnungsvollen Jüngling". Wandlungen des Jugendlebens im 18. Jahrhundert* (Heidelberg: Quelle and Meyer, 1965); Michael Mitterauer, *Sozialgeschichte der Jugend* (Frankfurt a.M.: Suhrkamp, 1986); Peter Dudek, "Geschichte der Jugend," in *Handbuch der Kindheits–und Jugendforschung*, ed. Heinz-Hermann Krüger and Cathleen Grunert (Opladen: Leske + Budrich, 2002), 333–49.

19   Horn, *Was ist Jugend*, 4f.

20   "Risico," in Johann Georg Krünitz, *Oekonomische Encyklopädie oder allgemeines System der Staats-, Stadt-Haus-, und Landwirthschaft*, vol. 125 (Berlin: Joachim Pauli, 1818), 23.

21   "Riskieren," in *Deutsches Wörterbuch von Jacob Grimm und Wilhelm Grimm*, 16 vols (Leipzig: S. Hirzel 1854–1960), vol. 14, 1042, http://germazope.uni-trier.de/Projects/WBB/woerterbuecher/dwb/ (accessed February 19, 2009).

22   "Risiko," in *Meyers Lexikon online* (2007), http://lexikon.meyers.de/meyers/Risiko.

23   "Risk," in *The Oxford English Dictionary*. 2nd ed., prepared by J.A. Simpson and E.S.C. Weiner (Oxford: Clarendon Press, 1989), 987.

24   "Risk," in *A New English Dictionary on Historicle Principles*, vol. VIII. Founded mainly on the materials collected by the Philological Society, ed. Sir James A.H. Murray (Oxford: Clarendon Press, 1910), 714.

25   *Oxford English Dictionary*, 987.

26   Cf. *Successful Services for our Children and Families at Risk* (OECD: OECD Publishing, 1996); *Co-ordinating Services for Children and Youth at Risk. A World View* (OECD: OECD Publishing, 1998).

27   Before the *International Standing Conference for the History of Education* (ISCHE 29) in, 2007 in Hamburg, there had already been a conference of the *History of Education Society* (UK) on the subject in Oxford in 1993; a further conference on *Children and Youth at Risk and Taking Risks* is currently being organised by the *Society for the History of Children and Youth* at the University of California at Berkeley while the *European Educational Research Association* (EERA) hosts a *Children and Youth at Risk and Urban Education* network (Network 5).

28   Hugh Cunningham, "The Rights of the Child from the Mid-Eighteenth to the Early Twentieth Century," in *Aspects of Education: Children at Risk*, no. 50 (Hull: Institute of Education, University of Hull, 1994), 2–16, 2f.

29   *Allgemeines Landrecht für die Preußischen Staaten von 1794*, ed. Hans Hattenhauer (Frankfurt a.M: Alfred Metzner, 1970), II, 20, § 2; for England cf. Cunningham, *The Rights of the Child*, 3f.

30   Cf. ALR I, 6, §§ 104, 105.

31   Ibid. I, 1, §§ 10–12.

32   John Locke, *Some Thoughts Concerning Education* (1692), section 138. Modern History Sourcebook, http://www.fordham.edu/halsall/mod/1692locke-education.html (accessed February 19, 2009).

33   Cf. Prout, *The Future of Childhood*, 7.

34   "Teurer Nachwuchs," *Frankfurter Rundschau*, no. 187, August 12, 2008, 6f.

35   "Armutsbericht der Bundesregierung. Tiefe Kluft zwischen Arm und Reich," *ARD Tagesschau*, May, 19, 2008, http://www.tagesschau.de/inland/armutsbericht4.html (accessed February 19, 2009).

36   Grossberg, Lawrence. "*Feinde der Gesellschaft*. Gespräch mit Matthias Dusini und Klaus Taschwer," *Freitag*, no. 37, September 8, 2000, http://www.freitag.de/2000/37/00371701.htm (accessed February 19, 2009); cf. Lawrence Grossberg, *Caught in the Crossfire: Kids, Politics, and America's Future* (Boulder, CO: Paradigm Publishers, 2005).

37   Cf. Prout, *The Future of Childhood*, 19ff.

38   Jürgen Link, *Versuch über den Normalismus. Wie Normalität produziert wird*. 3rd revised ed. (Göttingen: Vandenhoeck und Ruprecht, 2006), cf. also Michel Foucault, *Geschichte der Gouvernementalität I. Sicherheit, Territorium, Bevölkerung: Vorlesung am Collège de France, 1977–1978* (esp. Vorlesung III, 25. Jan., 1978, 87–133), ed. Michel Sennelart (Frankfurt a.M.: Suhrkamp, 2006).

39   "Norm," in *Deutsches Wörterbuch*, vol. 13, 899.

40   Ibid.

41   Krünitz, *Oeconomische Encyklopäddie*, vol. 102, 1806, 679.

42   Link, *Versuch über den Normalismus*, 20.

43   Ibid., 359.

44   Krünitz, *Oeconomische Encyklopädie*, vol. 102, 679.

45   Link, *Versuch über den Normalismus*, 179.

46   Jürgen Link, "Zum diskursanalytischen Konzept des flexiblen Normalismus. Mit einem Blick auf die kindliche Entwicklung am Beispiel der Vorsorgeuntersuchungen," in *Ganz normale Kinder. Heterogenität und Standardisierung kindlicher Entwicklung*, ed. Helga Kelle and Anja Tervooren (Weinheim and Munich: Juventa Verlag, 2008), 59–72, 69.

47   Ibid., 59.

48   André Turmel, "Das normale Kind: Zwischen Kategorisierung, Statistik und Entwicklung," in Kelle and Tervooren, *Ganz normale Kinder*, 17–40; cf. also André Turmel, *A Historical Science of Childhood: Developmental Thinking, Categorization and Graphic Visualization* (Cambridge: Cambridge University Press, 2008).

49   Cf. Turmel, *Das normale Kind*, 26.

50   On the child study movement in the USA and developments in other countries cf. Marc Depaepe, *Zum Wohl des Kindes? Pädologie, pädagogische Psychologie und experimentelle Pädagogik in Europa und den USA, 1890–1940* (Weinheim: Deutscher Studien Verlag; Leuven: University Press, 1993), esp. 49–130.

51   Cf. esp. Jeroen Dekker, *The Will to Change the Child: Re-education Homes for Children at Risk in Nineteenth Century Western Europe* (Frankfurt a.M.: Peter Lang, 2001), 101–28.

52   On Galton and his experiments cf. Link, *Versuch über den Normalismus*, 233–43.

53   Annette Miriam Stroß, "Der Schularzt – Funktionalität und Normierungstendenzen eines neuen Berufsfeldes im 19. Jahrhundert," in Kelle and Tervooren, *Ganz normale Kinder*, 93–105, 97. In

change in German-speaking Switzerland cf. Monika Imboden, *"Die Schule macht gesund". Die Anfänge des schulärztlichen Dienstes der Stadt Zürich und die Macht hygienischer Wissensdispositive in der Volksschule 1860–1900* (Zürich: Chronos, 2003).

54 "Verwahrlosung," in *Encyklopädisches Handbuch der Pädagogik*, ed. Wilhelm Rein, vol. 9, 2nd ed. (Langensalza: Beyer, 618–31); not least the length of the article bears witness to the perceived seriousness of the issue.

55 Helga Kelle and Anja Tervooren, "Kindliche Entwicklung zwischen Heterogenität und Standardisierung eine Einleitung," in Kelle and Tervooren, *Ganz normale Kinder*, 7 14, 9.

56 Parallel to the contributions in this volume a selection of papers will be published in Christine Mayer, Ingrid Lohmann and Ian Grosvenor, eds, *Children and Youth at Risk – Historical and International Perspectives* (Frankfurt a.M.: Peter Lang, 2009).

57 On this issue see also the conceptional thoughts outlined in Catherine J. Kudlick, "Disability History: Why We Need Another 'Other'," *American Historical Review* 108, no 3, http://www.historycoop-erative.org/journals/ahr/108.3/kudlick.html (accessed February 19, 2009).

58 Cf. e.g. Sally Lubeck and Patricia Garrett, "The Social Construction of the "At-Risk" Child," *British Journal of Sociology of Education* 11, no. 3 (1990), 327–40; Diane Wishart, Alison Taylor and Lynette Shultz, "The Construction and Production of Youth 'At Risk'," *Journal of Education Policy* 21, no. 3 (2006), 291–304.

59 Cf. e.g. *Vom Bauhaus nach Terezin: Friedl Dicker-Brandeis und die Kinderzeichnungen aus dem Ghetto-Lager Theresienstadt*, ed. Georg Heuberger (= Ausstellung des Jüdischen Museums der Stadt Frankfurt am Main, 25. April – 28. Juli, 1991) (Frankfurt a.M.: Jüdisches Museum, 1991); *Kinderzeichnungen und Gedichte aus Theresienstadt, 1942–1944* (Praha: Státni Zidovsé Museum, 1959).

60 Cf. Barry M. Franklin, *From Backwardness to At-Risk: Childhood Learning Difficulties and the Contradictions of School Reform* (New York: State University of New York Press, 1994).

Chapter 26

Kathleen S. Uno

CHILD-REARING IN THE
NINETEENTH CENTURY

THIS CHAPTER EXPLORES THE CARE and socialization of children in nineteenth-century Japanese households and extrafamilial institutions in order to assess the implications of preexisting patterns of reproduction for Japanese acceptance of day-care centers in the early twentieth century. In the mid-nineteenth century very few institutions provided care and education for children outside a household setting, although formal schooling had begun to flourish. Within the household, early modern willingness to entrust infants and toddlers to nonmaternal caregivers such as male and female kin and servants persisted after the Meiji Restoration of 1868 despite the introduction of Western notions of motherhood assuming the superiority of infant care by the biological mother. After the Restoration, the number and importance of extrafamilial institutions steadily increased, but important continuities in urban and rural household organization prevented drastic changes in the treatment of children. The elementary school, the most ubiquitous new institution, enrolled youngsters above the age of six, while kindergartens, day nurseries, and later day-care centers took in children under that age.

Because households dominated the care and socialization of children, especially infants, at the beginning of the modern era, this chapter focuses on the treatment of children in late nineteenth century and early twentieth century households more than on reproduction in extrafamilial institutions. In contrast to the norms in Japan today, there is considerable evidence of willingness to resort to multiple caregivers for infants and toddlers in households of all classes in the nineteenth century, which in turn set the stage for the favorable reception of day-care centers—facilities where nonmaternal caregivers provided all-day care and education for young children after their establishment at the dawn of the twentieth century.

Household child care in the nineteenth century

The development of growing numbers of extrafamilial institutions for children is a hallmark of post-Restoration Japanese society; nonetheless, it would be a mistake to overemphasize the speed and magnitude of changes in either organizations or individual practices. In pre-1868 Japan the care and socialization of children took place to a great extent in households, but by the end of the early modern period increasing numbers of male and female children attended educational institutions. And well into the modern era, despite high nominal rates of school enrollment, in average and poor rural and urban households, parents and children often gave higher priority to household or wage-earning activities than to regular class attendance.

At the beginning of the modern era abolition of the four hereditary class distinctions accorded warriors (samurai), artisans, merchants, and peasants freedom of occupation and residence, but thereafter the vast majority of Japanese continued to gain a livelihood by means of small farm, retail, or manufacturing enterprises. Their household businesses relied largely on unpaid family labor for both domestic and productive work, and family survival also required assistance from local community organizations based on household membership, much as it had before 1868. Rural areas did not escape progress; the coming of improved roads, railways, newspapers, telegraph lines, and schools during the modern era linked villages to the metropole. Yet labor-intensive, unmechanized cultivation by farm families on tiny plots of land still characterized agriculture, the basic source of rural livelihood.[1] Those whom the land could not support migrated to find employment in towns and cities, as many had done before the Restoration.

After 1868 most city dwellers continued to live and work in households operating small enterprises, although by the beginning of the twentieth century a number of traditional trades had fallen into decline.[2] Nonetheless, to assert that life and labor for ordinary villagers and townspeople retained much of their early modern character is not to posit timeless, unchanging rural and urban life.[3] Changes in the household division of labor, attitudes toward formal education, social mobility, and social relations had been occurring throughout the nineteenth century, but economic and demographic conditions, customary forms of socialization, ideological institutions, and legal codes limited the range of change.

The continued predominance of small-enterprise households in the city and countryside throughout the modern period accounts for much of the continuity in the treatment of children. In the early modern period the lion's share of child-rearing, both care and socialization, occurred in household units, with the education of some children taking place outside the household in various types of schools. Many children acquired most or all of the vocational training, social skills, and general knowledge necessary for adult life through socialization within households. In wealthy households, youngsters might learn from servants or tutors, while poor or prosperous children placed out as apprentices or domestic servants acquired their trade, manners, and social place from the master, mistress, and other residents of their employer's household. Before the Restoration there were almost no specialized institutions that cared for children, but an expanding network of domain schools, private Confucian academies, and temple schools (terakoya) provided a variety of skills ranging from basic or advanced literacy to arithmetic, calligraphy, and moral lessons.[4] However, by the late 1890s, thirty years into the modern period, rising enrollment rates indicate that far more children were being socialized by extrafamilial institutions as they attended the nationwide network of public elementary and higher schools.

In the late nineteenth century household priorities exerted great influence on the internal division of labor, including the task of minding young children. In urban and rural and rich and poor families, young mothers lacked extensive authority over child-rearing if older members were present, and they shared the care and education of even infants and toddlers with other household members. The male household head or senior household members, rather than the mother, generally made important decisions about the care and education of children. The care of young children was regarded as a simple, light task. It was often performed by older children, the elderly, and full-time and part-time servants, freeing mothers for tasks requiring greater skill, strength, or endurance. Rather than devoting most or all of their time to child care, young married women in poor and ordinary households engaged in productive activities such as agriculture, handicrafts, or even wage labor, while in wealthy households they waited on their husband or in-laws, supervised servants, tended family members' wardrobes, and oversaw inventories of household possessions.[5]

The household context of child care: structure and values

The basic setting for reproduction was the household, or *ie*, a form of stem family.[6] Lutz Berkner has defined the stem family as

> a specific type of extended family organization in which only one child marries while remaining at home to inherit the family property and the other children either leave to establish their own families elsewhere or stay in the households as celibates.[7]

Thus a complete stem family consisted of adult couples of two or more generations, the head, wife and children, and the head's parents.[8] In Japan, servants and apprentices were included as *ie* members of inferior status.[9]

The *ie*, however, was more than a coresident kin group. It was a corporate entity that prized its own permanence—the eternal preservation of its status, name, and property. The term "*ie*" therefore carried a range of historical and cultural connotations

> corresponding closely to the varying meanings of our word "house." It may refer to the physical structure, the domicile; to the residents of the domicile, the household; or to the family line, as in the English House of Windsor. . . . It is on this last broader level that it acquires the rich shading of social and ethical value implications important to Japanese society.[10]

Whether translated as "household," "family," or "house" (I prefer the former), the term "*ie*" denotes a corporate unit comprised of past, present, and future generations. Of great importance to the fate of day-care in Japan was the fact that the overriding *ie* goal of household continuity shaped all aspects of reproduction in the family, including procreation, child care, and the education of children.

Children were essential to the achievement of an *ie*'s immortality—the eternal presence of descendants to pay respects to the ancestors, the maintenance of household prosperity, and the preservation of family status in the local community. In most regions during the late Tokugawa and early Meiji periods, parents named the eldest son the successor and sole heir to household property. Alternative practices included assumption of the headship by the youngest son as well as succession by the eldest child and spouse, the latter involving adoption of the husband of a daughter if she were the eldest offspring. Official toleration of variation in succession practices terminated in 1898, when the family section of the newly adopted Civil Code prescribed the succession of the eldest son with rare exceptions.[11] Long-standing local customs did not change overnight; however, after 1898 the birth of a son became more widespread as the goal of procreation.

Emphasis on intergenerational continuity meant that the parent-child relationship, rather than the husband-wife relationship, formed the axis of the Japanese family. The primary aims of marriage were providing the *ie* with an heir, obtaining additional labor for the household, and advancing the household's status or material interests, rather than the uniting of bride and groom in a companionate relationship. Marriage "represented the union of man and woman for the purpose of obtaining a successor to maintain the continuity of Ancestor-worship."[12] Children were precious since they literally embodied the future of the house, but the future successor was far more important than the other offspring in the eyes of adult family members. The heir generally received special treatment ranging from more attention, affection, and praise to better food and clothing than the other children.

In the modern era, parents and grandparents often rejoiced at the birth of a male child, who would in turn grow up to wed and father a successor. A bride who did not soon bear a child could be divorced and sent back to her natal family. If a divorce took place for other reasons, as a rule the household, not the mother, kept the offspring of the marital union. This customary practice was reinforced by law after 1898.[13] Household interests took priority over the bond between mother and child; therefore children belonged to the *ie* rather than to their mothers. Families could hire wet nurses or call on lactating neighbors for assistance in order to raise unweaned infants who were separated from their mothers by divorce.

However, besides the birth of a successor to a mother in the *ie*, adoption also constituted a socially acceptable means of maintaining household continuity. That is, children could be adopted to carry on the household in absence of a natural heir. If an *ie* had daughters but no son, the household head might adopt a daughter's husband as future successor and heir. For childless households, one strategy involved first adopting a girl, then adopting her husband when she married some years later. Alternatively, heirless families could adopt an adult married couple to maintain household continuity. The latter practice indicates greater concern with maintenance of the family as a corporate unit than with continuity of blood lines.[14] In fact, success-oriented merchants sometimes bypassed dull or extravagant natural sons, instead adopting adult employees with greater business acumen as heirs.[15] Households resorted to adoption when natural succession proved impossible or impractical; nonetheless, the birth and rearing of children born into an *ie* was a simpler means of safeguarding the household's vital long-term interests.

If authority over child-rearing and participation in the task of child-rearing itself were not distributed in a way that minimized disputes, discord over child care might jeopardize *ie* continuity. Therefore, in three-generation households the junior wife, a newcomer to her husband's household with questionable loyalties to it, played a limited role in the care and education of the children she bore.[16] Instead, the household head and senior generation—the mother- and father-in-law—had authority over child-rearing, especially the upbringing of the heir.[17] Despite giving birth to new family members, including the heir, a young woman who had married virilocally was not quickly accepted as a household member, and she consequently could exercise little influence over the rearing of her own children, especially the heir, in an extended household.

The task of child care

Besides household goals, assumptions about how children should be treated and what they needed shaped the distribution of child-rearing work among various household members. Children did not receive elaborate care in ordinary nineteenth-century Japanese households, perhaps because other tasks were often so demanding that family members had little time left over to care for children. When an infant was present, child care, like a multitude of other household chores, had to be performed daily, but the minding of infants and young children was regarded as a fairly simple chore, not as a complex and weighty duty with grave and indelible consequences for future mental, moral, and psychological development. In wealthy families wet nurses provided constant care for infants, while nannies, baby-sitters, or boy apprentices watched toddlers and older children. In poor and ordinary farm families and urban households babies up to age three rode around on the backs of siblings or grandparents, freeing mothers to labor at essential tasks during the day and when necessary into the night. Strapping the infant onto the back of the caregiver, with its head facing forward, also protected the baby from wandering off or hurting itself.[18] The caregivers brought nursing infants to the mother for feeding in average households, while among the rich the wet nurse provided essential nourishment. In short, care focused on the infant's basic physical well-being—its feeding and safety—rather than on painstaking cultivation of its psychological or intellectual development.

Multiple caregivers in ordinary families

Lacking the means to hire caregivers for their children, ordinary families generally depended on their own members to care for young children to free mothers for productive and managerial tasks in the household. Since the senior wife in a three-generation family (the *shufu*, or housewife) wielded authority over household affairs, she typically minded the young children and supervised their upbringing while the junior wife engaged in long hours of handicraft work, strenuous farm labor, or heavy household tasks. Alternatively, other family members such as older children or the retired household head might also tend infants and toddlers.

Women and older children watched over infants and taught their juniors social and vocational skills, but male household heads and fathers[19] were not exempt from reproductive tasks. The fact that boys generally learned occupational skills from older males in the household meant that heads of households, fathers, and grandfathers were largely responsible for the socialization of boys, and above all for the proper rearing of the heir. The household head had a considerable stake in the upbringing of at least one child, since he had the responsibility of finding a suitable successor to take over the heavy responsibilities of continuing the family line, venerating the ancestors, preserving the household occupation and its property, maintaining its status, and representing it to the outside world.

Several early Meiji accounts describe fathers' involvement in child care and their emotional investment in children. First, one intrepid Englishwoman, Isabella Bird, who journeyed through villages in northeast Japan during the 1870s, before the interior was opened to travel by foreigners, reported that

> Both fathers and mothers take pride in their children. It is most amusing about six every morning to see twelve or fourteen men sitting on a low wall, each with a child under two years in his arms, fondling and playing with it, and showing off its physique and intelligence. . . . At night, after the houses are shut up, looking through the long fringe of rope or rattan which conceals the sliding door, you see the father who wears [next to] nothing . . . in the "bosom of his family," bending his ugly, kindly face over a gentle-looking baby, and the mother, who more often than not has dropped the kimono from her shoulders, enfolding two children destitute of clothing in her arms. For some reason they prefer boys, but certainly girls are equally petted and loved.[20]

This description suggests that a father's authority over family affairs did not preclude involvement in child care. In fact, in households with several young children and no older siblings or grandparents to baby-sit, the father's assistance with child care may have been a necessity.

Second, in her autobiography, former textile worker and union activist Takai Toshio (b. 1902) recalled her father's nurturant role during her childhood. She remembered her father as kinder than her mother, and her memoirs record his devoted efforts to ensure the survival of her younger brother. Takai's family was poor; they had migrated from an overpopulated village in central Honshu to live by themselves on forest land where her father made charcoal. They lived in a flimsy hut, with barely adequate food and clothing. Despite their poverty, her father was determined to raise his infant son to become a strong, healthy boy. When his son started eating solid foods at age one, Takai's father began to hunt rabbit, fish, and fowl as dietary supplements. He grilled his daily catches over an open fire and fed them to his son. The father also gave these treats to Takai and her younger sister, but he did not begin to prepare these special foods until after the son was born.[21] Takai's account as well as Bird's observations suggest that even in households without property or an adequate livelihood, fathers could develop an intense emotional attachment to their successors and that such strong paternal sentiments could lead to direct involvement in the care of young children.

Mothers were not the sole caregivers of infants and young children, for a number of reasons. First, although a mother had much authority over child-rearing and household affairs in poorer two-generation households consisting of only the head, wife, and children, her necessary involvement in income-earning activities such as agriculture, by-employments, sales and management, manufacturing, or wage work and in domestic chores left little or no time or energy for child care. As mean household size was about five persons during the prewar era, and slightly over half of the households consisted of only two generations, large numbers of women, particularly those of the lower classes, were likely to experience motherhood in a two-generation household.[22] Yet in two-generation households, the greater authority of a young mother over child care and other household matters was counterbalanced by the disadvantage of not having an older female, that is, a mother- or sister-in-law, to assist with the heavy burdens of housework, child tending, and productive work. Thus in poor and average households children were frequently called on to assist with household chores and productive labor.

Second, when a senior generation was present in the household, the junior wife's work and her relationship with her children were subject to supervision by her in-laws, especially her mother-in-law, who as mistress of the household typically dictated how cleaning, food preparation, laundry, consumption, and servants' labor as well as child-rearing should be done. According to the logic of the *ie*, a newcomer such as the young mother ought not be entrusted with control over its precious children, the embodiment of the household's supreme goal of intergenerational continuity. Therefore, if *ie* members with higher status, such as her husband, parents-in-law or sisters-in-law, chose to make decisions about a child's upbringing, as was often the case, the young wife (*yome*) had to defer to their wishes. And even after a junior wife assumed the position of housewife after her mother-in-law's retirement, force of habit, filial piety, and deference might limit her authority in household management and child-rearing until the death of the senior woman.

Mikiso Hane states about the junior wife in a rural areas during the modern era:

> A young wife was treated as an outsider and as the lowliest member of the family until her mother-in-law got too old to run the household. . . . A young wife had to be the first to rise and the last to go to bed. She had to get up at three or four in the morning to cut grass for the horse or ox, work all day, and do the washing late at night after the others had gone to sleep. She had to resign herself to spending little time with her own children, because their care was taken over by her mother-in-law, sister-in-law, or the grandmother of the family."[23]

In metropolitan areas as well, mothers-in-law had more authority over child-rearing than mothers themselves in three-generation households. Reflecting on prewar and early postwar practices, Japan's Dr. Spock, Matsuda Michio, recalled that for the baby's first office visit, "[i]n the past, the mother-in-law commonly carried the newborn baby. The mother herself followed behind."[24]

Hane also notes one of the affective consequences of the young mother's pattern of activities, which reflected the value of her labor and her lack of power in the *ie*. Prolonged daily caregiving by others had great impact on the emotional dynamics of the mother-child relationship in a three-generation household:

> All the spare time the young wife had was to be devoted to work. Caring for her children was an indulgence. One young girl recalled that her mother had to be deliberately cool toward her children so that they would go to her mother-in-law or sister-in-law for attention. As a result, the girl came to look upon her mother as a cold, forbidding person. One day, when she was three or four years old, she watched her mother weeping after being tormented by her in-laws. Seeing the child, her mother called her to her side, but the little girl was afraid to go to her. When her mother told her that she loved her, she blurted out, "Do you mean it?" The mother realized that she had turned her daughter into a stranger in her effort to be a good *yome*.[25]

Senior *ie* members, especially the mother-in-law, expected the *yome* to apply herself diligently to housework, agricultural tasks, and by-employments from morning until night with no complaints, a work regimen that left the young wife scant time to devote to child-rearing.

If a grandmother wished to raise the heir or another child, the young wife's duty was to yield to her mother-in-law's wishes. It is likely that grandmothers frequently chose to take charge of their grandchildren. It was part of their duty to the household, and also compensation for not rearing their own children when they had been *yome*, A grandchild also provided companionship if the grandmother lived in a separate residence. Finally, exercising authority over the grandchild and young wife gave the grandmother a chance to assert her hard-won prerogatives as a senior *ie* member. The above story of the young girl treated coldly by her natural mother is one such case. The childhood of Kawakami Hajime, a noted Marxist scholar born in 1879 to a rural samurai household in south-western Japan constitutes another.[26] Although his mother was alive, as the heir Kawakami was brought up from infancy by his grandmother. One biography of Kawakami records:

> A picture . . . taken when Hajime was about three shows him resting against his grandmother's knee, as she sits holding one of his hands in her lap, while his mother, only about twenty at the time stands demurely to one side. The picture symbolizes the relative roles played by these two women in Hajime's early life.
>
> Grandmother Iwa was fifty-two years old when Hajime was born, and with her daughter-in-law to serve her, she now had leisure time and some savings to lavish on her eldest grandson. By dint of hard work, she had managed to acquire enough money to build separate quarters for herself attached to the original family house. Sunao [Hajime's father], his wife, and his second son lived in the old house, while Hajime slept in Iwa's room. This arrangement was a common practice among Japanese families; especially after the birth of a second child, it was not unusual for the first-born to become "grandmother's child." . . .
>
> Iwa doted on her grandchild. She picked him up as soon as he started to cry and walked back and forth in the garden to comfort him. . . . When he was still learning to crawl, she scattered sweet cakes on the floor to encourage him. Wherever Iwa went—to the theater, on picnics, sight-seeing at local shrines or Buddhist temples—she took her grandson along.[27]

In households of modest means, grandmothers such as Kawakami's could devote themselves to child-rearing, leaving the task of running the household to the young wife.

Even grandfathers looked after babies and toddlers. Like fathers and grandmothers, fondness may have motivated some grandfathers to take care of their grandchildren. So, too, might a sense of responsibility for the upbringing of the heir lead grandfathers to tend male grandchildren. On the other hand, a grandfather in a household with few able-bodied adults may have been the only person the household could spare for the relatively light work of baby-sitting.

The renowned ethnographer Miyamoto Tsuneichi, born in Yamaguchi Prefecture in 1907, remembers that even though he was quite young when he used to go to the fields and forest lands with his grandfather, the old man gently began to mold him into a good farmers' son. Miyamoto would ride on his grandfather's back when the old man had no bundles to carry. After arriving at the destination, he was free to wander about while his grandfather worked, but recalled that "when I scampered back from playing in nearby hills, I was relieved to see him there at work. He would encourage me to work too by saying, 'If you pull even one sprig of grass, it helps [my work] by that much.' "[28] The grandfather kept an eye on his grandson while doing other chores, and at the same time taught him wholesome attitudes toward work.

Besides parents and grandparents, older children cared for infants and toddlers in ordinary rural and urban families. Children of both sexes between ages seven and fourteen worked at useful housekeeping and productive tasks such as cutting grass, sweeping, finding firewood, weeding, and plaiting straw cords, and they tended younger brothers and sisters as well. In impoverished families, children might begin to baby-sit siblings at age three or four.[29]

Boys as well as girls minded young children. Katayama Sen, a Meiji socialist born to a prominent family in an Okayama village, recalls that his brother, only four years his senior, as well as his grandmother and aunt, took care of him during his early childhood, while his mother farmed the family lands.[30] A 1900 survey of higher elementary students in a rural hamlet near Yokohama conducted by their teacher revealed that many thirteen-year-old boys helped with both baby tending and housework. The teacher summarized the boys' activities in the following way:

> Boys' daily work [included] 1) cultivating paddies and dry fields, 2) babysitting, 3) indoor and outdoor cleaning, 4) drawing water . . . 5) cleaning lamps, 6) braiding ropes or straw sandals, 7) preparing the bath, 8) doing errands, 9) gathering fertilizer, and 10) reviewing lessons or 11) looking at the newspaper, and 12) other [tasks].[31]

The social acceptability of child-tending by boys is suggested by the praise heaped on one mid-Meiji elementary school student in a novel by Chiba Hisao. Taima Tsuneyoshi, an eleven-year-old fifth son, was praised by school officials in his town for

> being obedient, not quarrelling with others, whether at school or not, and having good character, minding the teachers' instructions well while at school, and having never been punished for violating school rules. At home, he did not contradict his parents, and had reportedly never angered them or been scolded by them. . . . He always reviewed his lessons after school, but after that, plaited rope to supplement the family finances, and was never lazy. Furthermore, he sometimes babysat his nephew (aged 7) and acted as a scarecrow in the rice fields. . . . Due to the family's financial condition, his parents apprenticed him to a certain shop . . . but the master released him from service because he wore

a melancholy look day and night. . . . [H]e was very happy to return home again
. . . and his parents sent him to school once more.[32]

School authorities excused Taima's failure as an apprentice, instead lauding his conduct at home and at school, including his work as a baby-sitter. The male writer of the novel's afterword, who grew up in a rural hamlet, also recalls having his baby sister, ten years younger, bound to his back.[33]

Multiple caregivers in elite households

Family members besides mothers cared for infants and toddlers on a daily basis in ordinary rural and urban households; nonmaternal care was also widespread in wealthy households. In rich households, however, the alternate caregivers were hired child baby-sitters, wet nurses, nannies, or apprentices rather than other family members. Despite the introduction of Western conceptions of womanhood emphasizing the critical role of mothers in raising children and the companionate relationship of spouses as the basis for marriage, many aspects of household goals and organization—the aim of household immortality, the junior wife's lack of authority, and work patterns—changed little or not at all in both prosperous and poor families after 1868. These values in turn kept alive many early modern conceptions of child care and motherhood.

In wealthy enterprise households, lingering early modern Confucian family ideals also undermined notions of increased maternal responsibilities for children; authority was vested in the household head and the senior generation, not in the young wife who gave birth to the next generation. Over time new views of womanhood and child-rearing slowly gained greater influence, particularly in the ranks of the new urban middle class, salaried workers, and their families. And as workers leaving the villages gravitated toward freer forms of labor, a growing shortage of domestic servants in the modern era contributed to a slow decline in the practice of employing nonmaternal caregivers.

In rich households, discourses of early modern written culture as well as the logic of the *ie* weakened a mother's authority over her children. By the middle of the early modern period, wealthy urban merchants and prosperous peasants had begun to absorb Japanese Confucian thought, formerly limited to the ruling warrior class, and the influence of these ideas lingered into the modern era. Popular Confucian tracts for women such as Kaibara Ekken's "Onna Daigaku" (Greater learning for women) emphasized female inferiority. According to Kaibara, women were afflicted with seven vices; female moral deficiencies were so extensive that only with considerable difficulty could women conduct themselves well enough to be models of virtuous conduct for children. The advice books admonished young brides to serve their in-laws faithfully, to practice frugality and modesty, and to learn to manage household and servants well, but they scarcely mentioned the responsibilities of motherhood. The lengthy instructions regarding a *yome*'s duty to her husband's parents and siblings suggest that obedience to in-laws in her new household was more important than child care for a young Japanese woman.[34]

Some popular Confucian-influenced writings advised households on how best to educate children. These tracts commonly warned "fathers and elder brother" (*fukei*) or "fathers and mothers" (*fubo*) to take care to choose a suitable tutor for the child. Almost never was advice regarding education and child-rearing addressed to mothers alone.[35] Women did in fact play important roles in child care as wet nurses, nannies, baby-sitters, and mothers, but notions of female inferiority precluded strong female authority over child-rearing and, at least in theory, argued against allowing women the major role caring for children. These tracts delegated ultimate responsibility for children's upbringing to male figures, since Confucian logic dictated that children, especially boys who would assume positions of influence in society, be reared by virtuous men instead of inferior females. In fact, because boys studied under male tutors and learned much about their future occupation from fathers, master craftsmen, or successful merchants, they had much more contact with men than did girls, who were not destined to become leaders in the household or in society and could therefore be relinquished to female mentors. Social norms, then, in theory and in practice placed little emphasis on mothers as autonomous or primary nurturers of infants and young children.

Thus despite the presence of servants, mothers in wealthy households tended to many household tasks, because female idleness was scorned, but child-rearing was not one of their central duties. Unlike lower-class women, mothers in prosperous families did not as a rule participate directly in income-earning activities. Their work for the household, waiting on their husband and in-laws and supervising clothing, household decor, and kitchen supplies as well as servants, left them little time to spend with their offspring.[36]

The lack of extensive daily contact between mother and children, however, caused no anxiety among the adults in the household—neither household head, parents, grandparents, nor servants. Instead, in prosperous households infant care was routinely assigned to child baby-sitters (komori) or apprentices for part or all of the day, while as a mark of social distinction, very rich families hired full-time servants such as wet nurses or nannies to specialize in child care.

The komori was usually a youngster from a poor family. Instead of helping their own families, studying, or playing, poor children hired out as baby-sitters and spent their daytime hours tending infants in the masters' households. Sugō Hiroshi's historical novel set in the rural Koriyama district of Fukushima Prefecture recounts how boys from impoverished households were hired as live-in baby-sitters; in a lower-class Tokyo district, Sangorō, a sixteen-year-old rickshaw puller's son, sometimes provided unpaid child care for his land-lord's infant by strapping the child to his back.[37] In a village in Saitama Prefecture, poor tenant farmers sent out their daughter, Kichi, to work as an unpaid komori for the landlord; by doing so, she drained less of the family's meager resources, because she received two out of three daily meals at her employer's house. She continued to work as a nonresident komori from age seven to ten, until she grew old enough to do field work.

A description of Kichi's daily routine reveals in some detail the nature of a baby-sitter's duties and the type of care the infant received. Kichi set off for the landlord's residence soon after breakfast seven days a week, then trudged home late at night after finishing a skimpy dinner of leftovers at her employer's. Her work consisted of carrying the landlord's baby on her back all day, except when the child was being fed. The baby pulled her hair, and the young wife criticized Kichi's eating habits. Little Kichi complained, but her mother replied that the family was lucky she was able to baby-sit for the landlord. When Kichi graduated to field work at the age of ten, her younger sister took her place as komori.[38] Well into the 1930s, rural households continued to make use of komori to care for infants while their mothers worked in the fields.[39]

Some children moved away from home to serve as live-in baby-sitters in nearby towns or distant cities. One woman recalled:

> I was born in 1887 as the oldest daughter in a poor farm family in . . . a village in the watershed of the Yodogawa River in Kochi prefecture. I didn't go to elementary school. At twelve, I went into service as a komori in a paper-maker's household. At eighteen, I became a full-fledged paper-maker . . . and sent home nearly all my wages to help the family finances.[40]

Although hired baby-sitters usually came from poor households, occasionally motives other than poverty led parents to place children in other households. For example, the father of one eight-year-old girl from Niigata Prefecture arranged for her employment as a *komori* for a factory owner's family in neighboring Nagano Prefecture to help her escape mistreatment by her stepmother.[41]

Rather than the joys and satisfactions of nurturing precious infants, baby-sitters' songs reveal the misery and resentment of modern *komori*. Former *komori*, when interviewed in their old age by Mariko Asano Tamanoi, recalled singing, "One, we are all bullied. Two, we are all hated. Three, we are all forced to talk. Four, we are all scolded. Five, we are all forced to carry babies who cry a lot. Six, we are all fed with terrible food. Seven, we are all forced to wash diapers in the cold water of the river. Eight, we are all impregnated and shed our tears. Nine, we are all persuaded to leave, and finally, ten, we all must leave," But baby-sitters could get even with their employers for the unpleasant work and any sexual liberties that might be taken: "Listen, my master and mistress. If you treat me bad, I may exert an evil effect on your kid."[42]

In urban settings the duties of apprentices often included baby-sitting and household chores such as boiling breakfast rice and sweeping floors, as much as productive work. Boys generally became apprenticed to merchants or master tradesmen between the ages of ten and thirteen, although some from poor families might enter service as young as seven or eight. One historian of childhood describes the first stage of an artisan's apprenticeship in the following way:

> When a child was bound out, he lived with the master's family. At first, he began by doing household chores such as drawing water, boiling rice, cleaning the yard, heating the bath, running errands, and baby-sitting. After that he learned the trade, beginning with carrying and arranging tools.[43]

A lacquer craftsman from Wajima on the Japan Sea explained that for the first three years a new apprentice's life consisted of baby-sitting and doing household chores such as drawing water, changing outhouse buckets, and straightening up the workplace. One plasterer from Sagamihara City, Kanagawa Prefecture, who became an apprentice in 1914 at age thirteen, recalled that his early duties included minding the master's child:

> I became a plasterer because my father thought that as the oldest son I ought to be prepared to head the family business. . . . Until another junior apprentice entered the household, I had to do miscellaneous chores. I helped prepare meals, babysat, washed the baby's diapers, massaged the master's shoulders, and ran errands for the craftsmen and master. Since the master also farmed, I had to do agricultural work, too. I waited on the master during meals, so it was important to be able to eat faster than he did.[44]

Although not all apprentices engaged in child care, the training of young, unskilled apprentices invariably commenced with easily performed chores. The fact that artisans lumped child care, housework, and errands together, delegating them to neophytes, suggests that they regarded these types of work as menial but necessary tasks in household activities.

Families in the upper ranks of society commonly employed wet nurses (*uba*) to care for infants, a tradition that existed for centuries in Japan.[45] For this reason, very rich families hired full-time servants who specialized in child care as a mark of social distinction. Early modern literary evidence suggests that wet nurses (also called nursemaids) stayed with their charges at least until they reached age three or four.[46] Child-rearing tracts of the day included sections on criteria for selecting *uba* of good character.[47] Authors of these advice books took for granted that caregivers other than the mother would tend young children, Although it was expected that an *uba* or nanny would care for children in rich households,[48] tensions could exist between the pecuniary motivations of lower-class wet nurses and the desire of parents for attentive care for their beloved child or between the nurturing and affection a wet nurse felt she owed to her employer's as well as her own child. Recognizing this gap between expectations of employed and employer, Saikaku, a renowned early modern writer, declared (with some hyperbole), "People say that the three great scoundrels are pack-horse drivers, ship's captains, and wet nurses," since only young women with "the most naive notion of how to raise a child" or gold diggers became wet nurses.[49] The practice of wet-nursing reveals that neither upper- nor lower-class mothers were expected to care for their own infants. Not only did rich mothers largely place their babies in the hands of hired caregivers, but each *uba* had to give up nurturing her own child. A wet nurse had the choice of hiring a foster mother for her own baby, or leaving her infant with the father, who in turn would depend on a live-out, hired wet nurse nearby or the voluntary help of a nursing neighbor to suckle the newborn. Although this form of employment improved the finances of the *uba*'s household, she endured the disadvantages of separation from her husband, the endangerment of her own child's survival, and confinement to the home of her employer.[50]

Wet nurses freed wealthy mothers from the daily toil of feeding, carrying, and bathing young children. Yet the difference in status between child and nanny might be problematic. Early modern advice tracts warned parents to take care in selecting an *uba* in order to avoid improper moral influences on their offspring. Other difficulties might arise for the employer due to status differences between hired nurturer and child. In the opening scene of Chikamatsu Monzaemon's early modern puppet play, "Yosaku of Tamba," the daughter of a feudal lord causes a great stir by refusing to travel north to wed. Her governess, a woman of the warrior class, and other retainers beg her to set forth, but since they are lower ranking, they cannot compel her to begin the journey.[51] Despite disparities in social status, extremely close, lasting bonds might develop between a wet nurse and the child she nursed.[52]

Robert Danly's sketch of the tragic, fleeting life of the renowned Meiji writer, Higuchi Ichiyō, reveals deep affective ties that developed between an *uba* and her charge, but it also shows that the nurturing of the employer's infant came at the expense of the wet nurse's baby. Ichiyō's parents, Noriyoshi and Ayame, descended from wealthy peasants, fled relatively secure lives in their village for a marginal existence in Edo (now Tokyo) in order to marry shortly before the Meiji Restoration. After Ayame bore a child, Noriyoshi's patron, Mashimo, assisted the penniless couple by arranging a prestigious position for Ayame as an *uba* in a prominent samurai family:

> Mashimo . . . saw to it that the young bride was properly established in her new home. He sent baby clothes when her daughter Fuji, named for Mashimo's wife, was born on 14 May. And he arranged for Ayame to serve as a wet nurse once she had recuperated from the birth. On 24 June, Ayame left Noriyoshi and the newborn Fuji in Koishikawa for the time being and went off to the Yushima estate of Inaba Daizen, a *hatamoto* [direct shogunal retainer] whose daughter, Ko, Ayame was to nurse . . . .
>
> Taki [Ayame's new name bestowed by Inaba] was constantly reminded of her inferior position. When nursing the Inaba child, deference required her to place a piece of tissue over her mouth, lest she breathe on "the little princess." She paid for the privilege of serving the exalted child by being forced to put her own baby out to nurse and to endure long absences from her new husband.[53]

For seven years, until the family's economic situation improved, Taki lived at the Inaba estate separated from her husband and daughter [Fuji, later known as Ichiyō]. Deep bonds of affection between Taki and Ko survived Taki's departure from the Inaba household. Ko regarded Taki "almost as a mother," and years later nurse and nursling continued to keep track of each other's whereabouts.[54]

In the modern era, elite families in urban and rural regions continued to employ wet nurses. In an 1876 work, one of the first introducing kindergartens to Japan, Kuwada Shingo scathingly remarked that "[t]he *yome* [young wives] in noble and wealthy households always wear makeup and fine garments, but they know nothing about how to rear children. They only give birth, and without ever laying hands on the child, turn it over to an insincere wet nurse."[55] Journalist and educator Fukuzawa Yukichi, who married in 1861, recalled that his wife nursed the first five of her nine children herself, but thereafter hired an *uba*.[56] Writer Dazai Osamu, born in 1909 to a prominent rural family in Aomori Prefecture, was reared by his aunt and hired caregivers because his mother was sickly. He recalls that

> [b]ecause my mother was in poor health, I never drank a drop of her milk, but was given to a wet nurse as soon as I was born. When I was two years old and tottering about on my own, I was taken away from her and put in the care of a nanny—Take. At night I would sleep in my aunt's arms but during the day I was always with Take. For the next five years, until I was about seven, she raised me.
>
> And then one morning I opened my eyes and called for Take, but Take did not come. I was shocked. Instinctively I knew what had happened. I wailed, "Take has gone! Take has gone!" I sobbed, feeling as if my heart would break; and for two or three days all I could do was cry. Even today I have not forgotten the pain of that moment.[57]

A 1913 survey of servants in Tokyo revealed that wealthy households were still hiring wet nurses, mostly country or lower-class city girls, who in turn employed someone else to care for their babies during their term of service. Wet nursing appears not to have been an easy occupation, because the survey also noted that *uba* rarely completed their contracts. One wonders about these women: Did they leave because they were treated badly, or did they want to return to their own children or husbands, or did they leave for other employment in the city?[58]

The character of late nineteenth century child care

In sum, not just mothers, but other household members ranging from grandparents and fathers to siblings and several types of servants commonly provided daily care for infants and toddlers in nineteenth-century Japanese households. While younger adult males were less likely to provide all-day care for young children, household heads and retired household heads (grandfathers) had much incentive to spend time with at least one child, since they were obliged to train a successor. Not only did the presence of a mother-in-law or servants diminish contact between mother and child and reduce the authority of a mother over her offspring, but the father and father-in-law, too, could limit her freedom to raise the children as she wished. Especially in the literate classes, old ideas tended to undermine mothers' relationships with their children, because early modern advice tracts held that women's many faults impeded their ability properly to socialize children. Children would become better adults if reared by more virtuous males.

Viewed from a contemporary perspective, this pattern of multiple caregivers may appear to have deprived a Japanese baby of a mother's tender care. In fact, two major advantages of this infant care method are first that it allowed mothers of very young children to participate in productive labor and second that it offered infants a considerable degree of security. The Japanese child under three spent most or all of its waking hours strapped to the back of the caregiver, generally the same sibling, grandparent, or servant, each day. The baby was safe and emotionally secure, because it was protected from physical harm, was never alone, and experienced constant, reassuring physical contact with its caregiver. The child was unbound from the baby-sitter's back and brought to nurse at its mother's breast for feeding. The infant was also unstrapped for elimination, but mistakes in timing meant that the caregivers not infrequently became wet or soiled.

Robert Smith and Ella Lury Wiswell's observations of Suye Village indicate that reliance on multiple caregivers persisted into the mid-1930s in parts of rural Japan, although by this time boys had been largely excluded from infant care. Wiswell's field notes indicate that grandmothers, older sisters, and teenage girl baby-sitters carried infants and young toddlers around on their backs during the day. The baby-sitters watched three-to six-year-olds play together in groups. These older toddlers ran to the caregiver or whoever else was near— sibling, grandparent, mother, father, or neighbor—for comfort or protection. Mothers breast-fed their youngest children, who slept by mother at night, and they also nursed babies of others when the mother was not nearby. Other cosleeping arrangements were also practiced; young children often slept next to fathers, siblings, or grandparents. Thus in addition to mothers, family members or *komori* kept young children reasonably secure and safe.[59]

Post-Restoration changes

As we have seen, throughout the nineteenth-century nonmaternal caregivers spent as much or more time than mothers in caring for and educating children, including infants, in households of all classes. However, after the 1868 Meiji Restoration, as part of a concerted effort to catch up to the West, the modern Japanese state promoted the creation of new social institutions to consolidate its authority and to strengthen the nation. The new economic and educational institutions—factories, government offices, and schools—made demands on the time and energy of household members that reshaped the household division of labor, including participation in child care. Students attending school and wage-earning members of the family were away for long hours nearly every day, thus preventing them from engaging in baby tending and other domestic activities during working hours.

The new educational institutions affected reproduction in the family in two ways. First, the activities taking place in schools, and to a degree those in kindergartens, replicated some household functions, because they offered children and older youth vocational and moral training for their future roles in society. Second, daily absence from the household for many hours made it impossible for older children attending school to play a major role in child care at home. In founding the public schools and mandating first four, then six, years of education for children of both sexes, the government sought to alter the socialization process to foster state goals. However, the negative impact of compulsory education on the household division of labor and family livelihood stirred resistance to state policy, mainly among ordinary households that depended on children's household or wage-earning labor to survive. The government adopted various strategies such as reducing the duration of compulsory education, lowering tuition rates, and founding special institutions to educate poor children to soothe aggrieved families, but it continued to promote school enrollment and to send out truant officers to compel school attendance. By the early twentieth century enrollment rates suggest that ordinary families throughout the nation had come to accept compulsory schooling.

In the home, care of young children by persons other than mothers was common to all levels of nineteenth-century Japanese society, but with the growth of trade and industry after 1890, a new pattern of child care began to emerge in city households that were no longer productive units. Particularly influential were the family patterns of the new urban middle-class households whose bread-winners filled the expanding ranks of salaried employees, although the new middle class remained a minority of Japan's population during the prewar era. The upper reaches of the new salaried class included influential professionals such as journalists, educators, bureaucrats, technicians, and managers, and in their homes, women and children became dependent consumers as the family shed many of the productive tasks that women and sometimes children continued to perform in rural and urban enterprise households. The old pool of caregivers shrank as cities grew, since urban families on average contained fewer members than rural households.[60]

Children and fathers who went out to schools and workplaces during the day of course were not available to care for infants. In villages, towns, and metropolitan districts where mothers in peasant, merchant, and artisan families still worked, other family members continued to provide care for babies. Thus old family and child-care patterns coexisted with the new; however, as the ranks of new middle-class families continued to swell during the twentieth century, practitioners and advocates of the new patterns increased.

Modern schools and child care

Examination of the impact of modern schools on the process of reproduction in late nineteenth century Japanese households reveals that the policy of universal compulsory education, begun in 1872, worked against the custom of having older children, hired baby-sitters, and apprentices look after the youngest family members. Child-care practices were little affected at first, because families refused to enroll their youngsters, resulting in low school attendance in early Meiji. In 1873, the overall enrollment was a mere 28 percent; twelve years later it had risen only to 49 percent.[61] At the time many average Japanese perceived schools to be detrimental to the interests of their families and localities because schooling was costly, with new local taxes assessed to support public schools. Moreover, children attending schools paid tuition. In fact, education was a double burden for ordinary households because schools drained cash from household coffers and robbed them of the use of older children's labor during prime daylight hours for a period of four to six years. For these reasons, it is not surprising that families of limited means were reluctant to enroll children in schools. Resistance took an active form in some areas during the early Meiji as protestors razed and set fire to schools.[62]

Despite resistance, however, the government maintained its compulsory education policy, because schooling was crucial to shaping the character and talents of future citizens of the new Japan. Through various means educational authorities raised school attendance levels: they threatened with truant officers, they cajoled by offering special schools that allowed children to work—night schools, industrial schools, tuition-free pauper's schools, and baby-sitters' schools (*komori gakkō*). Over time the carrot-and-stick method proved to be fairly effective; by the late Meiji period school enrollment rates had reached 98 percent.[63] Yet registration rates painted a rosier picture than reality. Autobiographies and oral histories reveal that children of all ages were routinely kept home from school when their families required extra labor:

> [M]y family [was] a farm family. I had five brothers and sisters, but one died young. I went to four years of elementary school, but baby-sitting, baby-sitting. . . . [I]f I calculate it, I actually attended only three full years. I can barely read the syllabary.[64]

Observers were also struck by the low rates of school attendance of urban poor.[65]

Local educational authorities created baby-sitters' schools (*komori gakkō*) as a means of increasing elementary school enrollment. The state was not willing to neglect even lower-class children in its quest to mold loyal, obedient, patriotic citizens through education in state-monitored schools. The nationwide establishment of these schools indicates that large numbers of families could not dispense with children's help in productive and reproductive labor, including the care of infants, by enrolling them in regular public schools. The employment of *komori* in the late 1880s and 1890s was so widespread that it called for special policy measures.[66] *Komori* could bring the infants in their care to baby-sitters' schools, but since the schools' primary aim was to educate children in the elementary grades rather than preschoolers, the facilities for infants were very limited. At the time, the provisions for children under six were as simple as letting *komori* or siblings take turns minding the toddlers in a separate room adjoining the classroom. A few exceptionally well equipped baby-sitters' schools had separate programs and teachers for the preschoolers.[67]

The efforts of the state to mold solid future citizens extended not only to older working children such as *komori*, farm children, and factory operatives; the state encouraged development of new institutions to educate children under age six as well. In creating the modern educational system in 1874 based on Western models, the Meiji government mandated the founding of kindergartens (*yōchien*) as well as elementary schools and higher institutions of learning; and for a similar reason—to improve the quality of the nation's manpower. The first *yōchien* opened in 1876, a few years after the national school system and compulsory education were established early in the Meiji period. It aimed to develop the intellectual abilities of preschool children aged three to six.[68]

The state viewed kindergartens positively, since they fostered early development of the abilities of future citizens. Implicit in the government's endorsement of these schools as well as other educational institutions was the assumption that learning at home from parents or tutors was insufficient to socialize citizens for participation in a modern nation. However, government interest did not extend to funding the construction of kindergartens. Their establishment was left largely to private initiative, as building a nationwide network of elementary and higher schools had higher priority. Public and private kindergartens charged tuition, which tended to limit enrollment to children from wealthy families. The curriculum, which fairly often included foreign languages and Western etiquette, appealed little to lower-class families. The regulations promulgated in 1899 by the Ministry of Education limited kindergarten classroom time to five hours per day, ensuring that operating hours were too limited to permit the schools to care for children while their parents worked.[69]

Attended by a tiny percentage of the nation's preschoolers, kindergartens exerted little influence on the household division of labor or attitudes toward institutional care of children during the late nineteenth century. As these institutions were viewed in the West as training grounds for future mothers, to some extent their diffusion fostered Western conceptions of strong maternal responsibility for the care of young children among the middle-class girls and women who were the mainstays of kindergartens' staff and possibly among the parents of the students as well.

Class differences in child-rearing change

The separation of workplace and home and compulsory education had an uneven impact on the domestic life of different classes. The practices of the wealthiest families were little affected, since they could still hire private tutors, wet nurses, and governesses to raise their offspring, although criticism of these practices emerged after the 1870s. New middle-class wives' share of housework and child care increased as their children attended school instead of helping with domestic chores and as the supply of domestic servants declined. Supported by their husbands' salaries, these wives of officials, office workers, and teachers became specialists in domestic work, while busy, productive women in the enterprise households of the old middle class—ordinary merchants, middling farmers, and craftsmen or small manu-facturers—remained at home to engage in housework and child care as well as income-producing labor according to household needs, much as they had in the early modern era. Families in the lower ranks of rural and urban society generally needed the earnings of women and children to survive. If all able-bodied members worked to support the household, as in the early modern era, it sometimes left neither working adults nor older children with time to spare to tend small children.[70]

Previously, the household had been the locus of productive and reproductive work; now for an increasing number of families child care, consumption, and leisure activities—but not income-earning activities—took place at home. As the modern sector grew, the expansion of employment at large-scale economic organizations refashioned the household division of labor by decreasing the number of family members available for tasks performed at home, including child care. The fact that male wages were nearly always higher than those of married females provided an economic incentive for men rather than women to work at outside occu-pations.[71] In the middle classes, as school attendance removed older children from the home, mature women and children too young to work or attend school tended to remain at home together.

Among the lower classes, the meager earnings of workers, petty traders, and casual laborers did not permit wives to specialize in housework and child care. Some lower-class women took in piecework at home; others went to work in factories, small businesses, and in certain trades. Young women working outside the home found it difficult to manage child care for infants and toddlers. During the early 1890s a few factory day nurseries, called *kōjō takujisho* (literally, places at factories caring for children), were established to care for the young children of miners and factory operatives.[72] In contrast to *yōchien* and day-care centers (although the latter had not yet appeared in Japan), the factory day nurseries provided custo-dial care—attending mainly to preschoolers' physical needs such as sleep, food, and safety. The goal of the industrial nurseries was to increase the productivity of married female workers by removing children from work areas, not improving the infants' educational or moral development.[73] Although factory day nursery programs may seem inadequate from a modern point of view, they constituted a little-known early institutional effort to cope with the child-care problems of wage workers during industrialization.[74]

The rise of industry in late nineteenth and early twentieth century Japan expanded the demand for homeworkers as well as factory operatives. Women in lower-middle and lower-class urban families frequently took in piecework (*naishoku*) at low rates to supplement family income.[75] Yet work at home could also interfere with child care. The time regimens of home-work and factory labor were more rigid than the work schedules of family enterprises. Factory workers could not take breaks to tend to their children, while homeworkers were subject to the demands of subcontractors, who tended to dump large consignments with tight deadlines on their workers. Female homeworkers sometimes had to work all night and had to enlist their children's help to complete orders on time. When hurrying frantically to finish a consignment, mothers had little, if any, spare time or energy for minding their children.

The rise of new economic and educational institutions after the Restoration inadvert-ently affected child care in the home. Concerted efforts to change child-rearing attitudes and practices commenced around the turn of the century. The new ideas diffused first among the middle and upper classes through higher education and the mass media. Private educators and education ministry officials took up this cause in the 1890s, displaying marked enthusiasm for the task following the 1894–95 Sino-Japanese War. The need to mobilize women for national service, especially during wartime, led educators to reevaluate women's nature and capabilities. Women were found best suited to fill supportive roles at home, but they now had to be capable of substituting for men in wars or emergency situations. In 1899 *ryōsai kenbo* (good wife, wise mother), a redefinition of Japanese womanhood, became the cornerstone of the curricula of girls' higher schools attended by daughters of the elite, but it was not explicitly introduced into the curricula of elementary schools until the 1911 revision of the ethics textbooks.[76]

From long before the 1868 Restoration, Japanese families had expected the mistress of the house to be a diligent, shrewd, and dedicated household manager; the new element in *ryōsai kenbo* was its emphasis on motherhood—the married adult woman's indispensable role as the nurturer and above all the socializer of children. No longer was female inferiority grounds for denying women, even young wives, a major role in the education of children. In expecting lower-class mothers to raise industrious and loyal citizens and middle-class women carefully to rear future leaders, the state's new views of womanhood nominally entrusted women with unprecedented responsibility for shaping the destiny of nation and society.[77]

Significantly, the state failed to endorse the child-rearing roles of other household members; by default, it assigned the chief responsibility for the care and training of children to mothers alone. This was in part a response to changing social realities, and in part a reflection of the aims of the state. Children now went out to school, and men, especially urban men, commuted to their workplaces outside the home;[78] neither was expected to be at home during most of the daytime hours. It is likely that parents-in-law were passed over as major providers of child care in recognition of the fact that young women educated under the new regime were more likely than the older generation to train children to give their allegiance to the state rather than household, local community, and province—the key social units of yesteryear. In addition, the fact that new households formed by migrants to the cities often lacked parents-in-law may also have influenced the upgrading of the role of the mother.

However, granting greater authority over child-rearing to mothers as opposed to mothers-in-law, inherent in the "good wife, wise mother" formulation, contradicted another ideological initiative of the Meiji state and the private ideologues who supported it: the family-state (*kazoku kokka*) ideology, formulated in the same era. The values of the family-state stressed filial piety to parents for children and submission to parents-in-law as surrogate parents for women in virilocal marriages as a means of demonstrating loyalty to the emperor. In other words the more positive evaluation of married women's domestic and public capacities implied by the state's endorsements of "good wife, wise mother" undercut other ideological persuasions instructing a married woman to be subservient to her husband or coresident parents-in-law in the patrilineal stem family established by the 1898 Civil Code.[79]

Although the educational system became the major means for diffusion of a new vision of womanhood associated with novel child-care attitudes and practices many Japanese women failed to become model *ryōsai kenbo*. The stumbling block was motherhood rather than housewifery. The problem was that the conditions of life in a high proportion of households favored continued reliance on the traditional pool of caregivers, freeing mothers for productive work at home or elsewhere. Busy wives of ordinary laborers, farmers, craftsmen, shopkeepers, and petty manufacturers could not devote more time to their children without undermining their families' precarious economic security.

It is likely that the increasing separation between home and workplace and between home and school from the turn of the century had a more significant impact on lower-class families than did the rise of new conceptions of womanhood. In metropolitan areas diminished control over the deployment of family labor and decreased flexibility in work routines as well as irregular employment, low wages, and long working hours prevented lower-class parents from devoting much effort to child care. And as in the previous era, the physical aspects of the lower-class urban environment, with its lack of open space, its dank, dilapidated, overcrowded housing, and its poor sanitary facilities, created health and safety hazards for children and adults alike. By the middle of the 1880s lower-class children living in the squalor and stench of urban slums began to evoke pity and concern among humanitarians and social reformers. The sight of packs of youngsters roaming the slum streets begging, rummaging through garbage to find food, and engaging in petty theft and rowdy behavior spurred reformers and officials to try to find a means of coping with the issue of unruly lower-class children. The institutional response to the problems posed by neglected or unsupervised lower-class youths began with orphanages and reformatories after the 1870s. Next came special elementary schools and day-care centers after the 1890s, followed by infant and maternal health programs after World War I.

Amid increasing concern about the undesirable social consequences of industrialization at the turn of the century, humanitarians sought to relieve the suffering of poor youngsters. Some of them hoped for general improvement in the home environment of the urban lower classes. Officials worried about the impact of industrialization for different reasons. Their primary concerns were preservation of social order and increasing economic productivity. To attain these ends, they helped create programs and institutions promoting values such as diligence, savings, discipline, and self-reliance in all citizens, especially the urban poor and working classes. Sharing similar concerns, twentieth-century advocates of institutional child care were quick to assert that day-care centers could contribute to the future development and stability of Japanese society and that they could offer two additional benefits—improvement of the urban lower-class household and betterment of the present and future lives of poor children. At the beginning of the twentieth century traditional tolerance for multiple caregivers allayed distrust of day-care centers as institutions nurturing young children outside the home. But in the long run positive support for institutional child care flourished because day-care programs promised benefits not only to poor children, but to their parents, households, and above all, to the entire society and nation.

Notes

1   Regarding continuity and change in farming and village life, see Thomas C. Smith, *Agrarian Origins of Modern Japan*, 208–10; and Daikichi Irokawa, *The Culture of the Meiji Period*. As late as 1930 a majority of the labor force was employed in household enterprises. Uno, "Women and Changes," 18. Even in the early postwar years the percentage of the labor force in the "self-employed" and "family worker" categories totaled 59 percent in 1950 and 35 percent in 1960. Robert E. Cole and Kenichi Tominaga, "Japan's Changing Occupational Structure and Its Significance," 59, 64–65.

2   Fukutake Tadashi, *The Japanese Social Structure: Its Evolution in the Modern Century*, 18, 21.

3   Irokawa, *The Culture of the Meiji Period*, provides a sensitive, detailed account of many aspects of early Meiji rural change, but Western-language accounts of the social and cultural life of ordinary urbanites in the prewar era have yet to be written.

4   See Ronald P. Dore, *Education in Tokugawa Japan;* Herbert Passin, *Society and Education in Japan*; and Richard Rubinger, *Private Academies of Tokugawa Japan*. Sons of high-ranking or wealthy families—both warrior and commoner youth—attended the domain schools and Confucian academies; children of less prosperous households attended the village and city schools. Regarding women's education, see Kikue Yamakawa, *Women of the Mito Domain: Recollections of Samurai Family Life*, trans. Kate Wildman Nakai.

5   See also Uno, "Women and Changes," 22–30.

6   It was clearly established as the legal norm by the Civil Code of 1898. However, conflicting views in Japanese scholarship suggest that the nineteenth-century urban and rural lower classes may not have accepted the stem family with inheritance and succession by primogeniture as a normative household form. Uno, "Women and Changes," 23; Uno, "Japan," 390, 404.

7   Lutz Berkner, "The Stem Family and the Developmental Cycle: An Eighteenth Century Example," 399.

8   Or alternatively, before retirement of the head's father, the household might consist of a head, wife, and successor, plus successor's wife, children, and siblings. However, a household might be comprised of a single generation—the head and his wife—or two generations, i.e., head, wife, and children, due to poverty, divorce, or death.

9   Length and quality of service might improve their status as household members. For example, trusted elderly servants as well as parents might instruct children in proper behavior and household customs. See Kathleen Uno, "Questioning Patrilineality: On Western Studies of the Japanese *Ie*," 569–94. On the dynamics of the early modern household in its social context, see Herman Ooms, *Tokugawa Village Practice: Class, Status, Power, Law*.

10   Richard K. Beardsley, John W. Hall, and Robert E. Ward, eds., *Village Japan*, 217. In contrast to *ie*, the term *"katei,"* rendered as "home" or "family," or occasionally "household," refers to the family as a social unit or set of domestic relationships developing from coresidence. *Setai*, or "household," refers to a domicile or residential unit. See also Ronald Dore, *City Life in Japan*, ch. 8–10, ch. 20; Susan Orpett Long, *Family Change and the Life Course in Japan*, 7–31; Uno, "Questioning Patrilineality," including the bibliography. Regarding the genesis of the middle-class *katei* in the modern period, see in English Yūko Nishikawa, "The Changing Form of Dwellings and the Establishment of the (Home) in Modern Japan," and Jordan Sand, "At Home in the Meiji Period: Inventing Japanese Domesticity"; lower-class developments are presented in Miyake, "Female Workers of the Urban Lower Class," and Uno, "One Day at a Time."

11   Harumi Befu, *Japan: An Anthropological Introduction*, 41. The law permitted the disowning only of retarded, mentally ill, or incurably profligate eldest sons.

12   Nobushige Hozumi, *Ancestor-Worship and Japanese Law*, 130. Hozumi stated that if the estate could support only one heir, the other children were not allowed to marry unless they obtained the means to support a household. During the late Tokugawa period girls generally married into other households; boys who remained at home or left the household as apprentices or servants frequently did not marry. Ibid., 138.

13   For this reason, anthropologist Chie Nakane has argued that the *ie* should be considered a corporate group, not a kinship group. *Kinship and Economic Organization in Japan*.

14   Ibid.

15   See Uno, "Questioning Patrilineality," 576–77; 589, notes 25–26.

16   The junior wife, the wife of the heir and successor, was also called the "young wife" or *yome*. Until retirement of the senior couple, her mother-in-law (*shūtome*), was called the "housewife," or in Japanese, *shufu* or *kaka*.

17   The authority of the adopted son who became household head was, however, weaker than that of a natural son who succeeded his father; as an insider, the wife of an adopted heir might possess considerable authority in business affairs as well as household matters. One would also expect such women to have had a strong voice in the rearing of their children, although I have not been able to find concrete evidence of this.

18   In her 1935 observations of social life in Suye, a rural hamlet in Kyushu, Wisell notes that when a new baby was born, the next-youngest child stopped nursing and began to sleep beside another household member besides the mother. During the day infants and the next-youngest children were carried around most frequently by sisters, grandmothers, and girl baby-sitters, but also by brothers. Fathers played a fairly active role in raising children. Smith and Wiswell, *The Women of Suye Mura*, 202–53.

19   The father of an infant might or might not be the household head, just as his wife, the child's mother, might or might not be the mistress of the household (the housewife or senior wife).

20   Isabella Bird, *Unbeaten Tracks in Japan*, 74. Bird traveled through villages in northeast Honshu in 1878 before foreigners were permitted to travel freely in Japan. Hideo Kojima, "Childrearing Concepts as a Belief-value System of Society and Individual,"

21   Takai Toshio, *Watashi no jokō aishi*, 8–9. Takai's account as well as Bird's observations suggest that even in households without livelihood or property, father could develop a strong emotional attachment to their successors, and that such paternal sentiments could lead to direct involvement in the care of young children.

22   Limited demographic data are available for the modern era, especially between 1870 and 1920. Mean household size (MHS) averaged 4.65 in 1870, 4.89 in 1920, 4.98 in 1930, and 5.00 in 1940. Rural-urban differentials are 4.99 rural MHS and 4.47 urban MHS for 1930 and 5.25 rural MHS and 4.62 urban MHS for 1940. Chie Nakane, "An Interpretation of the Size and Structure of the Household in Japan over Three Centuries," 523, 531. Regarding household composition in 1920, 53.2 percent of the nation's households consisted of two generations, while 27 percent consisted of three generations and 17.7 percent of one generation. In 1920 in rural counties respective figures were 52.2, 29.8, and 15.7 percent, and in the six great cities, 59.5, 12.8, and 27.4 percent. Irene Taeuber, *The Population of Japan*, 106.

23   Hane, *Rebels, Peasants, and Outcastes*, 83.

24   Dr. Matsuda also observed that "[n]owadays it is the young mother herself who carries the baby into the clinic. She is usually followed by her husband." Matsuda Michio, *Oyaji tai kodomo* (Tokyo 1966), cited in Hiroshi Wagatsuma, "Some Aspects of the Contemporary Japanese Family: Once Confucian, Now Fatherless?" 189; 206, note 27.

25   Hane, *Rebels, Peasants, and Outcastes*, 83. See also the discussion on grandmothers and child-rearing later in this chapter.

26   Despite its samurai status, I have treated the Kawakami household as an ordinary household, because it lacked sufficient income to hire servants to care for the children.

27   Gail Bernstein, *Japanese Marxist: A Portrait of Kawakami Hajime 1879–1946*, 6. Regarding grandmother's child in contemporary Japan, see Joy Hendry, *Becoming japanese: The World of the Preschool Child*, 24, 48, 52–53, 55; and Ezra Vogel, *Japan's New Middle Class*, 224–26.

28   Tanaka Katsubumi, "Ie de hataraku kodomo," 245.

29   Kobayashi Hatsue, *Onna sandai*, 97–98.

30   Hyman Kublin, *Asian Revolutionary: The Life of Sen Katayama*, 11–17.

31   Tanaka, "Ie de hataraku kodomo," 246–48.

32   Chiba Hisao, *Meiji no shōgakkō*, 273–74.

33   Sugō Hiroshi, *Komori gakkō*.

34   Ishikawa Matsutarō, *Onna daigakushū*. In English, see Basil Chamberlain, *Things Japanese: Being Notes on Things Connected with Japan*, 67–76 or Atsuharu Sakai, "Kaibara Ekiken and 'Onna Daigaku,'" 43–56.

35   Yamazumi Masami and Nakae Kazue, *Kosodate no sho*, vols. 1–2.

36   Uno, "Women and Changes," 27–30; Yamakawa, *Women of the Mito Domain*, 19–23, 39–61, 85–100.

37   Sugō, *Komori gakkō*, 6–25; Ichiyō Higuchi, "Child's Play," in Robert Danly, ed. and trans., *In the Shade of Spring Leaves: The Life and Work of Higuchi Ichiyo, A Meiji Woman of Letters*, 276, 261–62; originally published in 1895–96 as "Takekurabe."

38   Kobayashi, *Onna sandai*, 10, 12.

39   Smith and Wiswell, *The Women of Suye Mura*, esp. 146–47, 234–36.

40   Tanaka, "Ie de hataraku kodomo," 257.

41   Ibid. The girl left home in 1905.

42   Tamanoi, "Songs as Weapons," 808–9.

43   Nishimura Kōichi, "Shokunin no ko—totei kara oyakata made," 80, 91, 104.

44   Ibid., 91, 104.

45   For example, see Richard Bowring, ed. and trans., *Murasaki Shikibu: Her Diary and Poetic Memoirs: A Translation and Study*; and Helen Craig McCullough and William H. McCullough, trans., *A Tale of Flowering Fortunes*.

46   Ihara Saikaku, *Some Final Words of Advice*, trans. Peter Nosco, 226. However, early modern wet nurses or nannies might also serve until the betrothal of their charges, or after. Chikamatsu Monzaemon, "Yosaku of Tamba," 91–98; Etsu Inagaki Sugimoto, *A Daughter of the Samurai*, 84–85, 96–97.

47   See Yamazumi and Nakae, *Kosodate no sho*, 73–79, 95–99.

48   See Sugimoto, *A Daughter of the Samurai*, 3, also 7–16, 21–22, 84–85; and Shidzuee Ishimoto, *Facing Two Ways*, 23.

49   Ihara, *Some Final Words of Advice*, 225–26.

50   Ibid., 228–29; Robert Danly, "A Brief Life," in Danly, ed. and trans., *In the Shade of Spring Leaves*, 7; Ihara Saikaku, *This Scheming World*, trans. Takatsuka Masanori and David C. Stubbs, 80–81.

51   Chikamatsu, "Yosaku of Tamba," 91–98.

52   Sugimoto, *A Daughter of the Samurai*, esp. 1–35; Chiyoko Higuchi, "Lady Kasuga, Mother of Shoguns," 38–42.

53   Danly, "A Brief Life," 7.

54   Ibid., 28, 43.

55   Kuwata Shingo, *Osanago no sono* (1876), cited in Ichibangase, et al., *Nihon no hoiku*, 15.

56   Fukuzawa Yukichi, *The Autobiography of Yukichi Fukuzawa*, 297–98.

57   Osamu Dazai, *Return to Tsugaru: Travels of a Purple Tramp*, xv–xvi, 152–54.

58   Hachihama Tokusaburō, "Keian no kenkyū," 230.

59   Smith and Wiswell, *The Women of Suye Mura*, 202–53.

60   For example, Cole and Tominaga estimate that male and female professional, managerial, and clerical employees comprised 12 percent of the labor force in 1920 and 13.6 percent in 1930. Cole and Tominaga, "Japan's Changing Occupational Structure," 60. However, the new middle class exerted social and cultural influence beyond its numbers because its ranks included journalists, writers, schoolteachers, professors, and government officials.

Demographic as well as economic factors account for the scarcity of parents-in-law in urban households. Parents of rural migrants who established families in the cities tended to remain in the village with the *ie* successor. National figures on earlier household composition are unavailable, but Toda Teizō's *Kazoku kōsei*, the classic analysis of the 1920 census results, revealed that while 67.9 percent of rural (*gun*) households consisted of one- or two-generation households and 29.8 percent consisted of three-generation households, the corresponding figures for the six great cities were 86.9 and 12.8 percent. Cited in Taeuber, *The Population of Japan*, 106. (Female labor was negligible in 1920, but it comprised roughly 6 percent of the clerical category in 1930.) See also Kinmonth, *The Self-Made Man*, 279–80. Regarding household size, see Nakane, "An Interpretation," 531.

61   Naka, 86, 93.

62   Masaaki Kosaka, *Japanese Thought in the Meiji Era*, trans. David Abosch, 84.

63   In 1900 the overall enrollment rate was still only 82 percent, but in 1909 it leveled off and remained at about 97 percent. Kami Shōichirō, "Honryū no naka no gakkō kyōiku," 100.

64   Tanaka, "Ie de hataraku kodomo," 245.

65   "Nippori-chō jidō shūgaku jōkyō chōsa ni tsuite," 57–58; "Jidō kyōyō chōsa," 51, 56–58.

66   The first *komori gakkō* was founded in 1883. In 1891 many schools of this type were founded in Aichi and Nagano Prefectures. In 1899 a national educators' association recommended that *komori gakkō* be established at all public elementary schools. Thereafter, curriculum plans to implement this recommendation were drawn up in various prefectures ranging from the south of Kyushu to the northern central areas of Japan's main island, Honshu. The *komori gakkō* disappeared after World War II. Tanaka, "Ie de hataraku kodomo," 265–66. See also Tamanoi, "Songs as Weapons." Similarly, special factory and evening schools for children employed in other occupations were established around the turn of the century. Tanaka, "Ie de hataraku kodomo," 267–72.

67   See Ichibangase, et al., *Nihon no hoiku*, 2, 20; Urabe, et al., *Hoiku no rekishi*, 4–5; and Kōzu Zenzaburō, *Kyōiku aishi*.

68   *The gakusei*, the 1874 edict establishing Japan's centralized educational system, provided for the founding of *"yōchi shōgaku,"* best translated as nursery schools. Urabe, et al., *Hoiku no rekishi*, 3.

69   Monbushō rei dai sanjūnigō, "Yōchien hoiku oyobi setsubi kitei," issued June 28, 1899, cited in Urabe, et al., *Hoiku no rekishi*, 34–35.

70   This was true for both rural and urban lower-class families; however, urban families could not obtain supplementary food or fuel from the land. Also, weaker ties to their landlords made it more difficult for lower-class city dwellers to obtain paternalistic aid.

71   For example, E. Patricia Tsurumi documents 1901 wage differentials by gender at cotton spinning mills in Kansai, Japan's great industrial area, in *Factory Girls*, 149, table 8.2.

72   Evidence concerning the *kōjō takujisho* is sparse, but records indicate that many of the earliest operated at mines. See, for example, Fukuoka-ken shakai jigyō kyōkai, *Fukuoka kenka shakai jigyō*.

73   Kami Shōichirō and Yamazaki Tomoko, *Nihon no yōchien: Nihon no yōji kyōiku no rekishi*, 129–44.

74   The virtual absence of references to factory day nurseries in welfare and educational journals indicates that they did not capture the attention of turn-of-the-century social reformers as day-care centers did, most likely because day nurseries did not attempt to reform children's or parents' character or to improve home life.

75   The two groups did different types of work. Lower-middle class women performed skilled or semiskilled work such as embroidering handkerchiefs and finishing garments. Lower-class women did unskilled work such as gluing paper bags and attaching sandal thongs. See Uno, "One Day at a Time."

76   Fukaya Masashi, *Ryōsai kenbo no kyōikushugi*; Uno, "Origins of 'Good Wife, Wise Mother.'"

77   One can compare Japan's *ryōsai kenbo* and with the U.S. "republican motherhood" of the federal era; however, as prewar Japan was a constitutional monarchy, one might call *ryōsai kenbo* "imperial motherhood." See Mary Beth Norton, *Liberty's Daughters: The Revolutionary Experience of American Women, 1750–1800*; Linda Kerber, *Women of the Republic: Intellect and Ideology in Revolutionary America*; and Cott, *The Bonds of Womanhood*. See also Sievers, *Flowers in Salt*, esp. 112–13.

78   As industrialization proceeded, wage work in the new economic organizations outside the home was defined as men's work.

79   As filial piety to coresident parents or parents-in-law was of greatest importance, wives whose husbands had been adopted into the bride's household (housedaughters) were not obliged to serve their husbands' parents. Rather, their husbands were obliged to obey their adoptive parents, who were at the same time their parents-in-law. Additional study of the dynamics of these relationships in concrete cases is needed. The 1898 Civil Code disregarded regional variations, mandating primogeniture, male succession, and thus the patrilineal stem family as the basic household unit throughout Japan.

Chapter 27

Ellen Schrumpf

FROM FULL-TIME TO PART-TIME: WORKING CHILDREN IN NORWAY FROM THE NINETEENTH TO THE TWENTIETH CENTURY

Norwegian childhood politicized

AS THE NINETEENTH CENTURY gave way to the twentieth, Norway was in the midst of a sweeping modernization. Characteristic signs of modernization were specialization, division of labour, rationalization in society and in the work place, new social classes, individualism and the breaking away from nature, kin and one's destiny. Massive reforms were put into effect to build a modern Norway – with much of this reform zeal directed at the child and childhood. One example comes from the Central Office of Statistics, which was set up in 1875 with a brief to produce an overall view of the country's development and structure, as a basis for the planning of tomorrow's society. The first major task given to its Secretary was to discover the extent of child labour and to prepare legislation on this issue. Jacob Neumann Mohn's inquiry was the forerunner of the first labour law – the Factory Inspection Act of 1892. The most important features of this were that children under 12 years of age were forbidden to work in industrial undertakings and that work done by children and teenagers of between 12 and 18 years was to be regulated.[1]

The child and its childhood were also at the centre of major reforms in education. The Education Act of 1889 extended the duration of schooling and also the number of subjects in the elementary school curriculum. More school meant less work in a child's life. Furthermore, the laws were based on the principle of a common school for town and countryside.[2] *All* children were to be included, and the school was to be a mechanism for ironing out differences between the urban and rural communities and between social groups. Universality was also a core principle.[3] And the school was seen as an important element in nation building.

The principles of a school that town and country had in common, and of universality, presupposed that the State would look after the interests of the aberrant child. Therefore, in 1900 Norway became the first country in the world to set up an official child welfare agency. The law on the 'treatment of neglected children' was a trail-blazing one. Whenever the family, parents or guardians failed a child, the public authorities would step in and assume the responsibility.[4]

These are but a few of the many examples illustrating the great efforts made by the Norwegian authorities for children – at the turn of the 'children's century'.[5] The State became actively engaged in the development of a new childhood. The school and the public authorities took responsibility for and control of the child's upbringing at the expense of the family and the work place. Then as now it was universally accepted as a fundamental truth that the child was the father of the man and the mother of the woman, and that the child of today carried within it tomorrow's future. In a modern society it was important that the child's upbringing and development should be under official control. There were, however, differences of opinion about how childhood should be shaped. Consequently, it became politicized.

Childhood in Norway was undergoing a process of change, central to which was the changeover from work to school. That changeover is the theme of this chapter. Till then, work had been the most important socializing factor in a child's life. Through the social and cultural impact of the processes of work, the child was formed in terms of gender, age and social class. Now the school took over the role of the work place in shaping and socializing the child.

Children were a flexible labour force and took part in a wide range of paid and unpaid work inside and outside the home. Here we shall look first at children's *paid work*, starting with two statistical inquiries into the Norwegian children's participation in the work place. One was the already mentioned study of children's work carried out by Jacob Neumann Mohn in the years 1875–77.[6] The other was an inquiry into paid work among school children in Kristiania (Oslo) in 1912.[7] These provide the basis of the picture of children's paid work to be presented here: the kind of work undertaken by children, what they earned and how the work was organized. In addition, they provide the starting point for a discussion of the significance children's work had for the family, the society and for the child's development. Finally, the two inquiries will be brought together to highlight some of the important changes in children's work in the period 1875–1912.

Paid work was however only a small part of the work carried out by children inside and outside the household. Two actual accounts of childhood will give us an insight into the range, flexibility and totality of the tasks undertaken by children. They will tell us what the work meant to the child itself, and how it was remembered and retold in later life. Through their reminiscences the children assume the role they had in real life, and the one they have in this account of the experience of childhood. They were both participants and subjects and made an active contribution to their own development and to that of their families and local communities[8]. The child partly shaped him- or herself – and partly was shaped by others. Here we are dealing with Hans and Torleif, two boys who grew up in different parts of Norway – one before, the other after the turn of the century. Hans was born in 1865 in the rural community of Ulefoss. Torleif was born in the town of Porsgrunn in 1910.[9] The story of their childhood will both widen our perspective and help tie the statistics, representing the many thousands of anonymous children, to the experiences of two children's lives. They will help create a reality out of history and show just how the everyday life of a child and its upbringing in the family and in society worked out. But let us first look at the general picture.[10]

The child, work and school at the end of the nineteenth century

When the Department of the Interior gave Jacob Neumann Mohn the task of preparing a bill on 'the employment of children and young people for regular work outside the home,' he set to work with all the thoroughness and dedication expected of a senior public official at that time. By training Mohn was a lawyer. It was, however, through his work as a statistician he had gained a thorough understanding of the economic and social conditions in Norway. As he said himself, 'it was a matter of urgency that a carefully prepared and accurate account be drawn up of the extent and nature of the work currently carried out by the youth of our country.'[11] He also compiled a comprehensive account of other countries' laws on the subject. Furthermore, he made a thorough study of Norwegian schooling and surveyed the ways in which school and work had an impact on the child's life. In addition, he personally visited Norwegian factories to collect information on children's contact with and tasks in the work place. He visited one of the Danish factory inspectors to discover the impact of legislation in that country, and also referred to a large amount of written material, collected from the school directors in the towns, and from industrialists around the country, about the nature of the schooling and work experience of Norwegian children. Both the 1875 Census and the factory statistics from the 1870s were used. Thus, a perfectly solid piece of work accompanied the legislative proposal of 1878. It provided a good insight into the work carried out by Norwegian children.

Children's work in town and country

The main conclusion of Jacob Neumann Mohn's inquiry was that in the second half of the nineteenth century it was common practice for Norwegian children to work, and that they worked wherever there were opportunities for doing so. Consequently, children were to be found in a vast range of occupations. There were many similarities but also vast differences in what they did, both in the towns and in the countryside.

In 1875 over 13,000 children, aged 13–14 years, were registered in the rural districts as being in paid work outside the home. Jacob Neumann Mohn was well aware that his information was incomplete and that the totals in both censuses and the factory statistics were too low. He was, therefore, unable to say what percentage of all children were in paid work. It is not, however, the totals that are the most important. What Mohn's table [see original reading] gives us is the extent to which children were distributed across a wide range of different tasks and the differences between the sexes.

Surprisingly, Mohn found that in the rural districts more girls than boys were in paid work. The table shows that girls and boys had many activities in common: both went into service, worked in factories or herded animals. Some jobs were, however, clearly sex-specific. The running of errands was typically a boy's job – virtually no girls did it. Furthermore, only boys went to sea and worked on building sites, railways, roads and with timber rafting. On the other hand, we find only girl seamstresses and milkmaids working in the dairy. This suggests that both girls and boys followed in their parents' footsteps from childhood as to sexual division in the work place. As far as the rural districts were concerned, it seems that women took charge of the local and home-based work, while the men were occupied with activities further afield. Another significant feature is the tremendous variety of jobs undertaken by children. Children could make themselves useful and were to be found in just about every field of work: in the mines, in land and sea transport, in forestry, in the dried cod and fish processing industries, in craft and domestic industry, on building sites, on the docks, in cafes and inns.

Child workers were to be found as young as five or six years. Around 400, or 3 per cent of the more than 13,000 children, were under 10 years of age. Many of the very young were occupied in the home with outwork from the match factories. There, small boys and girls could be found, assembling and sticking matchboxes together.

Mohn had to admit that it was more difficult to establish the extent of children's work in the towns. The census returns were unreliable – so it was impossible to produce the same statistics as he had in the rural districts. But children's work was just as widespread and the range of tasks just as many. On one hand, many tasks were the same as in the countryside. Town children went into service, minded young children, herded animals, took part in potato picking, worked on farms and in gardens. In the coastal towns children were involved in the fisheries, and helped with the washing and drying of cod. On the other hand, factory work was more widespread among town children, and, in general, the towns could offer a wider range of work opportunities. Delivering messages was typically a child's occupation in the towns; also, delivering papers, taking food to the work place, carrying goods to and from the markets and quays, delivering beer. They were active in retailing in the market and on the streets. Children were paid to sweep streets, tend lights, chop wood and stack timber, bricks, etc. on the building sites. Children were often to be found loading ice, laying paving stones and acting as bricklayers' mates. They were in dance halls, restaurants and other places of recreation. They even worked as travelling acrobats, tightrope walkers and bareback riders. This part of Mohn's inquiry does not distinguish between male and female work, but one must reckon that, as in the countryside, the children's work in the towns was similarly sex specific – with the girls' work to a greater extent linked to the home.

The broad spectrum of work opportunities for children in town and country shows that their entry into the labour market was open and provided many opportunities for different types of work. It also suggests that children were an accepted element in the work place. In commenting on the participation of children, Mohn remarked:

> The above shows that child labour has penetrated, to a greater or lesser extent, most fields of activity in this country.[12]

The variety of tasks undertaken by children also suggests that they were flexible and that *flexibility* was one of their advantages in the labour market. In the early years of industrialization, output took place unevenly with a greater seasonal element than later. Moreover, adult workers were less committed to their work. Edvard Bull, the Norwegian social historian, argued that not tying one down to a particular work place was part of that independent streak, which was such a feature of unskilled day labourers in nineteenth century Norway.[13] Workers moved from one work place to another. The flexibility inherent in child labour helped to even out the irregularities in the working year, so that one did not end with a backlog. Children helped eliminate the bottlenecks in the production process. They went in and out of different jobs, taking work where they were needed. Work also suited the needs of the family and the household. The rhythm of children's work was decided by the family cycle and the possibilities offered by the labour market.[14] These constant changes broke down the boundary between life inside and outside the home. This flexibility and the loose links with the world of work are partly why it was so difficult to make a record of children's work. A statistical account of such a complex matter was *no* easy task.

The Department of the Interior had also given Jacob Neumann Mohn the task of highlighting the *unfortunate* aspects of child labour. He did not find many. Like his contemporaries he had no objection in principle to children working. Children's work was accepted as a good thing. It kept children occupied and contributed positively to their upbringing. In only a few areas was it felt necessary to regulate and/or forbid child labour: principally in factories, mining, crafts and herding. It was argued that much of the work in these areas damaged children's health. In both factories and workshops children were exposed to noise and accidents. Poorly clad shepherds and goatherds suffered from colds and lung ailments, when they were looking after animals during late, chilly autumn evenings. Apart from their health, children needed moral protection. Children's morals and their moral conduct were at stake when they worked in bars and other places of entertainment, or when, on a tour, they took part in public performances. Worries about health and morals were also in keeping with contemporary line of thought. A campaign on diet and hygiene was carried out across the country and, within a few years, the debate on morals and moral conduct was to become *the* major cultural conflict in Norway.[15] Health, hygiene and morality were important components in the creation of a modern Norway. Children were in the centre of this. They were especially in need of protection.

Children in the factories

When children worked in factories both their health and their morals were at risk. Not only were the premises dirty and polluted, the human environment also exposed the children to dangerous elements. Karl Marx, in writing of the unfortunate influences children working in industry were exposed to, had this to say:

> The crude language they heard from their tenderest years, the indecent and shameless behaviour, which unknowing and lost they grew up with, makes them lawless, depraved and slovenly for the rest of their lives.[16]

Daily contacts with a 'coarse and brutal' working class produced measures to control and protect the coming generation exposed to industrialization. Also, in Norway children's work in factories was the subject of special attention. In 1875 the country had little modern industry. Of a total of 45,000 industrial workers about 3,000 were children, i.e. around 7 per cent. Nevertheless, from 1870 the number of children working in industry had risen by 60 per cent. Mohn's inquiry was therefore conducted at a time when the extent of child labour was on the increase and seemed destined to reach a considerable size. This caused alarm in some quarters and was one reason the inquiry was set up. That children would put paid work before schooling, was also a cause for concern. Mohn discovered that, compared with other countries, there were a relatively large number of children in the Norwegian industry.

> Our factories, compared to those of other countries, appear to employ many, and in several important branches, very many children. (. . .) They are to be found more or less established in all of the most important kinds of industrial activity.[17]

Given that there was insufficient registration, Mohn found the following distribution of children working in factories [see original reading]. They were found in both the 'old' and the 'new' industries.

Factories were primarily the work places for boys. In all branches of industry more boys than girls were found.

Some industries stood out as having an especially large number of children employed. For instance, in 1875, every other worker in the tobacco industry was a child – with five times as many boys as girls. The balance between the sexes was more even in the match-making industry, where around one third of the workers were children. The share of children in the glass industry, was also high, and here there were virtually no girls. The total *number* of children was at its highest in the saw and planing mills, but the *proportion* was lower. And there were no girls in the sawmills.

At this time the saw and lumber industries were the country's most important industrial enterprises. The sawmill industry had a long history, reaching back to the sixteenth century. There was a long tradition of child labour in the industry.[18] One might argue that children were part of the old labour force and that the children working in industry, as registered by Mohn in the 1870s, were no new phenomenon. Rather it was the continuation of an old industrial tradition. This was prolonged in the newly 'industrialized' old enterprises and carried into the new.[19] A general explanation as to why some activities were open to many children, while others were open to boys but not to girls, is unlikely to be forthcoming. The explanations will be specific to particular industries and particular localities, based upon methods of production, technology and local work cultures, employment opportunities in each locality and the local traditions as to the upbringing of children. Methods of recruitment are also important. Often particular jobs were passed from one generation to the next. Boys and girls came into a factory next to their mother and father – as Mohn also observed.

> When one looks at the individual factory or the individual workplace, one usually finds that the workers employed there obtained employment for their children at the same enterprise or in the same place.[20]

A persistent feature of industrial work for children was that they were found everywhere. They worked in rope walks, in fish fertilizer factories, in spinning mills, brick works, breweries, the canning industry, nail making factories – to mention but a few of their activities. Most children working in factories were over 10 years of age. Six per cent were under 10. There was some division of labour by age and this had to do, among other factors, with the fact that some tasks demanded a certain amount of physical strength. Therefore, the somewhat older children were found in the factories. The youngest children were mostly at home, doing unpaid work. This applied also to girls. While the socialization of boys often took place in the company of their fathers in paid work, the girls learned their adult roles from their mothers in the household or in paid domestic service. The household was an important work place for many children and as both paid and unpaid workers, children played an important role in the family economy.

Children in the factories: hours of work, school and pay

Whether working at home or outside it, the child's job was to assist the adults. Children and adults worked as a team, each depended upon the other. A child's hours of work were therefore fixed. They had just as long a workday as the adults.

> The adults' activities are based upon the help they receive from the young so they cannot allow them more control over their time (. . .). In general, the children's work day is as fixed as that of the adults.[21]

Mohn found that in the 1870s the working day for children employed in factories in the countryside was between 10 and 11 hours. In the towns it was shorter, around 10 hours. If the children in the towns went to school every day, then they went to the factory either in the morning or the afternoon. They then worked 5–6 hours in every 24. In the countryside children went to school only every other day. Most children went to school two days a week and to the factory for four. Some had three days at school and three days in the factory. At several glassworks children worked every day and went to school in the evening. Some work was seasonal, for instance, at the sawmills. In the winter ice on the river hindered production and brought the mills to a standstill for various lengths of time. Thus, boys at the sawmills went to school in the winter and worked during the summer. When the mills were operating, they had to exploit all their resources to the utmost: the working day lasted 12 hours and a shift system operated. The children also worked shifts – including the night shift. At the Ulefoss Sawmill this was arranged as follows:

> The shift ran from 12 noon to 12 midnight – with the next from 12 midnight to 12 noon. It might happen, when there were two boys of the same age each doing a different shift, they had to be escorted to work, especially when it was dark. Usually, the mother took the one who began work at midnight and brought the other home.[22]

There were also many alternative arrangements. The allocation of time to school or work depended upon the nature of the work and whether the child was in a rural or an urban school. In general, a child's day was organized so that its time out of school was filled with work.

> Day after day a full day's work was done so that any time outside school hours was completely filled.[23]

The length of time filled by work and school was different for children in the town and in the countryside. Mohn found it to be as follows [see original reading].

If children attended school for the prescribed number of hours, then the child who worked at a factory in the town spent almost twice as much time at school as his country cousin. Moreover, children in the countryside spent five times as much time in the factory as in the school, while children in the town spent only slightly more than twice as much. The country child was thus to a greater extent a worker, and his urban counterpart, a scholar. On the other hand, both groups of children spent a long time every year in the factory. It was their main sphere of activity. Mohn, in any case remarked that in reality *all* children spent more time at work and less at school, because more often than not the latter was neglected in favour of the former. There were also similarities and differences in the life of the urban and rural child. One significant difference was that in the towns, children both attended school and went to work simultaneously throughout the year – unlike in the countryside where work and schooling was decided by the seasons. Children worked in the summer and went to school in the winter. Nevertheless, work and school were adjusted to fit the lives of all children. That many children played truant suggests that work often took precedence to schooling. Other reasons for missing school might be that the pupils lacked clothes and shoes, or it was a long way to school, or the parents were not concerned about their children's education at school. It might also be an expression of protest on the parents' part against the religious and ideological indoctrination to which the children were exposed at school.[24]

Children had just as long a working day as adults, but a shorter working year. Nor did they carry out the same work. For children had smaller physical frames, less strength and experience. So the work was adjusted to suit the child:

> As to the work to which the young are put in the factories, there is, in general, a natural limit, which is decided by their being less strong and having had less practise. The heavier work and the immediate control of the machines are not their concern. In the main, their job is, partly, to carry out lighter labour jobs for the adults and, partly, to perform various simple secondary operations, which, as a rule, still bear such a relationship to the main activity that they determine its success.[25]

Factory children were treated – and regarded – both as workers and as children. The fact that they worked a long day together with adults – and without any special protection under the law – shaped them as adults. Their more sporadic connections with the work place, their shorter work year, and that they were assigned special tasks, shaped them as children. In the factories the children were not responsible for the actual output. They assisted the adults. Yet they were an essential part of the production chain. They had to carry out their work at the right time and in the correct tempo so the productive process moved as it should. For example, at the sawmills the boys had to carry timber to the saw by the chute or carry finished beams and planks into the yard. There they tagged and stacked them. They swept the place, cleared away and chopped the scrap timber. They helped the sawmaster. They were an essential part of the production process – and thus they earned a position in the work place that was both meaningful and responsible. This was the foundation for the mutual respect adults and children had for each other – and for the children's sense of themselves as both useful and necessary. This sense of their worth of self was reinforced by the fact that children earned good wages for the work they did. Mohn discovered that the average income of a child working in a factory was high. In fact, he thought it was extraordinarily so, in relation to what the children did, and that employers found it unrenumerative.

> At least in this country, as well as elsewhere, one not infrequently hears or reads the comments of employers, to the effect that child labour is, in essence, of little value to them. Children are frequently taken on at the request of their parents, who want them to make themselves useful. This is especially so when their fathers work in the same place.[26]

It is difficult to judge the relationship between what children contributed by their labour and what they earned. But children could earn 160 kroner annually, and, if they worked every day, as much as 400 kroner. An adult worker earned around 800 kroner annually. In other words, a child working in a factory could earn up to half an adult wage. Such pay was more or less the same in both the countryside and in the town. There is no mention of differences in the wages paid to boys and girls. The implication of this is that at the end of a week in the factory, both girls and boys took home a relatively full wage packet, which might cover a considerable part of a family's expenditures. We can imagine several situations like this one:

> I got 0.75 kroner a day. When the season ended and my account was settled, I had 60 kroner. The manager scarcely trusted me to go home with the money. I was almost in tears. In the end I got the money. When I got home, I said to my dad: 'Now we'll go and buy some cotton cloth to make trousers and a jacket for me'. That came to 7–8 kroner. "The rest you can have to pay off some of our debt at the shop." I thought that would mean we would be creditworthy again, and that turned out to be the case.[27]

The good wages earned by children show that it was not a child's wage they received, in the sense that it was based on their age. The children were paid as workers. True, they were not fully mature workers. That is why they were not paid as much. But the work they did and the money they earned related to the tasks they undertook.[28] Children were paid according to their contribution. We have seen that when the boy, we have cited above, came home from the sawmill with his first pay packet, his contribution had a significant impact on his family's economic well-being. However, it is also possible that it had a social and cultural impact as well. It meant something for the child's position in the community and in the family. It had an influence on child-adult relationships. Pay said something about the child as a child – and as a worker. It shaped a child's identity and self image.

To sum up, we can suggest that Jacob Neumann Mohn's inquiry into child labour in Norway in the 1870s sprang from a time and a culture in which work was a way of life. To most people life meant work – and work gave both meaning and content to one's existence. Work was economically necessary, but it was also a norm and a *mentalité* that embraced all; women and men, children, adults, the elderly.[29] A family's economy and livelihood were based on work. In cooperating around this purpose, its members became a social and cultural entity. Through work children were given practical skills, they acquired social roles and were shaped culturally. What they learned was mostly through practical work and less from school, although the actual balance between the two depended on whether one grew up in the town or in the country, and whether one was a boy or a girl. Their entire upbringing was based on the kin group and under the family's control. A whole way of life was transmitted from one generation to the next. This transfer – through work and with the child as the central link – was at the heart of family formation, and the development of society as well.[30]

Schoolchildren in Kristiania, 1912: work and school

A generation later, in 1912, a large questionnaire-based inquiry was carried out among Kristiania's schoolchildren, to find out the extent to which they took part in paid work.[31] This initiative was taken by the Kristiania School Board. Class teachers were responsible for collecting the information from their pupils. Therefore, educational authorities and the teachers had a central role in this inquiry. The results showed that children continued to do paid work, with one in five schoolchildren in Kristiania engaged in it: one in three boys and one in ten girls[32]. Although children worked, they also attended school each day. Work was adjusted to their schooling. The majority went to school in the morning and worked in the afternoon. Three out of four working boys were errand boys – one-half of the girls were in service. Only 2 per cent of the children worked in factories. Otherwise, we find children working in cinemas, theatres, cafés and restaurants, in shops, and with veterinarians.[33]

On average the children worked between three and five hours a day, with the boys doing slightly more than four hours, the girls around three. The boys had the better wages: 2.40 kroner a week or 120 kroner a year. The girls earned about half as much. The difference was greater than the difference in the working hours would indicate. The work of girls was not valued as much as that of boys. This was part of the general sexual division of renumeration levels – of which children's work was but a part. Within this, the girls' roles and tasks were regarded as less significant than those of the boys.[34] Boys were closer to the heart of the money economy and to the support of their families, both in the long and short term. Most girls were in service. This had become a job for females and was one of the poorest-paid occupations – for adults and for children.

There was a big difference between the pay of children and adults. For example, in 1914 an adult pottery worker earned 800 kroner annually and a skilled craftsman about double that amount.[35] In other words, while a well-paid boy in 1875 *could* earn as much as around one-half of an adult worker's pay, the gap between the two had widened considerably by 1912. By then adult workers earned often many times as much as well-paid elementary school children in the towns. The main reason for this was that the total hours the children spent working had been drastically reduced by 1912. At that date children were part-time workers. Their *hourly rate* was however relatively high, and the less hours they worked the higher it was. Thus, a boy who worked less than one hour a day earned almost three times as much per hour (19 øre) than one with a working day of between six and eight hours (7.2 øre). Taken as a whole, however, children working part-time in 1912 were able to contribute a significantly smaller sum to the maintenance of their families. To board and lodge a child cost

5.25 kroner a week, according to Kristiania's Local Health Insurance Board.[36] The average pay of a boy was 2.40 kroner, which would barely cover half of this expenditure. Children working part-time were far from able to support themselves. This applied especially to girls. Thus, the children's pay meant far less for both the family and the child than it had a few decades earlier, when they were well able to support themselves on the wages they earned.

Even in 1912 some children did paid work at a very young age. Almost 300 children were seven years or younger when they began their working lives. Some of the elementary school pupils said they had been as young as three years of age. But the older the children were the more work they did, adjusting it to their school work. Although school took up much more of a child's day than it had some decades earlier, there is no evidence to suggest any conflict between work and school. Teachers, when asked if they felt that paid work meant that school work was neglected, somewhat surprisingly replied that it did not seem to affect attendance or cause any significant problems. Less attention might be paid to homework and if the combination of school work and paid work was too long, then this reduced the child's time for rest and play. But the teachers stressed that work was good for children. They became accustomed to orderliness, obedience and punctuality. Children learned to use their time to the best advantage, to make the most of it. Work kept children off the streets and helped to keep them in check. In fact, school and work was an ideal combination. Children learned both abstract and practical skills and adjusted to the demands of society with good morals and an effective use of their time. The inquiry had to admit that the children who worked were often the best pupils in the class.

> A short period of work each day must be regarded as a good thing, especially for children aged 11–12 years and above. Children get accustomed to orderliness and obedience and they gain routine in how to use their time. Besides, work keeps them out of mischief on the streets. Many schoolmasters and schoolmistresses say that children who work are often the most diligent and the brightest of their pupils. (. . .) It is worth noting that the abovementioned Danish inquiry of 1908 was not able to show that gainful employment had any unfortunate impact on teaching. The inquiry asked if a pupil belonged to the brightest, middle or weakest third of the class. That no result was forthcoming from this was explained by the State Office of Statistics as due to the fact that employers preferred to take on children who were the best equipped, mentally and physically. This was, as indicated above, what was found by this inquiry.[37]

In the 1870s it was the schools that had warned of the unfortunate impact of work on a child's schooling.[38] In 1912 teachers had to acknowledge that children who worked were among the schools' best equipped, both mentally and physically, and that work in no way adversely affected a child's health, at least not the boys. Boys who worked were less likely to be ill than those who did not. However, for girls the reverse was the case. That was not because of work itself but its nature and where it took place, often it was indoors.

> On the other hand, the state of health of the girls who work is much worse than it is among those who do not. (. . .) That the situation is so much worse for girls is more likely due to the indirect results of the work than to the work itself, and especially the fact that working girls are more often required to remain indoors.[39]

While boys ran about in the fresh air as delivery and messenger boys, the girls' health was weakened in badly ventilated houses and often through heavy physical work. Common to boys and girls, however, was exposure to *moral* dangers at work. Certain moral limits were not to be transgressed. Girls should not work for men living alone. It was also not proper that either girls or boys model for artists, work for hotdog sellers at night, or work in the entertainment business. If these limits were observed, however, work could actually strengthen a child's moral sense.

The best pupils, mentally and physically, in the school class were working. Neither socially nor economically were all Kristiania's child workers badly off. Kristiania was divided along social lines into a better-off West End and a working-class East End. The child workers were almost equally divided between schools in the two areas. If anything, children attending schools in the centre and west of the town were more likely to have jobs than those from the east side. This distribution was also reflected in the social classes to which the working children belonged. In families where the main breadwinner was self-employed, one in five boys had paid work. Approximately the same proportion did so where the main breadwinner was a factory worker. In the families of senior public servants, however, only one in ten boys was in paid work.[40] This suggests that it was cultural influences, in the form of *mentalité* and childrearing principles – rather than purely economic considerations – that were at the root of many families' desire that their children should, or should not, work. In other families, however, economic necessity might be more pressing. This was, for example, the case where single women were the family's main breadwinner. Usually, they worked in badly paid women's jobs such as sewing, laundering and cleaning. That one in three children in such families had paid work was probably the result of economic need.

Children in work from 1875–1912: continuity and change

By placing the two inquiries together, we can compare their findings. The comparison must be carried out with care for the two inquiries are very different from each other. This applies to both the children who were the subject of the inquiries and the way the inquiries were carried out. In quantitative terms both are flawed and not at all comparable. But the qualitative elements give us an insight into contemporary views on children's work and its significance for society for the family and the child's upbringing. It is then based on this qualitative material that a comparison will be made and a summing up attempted.

The picture is one of *work* as an important feature of childhood. This was the case throughout the period 1875–1912. At the beginning of the period, work itself was the way a child entered adulthood. Children assisted adults. They worked side by side. Often children occupied an essential place in the production process. In addition, they were flexible, with flexibility as their supreme advantage – from a work point of view. Through their place in the labour force they were integrated into society and family, both socially and culturally. Through work they became useful and significant.

Throughout the period children tackled a wide range of jobs. They were everywhere that work was to be found and they were paid for the work they did. As full-time workers they were paid well, especially the boys. At the beginning of the period children could more than support themselves through the wages they contributed to the family economy. Later a reduction in the number of hours they worked meant their pay and contribution to the family fell sharply.

Recruitment was wide-ranging. This appears clearly from the 1912 inquiry. It was not just children from the poorest families who had paid work, but also children from the families of senior public officials and the self-employed. Money was not always the reason why parents wanted their children to work. Rather an important explanation lay in the fact that work was the norm. It accorded with the principles of childrearing.

Changes in children's work had above all to do with changes in hours of work. The length of the working day fell. While it was common in the 1870s for this to last 10 hours, by 1912 merely a small proportion of children's work lasted for such a long day.[41] There was less room for work in a child's life, more for school and organized, or unorganized, leisure time. Yet there continued to be many children in the towns, and probably even more in the countryside, who still had paid work in 1912. Children's work continued to be socially acceptable. But it now took second position in a child's life.

Child labour also changed its character. Whereas Jacob Neumann Mohn had found an enormous number of children in factories in the 1870s, very few remained there in 1912.[42] By that date children working full-time and children working in industry were virtually a thing of the past. Essentially, children were now part-time workers as domestic servants or employed in the service sector generally. The work was child-specific, organized outside the family and cut off from the world of adult labour. It did not provide children with a training for future work. The school was now the most important agent of socialization for the child, at least in the towns. It filled a child's day: 'Since then (1870s – my note) schooling has increased dramatically. So to work 14 hours in 24, as then, would simply not be possible, was how document No. 36 summed up the matter.[43] While in the 1870s it had been the school authorities who had taken the initiative to ensure that child labour was regulated and adjusted to the needs of the school, by 1912 teachers were happily able to say that the school had now taken first priority in a child's life. The working child had become the schoolchild.

These two inquiries have described the character of children's work, its organization and its place in the life, of the child, the family and society at large. They have also shown the changes that occurred. So far, our story has been about the many and about child labour seen from the outside. By writing down the reminiscences of individual workers it is, however, possible to link our quantitatively based story to a qualitative assessment, a view from the inside – as expressed by two boys who lived through it. What place did work have in their lives? What meaning did it have for those who actually experienced it? The children are called Hans and Torleif. Based on their accounts we shall reconstruct and compare two children's lives. But we shall also widen the perspective. Our analysis of the childhood of Hans and Torleif will enable us to construct two models: one of the child in the traditional society, the other in the modern. Thus, their stories will deepen our understanding of their lives and contribute to a greater understanding of the development of the modern child.

Two accounts of childhood

Hans Olsen Solvold was born in 1865 in Holla, Telemark country. He grew up in a family attached to the Ulefoss Sawmill towards the end of the last [nineteenth] century, his father being a master sawyer. His mother was from Kviteseid and had worked on a mountain farm before she married and moved to the sawmill. The family lived on a cotter's holding, belonging to the home farm at Ulefoss. There were six children of which five grew up in reasonable comfort. They lived in a house that was standard for that time at Ulefoss. There were a living room and a kitchen. The children lay two or three in a bed, a homemade affair filled with straw and wood shavings. Fleas were thriving in beds like this. The everyday fare included flat-bread, homebaked rye bread, porridge, herring and potatoes. They kept a pig, which was killed in the autumn. So on Sundays and feast days they had meat or fried pork. Their clothes were made of linen or homespun cloth. Hans's mother made his clothes. They had leather shoes in the winter, but in summer they went barefoot.

The livelihood of the family was quite adequate, it was said. It was many-sided too, with the whole family contributing. Hans began to work at an early age. He was flexible and stepped in where he was needed. At first he worked at home with his mother. He watched the cows, worked on the arable land and chopped wood. He was seven years old when he began to go to school. At eight and a half he began work with his father – a master sawyer – at the sawmill. He was a boy-helper. He worked 12 hours a day earning about 60 øre. With this he could buy either a kilo of pork, half a kilo of butter, 10 kilos of potatoes or six loaves.[44] It would seem that Hans could more than satisfy his own nutritional requirements. The sawmill was in operation during the summer half of the year. It ceased production in the winter, at which time Hans went to the work's school. The school was a small, red-timbered building situated among the houses of the workers and the work's buildings. The school was open every other day from 9.00 am to 3.30 pm with a one-hour break in the middle of the day. This private work's school was a good one. Hans recalled that the teachers were strict, but clever. He learned to read and write and do arithmetic. He studied a bit of religion, some geography and some history. But he had no practical subjects. When they were introduced, following the 1889 Education Act, they were for a long time taught outside the normal school hours. The subject gymnastics was not introduced until 1910.[45] Practical things were learned outside the school. School was a place for book learning only. At 14 Hans was confirmed. That was the end of his schooling and he began to work full-time at the sawmill like the other adult workers. He lived at home until his marriage in 1893. He was then 28. His parents managed his money until he was 20 years of age. After that he paid for his own upkeep.

Torleif Albretsen was born in 1910, a generation and a half later, in the town of Porsgrunn also in Telemark country. His father was a jack of all trades and changing jobs often. He worked in a bicycle factory, trained to become a baker and ended as a stevedore for Norsk Hydro. His mother stayed at home. She and her husband had six children, two of whom died of tuberculosis. The family occupied a small house on the east side of Porsgrunn. It contained a kitchen, living room and bedroom downstairs and two small rooms in the loft. The living room was only used on special occasions. Electricity was installed, but water and the lavatory were outside. They had a pig and hens in the back garden. There was also an outhouse. Torleif's father fished and sold a little of what he caught. His mother was clever at everything she did, said Torleif. She made the boys' suits. They had enough to be able to share with others, if the need arose. A parish nurse lived nearby and she would generally come with an empty container on the days she knew they had freshly made soup.

For seven years Torleif went to the elementary school on Porsgrunn's east side. It was a custom-built general school in large new buildings of a modern design. When he was between 10 and 12 years of age, Torleif began to use his leisure time to deliver newspapers, along with his brother. He earned 25 kroner a month. He kept five kroner and gave his mother the rest to save. It was to be used to buy his clothes. One thing he had learned. If he were going to buy anything he would pay cash. Finished with elementary school, many of Torleif's friends went on to secondary school. He did not. He said he was dyslexic. He wanted to go to sea, but his mother was against it. Instead, aged 15, he began work at the in porcelain factory Porsgrunn. He was employed as a painter and did straw patterns. He earned good money as an apprentice painter: 40 øre an hour. That was half of what a fully trained man received. Some of his wages went to pay for his keep at home, the rest he kept himself, for visits to the cinema and other places of entertainment. He lived at home until he was married, aged 27.

This is a brief account of the childhood of two boys and children, as they remembered and later retold it. Their accounts fitted well in the picture painted by the statistical inquiries into childhood. Like the children in the statistics, Hans and Torleif *both* went to school *and* to work. Furthermore, both contributed to a livelihood made up of many different jobs. At first they contributed through unpaid work in the home. There they worked with their mother, lending her a hand as needed. She was responsible for a wide range of household jobs, involving many types of productive and reproductive work. She needed the labour the children could provide. Later they went out to work, their earnings going to support the family's economy.

They had much in common, but there were also important differences. To a large extent these stemmed from the difference between a more traditional childhood based on work and a more modern one based on school. Allowing for the fact that the individual child's life was made up of the present and the past, and that both the traditional and the modern contributed to the process, we call childhood, we shall nevertheless analyse the two experiences based on this one overriding perspective: that their childhood was a product of the tension between the traditional and the modern.

So far as *work* was concerned it stood at the heart of Hans's life as a child and took more of his *time*. Hans belonged to a culture where work was a way of life, and since he was quite small, his day was filled with a variety of jobs. They began with his working at home alongside his mother. Later he went out to do paid work at the sawmill. He also went to the school at the works. School was important but work came first. School was adjusted to his working life, adapted to it. It functioned only on a seasonal basis – and then every second day.

School took up most of Torleif's childhood from the age of seven to fifteen. It operated every day and throughout the year. Torleif also worked, but either before or after school. School came first. As for the time they filled, school and work swapped places in the childhood experiences of Hans and Torleif. While work took the leading role in Hans's life, school did so for Torleif. After seven years of elementary school, Torleif, a working class child, could have continued, but because of his dyslexia he was convinced that he did not have the necessary qualifications for secondary school.

Work then played a different part and had a different meaning for the two boys' childhood. Hans was well trained for his future job and socialised into adult life in the widest possible sense through work. He was employed at a sawmill where the work passed, as an inheritance, from one generation to the next. He worked together with his father. Thus the practicalities of work, its social roles and culture were transferred from father to son. The foundation for continuity and stability in both the family and society lay in the work recruitment and work training.

Torleif's early work experiences were not a part of family-based, practical training. Consequently, Torleif's father had neither control of nor influence upon his son's work training and introduction to adult roles.[46] Training and socialization were to a much greater extent outside the family's control and placed in institutions where adult professionals had a hand in the child's training. These professional educators were above all teachers, but psychologists, doctors and psychiatrists also came to have an important place in a child's life. The child and childhood were subjected to scientific analysis, simultaneously as they were institutionalized. One imagines that with such a development feeling for kin would be weakened, and the family itself would take on a different role and meaning in a child's life.[47]

Nevertheless, Torleif did gain useful work experience as a newspaper boy. He had to learn how to dispose of his time and get used to the rhythm of work. He had to learn to be punctual and responsible as far as money was concerned. Through his work he was socialized into an urban, industrial society's rhythms, roles and *mentalité*. But this work did not lead to a particular occupation in the future. As a newspaper boy Torleif worked in specifically a child's job, as did the children in the Kristiania inquiry. What is more, he worked in a typical boy's job in towns around the turn of the century. Not until he was 15 did he begin to work in the place that was to be his future, namely the porcelain factory. Torleif's career both at school and at work, reflected the provisions of the new education and factory acts.

So the school was more important to Torleif's upbringing. It also had a different function and meaning in the lives of the two children. At the work's school in Ulefoss, Hans acquired a knowledge of the basics. Practical subjects had no place there. The school and the community were bound together as one. The little school house did not even look very different from the other houses in the sawmill's environs.

The school played quite a different role in the urban society of Porsgrunn. It was both more pervasive and more restrictive. For example, attendance was more strictly controlled. Absence led to parents being called before the school board, and repeated absenteeism was punished with fines.[48] In many ways the Porsgrunn school was a cultural system that drew Torleif away from his roots in the family and neighbourhood.[49] The modern school buildings on Porsgrunn's east side were large, even monumental. One imagines that Torleif and his parents must have felt strange and of little consequence when they walked into the Porsgrunn school grounds.[50]

Torleif spent much of his childhood at school. There he acquired abstract and theoretical knowledge and some practical skills. Through the learning process itself he was shaped as an individual. To learn to read and write lays the foundation of an identity and defines one as an autonomous individual. Torleif was turned inwards focusing on himself. "Children are perforce withdrawn from face-to-face communities," Barbara Finkelstein says about learning from the book.[51] The school also promotes the merits of rationality, individualism and precision. The foundation of the school itself was the idea of enlightenment and a belief in reason. The foundations of individualism were best laid by competition for top marks between the pupils themselves. Torleif failed there because he was dyslexic. The strict demands of the timetable itself promoted punctuality. For Torleif the school bell was a source of authority. That it had a powerful hold on the children was shown by the way they fell into straight lines as soon as they heard its ring.[52] There was no school bell at Ulefoss. Hans and the other children were called in by the teacher.

Torleif was probably less physically tired than Hans, though mentally more so, when he went to bed at night. But the body was also an important instrument in modern culture. It had to be kept strong, in fighting trim, unflinching and able to reproduce itself.[53] Physical education was introduced into the school as a compulsory subject – an hour a week on Torleif's timetable.[54] The new athletics movement aimed at enrolling working class children in the conquest of the body. *Porsgrund Gymnastics Club* was established in 1880, and by the turn of the century, associations and clubs covered most forms of athletics, gymnastics, skiing, skating, swimming, rowing, wrestling, football and track events.[55] There was no gymnastics at school for Hans. At Ulefoss it was thought unnecessary and was not introduced as a school subject until 1910.[56]

Children's pay also had a different role and a different meaning in the lives of Hans and Torleif. It moulded them differently. The money Hans earned went in full into the family's common purse until he was well into his twenties. Personally he had nothing at his disposal. Indirectly, however, he could take pleasure in the fact that what he earned served to increase the family budget. The traditional family economy based on all pay going into a common purse shaped it into a collectivity. Nevertheless, it also had a significance for Hans's view of himself as someone who was both useful and needed.

As far as Torleif was concerned he kept a part of his pay and used it for pleasure. The rest was laid aside to be used to buy his clothes. When he became an adult he continued to live at home and paid his parents for his upkeep. Consequently, his pay was to a greater extent his own, even though it also eased the family budget somewhat. Nevertheless, his pay had a different orientation to that of the family income economy. It was geared to Torleif's person and contributed to a greater extent to shape him as an individual.

Torleif belonged to a more modern family in which the housewife and children were assigned specific jobs. The mother was to make sure that Torleif and the other children grew up in a healthy, hygienic, natural, private, loving and sheltered environment.[57] It was possible for her to accomplish this because the family was *materially* so much better off than the working class family in Ulefoss. Torleif, as he grew up, had a more varied diet, he was dressed in clothes brought at the shop, and his home was more spacious. But there was a cultural side to this higher material standard. New and increased demands were made on childrearing. In as much as Torleif's father occupied a less central role in the socialization of his children, because his sons did not work beside him, so the mother became the central figure. Mother and child formed the ideological and emotional core of the modern family. Childrearing was to advance an inner harmony and social responsibility.

The working class family embraced new ideals: it should be proud and respectable. One expression of this was that Torleif's family had 'a room for best use'. It symbolized the fact that the family had more than absolutely necessary: a room that was not used every day, but only for special occasions. Another feature underlined by Torleif was that his family did not depend on support from others and had sufficient means to give – out of feelings of common human concern – to others in need. In keeping with this it was also important that the family paid cash for whatever was bought. Torleif's family was then representing of a proud and respectable working class.[58]

It has been argued that the respectable working class family had been transformed into 'bourgeoisie' and, thus, the modern child was a middle class child. Possibly the process of becoming bourgeoisie for the working class family in Porsgrunn could be explained by the fact that it was exposed to an ideological pressure exerted through an all-pervasive campaign covering housekeeping, looking after children, diet, hygiene and education. The campaign was especially directed towards working class women with new behavioural norms and ideals. Its bourgeois message had clear moral overtones.[59] It was disseminated through many channels around and after the turn of the century: through local papers, magazines and other publications – from one woman to another in the many local charitable and philanthropic organizations, within the Labour movement and through the school.[60] Dissemination might also occur in more subtle ways. The working class espoused the bourgeois way of life and behaviour merely by observing it and following suit. The Norwegian social historian, Edvard Bull, suggested that servant girls probably played an important role in transferring domestic ideals from the middle class home to their own homes.[61]

It is unlikely, however, that Torleif's family either directly or passively assumed a middle class stock of values and a middle class culture. Orvar Löfgren argues that the middle class message was received in different ways by the working class and was remodelled to conform with the working class family's own dreams, expectations and practices. Traditional, cultural resources were used and changed to meet a new situation.[62] In such a way new forms of behaviour and new ways of life were expressed differently and given a new meaning by the working class. In Torleif's family it was a matter of living a respectable family life in a pretty, orderly home – with a stay-at-home housewife, a father who worked outside the home and a limited number of children who were healthy, wholesome, clean and went to school. A more instrumental relationship to life replaced a fatalistic one. The parents took the fate of their children into their own hands. They sent them to school. This was not necessarily an expression of a desire for their children's social and economic advancement. It was just as much the parents' wish to ensure a secure future for their children based on visions and desires in the broadest sense. Earlier, they had been at pains to ensure that their children acquired the skills necessary to hold down a specified job. As time passed schooling became a norm and a necessity.

Hans and Torleif had their identities shaped both by work and school. But identity was more than knowing what rules applied and what forms of behaviour were acceptable in different circles. Identity was also a question of becoming skilled in how to behave, and in the body language expected of a child. Through practice and action Hans and Torleif took part in the shaping of childhood within the framework set by the family and society.[63] The frame-works were different, just as the frameworks for children in the two statistical inquiries were different. Thus, Hans and Torleif and the many children in the statistics had different child-hoods. To be a worker's child in a rural and traditional industrial society was to have quite a different life from that of a worker's child in a modern, industrialized, urban society. The two accounts of childhood and the two statistical inquiries also contain a time element and tell us something about historical change. Therefore, to grow up after the turn of the century was quite different from the decades before.

Conclusion: the modern child is a child of the school

Hans and Torleif and the thousands of Norwegian children included in the 1875 and 1912 inquiries grew up and lived for most of their lives, though for different lengths of time, in the family, at work outside the household and at school, in a society that went through vast changes in working life, social structures, the household and the family. The child and child-hood were at the centre of these processes of change. According to Edvard Bull, it is precisely the relationship between the generations – that is to say the way childhood is organized – that is one of the most central of all historical phenomena.

> The relationship between the generations is one of the most central of all histor-ical phenomena. The development of society – even 'historical development' – cannot happen without a constant transfer of experience and entire patterns of social life from generation to generation. The mechanics of this transfer must be of interest to the historian that is to say the structure of upbringing and the relations between adults and children, old and young.[64]

Here we have told a story of great variety, of similarities and differences, of changes in chil-dren's work and of the conditions under which they grew up – within a period around the turn of the century. Work undoubtedly became a smaller part of childhood. Norwegian school children sat at their desks for several additional hours after the turn of the century than they had done before. Normatively the school gained ground too. At the end of the century, the debates over the major legislative activity concerning the regulation of children's work and the extension of schooling, created the conditions upon which new ways of thinking were based. That children should not work but should go to school won acceptance and became one of the basic norms of modern society. In the long term this interest in children and in childhood changed the pattern of thought. It was not that one pattern replaced another. Different and complex patterns existed side by side and simultaneously in the child's life, the family and the community.[65] That is to say, the childhood focused on work and also that focused on school existed side by side within the mental structures.

In modern society the child's life became more separate from that of the adult. The State took charge of the child with progressive legislation and by building its own institutions for children, above all the school. However, the modern child was also an organized child. In organizations designed specifically for children, they were introduced to particular roles and ways of behaviour. Simultaneously, as the child was made public and institutionalized, modern childhood is characterized by a process of *familiarization*, an encircling of the child by the family, and a growing intimacy of family life.[66] This development provided the conditions for the growth of a specific child culture. Here the codes and behaviour patterns of childhood were acquired, the identity of the child – regarding age, sex and social class – was formed. The child learned that he or she was *different* from other children.[67] This applied to gender.

Yet age became especially important in the formation of the modem child.[68] Birthdays were the object of great attention and the fact that children at school were separated by age, and that factory legislation focused on age, defined the child in a new way.

A childhood of schooling was a norm that won strong support. Nevertheless, children continued to work. Often school and work were combined, as with the children in Kristiania in 1912. The child was a *schoolchild and a covert part-time worker*. Children's work has become invisible in our own times and within our own culture.[69] Making something invisible is an expression of cultural prejudice. That occurs also when – in our part of the world – we moralize and condemn the practices of other countries and cultures concerning children's work. The story of child labour in our own industries is similarly handled – with clear moral overtones in the historical literature.[70] In working with the history of childhood we must adjust our sights and become conscious of our prejudices. Children's work must be understood and explained within the cultural and historical context of which it was a part.

Notes

1   Norway was a late starter in this area. Denmark made a similar law in 1873, while Sweden had a law making night work illegal for children and young people as early as 1853.

2   There was a long tradition for different acts for urban and rural schools. There were still two laws in 1889, one for the towns and one for the rural districts. Nevertheless, by then the aim was to make them as similar as possible. The principle of one school for all was upheld more strongly in Norway than in the other Nordic countries, or, for that matter, in European countries generally. See Jordheim 1984, p. 91.

3   On universatility as a principle of Norwegian social policy, see Seip 1984, pp. 185–86.

4   See Stang Dahl 1978.

5   For more on this, see Seip 1984, chapter 10.

6   Mohn 1878.

7   The inquiry was undertaken by a committee appointed by the Kristiania School Board. The committee was also to prepare proposals for changes in the Elementary School Act. Document No.36 1912–13.

8   James and Prout 1990, p. 8.

9   Hans Olsen Solvold was interviewed by Edvard Bull in 1953. The transcript can be found in the Arbeiderminne samlingen (collection of worker reminiscences), Department of History, University of Trondheim. Torleif Albretsen was interviewed by the author of this chapter. The audio-tape can be found in the Labour Movement's Archives in Telemark.

10   Childhood and upbringing were sexually conditioned. It would, therefore, have been desirable if one of the children had been a girl. Unfortunately, only boys appear in the Ulefoss and Porsgrunn material. This was in part because worker reminiscences were only collected from among industrial workers, with the result that girls were excluded.

11   Mohn 1878, p. 3.

12   Mohn 1878, p. 6.

13   Bull 1985, p. 319

14   On the flexibility of child labour and the needs of the family, see, for example, Hareven 1982, p. 213. On the family cycle, economy and work, see Fløystad 1979.

15   See, for example, Avdem and Melby 1985.

16   Marx 1983, p. 116.

17   Mohn 1878, p. 8.

18   See Schrumpf 1997, chapter 3.

19   The extent to which children working in industry was a mark of change or continuity was discussed by contemporaries and subsequently by historians. See, for example, Olsson 1980. Olsson argues that it did in fact represent a break with pre-industrial child labour.

20   Mohn 1878, p. 31.

21   Mohn 1878, p. 14.

22   Isak Lindalen's account of his father Ole Pedersen Lindalen, born 1859.

23   Mohn 1878, p. 15.

24   Dokka 1879, p. 32.

25   Mohn 1878, p. 28.

26   Mohn 1878, p. 31.

27   Cited by Bull 1953, p. 32.

28   On age and task orientated work, see Thompson 1967.

29   On work as a way of life, see Slettan 1989, and on the *mentalité* of work, see Thorsen 1993, p. 22.

30   Bull 1979, p. 35.

31   The answers related to 1. February 1912 and covered 85 per cent of schoolchildren in the city. The Board reckoned that 'the inquiry covered just about all productive employment carried out by schoolchildren in Kristiania'. Document No.36 1912–13, p. 9.

32   More precisely 30 per cent of the boys and 12 per cent of the girls in the elementary schools. All paid work inside or outside the home as per January 1912, or in the course of the last school year, was included.

33   Document No.36 1912–13, p. 29.

34   On the sexual division, see Blom 1994, p. 40.

35   Schrumpf 1996, Chapter 5.

36   Document No.36 1912–13, p. 37.

37   Document No.36 1912–93, pp. 40, 43.

38   Bull 1984, p. 81.

39   Document No.36 1912–13, p. 22.

40   The inquiry is not wholly reliable for other than the working class. This was because a greater number of children from the other classes were educated in state (as opposed to local authority) or private schools. These were not included in the inquiry and totalled around 7,000 children.

41   The figures show that in 1871 around one in three boys and one in four girls worked for 10 hours a day or more. By 1912 the percentages had fallen to 0.07 and 0.17 respectively. Document No.36 1912–13, p. 52.

42   The figures show that in 1871 some 3.8 per cent of boys and 1.5 per cent of girls in Kristiania's elementary schools, worked in factories. By 1912 the percentages had fallen to 0.42 and 0.08 respectively. Document No.36 1912–13, p. 52.

43   Document No. 36 1912–13, p. 52.

44   *Historical Statistics* 1968.

45   Ytterbø 1957, pp. 225–26.

46   On this kin-based learning, see, for example, Seccombe 1993, p. 18.

47   One consequence of changes in kin feelings has been described by Edward Shorter thus: 'whereas once people had been able to answer such questions as "who am I" by pointing to those who had gone before and would come after, in the twentieth century they would have other replies.' Shorter 1975, p. 4.

48   Minutes of the Porsgrund School Board 1890–1900.

49   On differences in the child's experience of school in urban and rural districts, see Finkelstein 1979.

50   On the significance of school architecture, see Coninck-Smith 1992.

51   Finkelstein 1979, pp. 114–15.

52   The role of the school bell for childhood in the modern period is emphasized by Sutherland 1993, Chapter 10.

53   On the body in middle class culture, see Rudberg 1983, pp. 163–64.

54   Minutes of the Porsgrund School Board 1890–1900.

55   Tønnessen 1957, p. 501.

56   Ytterbø 1957, pp. 225–26.

57   An important advocate of this new view of the family, the child and childrearing was the Swedish Social Democrat, Ellen Key. She influenced Social Democrats, popular communicators and educationalists throughout Scandinavia. See Ambjørnsen 1981, pp. 43–44 and Gordon 1988. She argued that the new way of bringing up children strengthened women's role and enhanced a woman's sphere of influence.

58   On respectability and the working class family, see Seccombe 1993, p. 206.

59   See for example Avdem and Melby 1985.

60   Anna Davin argues that the school's most important aim was to convey the middle class view of the family to working class children and so create a new generation of parents, especially mothers, Davin 1982, p. 643.

61   Bull 1985.

62   Löfgren 1982. In the same way Liv Emma Thorsen argues that the cultural identity of young girls of farming stock was strengthened rather than weakened when meeting that of the middle class. See Thorsen 1993, p. 83.

63   See James and Prout 1990, p. 8.
64   Bull 1970, p. 35.
65   On the procedural character and separability of *mentalités,* see Thorsen 1993, p. 20.
66   Qvortrup 1990, p. 48.
67   On similarities and differences in the forming of the child in gender terms in early modern times, see Sandmo 1995.
68   See Chudacoff 1989.
69   See Anne Solberg's chapter in this book [see original reading].
70   See Schrumpf 1993 and 1996.

Unpublished sources

–   Forhandlingsprotokoll for Porsgrund Skolestyre 1890–1990. Porsgrunns byarkiv.

–   Protokoll for Tilsynsutvalget ved Ulefos brugs Skole 1890–1920. Ulefos Brugs arkiv.

–   Muntlige kilder:

–   Hans Olsen Solvold, født 1865 på Ulefoss. Arbeiderminnesamlingen Universitetet i Trondheim.

–   Torleif Albretsen, født 1910 i Porsgrunn. Arbeiderbevegelsens arkiv i Telemark.

–   Isak Lindalens beretning om sin far, Ole Pedersen Lindalen, født 1859 på Ulefoss. Arbeiderminnesamlingen Universitetet i Trondheim.

Published sources

–   Dokument nr. 36 (1912–13). Erhvervsmæssig arbejde blandt skolebarn i Kristiania.

–   *Mohn, Jacob Neumann* (1875). Angaaende Børns og Unge Menneskers Anvendelse til Arbeide udenfor Hjemmet. I Stortingets forhandlinger 1883, del III. Kristiania.

Literature

Ambjørnsen, Ronny, (1981): "Barnets fødsel". In Clausen, C. (red)(1981). *Barndommens historic.* København.

Avdem, Anna og Melby, Kari, (1985): *Oppe først og sist i seg. Husarbeid i Norge fra 1850 til i dag.* Oslo.

Blom, Ida, (1984): "Barneoppdragelse". In Hodne, B. & Sogner, S. (red)(1984). *Barn av sin tid.* Oslo.

Blom, Ida, (1994): *Det er forskjell på folk før som nå. Om kjønn og andre former for sosial differensiering.* Oslo.

Bull, Edvard, (1953): *Arbeidervern gjennom 60 år.* Oslo.

Bull, Edvard, (1970): "Historisk vitenskap foran 1970-årene". In Edvard Bull (1981). *Retten til en fortid.* Oslo.

Bull, Edvard, (1984): "Barn i industriarbeid". In Bjarne Hodne & Sølvi Sogner (ed.). *Barn av sin tid.* Oslo.

Bull, Edvard, (1985): "Arbeiderklassen blir til". 1 in *Arbeiderbevegelsens historie.* Oslo.

Chudacoff, Howard, (1989): *How old are you? Age Consiousness in American Culture.* Princeton.

Coninck-Smith, Ning, (1992): "Copenhagen Children's Lives and the Impact of Institutions c. 1840–1920". *History Workshop Journal.*

Dahl, Tove Stang, (1978): *Barnevern og samfunnsvern. Om stat, vitenskap og profesjoner under barnevernets oppkomst i Norge.* Oslo.

Davin, Anna, (1982): "Child Labour, the Working-Class Family, and the Domestic Ideology in 19th Century Britain". In *Development and Change*, vol. 13. Number 4 October 1982.

Dokka, Hans-Jørge, (1979): "Barn i skolen". In *Forskningsnytt* nr. 4–1979. Oslo.

Finkelstein, Barbara (ed), (1979): "Reading, and Writing, and the Acquisition of Identity in the United States: 1790–1860". In Barbara Finkelstein (ed.)(1979). *Regulated, Children/ Liberated Children. Education in Psychohistorical Perspective*. New York.

Fløystad, Ingeborg, (1979): "Vi lærte tidlig å" arbeide!". In *Forskningsnytt* nr. 4–1979.

Gordon, Linda, (1988): *Heroes of Their Own Lives. The Politics and History of Family Violence*. Boston 1880–1960. New York.

Hareven, Tamara, (1982): *Family time & Industrial Time*. Cambridge.

Historisk Statistikk, 1968.

James, Allison & Prout, Alan (ed.), (1990): *Constructing and Reconstructing Childhood. Contemporary Issues in the Sociolocical Study of Childhood*. London.

Jordheim, Knut, (1984): "Skolens rolle". In Hodne, Bjarne and Sogner, Sølvi (ed.)(1984). *Barn av sin tid*. Oslo.

Löfgren, Orvar, (1982): "The Swedish Family": a Study of Privatisation and Social Change since 1880". In Thompson, Paul & Burchardt, Natasha (ed.)(1982). *Our Common History. The Transformation of Europe*. London.

Marx; Karl, (1983): *Kapitalen*. Oslo.

Olsson, Lars, (1980): *Då barn var lönsamma*. Stockholm.

Qvortrup, Jens, (1990): "Børn forgår barndommen består. På sporet af en barndommens sociologi": *In Dansk Sociologi* nr. 1, 1990.

Rudberg, Monica, (1983): *Dydige, sterke og lykkelige barn – ideer om oppdragelse i borgerlig tradisjon*. Oslo.

Sandmo, Erling, (1995): "Et virkelig mandfolk". Teorier om kjønn i det tidlig-moderne Europa. In *Svensk historisk tidskrift* nr. 4–1995.

Schrumpf, Ellen, (1993): "Synet på industrielt barnearbeid – et opgjør med elendighetshistorien": In (Norsk) *Historisk tidsskrift* nr. 2, 1993.

Schrumpf, Ellen, (1994): "Familien i erindring". In *Historie. Populærhistorisk magasin* nr. 2, 1994.

Schrumpf, Ellen, (1996): "Barnearbeid og vestlig arroganse". Kronikk in *Aftenposten* 10. januar 1996.

Schrumpf, Ellen, (1997): *Barnearbeid – plikt eller privilegium? Industrielt barnearbeid i to norske industrisamfunn omkring århundreskiftet*. Kristiansand.

Seccombe, Wally, (1993): *Weathering the Storm. Working-class Families from the Industrial Revolution to the Fertility Decline*. London.

Seip, Anne-Lise, (1984): *Sosialhjelpstaten blir til. Norsk sosialpolitikk 1740–1920*. Oslo.

Shorter, Edward, (1975): *The making of the Modern Family*. New York.

Slettan, Dagfinn, (red.) (1989). *Bondesamfunn i oppløsning? Trønderske bondesamfunn 1930–1980*. Trondheim.

Sutherland, Neil, (1993): *Growing up. Childhood in English Canada From the Great War to the Age of Television*. Upublisert manus. University of British Columbia.

Thompson, Edvard P., (1967): "Time, Work-Discipline, and Industrial Capitalism". In *Past & Present* no. 38, 1967.

Thorsen, Liv Emma, (1993): *Det fleksible kjønn. Mentalitetsendringer i tre generasjoner bondekvinner 1920–1985*. Oslo.

Tønnessen, Joh. N., (1957); *Porsgrunns historie 1807–1920*. Oslo.

Ytterbø, S., (1957): *Holla II*. Skien.

Chapter 28

Mary E. Odem

STATUTORY RAPE PROSECUTIONS
IN CALIFORNIA

IN APRIL 1915, OAKLAND POLICE arrested George Fields, a young man of
nineteen years who worked as a jitney bus driver, on a charge of statutory rape. George
sat in the county jail for several weeks until his case was heard in the Alameda County
Superior Court. Law enforcement officials also apprehended his female partner, thirteen-
year-old Louise Blake, and placed her in the county detention home for wayward girls to
await the trial. Louise admitted to court officials that she had engaged in sexual relations with
the defendant on several occasions. At first George denied any sexual involvement with her
but later pleaded guilty to the charge. At the sentencing hearing, the county probation officer
recommended probation for the defendant. The young man, he informed the judge, "had
previously borne an excellent reputation," while his female partner in the case "was not a
pure girl." The officer concluded, "The circumstances of this case are such as would test the
moral backbone of persons far better equipped to resist than he had been." Persuaded by this
reasoning, the judge granted the young man probation.[1]

The case of George Fields and Louise Blake, along with others heard before the Alameda
County Superior Court and the Los Angeles County Juvenile Court, allow us to explore how
the criminal justice system responded to the age-of-consent law. (See Appendix for more
information on these case records [see original reading].) Many male court officials were
deeply ambivalent about the new legislation and the assumptions on which it was based.
Moral reformers had been able to persuade legislators to raise the age of consent but could
not ensure that the legal system would enforce the law as they had intended. Like the probation officer and judge in the Fields case, many court officials did not accept the model of
female sexual victimization promoted by purity reformers, nor did they share the reformers'
commitment to a single standard of morality for both sexes. Rather, they held to a different
moral code that tolerated sexual license on the part of men yet expected women to remain
chaste. Informed by such attitudes, courts were reluctant to apply the criminal penalties the
law called for, particularly in cases in which, like George Fields, the male offenders were
young and white and their female partners were thought to be immoral.

With the passage of age-of-consent legislation, the state assumed an active role in monitoring the sexual behavior of working-class women and girls and their male partners. Police
officers patrolled train stations, amusement parks, cafés, and dance halls in search of suspected

immoral behavior. They also conducted periodic raids of downtown hotels and arrested couples who had violated the law. Adult men arrested for statutory rape typically were detained in the county jail until a preliminary examination could be held in one of the police or justice courts in the county.

At the preliminary hearing, the judge sought to determine if there was sufficient evidence to hold the accused man for trial in superior court, which was the central criminal court for counties in California. Both the prosecution and the defense were permitted to call witnesses for examination and cross-examination. Once the judge decided that prosecution should go forward, which was the outcome in most cases, he set bail to guarantee the defendant's appearance at superior court. If the defendant could not raise bail, he remained confined in the county jail until the trial.[2] At least 36 percent of those charged with statutory rape in the Alameda County Superior Court spent anywhere from one week to six months in jail while awaiting trial.[3]

Although the age-of-consent law was intended to "protect" young women, the prosecution of statutory rape cases proved to be a punitive process for them as well as for the male defendants. Young women and girls were frequently confined in the county detention home for delinquent youth to await court hearings. While in detention, all girls were subjected to compulsory pelvic exams to determine whether they were virgins. If the physician found evidence of sexual experience (a ruptured hymen or relaxed vaginal opening), the girls faced rigorous questioning about their sexual activities by female probation officers, who pressured them to reveal the names of their sexual partners, then turned these names over to the police. During a cross-examination in a police court in Alameda County, the defense attorney asked one girl why she had filed a complaint against the defendant. The girl responded:

> A: They made me tell.
> Defense: Who made you tell?
> A: Miss Rich [probation officer at the detention home] . . . .
> Defense: Well, did you tell her you had had sexual intercourse with anyone?
> A: Well, she knew it after I was examined. . . .
> Defense: How did she happen to have you examined by a doctor?
> A: Well, as far as I know, all the girls are who go there.[4]

These inquiries sometimes led to the arrest of several young men for the rape of one girl. In one such case, an unmarried, pregnant teenager, Mary Reed, told the probation officer that the father of her unborn child was a young man she had been dating steadily for the past year. Under questioning by the probation officer, she also confessed to sexual intimacy with several others prior to her current relationship. Rape complaints were filed against all of the young men, even though Mary insisted she only wanted her child's father arrested.[5]

Young women involved in statutory rape cases faced long interrogations about their sex lives at the preliminary hearing. The hearings were meant to determine if sufficient grounds existed to prosecute the defendant, but they usually focused on the moral character of the female witness, too. Male defendants were not required to testify in these hearings, and the vast majority did not. But the young women were routinely questioned by both the prosecution and defense attorneys about their sexual relationships with the accused and usually about past sexual experiences as well. Topical questions included: Where and when did the sex act occur? How did you become undressed? Where did he touch you? What type of underwear were you wearing? What did you say during intercourse? How many times did you have intercourse? The experience was humiliating for many young women and girls, who were compelled to give explicit details of their sexual activities, as in the following exchange between the prosecutor and one female witness:

Prosecutor: And he got on top of you?

A: Yes sir . . . .

Prosecutor: How were your legs when he had this act of sexual intercourse with you, were they close together or apart?

A: They were apart.

Prosecutor: And how did they get apart, you put them apart yourself, Didn't you?

A: No sir.

Prosecutor: Sure about that?

A: Yes sir.

Prosecutor: Who put them apart?

A: He did . . . .

Prosecutor: What were you doing when he put them apart?

A: Nothing.

Prosecutor: Where were your hands when he put them apart?

A: Down at the side.

Prosecutor: What did you say during the time he was putting your limbs, your legs, apart?

A: Didn't say anything.[6]

In response to these questions, many young women and girls spoke in low voices and gave short, one-word answers whenever possible. One teenage girl expressed the pain and embarrassment that many felt before this type of examination: "Really I don't wish to tell it all," she told the judge. "It humiliates and disgraces me and I don't want to." When the judge threatened to pronounce her in contempt of court and send her to the city jail, she said, "You will have to send me, I can't tell it."[7] One fifteen-year-old African American girl, who had run away from home and moved in with a young man, was asked repeatedly for specific details about her sexual relationship with the defendant. When asked, "What did he do to you when he got into bed with you?" she responded impatiently, "Do you expect me to tell the whole history of my life? . . . I am not going to tell the whole history of my life." After the trial of her male partner in superior court, the district attorney complained that "the little girl was a very unwilling witness while on the stand and did everything possible to shield him, as she said she expected to marry him."[8]

One of the central questions raised in the preliminary hearings was whether the female witness had consented to the sexual act. This issue should have been immaterial in cases of statutory rape, because the law prohibited sexual intercourse with female minors, regardless of their consent. Nonetheless, judges routinely allowed attorneys to question female witnesses about their willingness to engage in sex. When the defense attorney in one case asked a female witness if she had consented to sex with the defendant, the prosecutor objected: "It is absolutely immaterial, Your Honor. The question is whether he had an act of sexual intercourse or not and how he obtained that is not a matter for us here." The judge, in this case and numerous others, demonstrated a marked ambivalence about the issue. He admitted that the question was immaterial but nevertheless permitted the defense attorney to continue his line of questioning: "While I don't believe it is relevant, if you want to ask any direct question as to whether he overpowered her by force or anything of that kind at the time of the act, you may do so."[9]

During another hearing, the judge himself asked the young female witness: "Whatever you did, you did of your own free will?" When she responded affirmatively, the judge demanded: "Well how did you happen to complain against him, then?" The prosecutor became exasperated with the judge's disregard for the law: "Don't you know what the statute is, Judge?" "Yes, I know all about it," he replied, "but I am not so touchy upon this subject [that I can't] try to find out some of the reasons which I have been fishing for since this statute has been changed." The judge continued to badger the witness: "What did you go in the house for? . . . What did you take your clothes off for and go to bed with him? . . . Did you know what you were going to get when you were undressing yourself?"[10]

It is understandable that judges would want to distinguish between forcible and consensual intercourse; a major problem with the age-of-consent law was that it conflated the two by denying women under eighteen years of age the capacity to consent to sex. But judges and attorneys went well beyond establishing consent. They viewed a young woman's willingness to engage in sex as a sign of moral depravity, and they often harassed such young women and girls in court hearings, labeling them "depraved," "wayward," or "loose" and blaming them for the moral transgression.[11]

Like male legislators who had opposed the age-of-consent campaign, some judges and court officials reversed the seduction narrative promoted by moral reformers by portraying teenage girls as temptresses who had lured young men into wrongdoing. In one case, a twenty-three-year-old defendant, employed as a streetcar motorman, had engaged in sex with a teenage girl whom his roommate had met on the street and invited to their apartment. The girl explained in court that she did not want to have sex with the young man and told him so, but she did not actively resist his advances. She had recently left the home where she had been employed as a domestic, was stranded with no money, and needed a place to spend the night. Later the next day, probation officers apprehended and questioned the girl and had the man arrested for statutory rape. Upon hearing the case, Judge Frank B. Ogden of the Alameda County Superior Court claimed that the male defendant was the true "victim" in the case. "A man is a man under those circumstances," he explained. "With a girl over the age of 16 years and of mature appearance it would be pretty hard for a man indeed to so control himself as to eliminate himself from all present danger . . . and under the circumstances it would be a pretty strong man who could escape, a pretty strong man."[12]

In a similar case, a young man of twenty years was arrested for having sexual intercourse with a sixteen-year-old girl who had recently run away from home. She met the defendant at a café, where he worked as a janitor. At his request, the girl agreed to stay at the apartment he shared with several friends until she could find work. During that time the couple formed an intimate relationship. In his report on the case, the probation officer for the court called the young woman "the instigator of the acts" and argued that "there ought to be some protection of youths of his age against girls who get into their beds."[13] The image of female entrapment constructed by court officials, like the seduction narrative of the reformers, served mainly to obscure the actual lived experiences of young working-class women and girls.

Even in cases of forcible assault, judges sometimes scolded the female victims for tempting defendants into immoral behavior. In one instance, sixteen-year-old Ruby Haynes was raped by a young man she had been dating. On their way home from the nickelodeon one evening, the young man pushed Ruby into the yard of a vacant house and demanded that she have sex with him. When she refused, he threw her to the ground and raped her. The judge became impatient with Ruby during the preliminary examination and demanded to know why she had not put up a stronger resistance: "Why didn't you scream, that's what I don't understand. Why don't these girls scream out? Why do you lend yourself to the proposition?"[14] Such encounters, now defined as acquaintance rape, did not fit the court's definition of forcible assault.[15] In the eyes of court officials, Ruby had invited the assault by going out unescorted with a young man she only recently met. She had violated what they considered appropriate codes of conduct for respectable women, thereby becoming "fair game" for men. In commenting on Ruby's case, the judge said, "Wherever she went and whatever she did with that man was voluntary, no force to it at all; she knew what she was going to get when she got it."[16]

Officials responded in a similar fashion to a fourteen-year-old Portuguese girl who was sexually assaulted by the janitor in the cannery where she worked. At the end of a workday this janitor, a twenty-two-year-old man, asked the girl to come into an office. When she did, he pushed her to the floor, held his hand over her mouth to keep her from screaming, and raped her. Once the defendant pleaded guilty, the county probation officer recommended that he be granted probation. "She was an inexperienced girl, it is true, and entitled to protection," the male probation officer stated, "but her willingness to accompany [the defendant] into the office alone, placed him under special temptation." The judge apparently agreed with this reasoning, because he granted the man probation.[17]

At other times, judges might claim that young women and girls had not resisted strongly enough. The court scolded one thirteen-year-old who had been sexually abused by her twenty-seven-year-old brother: "Why did you let him do this, [Pearl], you knew that it was naughty, didn't you? Didn't you know that he hadn't any right to do it to you?. . .Why did you let him?" Pearl tried to explain that the acts were committed against her will: "I couldn't do anything against him. We were the only ones home."[18] In cases like these, the victims of forcible rape were made to feel that *they* had done something wrong and immoral and had somehow invited the attack.

Questions in preliminary hearings furthermore were not confined to the specific sexual encounter or relationship with the accused man. Rather a young woman's entire sexual past was put on display in the courtroom. By the late nineteenth century it had become routine, in rape trials involving adult women, to permit the defense to introduce evidence about the victim's prior sexual experience in an attempt to discredit her before the jury. This practice stood in stark contrast to the handling of male defendants in rape cases. Courts prohibited similar inquiries into a male defendant's sexual history, arguing that such evidence would unfairly prejudice the jury against him. Judges allowed such questions about rape complainants because they held that a woman's sexual past was related to a key issue: whether she had consented to the sexual act. The assumption was that if she had consented to sexual relations in one situation, she was likely to do so in others.[19] As one state appeals court judge pronounced in 1915: "No impartial mind can resist the conclusion that a female who had been in the recent habit of illicit intercourse with others will not be so likely to resist as one who is spotless and pure."[20]

The practice of questioning rape complainants about their sexual pasts was eventually incorporated into standard legal texts on evidence. According to John H. Wigmore, the leading legal scholar on the law of evidence at the time, "When the woman consents to the act, no crime of rape is committed; on such a charge, then, the main issue often is whether the woman did consent. Here the woman's disposition to unchastity would have probative value, and would be admissible on behalf of the accused."[21]

But even after it had become standard legal practice in rape trials to question adult women about past sexual acts, such tactics were still considered improper in cases involving underage females. As Wigmore wrote, "But in a trial for a sex offense where the woman's consent is immaterial and not in issue, it follows that the woman's unchastity would also be immaterial, e.g., a charge of carnal knowledge of a minor (usually miscalled in the statutes 'rape under age' or 'statutory rape')."[22] Despite this rule, it was nonetheless a common practice in Alameda courts to question underage female witnesses about their sexual experience. Some judges did prohibit such questions. One interrupted a defense attorney when he asked the young woman on the stand about her sexual relations with men other than the defendant. "You can't ask her that, [Mr. Brown], she might be a common prostitute, but being under 18 years of age her mouth is closed by law."[23] But other judges were quite willing to bend the rules of evidence. When the prosecution objected to a question about the previous sexual experience of one female witness, Judge Weinmann overruled the objection, explaining, "I will allow a certain number of questions bringing out that side of it, because I think it is no more than fair, while I don't think it is strictly legally admissible."[24] Some judges actually introduced questions themselves about the sexual pasts of female witnesses. Judge George Samuels, for example, asked one teenage girl, "You understood what it was all about, it wasn't your first time? . . . You had been out with these boys more or less quite a number of them right along, that is right isn't it?"[25]

Alameda court officials clearly interpreted the purpose of age-of-consent legislation differently than women reformers did. They saw the law as a tool to be used not so much to protect women from sexual harm as to protect the interests of fathers, future husbands, and the state. According to this view, fathers needed to preserve the chastity of their daughters in order to uphold the family name and reputation and to ensure the daughters' marriageability. One judge chastised a male defendant charged with statutory rape for injuring the father's home and family name by having intercourse with his daughter. According to several judges, the state also had a great interest in the preservation of female chastity. It was necessary, they argued, to ensure the production of a healthy, moral citizenry. Judge Mortimer Smith explained that the "philosophy" behind the law was "that the country depends upon its women to produce good citizens, and a woman who is debauched, that has its effect upon the mind of every child that is born to her and therefore, a sound public policy demands that no man shall have intercourse with a woman under the age of 18 unless he is married to her, and if he does so, that he interferes with the well-being of the community."[26] In a similar vein, Judge Frank Ogden stated that the law aimed "to conserve the woman who is the mother of the children and of the future generations called upon, perchance to rule and govern the state."[27]

Given their understanding of the law and its purpose, it makes sense that court officials were preoccupied with the moral character and sexual experience of young women in statutory rape cases. They deemed sexual intercourse with an "unchaste" girl a less serious offense than the same act with a "chaste" girl. The former was already "ruined," already a liability to her family and a danger to the state, and apparently did not deserve the same legal protection as the latter. One defense attorney stated in court that a man who had relations with a sexually experienced girl, while technically guilty of rape, "has not committed a crime that is as heinous as it would be if he had raped a pure girl."[28] Even the prosecuting attorney expressed this view in the case of a young man of nineteen years charged with the statutory rape of a pregnant fifteen-year-old girl. "This boy is a pretty respectable boy," the prosecutor explained in court. "This girl has been running around with many people, Judge. It is one of those cases where it is too bad that any complaint had been filed at all."[29]

The trial records from Alameda County clearly demonstrate that the sexual double standard still held sway in the courtroom. Male judges, attorneys, and probation officers were impervious to the ideals of male continence and a single standard of morality for men and women, so ardently promoted by purity reformers. Court officials continued to act on traditional views of male and female sexuality. As one judge stated, "The passions concerned are the strongest to control in men, it has been ordained so."[30] The general stance taken in the courtroom was that it was man's nature to be lustful and woman's responsibility to maintain moral standards. Men were expected to "sow their wild oats" during their youth. They could engage in illicit sex and still remain respectable, but when a young woman made a slip of this kind, she was considered permanently "ruined"—a moral threat to society.

Moral reformers in California and elsewhere became increasingly frustrated by the failure of the legal system to enforce the age-of-consent law as they had envisioned, and they pursued various strategies to counter the reluctance of law enforcement officials. In San Francisco and Oakland, members of the Woman's Christian Temperance Union (WCTU) organized to locate violators of the law and pressure courts to prosecute these "cases of outraged girlhood." Rose French of San Francisco was particularly active in this campaign.

According to a report issued by the WCTU of Northern California, French helped to initiate numerous prosecutions of male sex offenders.[31] Purity reformers in other parts of the country also worked to ensure the enforcement of age-of-consent legislation. Members of the American Purity Alliance joined forces with the New York Society for the Prevention of Cruelty to Children to find and prosecute men who had sexual intercourse with underage females. Women's clubs in Chicago established a special organization, the Protective Agency for Women and Children, that brought cases of rape and seduction to the attention of the police and the courts. Members of the agency encouraged young women to file complaints and offered them legal assistance in the prosecution of their cases.[32]

Clubwomen also monitored trials of men charged with sex offenses. Women's organizations in Oakland, for example, arranged to have their members in daily attendance at the 1906 trial of a man who was accused of assaulting a young woman.[33] Their object was to provide emotional support for the women who had to testify in court and to assert their moral influence in a courtroom dominated by men. The Protective Agency for Women and Children carried out this work on a regular basis in Chicago courts. According to the *Union Signal*, the official publication of the National WCTU, members of the agency "have repeatedly gone to the police court, and stood by the girl through all the trying ordeal. Their presence changes the moral tone of the police court, and imparts courage to the timid girl whose very innocence confuses her in the presence of strange, sneering men."[34]

Although important, this type of moral support in the courtroom was limited in what it could accomplish. Organized clubwomen came to believe that they needed to have real power within the political and legal systems to influence the prosecution of sex offenses. Political enfranchisement would enable them to shape legislation and to elect judges and prosecutors who were sympathetic with their goals. Concern about sex crimes helped to fuel the burgeoning suffrage movement of the late nineteenth and early twentieth centuries, and it was a key issue for California suffragists. After they won the vote in 1911, one of their first legislative goals was to raise the age of consent from sixteen to eighteen.[35]

Once that goal was achieved, clubwomen and reformers used their newly acquired political voice to recall a San Francisco police court judge because of his lenient treatment of male sex offenders. The recall effort began in 1913, when Judge Charles Weller lowered the bail of a defendant charged with the rape of a young woman. The accused man made bail; shortly thereafter he left the city and was never located by law enforcement officials. Angered by the judge's action, clubwomen investigated his record and found that Weller consistently set low bail for rape suspects and dismissed cases in face of what they considered incriminating evidence. They formed the Weller Recall League and circulated petitions to have the recall placed on the ballot for the next election. The struggle to oust Weller became a cause célèbre for clubwomen throughout the state.[36] The California Federation of Women's Clubs threw its support behind the campaign and printed the following statement from the Recall League in its journal, the *Woman's Bulletin*: "We are working steadily and faithfully that this condition of injustice and immorality we have inherited from the fathers in our city, who have allowed this system of vice to grow, may be uprooted by the mothers of our city and be supplanted by courts of justice which do not belie their names and where a girl's virtue may be considered the foundation of good citizenship."[37] Recall proponents gathered enough support to defeat Weller and to elect another judge, Wiley Crist, who pledged to use his office to protect womanhood.

After the success of the recall campaign, women reformers in California broadened their quest for authority in the courtroom by demanding the right to sit on juries. The California Civic League (earlier the California Equal Suffrage Association) organized its members to lobby for a state law that would extend jury service to include women. The absence of women on juries, they argued, prevented fair rulings, particularly in the prosecution of sexual offenses. As one female activist explained, "Women witnesses, often young, often wronged, often ignorant, need the protection of their own sex in the hour of trial as well as of temptation."[38] Their efforts finally paid off in 1917 with the passage of the Woman Jury Bill, which made California one of the first states to legalize women jurors. The actual implementation of this bill, however, comprised an ongoing struggle between women reformers and a reluctant criminal justice system.[39]

The reformers' concerns about sexual offenses evoked greater sympathy from male justices on the juvenile court. The juvenile court was a product of the late-nineteenth- and early twentieth-century movement to reform the criminal justice system. Established in California in 1903, the juvenile court removed youths from the adult criminal justice system and handled them in special courts designed to address their particular problems. The first judges on the Los Angeles Juvenile Court had played an important role in the foundation of this system, and they shared many of the goals and ideals of women reformers. Curtis D. Wilbur, who served on the court from 1903 to 1913, helped to draft the Juvenile Court Law of California. He and Judge Sidney Reeve, who served on the court from 1915 to 1921, worked closely with women activists in Los Angeles to enact and enforce penal reform measures.[40]

Under Judges Wilbur and Reeve, the prosecution of statutory rape proceeded very differently than in the adult criminal court of Alameda County. In court hearings Wilbur and Reeve spoke out against the double standard of morality and chastised young male moral offenders for their wrongdoing. Judge Reeve sounded remarkably similar to women moral reformers when he scolded one young man for having sexual relations with a teenage girl: "There is not a meaner beast on earth than a fellow who will start a girl or try to induce a girl who has been a good girl before on a career of that kind. He is the meanest kind of cuss, just a low down cuss, just a little beast; and that is what you have been."[41] When another teenage boy charged with statutory rape appeared before him, Judge Reeve lectured about the dangers that illicit activity posed for future generations: "The life that you lead from the time you start in past the period of adolescence up to the time you die, is reflected in future generations two-fold. I want to tell you that. And just through parties such as were pulled off here, through associations such as are pulled off here, conditions develop where we have the defective and we have the blind—they are with us all the time and you can put them all right down to just carelessness."[42]

During these juvenile court hearings judges tried to impress upon young men the importance of the single standard of morality, to instruct them that men as well as women had a responsibility to remain chaste. When one sixteen-year-old boy tried to excuse his behavior by claiming his female partner was "of easy morals," Judge Reeve scolded him: "Now, there are no two standards in this world; there is only one. It doesn't make any difference if this girl had sexual intercourse with 20 men, it wouldn't lessen your offense under the law. But the part I hate to see is that when these boys get in trouble, they say, 'Well, I was not as much to blame as the girl.' " Reeve went on to remark, "You might be in the eyes of some boys a hero, but you are not. . . . Supposing some fellow went along and did what you did to this girl, to your sister."[43] To emphasize the seriousness of the offense, judges often made male youths read aloud the law on statutory rape, particularly the section stating that a man found guilty of this crime faced up to fifty years in prison. (In California, the penalty for both forcible rape and intercourse with girls under sixteen was a maximum of fifty years; the punishment for intercourse with girls between sixteen and eighteen was either confinement in the county jail for not more than one year or in the state prison for not more than fifty years.)[44]

In their pursuit of male sex offenders, the juvenile courts met with resistance from police departments and from the adult criminal justice system. Judge Reeve became particularly disturbed in one instance when the police and the district attorney failed to follow up a complaint that had been filed against a nineteen-year-old sailor. According to the report filed by a probation officer for the juvenile court, the sailor had engaged in sexual relations with one teenage girl in Los Angeles and was responsible for the pregnancy of another young woman he had dated earlier. Judge Reeve criticized the leniency shown to male offenders by the police: "Now the great difficulty is that it seems the double standard is very prominently fixed in the eyes of the Police Department and they want the girl filed on and put away and they want to let the boys be turned loose. I don't believe in it and never have believed in it. I don't believe there is any boy that has ever been tied up and forced to commit an act of this kind."[45] In an effort to correct police bias and to send a message to other young men, Reeve sentenced the sailor to one year in a reform school.

Most young men prosecuted for statutory rape in the Los Angeles Juvenile Court, however, did not face institutional confinement, because juvenile offenders were not subject to the same criminal penalties as their adult counterparts. Judges for the juvenile court were expected to devise a sentence appropriate to each individual case, based on the youth's character, attitude, and family background, as well as the particular offense he committed. Juvenile officials tried to avoid the incarceration of young criminal offenders whenever possible. The favored form of correctional treatment was probation, which aimed to rehabilitate delinquent youth in their own homes under the supervision of a probation officer.[46] The court's handling of statutory rape cases generally followed a predictable pattern. After administering a severe scolding in the court hearing, judges typically released the young men from detention and placed them on probation. Of the twenty-three defendants charged with statutory rape before the Los Angeles court in 1920, more than four-fifths (82 percent) were placed on probation and less than one-tenth (9 percent) were sent to reform institutions. The remaining cases were either dismissed or sent to adult criminal court.

Those convicted in adult criminal court were more likely to be incarcerated than were juvenile offenders, but they, too, had a decent chance of receiving probation. Adult probation, introduced in California in 1903, offered an alternative to imprisonment in felony cases. It became common for defendants to plead guilty in the hopes of receiving a lighter sentence, preferably probation.[47] Forty-eight percent of the defendants charged with statutory rape in the Alameda County Superior Court between 1910 and 1920 pleaded guilty. Another 13 percent were acquitted by a jury, 16 percent were convicted, and 15 percent of the cases were dismissed before going to trial (see Table 4 [see original reading]).[48] The high number of guilty pleas indicates the growing use of plea bargains in which the defendant made a deal with the prosecution, promising to plead guilty in return for a lesser charge or a reduced sentence. Many defendants entered a guilty plea immediately; others first pleaded not guilty and later changed their plea to guilty, a sign of probable bargaining between the defense and prosecution.[49] Defendant's hopes of receiving probation were often fulfilled. Approximately half (49 percent) of those found guilty of statutory rape in the Alameda County Superior Court were granted probation (see Table 5 [see original reading]).[50]

Various factors—including the defendant's age, the nature of the sexual encounter (whether or not force was used), the moral character of the female witness, and the defendant's race and ethnicity—determined whether convicted men would receive probation or incarceration. In particular, judges were far less likely to send younger men to prison or jail. Sixty-four percent of convicted defendants age thirty or younger were placed on probation, while just over a third (36 percent) were incarcerated in prison, jail, or reform school,[51] In contrast, approximately one-fifth (22 percent) of the convicted defendants over age thirty received probation, while nearly four-fifths (78 percent) were incarcerated.[52] Courts tended to be lenient with young offenders because, as one official explained, "With a youth up to the early twenties a slip of this kind can be condoned."[53] The age of a twenty-one-year-old defendant clearly influenced Judge William Donahue's decision to grant him probation. As Donahue explained, "In your case you are young. I can understand why a man of the age of twenty-one only, and the girl was about seventeen, how that could occur, and there might be extenuating circumstances. If you were an older man I would not place you upon probation. I would send you to prison. But seeing you are a young man I am going to give you probation."[54]

Superior court judges were also less likely to order incarceration in cases in which the female partner had consented to intercourse. Sixty-six percent of those convicted of statutory rape in consent cases were granted probation, and 32 percent were sent to prison or jail.[55] But only 17 percent of those found guilty in cases involving forcible rape were placed on probation, while 73 percent were incarcerated in prison or jail (see Table 5 [see original reading]).[56]

Even in cases of forcible assault, judges typically showed more concern for the loss of female chastity than for the physical and emotional harm done to young women and girls. Male perpetrators received harsh sentences not so much because they had raped a young girl, sometimes with violence, but because they had destroyed her moral purity. After sentencing one man to prison for raping an eight-year-old girl, the judge lamented that she was now "marred and marked . . . with the stigma that will attach to her in the future."[57] In another case, a fifteen-year-old girl was raped by her male employer in the home where she worked as a domestic. The judge sentenced the man to prison, but he expressed little interest in the harm done to the girl, instead stressing the importance of female chastity for the creation of a racially and morally pure social order. "[O]ur children, our girls," he stated to the defendant, "should be kept clean from contamination so they can become mothers of a better race. It devolves upon the court to sentence you, and after you have gained your liberty I hope that you may come out a better man."[58]

When determining sentences, court officials also took into account what they judged to be the moral character of the female witness. Young women were deemed immoral on a variety of grounds: if they had consented to sex; if they had previous sexual experience; if they engaged in what was considered inappropriate behavior for respectable women, such as walking the streets at night, going out alone with men, drinking liquor in cafés, or living away from home. Judges frequently granted lenient sentences to defendants in cases involving young women of suspect character. Judge J. D. Murphey based his decision to award probation to one defendant on the supposed immorality of the fourteen-year-old female witness. The defendant had met the teenager and her girlfriend at a dance and invited them to stay in his hotel room for the night. After studying the case, Judge Murphey ordered the man released from custody and placed on probation: "The record appears to me to sustain the proposition very fairly that these girls themselves were not good at all. They were wayward girls and disposed to do anything probably, and while, understand, it is not any excuse from a legal point of view, [Anderson], it may in a way assist the Court upon the recommendation of all your friends to see its way clear to grant you this requested probation."[59]

The dubious character of the fifteen-year-old female witness in another case led Judge James G. Quinn to grant probation to a fifty-seven-year-old man. Quinn stated in court that "this is the first case of a serious nature such as this, with a man of this age, where probation has even been considered." The older man deserved leniency, he explained, because the teenage girl "has the appearance of being a much older woman," and "her habits and morality are not alone questioned, but are absolutely proved to be bad."[60]

Other factors that influenced sentencing decisions in the Alameda County Superior Court were the ethnicity and race of the defendant. It is impossible to provide firm statistical evidence of the relation between sentence and ethnic background because court records do not consistently indicate the ethnicity or birthplace of male defendants. The court transcripts do, however, suggest that judges took this factor into account. Louis Albertoli, a twenty-four-year-old Italian immigrant, faced deportation and a five-year prison sentence for having sex with a fourteen-year-old girl who lived in his neighborhood. In handing down his decision to incarcerate the young man, Judge Ogden explained that American society could not afford to tolerate the supposedly degraded customs of certain immigrant groups:

> I do not feel that we ought to have people come to this country unless they are able and willing to abide by our laws. I realize that in some foreign countries the same code of morals is not present that is present in this country. . . . It is a fact that in some of the countries today a man can forcibly take his woman that he looks to and wants to have for his own and these consider it a marriage, but of course, we do not call those countries civilized, but as I said before if we permit these customs to prevail upon this soil instead of having the higher code of ethics, we would descend to the code of ethics and morals of the other communities.[61]

A stronger case can be made for the role of race in shaping sentencing decisions. Both statistical data and court transcripts indicate that African American men were more likely to be incarcerated for engaging in sex with female minors than were white defendants. All five of the African Americans prosecuted for statutory rape in Alameda County during these years received the court's harshest punishment—incarceration in the state prison. In one of these cases, a young black man, Raymond Thompson, was arrested when he was found living with Lucy Somers, a black teenager of fifteen years. Lucy had left her aunt's home and decided to move in with Raymond. The couple had known each other for several months and hoped to marry soon, despite the aunt's objections. Like most defendants in similar cases, Raymond pleaded guilty in the hope of receiving lenient treatment. At the sentencing hearing, his attorney urged the judge to grant Raymond probation. He explained that the couple wanted to marry and that Raymond was currently employed in a good job as a barber and was capable of supporting a wife. But in contrast to other cases of this nature, the prosecutor pressed hard for a prison sentence. He pointed out that Raymond had been married before and was therefore unreliable as a husband.

The prosecutor also made an issue of Raymond's race in presenting his case for incarceration. A stiff sentence, he argued, would serve to warn the black community to reform their supposedly lax and immoral habits. "It is about time that we should educate these colored people and tell them that they have to obey the laws," the prosecutor explained to the judge. The defense was quick to point out that white defendants typically received probation even in violent cases: "For the last two years, I can show fifteen cases where the circumstances and facts have been of the most aggravated character in rape cases where white people have had probation, but the trouble is that Mr. Smith [prosecutor] is biased against the probation proposition." The defense attorney also made use of racial stereotypes in presenting his case to the judge. He argued that the court should not expect blacks to maintain the same moral standards as whites. In the end, the prosecutor's arguments proved more persuasive, and the judge sentenced Raymond to ten years in San Quentin.[62]

The court clearly had different standards for black or foreign-born and for native-born white defendants. Judge Ogden, who sent Louis Albertoli to prison, granted probation to a twenty-three-year-old white man in a similar case because he believed the man was the true "victim." It would require a very strong man, he had explained, to escape from the trap set by the sixteen-year-old female witness.[63] When a white man had sex with an underage female, he was seen as the victim of her loose and immoral ways. When an immigrant or African American man did the same, he was labeled a product of an uncivilized and depraved racial group.

As all these cases show, the actual enforcement of age-of-consent legislation in California had consequences that moral reformers had not intended and could not control. Most male police and court officials in the criminal justice system showed little concern for, if not outright hostility to, the reformers' goals of ending the double standard and male sexual privilege. In their hands, enforcement of the law became a punitive process for the young women and girls it was meant to protect, as they faced possible confinement in detention centers and reformatories and had to endure grueling interrogations by male judges and attorneys who frequently labeled them promiscuous and immoral. Furthermore, officials used the law to reinforce racial bias within the legal system by targeting African American and immigrant men for the harshest forms of punishment.

Notes

1   Alameda County Superior Court, Oakland, Calif., Case No. 6042 (1915). Cases are hereafter referred to as Alameda Case No. 6042 (1915). In all chapters that draw on original case files, I have changed the names of the young women, male partners, family members, and others involved in the cases but have attempted to retain their ethnic distinctions.
2   For an excellent discussion of the operation of the criminal justice system in Alameda County in the late nineteenth and early twentieth centuries, see Friedman and Percival, *Roots of Justice*.
3   For these cases, N = 112. See Appendix for further information on the calculations in this chapter.
4   Alameda Case No. 5530 (1913).
5   Alameda Case No. 5670 (1914); Case No. 5676 (1914); Case No. 5705 (1914); Case No. 5706 (1914).
6   Alameda Case No. 5540 (1913).
7   Alameda Case No. 5624 (1913).
8   Alameda Case No. 6672 (1917). For another example of resistance by female witnesses, see Alameda Case No. 5663 (1914).
9   Alameda Case No. 6332 (1916).
10 Alameda Case No. 5773 (1914). For other cases in which questions about the witnesses' consent were permitted, see Alameda Case No. 5515 (1913); Case No. 5731 (1914); Case No. 5734 (1914); Case No. 5844 (1914); Case No. 6859 (1918); Case No. 6332 (1916); Case No. 6346 (1916).
11 Alameda Case No. 6734 (1917); Case No. 5501 (1913); Case No. 5707 (1914).
12 Alameda Case No. 5821 (1914). On the harassment of women and girls in rape and seduction trials in Ontario in the late nineteenth and early twentieth centuries, see Dubinsky, *Improper Advances*, pp. 22–31, 77–79.
13 Alameda Case No. 7231 (1919).
14 Alameda Case No. 5657 (1914).
15 For feminist analyses of acquaintance rape, see Estrich, *Real Rape*; Warshaw, *I Never Called It Rape*; Parrot and Bechhofer, eds., *Acquaintance Rape*.
16 Alameda Case No. 5657 (1914).
17 Alameda Case No. 5844 (1914).
18 Alameda Case No. 6859 (1918). On the treatment in rape trials of the issue of women's resistance to sexual assault, see Friedman, *Crime and Punishment*, pp. 216–17; Estrich, *Real Rape*, pp. 29–41.
19 Nemeth, "Character Evidence in Rape Trials"; Estrich, *Real Rape*, pp. 47–53; Wigmore, *Student's Textbook*, pp. 59–64, 88–91; Wigmore, *Treatise on the System of Evidence*, 1:125–32.
20 *Lee v. State*, 132 Tenn. 658 (1915).
21 Wigmore, *Student's Textbook*, p. 63; see also Wigmore, *Treatise on the System of Evidence*, 1:130.
22 Wigmore, *Student's Textbook*, pp. 63–64; Wigmore, *Treatise on the System of Evidence*, 1:131–32.
23 Alameda Case No. 5657 (1914).
24 Alameda Case No. 6346 (1916).
25 Alameda Case No. 5706 (1914). For other cases in which questions about prior sexual acts were permitted, see Alameda Case No. 4979 (1911); Case No. 5676 (1914); Case No. 5732 (1914); Case No. 5695 (1914); Case No. 6428 (1916); Case No. 6631 (1917).
26 Alameda Case No. 5920 (1914).
27 Alameda Case No. 6546 (1917).
28 Alameda Case No. 4979 (1911). For a discussion of the differential treatment of "chaste" and "unchaste" females in rape trials, see Friedman, *Crime and Punishment*, p. 217; Estrich, *Real Rape*, p. 49.

29   Alameda Case No. 6084 (1915).

30   Alameda Case No. 5562 (1913).

31   Spencer, *History of the Woman's Christian Temperance Union*, pp. 67–68

32   "The Amended Penal Code—First Successful Case of Prosecution," *Philanthropist*, February 1888, p. 4; Anna Rice Powell to Elizabeth Gay, March 21, 1898, Sidney Howard Gay Collection, CU; "For the Better Legal Protection of Young Girls," *Philanthropist*, March 1891; "The Protective Agency for Women and Children of Chicago," *Union Signal*, October 6, 1887, p. 8; Protective Agency for Women and Children, *Annual Reports*, 1887–91. On the Protective Agency for Women and Children in Chicago, see Pleck, "Feminist Responses," pp. 465–69; Pleck, *Domestic Tyranny*, pp. 95–98.

33   *Berkeley Reporter*, March 21, 1906, p. 1.

34   "Protective Agency for Women and Children of Chicago."

35   *Woman's Bulletin*, June 1912, p. 15; ibid., February 1914, pp. 21–22; Gibson, *Record of Twenty-five Years*, pp. 181–83.

36   On the recall campaign, see "The Recall League of San Francisco," *Woman's Bulletin*, April 1913, p. 13; Weiss, "Feminine Point of View."

37   "Recall League of San Francisco," p. 13.

38   Quoted in Weiss, "Feminine Point of View," p. 18. On the movement to put women on juries in the United States, see Friedman, *Crime and Punishment*, pp. 419–21.

39   Weiss, "Feminine Point of View," pp. 17–23.

40   On Curtis D. Wilbur, see Bates, ed., *History of the Bench and Bar*, p. 556; Curtis D. Wilbur File, California State Library, Sacramento, Calif. On Sidney Reeve, see McGroarty, *Los Angeles*, 2: 113–14. On the Progressive Era juvenile court movement, see Rothman, *Conscience and Convenience*, chaps. 6–8; Schlossman, *Love and the American Delinquent*, chap. 4.

41   Los Angeles Case No. 17619 (1920).

42   Los Angeles Case No. 17299 (1920).

43   Los Angeles Case No. 16196 (1920).

44   Kerr, *Consolidated Supplement*, sec. 264, p. 2066.

45   Los Angeles Case No. 15969 (1920).

46   Rothman, *Conscience and Convenience*, pp. 218–19; Schlossman, *Love and the American Delinquent*, pp. 60–66.

47   Friedman and Percival, *Roots of Justice*, pp. 224–28; Friedman, *Crime and Punishment*, pp. 406–9.

48   For these cases, N = 112.

49   Friedman and Percival, *Roots of Justice*, pp. 179–81; Friedman, *History of American Law*, p. 576.

50   For these cases, N = 75.

51   For these cases, N = 50.

52   For these cases, N = 23.

53   Alameda Case No. 5688 (1914).

54   Alameda Case No. 5563 (1913).

55   For these cases, N = 50.

56   For these cases, N = 23.

57   Alameda Case No. 5620 (1913).

58   Alameda Case No. 5688 (1914).

59   Alameda Case No. 5501 (1913).

60   Alameda Case No. 6929 (1918). For other cases in which judges discussed the "immoral" character of the female witness as an important factor in granting probation, see Alameda Case No. 5707 (1914); Case No. 5540 (1913); Case No. 5732 (1914); Case No. 5799 (1914); Case No. 6042 (1915); Case No. 6084 (1915); Case No. 6929 (1918); Case No. 7231 (1919); Case No. 7550 (1920).

61   Alameda Case No. 6008 (1935).

62   Alameda Case No. 6672 (1917).

63   Alameda Case No. 5821 (1914).

Chapter 29

Neil Postman

THE DISAPPEARING CHILD

To THIS POINT, MY EFFORTS HAVE BEEN directed at describing how the symbolic arena in which a society conducts itself will either make childhood necessary or irrelevant. I have, in particular, tried to explain how our new and revolutionary media are causing the expulsion of childhood after its long sojourn in Western civilization. It remains for me to put forward some of the direct evidence that this expulsion is indeed well under way.

The evidence for the disappearance of childhood comes in several varieties and from different sources. There is, for example, the evidence displayed by the media themselves, for they not only promote the unseating of childhood through their form and context but reflect its decline in their content. There is evidence to be seen in the merging of the taste and style of children and adults, as well as in the changing perspectives of relevant social institutions such as the law, the schools, and sports. And there is evidence of the "hard" variety—figures about alcoholism, drug use, sexual activity, crime, etc., that imply a fading distinction between childhood and adulthood. However, before presenting or pointing to any of it, I am obliged to acknowledge that the conjecture advanced in this book as to *why* this is happening cannot be proved, no matter how much evidence is marshaled in its favor. This is so not only because conjectures or theories can never be proved, even in the physical sciences, but also because in any effort at social science the very idea of proof or refutation is so encrusted with ambiguities and complexities that one can never be sure if the evidence has left a conjecture standing or has laid it low or is just plain irrelevant.

To illustrate: It has been claimed that the onset of puberty in females has been falling by about four months per decade for the past one hundred and thirty years, so that, for example, in 1900 the average age at which menstruation first occurred was approximately fourteen years, whereas in 1979 the average age was twelve years.[1] I rather fancy this statistic because, if true, it suggests that the contraction of childhood began to occur even in physiological terms shortly after the invention of the telegraph; that is, there is an almost perfect coincidence of the falling age of puberty and the communications revolution. I should therefore love to offer this as evidence in favor of my argument, but I rather think there are better explanations available, particularly those having to do with changes in diet.

To take another example: It is a certainty that the American household is shrinking. Today, there are only 2.8 persons per household, as compared to 4.1 in 1930. Or to look at it from another direction, in 1950, 10.9 percent of American households had only one person in them. Today, the figure is 22 percent.[2] Americans are not only having fewer children but apparently are spending less time nurturing them at home. Is this an effect of our changing communication environment? I believe it is, but one would be foolish to deny the contribution of other factors such as the increased affluence of Americans, their incredible mobility, the women's liberation movement, etc. In other words, as in this example, not only may there be multiple causation but, as in the first example, there well may be other theories to explain the facts. After all, in trying to account for changes in social organization or, indeed, for any cultural tendencies, there are many points from which one may embark. Marxists and Freudians, for example, would have ready explanations as to why childhood is disappearing, assuming that they agreed the evidence shows it is. Sociobiologists, anthropologists and—who knows?—perhaps even Scientific Creationists will not find themselves dry on the issue either. I have chosen the explanation offered in this book [see original reading] because insofar as any single perspective can be said to be tenable, this one best explains the facts. Indeed, nothing seems more obvious to me than that childhood is a function of what a culture needs to communicate and the means it has to do so. Although economics, politics, ideology, religion, and other factors affect the course of childhood—make it more or less important—they cannot create it or expunge it. Only literacy by its presence or absence has that power. I shall not, however, reargue this idea here. I wish only to say that I believe the idea is plausible, that it has at least a modest recommendation from the facts of history, and that it is supportable by present trends. The purpose of this chapter is to show that childhood *is* disappearing. After considering the evidence, the reader, inevitably, will decide if my theory is useful.

I should like to start, then, by calling attention to the fact that children have virtually disappeared from the media, especially from television. (There is absolutely no sign of them on radio or records, but their disappearance from television is more revealing.) I do not mean, of course, that people who are young in years cannot be seen. I mean that when they are shown, they are depicted as miniature adults in the manner of thirteenth- and fourteenth-century paintings. We might call this condition the Gary Coleman Phenomenon, by which I mean that an attentive viewer of situation comedies, soap operas, or any other popular TV format will notice that the children on such shows do not differ significantly in their interests, language, dress, or sexuality from the adults on the same shows.

Having said this, I must concede that the popular arts have rarely depicted children in an authentic manner. We have only to think of some of the great child stars of films, such as Shirley Temple, Jackie Coogan, Jackie Cooper, Margaret O'Brien, and the harmless ruffians of the Our Gang comedies, to realize that cinema representations of the character and sensibility of the young have been far from realistic. But one could find in them, nonetheless, an ideal, a *conception* of childhood. These children dressed differently from adults, talked differently, saw problems from a different perspective, had a different status, were more vulnerable. Even in the early days of television, on such programs as *Leave It to Beaver* and *Father Knows Best*, one could find children who were, if not realistically portrayed, at least different from adults. But most of this is now gone, or at least rapidly going.

Perhaps the best way to grasp what has happened here is to imagine what *The Shirley Temple Show* would be like were it a television series today, assuming of course that Miss Temple were the same age now as she was when she made her memorable films. (She began her career at age four but made most of her successful films between the ages of six and ten.) Is it imaginable except as parody that Shirley Temple would sing—let us say, as a theme song—"On the Good Ship Lollipop"? If she would sing at all, her milieu would be rock music, that is, music as much associated with adult sensibility as with that of youth. (See Studio 54 and other adult discos.) On today's network television there simply is no such thing as a child's song. It is a dead species, which tells as much about what I am discussing here as anything I can think of. In any case, a ten-year-old Shirley Temple would probably require a boyfriend with whom she would be more than occasionally entangled in a simulated lover's quarrel. She would certainly have to abandon "little girl's" dresses and hairstyles for something approximating adult fashion. Her language would consist of a string of knowing wisecracks, including a liberal display of sexual innuendo. In short, *The Shirley Temple Show* would not—could not—be about a child, adorable or otherwise. Too many in the audience would find such a conception either fanciful or unrecognizable, especially the youthful audience.

Of course, the disappearance from television of our traditional model of childhood is to be observed most vividly in commercials. I have already spoken of the wide use of eleven- and twelve-year-old girls as erotic objects (the Brooke Shields Phenomenon), but it is necessary to mention one extraordinary commercial for Jordache jeans in which both schoolgirls and schoolboys—most of them prepubescent—are represented as being driven silly by their undisciplined libidos, which are further inflamed by the wearing of designer jeans. The commercial concludes by showing that their teacher wears the same jeans. What can this mean other than that no distinction need be made between children and adults in either their sexuality or the means by which it is stimulated?

But beyond this, and just as significant, is the fact that children, with or without hyperactive libidos, are commonly and unashamedly used as actors in commercial dramas. In one evening's viewing I counted nine different products for which a child served as a pitchman. These included sausages, real estate, toothpaste, insurance, a detergent, and a restaurant chain. American television viewers apparently do not think it either unusual or disagreeable that children should instruct them in the glories of corporate America, perhaps because as children are admitted to more and more aspects of adult life, it would seem arbitrary to exclude them from one of the most important: selling. In any case, we have here a new meaning to the prophecy that a child shall lead them.

The "adultification" of children on television is closely paralleled in films. Such movies as different as *Carrie, The Exorcist, Pretty Baby, Paper Moon, The Omen, The Blue Lagoon, Little Darlings, Endless Love*, and *A Little Romance* have in common a conception of the child who is in social orientation, language, and interests no different from adults. A particularly illuminating way in which to see the shift in child film imagery that has taken place in recent years is to compare the Little Rascals movies of the 1930s with the 1976 film *Bugsy Malone*, a satire in which children play the roles of adult characters from gangster movies. Most of the humor in the Little Rascals films derived its point from the sheer incongruity of children emulating adult behavior. Although *Bugsy Malone* uses children as a metaphor for adults, there is very little sense of incongruity in their role playing. After all, what is absurd about a twelve-year-old using "adult" language, dressing in adult clothes, showing an adult interest in sex, singing adult songs? The point is that the Little Rascals' films were clearly comedy. *Bugsy Malone* comes close to documentary.

Most of the widely discussed changes in children's literature have been in the same direction as those of the modern media. The work of Judy Blume has been emulated by many other writers who, like Ms. Blume, have grasped the idea that "adolescent literature" is best received when it simulates in theme and language adult literature, and, in particular, when its characters are presented as miniature adults. Of course, I do not wish to give the impression that there are currently no examples in children's literature (or, for that matter, in television or movies) of children who are emphatically different from adults. But I do mean to suggest that we are now undergoing a very rapid reorientation in our popular arts in regard to the image of children. One might put the matter, somewhat crudely, in this way: Our culture is not big enough for both Judy Blume and Walt Disney. One of them will have to go, and as the Disney empire's falling receipts show, it is the Disney conception of what a child is and needs that is disappearing.[3] We are in the process of exorcising a two-hundred-year-old image of the young as child and replacing it with the imagery of the young as adult.

Although this is exactly what Ms. Blume, our modern filmmakers, and TV writers are doing, no moral or social demerit may be charged against them. Whatever else one may say in criticism of our popular arts, they cannot be accused of indifference to social reality. The shuffling black, the acquisitive Jew, even (to some extent) the obedient and passive wife, have disappeared from view, not because they are insufficiently interesting as material but because they are unacceptable to audiences. In a similar way, Shirley Temple is replaced by Brooke Shields because the audience requires a certain correspondence between the imagery of its popular arts and social reality as it is experienced. The question of the extent to which, say, television reflects social reality is a complex one, for there are times when it lags slightly behind, times when it anticipates changes, times when it is precisely on target. But it can never afford to be off the mark by too great a margin or it ceases to be a popular art. This is the sense in which we might say that television is our most democratic institution. Programs display what people understand and want or they are canceled. Most people no longer understand and want the traditional, idealized model of the child because that model cannot be supported by their experience or imagination.

The same is true of the traditional model of an adult. If one looks closely at the content of TV, one can find a fairly precise documentation not only of the rise of the "adultified" child but also of the rise of the "childified" adult. Television is as clear about this as almost anything else (although, without question, the best representation of the childlike adult is in the film *Being There*, which is, in fact, about the process I am describing). Laverne, Shirley, Archie, the crew of the Love Boat, the company of Three, Fonzie, Barney Miller's detectives, Rockford, Kojak, and the entire population of Fantasy Island can hardly be said to be adult characters, even after one has made allowances for the traditions of the formats in which they appear. With a few exceptions, adults on television do not take their work seriously (if they work at all), they do not nurture children, they have no politics, practice no religion, represent no tradition, have no foresight or serious plans, have no extended conversations, and in no circumstances allude to anything that is not familiar to an eight-year-old person.

Although students of mine who are dedicated TV watchers have urged me to modify the following statement, I can find only one fictional character regularly seen on commercial television, Felix Unger of *The Odd Couple*, who is depicted as having an adult's appetite for serious music and whose language suggests that he has, at one time in his life, actually read a book. Indeed, it is quite noticeable that the majority of adults on TV shows are depicted as functionally illiterate, not only in the sense that the content of book learning is absent from what they appear to know but also because of the absence of even the faintest signs of a contemplative habit of mind. (*The Odd Couple*, now seen only in reruns, ironically offers in Felix Unger not only an example of a literate person but a striking anomaly in his partner, Oscar Madison—a professional writer who is illiterate.)

A great deal has been written about the inanity of popular TV programs. But I am not here discussing that judgment. My point is that the model of an adult that is most often used on TV is that of the child, and that this pattern can be seen on almost every type of program. On game shows, for example, contestants are selected with great care to ensure that their tolerance for humiliation (by a simulated adult, the "emcee") is inexhaustible, their emotions instantly arousable, their interest in things a consuming passion. Indeed, a game show is a parody of sorts of a classroom in which childlike contestants are duly rewarded for obedience and precociousness but are otherwise subjected to all the indignities that are traditionally the schoolchild's burden. The absence of adult characters on soap operas, to take another example, is so marked that as of this writing a syndicated "teen-age" version of a soap opera, called *Young Lives*, has been embarked upon as if to document the idea that the world of the young is no different from the world of the adult. Here television is going one step further than the movies: *Young Lives* is *Bugsy Malone* without satire.

All of this is happening not only for reasons suggested in the last three chapters [see original reading] but also because TV tries to reflect prevailing values and styles. And in our current situation the values and styles of the child and those of the adult have tended to merge. One does not have to be a sociologist of the familiar to have noticed all of the following:

The children's clothing industry has undergone vast changes in the past decade, so that what was once unambiguously recognized as "children's" clothing has virtually disappeared. Twelve-year-old boys now wear three-piece suits to birthday parties, and sixty-year-old men wear jeans to birthday parties. Eleven-year-old girls wear high heels, and what was once a clear marker of youthful informality and energy, sneakers, now allegedly signifies the same for adults. The miniskirt, which was the most embarrassing example of adults mimicking a children's style of dress, is for the moment moribund, but in its place one can see on the streets of New York and San Francisco grown women wearing little white socks and imitation Mary Janes. The point is that we are now undergoing a reversal of a trend, begun in the sixteenth century, of identifying children through their manner of dress. As the concept of childhood diminishes, the symbolic markers of childhood diminish with it.

This process can be seen to occur not only in clothing but in eating habits as well. Junk food, once suited only to the undiscriminating palates and iron stomachs of the young, is now common fare for adults. This can be inferred from the commercials for McDonald's and Burger King, which make no age distinctions in their appeals. It can also be directly observed by simply attending to the distribution of children and adults who patronize such places. It would appear that adults consume at least as much junk food as do children.[4] This is no trivial point: it seems that many have forgotten when adults were supposed to have higher standards than children in their conception of what is and is not edible. Indeed, it was a mark of movement toward adulthood when a youngster showed an inclination to reject the kind of fare that gives the junk-food industry its name. I believe we can say rather firmly that this marker of the transition to adulthood is now completely obliterated.

There is no more obvious symptom of the merging of children's and adults' values and styles than what is happening with children's games, which is to say they are disappearing. While I have found no studies that document the decline of unsupervised street games, their absence is noticeable enough and in any case, can be inferred from the astonishing rise of such institutions as Little League baseball and Pee Wee football. Except for the inner city, where games are still under the control of the youths who play them, the games of American youth have become increasingly official, mock-professional, and extremely serious. According to the Little League Baseball Association, whose headquarters are in Williamsport Pennsylvania, Little League baseball is the largest youth sports program in the world. More than fourteen hundred charters have been issued, over two and a half million youngsters participate, from ages six to eighteen. The structure of the organization is modeled on that of major league baseball, the character of the games themselves on the emotional style of big league sports: there is no fooling around, no peculiar rules invented to suit the moment, no protection from the judgments of spectators.

The idea that children's games are not the business of adults has clearly been rejected by Americans, who are insisting that even at age six, children play their games without spontaneity under careful supervision, and at an intense competitive level. That many adults do not grasp the significance of this redefinition of children's play is revealed by a story that appeared in *The New York Times*, July 17, 1981. The occasion was a soccer tournament in Ontario, Canada, involving four thousand children from ten nations. In one game between ten-year-old boys from East Brunswick, New Jersey, and Burlington, Ontario, a brawl took place "after fathers had argued on the sidelines, players had traded charges of rough play and foul language, and one man from Burlington made a vulgar gesture." The brawl was highlighted by a confrontation between the mothers of two players, one of whom kicked the other. Of course, much of this is standard stuff and has been duplicated many times by adults at "official" baseball and football games. (I have myself witnessed several forty-year-old men unmercifully "riding" an eleven-year-old shortstop because he had made two errors in one inning.) But what is of most significance is the remark made by one of the mothers after the brawl. In trying to put the matter in perspective, she was quoted as saying, "It [the brawl] was just 30 seconds out of a beautiful tournament. The next night our boys lost, but it was a beautiful game. Parents were applauding kids from both teams. Over all, it was a beautiful experience." But the point is, What are the parents doing there in the first place? Why are four thousand children involved in a tournament? Why is East Brunswick, New Jersey, playing Burlington, Ontario? What are these children being trained for? The answer to all these questions is that children's play has become an adult preoccupation, it has become professionalized, it is no longer a world separate from the world of adults.

The entry of children into professional and world-class amateur sports is, of course, related to all of this. The 1979 Wimbledon tennis tournament, for example, was marked by the extraordinary performance of Tracy Austin, then not yet sixteen, the youngest player in the history of the tournament. In 1980, a fifteen-year-old player made her appearance. In 1981, a fourteen-year-old. An astonished John Newcombe, an old-time Wimbledon champion, expressed the view that in the near future twelve-year-old players may take the center court. But in this respect tennis lags behind other sports. Twelve-year-old swimmers, skaters, and gymnasts of world-class ability are commonplace. Why is this happening? The most obvious answer is that better coaching and training techniques have made it possible for children to attain adult-level competence. But the questions remain: Why should adults encourage this possibility? Why would anyone wish to deny children the freedom, informality, and joy of spontaneous play? Why submit children to the rigors of professional-style training, concentration, tension, media hype? The answer is the same as before: The traditional assumptions about the uniqueness of children are fast fading. What we have here is the emergence of the idea that play is not to be done for the sake of doing it but for some external purpose, such as renown, money, physical conditioning, upward mobility, national pride. For adults, play is serious business. As childhood disappears, so does the child's view of play.

This same tendency toward the merging of child and adult perspectives can be observed in their tastes in entertainment. To take an obvious example: The 1980 Nielsen Report on Television reveals that adults (defined as people over the age of eighteen) rated the following as among their fifteen most favored syndicated programs: *Family Feud, The Muppet Show, Hee Haw, M*A*S*H, Dance Fever, Happy Days Again*, and *Sha Na Na*. These programs were also listed among the top fifteen most favored by those between the ages of twelve and seventeen. And they also made the favored list of those between the ages of two and eleven! As for (the then) current shows, the male adult group indicated that *Taxi, Mork & Mindy, M*A*S*H, Three's Company, ABC Sunday Night Movie*, and *The Dukes of Hazzard* were among their favorites. The twelve-to-seventeen age group included the same shows.[5] In the 1981 Nielsen Report, adult males favored six syndicated programs (out of ten) that were the same as those favored by the twelve-to-seventeen age group, and four (out of ten) that were the same as the two-to-eleven age group.[6]

Such figures are painful to contemplate but are entirely consistent with the observation that what now amuses the child also amuses the adult. As I write, *Superman II, For Your Eyes Only, Raiders of the Lost Ark*, and *Tarzan, the Ape Man* are attracting customers of all ages in almost unprecedented numbers. Twenty-five years ago, such films, which are essentially animated comic strips, would have been regarded as children's entertainment. Not as charming, innocent, or creative as, say, *Snow White and the Seven Dwarfs* but nonetheless clearly for a youthful audience. Today, no such distinctions need to be made. Neither is it necessary to distinguish between adult and youthful taste in music, as anyone who has visited an adult discotheque can attest. It is still probably true that the ten-year-old-to-seventeen-year-old group is more knowledgeable about the names and styles of rock groups than are those over the age of twenty-five, but as the declining market for both classical and popular "adult" music suggests, adults can no longer claim that their taste in music represents a higher level of sensitivity than teen-age music.[7]

As clothing, food, games, and entertainment move toward a homogeneity of style, so does language. It is extremely difficult to document this change except by repairing to anecdotes or by asking readers to refer to their own experience. We do know, of course, that the capacity of the young to achieve "grade level" competence in reading and writing is declining.[8] And we also know that their ability to reason and to make valid inferences is declining as well.[9] Such evidence is usually offered to document the general decline of literacy in the young. But it may also be brought forward to imply a decline of interest in language among adults; that is to say, after one has discussed the role of the media in producing a lowered state of language competence in the young, there is still room to discuss the indifference of parents, teachers, and other influential adults to the importance of language. We may even be permitted the assumption that adult control over language does not in most cases significantly surpass children's control over language. On television, on radio, in films, in commercial transactions, on the streets, even in the classroom, one does not notice that adults use language with more variety, depth, or precision than do children. In fact, it is a sort of documentation of this that there has emerged a small industry of books and newspaper columns that advise adults on how to talk as adults.

One may even go so far as to speculate that the language of the young is exerting more influence on adults than the other way around. Although the tendency to insert the word *like* after every four words still remains a distinctive adolescent pattern, in many other respects adults have found teen-age language attractive enough to incorporate in their own speech. I have recorded many instances of people over the age of thirty-five, and from every social class, uttering, without irony, such phrases as "I am into jogging," "Where are you coming from?" (to mean "What is your point of view?"), "Get off my case," and other teen-age locutions. I must leave it to readers to decide if this tendency is confirmed by their own experience. However, of one thing, I believe, we may be sure: Those adult language secrets to which we give the name "dirty words" are now not only fully known to the young (which may always have been the case) but are used by them as freely as they are by adults. Not only on the soccer field in Ontario but in all public places—ball parks, movie theaters, school yards, classrooms, department stores, restaurants—one can hear such words used comfortably and profusely even by children as young as six years old. This fact is significant because it is an example of the erosion of a traditional distinction between children and adults. It is also significant because it represents a loss in the concept of manners. Indeed, as language, clothing, taste, eating habits, etc., become increasingly homogenized, there is a corresponding decline in both the practice and meaning of civilité, which is rooted in the idea of social hierarchy.[10] In our present situation, adulthood has lost much of its authority and aura, and the idea of deference to one who is older has become ridiculous. That such a decline is in process can be inferred from the general disregard for rules and rituals of public assembly: the increase in what are called "discipline problems" in school, the necessity of expanded security at public events, the intrusion of the loudest possible radio music on public space, the rarity of conventional expressions of courtesy such as "thank you" and "please."

All of the foregoing observations and inferences are, I believe, indicators of both the decline of childhood and a corresponding diminution in the character of adulthood. But there is also available a set of hard facts pointing to the same conclusion. For example, in the year 1950, in all of America, only 170 persons under the age of fifteen were arrested for what the FBI calls serious crimes, i.e., murder, forcible rape, robbery, and aggravated assault. This number represented .0004 percent of the under-fifteen population of America. In that same year, 94,784 persons fifteen years and older were arrested for serious crimes, representing .0860 percent of the population fifteen years and older. This means that in 1950, adults (defined here as those over and including fifteen years of age) committed serious crimes at a rate 215 times that of the rate of child crime. By 1960, adults committed serious crimes at a rate 8 times that of child crime; by 1979, the rate was 5.5 times. Does this mean that adult crime is declining? Not quite. In fact, adult crime is increasing, so that in 1979 more than 400,000 adults were arrested for serious crimes, representing .2430 percent of the adult population. This means that between 1950 and 1979, the rate of adult crime increased three-fold. The fast-closing difference between the rates of adult and child crime is almost wholly accounted for by a staggering rise in child crime. Between 1950 and 1979, the rate of serious crimes committed by children increased 11,000 percent! The rate of nonserious child crimes (i.e., burglary, larceny, and auto theft) increased 8,300 percent.[11]

If America can be said to be drowning in a tidal wave of crime, then the wave has mostly been generated by our children. Crime, like most everything else, is no longer an exclusively adult activity, and readers do not need statistics to confirm this. Almost daily the press tells of arrests being made of children who, like those playing tennis at Wimbledon, are getting younger and younger. In New York City a nine-year-old boy tried to hold up a bank. In July 1981, police in Westchester County, New York, charged four boys with sexual assault of a seven-year-old girl. The alleged rapists were a thirteen-year-old, two eleven-year-olds, and a nine-year-old, the latter being the youngest person ever to be accused of first-degree rape in Westchester County.[12]

Ten- to thirteen-year-olds are involved in adult crime as never before. Indeed, the frequency of serious child crime has pushed youth crime codes to their limits. The first American juvenile court was established in 1899 in Illinois. The idea could come to its end before the century is out as legislators throughout the country hurriedly try to revise criminal laws so that youthful offenders can be treated as adults. In California a study group formed by the attorney general has recommended sending juveniles convicted of first-degree murder to prison rather than to the California Youth Authority. It has also recommended that violent offenders sixteen years old and younger be tried as adults, within the court's discretion.[13] In Vermont the arrest of two teen-agers in connection with the rape, torture, and killing of a twelve-year-old girl has driven the state legislature to propose hardening the juvenile codes.[14] In New York, children between the ages of thirteen and fifteen who are charged with serious crimes can now be tried in adult courts and, if convicted, can receive long prison terms. In Florida, Louisiana, New Jersey, South Carolina, and Tennessee, laws have been changed to make it easier to transfer children between the ages of thirteen and fifteen to adult criminal courts if the crime is serious enough. In Illinois, New Mexico, Oregon, and Utah, the privacy that usually surrounds the trials of juveniles has been eliminated: newspaper reporters may now regularly attend the proceedings.[15]

This unprecedented change in both the frequency and brutality of child crime, as well as the legislative response to it, is no doubt attributable to multiple causes but none more cogent, I think, than that our concept of childhood is rapidly slipping from our grasp. Our children live in a society whose psychological and social contexts do not stress the differences between adults and children. As the adult world opens itself in every conceivable way to children, they will inevitably emulate adult criminal activity.

They will also participate in such activity as victims. Paralleling the assault on social order *by* children is the assault by adults *on* children. According to the National Center on

Child Abuse and Neglect, there were 711,142 reported cases of child abuse in 1979. Assuming that a fair amount of child battering goes unreported, we may guess that well over two million instances of child abuse occurred that year. What can this mean other than that the special status, image, and aura of the child has been drastically diminished? It is only half an explanation to say that children are beaten up because they are small. The other half is that they are beaten up because they are not perceived as children. To the extent that children are viewed as unrealized, vulnerable, not in possession of a full measure of intellectual and emotional control, normal adults do not beat them as a response to conflict. Unless we assume that in all cases the adult attackers are psychopaths, we may conclude that at least part of the answer here is that many adults now have a different conception of what sort of a person a child is, a conception not unlike that which prevailed in the fourteenth century: that they are miniature adults.

This perception of children as miniature adults is reinforced by several trends besides criminal activity. For example, the increased level of sexual activity among children has been fairly well documented. Data presented by Catherine Chilman indicate that for young white females the rise has been especially sharp since the late 1960s.[16] Studies by Melvin Zelnick and John Kantner of The Johns Hopkins University conclude that the prevalence of sexual activity among never-married teen-age women, among all races, increased by 30 percent between 1971 and 1976, so that by age nineteen, 55 percent have had sexual intercourse.[17] We may safely assume that media have played an important role in the drive to erase differences between child and adult sexuality. Television, in particular, not only keeps the entire population in a condition of high sexual excitement but stresses a kind of egalitarianism of sexual fulfillment; sex is transformed from a dark and profound adult mystery to a product that is available to everyone—let us say, like mouthwash or underarm deodorant.

One of the consequences of this has been a rise in teen-age pregnancy. Births to teen-agers constituted 19 percent of all the births in America in 1975, an increase of 2 percent over the figure in 1966. But if one focuses on the childbearing rate among those of age fifteen to seventeen, one finds that *this is the only age group whose rate of childbearing increased in those years, and it increased 21.7 percent.*[18]

Another, and grimmer, consequence of adult-like sexual activity among children has been a steady increase in the extent to which youth are afflicted with venereal disease. Between 1956 and 1979, the percentage of ten-to-fourteen-year-olds suffering from gonorrhea increased almost threefold, from 17.7 per 100,000 population to 50.4. Roughly the same increase is found in the fifteen-to-nineteen-year-old group (from 415.7 per 100,000 to 1,211.4). The traditional restraints against youthful sexual activity cannot have great force in a society that does not, in fact, make a binding distinction between childhood and adulthood. And the same principle applies in the case of the consumption of drugs. For example, the National Institute on Alcohol Abuse and Alcoholism concludes that a substantial number of fifteen-year-olds drink "considerable amounts." In one study of the drinking habits of tenth-to-twelfth-graders, almost three times as many males indicated they were "heavier" drinkers (meaning they drink at least once a week and consume large amounts when they drink) than those who indicated they were "infrequent" drinkers (meaning they drink once a month at most and then in small amounts). Alcoholism, once considered an exclusively adult affliction, now looms as a reality for our new population of miniature adults. Of other drugs, such as marijuana, cocaine, and heroin, the evidence is conclusive: American youth consume as much of it as do adults.[19]

Such figures as these are unmistakable signs of the rise of the "adultified" child, but there are similar trends suggestive of the rise of the "childified" adult. For example, the emergence of the "old persons' home" as a major social institution in America bespeaks of a reluctance on the part of young adults to assume a full measure of responsibility for their parents. Caring for the elderly and integrating them into family life are apparently perceived as an intolerable burden and have rapidly diminished as adult imperatives. Perhaps more significant is the fact that the present generation of young adults is marrying at a dramatically lower rate and having fewer children than their parents' generation. Moreover, their marriages are not as durable. According to the National Center for Health Statistics, parents are getting divorced at twice the rate they did twenty years ago, and more children than ever before are involved in marital dissolution: 1.18 million in 1979 as compared to 562,000 in 1963. Although we must assume multiple causality for such a trend, including what Christopher Lasch calls the rise of the narcissistic personality, we may fairly claim that it indicates a precipitous falling off in the commitment of adults to the nurturing of children. The strongest argument against divorce has always been its psychological effect on children. It is now clear that more adults than ever do not regard this argument to be as compelling as their own need for psychological well-being. Perhaps we might even say that, increasingly, American adults want to be parents of children less than they want to be children themselves. In any case, children have responded to this new mood by, among other things, running away in droves. According to the FBI, 165,000 children were taken into custody by police in 1979. It is assumed that at least three times that number went undetected.

In the face of all this one would expect the rise of a "philosophy" of sorts to justify the loss of childhood. Perhaps there is a principle governing social life that requires people to search for a way to affirm that which is inevitable. In any case, such a philosophy has, indeed, emerged, and we may take it as evidence of the reality it addresses. I refer here to what is sometimes called the Children's Rights Movement. This is a confusing designation, because under its banner are huddled two conceptions of childhood that are, in fact, opposed to each other. One of them, which I do *not* have in mind in these remarks, believes that childhood is desirable although fragile, and wishes to protect children from neglect and abuse. This view argues, for example, for the intervention of public authority when parental responsibility fails. This conception of childhood dates back to the nineteenth century and is simply a widening of the perspective that led to child labor laws, juvenile crime codes, and other humane protections. *The New York Times* has referred to those who stand up for this idea as "child savers."

The other conception of "child's rights" rejects adult supervision and control of children and provides a "philosophy" to justify the dissolution of childhood. It argues that the social category "children" is in itself an oppressive idea and that everything must be done to free the young from its restrictions. This view is, in fact, a much older one than the first, for its origins may be found in the Dark and Middle Ages when there were no "children" in the modern sense of the word.

As is frequently the case in such matters, we have here a "reactionary" position being advanced by those who think of themselves as "radicals." In any case, these are people who might be called "child liberators." Among the earliest of them was Ivan Illich, the brilliant social critic, whose influential book *Deschooling Society* (1971) argued against compulsory schooling not only on the grounds that schools were unimprovable but, even more, that compulsory schooling effectively bars the young from fully participating in the life of the community; that is, prevents them from being adults. Illich redefined the relationship of children to school by insisting that what most people see as a benevolent and nurturing institution is instead an unwarranted intrusion in the life and learning of a certain segment of the population. The force of Illich's argument derives from the fact that information is now so widely distributed, available from so many sources, and codified in ways that do not require sophisticated literacy that the school has lost much of its meaning as the fountainhead of learning. Moreover, as the distinction between childhood and adulthood becomes less marked, as children less and less have to *earn* adulthood, as less and less is there anything for them to *become*, the compulsory nature of schooling begins to appear arbitrary.

This impression is intensified by the fact that educators have become confused about what they ought to be doing with children in school. Such ideas that one ought to be educated for the greater glory of God or Country, or even for the purpose of beating the Russians, lack both serious arguments and advocates, and many educators are willing to settle for what Marx himself would have emphatically rejected: education for entry into the marketplace. This being the case, a knowledge of history, literature, and art, which once was the mark of an educated adult, recedes in importance. Moreover, it is not as well established as many think that schooling makes an important difference in one's future earning power. Thus, the entire edifice of our educational structure is laced with dangerous cracks, and those who would demolish the structure altogether are by no means misinformed. Indeed, there is a sense in which their proposals are redundant. As childhood disappears, so must schools. Illich does not have to write a book about it so much as merely wait.

All of this is the theme of John Holt's *Escape from Childhood*. In this and other books he argues for the liberation of the child from the constraints of a three-hundred-year-old tradition of bondage. His arguments are broadened—that is, taken to their logical conclusion—in Richard Farson's extraordinary book, *Birthrights* (1974). Farson argues that the child's right to information, to his or her own choice of education, to sexual freedom, to economic and political power, even to the right to choose his or her own home environment, must be restored at once. "We are not likely to err," he says, "in the direction of too much freedom."[20] Farson, who is not unaware of the history of childhood, evidently finds the fourteenth and fifteenth centuries a suitable model for the ways in which the young ought to be integrated into society. He believes, among other things, that the principal objection to incest is that people are made to feel unreasonably guilty about practicing it; that all sexual behavior should be decriminalized, including sex between adults and children; that arrangements need to be made to permit children to live wherever and with whom they wish, including "homes" governed by themselves; and that children must be given the right to vote "because adults do not have their interests at heart and do not vote in their behalf."[21]

Such a child's rights movement as this may be said to be a case of claiming that the disease is the cure. Expressed more neutrally, what this sort of advocacy represents, as noted, is an attempt to provide a rationalization for what appears to be an irreversible cultural tendency. Farson, in other words, is not the enemy of childhood. American culture is. But it is not a forthright enemy, in the sense that one might say, for example, that America is against communism. American culture does not *intend* to be against childhood. In fact, the language we use to talk about children still carries within it many of the assumptions about childhood that were established in the eighteenth and nineteenth centuries. Just as our language about war preserves the idea of a nineteenth-century war, when, in fact, such an idea today is preposterous, our language about children does not match our present social reality. For in a hundred years of redesigning how we communicate, what we communicate, and what we need to be in order to share in it all, we have reached the point of not needing children, just as we have reached the point (although we dare not admit it) of not needing the elderly. What makes Farson's proposals so horrifying is that without irony or regret he reveals the future.

Notes

1   See Leonide Martin's *Health Care of Women*, p. 95. However, this widely held belief has been challenged by Vern L. Bullough of the State University of New York at Buffalo. See "Drop in Average Age for Girls' Maturing Is Found to Be Slight," *The New York Times*, July 11, 1981, p. 17.

2   See George Masnick and Mary Jo Bane's *The Nation's Families: 1960–1990* for documentation of the decline of household members and the rise of the single-member household.

3   For documentation and analysis of the decline of the Disney empire, see "Wishing Upon a Falling Star at Disney," *The New York Times Magazine*, November 16, 1980.

4   McDonald's insists on keeping private its figures as to how much of its food different age groups consume. The best I could get from them is the statement that young adults with small children are the largest group among those who patronize McDonald's. The categories McDonald's inventories are small children, "tweens," teens, young adults, and seniors.

5   These figures are from *Nielsen Report on Television 1980*.

6   *Nielsen Report on Television 1981*. Both this report and the 1980 report are available upon request to A. C. Nielsen Company, Nielsen Plaza, Northbrook, Illinois 60062.

7   According to RCA, the largest producer of classical music recordings, in the early 1960s the company released approximately eight new recordings a month. Today, that figure is down to four. A spokesman for RCA claims this situation is similar for every other company in the business. RCA also concedes that there has been a steady decline in the share of the market of both classical music and sophisticated popular music. Today, classical music, opera, and chamber music account for about seven percent of all sales. The rest is mostly rock, country, and jazz.

8   Among the many studies documenting this decline is one conducted by the California Department of Education in 1979. Seniors tested under the California Assessment Program continued to perform (as they had in 1978) sixteen percentage points below what the testing industry says is the national average for reading.

9   In a report released in 1981, the National Assessment of Educational Progress revealed that the inferential reasoning of thirteen-year-olds declined throughout the period of the 1970s.

10   For an excellent historical analysis of these relationships, see Sennett's *The Fall of Public Man*.

11   These figures were compiled by using the 1950 and 1970 Uniform Crime Report (published by the FBI) and the 1950 and 1970 census.

12   See the New York *Daily News*, July 17, 1981, p. 5.

13   See the United Press International report of June 22, 1981.

14   See the New York *Daily News*, July 17, 1981, p. 5.

15   For a comprehensive review of the changing attitudes toward child crime, see *The New York Times*, July 24, 1981.

16   Cited in Melvin Zelnik and John Kantner's "Sexual and Contraceptive Experience of Young Unmarried Women in the United States, 1976 and 1971," *Family Planning Perspectives*, Vol. 9, No. 2 (March/April 1977), pp. 55–58.

17   See Zelnik and Kantner, above.

18   See Stephanie Ventura's "Teenage Childbearing: United States, 1966–75," *The Monthly Vital Statistics Report*, a publication of the National Center for Health Statistics.

19   See "Student Drug Use in America, 1975–80," prepared by Lloyd Johnson, Jerald Bachman, and Patrick O'Malley of the University of Michigan Institute for Social Research. It is available from the National Institute on Drug Abuse, Rockville, Maryland 20857.

20   Farson, p. 153.

21   Farson, p. 179.

Index